Designing XML Databases

Designing XML Databases

MARK GRAVES

Prentice Hall PTR, Upper Saddle River, NJ 07458
www.phptr.com

Library of Congress Cataloging-in-Publication Data

Designing XML databases / Mark Graves.
p. cm.
Includes index.
ISBN 0-13-088901-6
1. XML (Document markup language) 2. Database management. I. Graves, Mark. II. Title.

QA76.76.H94 G7338 2001
005.7'2--dc21 2001021472

Editorial/Production Supervision: *Laura Burgess*
Acquisitions Editor: *Mark L. Taub*
Editorial Assistant: *Sarah Hand*
Marketing Manager: *Bryan Gambrel*
Manufacturing Buyer: *Maura Zaldivar*
Cover Design: *Anthony Gemmellaro*
Cover Design Direction: *Jerry Votta*
Interior Design: *Gail Cocker-Bogusz*

Prentice-Hall, Inc.
Upper Saddle River, NJ 07458

Prentice Hall books are widely used by corporations and government agencies for training, marketing, and resale.

The publisher offers discounts on this book when ordered in bulk quantities. For more information, contact:
Corporate Sales Department,
Phone: 800-382-3419; FAX: 201-236-7141
E-mail: corpsales@prenhall.com; or write:
Prentice Hall PTR; Corp. Sales Dept.
One Lake Street; Upper Saddle River, NJ 07458

Printed in the United States of America

10 9 8 7 6 5 4 3 2 1

ISBN 0-13-088901-6

Pearson Education LTD.
Pearson Education Australia PTY, Limited
Pearson Education Singapore, Pte. Ltd
Pearson Education North Asia Ltd
Pearson Education Canada, Ltd.
Pearson Educación de Mexico, S.A. de C.V.
Pearson Education—Japan
Pearson Education Malaysia, Pte. Ltd

To Ellen,
for her support and encouragement

Contents

9

Indexing 458

10

Implementation 480

Appendix A

Appendix B

Appendix C

together. Some advanced techniques are described in this book and the presentation is fairly dense in those areas.

The book covers:

- How to design a schema for an existing XML DBMS beginning with the concepts of the field being modeled and resulting in compatible schemas for XML documents, relational databases, and object-oriented applications.
- How to store XML data in a relational DBMS, object-oriented DBMS, or flat files, and how to make decisions on which approach to choose.
- How to design a system architecture that contains an XML database, Web server, and user applications.
- How to develop a user interface for XML data accessed via a Web browser or Java application.
- How to query an XML database and what algorithms support XML database querying.
- How to create a native store for an XML DBMS.

In addition, a theoretical foundation is presented for XML databases, querying, and interdocument links.

Some history on how this book came about may be helpful. When I was in graduate school, I heard someone say that it took about 10 years for database technology to go from academic research to industry. I decided that I might be able to get a head start by focusing on the application of database theory to real-world problems. At the same time, the Human Genome Project was starting, and I found it fascinating to contribute to the unique endeavor to understand biologically what makes us human. Along the way, I discovered what worked for databases and what did not.

My dissertation described a way to interconnect data that grew out of ideas in artificial intelligence, hypertext systems, and databases. The premise was that systems of interconnected links could be treated as a database (or knowledge base), and that well-defined operations could be performed on the somewhat fuzzy entanglement of links. For lack of a better term, I called the connection of interconnected links a Web, the operations on them Spiders, and the whole system a Weave. However, in the early 1990s, there was no practical application for such a bizarre system, other than in artificial intelligence knowledge models, natural language processing, and interesting enough, the very early stages of computational biology.

I decided to begin work on capturing the interconnection of biological information in this system, and went to Baylor College of Medicine as a postdoctoral researcher in the very first computational molecular biology group. There I discovered that the graph-like structure of the links was very similar to the mechanisms biologists were developing to describe the relationship of interactions in the cell. My ideas were refined to support the graph-like interactions in biological data and incorporated into larger database systems.

About that time, another group developed a hypertext system called the World Wide Web that was geared toward exchanging text and images across the Internet, which was gaining in popularity. Although similar to what I was working on because of some of the shared hypertext ideas, its language, HyperText Markup Language (HTML), was geared more toward presentation and less toward data. It was applicable to user interfaces for a scientific database, but not applicable at all for capturing scientific data.

At the same time, the Human Genome Project was becoming more visible to biotech and pharmaceutical companies who started hiring almost every person in the very small, very new, and esoteric field of using computers to manage the rapidly growing biology data, called bioinformatics. I went to industry and began integrating what I had learned with even larger relational databases and delivering that data via Web browsers. Then, in 1998, the World Wide Web Consortium proposed a recommendation for a HTML-like language for data, called Extensible Markup Language (XML), which provided a flexible syntax for representing hierarchical data.

Since then, I have been adopting XML as the language for representing data and integrating that with commercial relational database management systems (DBMSs) in the framework I had been using for 10 years. This book pulls together what I learned during that time. In particular, I have strived to include techniques from databases that are particularly useful for XML and may not be accessible in other resources.

As it is rare for a technical book to be read from beginning to end, the following chapter groups may be useful. To:

- Effectively use an existing XML DBMS, see Chapters 1, 2, 5, 7, and 10.
- Purchase an XML DBMS or components of a solution, see Chapter 6. Chapters 1, 4, and 5 provide background material for understanding Chapter 6.
- Use an existing flat file, relational, or object-oriented DBMS with XML, see Chapters 2, 3, 4, 5, 7, 8, and 10.
- Obtain a manager's overview of XML database technology, see Chapters 1, 6, and 10. Chapters 2 and 5 provide background material for understanding Chapter 10. Chapter 4 provides some project alternatives.
- Create or enhance an XML DBMS, see Chapters 3, 4, 8, and 9. Other chapters provide background material.
- Learn all about XML databases, see all the chapters.

Introduction

- Are XML databases a perfect marriage of Web and database technologies?
- Will the marriage last?
- Is it a flash-in-the-pan, destined to end as soon as the incompatibilities become apparent?
- Or, is it a long-term commitment where each technology supports and strengthens the other?

1

This book provides an introduction to XML database technology: How to design the databases, how to build the systems to manage the databases, and how to leverage those systems in the real world. In addition to the requisite toy examples, many examples are drawn from the field of biology and provide a complex, yet reasonably understood application area in which to discuss the intricacies of XML database design.

This chapter provides an introduction to XML and databases and begins to address questions such as:

- What are XML databases?
- How can I use them? Design them? Build them?
- What technologies are available?
- What are their strengths and limitations?

XML databases can integrate Web technologies and database systems through three scenarios:

1. XML documents can be stored in a relational or object-oriented database management system (DBMS) by translating the documents into relations or objects.

2. Database software can present existing relations or objects in a database as XML.
3. A new DBMS can be created with a data model based on XML.

In this book, database systems are described to address these tasks and processes are described to support them. Good design is stressed through the integration of theoretical foundations and practical considerations. The primary focus is on a strong system architecture with applications drawn from a variety of domains.

1.1 XML

1.1.1 What Is XML?

XML stands for Extensible Markup Language. It is a language for representing data as a string of text that includes interspersed "markup" for describing properties of the data. Using markup allows the text to be interspersed with information related to its content or form.

The markup occurs predominately as *tags* that are distinguished from the *character data* (unmarked up text) by surrounding them with angle brackets "<" and ">" like "<this>". Thus as a string, a document consists of tags and character data; these are combined to form elements. An *element* starts with a start tag and ends with an end tag. The end tag has the angle brackets and a slash "/" to distinguish it from a start tag, like "</this>". The tags are <keyword>interspersed</keyword> within the text being marked up, and the region of text from a start tag to its end tag is an element; in this sentence "<keyword>interspersed</keyword>" is an element.

Specifically, markup provides a mechanism for adding meta-content and structure information to a document. Tags provide a mechanism for annotating the character data within an element. An element is the basic building block of XML. Elements may contain other elements nested within them, called *subelements.* A document consists of a single outermost (or top-level) element, which contains other elements and/or character data, and each subelement can contain other sub-subelements interspersed with character data, and so on. An example XML document is given in Example 1–1. This document consists of the "<?xml version="1.0">" processing

Example 1–1 : An Example XML Document

```
<?xml version="1.0"?>
<story>
<para>
John and Bob were walking down to the lake to go fishing. They enjoyed
fishing together and had been going regularly for almost twenty
years. Today was different. There was a man already in their spot with
his line in the water.
</para>
<para>
John and Bob walked around the man and shifted down the shore to the
side of a little inlet. It was not as good of a spot, but they had
done well there years ago, and it would do.
</para>
<para>
John and Bob each cast their line in the water. John using the same
rod he always had, and Bob using the new graphite one his son got him
for his birthday. John got a tug on the line and reeled in a 7-inch
rockfish. It was too small to keep, and John tossed it in the water.
</para>
<para>
The fish was glad to be alive when it hit the surface of the lake and
could breathe the water again. In relief, the fish started swimming
furiously and  yelled out to the rest of the lake, "Hello World!!!".
</para>
</story>
```

instruction followed by the element “<story>…</story>”. The “story” element has a start tag “<story>” and an end tag “</story>”. The “story” element contains four elements, each of which is labeled with “para” tags.

An XML document consists of an element (with its subelements). Nested elements may also be used to describe part of another element. The graphical markup in Figure 1–1 can be presented as XML as shown in Example 1–2. A hierarchy of markup is created for the annotations.

The two example documents also illustrate two features of XML. The first feature is that a document can be marked up and still be understood; in effect, adding XML markup preserves the information in the document. The second feature of XML is that it can represent hierarchical (nested) information. Thus, XML markup can add information to a document about its content and structure.

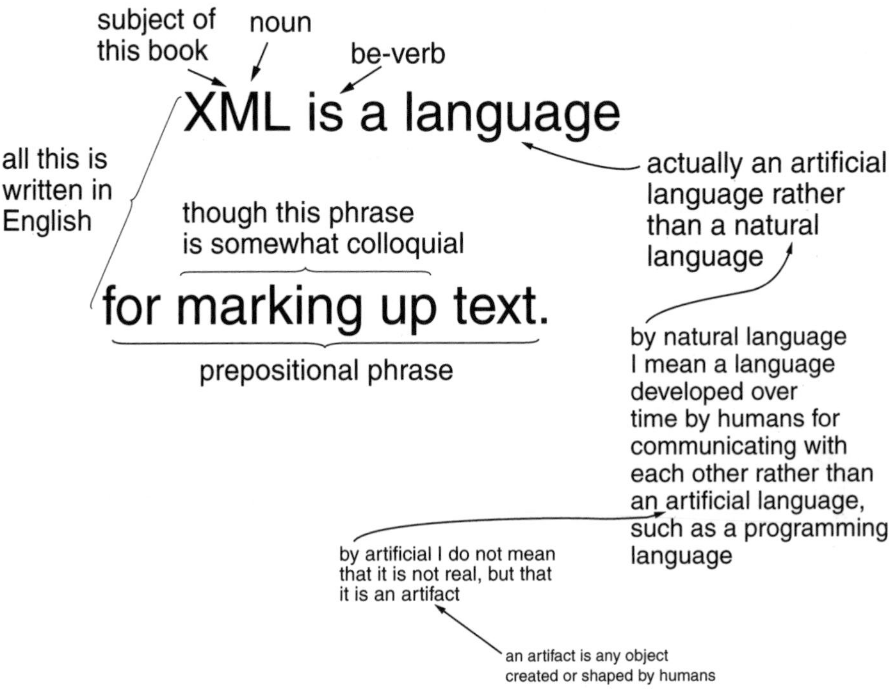

Figure 1–1 Marked-up text

A collection of elements with the same properties is called an *element type*. Element types are distinguished by giving the tag of those elements a unique name (sometimes called the tag name). For example, each "<para>" tag in the example identifies a member of the "para" element type, and "<a>", "<a href="there">", and <a index="1"> are all start tags of the element type named "a". Type in XML is used in the same way as in programming languages, where "1", "2", "3" are members of the data type named "integer".

Some programming languages have extensible data types, such as object-oriented programming languages like Java. If you create an object class called "color", it may have instances with names "red", "blue", "yellow", "green", and "violet". One benefit of the extensibility of object-oriented programming languages is that you do not have to overload other data types, such as stating that the number "1" represents "red", the number "2" represents "blue", and so on. In the same way, the extensibility of XML avoids the overloading of HTML, where "<b>" (for bold), sometimes repre-

Example 1–2 : An Example of XML Markup

```
<?xml version="1.0"?>
<sentence language="English">
<subjectOfBook><noun>XML</noun></subjectOfBook><verb type="be">is</
verb> a
<annotation>
  <text>language</text>
  <note>
    actually an artificial language rather than a
    <annotation>
      <text>natural</text>
      <note>
        by natural language I mean a language developed over time
        by humans for communicating with each other rather than an
<annotation>
          <text>artificial</text>
  <note>
    by artificial I do not mean that it is not real,
            but that it is an
    <definition>
      <text>artifact</text>
      <def>
        an artifact is any object created or shaped by humans
      </def>
            </definition>
  </note>
</annotation>
language, such as a programming language
      </note>
    </annotation>
    language
   </note>
</annotation>
<prepPhrase>for <colloqial>marking up</colloqial> text</prepPhrase>.
</sentence>
```

sents emphasis, sometimes represents section header, and sometimes represents a keyword search result. In XML, the element types are extensible, thus, you can create a new element type named “color”, or “keyword”, or “babyPicture”. These element types have attributes, which are represented as part of the tag, such as <color rgb=“110”> or <story language=“English” keyword=“fish”>. An *attribute* consists of a name-value pair.

XML provides an extensible mechanism for annotating and marking up character data. This extends the kinds of information that can be associated with data in documents and in databases.

1.1.2 Where Does XML Come from?

The first markup language, GML, was invented in 1969 and was used primarily to support document processing applications. In 1974, Standard Generalized Markup Language (SGML) was invented and from 1978 to 1980 it was refined and developed by the International Standards Organization to meet requirements for system independence and international exchange. These requirements necessitated a wide range of options for dealing with the disparate systems that existed at the time.

HTML is an application of SGML intended for simple, device-independent rendition and hyperlinks. XML, in contrast, is a configuration of SGML designed in the late 1990s to provide the extensibility of SGML in the World Wide Web environment. XML, unlike full SGML, allows no options. It supports only the choices made for the Web and is therefore easier to learn and to use.

SGML was designed to permit the separation of content from presentation. HTML mixed content, presentation, and process in the same framework, which made the documents more difficult to work with and maintain. XML, and its related standards, encourage the separation of content as abstract *element types,* presentation as formatting objects (a specific set of element types), and process as stylesheets. Each dimension can be developed independently without the compromises needed in a monolithic framework.

XML is designed to be delivered via the Web. Data is represented using the structure of an XML document. The elements and attributes provide useful *meta-data*—data about data—and structure the data in a way that can be transported across the Web, manipulated by different applications, and transformed to meet differing needs.

1.1.3 Why Use XML?

XML, as a configuration of SGML, was originally designed to meet the challenges of large-scale electronic publishing by isolating content from formatting. Separating the content of a document from how it is to be formatted simplifies development and maintenance. Different people (or teams) with different expertise can work independently on the information captured in a document and on the format, style, and aesthetics.

XML is also proving useful in *data exchange*. XML can be used to exchange the data on the Web between applications or between applications and users. XML by itself is not intended for presentation to an end user, but when used in conjunction with stylesheets (which provide presentation), XML documents may be easily viewed. XML documents provide a way to capture the data, and stylesheets—such as eXtensible Stylesheet Language (XSL) or Cascading Style Sheets (CSS)—provide mechanisms for transforming the XML to HTML (or other renditions). XSL and CSS provide control over the presentation of XML in Web browsers.

Another key advantage of XML is its ability to integrate data and documents. Most languages are designed to be better at expressing the rigid, absolute content and structure of data *or* the flexible, free-form text of documents, but XML does *both* equally well. It can capture scientific or financial data as well as format a love letter for sending via email, or it can be used to publish a poem. XML can not only represent data and free form text, it can do both in the same document. Long comments or complete scientific papers can annotate a single piece of data in a large, complex data set, and scientific papers can have large, complex, hierarchical data sets embedded within the document.

XML is designed to communicate content in a flexible and extensible representation. Thus, descriptions of the data can be iteratively refined as the underlying domain changes. This makes XML particularly useful for areas whose knowledge has a complex organization that undergoes frequent revision. Some of the early adopters of XML technology include scientific areas, such as biology, chemistry, and mathematics. Scientific standards exist in those areas based on XML, namely, BioML, CML, and MathML, respectively. Thus, fairly complex domains can be represented reasonably well using XML.

The two key aspects of XML over other data exchange languages are that it is fairly expressive and extensible. In effect, you can say what you want to say on the topic you choose. It also has a consistent syntax that makes it easy to parse (and to write parsers for). Thus,

- XML can capture the kind of information that is exchanged between applications.
- XML documents can be tailored to fit very specific needs.
- XML parsers and other generic tools are already available.

XML can be used to represent the content of Web pages with stylesheets used to define the processing. The Web pages may be static or dynamic, such as online catalogs. Even in static Web pages, the separation of content from presentation may simplify development and reduce the size of the pages. Dynamic Web pages are much easier because the content can change as needed, while the stylesheet remains static. Very different presentations are possible using the same stylesheet when appropriately conditioned on the content. For example, data might vary from a large table to a single instance, and the presentation can be tailored to respond with different formatting.

XML documents can be published in a variety of forms: HTML, PDF, Postscript, and so on. Although this book focuses on the use of XML to represent data for database applications, XML still provides an effective language for representing information to be presented to users.

There are several cases when you should seriously consider the use of XML. XML should be used when you need to present data to both users and applications. The same document can be presented using stylesheets to the user and be parsed and manipulated by the applications. It is much easier to use the same document than to develop a separate representation for users and applications.

XML should be used when you desire a simple user interface. A simple stylesheet can be defined to present an XML document and support navigation of it by the user. The work required for a simple stylesheet is negligible compared to other approaches that require parsing another data format and creating a browsing application.

XML should be used when you need to exchange data between applications, particularly when the structure of the data changes. There are times when XML may not be the best choice. If the data is always of a simple format, such as a table, it may be more efficient to use a simpler representation. If for some reason you want to have these alternatively formatted documents also available in XML, the document can be wrapped as a single top-level element and a CDATA section, which prevents the body of the document from being parsed by the XML parser.

When the data structure is not simple, XML may be needed to store complex relationships. Many complex relationships can be captured in XML. If the relationships are very complex, or not completely understood in detail, significant effort may be necessary to model the relationships before deciding on the structure to best use in the XML representation. This topic is addressed more fully in Chapter 2.

As described previously, XML is particularly useful when you need to merge database data with the content of a publication. You can develop separate representations for the data and the publications, then combine them into an XML document.

There are also business reasons to use XML. It is supported by Web browsers, which, because they are already pervasive, reduces the cost of delivery. XML—as a World Wide Web Consortium (W3C) Recommendation—has a level of insurance for development of larger systems, because larger software companies, such as Microsoft, IBM, Sun, and Oracle are supporting the technology. These reasons are particularly important for databases, as large database systems can be expensive and a substantial portion of the enterprise may depend on them.

The W3C provides a list of other business reasons from their Web site (*www.w3c.org*). XML will:

- Enable internationalized media-independent electronic publishing
- Allow industries to define platform-independent protocols for the exchange of data, especially the data of electronic commerce
- Deliver information to user agents in a form that allows automatic processing after receipt
- Make it easier to develop software to handle specialized information distributed over the Web
- Make it easy for people to process data using inexpensive software
- Allow people to display information the way they want it, under stylesheet control
- Make it easier to provide meta-data—data *about* information—that will help people find information and help information producers and consumers find each other

unique identifier to a physical block in the database file. There are many complex variations to efficiently create that mapping.

A simpler mechanism for storage is called a *flat file database.* In a flat file database, data is divided among text files and directory structures instead of file blocks and mapping structures. The files are usually much larger than the size of an individual block, and so must be searched, which is slower. The advantage of the flat file database is that the text files can also be accessed by other applications, such as text editors, find tools, browsers, and scripting languages. Flat file databases have been used for "pseudo-relational" DBMSs, where each table is stored as an individual file, and some (but not necessarily all) relational operations are provided. The biggest limitation of flat file databases is that it has been almost impossible to find a file format that is even remotely intuitive enough to allow browsing, can capture complex hierarchical structures, can be broken into meaningful file-size pieces, and can also work with applications. Now, XML addresses these issues, and flat file databases are feasible based on XML.

1.2.2 What Is an XML Database?

An XML database is a collection of XML documents that persist and can be manipulated. Historically, documents were developed for communication between humans. With the advent of computers, documents may also be used for computer-computer communication, human-computer communication, or computer-human communication. Each of these communication paradigms has its own requirements, such as aesthetics, tolerance for ambiguity, preciseness, and flexibility.

XML documents tend to be either document-processing-oriented or data-processing-oriented. *Document-processing-oriented documents* are those in which XML is used for its ability to capture natural (human) languages, such as in user's manuals, static Web pages, and marketing brochures. They are characterized by complex or irregular structure and mixed content and their physical structure is important. The processing of the document is focused on the final presentation of the information to the user; thus, they may be called presentation-oriented documents. *Data-processing-oriented documents* are those where XML is primarily for data transport. These include sales orders, patient records, and scientific data. The physical structure of data-processing-oriented documents, such as the order of elements or whether data is stored in attributes or subelements, is often unimportant. They are characterized by highly-regular structure with many repetitions of those data structures. The processing of the document is usually focused on its use and exchange by applications; thus, they may be called message-oriented documents. Document-processing-oriented and data-processing-oriented documents are sometimes called document-oriented documents versus data-oriented documents, respectively, but those terms are ambiguous as every document always contains data.

One purpose of this book is to extend the data processing paradigm for databases to handle the richer structure typically found in some document-processing-oriented documents. The structure of document-processing-oriented documents may be more flexible than the structure of data-processing-oriented ones. For example, the structure of English prose has a much richer grammar than the structure of tab-delimited files. Data-processing-oriented documents tend to have many repetitions of the same constructs without exception. XML provides a language for capturing the nested hierarchies of XML elements that extends the regularities that are easily captured by traditional databases.

The distinction between data-processing-oriented or document-processing-oriented XML documents can be subtle, and some documents, such as dynamic Web pages with descriptive text and data, could be viewed either way. However, the operations that are desired on the documents will vary. In a document-processing-oriented document, desired operations include retrieving the entire document, searching for a word, finding previous words or following words, modifying a section, or reordering a section. In a data-processing-oriented document, desired operations include retrieving a specified fragment of the document, searching for a particular combination of elements and data, modifying or deleting a single element or a single piece of data, or adding a new element to the document. Some desired operations are shared between the two orientations, such as determining the outline of the element structure or navigating the document in order to perform some other operation.

XML databases are a collection of data-processing-oriented documents. The operations provided by the XML database are geared more toward data manipulation than text processing. Text processing systems based on SGML are fairly mature and may provide features for manipulating XML documents. Chapter 3 describes in more detail what those operations might be. In practice, it may also be useful to provide some text processing commands in an XML DBMS to simplify the manipulation of document-processing-oriented documents or sections of documents.

There are at least three ways that XML can be used within a Web database system.

1. Data can be accessed via a Web server from a flat file database that stores data as XML documents. Not only can a Web server provide access to document-processing-oriented XML documents, for which it was designed, it can also provide access to the organized data-processing-oriented XML documents of a flat file database.
2. Data can be accessed through a Web server interface to a traditional database and formatted as XML when retrieved. For example, reports from queries on a relational DBMS can be formatted as XML.
3. Data can be accessed through a Web server interface to an XML DBMS.

1.3.1 Flat File Database

An XML flat file database provides hierarchical access to data first through the directory structure of a file system, then through the element structure of XML documents.

The advantages of a flat file database are that it is small, easy to build and maintain, and easy to access with other tools. Disadvantages of flat file databases are that the data is not as well protected and is harder to query. Flat file databases also do not usually provide concurrency control, data locking, or recovery facilities. In developing an XML flat file database, decisions must be made about what is captured by the directory structure and what is captured by the structure of the XML document, as the following example illustrates.

Rudolph's Christmas Tree Farm is setting up a Web site to allow customers in the adjacent urban area to order Christmas trees via the Web for delivery. Rather than cut the trees in November and sell them wholesale to the inner-city Christmas tree retailers, Rudolph's can rent a couple of extra trucks, hire a couple of drivers, and deliver freshly cut trees to different parts of the city throughout late November and December. Because the trees are freshly cut and delivered directly from the farm, customers might even pay a premium over the normal retail price. From a business perspective, there is a trade-off in maximizing the number of trees sold direct (for a higher profit) while minimizing the lost revenue from not having sold the trees wholesale. Because Rudolph's has never sold Christmas trees via the Web before, they have no prior data and decide to set up an adjustable pricing scheme that varies based on demand, inventory, and days before Christmas. This eliminates the possibility of having static Web pages, as the price information must vary. Because this is a new, high-risk, seasonal venture, they don't want to invest in a large inventory database application to support the site.

A flat file database is designed, as shown in Figure 1–4, that contains customers, products, and sales. A directory is set up on a Web server to contain the data. The next step is to decide which relationships are captured by the directory structure and which are captured by the XML documents. One extreme would be to have all the information captured in a directory structure, with files containing only a single piece of information. This is a fine-grained flat file database, because the data is finely ground into many small pieces. A database explorer for the fine-grained database is shown in Figure 1–5. The other extreme would be to have one XML document that contains the entire database. This is a very coarse-grained flat file database, because the data is very coarsely ground into a few large pieces, namely one piece. An example coarse-grained database of one XML document is given in Example 1–3. A more moderate approach is to have each customer, product, and transaction as a single file. This is a medium-grained flat file database. An example medium-grained database of one XML document is given in Figure 1–6.

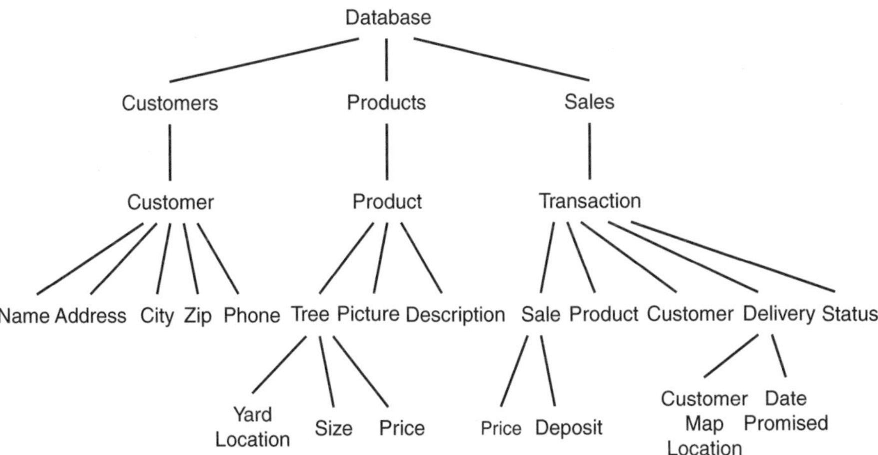

Figure 1–4 Rudolph's Christmas tree database

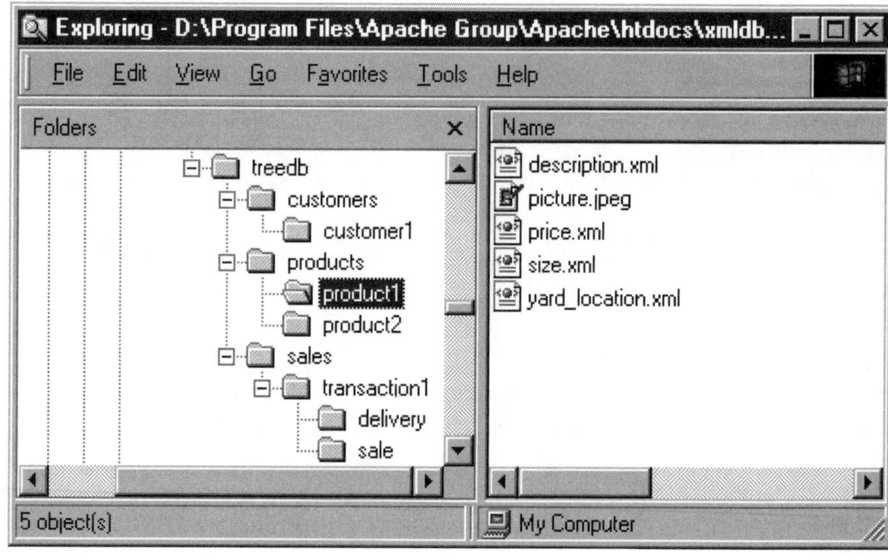

Figure 1–5 Fine-grained Christmas tree database

Example 1–3 : Coarse-grained Christmas Tree Database

```
<?xml version="1.0"?>
<treedb>
 <customers>
  <customer id="1">
   <name>Ebenezer Scrooge</name>
   <address>7 Main Street</address>
   <city>Anytown</city>
   <zip>12345</zip>
   <phone>6785559823</phone>
  </customer>
 </customers>
 <products>
  <product id="1">
   <tree>
    <yard_location>3F2</yard_location>
    <size>8</size>
    <price>59.95</price>
   </tree>
   <picture img="1.jpeg"/>
   <description>Beautiful fir tree with solid body and smooth shape.</
description>
```

```
  </product>
  <product id="2">
   <tree>
    <yard_location>2A6</yard_location>
    <size>6</size>
    <price>39.95</price>
   </tree>
   <picture img="2.jpeg"/>
   <description>Clean young tree with full coverage.</description>
  </product>
 </products>
 <sales>
  <transaction id="1" status="open">
   <sale>
    <price>39.95</price>
    <deposit>20.00</deposit>
   </sale>
   <customer id="1"/>
   <product id="2"/>
   <delivery>
    <customer_map_location>689A5</customer_map_location>
    <date_promised>1223</date_promised>
   </delivery>
  </transaction>
 </sales>
</treedb>
```

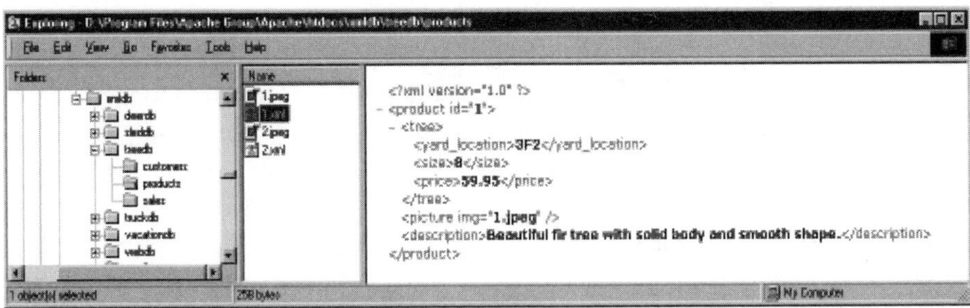

Figure 1–6 Medium-grained Christmas tree database

The order system is set up to provide the customer a variety of delivery dates based on address and zip code. It also organizes the XML file for each product in "available" and "sold" directories and moves the product file from the "available" to "sold" directory upon completion of the sale. A script is written to go through the transactions every night and create summary reports for pricing. Another script is written to adjust the price of all unsold products by a certain percentage. Finally, a script is written to generate a report of all trees to be delivered on a specified date, with customer names, addresses, and phone numbers, sorted both by location of the tree in the yard and by the customer's map coordinate.

1.3.2 Relational DBMS

An XML interface to a relational DBMS provides access to robust database technology with the advantages of XML delivery. It is especially useful when a relational database already exists. The main disadvantage is that the representation of the data is limited to relations, which may be an issue for some domains. There is a mismatch between what the relation and the XML element can represent, because the XML element has more inherent flexibility than the relation. A relation (or row in a table) consists of a fixed number of characteristics (or columns), and each characteristic consists of one data item, while an XML element can contain an arbitrary number of characteristics (as subelements or attributes) and each subelement may contain more than one data item. The relation can be easily expressed in XML, but loading data from an arbitrary XML document into a relational database may be difficult. You may need to modify the relational schema to allow for more variation in the structure of the data than is typically provided. For example, to capture multiple occurrences of sub-elements with the same element type, it may be necessary to create a separate relation to capture that set of data and linking it to the original relation. This can increase the complexity of the relational database, suggesting that it may be time to consider using an XML DBMS.

One of the advantages of using a relational DBMS is that complex queries may be written in SQL, the standard query language for relational DBMS. The reports may be formatted as XML to provide many views on the underlying data. In particular, this is useful when multiple applications require particular views on the database. The applications can query the database for the particular information required in a structure that mimics the data structures of the application; receive the data as XML; and insert the data fairly easily into the data structures or objects. For example, if an object-oriented tracking application requires data from a complex customer, product, and sale transaction database, it can perform a complex query to retrieve the data as an XML document that closely mimics the object model developed for the application, even if it is considerably different from how data is stored in the database.

Other advantages of using a relational database include its easy interoperability with other relational databases, sophisticated transaction management and recovery mechanisms, and numerous tools that support the technology. Using an XML interface to a relational database is especially appropriate when the database must be accessed by applications that interact with other relational databases.

Developing an XML interface to a relational database is described in Chapter 5.

1.3.3 XML DBMS

An XML DBMS provides direct access to XML documents and fragments of documents and the ability to query across those documents and fragments. Using an XML DBMS is especially appropriate when capturing the data from a domain with complex hierarchical relationships, such as scientific databases, large organizations, and manufacturing systems.

An XML DBMS may be built from scratch, bought, or built on top of another DBMS. Building an XML DBMS from scratch requires special attention to memory management and efficient access of document fragments. This is discussed in Chapter 9. Buying an XML DBMS may be the best solution when an existing XML DBMS meets project needs and there is no legacy data. Commercial systems are described in Chapter 6. Building an XML DBMS on top of another DBMS is quicker and provides many of the benefits of the underlying DBMS used for storage. It may also be easier to integrate with existing applications and legacy data. Building an XML DBMS using relational or object-oriented DBMSs for storage is described in Chapter 4, and accessing those systems via Web interfaces is described in Chapter 5.

In particular, building an XML DBMS on top of a relational DBMS has many advantages. The data is as robustly protected as any data in a relational DBMS; it may be accessed through all existing applications to a relational database, including query tools, browsers, explorers, data loaders, and data exporters; and it may be integrated with existing legacy data in queries and views. It is also useful when some of the data is best captured in a relational form, or through tools that assume an underlying relational database.

For example, if Rudolph's Tree Farm's Web site were a shining success, then the next year they may want to purchase accounting software to manage the sales transactions. The accounting software is from a stodgy, ultraconservative company that has not updated the software in years, but it has

1.5.2 General Sites

Some general XML sites are:

- *www.xml.com*—Lots of XML
- *msdn.microsoft.com/xml/*—Microsoft's XML home page with tutorials
- *www.ibm.com/developer/xml/*—IBM developerWorks XML overview
- *xcentral.alphaworks.ibm.com/xmlguide.html*—Another IBM XML site
- *www.ddj.com/topics/xml/*—Dr. Dobb's Journal XML site
- *www.builder.com/Authoring/XmlSpot/*—CNET main XML site with lots of links
- *www.oasis-open.org/cover/xml.html*—Robin Cover's site on XML (or *www.oasis-open.org/cover/* the site on SGML/XML); everything you always wanted to know about XML, but didn't know enough to ask
- *www.xmlinfo.com*—More information on XML
- *www.xml101.com*—Links, articles, and tutorials
- *www.xmlpitstop.com*—XML Developer's site
- *www.csclub.uwaterloo.ca/u/relander/XML/*—Overview of XML resources
- *www.xmltimes.com*—News of the XML world and tutorials
- *www.xmlbooks.com*—List of XML books in print

1.5.3 XML Portals

- *www.xmltree.com/xmlTree*—A directory of XML content on the Web; provides search capabilities to many examples
- *www.schema.net*—A directory of domain-specific XML specifications
- *www.xml.com/pub/Guide/Directories*—A directory of sites that carry listings of XML-based Web sites
- *www.xml.org*—An XML portal that registers XML specifications, schemas, and vocabularies

1.5.4 XML Tools

In addition to the tools listed at the general XML Web sites, the following sites have some specific information on XML tools

- *www.xmlsoftware.com*—A listing of XML software
- *xml.apache.org*—Apache's XML site

1.5.5 XSL

Some sites to gain more information about XSL are:

- *www.xmlinfo.com/xsl/*—XSL The Extensible Stylesheet Language at XMLINFO
- *www.xml101.com/xsl/*—XSL Tutorial
- *msdn.microsoft.com/xml/XSLGuide/*—Microsoft's XSL site
- *www.xmlsoftware.com/xsl/*—XSL Editors - Tools at XMLSOFTWARE
- *www.w3.org/Style/XSL/*—Home page for W3C XSL activity
- *www.w3.org/TR/xsl/*—XSL Specification
- *www.dpawson.freeserve.co.uk/xsl/xslfaq.html*—XSL Frequently Asked Questions
- *www.mulberrytech.com/xsl/xsl-list/*—Mulberry Technologies, Inc. XSL-List—Open Forum on XSL

1.5.6 W3C Documents

- *www.w3.org/XML/*—Main W3C site for XML
- *www.w3.org/XML/Activity*—Provides an overview of W3C XML Activity
- *www.w3.org/TR/REC-xml*—Official XML Specification
- *www.w3.org/TR/*—Lists all W3C Technical Reports and Publications
- *www.w3.org/DOM/Activity.html*—Provides an overview of W3C activity for DOM
- *www.w3.org/Style/XSL/*—Home page for W3C XSL activity

XML Specifications include:

Schema Design

- How can I store XML in a database?
- What does the database look like?
- How do I design it?
- What language should be used for designing XML databases?
- How do I determine what the XML should look like?

2

In developing a new XML database, it is important to understand how the data will be captured in the DBMS. The initial and most influential interaction between users and the DBMS will be in designing schemas for the database. A *schema* is the description of what the data in the database looks like. It is the blueprint for the database and describes the content of the database. As in a blueprint, it does not look very much like a building, but to the trained eye, it communicates what form the building will take.

Understanding schemas is especially important in developing Web databases because the database schema tends to have a greater impact on the end user's perspective than, for example, in a large, complex financial database behind an application of 50,000,000 lines of code. Part of that tendency is self-selection: The applications chosen for Web delivery tend to be simpler applications, which are delivered to a variety of users across many platforms. Hopefully, one would not be developing a Web-delivered database for astronauts to use in landing the space shuttle.

Another reason to understand schema design is for developing applications that access the database. A good design for a schema in the database can also drive the description of the domain for the variety of applications that use the database.

In this chapter, a database design method is described. The best place to start designing a database is from the description of the domain as seen by an expert or user, not the database developer. The basic framework consists of three steps. First, a modeling language, which is easy for the domain expert to use, is used to describe the domain. Then the description is translated into something that the database developer needs and understands. That is then translated into something the computer understands and needs to function.

2.1 Database Design

Database design is a multi-step process and each step requires different areas of expertise. As in engineering, architecture, fabric design, graphic arts, or really any design area that is complex enough to require planning, the process begins with understanding the requirements:

- What needs to be done?
- What is the scope of the project?
- What are the boundaries of the project?

The process then moves on to understanding what is within that scope:

- What do I have to work with?
- What is the domain?
- What are the constraints on the design?
- What design constructs, which I know, are appropriate?

The design process then moves from design toward implementation:

- What are the implementation constraints?
- How will what I know about the tools and resources affect this design?
- What is practical to implement?

Finally, implementation begins.

From scratch design is rarely sufficient in practice. There are usually existing databases, nonfunctional requirements, regulations, political constraints, trees, large rocks, hills, existing color schemes, supplier constraints, and so on, that must be addressed in realistic design. However, in database development, the most important constraint is the domain, so the best approach is to forget about existing designs and practical constraints and design a schema based solely on the domain first, then go back and revise the design to incorporate existing systems.

Early on in the process, the design depends heavily on the domain being modeled. What is in the domain? What area is to be captured? How are the concepts in the domain related? What is the purpose of the database? What are the essential features and characteristics of concepts that must be captured for that purpose? These questions are best answered by someone with a lot of knowledge in the area being modeled. This person is referred to as the domain expert.

Later in the process, the design depends primarily on understanding the database technology used. What database technology should be used? In what form should the technology be used? Are there additional technologies needed? Of the different technical options, which is best for the current situation? These questions are best answered by the database developer, who has the expertise necessary to effectively use the database tools available.

Database design is the process of developing a schema for a DBMS that captures the data for a database. There are many design strategies, but one of the clearest is a multi-step process that begins with the concepts of the domain to be captured and iteratively incorporates more database-specific decisions. A three-step database design process is described as consisting of conceptual, logical, and physical design. These steps incorporate the concepts of the domain, the data model of the DBMS, and implementation decisions that depend on the DBMS used, respectively.

The first step in designing a database schema is called *conceptual modeling*. The concepts of a domain are captured in a schema called the *conceptual schema*. The domain expert can understand the conceptual schema because it has in it the concepts with which the expert is familiar, and it does not have any of the technical aspects of the database with which the expert has no particular knowledge or interest. The database developer can understand the conceptual schema because it is a schema that the developer has the training to understand without knowing or caring about what the concepts are or how they are used.

As in any abstract design, the modeling language chosen can greatly affect the ability of the modeler to appropriately capture the essential form and nuances of the domain. Performing conceptual modeling as an independent phase of design allows a modeling language to be chosen that is appropriate for the domain. An entity-relational data modeling language is often chosen for business applications that will be implemented in a relational database, but it can overly restrict the conceptual model and is rarely appropriate for implementations other than a relational database.

Logical design is taking what was developed by the domain expert and turning it into something the database developer can use. It takes the domain concepts and turns them into database constructs. The logical design process is, in a word, a *logical* process. The somewhat fuzzy domain information is sifted down and squeezed into a logical, often mathematically precise, framework called the (logical) data model. Although some nuances of the domain are often lost, the resulting database will be efficient and useful if modeled appropriately.

Any data model can be used as the logical data model for a DBMS, including data models based on relations, objects, graphs, trees, semantic networks, restricted first order predicate logic, symbols, sets, pointers, or abstract algebra. Each data model has strengths and weaknesses that make it more useful for one domain than another. For example, relations are great for financial applications where accountants have made sure that everything will fit into a spreadsheet; objects are good for CAD/CAM where engineers have connected parts together in very practical, though not necessarily elegant ways; graphs are great for molecular biology where everything is connected in some way to everything else. But, if you don't know exactly what the domain is and don't have the resources to build a custom DBMS for a domain, there are basically three choices: relations, objects, and, because you bought this book, XML. (By the way, if you think creating new data models for individual domains is a fascinating idea, check out my dissertation (1993); it may also be helpful if you have insomnia.)

Physical design is taking the mathematically clean data model and making it work on the computer within the constraints of the hardware, operating system, and DBMS. Lots of tradeoffs, details, and optimizations are worked out at this stage. The focus of the physical design stage is performance and implementation. Sometimes additional details of the domain may be included that did not affect the overall design enough to be included in the logical data model. However, these details are often essential to the proper functioning of the database. These "business rules" include domain details like, when making a withdrawal from one account, a deposit of the same amount must be made to another, or that a particular table will contain 23 billion entries. In summary, conceptual design is similar to carrying on an interesting conversation to design a new building, logical design is similar to developing a plan with blueprints and engineering diagrams, and physical design is figuring out how to get the drywall up two flights of steps.

You can use XML, as a language, in any of the three stages of design. For example, you can

- Use XML as a conceptual modeling language and create a relational or object-oriented database from it.
- Use XML as a logical data modeling language used by an XML DBMS, such as eXcelon.
- Use XML as the physical data modeling language used to specify a schema, such as using XML Schema to create a database.

However, in this book I will primarily focus on the use of XML as a logical data modeling language.

2.2 Conceptual Modeling

Conceptual modeling is the process of describing a domain independently of any DBMS. The goal is to capture the essential aspects of the domain without making premature decisions about how the domain will be mapped into the implementation structure.

2.2.1 Graph Conceptual Model

Sometimes it is useful to have a more flexible and less precise modeling language for conceptual modeling than is used for the logical modeling. A more "conceptual" language focuses effort on the essentials of the domain and alleviates premature effort spent working on the details of the implementation. A conceptual modeling language for XML should have more structural flexibility than the hierarchical structure of XML and retain the mathematical abstraction of XML documents as a collection of trees. At the same time, the conceptual language should not be too different from the language for the logical XML data model. Thus, the conceptual model can be easily used for design and still be translated into the precise formalisms that define XML. Graph languages meet these requirements, and a graph conceptual model is defined in this section.

mation. Each word will eventually translate into a large, complex computational structure and may be central to a significant project; so, each word should capture and accurately describe significant information. If you are familiar with other modeling formalisms, avoid introducing bias about how a concept may be modeled, such as inheritance or aggregation (at least at first), as these are decided upon later in the process. An edge may also have a cardinality constraint that provides restrictions on the quantity of items the edge may connect in a database. Do not be too concerned about the style for the first database. You may want to try practicing with something fun if the modeling process is new to you; the later steps in database design should inform the learning process and improve subsequent modeling.

A graph conceptual model is a formal system that represents the concepts and relationships of a domain as a graph. One way to describe the domain as a graph is as follows:

- A *graph* is a collection of concepts, labeled edges, and cardinalities.
- *Concepts* are the nodes of the graph and model the simple concepts and relations of the domain.
- *Labeled edges* connect two concepts and model the characteristics of a concept and the binary relations of the domain.
- *Cardinalities* are a pair of positive integers associated with an edge. A cardinality may be the term "Many" (denoted by an "*") instead of an integer. The "Many" cardinality typically refers to zero or more occurrences, but the cardinality "One-or-More" may be denoted by a "+". If a cardinality is omitted, it is assumed to be "1".

An example of information that might be stored in a Rolodex is shown in Figure 2–3. A person has a name, email, phone number, company, and address. In a simple example, the labels for the edges and the nodes are the same. However, if the person had a fax number or pager, those characteristics would still refer to the "phone number" concept (as shown in Figure 2–4). The address concept of Figure 2–3 has multiple address lines, city, state, and zip. The multiple address lines are denoted by the "*" next to the "line" concept on the "line" edge, though the number of address lines could have been restricted to two lines, which would have been denoted by a "2" instead of an "*".

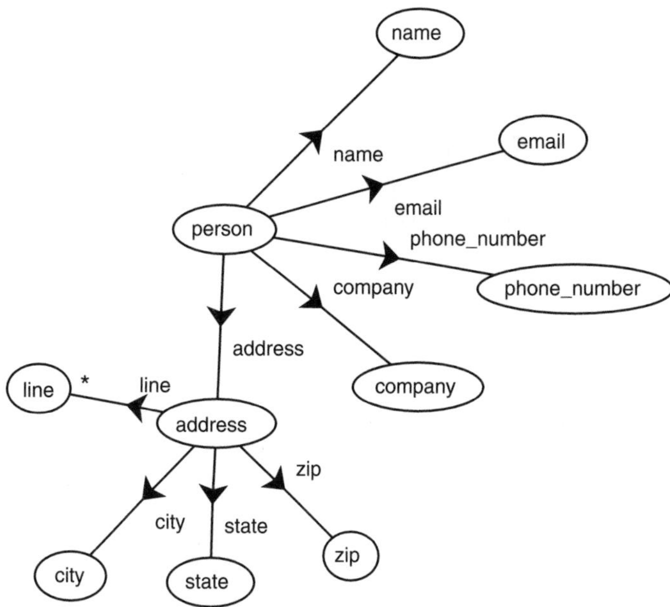

Figure 2–3 Rolodex graph conceptual schema

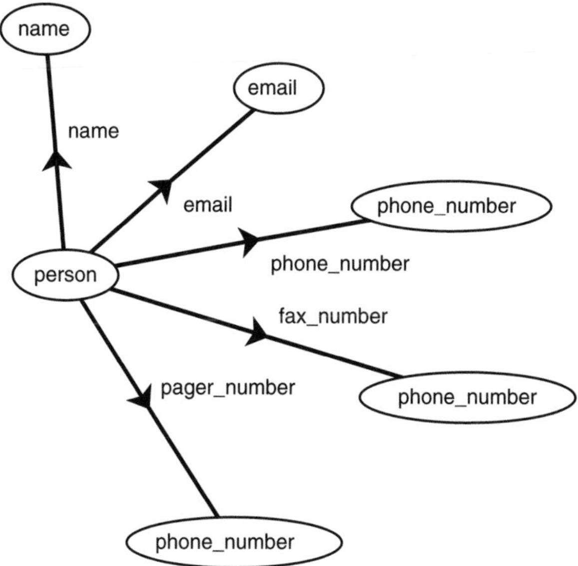

Figure 2–4 Person graph conceptual schema

Figure 2–5 shows cardinality constraints between a person and a name for the four common cardinalities:

a. 1-to-1 cardinality—Each person has one name.
b. 1-to-Many cardinality—Each person may have many names.
c. Many-to-1 cardinality—Many people may share one name.
d. Many-to-many cardinality—Many people may share many names.

In all the cases, the "1" cardinality is omitted from the diagram.

A graph conceptual schema describing an employee in a department is presented in Figure 2–6. An employee has a name, employee number, salary, commission, job, hire date, manager, and department. A manager is also an employee and has many employees. Note that the employee concept has a manager characteristic, so the arrow is directed from the employee to the manager, and thus the "many" cardinality is at the source of the edge. Many employees may be in a department, and a department has a number, name, and location.

Using graphs as a conceptual model offers several advantages. Graphs are visual, nonlinear, and flexible with respect to operations such as layout,

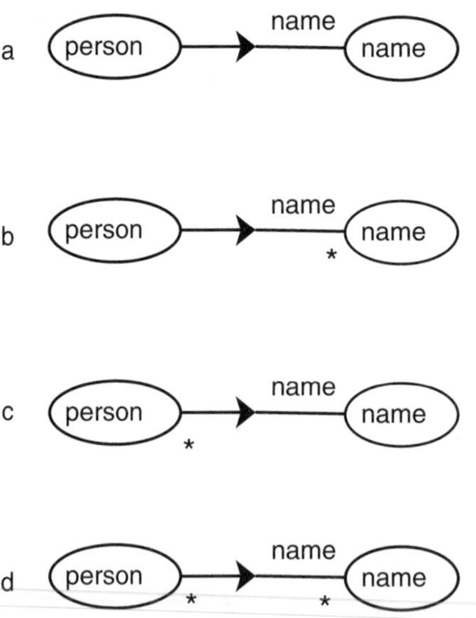

Figure 2–5 Example graph cardinalities

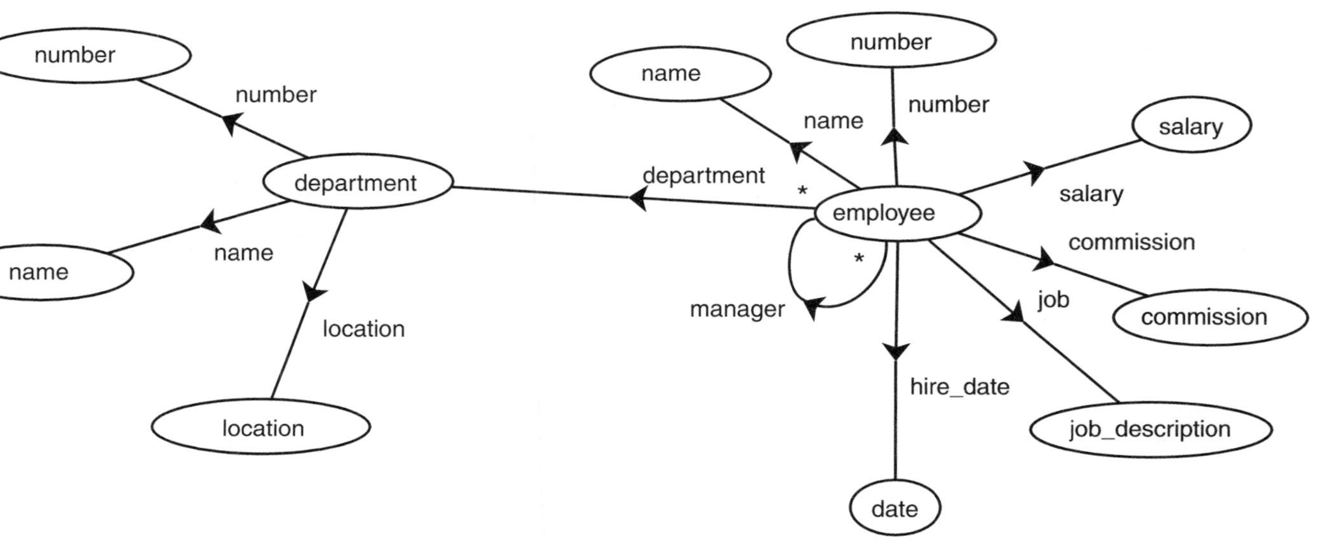

Figure 2–6 Employee graph conceptual schema

organization, adding concepts, adding characteristics, deleting concepts, and deleting characteristics. Graphs are easy to modify while developing a schema and are easy to understand and translate into a logical schema.

A graph conceptual model is used to capture data for XML databases because it is understandable by domain experts, is useable by database developers, and completely captures the structure of XML with a little wiggle room to easily handle more complex structures. Graphs are used to capture the structure of natural language in artificial intelligence, used by children to describe domains for evaluation by educational psychologists, and used by molecular biologists to model the complex interaction of cellular processes. In addition to being understandable by people, the language of graphs is also specific and precise enough to be translated easily, accurately, and efficiently into a database-specific language. Domain experts tend to need a slightly more expressive language to capture information in a domain than a nonexpert would assume. For example, in high school biology you may have learned the King Phillip Can Order Funny Goose Soup taxonomy (also known as Kingdom, Phylum, Class, Order, Family, Genus, Species). After taking a computer science data structure class, you would call this a tree (i.e., the computer science hierarchical tree, not the *Dicotyledoneae Fagales* variety), but the biologists who develop those taxonomies are aware of so many exceptions to the hierarchical tree, they need a directed, acyclic graph to keep them straight. To develop a linear order of genes on a chromosome, they need a cyclic graph, and to develop a (temporal) ordering of biochemical pathways, they need something even more complicated. Physics can need even more wiggle room, with as many as 10 dimensions to describe our three (or four), and economists need so many dimensions they do not even count them. In summary, for many domains, the modeling language needs to be more general than the language used by the DBMS. There are many formalisms that are more general than graphs that could be used for capturing XML, some of which are very interesting, but if someone starts talking about building a Web database for a domain that requires hyper-graphs, knots, or higher order monads, my advice is to negotiate a time-and-materials contract instead of a fixed-price contract and to avoid committing to firm deliverable dates.

2.2.2 Graph Conceptual Modeling Process

Although some people can intuitively draw the graphs, the following process may be used to provide structure to the elucidation. You can develop a graph conceptual model through a seven-step process. One advantage of this process is that it can be carried out with minimal knowledge of database systems, and the resulting schema is understandable by domain experts without specialized training.

I present the entire process first, and then I present it in the context of an example.

1. **List the domain concepts and complex relationships.** Concepts are real-world objects, relationships, or events. Syntactically, these are the nouns in a description of a domain.
2. **Connect domain concepts by creating simple sentences that describe relationships in the domain.** The simple sentences should describe characteristics of a domain concept or connect two domain concepts with a linking word or phrase, such as "Employee has a name", "Paragraph format has a font", or "Supervisor manages an employee". Linking phrases are descriptions of the interaction of the two domain concepts and should describe the relationship clearly. If a relationship is needed between more than two concepts, then you can add that relationship to the list in Step 1.
3. **Select major concepts in the domain from the list.** Concepts should be included that are fundamental to the domain or that occur in several of the simple sentences created in Step 2.
4. **Draw the major concepts as nodes in a conceptual schema.** Use a blank sheet of paper or whiteboard to draw the major concepts as nodes with ovals around the words. Concepts that are closely related are best drawn relatively close to each other on the surface.
5. **Draw the simple sentences as edges in the graph.** There are two ways to draw the characteristics of the domain concept, depending on style and space on the surface. The most complete way is to draw the characteristic as an oval representing a new concept and connect the domain concept to the characteristic with a directed edge and label the edge with the name of the characteristic. For example, draw "Employee has a name" by connecting "Employee" to "Name" with an edge labeled "Name", dropping the "has a" part of the linking phrase for simplicity. The second way to draw a characteristic is to omit the oval representing the characteristic when the

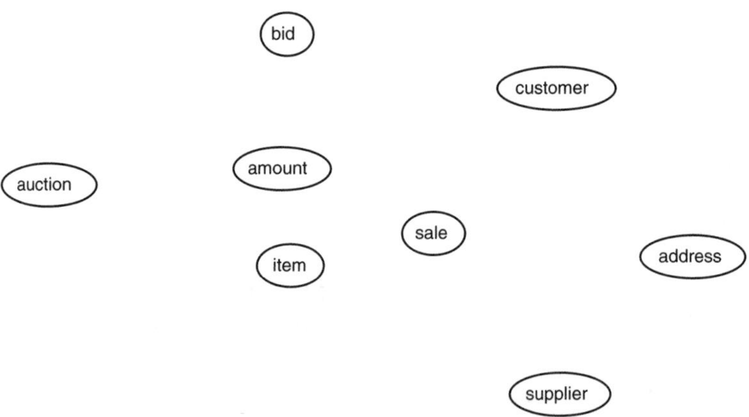

Figure 2–7 Major concepts in an electronic auction graph conceptual schema

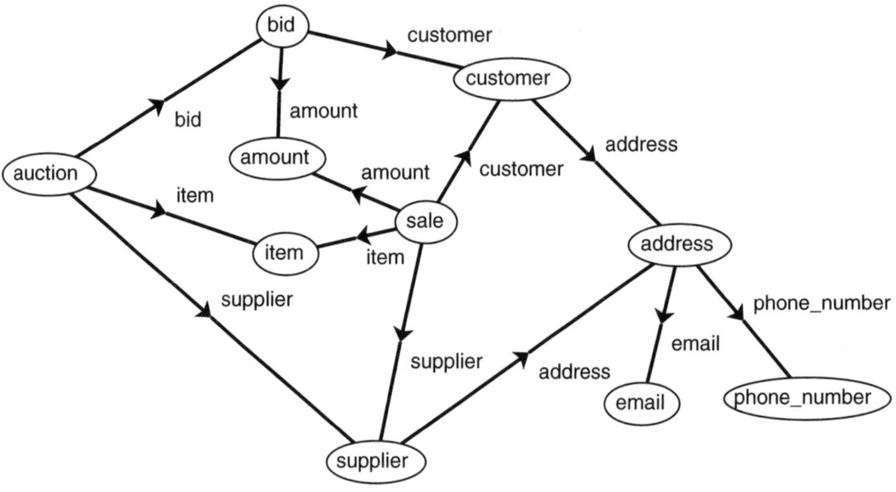

Figure 2–8 Electronic auction graph conceptual schema without cardinality constraints

6. **Add cardinality constraints to the edges.** This is shown in Figure 2–9. Information is added that an auction is a collection of bids, that a customer can bid and purchase more than one item, and that a supplier can provide more than one item.

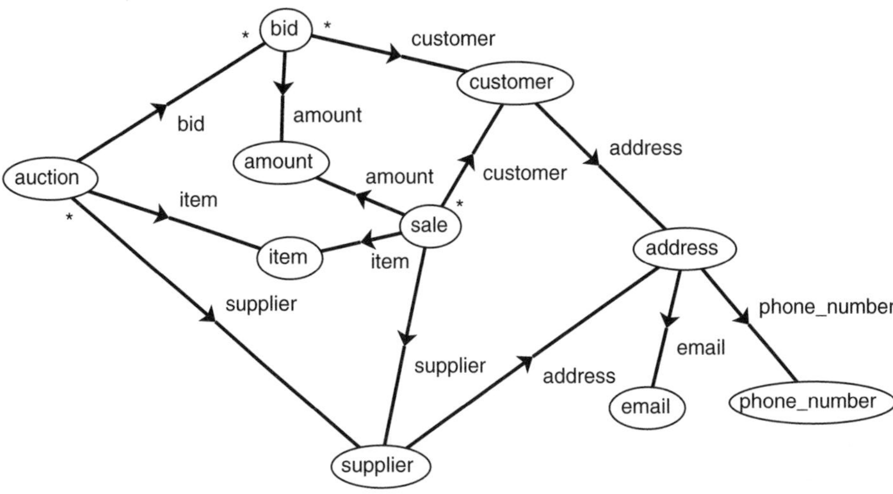

Figure 2–9 Electronic auction graph conceptual schema

7. **Revise the schema by examining the domain.** Additional information could be added, such as a fax number, pager, cell phone, or Web address.

The resulting diagram has two essential benefits. First, it can be understood by anyone familiar with the electronic auction domain. Second, it can be translated in a straightforward way to a database schema. Thus, it provides a clear point of communication between the domain expert and database developer.

2.2.3 Conceptual Modeling Issues

In practice, two issues that may arise in conceptual modeling are (a) whether the domain is modeled from a process-oriented or data-oriented perspective and (b) what level of abstraction is chosen for the modeling.

2.2.3.1 Process-Oriented versus Data-Oriented

The conceptual modeling process can be used to elucidate the relationships in a domain from either a process-oriented or data-oriented perspective. Most databases capture a domain from a data-oriented perspective.

However, a common exception is when the database is to support a process, such as workflow.

For example a domain, such as *molecular genetics,* which studies the processes related to deoxyribonucleic acid (DNA) replication, transcription, and translation, can be modeled from either perspective. The process-oriented perspective is appropriate when investigating the molecular interactions that comprise the fundamental processes involving genetic material. The data-oriented perspective is appropriate when using the results of that investigation for further exploration. Read on to see how both perspectives are modeled.

Genetic information is stored in every living cell in the form of DNA. DNA encodes the information needed to produce proteins that take part in and regulate all aspects of cellular life, including the mechanisms for replicating DNA when the cell divides. The mechanism for making proteins from DNA involves transcription of a stretch of DNA into ribonucleic acid (RNA), then translating the RNA into a polymer of amino acids to form a protein. The primary protein involved in DNA replication is DNA polymerase, while the mechanism for transcription involves RNA polymerase. Translation involves ribosomes and transfer RNA.

A process-oriented perspective could lead to the following conceptual modeling.

1. **List the domain concepts and complex relationships.** The concepts are:
   - DNA
   - RNA
   - Protein
   - DNA polymerase
   - RNA polymerase
   - Ribosome
   - Transfer RNA

2. **Connect domain concepts by creating simple sentences that describe relationships in the domain.** Check that the sentences capture the domain at the required level of accuracy. Recall that this step is being performed by the domain expert.
   - DNA polymerase replicates DNA.
   - DNA polymerase synthesizes DNA.
   - RNA polymerase transcribes DNA.
   - RNA polymerase synthesizes RNA.

- Ribosome translates RNA.
- Ribosome synthesizes protein.
- Ribosome requires transfer RNA.

3. **Select major concepts in the domain from the list.** In such a small domain description, all the concepts are major. For this example, those that occur more than once in the sentences are listed.
   - DNA polymerase
   - DNA
   - RNA polymerase
   - RNA
   - Ribosome
4. **Draw the major concepts as nodes in a conceptual schema.** See Figure 2–10.
5. **Draw the simple sentences as edges in the graph.** See Figure 2–11.

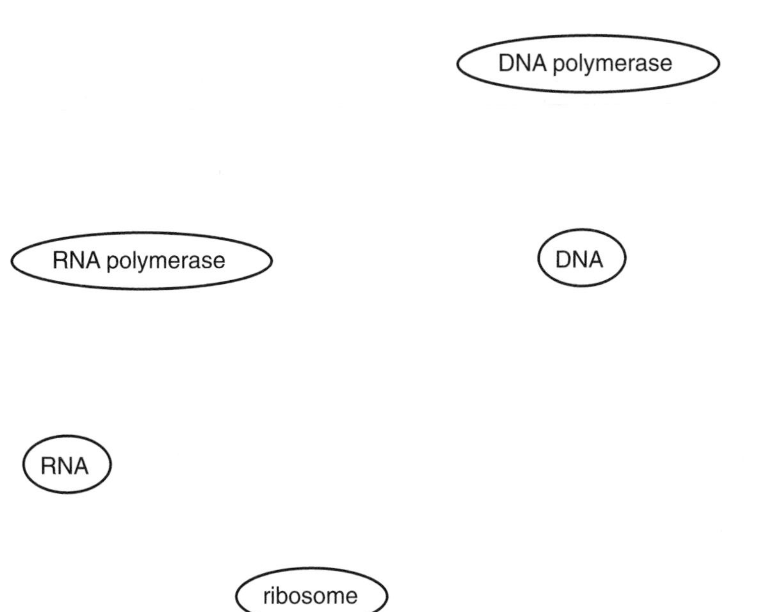

Figure 2–10 Major concepts in a molecular genetics graph conceptual schema

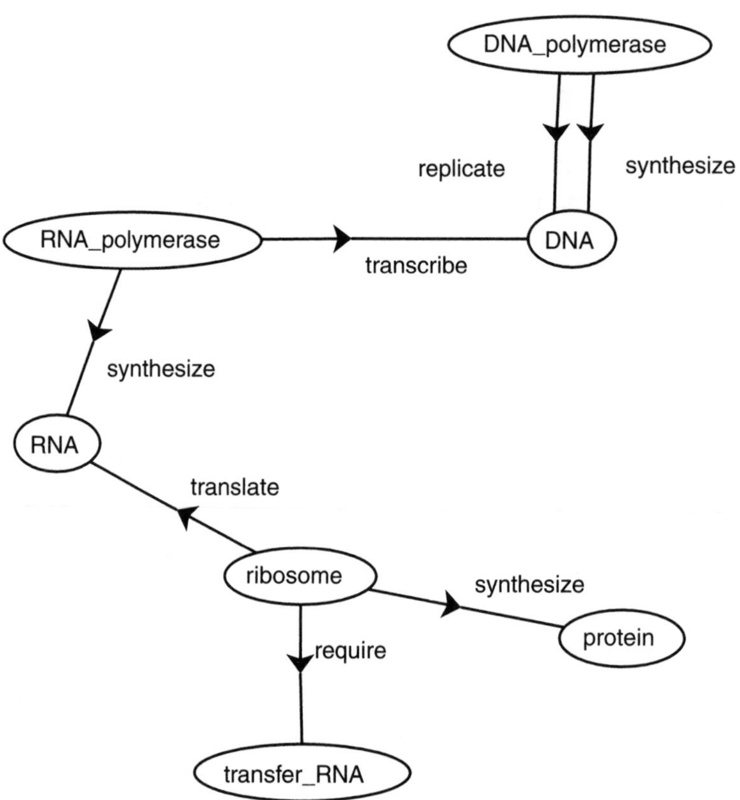

Figure 2–11 Molecular genetics graph conceptual schema

6. **Add cardinality constraints to the edges.** All of the cardinality constraints are many-many relationships.
7. **Revise the schema by examining the domain.** Much information could be added to the conceptual schema from a richer description of the molecular biology.

In using genetic information in other databases, information about genes and proteins are stored. DNA is a polymer of sugar molecules. Each sugar molecule is attached to one of four nucleic acids, called a base molecule. A relatively short region of DNA—or a sequence of bases—is transcribed into RNA and then translated into a protein. This is called a gene. A protein is a polymer of amino acids. The sequence of amino acids is directly related to the sequence of the bases of the gene. A database using genes and proteins would also store their respective sequences and names.

A data-oriented perspective could lead to the following conceptual modeling.

1. **List the domain concepts and complex relationships.** The concepts are:
   - Gene
   - Protein
   - Gene name
   - Gene sequence
   - Protein name
   - Protein sequence

2. **Connect domain concepts by creating simple sentences that describe relationships in the domain.**
   - Gene has a gene name.
   - Gene has a gene sequence.
   - Protein has a protein name.
   - Protein has a protein sequence.
   - Gene encodes for a protein.

3. **Select major concepts in the domain from the list.** For this example, those that occur more than once in the sentences are listed.
   - Gene
   - Protein

4. **Draw the major concepts as nodes in a conceptual schema.** The figure would consist of two ovals: one labeled "gene" and another labeled "protein".
5. **Draw the simple sentences as edges in the graph.** See Figure 2–12.
6. **Add cardinality constraints to the edges.** All of the cardinality constraints are one-to-one relationships.
7. **Revise the schema by examining the domain.** Much information could be added to the conceptual schema. In addition, the "encodes" relationship should be expanded.

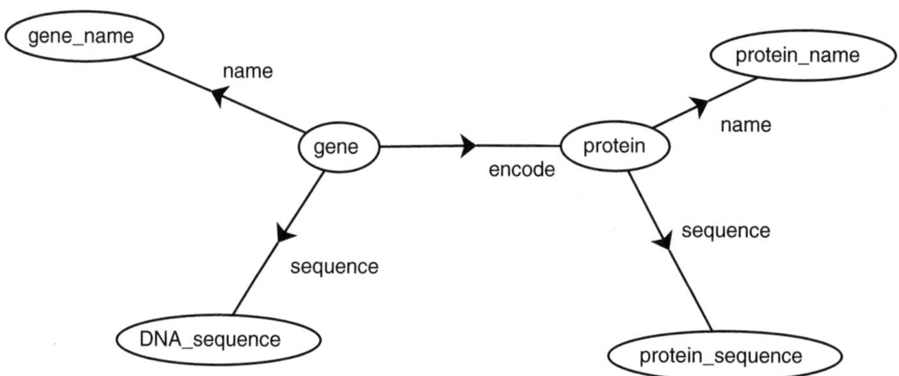

Figure 2–12 Gene/protein graph conceptual schema

2.2.3.2 Levels of Abstraction

One issue that arises in conceptual design that has a large downstream impact is the level of abstraction chosen in describing the domain. For example, in describing medical records, an illness could be described as an "illness" concept with a "type" describing the illness, or each illness could be described as an individual concept. Choosing the appropriate level of abstraction is significant and is based on how the resulting database will be defined and used in the application. For medical billing, a string or code distinguishing a broken arm from a migraine may be sufficient, but for an endocrinology research project, there may be a vastly different structure needed to capture the information associated with Type I and Type II diabetes. What structure is needed to distinguish the concepts? If all the concepts can be modeled with an identical structure (including data types) without domain confusion, then they can be a single concept in the conceptual schema. Most cases can be resolved simply by looking forward without becoming distracted by implementation issues. In general, the most concrete structures that completely capture the domain are best.

For example, to capture the information that "William Shakespeare wrote plays," several databases could be developed at various levels of abstraction depending on the application. Figure 2–13 depicts four levels of abstraction ranging from the most generic to the most specific:

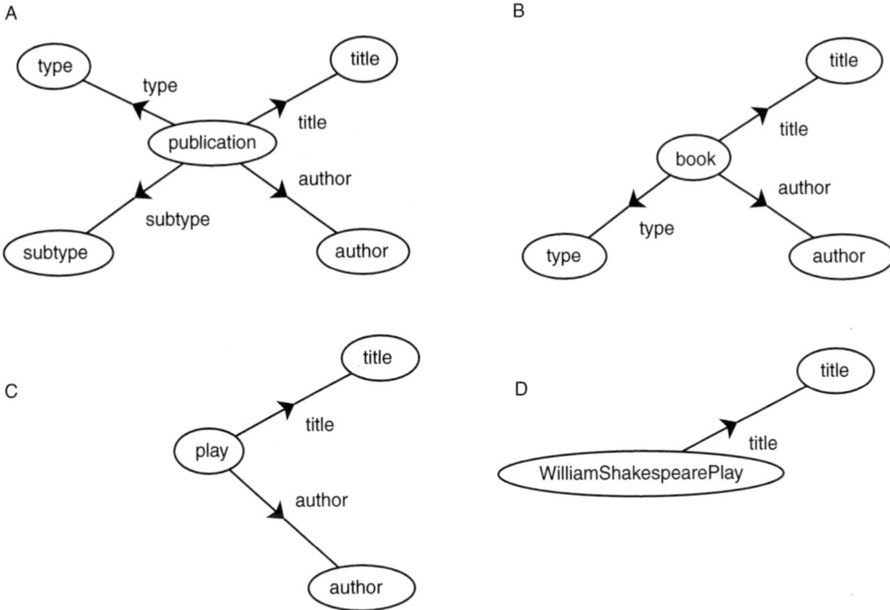

Figure 2–13 Four levels of abstraction for William Shakespeare's plays

a. Publication—Probably too generic for most applications, except for a Library of Congress catalog. An indication of the level of abstraction is the use of two levels of types.
b. Book—Still generic. It may be appropriate for a library.
c. Play—An appropriate level of abstraction for most applications.
d. William Shakespeare Play—Probably too specific except for a literary critic's database.

The four schemas might describe the following XML documents, each of which capture the information that William Shakespeare wrote a play called *Romeo and Juliet*, at a different level of abstraction.

```
<publication type="book" subtype="play" title="Romeo and
      Juliet" author="William Shakespeare"/>

<book type="play" title="Romeo and Juliet" author="William
      Shakespeare"/>
```

```
<play title="Romeo and Juliet" author="William Shakespeare"/>

<WilliamShakespearePlay title="Romeo and Juliet"/>
```

A way to find the appropriate level of abstraction is to examine the scope of the characteristics. In a different example, if ISBN numbers, publishers, and price information were included in the description and the information that these works are plays was dropped, then using the "book" representation would be more appropriate.

As an additional example, from Figure 2–11, the "DNA" and "RNA" may be appropriately replaced with "gene" and "messenger RNA" as shown in Figure 2–14, depending on the application.

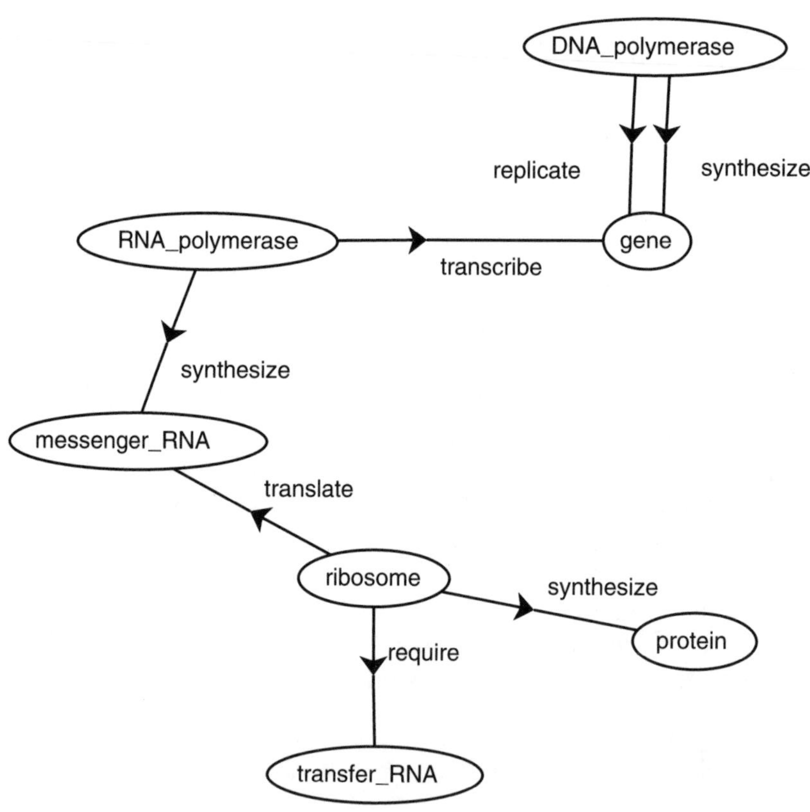

Figure 2–14 More specific molecular genetics graph conceptual schema

2.2.4 XML Conceptual Model

Although the primary point of this chapter is to describe how to use conceptual modeling to develop a schema for an XML database, it is also useful—as an aside—to examine how XML could be used as a conceptual modeling language to develop a database with a simpler structure. Using XML as a conceptual modeling language is described in this section, but not used anywhere else in this book.

XML can be used as a conceptual modeling language to capture the aggregate information of a hierarchically structured domain without inheritance. For example, a traditional biology taxonomy or parts of a book could be captured, as in Example 2–1 or Example 2–2, respectively. A fairly useful model can be developed with a few reasonable conventions, as follows:

- An XML conceptual schema consists of a collection of XML elements.
- Empty attribute values represent unrestricted attribute values.

Example 2–1 : Simple Conceptual Schema of Biology Taxonomy Represented in XML

```
<kingdom name="">
  <phylum name="">
    <class name="">
      <order name="">
        <family name="">
          <genus name="">
            <species name="">
            </species>
          </genus>
        </family>
      </order>
    </class>
  </phylum>
</kingdom>
```

Example 2–2 : Simple Conceptual Schema of Parts of a Book Represented in XML

```
<book title="" author="">
  <tableOfContents/>
  <chapter title="">
    <section>
      <subsection/>
    </section>
  </chapter>
  <index/>
</book>
```

For example, an XML conceptual schema describing employee relationships is presented in Example 2–3. The XML conceptual schema can be translated to a relational schema as follows:

a. Each element becomes a table (relation).
b. Each XML attribute becomes a column (relational attribute).
c. Each subelement of an element becomes a column in the table with a foreign key constraint to the table specified by the subelement.
d. All elements with the same name refer to the same relation (and any attribute or subelement relationships are merged).

Example 2–3 : Employee Conceptual Schema Represented in XML

```
<employee number="" name="" job="" hiredate="" commission="" salary="">
  <department number="" name="" location=""/>
</employee>
```

Example 2–3 can be translated to the following relations:

```
Employee(number, name, job, hiredate, commission, salary,
      department)
Department(number, name, location)
```

2.3 Logical Modeling

Logical design is the process of mapping a conceptual schema to a schema for the data model of the DBMS. Logical design is the most commonly emphasized aspect of the database design process. When the domain is well understood by the database designer, the data model of the DBMS is often used as the only modeling language. Tools that graphically present the schema of a database facilitate that process. However, when a conceptual model is used, the logical design stage consists primarily of translating the conceptual schema to a logical schema in a way that accurately captures the domain and effectively uses the constructs of the logical data model. The logical data model is usually more restricted in functionality and more rigid than the conceptual model. For example, the conceptual modeling languages entity-relational and semantic network more simply capture collections of many-many relations than the relational or object-oriented model, because they provide simple constructs for those collections. (These data models are described briefly in Section 3.5.1.)

Before describing the creation of an XML logical schema from a graph conceptual schema, I describe translation of graph conceptual schemas to entity-relation diagrams, relational schemas, and object models. These brief methodologies explain the process using more familiar technology and may also be used when relational or object-oriented technologies are used as part of an XML database system. Developing a database schema and an application's object model from the same conceptual schema that the XML markup is created from is one way to more closely align the representations of the domain in the database and the applications. For example, assume you had a relational DBMS that stored data for a project; the data is then translated into XML and transported to an application written in an object-oriented language (such as Java). Next year you want to transition part of the project data to an XML DBMS and increase the number of applications in the system. One goal is to keep the application interfaces as clean as possible, in effect to reduce the translation effort needed between the parts of the system. By designing the graph conceptual schema up front, you may use the same conceptual schema to define the relational database, the XML transport document, the object-oriented applications, and later the XML database.

2.3.1 Entity-relation Diagram

Entity-relation diagrams are often used as a conceptual model for relational databases. For the readers familiar with entity-relation diagrams, there is a simple method to translate a graph conceptual model to an entity-relation diagram. To translate from a graph conceptual schema to an entity-relation diagram, decisions are made on the importance and use of the concepts, and those descriptions are encoded in the entity-relation diagram. Three decisions are made:

- What are the principal concepts?
- Which concepts are fundamentally dependent on other concepts in the domain for their existence?
- Which concepts add descriptive detail?

To translate a graph conceptual schema to an entity-relation diagram, the concepts from the conceptual schema are separated into three classes as follows:

- Principal concepts are described as entities.
- Concepts that do not have their own essential independence in the domain are described as relationships.
- Concepts that add detail are described as attributes.

2.3.2 Relational Schema

There are two ways to translate from a graph conceptual schema to a (logical) relational schema. The translation can use an entity-relation diagram as an intermediate step or not.

To translate a graph conceptual schema to a relational schema, you can create an entity-relation diagram as an intermediate step using the process of the previous section. Translating an entity-relation diagram to a relational database is fairly well understood and other books are available on it.

You can also translate directly from a graph conceptual schema to a relational schema by following these rules:

- Each concept that can be an atomic value becomes an atomic value. An *atomic value* is one that does not need other values to have meaning in the representation of the domain. Typically, concepts with no characteristics of their own become atomic values. All other concepts become relations. To create a primary key, additional domain information may be required. Three approaches to creating a primary key are: allowing for multi-column primary keys, using a single column for a primary key when possible and otherwise creating a unique identifier, and always creating a unique identifier, possibly a unique number.

- Each edge with cardinality One-to-One becomes a column in the relation corresponding to the concept at the source of the edge. The edge label becomes the name of the attribute. If the destination concept is also translated as a relation, a foreign key constraint is also created. If the destination concept is translated as an atomic value, a unique constraint may be added to the column.
- Each edge with cardinality Many-to-1 or 1-to-Many becomes an attribute of the relation corresponding to the "Many" cardinality. For example, if a department has many employees, the employee table refers to the department. If the destination concept has the "Many" cardinality and would otherwise be an atomic value, an auxiliary "helper" table is created with attributes that refer back to the primary key of the source relation and an attribute with the atomic value. In any case, a foreign key relationship is created.
- Each edge with cardinality Many-to-Many becomes a joining table with attributes referring to the primary key of the relation corresponding to the connected concept. Two foreign key constraints are created on the joining table.

For example, the Employee conceptual schema of Figure 2–6 can be turned into a logical relational schema.

The logical schema is specified in the following format:

```
RelationName( columnName1 DOMAIN_NAME_1 , columnName2
     DOMAIN_NAME_2 )
```

An employee logical schema is:

```
Department(dept_number DEPT_NUMBER, dept_name DEPT_NAME,
     dept_location DEPT_LOCATION)
```

```
Employee(emp_number EMP_NUMBER, emp_name EMP_NAME, salary
      SALARY, commission COMMISSION, job JOB_DESCRIPTION,
      hire_date DATE, manager EMPLOYEE, department DEPARTMENT)
```

Primary and foreign keys are added to the relational logical schema:

- Primary key of "Department" table is "dept_number".
- Primary key of "Employee" table is "emp_number".
- The "department" column in "Employee" table refers to the primary key, "dept_number" in "Department".

After you create the relational schema, you may be able to simplify the schema further by using additional domain constraints.

2.3.3 Object Model

To translate from a graph conceptual schema to an object model, the following process may be used.

- Revise the conceptual model by being more specific about the cardinalities. Use a range or set of numerals if those are known, and distinguish a "Many" constraint that is zero or more (denoted by an asterisk "*"), and one that is one or more (denoted by a plus sign "+"). Optional characteristics can be denoted with "0", "0..1", "?", "opt", or a dashed-edge line. Draw additional diagrams that illustrate various configurations of characteristics if those occur.
- Each concept that has characteristics becomes a class in a class diagram.
- For each characteristic of a concept, it becomes an association if its cardinality may be greater than one or if additional domain information suggests that an association be created. Otherwise, the characteristic becomes an attribute if its cardinality (multiplicity) is "1" or optional.
- Concepts that do not have characteristics (i.e., no edge labels protruding) become either attributes or associations. These unrefined concepts may become new (empty) classes, built-in classes, or subtypes. For example, a "Name" might become a "String" or a subtype of String.

- When there are a variety of configurations for a concept, generalization may be useful.

Creating intermediate diagrams to translate a graph conceptual schema to an object model can be very helpful. In addition to the expanded cardinalities, two additional diagrams that are useful are the domain object diagram and the aggregation tree.

The domain object diagram captures the concepts in the conceptual schema that are central to the domain. These central concepts are drawn as classes in the class diagram. A domain object diagram is simply a graph conceptual schema with the less important concepts dropped from the diagram. It shows the relationships between the objects in the domain. One approach is to drop all concepts that have one incoming edge and no outgoing edge (and the edges with no destination concept).

An aggregation tree is created from the domain object diagram. When one object depends on another for its existence in the domain, the relationship is captured in an aggregation diagram. Aggregation (in this context) is a relationship between an object and other objects in the domain, where the description of an object is based on the other objects. The aggregation diagram describes domain objects that play an attribute role in the conceptual diagram but must be modeled as separate objects because they have their own attributes. For example, if a department depends on having a manager and staff for its existence, then that would be captured as an aggregation. If within the domain context, it were possible to have a department without a manager and staff (possibly newly created), then those relationships would be considered attributes instead of aggregations. One way to distinguish aggregation from associations is to write a definition of the domain concept. The terms needed to define the concept are in an aggregation relationship, and the other relationships are probably associations.

An example illustrates the process. In molecular biology, filter hybridization experiments consist of probing a piece of DNA (called a probe) against another piece of DNA (called the target) that is immobilized on a filter (a piece of tightly woven cloth). If the two pieces of DNA are suitably close inverses of each other, they will stick together (hybridize) under appropriate conditions. This can be used to identify an unknown piece of DNA (the probe) by comparing it with lots of pieces of known DNA (the targets on the filter). In this experiment, the probe and filter are aggregations because the experiment cannot exist without them, while the name of the person who did the experiment would be an association because the experiment could be described without knowing the person who performed the experiment. In practice, beware of any lengthy discussion about the semantics of domain objects, which can become quite involved, because only a pragmatic definition sufficient to capture the domain for a specific software product is required.

A graph conceptual schema for the filter hybridization example is shown in Figure 2–15. More specific cardinality constraints may be defined as shown in Figure 2–16 (which is identical with Figure 2–15 except for three cardinality constraints). From the conceptual schema, the peripheral concepts are dropped to create a domain object diagram in Figure 2–17. From the aggregation relationships, the aggregation tree in Figure 2–18 can be created. For example, the "probe," "filter," and "hybridization" concepts are essential for the existence of the (filter hybridization) experiment, but the "investigator" is not essential and is thus not part of the aggregation: The

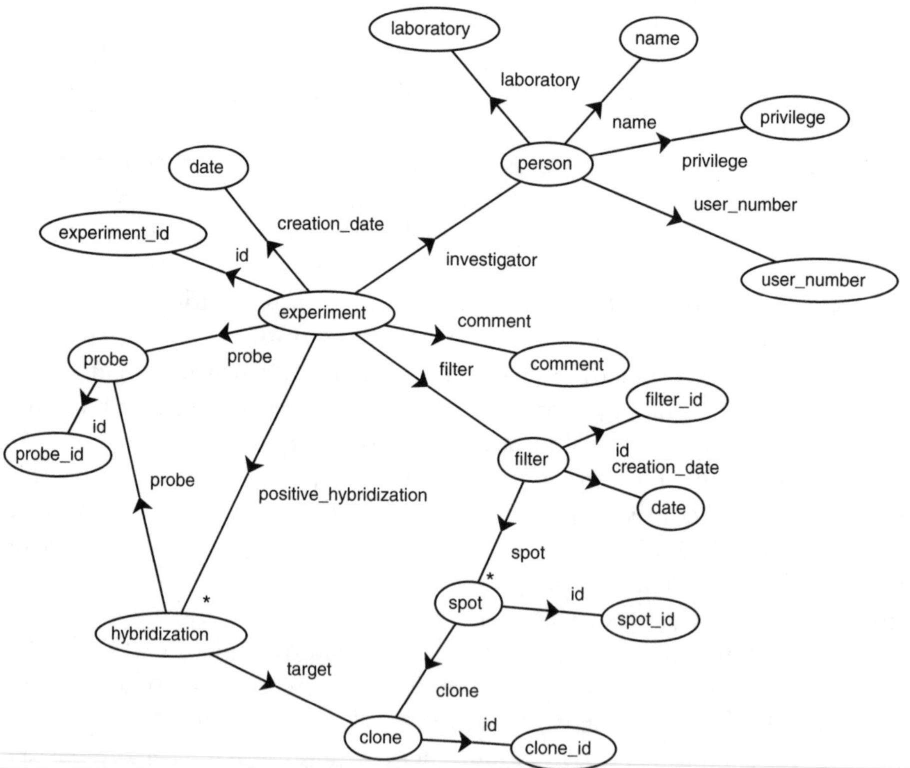

Figure 2–15 Filter hybridization graph conceptual schema

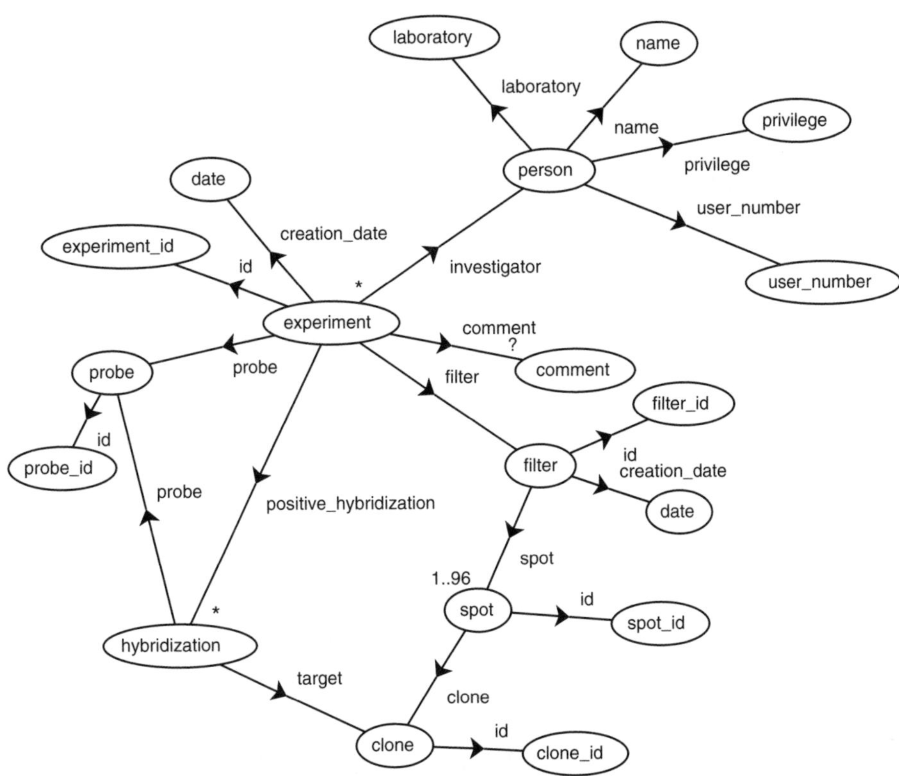

Figure 2–16 Filter hybridization schema with cardinality constraints

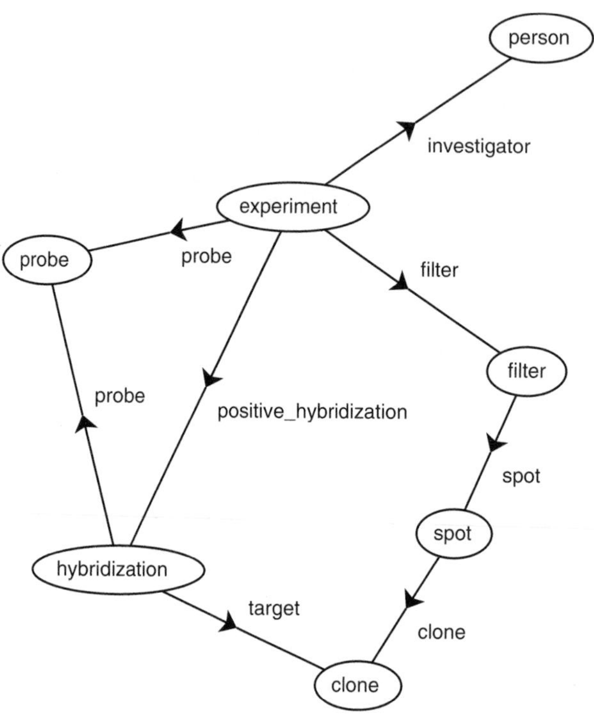

Figure 2–17 Domain object diagram for filter hybridization experiment

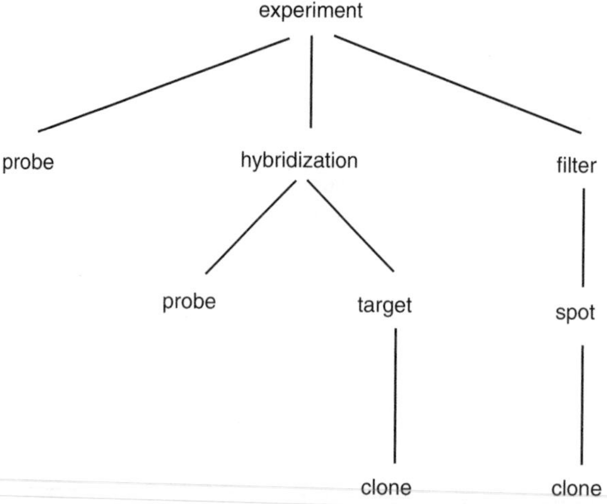

Figure 2–18 Aggregation tree for filter hybridization experiment

experiment could exist in the domain without the investigator known, but the experiment information would be incomplete without the reagents (probe and target) or results (hybridization).

From drawing the conceptual diagram, cardinality information, domain object diagram, and aggregation tree, many of the decisions needed for an object model have been made. These decisions can be captured in a modeling language for objects such as Unified Modeling Language (UML), and the preliminary diagram can then be refined based on principles of good object-oriented development. A UML diagram for filter hybridization is given in Figure 2–19.

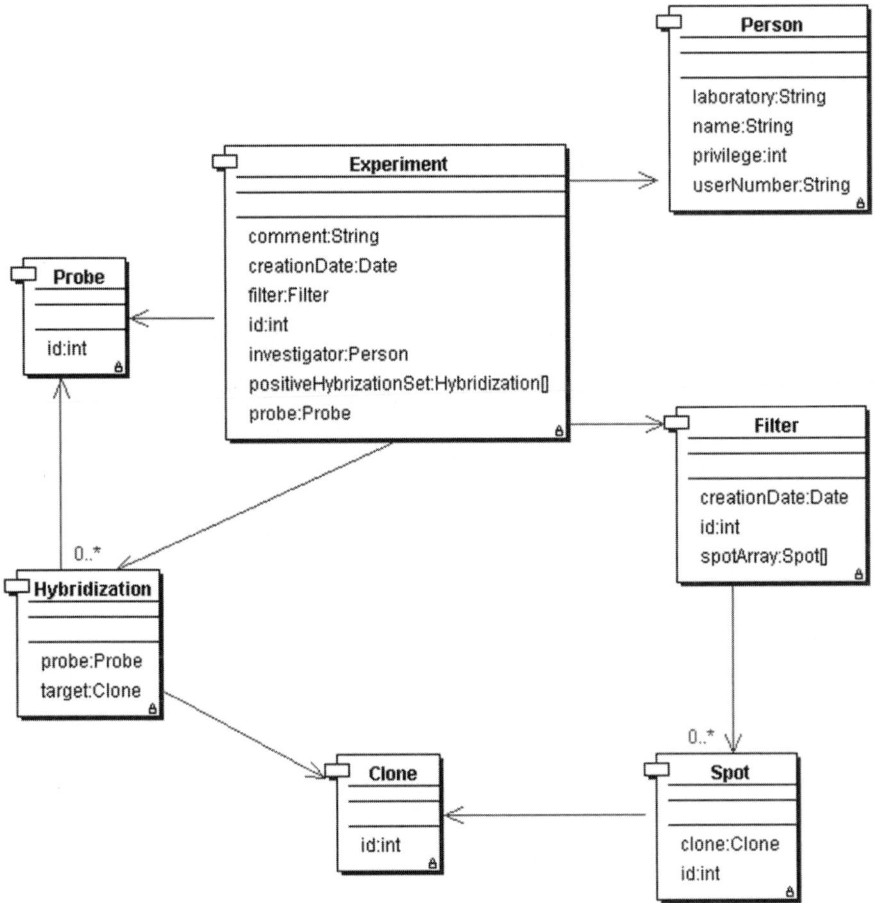

Figure 2–19 UML diagram for filter hybridization experiment

UML is a standard way to draw diagrams of object-oriented designs. It was derived from three earlier object-oriented design methodologies by the developer of those methodologies to combine the strengths of each approach and was standardized by Object Modeling Group (OMG). In this book, only the class diagrams from UML are used. Those diagrams present the name of a class, its attributes, and operations. The diagram also shows relationships between instances of classes (called associations), cardinality constraints on those associations, and generalizations (inheritance relationships). The associations are diagrammed with a simple arrowhead and the generalizations are diagrammed with an open triangle arrowhead. (The embedded rectangle and lock icons are artifacts of the software I used to draw the diagrams and are not part of UML.)

It is also possible to use the graph conceptual modeling within an existing object framework. Use rectangular boxes labeled with the names of existing objects as part of the conceptual modeling process. The graph/object hybrid modeling can then continue making use of existing objects where appropriate.

2.3.4 XML Logical Schema

Unfortunately, there is not an accepted schema language for modeling XML at the logical design level. The language for Document Type Definition (DTD) and XML Schema Definition Language (XSDL) are more suited for physical design and are described in Section 2.4.1. However, those document type or document schema definitions can be created from the process described as follows. In creating an XML logical schema, you may want to use the diagrams from the object modeling process of the previous section: conceptual diagram, cardinality information, domain object diagram, and aggregation tree. Three alternatives to representing an XML logical schema are presented later.

An XML logical schema can be created from a graph conceptual schema through the following steps.

- Each node becomes an element type with the same name.
- When a characteristic refers to a concept with no protruding edges (or exactly one identifying characteristic, such as "Name"), it may be either an attribute or a subelement type. If a characteristic depends on the concept for its existence in the domain and has cardinality 1:1 or Many:1, it becomes an

> attribute. Otherwise, it becomes a subelement. For example, in the Rolodex domain (from Figure 2–3), "Name", "Email", and "Phone Number" become attributes, and "Company" becomes a subelement. If more detail is later added to the domain, then subelements may acquire attributes or subelements.

The filter hybridization example from Figure 2–15, can be translated into a schema definition using XML, as shown in Example 2–4. The empty elements and attributes denote unrestricted values. Note that this schema uses an "empty" XML document to describe a collection of documents that include that form. A more informative schema is given in Example 2–5 based on the syntax of XSDL, but more readable. Example 2–6 is a hybrid approach of the two examples using XML Namespaces to augment the empty document with type information, much as XSL adds processing instructions to a template. Any one of the three may be useful in different database designs.

Example 2–4 : Filter Hybridization Example Represented as Empty XML

```
<experiment id="" creation_date="" comment="">
  <investigator>
    <person name="" privilege="" user_number="">
      <laboratory/>
    </person>
  </investigator>
  <probe id=""/>
  <filter id="" creation_date="">
    <spot id="">
      <clone id=""/>
    </spot>
  </filter>
  <positive_hybridization>
    <hybridization>
      <probe/>
      <target>
        <clone/>
      </target>
    </hybridization>
  </positive_hybridization>
</experiment>
```

Example 2–5 : Filter Hybridization Example Represented Using XML Elements

```
<?xml version="1.0"?>
<schema>
  <element name="experiment">
      <element name="investigator">
          <element name="person">
              <element name="laboratory"/>
              <attribute name="id"/>
              <attribute name="creation_date" type="date"/>
              <attribute name="comment" minOccurs="0"/>
          </element>
      </element>
      <element name="probe">
          <attribute name="id" type="string"/>
      </element>
      <element name="filter">
          <element name="spot" minOccurs="1" maxOccurs="96">
              <element name="clone">
                  <attribute name="id"/>
              </element>
              <attribute name="id"/>
          </element>
          <attribute name="id"/>
          <attribute name="creation_date" type="date"/>
      </element>
      <element name="positive_hybridization">
          <element name="hybridization" maxOccurs="unbounded">
              <element name="probe"/>
              <element name="target">
                  <element name="clone"/>
              </element>
          </element>
      </element>
  </element>
</schema>
```

Example 2–6 : Filter Hybridization Example Represented as Empty XML with Attributes

```
<?xml version="1.0"?>
<schema xmlns:xs="http://www.xweave.com/xmlns/xmldb/xs1">
  <experiment>
      <investigator>
          <person>
              <xs:attribute name="id"/>
              <xs:attribute name="creation_date" type="date"/>
              <xs:attribute name="comment" minOccurs="0"/>
              <laboratory/>
          </person>
      </investigator>
      <probe>
          <xs:attribute name="id"/>
      </probe>
      <filter>
          <xs:attribute name="id"/>
          <xs:attribute name="creation_date" type="date"/>
          <spot xs:minOccurs="1" xs:maxOccurs="96">
              <xs:attribute name="id"/>
              <clone>
                  <xs:attribute name="id"/>
              </clone>
          </spot>
      </filter>
      <positive_hybridization>
          <hybridization xs:maxOccurs="unbounded">
              <probe/>
              <target>
                  <clone/>
              </target>
          </hybridization>
      </positive_hybridization>
  </experiment>
</schema>
```

In physical modeling, some of the choices for attributes and subelements may change. For example, attributes whose values contain characters not valid for attribute values could become subelements and encapsulated in a CDATA section, which avoids parsing errors by escaping those characters. Additionally, subelements that are simple and do not require independent existence may become attributes.

2.4 Physical Modeling

Physical design is the process of efficiently capturing the schema of the general logical data model into the constructs of the implementation language associated with the DBMS used. For example, a relational schema might denote an EMPLOYEE relation with attributes NAME (a string) and EMPLOYEE_NUMBER (a number). The corresponding physical schema might describe the EMPLOYEE table as having two columns: NAME (a unique string of varying length less than 30 characters) and EMPLOYEE_NUMBER (a number with exactly 4 digits in the range 1000 to 3999). Each stage in the design process incrementally incorporates additional domain knowledge and business rules as appropriate for the modeling language.

Physical modeling captures the practical aspects of the design. A variety of factors influence the physical design, including size of data, security, likely access patterns, susceptibility to change, possibility for reuse, and required speed of access. In addition to the issues that arise in database physical modeling, additional issues arise in creating a physical schema for XML that will be used for a database and data exchange. How will the design affect the transport of data using XML? What are standards that may be applicable? How will choices in the database schema affect applications? Are there limitations imposed by the desire to have the XML viewable through Web browsers? Do additional notations (data formats) exist that need to be embedded in the XML for efficiency or compatibility with existing systems?

In addition to the structural decisions about the data, there are additional decisions to be made about incorporating text into the database. Does text occur only as parsed character data in an element (data-processing-oriented view), or is unparsed text (consisting of data interspersed with markup) stored (document-processing-oriented view)?

Four questions regarding physical design are described in the next four subsections.

- Is an XML physical schema required? If so, what language is used to describe it?
- Is the document more data-processing-oriented (like a database) or more document-processing-oriented (like a document intended for publication)?

- How can the document be designed to improve processing space and time performance?
- Does information tend to be represented as attributes or as elements?

2.4.1 XML Physical Schema

One choice that you need to make in physical design is to decide whether to explicitly define a schema as part of the XML document and what mechanism to use to do so. Different mechanisms may be used for design, database development, and inclusion in a data document. When defining a schema in an XML DBMS, the decision is probably determined by the DBMS chosen.

The DTD notation is a part of the XML 1.0 Standard and may be used to define a schema. Using a DTD offers advantages because it may be used by current parsers. Books and resources are available on designing a DTD. However, a DTD cannot provide the level of type constraints that are typically desired for a database. For this reason, XML Schema was developed.

XML Schema is a W3C Recommendation (which is not finalized at this writing). It provides a means to specify the structure and data values that may occur in a document. Unfortunately, XML Schema was developed with the assertion that it was to be used for machine processing and that human readability was not to be considered. Thus, its schema definition language, XSDL, is useful to appropriately restrict software to a specified schema, but not to design the schema. Thus, you must use another mechanism (such as those provided earlier in the chapter) to design a schema. After you design a schema, you may create a physical schema definition in XSDL for a database (as discussed in Section 3.1.1).

The filter hybridization example of Section 2.3.3 is translated into a DTD in Example 2–7 and into an XSDL schema in Example 2–8.

A third possible schema choice is to not specify a schema as part of the document. The primary use of the schema is to validate the content of the document. If application-specific mechanisms are used to ensure document validity, the validation may be an unnecessary overhead. One philosophy is that robust system design requires that validation be performed between system components, and XML document parsing typically will take place at component boundaries. Another philosophy is that document validation does not provide a sufficient increase in robustness given its cost (possibly 20% additional parsing time).

Example 2–7 : Filter Hybridization Example Represented in XML DTD

```
<!ELEMENT experiment (investigator, probe, filter,
positive_hybridization*)>
<!-- many posititive_hybridization are possible -->
<!ATTLIST experiment
  id       CDATA #REQUIRED
  creation_date CDATA #REQUIRED
  comment       CDATA #IMPLIED>  <!-- comment is optional -->
<!ELEMENT investigator (person)>
<!ELEMENT person (laboratory)>
<!ATTLIST person
  name     CDATA #REQUIRED
  privilege CDATA #REQUIRED
  user_number CDATA #REQUIRED>
<!ELEMENT laboratory ANY>
<!ELEMENT probe EMPTY>
<!ATTLIST probe
  id       CDATA #REQUIRED>
<!ELEMENT filter (spot*)> <!-- a filter has many spots -->
<!ATTLIST filter
  id       CDATA #REQUIRED
  creation_date CDATA #REQUIRED>
<!ELEMENT spot (clone)>
<!ATTLIST spot
  id       CDATA #REQUIRED>
<!ELEMENT clone EMPTY>
<!ATTLIST clone
  id       CDATA #REQUIRED>
<!ELEMENT positive_hybridization (hybridization)>
<!ELEMENT hybridization (probe, target)>
<!ELEMENT target (clone)>
```

Example 2–8 : Filter Hybridization Example Represented in XML Schema

```
<schema>
<!-- clone and probe are used more than once, so they need named types -->
<complexType name="cloneType">
  <attribute name="id" type="string"/>
</complexType>
<complexType name="probeType">
  <attribute name="id" type="string"/>
</complexType>
<element name="experiment">
```

```
<complexType>
  <sequence>
    <element name="investigator">
      <complexType>
        <sequence>
        <element name="person">
          <complexType>
            <sequence>
            <element name="laboratory">
              <complexType>
                <any/>
              </complexType>
            </element>
            </sequence>
            <attribute name="id" type="string"/>
            <attribute name="creation_date" type="date"/>
            <attribute name="comment" type="string" minOccurs="0"/>
          </complexType>
        </element>
        </sequence>
      </complexType>
    </element>
    <element name="probe" type="probeType"/>
    <element name="filter">
      <complexType>
        <sequence>
        <element name="spot" minOccurs="1" maxOccurs="96">
          <complexType>
           <sequence>
            <element name="clone" type="cloneType"/>
            <attribute name="id" type="string"/>
           </sequence>
          </complexType>
        </element>
        </sequence>
        <attribute name="id" type="string"/>
        <attribute name="creation_date"  type="date"/>
      </complexType>
    </element>
    <element name="positive_hybridization">
      <complexType>
        <sequence>
        <element name="hybridization" maxOccurs="unbounded">
          <complexType>
```

```
                <sequence>
                <element name="probe" type="probeType"/>
                <element name="target">
                  <complexType>
                    <element name="clone" type="cloneType"/>
                  </complexType>
                </element>
                </sequence>
              </complexType>
            </element>
            </sequence>
          </complexType>
        </element>
      </sequence>
    </complexType>
  </element>
</schema>
```

2.4.2 Data-processing-oriented View versus Document-processing-oriented View

William Shakespeare said, "A rose by any other name would smell as sweet."

That was fine for the bard. He did not need to try to find the rose in a 4GB/sec Earth Observatory Satellite data stream. The rest of us need to organize and index.

Do we view the data as embedded somewhere within a document? Or, do we view the document as an organized representation of the data? Where is the emphasis: document or data?

In the document-processing-oriented view, a document is character data interspersed with elements. It is possible in the document-processing-oriented view to have a document with no subelements in it; this would be meaningless in the data-processing-oriented view. All the content of the document in the document-processing-oriented view is usually within the character data.

```
<author>William Shakespeare</author>said<quote>A <index
category="Shakespeare, William" subcategory="rose
quotation">rose</index> by any other name would smell as
sweet.</quote>
```

In the data-processing-oriented view, a document is a collection of "similar" elements. It is possible to have a document that consists only of empty elements; in that case, the content would be contained in the attributes of the elements; this would be meaningless in the document-processing-oriented view. Usually, elements will consist of either a collection of elements or a single character data region, in effect, there will be no interspersed character data and elements at the same level of the document tree.

```
<famousQuote author="William Shakespeare" name="rose">
  A rose by any other name would smell as sweet.
</famousQuote>
```

The advantages of the data-processing-oriented view are that it has a regular structure, is easier to access with simpler applications, and is compatible with existing DBMSs. It works well with a tight coupling to a DBMS and has more structural flexibility than most existing DBMSs. The disadvantage is that it does not capture documents with highly-irregular structure.

The advantages of the document-processing-oriented view are that it is very flexible, captures existing documents and Web pages, and is compatible with existing document processing systems. It works well with textual data that has an irregular structure, such as technical documentation, scientific literature, or newspaper articles. The disadvantage is that there is no regular structure to exploit in simplifying application development.

Usually, when existing documents must be manipulated, there is no choice which approach to take. Either there is a regular structure that may be exploited in a data-processing-oriented approach, or there is an irregular structure that must be scanned for information. When designing for a database system, the advantages of the data-processing-oriented approach for simpler, more efficient application development imply that a regular structure should be designed and a data-processing-oriented view should be chosen.

As an aside, I should clarify that text is structured in both the document-processing-oriented view and the data-processing-oriented view. Sometimes a distinction is made between the document-processing-oriented view (as unstructured text) and the data-processing-oriented view (as structured text), but it is more accurate to describe the structure in the data-processing-oriented view as having a regular structure. The text of an English paragraph, such as this one, is highly structured, and it may take an intelligent person several years to learn enough of the English grammar to determine whether a sentence is valid in the grammar and to understand it. Or not. The text of a document designed for data processing typically has a much more regular structure, with less variation and fewer rules necessary to parse the document unambiguously at a level to capture the structural (grammatical) relationships. There are operations that ignore the irregular structure of a document-processing-oriented document and impose a much simpler regular structure, such as copying the text to another document by treating the document as a sequence of characters, but those same operations can also be used on a data-processing-oriented document without capturing its structure.

There are no hard and fast rules of when a document fits within the data-processing-oriented approach, as it does depend upon the type of operations required. Following are some guidelines for when a document can be usefully accessed using a data-processing-oriented approach (and thus managed using a database).

- A relatively simple parser for the document can map the content to an appropriate data structure for the application.
- Every piece of data uniquely processed by the application is uniquely identified in the structure of the document. For example, a document describing the content of a spreadsheet would uniquely label each cell (or identify it by the document structure), but a document managed by a word processor would not uniquely label each word.
- All elements in a document consist of either a sequence of subelements or a character data region, but there is no mixed content.
- There are a small number of element types that have mixed content, and they fit within the previous guideline. For example, all the elements in a document fit within a regular hierarchy except for those contained within the "comment" element type.
- There are a large number of documents that have the same element hierarchy to some level in the hierarchy. For example, some of the elements are data-processing-oriented, even if the entire document is not. Even document-processing-oriented documents may be usefully accessed though data-processing-oriented operations if there are enough of them. For example, a database of all Web pages at some site with the fields: "title", "URL", and "body".

In this book, I use a data-processing-oriented approach. If existing document-processing-oriented documents must be captured and stored in the database, preprocessing may be used to extract a regular structure from the text. Preprocessing may range from simply wrapping a couple of tags around text to a complex natural language processing system that parses the text and extracts records containing the information. Albeit very interesting, preprocessing text to extract data for a database is outside the scope of this book.

2.4.3 Data Transport

A big advantage of using XML is that it can be used to transport data as well as store it. Unlike relations, objects, spreadsheets, and other data-processing-oriented storage mechanisms, XML does not need a special serialization process to transfer the data and its relationships. However, it is a good idea to minimize the translation needed between the XML database schema and the XML data transport schema when possible. There are several places where considering the full impact of a design decision can improve the overall performance of the system, while retaining a clean design.

A big disadvantage of using XML for data transport is that the tags in the document take up space. When the data in the document has a fixed, regular structure, the tags are redundant. In Example 2–9, the tags in the document account for 85% of the character space, with only 15% of the document being the data.

Decreasing the size of the data improves performance during transport to an application, reduces storage space necessary within the database, reduces time in retrieving a document or query result from a database, increases responsiveness in user applications that parse the data, and reduces memory necessary for applications and servers. The disadvantages to decreasing the size of data are that development time is spent on the task that may best be spent elsewhere; that unless the data is large, performance may not be noticeably improved; that the document may become cryptic leading to mistakes or increased time in future development or maintenance; and that the schema may become overly rigid and unable to adapt. During initial development, it is usually best to delay optimizations until the system is stable and then prioritize the optimizations.

One way to reduce the size of the data is to use short, but meaningful element type names. In much older systems, severe size and space limitations often drastically impacted the ability to create meaningful names. That limi-

Example 2–9 : XML File with Regular Structure

```
<?xml version="1.0"?>
<colors>
  <color name="Black" red="0" green="0" blue="0"/>
  <color name="Silver" red="C" green="C" blue="C"/>
  <color name="Gray" red="8" green="8" blue="8"/>
  <color name="White" red="F" green="F" blue="F"/>
  <color name="Maroon" red="8" green="0" blue="0"/>
  <color name="Red" red="F" green="0" blue="0"/>
  <color name="Purple" red="8" green="0" blue="8"/>
  <color name="Fuchsia" red="F" green="0" blue="F"/>
  <color name="Green" red="0" green="8" blue="0"/>
  <color name="Lime" red="0" green="F" blue="0"/>
  <color name="Olive" red="8" green="8" blue="0"/>
  <color name="Yellow" red="F" green="F" blue="0"/>
  <color name="Navy" red="0" green="0" blue="8"/>
  <color name="Blue" red="0" green="0" blue="F"/>
  <color name="Teal" red="0" green="8" blue="8"/>
  <color name="Aqua" red="0" green="F" blue="F"/>
</colors>
```

tation has been greatly relaxed, and programmers were encouraged to give up their old habits and create meaningful names. Then an overcompensation began, with programmers using 20–30 character variable names in short programs. The balance is to find short, meaningful element type names that can be easily understood but do not needlessly clutter the document. Similarly, weather reports were historically sent over very slow teletypes and very cryptic notations were developed to increase the amount of information transferred per unit time. For example, consider the somewhat cryptic phrase in a weather report for airplane pilots: "TSTMS IMPLY PSBL SVR OR GTR TURBC SVR ICG AND LLWS." Passengers in the airplane might prefer that the pilot receive something like "Danger!!! Danger!!! Thunderstorms imply possible severe or greater turbulence, severe icing, and low-level wind shears. Ignore this warning and your plane will be ripped into pieces, your wings will no longer work, and you will not be able to land safely." But with sufficient training, airplane pilots would probably be comfortable with "Warning: Thunderstorms imply possible severe or greater turbulence, severe icing, and low-level wind shears." You should develop element type names similarly with appropriate clarity. For example, instead of "<amtpu>" or "<amount_of_plutonium_in_shipment>" use "<amount_plutonium>".

Another way to reduce the size of the data is to use attributes instead of elements when clear that attributes would work, for example, when the value will never have a structure and will always be a string that does not require a CDATA section.

In addition to reducing the size of the data by modifying the document, the size of the transported document may be reduced by using data compression algorithms. An efficient compression algorithm over a slow network may decrease the overall time by compressing and uncompressing the document in less time than would otherwise be needed to transport the uncompressed document.

One way to increase parsing efficiency is to annotate the document. For example, recording the size of a collection as an attribute would simplify creation of an array to store items. However, for a large collection whose size is not previously known, creating the collection may be more complicated because items, or their XML descriptions, may need to be stored temporarily to count the items before emitting the size attribute and XML descriptions of the items.

Another way to increase parsing efficiency is to be aware of information dependencies in the data, especially with Simple API for XML (SAX) parsers. Placing information into the data stream before items that would depend on them for creation simplifies developing parsers, when those relationships can be formalized. SAX parsers are described in Appendix B. For example, when transporting a hierarchical collection of items, placing parent items consistently before child items can substantially reduce the time needed to recreate the hierarchy.

Most optimizations are best performed after you obtain experience with the applications, but careful planning in the design of optimizations, when appropriate, can drastically improve application performance and acceptance.

2.4.4 Attribute versus Embedded Element Tradeoff

When should information be encoded as attributes and when should an embedded element (subelement) be created? A variety of factors may influence the decision including personal preference and style. A simple example is:

- <book title="Call of the Wild" author="Jack London"/>
- <book><title>Call of the Wild</title><author>Jack London</author></book>

In the first, the *attribute-oriented* approach, all content is contained in the attributes that can be, no unnecessary elements are created, and the cardinality relationship that a book has one title and one author is made explicit (even if not necessarily true).

In the second the, *element-oriented* approach, all content is in the elements and maximum flexibility is achieved.

In particular circumstances, any of the following may also be appropriate:

- <book author="Jack London">Call of the Wild</book>
- <book author="Jack London><title>Call of the Wild</title></ book>
- <book title="Call of the Wild"><author>Jack London</ author></book>
- <book><title>Call of the Wild</title><author><firstName> Jack</firstName><lastName>London</lastName></author> </book>

2.4.4.1 Philosophies

Underlying the approaches are different philosophies about the purpose of the attributes.

The attribute-oriented approach uses attributes where possible. It makes the document easier to understand and can make applications more efficient. The attribute is simpler than the embedded element and may provide additional information, such as constraints on cardinality and data type. The attribute name also provides a mechanism to make explicit the role of the content within the context of the element.

The element-oriented approach uses elements for all content. Attributes are used only for meta-data and possibly annotations on the content. Meta-data are data about the content (e.g., the source of the data or its database unique identifier) that provide no additional information that is not already included (in some form) within the data. Annotations on a database are similar to footnotes in a text publication. Annotations expand the information contained by the content, but are not inherent in it (e.g., the content is derived from or similar to some other referenced content). Attributes may also be used for presentation information, such as the language the content is in or that the content is central to the document and should be included in a summary. This approach is particularly useful if the document should make sense with all markup removed.

A moderate approach is to use attributes for particular aspects of content, such as properties or intrinsic characteristics. Attributes may be used when the information is an integral part of the object represented by the element type, and embedded elements are used when the object it represents has an independent existence—for example, attributes are properties of the object, not parts or children of the object being modeled. Attributes may also contain control information, such as names or unique identifiers, for which it would be useful to obtain without iterating over the embedded elements.

At the risk of overly simplifying fundamental differences in design styles, the attribute-oriented practitioner views the attributes *practically* as an efficient mechanism to capture the same information that would be captured in elements. The element-oriented practitioner views the attributes and elements as *fundamentally* containing two types of information—markup and content, respectively—that should be kept separate. Either approach may be more appropriate in specific applications, and software that manipulates XML data should support either approach.

2.4.4.2 Primary Considerations

There are some characteristics of attributes and elements that suggest which should be used regardless of the approach chosen.

- Attributes provide minimal data type validation.
- Elements provide constraints on the structural content of the data items.
- Elements provide embedded structure. If the data item requires structure, then elements are the only choice. If the data item may require structure later, then elements are a better choice.
- Elements may have multiple values, and attributes are restricted to one value. Elements must be used if a collection of values is possible.
- Elements may be reference through a link. Thus, if the content may be *shared* between documents or document fragments, it should be captured in an element.
- Elements preserve white space.
- Attributes may have default values, when using a DTD.
- Elements are more convenient for large values or binary entities.

- Elements can contain quotes more easily.
- Unique identifiers for a data item are typically put in attributes.

2.4.4.3 Secondary Considerations

In addition to decisions based on the design philosophy and considerations of the content, there are considerations about the *use* of the document that may also bias the attribute-versus-embedded-element decision. Some of these secondary considerations are:

- The resulting file size may influence the decision. When large documents are used, attributes are preferable because they do not require an end tag and thus use less space.
- Attributes may be easier to access within the processing framework. In XML parsers for example, the attributes are immediately available within the context of the element.
- The processing speed may be faster for attributes in some applications. Typically, attributes may be accessed faster than the embedded elements because attribute processing does not require iterative (and recursive) processing but embedded elements do.
- The resulting application may treat elements and attributes differently. For example, the application may have assumed an element-oriented design philosophy and treat the elements as containing all the content and treating it with specialized processing.

2.5 Bibliographic Remarks

Wirfs-Brock, Wilkerson, and Wiener (1990) describes a process of object-modeling by writing a paragraph description of the domain and selecting the nouns. Developing simple sentences to describe binary relationships between concepts is also used in the NIAM (Nijssen's Information Analysis Methodology) data model.

Translating an entity-relation diagram to a relational database is described in Teorey (1994).

Conceptual modeling is introduced and described in Brodie (1984). It is related to domain analysis from software engineering, where aspects of the domain are modeled for use in multiple software applications (Prieto-Diaz & Guillermo, 1991).

Megginson (1998) describes creating DTDs.

I write about creating data models of new domains in Graves (1993).

2.5.1 References

Brodie, M. (1984). *On conceptual modelling: Perspectives from artificial intelligence, databases, and programming languages,* Springer-Verlag, New York.

Graves, M. (1993). *Theories and tools for designing application-specific knowledge base data models,* University of Michigan PhD dissertation, University Microfilms.

Megginson, D. (1998). *Structuring XML documents,* Prentice-Hall, Upper Saddle River, NJ.

Prieto-Díaz, R., & Guillermo, A. (1991). *Domain analysis and software systems modeling,* IEEE Computer Society Press, Los Alamitos, CA.

Teorey, T. (1994). *Database modeling & design* (2nd ed.), Morgan Kaufmann, San Francisco.

Wirfs-Brock, R., Wilkerson, B., & Wiener, L. (1990). *Designing object-oriented software,* Prentice-Hall, Upper Saddle River, NJ.

Theoretical Foundations

- How can I store all this XML data other than as a bunch of XML documents?
- How do users and applications access the data?
- What representations do I use? What do they look like?

3

For XML data to be stored in a DBMS, the type of data and the requirements it places on a DBMS must be clarified. This clarification forms the theoretical foundation of an XML DBMS. These theoretical foundations are explored in this chapter. Particular emphasis is placed on the foundational types and operations that an XML DBMS needs to support and how to model XML data using existing technologies.

First data types are defined, then a description of DBMSs is given in Section 3.2. Section 3.3 provides an overview of XML standards, and Section 3.4 begins providing the requirements for an XML DBMS. Section 3.5 is the bulk of the chapter: it describes data modeling and presents six possible data models for an XML DBMS.

3.1 Data Types

A *data type* is a set of values with operations on those values. For example, the "Number" data type consists of (a) the set of numbers—often within some range—and (b) operations on those numbers, such as addition, subtraction, multiplication, and division. Most programming languages have several data types. Some programming languages, such as C, have a collection of fixed data types, and proper use of those types is enforced through type constraints by the compiler. Object-oriented languages, such as Java, have an extensible collection of data types (called objects), a way to create new types (called class creation), a way to add operations to the types (called methods), and a programming language construct to create one type from another type (called inheritance). *Objects* can be defined as data types with inheritance.

A DBMS can be viewed as a system to manage the values of particular data types. A relational DBMS usually has relation, number, and string data types. There are the typical operations on numbers and strings, and the relation has operations for creating, selecting particular relationships based on their constituents, inserting relationships, deleting relationships, and so on. An XML DBMS has data types for elements, attributes, character data, and so on. An object-oriented DBMS has an extensible collection of data types with inheritance.

When a programming language is used to manipulate the data in a database, the process is easier when the programming language and database share data types than when they do not. Manipulating objects from an object-oriented database is easier in programming languages—such as C++ or Java—that have objects, than manipulating relations from a relational DBMS in those languages, because they do not have a relation data type in the language. This incompatibility between data types in a DBMS and in a programming language is called *impedance mismatch.*

One way to reduce the impedance mismatch is to modify the programming language by adding a relation data type to it (for example, adding a generic "Relation" object to Java with select, insert, and delete operations that automatically mirror the value in the data type). Additional data types (helper objects) would also be needed to capture the individual relationships of a relation.

A second way to reduce the impedance mismatch is to create a database-specific mapping from each member of a data type in the database to members of the closest data type in the programming language. For example, an individual relationship in a relational database may be mapped to a different "struct" in C or a specific class in Java. Although there is no generic mapping from the Relation data type in a database to the programming language, each relation in a database can be individually mapped.

Okay, but what about XML?

In a structured language, such as XML, it is useful to distinguish between the data typing of character data, such as strings and numbers, and the data typing of structure, such as what element type name or attribute is valid within the context of a specific element.

The values of XML are untyped, which means they can be any string. A DTD may be associated with a document to restrict the document's structure of elements and attributes. XSDL provides a mechanism to *specify* both the structure of the document and the data type of the values. In addition to the data type definitions defined as part of XSDL, it may be useful to have an understanding of data type structures and how they can *emerge* from a tagged data type, such as XML elements. Because XML data has a relatively rich structure, it is also possible to derive unnamed (and unspecified) types from the structure. This alternative approach can be useful to integrate the physical schema developed for an XML database and the data types of other components of the system, such as object-oriented applications.

3.1.1 XML Schema

The XML Schema standard provides a framework to define the data types used in XML. Without the data types, there is no standard way to describe constraints on valid data. For example, data types provide a way to distinguish that 1, 2, 3 are valid numbers and "a green tree" is not. In a document, "fourscore and seven" will probably be interpreted as a number when read by a human, but will probably not when read by a database application. Data types provide a framework to distinguish the valid values that may occur in a specific context.

Data types may be built-in or specified as part of the schema. Built-in data types provide for commonly used value spaces, such as strings, numbers, integer, decimal, boolean, date, time, time instance, time duration, or binary. User-defined data types are specified as part of the schema and may be further restrictions of the built-in types, such as a range of numbers or an explicitly enumerated list of strings. XML Schema's definition language, XSDL, provides several mechanisms for deriving new types by restricting existing (built-in or derived) types, such as strings of exactly n characters, strings of less than n characters, strings that match a regular expression, numbers that are greater than n, numbers less than n, numbers greater than or equal to n, or numbers less than or equal to n.

XSDL defines the types of elements and attributes in XML using elements with type names "element" and "attribute". For example, the following fragment may be represented in a schema:

```
<email from="" to="" subject="" date="">body</email>
```

This could be represented as:

```
<element name="email">
  <attribute name="from"/>
  <attribute name="to"/>
  <attribute name="subject"/>
  <attribute name="date" type="date"/>
</element>
```

In addition to the data types imposed on the character data values that occur *within* elements and attributes, there are additional structural restrictions imposed *on* the elements that may occur in a specific context and restrictions on the attributes and subelements that they may contain. Fairly complex constraints can be imagined, and although they are limited in the database implementation to the specification of XSDL, additional constraints may be specified as part of the project documentation and enforced procedurally as part of the database, application, or middle tier.

The decision whether to use XSDL or DTDs (or neither) depends upon the applications being developed and what is required by the DBMS. DTDs provide a mechanism for the receiving application or database of the XML document to understand what the structure of the document should look like. The receiver may wish to use that information to validate that the document does meet the type definition of the DTD and was not corrupted, or the receiver may use that information to allocate data structures for processing. However, the receiver may already know the structure or not care what the structure is. For example, the structure may be already specified or hard-coded into the application, or the receiver may examine the content of the document body without respect to the type definition. In those cases, a DTD is probably not necessary.

XSDL provides a mechanism to specify both the structure and data types of a document. Again, the receiver may need that information, already have it, or not care.

3.1.2 Emerging Structural Data Types

The data types of XML have more structural flexibility than the types of most programming languages. Elements may be manipulated by adding embedded elements, character data, or attributes, while objects do not allow for adding instance variables at run time, for example. Programming languages centered around the "List" data type, such as Lisp or Tcl/Tk, provide an easy mapping from elements to lists, but the mapping is not clean, because of the need to capture tag names and attributes and to distinguish elements from character data.

Usually the simplest mapping from XML to a programming language is to create a generic "Element" data type and map all elements to it. The "Element" data type can be created as a class in an object-oriented language or mimicked using data structures of a programming language without extensible data types. The "Element" data type would have operations for adding subelements, retrieving attribute values, and so on. This approach is the simpler mapping, but all subsequent programming must deal with the intricacies of the XML data type operations instead of directly with the properties of the XML element.

For example, consider searching XML documents from various vendors to purchase a car over the Web. After all the information is mapped into the "Element" objects, your program would need to walk through the objects looking for "automobile" elements with appropriate "make" and "model" attributes—possibly verifying certain features by examining subelements—before extracting the character data from the "price" element.

What is desirable would be to extract the information and map it to an "Automobile" object that collects only information about desired features, then iterates over the collection of objects finding the one with the lowest price. Although the mapping is more complex, the resulting programs will be simpler. As always there are tradeoffs, and the best approach depends upon whether you are purchasing one car for yourself or developing an automobile purchasing system. The extraction of an object from a complex XML element is described in the next section and the mapping from documents to a generic "Element" type is described in detail in the remainder of the chapter.

3.1.3 Schema-driven Applications

There are two steps to developing an object as a view on the XML data. The first step is to simplify the structure of the XML to fit the record-oriented structure of an object. The second step is to develop the appropriate access methods on the object.

The structure is simplified by creating a set of mapping rules from the tree-oriented XML structure to the locally flat record structure of the object. *Mapping rules* describe how the elements and attributes of an XML document are used to create the fields of an object (and vice versa). By defining a list of mapping rules between XML documents and objects, generic code can be used to automatically create objects in an application from an XML document or to generate an XML document from the data objects in an application. A table of paths mapping the structure of Example 3–1 to the object fields of Example 3–2 is given in Table 3–1 using paths as specified by the XML Path Specification, where "@" denotes an attribute, "[]" denotes a constraint on the path, and "/*" denotes all the subelements of an element.

Example 3–1 : Automobile Example Document

```
<?xml version="1.0"?>
<automobile make="Toyota" model="Corolla" year="2001">
   <price>12489</price>
   <color>black</color>
   <feature category="radio">AM/FM/CD 4 speakers</feature>
   <feature category="doors">3-door hatchback</feature>
   <feature>4 cup holders</feature>
</automobile>
```

Example 3–2 : Automobile Object Specification

```
Automobile
   make      String,
   model     String,
   year      String,
   price     Number,
   color     String,
   radio     String,
   features  StringSet;
```

Table 3–1 Mapping from Automobile XML Document to Object Fields

Field	*Path*
make	@make
model	@model
year	@year
price	price

Table 3–1 Mapping from Automobile XML Document to Object Fields (continued)

color	color
radio	feature[category="radio"]
features (collection)	feature/*

The next step is to create access methods for the object fields, taking into account the cardinality of the fields and any helper objects needed. For example, the "feature" field of the "Automobile" object is a collection of features not included in previous fields and may be implemented using a generic collection object.

In more complex examples, a collection of objects may be necessary. Mapping rules may be created for each object. For example, suppose a collection of "automobile" elements were embedded in a "dealer" element with a "name" attribute and a "contact" embedded element, as in Example 3–3.

Example 3–3 : Automobile Dealer Example Document

```
<?xml version="1.0"?>
<dealer name="Honest Abe">
  <contact>
     <address>13 Automobile Way</address>
     <phone>800-555-1234</phone>
  </contact>
  <automobile make="Toyota" model="Corolla" year="2001">
     <price>12489</price>
     <color>black</color>
     <feature category="radio">AM/FM/CD 4 speakers</feature>
     <feature category="doors">3-door hatchback</feature>
     <feature>4 cup holders</feature>
  </automobile>
  <automobile make="Toyota" model="Celica" year="2003">
     <price>19995</price>
     <color>tan</color>
     <feature category="radio">AM/FM/CD 4 speakers</feature>
     <feature category="doors">2-door</feature>
  </automobile>
</dealer>
```

A "Dealer" object would be created from that element, as shown in Example 3–4. Each "Automobile" object would refer to that "Dealer" object. To simplify the specification of an object from a document, a base path may be specified for an object and a relative path from that base path for each field. The mapping rules are given in Table 3–2, where ".." denotes the parent element, as in the XML Path Specification.

Example 3–4 : Automobile Dealer Object Specification

```
Dealer
   name        String,
   address     String,
   phone       String,
   automobiles Set of Automobiles;
```

Table 3–2 Mapping from Automobile Dealer XML Document to Object Fields

Object	*Base Path for Object*	*Field in Object*	*Relative Path from Base*
Dealer	dealer	name	@name
Dealer	dealer	address	contact/address
Dealer	dealer	phone	contact/phone
Dealer	dealer	automobiles (collection)	automobile/*
Automobile	dealer/automobile	dealer	..
Automobile	dealer/automobile	make	@make
Automobile	dealer/automobile	model	@model
Automobile	dealer/automobile	year	@year
Automobile	dealer/automobile	price	price
Automobile	dealer/automobile	color	color
Automobile	dealer/automobile	radio	feature[category="radio"]
Automobile	dealer/automobile	features (collection)	feature/*

In developing the mapping rules for a collection of objects, the target of the rules may overlap. For example, the "Dealer" object may also track the makes for which it has automobiles, in which case the mapping rules for both "Dealer" and "Automobile" would refer to the "make" attribute of the "automobile" element. This would require a mapping rule from dealer "make" to "automobile/@make" as shown in Figure 3–1.

Mapping rules may be implemented in several ways. One way is to write an application that uses an XML parser to parse the XML and create the objects during parsing. Another way is to use XSL style sheets to implement the mapping rules. In using the style sheets, the elements may be rewritten into a specific (simpler) element, which can then be used by a more generic application to create the objects. It is also possible to combine the two steps by creating XSL style sheets that emit one of the following: code in a programming language to create the objects, an object creation specification in a specification language such as IDL, or an object creation specification in XML.

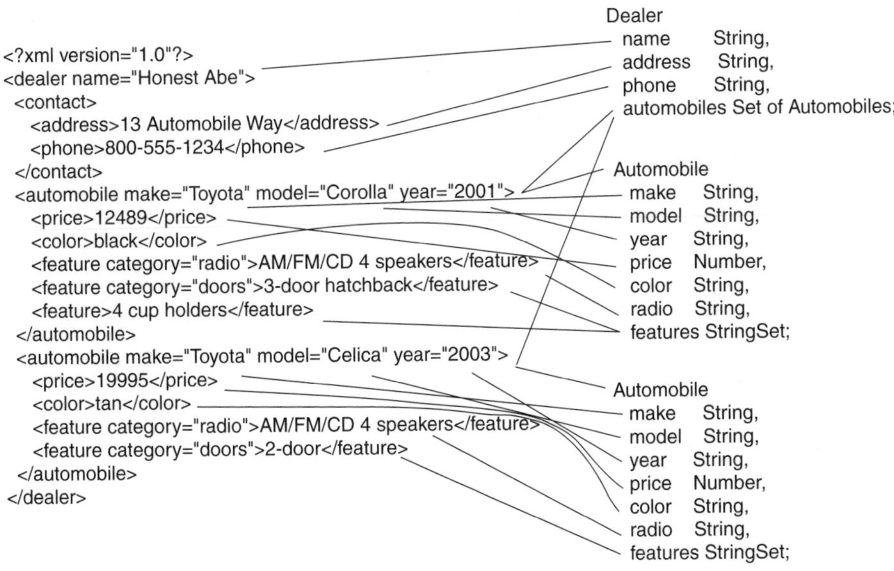

Figure 3–1 Mapping automobile document to objects

In addition to creating objects from an existing XML document, objects may be created to manipulate the data and write it back out in XML. A workflow process may also be created by a series of applications that parse the XML, manipulate it, and emit new elements into the stream that flows to the next application.

3.2 DBMSs

A common method to describe a DBMS system architecture is in terms of the interfaces to it. A DBMS can be described in terms of external, conceptual, and internal layers. These layers are built to support and provide the necessary functionality for application development, data manipulation and querying, and data storage, respectively. The external layer provides views to the end users and applications; the conceptual layer provides operations in the data model to store, query, and manipulate the data; and the internal layer provides the data structures that store and access the data. (These layers are depicted in Figure 3–2.) For example, in a relational database the

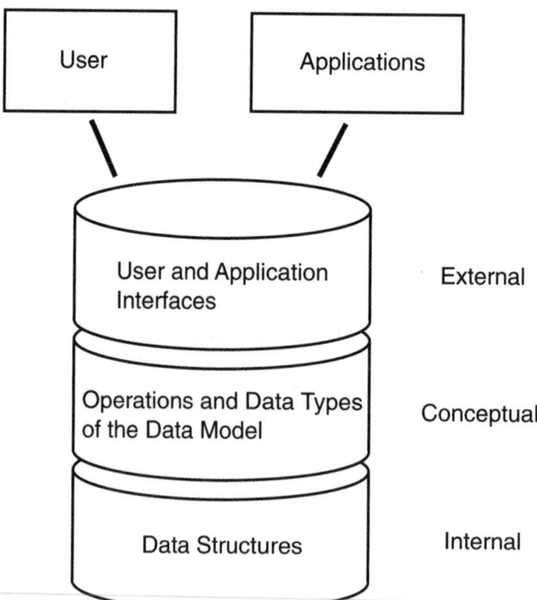

Figure 3–2 A three-layered database management system architecture

external layer might provide SQL and C interfaces; the conceptual layer provides the select, delete, update, and insert operations; and the internal layer provides the tables and index tree data structures that store the data in memory and on secondary storage.

These three layers of a DBMS architecture are similar in intention to the three stages of design in Chapter 2 in that they both attempt to isolate the user from the intricacies of the hardware and implementation. However, they are somewhat confusing in terminology. The external layer and conceptual design stage provide frameworks that meet the *user* needs as much as possible while still being capable of effective translation. The internal layer and physical design stage provide as much *detail* as possible to the respective developers without becoming overly burdensome with actual hardware-specific implementation. The middle conceptual layer and the logical design stage *connect* the user-oriented overview with the implementation-specific details through a precise, often mathematically rigorous, data-oriented framework.

In retrospect, database systems have been undergoing development since the 1960s, based on a steady progression of new technologies from other areas of computer science and commercial needs. Network and hierarchical databases were developed in the 1960s and became prevalent in the 1970s. Relational database theory was developed in the late 1960s, was implemented in working systems in the 1970s, and started to reach maturity in the 1980s. Object-oriented databases are based on ideas from programming languages from the 1970s, were developed into databases in the 1980s, and became robust enough for many real-world activities in the 1990s. Web database systems are based on ideas from the 1980s, were developed during the 1990s, and are becoming prevalent in the 2000s.

A layered architecture can be used to develop a DBMS for a new data model on top of an old one. For example, the underlying structures in relational DBMSs often resemble the pointers inherent in the first generation DBMSs, and logic (deductive) DBMSs store predicates as relations. Object-oriented DBMSs in particular provide a good framework on which to develop a DBMS for a new data model because of the full-function, object-oriented programming language they provide. However, relational DBMSs are more commonly available and may be a required technology for non-technical reasons.

Thus, a new logical data model can be developed for the conceptual layer of a new DBMS using the existing DBMS as the internal layer of the new DBMS. The diagrams in Figure 3–3 and Figure 3–4 may be helpful. Figure

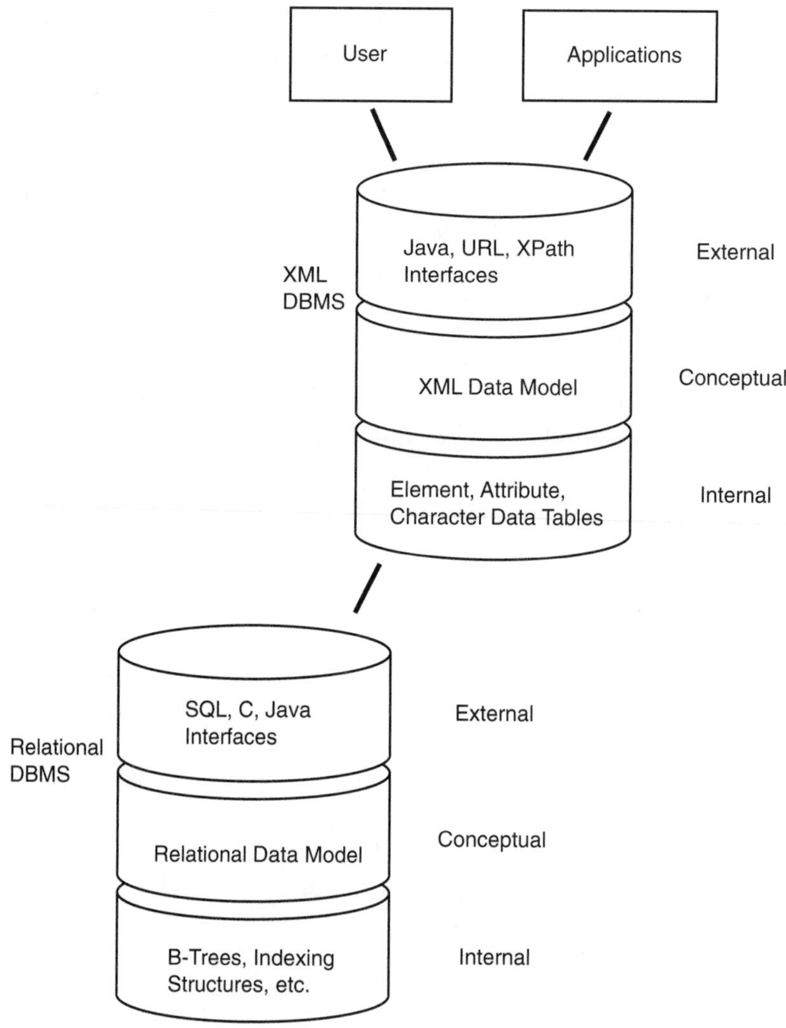

Figure 3–3 Developing an XML DBMS using a relational DBMS

3–3 shows the architecture of an XML DBMS built using a relational DBMS for storage. Figure 3–4 shows the architecture of an XML DBMS using an object-oriented DBMS for storage.

The purpose of the remainder of this chapter is to demonstrate how to develop an XML data model for the conceptual layer of the DBMS. The approach taken is to describe data modeling and develop six possible XML

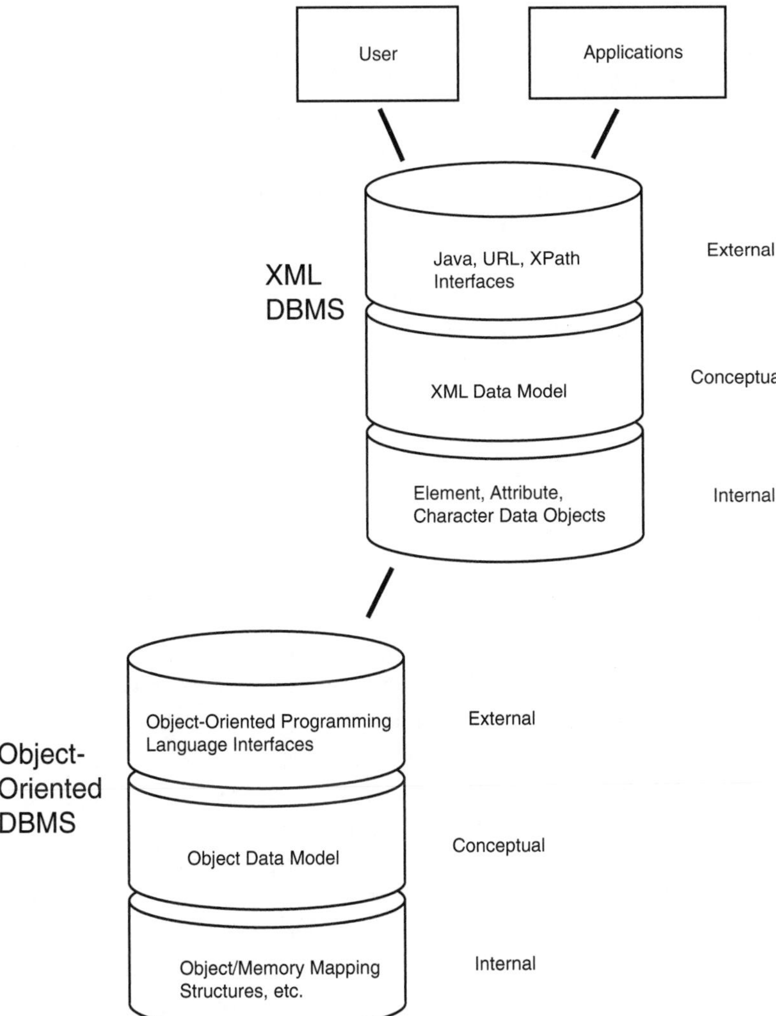

Figure 3–4 Developing an XML DBMS using an object-oriented DBMS

data models. Chapter 4 describes how to implement a data model using a relational (or object-oriented) DBMS for the internal layer. The external layer is described in the context of its use in Chapter 5.

Before delving into developing the foundations of an XML DBMS, it is useful to take a step back and examine the W3C standards that define XML and related technologies.

3.3 XML Standards

The World Wide Web Consortium (W3C) was created in October 1994 to develop technologies for the Web. W3C consists of more than 400 member organizations and it develops specifications, guidelines, software, and tools to lead the Web by developing common protocols that promote the Web's evolution and ensure its interoperability.

Much of this information is adapted from their Web site, *www.w3c.org*, which should be consulted for more recent, more accurate information.

TheW3C concentrates its efforts on three principal tasks:

- *Vision*—W3C promotes and develops its vision of the future of the Web. Contributions from researchers and engineers working for member organizations, from the W3C team, and from the entire Web community enable W3C to identify the technical requirements that must be satisfied if the Web is to be a truly universal information space.
- *Design*—W3C designs Web technologies to realize this vision, taking into account existing technologies as well as those of the future. The Web is an application built on top of the Internet and, as such, has inherited its fundamental design principles, which guide the work carried out within W3C activities.
    - *Interoperability*—Specifications for the Web's languages and protocols must be compatible with one another and allow (any) hardware and software used to access the Web to work together.
    - *Evolution*—The Web must be able to accommodate future technologies. Design principles such as simplicity, modularity, and extensibility will increase the chances that the Web will work with emerging technologies such as mobile Web devices and digital television, as well as others to come.
    - *Decentralization*—Decentralization is without a doubt the newest principle and most difficult to apply. To allow the Web to "scale" to worldwide proportions while resisting errors and breakdowns, the architecture (like the Internet) must limit or eliminate dependencies on central registries.
- *Standardization*—W3C contributes to efforts to standardize Web technologies by producing specifications (called

"Recommendations") that describe the building blocks of the Web. W3C makes these Recommendations (and other technical reports) freely available to all.

Work of the W3C on standards includes:

- HTML, the Web's hypertext markup language.
- XML, the Extensible Markup Language.
- DOM, the Document Object Model is an application programming interface that facilitates the design of active Web pages and provides a standard interface for other software to manipulate HTML and XML documents.
- CSS and XSL, style sheets for styling Web pages and supporting the separation of content and presentation.
- Related standards to XML, such as XPointer, XLink, and XPath.
- Standards based upon XML for a specific area, such as for marking up mathematics (MathML) or for creating synchronized multimedia presentations (SMIL).
- Other standards for graphics, the selection of rated content, meta-data, and the promotion of Web access for people with disabilities.

Several standards and standardization activities are part of the XML specification process, including XML Schema, XSL, XML Linking, XML Pointer, XML Path, XML Query, and XML Namespace. These are described in the next sections, along with DOM.

3.3.1 XML Schema (XSDL)

XML Schema provides a mechanism for declaring constraints on the use of markup within a document. The original XML 1.0 Standard provided an entirely different language for constraints: DTDs, which were derived from what was available in SGML. XML Schema provides a new constraint framework based on XML. XML Schema provides constraints on the XML document structure and data types though its definition language, XSDL.

XSDL is discussed briefly in Section 3.1.1, but not as much as one might expect from a book on XML databases. The reason is that XSDL is undergoing many changes, and it is not clear what it will look like or whether it will be a widely used standard. Other people—such as those developing XML databases—seem to have taken a wait-and-see attitude toward XSDL, too. Unfortunately, that means that there are not a lot of implementations to work with, which also decreases the likelihood of it becoming a standard.

Something like XSDL is necessary, and in this book I have tried to raise and discuss issues that would make XSDL (or a similar language) more understandable and useful. As a compromise, I have included a W3C primer on XML Schema as Appendix C. The primer accurately explains XML Schema as well as any resource does.

3.3.2 XSL

XSL is a language for expressing stylesheets. It consists of two parts:

- XSL Transformations (XSLT), which is a language for transforming XML documents.
- An XML vocabulary for specifying formatting semantics.

An XSL stylesheet specifies the presentation of XML documents by describing how those documents are transformed into XML documents that use the formatting vocabulary. XSL (or XSLT) can also be used to transform a document to a different XML document or an HTML document.

XSL is described more fully in Chapter 7.

3.3.3 XML Linking, Pointer, and Path

XML Linking provides mechanisms for hyperlinks. The hyperlinks include simple links—such as those available in HTML—and more complex links that may involve multiple documents. Links include references to external documents or resources as well as references within XML documents.

XML Linking Language (XLink) allows elements to be inserted into XML documents in order to create and describe links between resources. The language uses XML syntax to create hyperlinks. Unlike HTML, XLink links do not need to be stored within one of the documents they link. Links can be stored in a separate document and link explicit regions of other documents. The regions are referred to using the XPointer language.

XPointer allows XML resources to be linked into by another resource. An arbitrary region of an XML document may be referred to without respect to ownership or organization. XPointer uses a third specification, called XPath, which provides a way of specifying well-bounded regions, such as entire elements or lists of elements. XPointer uses XPath to define arbitrary regions by the use of spans (or regions). XPointer can refer to all the content between two points in a document, where the points are defined using XPath. Thus, an XPointer reference can refer to any contiguous region of any XML document accessible via a URL.

XPath is used as a foundation for both XPointer and XSL. XPath provides generic pointing expressions that can locate any node or set of nodes in an XML document structure. It is used in XSL to specify what part of a document is being matched and modified by XSL templates.

Querying documents that include links is addressed in Chapter 8.

3.3.4 XML Query

XML Query provides flexible query facilities to extract data from real and dynamically generated documents on the Web. The goal of the XML Query Working Group is to produce a data model for XML documents, a set of query operators on that data model, and a query language based on those operators.

XML Query Data Model defines a node-centric data model for XML that is specifically tailored to meet the needs of querying XML documents. The operations of the query system are defined by XML Query Algebra. The data model has the same intent as the data model based on DOM described in Section 3.5.5 but is defined in terms of mathematical functions that create trees from recursive application of a tree-creation function to a list of children trees. It rigorously defines a mathematical framework in which to develop queries.

The XML Query Data Model is built on XML Infoset, which is a model for XML. Query Data Model also incorporates post-schema validated XML Infoset and support for namespaces, XSDL data types, inter-document references, intra-document references, and collections of documents.

Data models for querying XML are discussed in Chapter 8.

3.3.5 XML Namespaces

A single XML document may contain elements and attributes that are defined for and used by multiple applications. Such documents pose problems of recognition and collision. Applications need to be able to recognize the tags and attributes that they are designed to process, even when some other applications use the same element type or attribute name. XML Namespaces provide a method for qualifying element and attribute names used in XML documents by associating them with namespaces.

This requires that document constructs have universal names whose scope extends beyond the document. XML Namespaces Specification describes a mechanism that accomplishes this. An XML namespace is a collection of names, identified by a Uniform Resource Identifier (URI) reference, which is a string of characters for identifying an abstract or physical resources. A URI includes both Uniform Resource Locators (URLs) and Relative Uniform Resource Locators.

Within an XML document, a namespace, such as "http://www.w3.org/TR/WD-xsl", can be associated with a element type name prefix, such as "xsl:", which can be used to distinguish elements of that namespace from other elements. Thus, element type names from different namespaces can be distinguished, such as "xsl:if" and "xperl:if".

3.3.6 DOM

DOM provides an interoperable set of classes and methods to manipulate XML documents (as well as HTML documents) from programming languages. A data model built using DOM is described in Section 3.5.5.

3.4 XML DBMS

XML DBMSs provide mechanisms to store, modify, query, and delete XML documents and elements stored in a database. A document can be stored in the database, modified in a variety of ways, queried based on its content, and deleted based on its identity. Documents may be modified by adding, modifying, or deleting elements in the document. The "document" itself provides a convenient mechanism to organize elements, but is not strictly necessary from a database perspective. Documents are, of course, necessary from a document-processing perspective.

An XML document might look something like:

```
<element1>
   <element2 attr1="value1" attr2="value2">
     Character Data A
   </element2>
   Character Data B
   <element3 attr3="value3" />
   Character Data C
</element1>
```

An XML document is defined by the W3C specification to contain seven types of constructs. Of the seven, the most relevant constructs are elements, attributes, and character data. An element is a section of the document bounded by a start tag, like <element1>, and an end tag, like </element1>. A document consists of one element that then contains all the remaining data in the document. Each element in the document contains an ordered collection of subelements interspersed with character data. Character data is another name for the text between the elements. By treating character data as separate constructs with the same level of identity and encapsulation as elements, the software and specification become simpler. An attribute is a property of elements that provides additional information.

Sometimes it may be useful to visualize the linear document as a tree structure. Each element and character data region can be visualized as nodes in a tree. Thus, in the previous example Element 2, Character Data B, Element 3, and Character Data C are all children of Element 1. The tree is depicted in Figure 3–5.

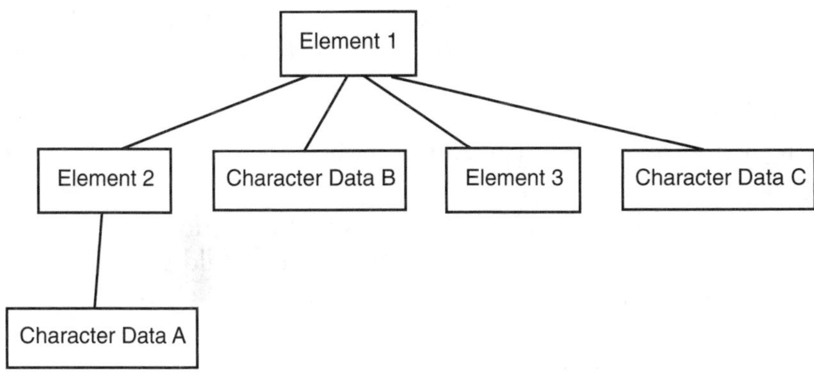

Figure 3–5 A tree depiction of a simple XML document

The first step in designing a relational schema for XML is to create a conceptual schema (as described in Chapter 2). The domain can be defined using the following definitions extracted from the XML specification:

- A document contains one (root) element.
- An element contains an element type name, a collection of attributes, elements, and character data where the order of elements and character data is retained.
- An attribute consists of a name and a value.
- Character data consists of strings in the document that are not tags or other markup.

To keep the presentation of database design simple, most of the information from the specification other than the tags and character data is ignored at this stage of design—namely, comments, processing instructions, references, and declarations. Only the basic information in a document is being captured.

3.4.1 Conceptual Schema

Using the design approach of Chapter 2, a graph conceptual schema can be created from the domain description. In this example, the domain is in the area of XML databases and thus contains considerable database terminology. A possible graph conceptual schema is shown in Figure 3–6, where an element contains collections of attributes, elements, and character data, and the interspersed order of the child elements and character data is tracked using an index number. In addition to the definition-driven modeling, a name characteristic is added to the document to make it easier to access the documents. In the conceptual schema,

- An (XML) *document* is defined to have a name and an element.
- An *element* is defined to have a type name, a collection of attributes, character data children, and element children.
- An *attribute* is defined to have a name and a value.
- A *child element* has an element (that it refers to) and an index number that orders it with respect to the other child elements and character data children.

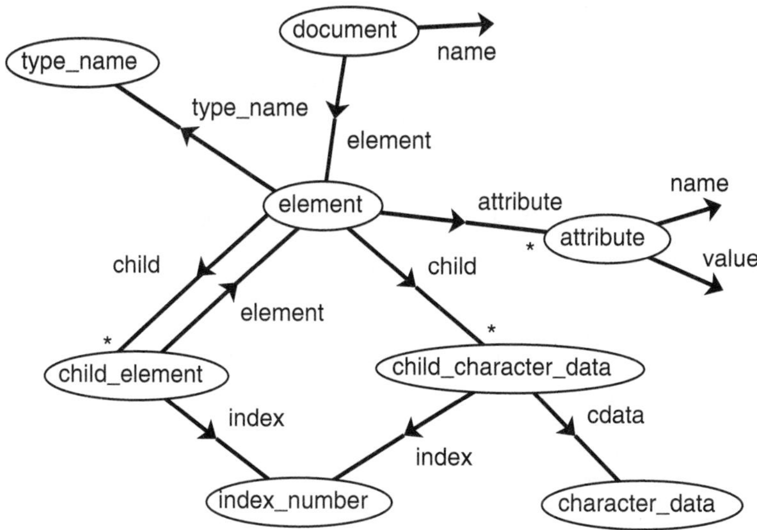

Figure 3–6 Simple graph conceptual schema for storing XML documents

- A *child character data* has a value, which is character data, and an index number that orders it with respect to the other character data children and element children.

From the conceptual schema, a relational or object-oriented schema can be created to develop an XML DBMS using a relational or object-oriented DBMS to capture the content of an XML document.

In addition to the description of what the data looks like, there needs to be a description of how the data may be used. First, we describe some example tasks that might be needed and then develop a collection of primitive operations that support those tasks.

3.4.2 Tasks

Many tasks may be performed by an XML database. Because you are reading this now, you may have some of your own ideas. Here is a list of eleven tasks—ranging from the most basic to fairly complex—that demonstrate some of the requirements for a data access language of an XML DBMS:

a. Store a document.
b. Retrieve a document.
c. Search for all elements with a given element type name.
d. Search for all elements with a given attribute value.
e. For the elements in (d), change the value of the attribute to be a specified string.
f. Search for all elements with a given element type name that contain exactly one character data child and the character data child consists of a given string.
g. Delete all the elements in (f).
h. Search for character data that contain a given string as a substring.
i. For the paths in (h), add a specified attribute to the leftmost element containing the character data region.
j. Replace all elements with a specified element type name that occur within the scope of an element with another specified element type name. For example, replace all tags named "para" with tags named "p" in the scope of an "html" tag.
k. Retrieve all elements with a specified attribute value that also occur as a specified attribute value of another specified element. For example, retrieve all "customer" elements with an attribute "salesperson" whose attribute value occurs as the value of the "name" attribute of a specified "salesperson" element.

The goal is to develop a DBMS (or storage system) that will support these and other similar tasks.

3.4.3 Operations

From the tasks and description of database functionality required, some example operations that might be needed are given for each data type. In addition, a new data type called "Database" is created to organize the global operations.

- Database
  - Add a document to the database.
  - Delete a document from the database.
  - Retrieve a document from the database given its name.
  - Search for all documents in the database given a particular set of constraints.

- Document
  - Add an element to a specific location in the document.
  - Delete an element from a specific location in the document.
  - Retrieve an element from a specific location in the document.
  - Retrieve all the elements and character data from a document in document order (in effect, regenerate the document).
  - Search for all elements in a document that satisfy a particular set of constraints.
  - Search the document for character data that matches a particular set of constraints (such as matching a string).
  - Replace an element at a specific location with another element or character data.
  - Replace character data at a specific location with other character data or elements.
  - Other operations—such as Copy or Edit—may be implemented using these operations.
- Element
  - All the operations of Document also apply to element: add/delete/retrieve a (sub)element to/from a specific location in the element, and so on.
  - Add an attribute to an element.
  - Delete an attribute from an element.
  - Retrieve an attribute from an element given its name.
  - Replace the value of an attribute in an element given its name.
  - Retrieve the *nth* child of an element.
  - Retrieve all children of an element.
- Character Data
  - Retrieve the text of the character data.
  - Retrieve the parent element of the character data.
- Query Constraint
  - Element type name equals (or does not equal) some value.
  - Attribute name equals (or does not equal) some value.
  - Character data equals (or does not equal) some value.
  - Element has a specified number of children (or less than, or greater than, or not equal to).

- Character data contains a specified string as a substring.
- Query constraint consists of two query constraints that must both be true (or either is true).
- Query constraint consists of one query constraint that must not be true.

These are some of the operations that may be useful for a DBMS. They are a description of what operations are appropriate for an XML DBMS based on an analysis of the tasks and serve as an informal set of requirements. To develop a design for an XML DBMS, a description is needed of what the data types are and how they may be manipulated. The best way to describe the *what* and *how* of a DBMS is a data model.

3.5 Data Modeling

A *data model* is a mathematical description of the representation language for a database.

A *model* is a construct created to capture some aspects of an entity. Model cars may look like real cars. Their wheels may or may not move, but models can demonstrate some differences between a Mustang and a Thunderbird. Precision airplane models are useful for testing airflow in a wind tunnel. Currently, a lot of modeling is done in the computer, but the principles are the same. When moving into the virtual world, the distinctions between the virtual and real become blurred, but we forget sometimes that the real is sometimes as artificial as the virtual. Plastic and steel are no more natural or less man-made than the image on a computer screen, they just happen to be more tangible. A computer model of a car may mimic more functionality than a physical model. Mathematical models provide the same biased functionality. They cleanly describe the properties of the system that are of particular interest and ignore others.

Why study data models? Why study data models when it is not part of a required course? Why choose to study data models? Why read about data models in a book when you could be elsewhere having fun? Data models are the requirement specifications for a DBMS. Again, not quite the same as reading for fun, but data models describe precisely and cleanly the necessary functionality of a DBMS, which is more fun to have than (1) developing a system without a requirements specification, (2) developing a system where the requirements keep changing out from under you, (3) developing a system where the requirements are so vague that they are open to (different) interpretations, (4) having your DBMS lose data, or (5) having your DBMS lose *your* data. Besides, imagine how much better the world would be if "a pervasively used personal computer operating system not mentioned here by name to avoid legal issues" had been developed to a clean and mathematically precise requirements specification. And, I will keep the mathematics to a minimum.

A data model describes the structure, function, and constraints of the data in a database. It provides a description focusing on the abstract, mathematical properties of the data—such as domains, data types, and ranges—and ignoring the concrete limitations imposed by a computer system. Thus, they are not useful when trying to figure out the details necessary to build a system to manipulate the database, but they are useful to provide a clean, concise overview when overwhelmed by the details and implementation.

In addition, the applications developed to access XML data in a general way may be rigorously specified by defining the operations that need to be supported as a data model. In other words, by having a data model defined for an XML database, the developers building applications that use the database can know precisely what the database will and will not support. This makes developing applications easier and makes the entire database system more productive and reliable.

A data model is defined in terms of its data types, operators, and constraints. Data types describe the basic building blocks of data, such as numbers, strings, sets, and relations. The operators describe how the data can be manipulated, such as adding two numbers or concatenating two strings. Constraints restrict which values of a data type can legally occur in the database—for example, that a set can contain numbers or strings, but not both, or that a relation can contain numbers or strings, but not sets or relations.

3.5.1 Existing Data Models

Relational databases were the first to be specified in terms of a data model by Codd in 1970. The data type for the relational model is the relation. The seven operators are select, project, join, product, union, difference, and intersection. There are two database-independent integrity constraints:

1. No component of the primary key of a base relation is allowed to accept nulls.
2. The database must not contain any unmatched foreign key values.

First, we will talk about what this means. By first understanding the relational data model (which is familiar), understanding the XML data model (which is new) will be easier.

The relational data model has one data type constructor: the relation. The relation is a type constructor that creates a set of relationships; each relationship (tuple) has an identical number of characteristics (attributes) in the same order. Each characteristic has a name and a domain (set of possible values). Those domains are usually modeled as data types. Each relationship thus contains an ordered collection of values, and each relation consists of an ordered collection of data types. One reason the relational model caught on was that it cleanly constrained all the relationships in a relation to have a similar abstract signature (*i.e.*, interface), instead of a lot of untyped pointers. Then, a small set of operations could be used to manipulate the relationships because the program knew exactly what to expect. But, that is too boring for the Web database, so we need to relax the restriction that the relationships be identical in structure but avoid the untyped free-for-all that existed before Codd cleaned up the database world. We will do that shortly, but now on with the operations of the relational model.

There are seven operations in the relational model:

- **Select** on one relation returns a collection of relationships based on a logical constraint (logical predicate), which all the returned relationships must satisfy. The logical constraints consist of logical and arithmetic operations on the data, such as that the value of a column is equal to 3. The logical constraints describe what must be true of the result of the query and should be distinguished from the database-specific integrity constraints (which all data in the database must satisfy) and the database-independent integrity constraints (which all databases in the relational data model must satisfy).
- **Project** on one relation and a set of column names returns a new relation with only those columns of the given relation.
- **Cartesian product** on two relations returns a new relation where the new relationships are a concatenation of every relationship in the first relation with every relationship in the second relation.
- **Join** on two relations restricts the result of their Cartesian product through an additional logical constraint (predicate),

such as equality. When an equality constraint is on two columns (one from each relation), the join is called a *natural join.*

- **Union** on two relations with the same number of columns (*arity*) returns a new relation with all the relationships from both given relations.
- **Difference** on two relations with the same arity returns a new relation with all the relationships of the first relation that are not in the second.
- **Intersection** on two relations with the same arity returns a relation with all relationships that occur in both given relations.

More information about the operations and examples of their use may be found in a relational database book (such as Ullman (1988)). The reason for examining them in an XML database book is that they provide a useful set of operations that can be extended to build an XML data model. Section 3.5.4 describes what the above operations mean if you change "relation" to "element tree," "column" to "attribute or element type names," and "relationship" to "element."

Additional operations are also needed to insert, update, and delete relationships in a relation, but historically these have not been specified by the relational data model. The relational data model describes how to combine existing relations to create other relations, and thus provides ideas on how to manipulate collections of XML elements.

In practice, no commercial database exactly matches any research data model, but the data models are a good mechanism to describe the basic function of the DBMS and serve as a basis of comparison between systems that claim to implement a particular data model.

The relational data model has been modified to describe the functionality of object-oriented databases, and these modifications have been incorporated in Object-Relational DBMSs (ORDBMSs). These modifications are also useful for modeling XML, but to understand them, you must understand relational database normal forms.

Normal forms are constraints placed on the kinds of relations that can occur in a relational database. They are a theoretical and somewhat obscure mechanism to address some very practical issues in relational database design. They address anomalies and potential inconsistencies that can occur with some relational designs.

The relational model has several normal forms, including first, second, third, Boyce-Codd, fourth, and fifth, which provide increasing restrictions on the way relations may be used to capture data. Relational design is primarily concerned with whether a database is in third normal form or Boyce-Codd normal form and minimizing the number of relations that are not in those normal forms for practical reasons. For XML databases, the two relevant normal forms are first normal form and fifth normal form.

First normal form requires that the domain of each attribute consist of indivisible values, such as a number or string, and not sets of values or embedded relations. The term "relation" generally implies that the relation is in first normal form, and traditionally relational DBMSs have only supported relations in first normal form. However, "relations" that are not in first normal form, called *non-first normal form relations,* are very useful for modeling objects or XML in a relational framework. Understanding first normal form is important for modeling XML because that restriction is assumed in all traditional relational DBMSs, but relaxing that restriction is necessary to model XML as relations.

Non-first normal form relations generalize the relational data model by removing the restriction that all relations refer to only atomic values and allow for embedded sets or relations. For many non-business domains, first normal form is too restrictive. Although developed to describe object and object-relational databases, these data models based on non-first normal form relations are useful for describing the embedding of subelements into elements.

A *fifth normal form relation* cannot be decomposed into any number of smaller relations without losing information should those relations be rejoined. To store the variant structure of XML elements in a relational DBMS supporting only first normal form relations, the structure of the XML element must be decomposed into its minimal constituents, which in the case of XML elements are binary relations. In other words, if the relational DBMS is not flexible enough to support the non-first normal form relations needed to capture XML elements, then each element structure must be decomposed, and because the element structure can vary, it must be completely decomposed (into fifth normal form).

In addition to the non-first normal form relation and fifth normal form relation, three data models are relevant to XML. They are the entity-relational, semantic, and graph data models, and they are briefly described here.

The entity-relational data model extends the relational data model by distinguishing among entities, which are the principal objects about which information is collected; attributes, which are the characteristics of the entities; and relationships between entities. The entity-relational model is used primarily for designing database schemas that are then implemented in a relational DBMS. Mapping data to XML from a database designed using entity-relation diagrams may be easier if those diagrams are used as part of the mapping process. There are tools that will implement a relational database from an entity-relation diagram automatically. Similar tools could be used to implement an XML Schema in a relational DBMS.

Semantic data models capture semantic information in a network of functional relationships. They originated from semantic networks that were developed as tools in artificial intelligence to represent the semantics of natural language using functional arcs or a small set of type constructors. They capture relationships such as generalization (is-a hierarchies), aggregation (part-of hierarchies), and data abstractions. Many of these constructs have been incorporated in object-oriented databases and programming languages, but the semantic data models provide a simpler foundation for those constructs that may be useful in XML databases.

Graph data models capture the structural information of a network of binary relations and thus are good data models to capture XML in fifth normal form relations. Graph data models have as their foundation the mathematical definition of a graph as a collection of nodes and edges. Graphs were described in Chapter 2 as a method for designing XML databases. Graphs also extend the linear limitation of an XML document to allow for interconnected fragments that allow fragments to be linked. Links are supported by the XML Link Specification and are discussed in Chapter 8.

The XML Specification (*www.w3.org/TR/REC-xml*) provides the data types and constraints that would be necessary for a data model. Because XML is a markup language, there are no explicit operations other than the ones for creating the elements in the data type, though querying operations are suggested through additional standards such as XSL and XPointer. Other data models may be developed based on Grove or other document-oriented models of forests (collections of trees). A variety of data models is possible depending upon the operations that are included, and the next six subsections describe six possible data models.

The data types and operations of a data model provide a rigorous specification of how XML documents and document fragments can be stored, retrieved, and manipulated in an XML DBMS. From this specification, an implementation can be developed that provides the XML DBMS functionality, as described in Chapter 4.

3.5.2 Simple XML Data Model

The goal of the next six subsections is to describe a variety of XML data models: a simple data model, a specification-oriented data model based on the W3C XML Specification, a relation-oriented data model based on the relational data model, a node-centric data model based on the W3C DOM, an edge-oriented data model based on an alternative mathematical description of a tree as a set of edges, and a generic data model that combines aspects of the other five.

This section introduces a simple data model, called (creatively) the Simple Data Model, which describes a very simple data model for XML. This data model demonstrates how to create a document of elements, attributes, and character data regions. An implementation of this data model would not capture all information in an XML document as defined by the W3C XML Specification, but could provide a simple mechanism to track the relevant content of the data exchanged between applications. Most of the data models in the remainder of this chapter will add to this one.

3.5.2.1 Types

The data types of the data model are:

- A *document* is defined to have one name and one (root) Element.
- An *element* is defined to have a type name, a collection of attributes, and an ordered collection of character data and elements. The character data and elements may be interspersed within the ordered collection.
- An *attribute* is defined to have a name and a value. Both the name and value are strings.
- *Character data* has a value, which is a string.

Three additional types are needed to capture (a) the shared property of character data and element types, which is that they can be children of an element, (b) a collection of attributes, and (c) an ordered collection of element children. Because both character data and elements are nodes in the element tree, and we will be adding more types of nodes in the following sections, we will call that union type "Node." (A data type union includes any instance of either data type and is analogous to a super-class relationship in an object-oriented programming language.)

- A *node* is a union of element and character data types.
- An *attribute set* is a collection of attributes.
- A *node list* is an ordered collection of nodes.

3.5.2.2 Operations

Operations are defined to add, delete, and retrieve data from the database. In this data model, no search or extensive query capabilities are included.

The operations for each type in the data model are listed shortly. Although you can use some very nice mathematical ways to describe the operations in a data model, the clearest practical presentation is probably to describe the name, parameters, parameter types, and result type of the operation along with a brief description. The convention is:

```
<operation name>( <type1> <parameter name 1> , … ) <result
type>
```

This is somewhat similar to the presentation used to describe operations in the Java programming language, though in Java the instance methods have an implied argument equal to the instance being called, which is explicit here.

From the data types and operations, an XML DBMS can be defined. One way to implement the DBMS would be in an object-oriented language, such as Java. The types can be defined as classes, and the operations as methods on the classes. The database-independent integrity constraints of the next section would need to be implemented within the body of the methods. The data models are presented in this book in a way that is similar to an object model or API, because object-oriented languages are good at defining new data types, and a data model consists of a collection of data types with constraints. Approaches to implement the data model using an existing relational or object-oriented DBMS are described in Chapter 4.

- Document
  These operations create and access documents.

```
newDocument(String name) Document
    Create a new document with unique <name>
createDocumentElement(Document document, String tag)
    Element
    Create the (root) document element for <document>
    with tag name <tag>, return the new element
```

```
getDocumentElement(Document document) Element
    Get (root) document element for <document>
getName(Document document) String
    Get the name of <document>
```

- Element

  The getTag operation retrieves the element type name.

```
getTag(Element element) String
    Get the tag (element type) name for <element>
```

The next operations *create* the attributes, character data regions, and subelements that an element may contain.

```
createAttribute(Element element, String name, String
    value) Attribute
    Add an attribute to an <element> with <name> and
    <value>, return the new attribute
createCharData(Element element, String data) CharData
    Add a character data region to the end of an
    <element> consisting of a string <data>, return
    the new CharData
createElement(Element element, String tag) Element
    Add a subelement to the end of an <element> with
    element type name <tag>, return the new subelement
```

The next operations *retrieve* the attributes, character data regions, and subelements that an element may contain. Access of the subelements and character data regions are combined into the getChild method. This allows the children of an element to be accessed without knowing which type of node they are. The Node type has an operation to distinguish the two types, and programming logic can use that operation to choose appropriate code to manipulate the subelement or character data region. Having one getChild method instead of separate getElement and getCharData operations also simplifies later data models that have additional types of nodes.

```
getAttribute(Element element, String name) Attribute
    Get the attribute of <element> with name <name>
getChild(Element element, Integer index) Node
    Get the child of <element> at <index>
```

The next operations *delete* the attributes, character data regions, and subelements that an element may contain.

```
removeAttribute(Element element, String name) Boolean
    Remove the attribute of <element> with name
    <name>, return true if the attribute existed
removeChild(Element element, Integer index) void
    Remove the child of <element> at <index>
```

The next operations extend the earlier child creation operations (for character data and element) by allowing an index to be specified into the list of children. These operations allow a new child to be inserted into the existing children at a specific location.

```
createCharData(Element element, String data, Integer
    index) CharData
    Add a character data region to <element>
    consisting of a string <data> at index location
    <index>, return the new CharData
createElement(Element element, String tag, Integer
    index) Element
    Add a subelement to <element> with element type
    name <tag> at index location <index>, return the
    new subelement
```

The next operations retrieve the collections of attributes or children that the element has. If a DBMS supports these operations, the retrieval of all attributes or children may be much more efficient than if the retrieval operations shown earlier are used that retrieve each attribute or child individually.

```
getAttributes(Element element) AttributeSet
    Get all the attributes of <element>
getChildren(Element element) NodeList
    Get all the children of <element>
```

- Attribute
  These operations access the individual attribute name-value pair that occurs in an element.

```
getName(Attribute attribute) String
    Get the name of <attribute>
getValue(Attribute attribute) String
    Get the value of <attribute>
setValue(Attribute attribute, String value) String
    Set the value of <attribute> to <value>
```

- Character data
  These operations access the character data regions that occur in an element.

```
getData(CharData charData) String
    Get the data string of <charData>
setData(CharData charData, String data) String
    Set the data value of <charData> to be <data>
```

- Node (union of element and character data)
  The getType operation allows applications using the DBMS to choose appropriate code depending upon the type of Node.

```
getType(Node node) String
    Get the type of <node> as a string, either
    'Element' or 'CharData'
```

- NodeList
  These operations allow a NodeList to be used.

```
getLength(NodeList nodeList) Integer
    Return number of nodes in <nodeList>
item(NodeList nodeList, Integer index) Node
    Retrieve from <nodeList> the node at location
    <index>
```

- AttributeSet
  These operations allow an AttributeSet to be used in the same way as a NodeList. Because order does not matter, better operations would be to define an iterator over the set, but that would needlessly complicate the data model because AttributeSet is only used as a helper type.

```
getLength(AttributeSet) Integer
    Return number of nodes in <AttributeSet>
item(AttributeSet attributeSet, Integer index)
    Attribute
    Retrieve from <AttributeSet> the attribute at
    location <index>
```

There are several ways to access data in a list, as suggested by such data structures as arrays, doubly-linked lists, enumerators, or Lisp lists. The array approach was chosen here for NodeList because it is used in the conceptual schema and is simple and efficient in a variety of storage implementations.

Most of the remaining data models will extend these operations. However, not all operations necessary for a DBMS are included in the data model, such as operations to start the DBMS, shut down the DBMS, find out if the DBMS is running, and find out how large the space used by the DBMS is. These operations depend upon the implementation of a DBMS and how it is used and maintained; a data model describes how the *database* is used.

3.5.2.3 Constraints

The constraints for the Simple Data Model are:

1. Each document name may occur only once. *Thus, the document names are unique and may be queried.*
2. All elements other than the document element have an element node as a parent. The document element has no parent. *Thus, the elements form a tree.*
3. No attribute name may appear more than once in an element. *This is required as part of the XML Specification. (There are some specified attributes, such as IDREFS, that have multiple values. These are not treated here, but they can be captured the same way as in the XML Specification: a space-delimited list.)*
4. The integer index is constrained to be the set of consecutive integers beginning from a fixed integer (such as 0 or 1) and to correspond to exactly one element in the collection. *This basically defines what it means to be an index, and that there are no gaps.*

3.5.3 W3C Specification-oriented XML Data Model

This section will be most accessible to readers already familiar with tree data structures and XML. The entire W3C specification is not used because the presentation would be overly complex; instead the namespace node type is not included. As presented, the data model could be used to capture XML documents without namespace information or ID/IDREFS (which still includes many applications). This data model may also be used in concert with the W3C specification to develop a full data model to capture the complete W3C XML Specification.

3.5.3.1 Types

An XML *document* consists of a tree. A *tree* is a collection of nodes where each *node* has at most one parent node and may have any number of ordered child nodes. (As was shown in Figure 3–5.)

Six kinds of nodes exist in an XML document:

- *Root node*—There is one root node in the document. The root node refers to the entire XML document resource. It has as children comment nodes and one element node called the document element node (sometimes confusingly called the element root node). In other data models in the book, the root node is considered identical to the XML document and comment nodes in the root node are not allowed.
- *Element node*—These are most of the tagged nodes of the document. Each element node has a name, one parent node, a collection of attribute nodes, and an ordered collection of element nodes, character data nodes, and comment nodes as children. The parent node may be either a root node or an element node, and every element node must have a parent.
- *Character data node*—These are the character data strings of maximal length within a document. If "<name>John Smith</name>" occurs in a document, then "John Smith" is a character data node. (The "maximal length" part of this definition ensures that everyone works with the same character data node and no one defines the character data nodes to be "John", " ", and "Smith", as would otherwise be allowed.) The XML Specification also defines a CDATA section that is a type of character data node where text strings are quoted.
- *Attribute node*—There is an attribute node for every name-value pair in an element. Multi-valued attributes (also called list attributes), such as IDREFS, are stored as a white-space delimited string.
- *Comment node*—A comment node consists of a text comment.
- *Processing instruction node*—A processing instruction node consists of a target and data. Processing instructions provide information such as the correct style sheet to use.

Namespace nodes are excluded from this data model as they interact heavily with the other nodes, would obscure the presentation, and are best understood in the context of the W3C specification.

3.5.3.2 Operations

Although several operations could be defined on the database, including those of the Simple Data Model in the previous section, there are three operations based on W3C activity that are particularly useful.

Each node has an operation "generateDocument" to generate the text with markups for that node. The W3C specification defines a similar function string-value without markup that is useful for displaying a document but may or may not be useful in developing a database. For the purposes of developing the data model, the string value of an element node consists of the name of the node, the attributes, and the concatenation of all child nodes with the appropriate XML syntax. Thus, the "generateDocument" value of the document (root node) is the text of the document *with* tags.

Each element node has an operation "path" that takes a path as specified in the XML Path Specification and returns a value or a node set. A value is either a number, boolean, or string. Processing is accomplished as in the XML Pointer Specification from W3C.

The document has an operation "transform" that takes as an argument an XSLT stylesheet and returns a document as the result. Processing is accomplished as specified in the XSLT Specification from W3C.

3.5.3.3 Constraints

For the data model, two constraints are necessary:

1. Only one element node has the root node as a parent. All other element nodes have an element node as a parent.
2. No attribute name may appear more than once in an element.

Several additional constraints are included in the XML Specification.

3.5.4 Relation-oriented XML Data Model

An XML data model is developed similar to the relational data model. This section will be the most accessible to those readers already familiar with relational databases. A theoretical foundation is laid for some of the operations in XML Path and XSL stylesheets in terms of the operations of the relational data model and SQL. This data model is most useful when extending a relational DBMS to include XML documents seamlessly integrated with relational data.

3.5.4.1 Types

The basic data type of the relational data model is the relation. In addition to the relation, additional data types are included in a database: the *relational database* itself (a collection of relations), a *domain* (a set of values), and a *column* (a labeled aspect of a relation that contains a value). A column takes its values from a domain; thus, domains describe the allowed values for a column. Domains may be numbers, strings, booleans, enumerated sets, and so on. This is necessary in the relational model to distinguish between columns that can be meaningfully joined. The data types of the relational data model—relational database, domain, column, and relation—are analogous to the data types of an XML data model—XML database, domain, attribute, and element. In the XML Specification, the only domain for XML values is character data, but the specification for XSDL provides additional domains.

One aspect of the relational data model that is essential in developing an XML data model is the way that collections are treated. The relational model provides a foundation for manipulating collections that the object-oriented data models do not provide. In the relational model, data is stored as a set of relations and the operations are oriented toward manipulating collections of relations, the object model has no predefined mechanism for creating collections of objects, and the operations are oriented toward manipulating individual objects. In the object model, the programmer must define a new object for each collection and choose the appropriate implementation mechanism. For example, instead of creating a new object "Set(Employee)" directly from the class Employee, a new class EmployeeRepository must be created as a sub-class of Vector, Hashtable, and so on. This greatly limits the usefulness of the object model for databases, which are intended for operation on large collections of entities. Some database vendors have included the collection operation from the relational model in their implementation of an object-oriented database, but these are almost universally restricted to one or two mechanisms for collecting homogenous objects. A big advantage of XML as a foundation for a data model is that it has a flexible mechanism for defining structures (like the object-oriented models) and a predefined approach to treating collections (like the relational model). In XML, hierarchical collections of markup (and character data) are modeled as a document.

Thus, in creating an XML data model from the relational data model, the primary decision process is in the way that operations on sets of identical relations are mapped to operations on a hierarchical tree of heterogeneous elements. Researchers have extended the relational model in two ways that need to be combined for XML. The first step is to extend the operations to a set of heterogeneous elements, and the second step is to extend those operations to a hierarchical tree.

Heterogeneous elements are those with varying structure. Early on it became necessary to allow for optional values in a relationship, so NULLs were added. It was a fairly kludgy solution, but because mathematicians bought into it and no one else had a better solution, developers were stuck with it. New operations are necessary on the columns of a relation capturing varying structure: Some columns can be repeated, thus each value in the relationship might become a set of values, or the order of the columns could be swapped around and even interspersed with the values of the other columns.

The second extension to the relational model necessary for XML is to allow for nested relations. A value in the relationship could be another relationship, thus adding deeper structure, like a tree. These are called non-first normal form relations and were described in Chapter 2. The two extensions can be combined so that a value can be captured as a relation. A concrete example should help clarify these steps and illustrate its relevance.

Consider a relation capturing meetings between a salesperson (S), a technical support person (T), and a client (C). Okay, so it's not that much more concrete. The domain of each column S, T, and C is not restricted and can be any string name. In the relational data model, the values of the relationships could have atomic string values, and a relation might look something like this:

S	*T*	*C*
Adam	Ben	Charles
Andy	Barbara	Candy

To simplify the description, a new parenthesized prefix notation for relationships is introduced for this example only. The relationship is described as:

```
{( <name of column 1> <value of column 1> ) (<name of column 2>
<value of column2>) ...}
```

Thus, the relation above is:

```
{(S Adam) (T Ben) (C Charles)}
    {(S Andy) (T Barbara) (C Candy)}
```

This may first be extended to allow for repeated column values and optional column values. For example, new relationships might be added as:

```
{(S Tom) (T Nancy) (T Jane) (T Sammy)}
    {(T Bill) (T Frank) (C Melanie) (C Jackie)}
```

Then the order of the columns can be relaxed and the values may be interspersed as in:

```
{(T Becky) (S Timmy) (S Hilton) (C Sammy)}
    {(T Betty) (S Rita) (T Hope) (C Ned) (C Ken) (S
    Frank)}
```

Another extension is to allow for nested relations, such as:

```
{(T {(first Ben) (last Smith)}) (S {(first Cindy)
    (last Jones)})}
{(C {(first Ann) (last Irwin)}) (C {(first Randy)
    (last Griffeth)})}
```

Because the syntax is becoming difficult to follow, we can change it with a more XML-like convention that the relationship is delimited with ≤name of relation≥ at the beginning and ≤/name of relation≥ at the end. Columns can be handled similarly with ≤name of column≥ instead of "(" at the beginning and ≤/name of column≥ instead of ")" at the end. Thus, the relations look like:

```
<r>
<t><first>Ben</first><last>Smith</last></t>
<s><first>Cindy</first><last>Jones</last></s>
```

```
</r>
<r>
<c><first>Ann</first><last>Irwin</last></c>
<c><first>Randy</first><last>Griffeth</last></c>
</r>
```

The goal is to map the relational operations to the heterogeneous trees in a way that the resulting operations make sense on the XML documents.

3.5.4.2 Operations

The same seven operators that were defined for the relational data model can be defined for the XML data model: select, project, join, product, union, difference, and intersection.

Select—In the relational model, select returns a new relation that contains a subset of the relationships (tuples) of the original relation that meet the constraints in the query. For a flat collection of heterogeneous relations, it would work to return tuples as long as they were tagged, but to perform a select on a tree of elements, the result needs to be a collection of trees (in effect a collection of elements). Select on a document returns a collection of elements that meet the constraints in the query; for example, constraints that the element type name does or does not equal some value, that attribute values meet some arithmetic or boolean condition, or that the character data contains or does not contain some string. To remain compatible with the select operation in the relational model, the select operation for XML should return one element that contains the collection of elements that meet the constraints in the query.

Project—In the relational model, project returns a new collection of relations where some of the columns of the relations have been dropped or reordered. For a flat collection of heterogeneous relations, a project operator could extract only those attributes that are shared between the relations. For example, the values of the attribute "name" or "size" of all elements in a heterogeneous collection could be extracted even though additional attributes or element type names might vary. For a tree, the project operation would need to access and create trees; for example, in Example 3–5 a new relation is created from a collection of circles, triangles, and rectangles to extract their bounding box subelements.

Another useful approach is to extend the project operation to consist of a collection of rewrite (project) rules that operate on the appropriate type of element. In a relational DBMS, the select and project operation are com-

Example 3–5 : Relational Projection of Simple Graphical Objects

```
-- Graphical objects in XML format
<circle radius="5">
  <point x="100" y="100"/>
  <boundingBox>
    <point x="95" y="95"/>
    <point x="105" y="105"/>
  </boundingBox>
</circle>
<triangle>
  <point x="100" y="80"/>
  <point x="80" y="100"/>
  <point x="120" y="100"/>
  <boundingBox>
    <point x="80" y="80"/>
    <point x="120" y="100"/>
  </boundingBox>
</triangle>
<rectangle>
  <point x="80" y="80"/>
  <point x="120" y="100"/>
  <boundingBox>
    <point x="80" y="80"/>
    <point x="120" y="120"/>
  </boundingBox>
</rectangle>

-- Projected onto *.boundingBox
<circle radius="5">
  <boundingBox>
    <point x="95" y="95"/>
    <point x="105" y="105"/>
  </boundingBox>
</circle>
<triangle>
  <boundingBox>
    <point x="80" y="80"/>
    <point x="120" y="100"/>
  </boundingBox>
</triangle>
<rectangle>
  <boundingBox>
    <point x="80" y="80"/>
    <point x="120" y="120"/>
  </boundingBox>
</rectangle>
```

bined in the SQL select statement. The initial clause of the SQL select performs the project and the SQL where clause performs the select operator (as well as possible joins). XSL templates (which are discussed in Chapter 7) may be viewed as rewrite rules that create a new tree and could be used in a manner similar to SQL. This is discussed briefly in Chapter 8. Currently, XSL does not support matching multiple element collections simultaneously so operations such as join that require two arguments could not be described in terms of XSL.

Cartesian product—In the relational model, Cartesian product creates one new relation from two existing relations. The new relation contains all the columns of both existing relations and creates relationships in the new relation by appending each relationship in the first relation with every relationship in the second relation. If the first relation had n relationships and the second one had m relationships, then the new relation will have $n \cdot m$ relationships.

On a heterogeneous flat collection of relations, the Cartesian product can operate on all the attributes. On trees, either (1) the Cartesian product could access and create a new element with two subelements: one from each of the two element collections being crossed, or (2) a new element could be created with a collection of new subelements that consist of all the subelements of the two element collections being crossed. Example 3–6 shows a Cartesian product of a collection of circle elements with a collection of color elements. In Alternative 1, a new element "colored_circle" is created with subelements "color" and "circle". In Alternative 2, a new element "colored_circle" is created with subelements "point", "bounding box", and "rgb". Either alternative may be useful depending upon the context. The XQuery algebra supports the first alternative.

Example 3–6 : Alternative Cartesian Products

```
-- Example Cartesian product
<cartesian_product result_collection="colored_shapes"
   result_element_type="colored_circle">
  <shapes>
    <circle radius="5">
      <point x="100" y="100"/>
      <boundingBox>
        <point x="95" y="95"/>
        <point x="105" y="105"/>
      </boundingBox>
```

```
    </circle>
    <circle radius="10">
      <point x="100" y="100"/>
      <boundingBox>
        <point x="90" y="90"/>
        <point x="110" y="110"/>
      </boundingBox>
    </circle>
  </shapes>
  <colors>
    <color name="Red">
      <rgb red="1" green="0" blue="0"/>
    </color>
  </colors>
</cartesian_product>

-- Alternative 1

<colored_shapes>
  <colored_circle>
    <circle radius="5">
      <point x="100" y="100"/>
      <boundingBox>
        <point x="95" y="95"/>
        <point x="105" y="105"/>
      </boundingBox>
    </circle>
    <color name="Red">
      <rgb red="1" green="0" blue="0"/>
    </color>
  </colored_circle>
  <colored_circle>
    <circle radius="10">
      <point x="100" y="100"/>
      <boundingBox>
        <point x="90" y="90"/>
        <point x="110" y="110"/>
      </boundingBox>
    </circle>
    <color name="Red">
      <rgb red="1" green="0" blue="0"/>
    </color>
  </colored_circle>
</colored_shapes>
```

```
-- Alternative 2

<colored_shapes>
  <colored_circle radius="5" name="Red">
    <point x="100" y="100"/>
    <boundingBox>
      <point x="95" y="95"/>
      <point x="105" y="105"/>
    </boundingBox>
    <rgb red="1" green="0" blue="0"/>
  </colored_circle>
  <colored_circle radius="10" name="Red">
    <point x="100" y="100"/>
    <boundingBox>
      <point x="90" y="90"/>
      <point x="110" y="110"/>
    </boundingBox>
    <rgb red="1" green="0" blue="0"/>
  </colored_circle>
</colored_shapes>
```

Join—In the relational model, join returns a new collection of relations that are built upon existing relations by creating a Cartesian product and restricting the product through additional arithmetic operations, such as equality. When the equality constraint is on two columns with the same domain, the join is called a *natural join.* As in the project operation on a heterogeneous flat collection of relations, it makes the most sense for the join operator to operate only on the attributes that are shared between the relation. On trees, the same alternatives to Cartesian product apply to joins: Either the join could access and create a tree with two subelements or a new element could be created with a collection of new subelements that consist of all the subelements of the two joined elements.

In the remaining three operations of the data model—union, difference, and intersection—there are two ways to define each operation depending upon whether a data-processing-oriented view or a document-processing-oriented view is taken (Section 2.4.2). If a document-processing-oriented view is taken, then the order of the elements in the document is essential and the set operations union, difference, intersection, and quotient need to be modified to preserve order. They then reduce to concatenation and document difference functions. If a data-processing-oriented view is taken, then the order of the elements is not important and may be declared irrelevant. In addition, duplications of data may be allowed or disallowed. If duplications are allowed, then the "set" data type is less appropriate than "bag", which by definition is a set that allows for duplications.

Although a "set" semantics may be more useful for developers working closely with a relational database—especially if XML is primarily used to transport data that is stored in relational form—in this chapter a "bag" semantics is used. RDBMSs usually implement a "bag" semantics, but most relational databases require a unique name for each item being modeled in the database, thus implying the equality operation necessary for a "set" semantics. A general mechanism to compare trees for equality can be time consuming in large documents. These equality comparisons are prevalent in the set operations union, difference, intersection, and quotient. Thus, although the "set" semantics may be theoretically cleaner, the "bag" semantics is more practical for large collections of element trees. If needed, a "set" semantics for a database can be enforced with database-specific integrity constraints (as is done in implementations of relational databases using primary keys and uniqueness constraints on a table).

Union—In the relational model, union operates on relations with the same arity. This restriction is not necessary with heterogeneous collections or trees that have a "bag" semantics. In those cases, the union operation can be implement as a concatenation of the two element collections. There is no need to check for duplications between the two collections—as in the union operation of sets—because duplicate elements are explicitly allowed in a document.

Difference—In the relational model, the difference in relations is between relations with the same arity. The (individual) relationships in the difference are the relationships in the first relation that are not in the second. This could be generalized to heterogeneous relations defining equality to mean that two relations must be identical in arity, attributes, and values. However, because the order of elements in a document is important, a better basis for the difference function is probably a document comparison program, such as Unix diff program, where documents are compared and the result is the text that occurs in the first document, but not the second document.

Intersection—In a document-processing-oriented view, the intersection is similar to the comparison made in the difference, except that the elements returned are those elements that occur in both documents. In a data-processing-oriented view, the order of elements is not important and each element is compared in some way to all other elements in the other document.

3.5.4.3 Constraints

There are two database-independent integrity constraints that can be defined similar to the ones in the relational model: (1) Every element must have a tag, and (2) Every element other than the root element must have exactly one parent.

3.5.5 Node-centric XML Data Model

The Node-centric XML Data Model is an object-oriented model based on the W3C DOM objects Attr, CharacterData, Comment, Document, Element, and Node. The DOM also has two ways of accessing the objects. The first way is through the constituent objects that correspond to the different nodes, namely, Element, CharacterData, and Comment. The second way is through operations primarily on the Node object (which the superclass of the Element, CharacterData, and Comment). The Node operations are more efficient in languages, such as Java, that require type casting. A disadvantage of a data model based on DOM is that it is typically inefficient for very large documents.

3.5.5.1 Types

The types of the Node-centric Data Model are based upon the Simple Data Model (Section 3.5.2.1) with the addition of the comment node from the W3C-oriented data model. The processing instruction node is not included to slightly simplify the presentation, but it is similar to the comment node.

- A *document* is defined to have one name and one (root) Element.
- An *element* is defined to have a type name, a collection of attributes, and an ordered collection of character data and elements. The character data and elements may be interspersed within the ordered collection.
- An *attribute* is defined to have a name and a value. Both the name and value are strings.
- *Character data* has a value, which is a string.
- A *comment* has a data value, which is a string.

In addition to the XML nodes, the DOM makes explicit the operations of a *node* data type and specifies the node object as a super-class of the element, character data, and comment nodes. The Node object provides access to the element tree through sibling relationships. The previous presentations have provided access to the tree through parent-children relationships, as does the Element object of DOM. Both kinds of relationships are depicted in Figure 3–7. The Simple Data Model (and Element object) provides access through the "parent" and "child" relationships, while the Node object of this data model provides access through the "parent", "nextSibling", and "previousSibling" relationships. The parent-children approach associates more information with the parent and may be best used with relation-based storage that tends to have lighter-weight entities (only the value). The sibling-parent approach associates more information with each child and may be best used with object-based storage that tends to have heavier entities (an object).

- A *node* refers to the document, the parent element, the previous sibling, and the next sibling.

In order to refer to ordered collections of nodes, a NodeList object is also needed.

- A *node list* consists of an ordered collection of nodes where each node is associated with an integer index. (Basically, an array of nodes.)

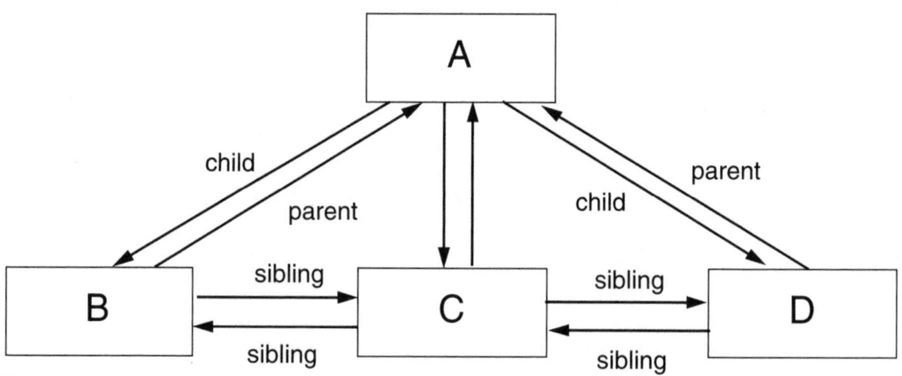

Figure 3–7 A tree depiction of parent–child and sibling relationships

3.5.5.2 Operations

- Document
  The elements, attributes, character data regions, and comments are associated with the Document type; in the Simple Data Model, they are associated with the Element type. In a Node-centric data model, the constituents of a document are associated with the document instead of an element and they are placed in the tree by operations on the Node type. Because of this, the "createDocumentElement" operation of the Simple Data Model is replaced with "setDocumentElement" here. In addition, a new operation "getElementsByTagname" is added.

```
newDocument(String name) Document
    Create a new document with unique <name>
getDocumentElement(Document document) Element
    Get (root) document element for <document>
setDocumentElement(Document document, Element element)
    void
    Set the (root) document element for <document> to
    be <element>.
createAttribute(Document document, String name, String
    value) Attribute
    Create an attribute in <document> with <name> and
    <value>, return the new attribute
createCharData(Document document, String value)
    CharData
    Create a character data region in <document>
    consisting of a string <data>, return the new
    CharData
createElement(Document document, String tag) Element
    Create an element in <document> with element type
    name <tag>, return the new element
createComment(Document document, String value) Comment
    Create a comment in <document> with text <value>,
    return the new comment
getElementsByTagname(Document document, String tag)
    NodeList
    Retrieve all elements in <document> with element
    type name <tag>
```

- Element

  The Element type operations differ from the Simple Data Model as follows: the creation operations are associated with the Document type and are no longer on the Element type; there are no operations using an index number; and the operation "getElementsByTagname" is added. The need for index numbers is replaced by the operations on the Node data type.

```
getAttribute(Element element, String name) Attribute
    Get the attribute of <element> with name <name>
getAttributes(Element element) AttributeSet
    Get all the attributes of <element>
getChildren(Element element) NodeList
    Get the children of <element> in order
getTagName(Element element) String
    Get the tag (element type) name of element
removeAttribute(Element element, String name) Boolean
    Remove the attribute of <element> with name
    <name>, return true if the attribute existed
removeChild(Element element, Node child) void
    Remove the child of <element> at <index>
getElementsByTagname(Element element, String tag)
    NodeList
    Retrieve all elements in <document> with element
    type name <tag>
setAttributeNode(Element element, Attribute attribute)
    void
    Add to <element> the <attribute>
```

- Attribute

  These operations are the same as the Simple Data Model

```
getName(Attribute attribute) String
    Get the name of <attribute>
getValue(Attribute attribute) String
    Get the value of <attribute>
setValue(Attribute attribute, String value) String
    Set the value of <attribute> to <value>
```

- Character data

  These operations are the same as the Simple Data Model.

```
getData(CharData charData) String
    Get the data string of <charData>
setData(CharData charData, String data) String
    Set the data value of <charData> to be <data>
```

- Comment
  The Comment type has the same operations as Character Data.

```
getData(Comment comment) String
    Get the data string of <comment>
setData(Comment comment, String data) String
    Set the data value of <comment> to be <data>
```

- Node (superclass of element, character data, and comment)
  The Node type has a more prominent role in this data model. The "getType" operation also occurred in the Simple Data Model, but all the other operations are new. They allow a tree of nodes to be created with siblings and parents.

```
getType(Node node) String
    Get the type of <node> as a string, either
    'Element', 'CharData', or 'Comment'
AppendChild(Node node, Node child) void
    Append to children of <node> the new node <child>
insertBefore(Node node, Node newNode, Node refNode) void
    In children of <node>, insert <newNode> before
    <refNode>
getOwnerDocument(Node node) Document
    Return the document to which <node> belongs
getParentNode(Node node) Element
    Get the parent element of <node>
getPreviousSibling(Node node) Node
    Get the previous sibling of <node>
getNextSibling(Node node) Node
    Get the next sibling of <node>
```

- NodeList
  These operations are the same as the Simple Data Model.

```
getLength(NodeList nodeList) Integer
    Return number of nodes in <nodeList>
item(NodeList nodeList, Integer index) Node
    Retrieve from <nodeList> the node at location
    <index>
```

- AttributeSet
  These operations are the same as the Simple Data Model.

```
getLength(AttributeSet) Integer
    Return number of nodes in <AttributeSet>
```

```
item(AttributeSet attributeSet, Integer index)
    Attribute
    Retrieve from <AttributeSet> the attribute at
    location <index>
```

3.5.5.3 Constraints

The first four database-independent integrity constraints are the same as the Simple Data Model. The constraints are:

1. Each document name may occur only once.
2. All elements other than the document element have an element node as a parent. The document element has no parent.
3. No attribute name may appear more than once in an element.
4. The integer index is constrained to be the set of consecutive integers beginning from a fixed integer (such as 0 or 1).
5. Each node has zero or one previous sibling. *This is the definition of sibling.*
6. Each node has zero or one next sibling. *This is the definition of sibling.*
7. Every child of a node has that (parent) node as its unique parent. *This provides integrity to the tree. The child and parent roles are inverses and the operations on a node should capture that.*
8. The owner document of a node is the same as the owner document of its parent. The owner document of a document element is the document for which it was created. *Thus, all the nodes in a tree belong to the same document. Otherwise you could insert a node from a different document into the tree.*

3.5.6 Edge-centric XML Data Model

When creating a data model based on a mathematical description, the emphasis placed on the mathematical concepts can greatly influence the implementation. A mathematical tree that underlies the XML document structure can be described as a restricted form of graph, which is a collection of nodes and edges where the edges consist of an ordered pair of nodes. Trees place the restriction onto graphs that there is a single root node, that all nodes are connected by edges, and that there are no cycles in the graph (i.e., there is only one way to get from one node to the other).

When mapping the structure of XML onto a mathematical tree, you can place emphasis on either the nodes or the edges, with very different results. For example, the element type names can be mapped as labels to either the nodes or the edges. In general, node-centric data models are best suited when it is useful to maximize the amount of information available when referring to a node, for example, when navigating a document tree within an object-oriented implementation. Edge-centric data models are best suited when accessing the relationships within a document or shared by documents, for example, when querying shared relationships across documents stored in a relational DBMS.

The document

```
<contact name="Joe Smith">
   <phone>
      <work>800-555-3456x789</work>
      <fax>888-555-9870</fax>
   </phone>
</contact>
```

could be represented by the relations in Table 3–3 where an internal node is represented as the concatenation of the number sign "#", the element type name, an underscore "_", and a unique number.

The Edge-centric Data Model is revisited in more depth in Chapters 8 and 9 on querying and indexing.

Table 3–3 Edges in a Personal Contact Document

Dimension	*Source*	*Name*	*Destination*
child	#root_0	contact	#contact_1
attribute	#contact_1	name	Joe Smith
child	#contact_1	phone	#phone_2
child	#phone_2	work	#work_3
child	#work_3	data	800-555-3456x789
child	#phone_2	fax	#fax_4
child	#fax_4	data	888-555-9870

3.5.6.1 Types

- A *document* is defined to have an ordered collection of edges and one internal node designated as the *root node.*
- An *edge* has a dimension, source, relation name, and destination where source and destination are each nodes.
- A *node* is either an internal node or a leaf node.
- An *internal node* is either the root node or an element node. An internal node has no explicit information other than a mechanism for distinguishing it from other internal nodes. The root node has one child that is the document element node. Having a separate root node in this data model allows the document element tree to be the destination of an edge (with the root as source) that gives the document element node's element type name (as the relation name).
- A *leaf node* can be an attribute or a character data region. A leaf node has a string value (either CDATA or PCDATA in XML Specification). If the leaf node is an attribute, it is attribute value. If the node is a character data region, the string value is the data. The leaf node type combines functionality to store a string value of the attribute type and character data region type of the other data models.
- An *edge dimension* is either "subelement", "child", or "attribute". The "child" dimension includes all children of an element, except for subelements; in this data model that would be only character data. In the "subelement" dimension, the relation name is the element type name; in the "attribute" dimension the relation is the element name; and in the "child" dimension, the relation name is "data".

A new edge dimension is added to the data model in Chapter 8 to handle XML Links for intradocument or interdocument links. It may also be useful to add a new dimension for ID/IDREF(S) attributes to capture intradocument links.

3.5.6.2 Operations

The operations are:

- Document

```
newDocument(String name) Document
    Create a new document with unique <name>
getName(Document document) String
    Get the name of <document>
newInternalNode(Document document, String tag) Element
    Create a new internal node for <document>
newLeafNode(Document document, String value) LeafNode
    Create a new leaf node for <document> with string
    value <value>
```

The root node is defined when the document is created.

```
getRootNode(Document document) Node
    Get root node for <document>
getRelationNames(Document document, Dimension
    dimension) Set of String
    Retrieve all relation names in <document> in
    <dimension>
newEdge(Document document, Dimension dimension, Node
    source, RelationName relationName, Node dest)
    boolean
    Add to <document> the edge in <dimension>
    consisting of <source>, <relationName>, and
    <dest>. Return true if the edge already existed.
delete(Document document, Dimension dimension, Node
    source, RelationName relationName, Node dest)
    boolean
    Delete from <document> the edge in <dimension>
    consisting of <source>, <relationName>, and
    <dest>. Return true if the edge did not exist.
```

The "edgeQuery" operation is key to the data model and is described in detail in Chapters 8 and 9 on querying and indexing.

```
edgeQuery(Document document, Dimension dimension, Node
    source, RelationName relationName, Node dest) List
    of Edge
    For <document>, return all edges in <dimension>
    that match the edge pattern constrained by
```

```
    <source>, <relationName>, or <dest>, any one of
    the three which may be NULL. If NULL, then that
    parameter is not constrained and can match any
    appropriate item in the database.
```

- Edge
  The "insertBefore" operation allows children to be moved. It has no effect on the attribute dimension.

```
insertBefore(Edge edge1, Edge edge2) void
    Move <edge1> to immediately before <edge2> in the
    document.
NextEdge(Edge edge) Edge
    Returns the next edge after <edge> in the
    document.
before(Edge edge1, Edge edge2) boolean
    Returns true if and only if <edge1> occurs before
    <edge2> in the document
```

- Node

```
getData(LeafNode node) String
    Returns the string data for leaf node <node>
```

- EdgeList
  These operations allow a EdgeList to be used.

```
getLength(EdgeList edgeList) Integer
    Return number of edges in <edgeList>
item(EdgeList edgeList, Integer index) Edge
    Retrieve from <edgeList> the edge at location
    <index>
```

3.5.6.3 Constraints

1. A document has one root node that is the child of no other node. *This is the definition of a root node.*
2. A root node has one child. *The child of the root node is the one document element.*
3. Edges in the child dimension all have the same relation name: "data". *This constraint ensures consistency between the relation names in the data dimension. If comments were added to the*

data model, then the constraint would be changed to: All edges in the child dimension are either "data" or "comment".

3.5.7 Generic XML Data Model

The Generic Data Model is derived from the previous data models and is used for the storage mechanisms described in the next chapter. It provides a basic data model for a variety of applications that can also be extended using more of the ideas in the previous data models.

3.5.7.1 Types

- A *database* is a collection of documents.
- A *document* is defined to have one name and one (root) Element.
- An *element* is defined to have a type name, a collection of attributes, and an ordered collection of character data and elements. The character data and elements may be interspersed within the ordered collection.
- An *attribute* is defined to have a name and a value. Both the name and value are strings.
- *Character data* has a data value, which is a string.
- A *comment* has a data value, which is a string.
- A *node* consists of a element, character data, or comment. In addition, a node refers to the document and the parent element (if it exists).
- A *node list* consists of an ordered collection of nodes where each node is associate with an integer index (basically, an array of nodes.)
- A *document list* consists of an ordered collection of nodes where each node is associate with an integer index.

In addition, there are types associated with constraints on which to query the database. These constraints are on the data to be returned by a query and differ from the database-independent constraints that are specified by a data model.

3.5.7.2 Operations

- Database
  The operations on the Database type are made explicit in the Generic Data Model.

```
newDatabase() Database
    Create a new database
newDocument(Database database, String name) Document
    Create a new document in <database> with name
    <name>
storeDocument(Database database, String body, String
    name) Document
    Store into <database> a new document with <body>
    and name <name>, return the new document
retrieveDocumentName(Database database, String name)
    Document
    Retrieve from <database> the document with name
    <name>
deleteDocument(Database database, Document document)
    Boolean
    Delete from <database> the <document>, return true
    if the document was originally there.
getAllDocuments(Database database) DocumentList
    Retrieve from <database> a list of all its documents
selectDocument(Database database, Constraint
    constraint) DocumentList
    Select from <database> all documents which satisfy
    <constraint>
```

- Document
  Two operations are added to the original Simple Data Model: (1) "generateDocument", generates the document text as suggested in the W3C Data Model and (2) a new operation "selectElement", is suggested by the Relation-oriented Data Model. The "selectElement" operation is more general than the "getElementsByTagname" of the Node-centric Data Model.

```
createDocumentElement(Document document, String tag)
    Element
    Create the (root) document element for <document>
    with tag name <tag>, return the new element.
getDocumentElement(Document document) Element
    Get (root) document element for <document>
```

```
getName(Document document) String
    Get the name of <document>
generateDocument(Document document) String
    Retrieve the body of <document>
selectElement(Document document, ElementConstraint
    elementConstraint)
    Select from <document> all elements which satisfy
    <elementConstraint>
```

- Element
  The first twelve operations for Element are the same as the Simple Data Model. The operations are taken from the Simple Data Model rather than the Node-centric Data Model, because the DOM Node operations are not likely to be efficient for large databases. Operations from the Edge-centric data model is not included as it is more useful for querying an existing document than storing one in a DBMS.

```
getTag(Element element) String
    Get the tag (element type) name for <element>
createAttribute(Element element, String name, String
    value) Attribute
    Add an attribute to an <element> with <name> and
    <value>, return the new attribute
createCharData(Element element, String data) CharData
    Add a character data region to the end of an
    <element> consisting of a string <data>, return
    the new CharData
createCharData(Element element, String value, Integer
    index) CharData
    Add a character data region to <element>
    consisting of a string <data> at index location
    <index>, return the new CharData
createElement(Element element, String tag) Element
    Add a subelement to the end of an <element> with
    element type name <tag>, return the new subelement
createElement(Element element, String tag, Integer
    index) Element
    Add a subelement to <element> with element type
    name <tag> at index location <index>, return the
    new subelement
getAttributes(Element element) AttributeSet
    Get all the attributes of <element>
getAttribute(Element element, String name) Attribute
```

```
    Get the attribute of <element> with name <name>
getChildren(Element element) NodeList
    Get all the children of <element>
getChild(Element element, Integer index) Node
    Get the child of <element> at <index>
removeAttribute(Element element, String name) Boolean
    Remove the attribute of <element> with name
    <name>, return true if the attribute existed
removeChild(Element element, Integer index) Boolean
    Remove the child of <element> at <index>
```

The operation "removeChild" (with parameter type Node instead of Integer) and the operation "moveChild" incorporate functionality suggested by the Node-centric Data Model.

```
removeChild(Element element, Node node) Boolean
    Remove the child of <element> which is <node>
moveChild(Element element, Node node, Integer index)
    void
    In <element>, move the <node> to empty location
    <index>
```

The operation "replaceChild" combines the functionality of "removeChild" and "moveChild" but may be implemented much more efficiently than the separate operations because the children of Element are indexed by contiguous integers in this data model rather than the sibling relationships of the Node-centric Data Model.

```
replaceChild(Element element, Node node, Integer
    index) Boolean
    In <element>, move the <node> to location <index>,
    return true if a node existed at that location
```

The "selectChildren" operation is suggested by the Relation-oriented data model.

```
selectChildren(Element element, Constraint constraint)
    NodeList
    Select from <element> all children which satisfy
    <constraint>
```

- Attribute
  These first three operations are the same as in the Simple Data Model and the Node-centric Data Model. The "getElement" operation is suggested by the "getParentNode" operation of the Node-centric Data Model.

```
getName(Attribute attribute) String
    Get the name of <attribute>
getValue(Attribute attribute) String
    Get the value of <attribute>
setValue(Attribute attribute, String value) String
    Set the value of <attribute> to <value>
getElement(Attribute attribute) Element
    Return the element to which <attribute> belongs
```

- Character data
  These operations are the same as in the Simple Data Model and the Node-centric Data Model.

```
getData(CharData charData) String
    Get the data string of <charData>
setData(CharData charData, String data) String
    Set the data value of <charData> to be <data>
```

- Comment
  These operations are the same as in the Node-centric Data Model.

```
getData(Comment comment) String
    Get the data string of <comment>
setData(Comment comment, String data) String
    Set the data value of <comment> to be <data>
```

- Node (superclass of element, character data, and comment)
  The "getType" operation comes from the Simple Data Model and the "getOwnerDocument" and "getParentNode" operations come from the Node-centric Data Model. The "getIndex" operation simplifies the sibling operations of the Node-centric Data Model in a manner similar to NodeList and may be more efficient for large databases.

```
getType(Node node) String
    Get the type of <node> as a string, either
    'Element', 'CharData', or 'Comment
getOwnerDocument(Node node) Document
```

```
    Return the document to which <node> belongs
getParentNode(Node node) Element
    Get the parent element of <node>
getIndex(Node node) Integer
    Get the index of <node> in its parent
```

- NodeList
  These operations are the same as the Simple Data Model.

```
getLength(NodeList nodeList) Integer
    Return number of nodes in <nodeList>
item(NodeList nodeList, Integer index) Node
    Retrieve from <nodeList> the node at location
    <index>
```

- AttributeSet
  These operations are the same as the Simple Data Model.

```
getLength(AttributeSet) Integer
    Return number of nodes in <AttributeSet>
item(AttributeSet attributeSet, Integer index)
    Attribute
    Retrieve from <AttributeSet> the attribute at
    location <index>
```

- Constraint
  Simple boolean operations are included to define constraints by combining other constrains. These operations come from the "select" operation of the Relation-oriented Data Model.

```
and(Constraint constraint1, Constraint constraint2)
    Constraint
    Return a constraint which is satisfied if and only
    if <constraint1> and <constraint2> are satisfied
or(Constraint constraint1, Constraint constraint2)
    Constraint
    Return a constraint which is satisfied if and only
    if <constraint1> or <constraint2> are satisfied
not(Constraint constraint) Constraint
    Return a constraint which is satisfied if and only
    if <constraint> is not satisfied
```

- CharDataConstraint (subclass of constraint)
  Simple operations are included to define character data constraints. These operations come from the “select” operation of the Relation-oriented Data Model. More operations are possible.

  ```
  dataEquals(String data) CharDataConstraint
      Return a constraint which is satisfied if and only
      if the data of a CharData equals <data>
  dataContains(String data) CharDataConstraint
      Return a constraint which is satisfied if and only
      if the data of a CharData contains <data>
  dataStartsWith(String data) CharDataConstraint
      Return a constraint which is satisfied if and only
      if the data of a CharData starts with <data>
  dataEndsWith(String data) CharDataConstraint
      Return a constraint which is satisfied if and only
      if the data of a CharData ends with <data>
  dataMatches(String regularExpression) CharDataConstraint
      Return a constraint which is satisfied if and only
      if the data of a CharData matches
      <regularExpression>
  ```

- ElementConstraint (subclass of constraint)
  Simple operations are included to define character data constraints. These operations come from the “select” operation of the Relation-oriented Data Model and from the W3C Specification-oriented Data Model.

  ```
  tagNameEquals(String name) ElementConstraint
      Return a constraint which is satisfied if and only
      if the tag name of an element equals <name>
  hasAttribute(String name) ElementConstraint
      Return a constraint which is satisfied if and only
      if an element has an attribute with name <name>
  hasCharData(CharDataConstraint constraint)
      ElementConstraint
      Return a constraint which is satisfied if and only
      if an element has a CharData which satisfies the
      <constraint>
  hasChild(Constraint constraint) ElementConstraint
      Return a constraint which is satisfied if and only
      if an element has a child which satisfies the
      <constraint>
  ```

```
hasChild(Constraint constraint, Integer index)
    ElementConstraint
    Return a constraint which is satisfied if and only
    if an element has a child at location <index>
    which satisfies the <constraint>
hasDescendent(Constraint constraint) ElementConstraint
    Return a constraint which is satisfied if and only
    if an element has a descendent which satisfies the
    <constraint>
hasMinNumChildren(Integer min) ElementConstraint
    Return a constraint which is satisfied if and only
    if an element has at least <min> children
hasMaxNumChildren(Integer max) ElementConstraint
    Return a constraint which is satisfied if and only
    if an element has at most <max> children
```

- DocumentList
  These operations allow DocumentList to be manipulated in a manner similar to NodeList.

```
getLength(DocumentList documentList) Integer
    Return number of documents in <documentList>
item(DocumentList documentList, Integer index) Document
    Retrieve from <documentList> the document at
    location <index>
```

3.5.7.3 Constraints

The constraints for the Generic Data Model come from the Simple Data Model and the Node-centric Data Model. The first four constraints come from the Simple Data Model and the last two come from the Node-centric Data Model. The constraints are:

1. Each document name may occur only once.
2. All elements other than the document element have an element node as a parent. The document element has no parent.
3. No attribute name may appear more than once in an element.
4. The integer index is constrained to be the set of consecutive integers beginning from a fixed integer (such as 0 or 1) and to correspond to exactly one element in the collection.
5. Every child of a node has that (parent) node as its unique parent.

6. The owner document of a node is the same as the owner document of its parent. The owner document of a document element is the document for which it was created.

3.6 Bibliographic Remarks

Date (1999) describes the architecture and functionality of DBMSs. Stonebraker (1998) provides an overview of database systems.

Ullman (1988) describes the relational data model and provides a theoretical overview of database systems from a relational database perspective. Codd was the first to describe databases in terms of data models. The first database to be described in that way was the relational data model (Codd 1970). He also developed later versions of the relational data model that impact current databases (Codd 1980, 1990).

More information about the attribute versus subelement trade-off has been collected at *www.oasis-open.org/cover/elementsAndAttrs.html.*

More information about theoretical foundations of XML may be found in Abiteboul (2000).

3.6.1 References

Abiteboul, S., Buneman, P., and Suciu, D. (2000) *Data on the Web: From Relations to Semistructured Data and XML,* Morgan Kaufmann, San Francisco.

Codd, E.F. (1970) "A Relational Model of Data for Large Shared Data Banks." *Communications of the ACM*, 13(6): 377–387.

Codd, E.F. (1980) "Data models in database management." In M. Brodie and S.N. Ziles, eds, *Proc. Workshop on Data Abstraction, Databases, and Conceptual Modelling*, June 1980. Also, ACM SIGMOD Record 11(2).

Codd, E.F. (1990) *The Relational Model for Database Management—Version 2,* Addison-Wesley, Reading, MA.

Date, C.J. (1999) *An introduction to database systems (7th edition),* Addison-Wesley, Reading, MA.

Stonebraker, M. and Hellerstein, J. (1998) *Readings in Database Systems (3rd edition),* Morgan Kaufmann, San Francisco.

Ullman, J. (1988) *Principles of database and knowledge-base systems, volume 1,* Computer Science Press, Rockville, MD.

Data Storage

- How can I store all this XML data other than as a bunch of XML documents?
- How do users and applications access stored data?
- What technologies can I use? How do I use them?

4

XML data can be stored in a DBMS that supports the manipulation and access of XML documents. Significant effort goes into protecting the data in commercial DBMSs to increase their robustness in a variety of situations. However, XML DBMSs are still new and not as mature as relational or object-oriented DBMSs, and this chapter focuses on developing a system architecture for an XML DBMS that leverages the more mature relational and object-oriented DBMSs. Particular emphasis is placed on how to integrate an XML storage facility into an existing technology platform. This chapter also serves as an introduction to developing a complete XML DBMS by describing the data storage aspects of XML data.

4.1 Storage Facilities

XML can be stored as a flat file, in an object-oriented database, or in a relational database. This section provides an overview of those three choices, and the remainder of the chapter focuses on storage in a relational database.

4.1.1 Flat File Database

A flat file is the simplest storage mechanism but does not support indexed queries or easy modification of a document. Relational and object-oriented databases provide flexibility in storing a document in pieces that allow for easy access of parts of a document. This can improve the efficiency of querying and modifying a document.

The easiest way to store XML data is in a single file that stores the entire XML document. The data can be readily accessed by a plethora of text editors and several XML tools. It is easily accessed from any programming language and is readily accessible from all XML parsers. Pretty much every XML book that mentions storage will consider this as a primary mechanism for storing an XML document. However, it is not the only mechanism, and for databases, it is not always the best.

For example, suppose you are working on data-mining software that finds relationships among sales transactions. You develop the software to take in a transaction, a big brother identifier of the customer such as checking account number or credit card number, and the items purchased. From this, your software can find patterns within what the customer buys and similarities with other customers with similar buying habits. The software can then suggest specialized marketing, such as half-price motor oil when purchasing beer and baby food. Your software is working great, and because you want it to be general, you make it work with this cool XML technology. Your VP of sales and marketing gets excited about it and lands a great contract with Wal-Mart, who wants to use it on its transaction database for last year. Everyone is really excited until you realize that the size of the XML document of transaction data upon which the software runs is 120 Terabytes. Your VP of sales and marketing does not even know what a Terabyte is. What do you do?

Suppose your XML document looked something like the document in Example 4–1, which collects information on the store, customer, items, and coupons of a transaction and omits information about price, checker, and date. Someone at Wal-Mart (who also thinks XML is cool) is willing to send you the data in that format but subdivided into many files with a separate file per store and month of the year. Each file will be an XML document with root element "<group store="" month="">". But, what you need is to search by customer or product UPC. Luckily, your system administrator knows a great Linux hacker who can set up a file system that will hold 200 Terabytes in 10 billion files using hard drives, DVDs, and optical disks. How do you organize the data? (*Disclaimer*: Do not try this at home.)

Example 4–1 : Collection of Sales Transactions for Data Mining

```
<collection>
   <transaction id="400100341">
     <customer>
        <credit_card number="4234567887654321"/>
     </customer>
     <store number="4567"/>
     <item upc="2460001001" qty="1"/>
     <item upc="1600042040" qty="2"/>
     <item upc="5928000020" qty="4"/>
     <coupon code="5928000100"/>
   </transaction>
   <transaction id="400100342">
     <customer>
       <checking_acct routing="344465456" acct="12345678"/>
     </customer>
     <store number="4567"/>
     <item upc="2460001002" qty="2"/>
     <item upc="1600024540" qty="2"/>
   </transaction>
   <transaction id="400100343">
     <customer>
       <cash/>
     </customer>
     <store number="4567"/>
     <item upc="2460001001" qty="1"/>
     <item upc="1645042940" qty="2"/>
     <item upc="5928000020" qty="1"/>
     <item upc="1645042876" qty="2"/>
     <coupon code="1645081140"/>
   </transaction>
</collection>
```

Flat file databases are a useful alternative to traditional DBMSs. Flat file databases can be as large as the operating system allows or as small as a single file. In the largest case, a general-purpose DBMS could be overwhelmed, and implementing a few specialized operations may be more efficient than relying on the generic operations that come with a general-purpose DBMS. In the smallest case, the functionality of the traditional DBMS may not be necessary, and the overhead may be burdensome. Even when the size is reasonable for a traditional DBMS, the operations may be inappropriate. When working with special-purpose operations, such as text search and temporal or spatial operations, they may be easier to implement on flat files.

One way to implement flat file databases is on top of the Unix file system. The Unix file system provides scripting and programming interfaces for prototypes, security, redundant storage, and indexed files. Most existing DBMSs are implemented as programs on top of a file system that store data in byte-addressable files, and most have versions that run in Unix and store data in Unix files. When working in a restricted environment—such as a Palm or other small, specialized device that has a Linux operating system—quite efficient and complex systems may also be implemented as modules in the Linux kernel. PalmOS also provides simple database functionality that may be used to implement more complex XML storage facilities.

For many applications, documents may be stored one per file in XML representation. For specialized applications, it may be useful to consider alternative storage formats such as a binary encoding, or using specialized characters, such as whitespace, to increase parsing efficiency with specialized parsers. These alternative formats for storing the element tree can improve queries on subelement relationships, although most flat file databases may be developed using generic XML parsers.

Usually, flat file databases will store large quantities of static data in a flat file database organized with one document per file. However, flat file databases have two relevant limitations: quick access and indexing. This also impacts the ability of a flat file DBMS to efficiently log updates and other transactions and to perform recovery. Sometimes, splitting documents into document fragments may be more efficient than storing an entire document in a file. For example, in the Wal-Mart application—because transactions are to be accessed individually—each transaction could be stored in separate file and named with a unique transaction identifier. A separate file can be created for each transaction. Each customer can have a separate file with a list of transaction identifiers in which the customer participated, and each UPC code can have a separate file with all transaction identifiers in which it was purchased.

A second approach is to group the transactions into an alternative grouping, such as the customer ID. In essence, a single index is created based on the most commonly accessed unique identifier. An alternative index, such as UPC code, would refer to the customer ID file and the transaction ID together as a way of accessing the data.

In order to generate the complete document, or even larger document fragments, each document fragment must have a way of referring to other documents. A simple mechanism for linking documents is to have a special element type name, for example, "include" with attributes that provide the necessary information to link to another document. In this example, the include element might have an "element" attribute with value "transaction" and an "ID" attribute with the transaction identifier as the value, for example:

```
<include element="transaction" id="12345"/>
```

These places where the document can be sliced into multiple document fragments are called *slice points*. When the slice points are already determined by the application, as in this case, the appropriate element type name may be used directly, such as:

```
<transaction id="12345"/>
```

In practice, this approach is too inefficient on the suggested scale because of time needed to access each file individually. However, the approach is useful on a smaller scale and will serve as a foundation for more complex storage schemes. Slice points can also be used to divide documents into fragments for storage in object-oriented or relational databases.

4.1.2 Object Database

Although several data models have been developed in Chapter 3 for which an object model could be created, two object models are particularly appropriate. The first is a subset of the Generic Data Model (developed in Section 3.5.7). The second is to use the Node-centric Data Model described in Section 3.5.5 with an XML DOM parser. An object database implementation of an XML DBMS is difficult to describe because there is not an implementation platform that is likely to be available to most readers, and unlike the relational database example in the next section, the differences between the implementation of the different object DBMSs makes porting specific examples more difficult. Thus, an overview of object-oriented implementation is provided here, whereas the next section provides details only in the context of a relational DBMS.

An object model can be defined in terms of the constructs of the XML data model; in effect, the terms that are defined in the XML specification, such as document, element, attribute, and character data. A document is an element. An element is made up of attributes and ordered character data and elements. An attribute has a name and value. Character data consists of strings in the document that are not elements.

Although a graph conceptual schema for XML was developed for what corresponds to the Simple Data Model in Section 3.5.2, it is useful to draw a more complete conceptual schema to correspond to the types of the Generic Data Model as will be stored in the object database. The conceptual schema is depicted in Figure 4–1. Recall that this is a conceptual schema for the particular engineered domain of XML storage systems using the same conceptual modeling language that is used for other application areas. These relationships between development tools are depicted in Figure 4–2.

The database design tools in Chapter 2 are used 99.9% of the time to develop a new application for an existing DBMS. However, they can also be used to develop a very specific kind of database software, namely a DBMS. These are not developed very frequently (0.1% of the time), but happen to be what this chapter and the previous chapter are about. The techniques in Chapter 2 will primarily be used to develop schemas for an XML DBMS (or other application), but because you are reading this chapter, you probably do not have a great XML DBMS that does everything you need. So you

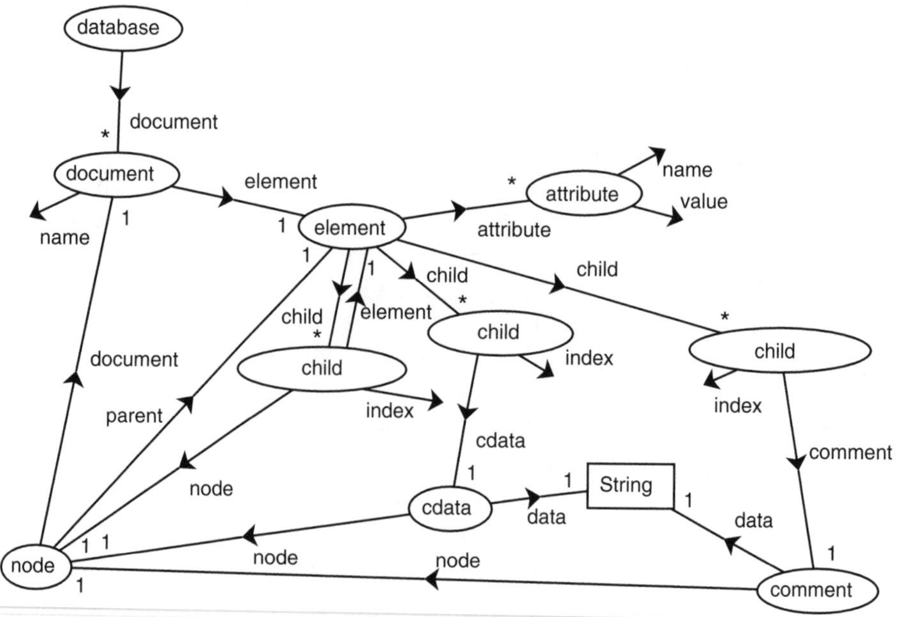

Figure 4–1 Generic graph conceptual schema for storing XML

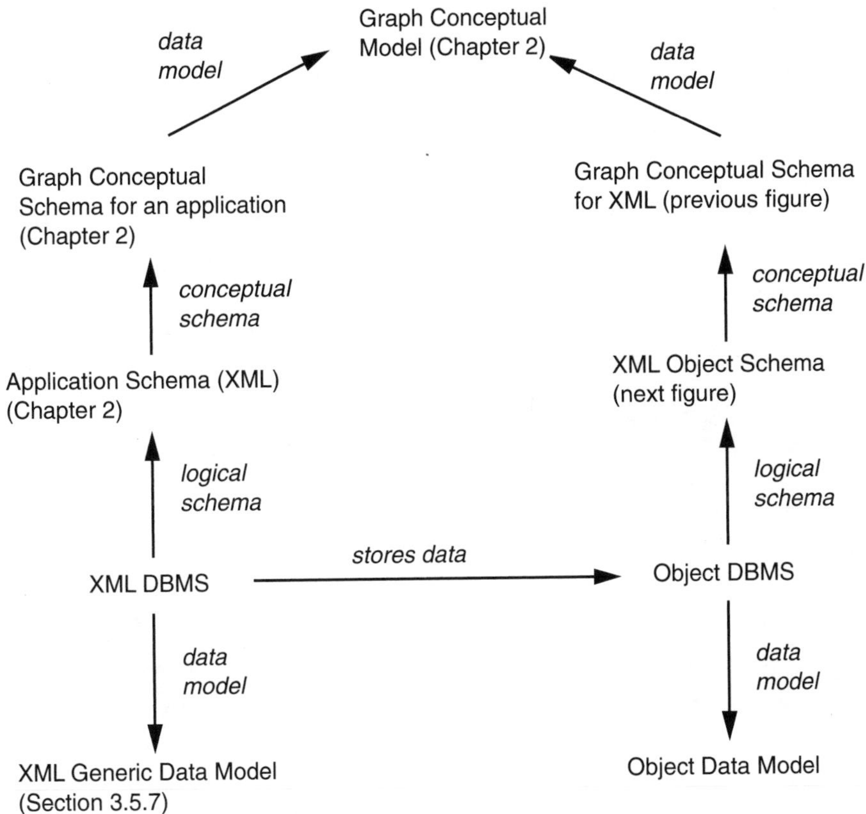

Figure 4–2 Relationships between schemas for general applications and XML database engineering application

need to build one, and this chapter describes how to do that easily. This step in the design process may be particularly confusing because you probably have not used the techniques of Chapter 2 to design a schema for your (yet to appear) XML DBMS (the 99.9% likely and more intuitive scenario). Furthermore, the domain of XML data structures is not the easiest schema to start with.

Using the design process of Chapter 2, the conceptual schema of XML data structures may be translated into a UML diagram for an object model. This model is depicted in Figure 4–3. Java code for interfaces implementing the XML storage is given in Example 4–2. Note that one modification is made in creating an object model from the data model: a new type called

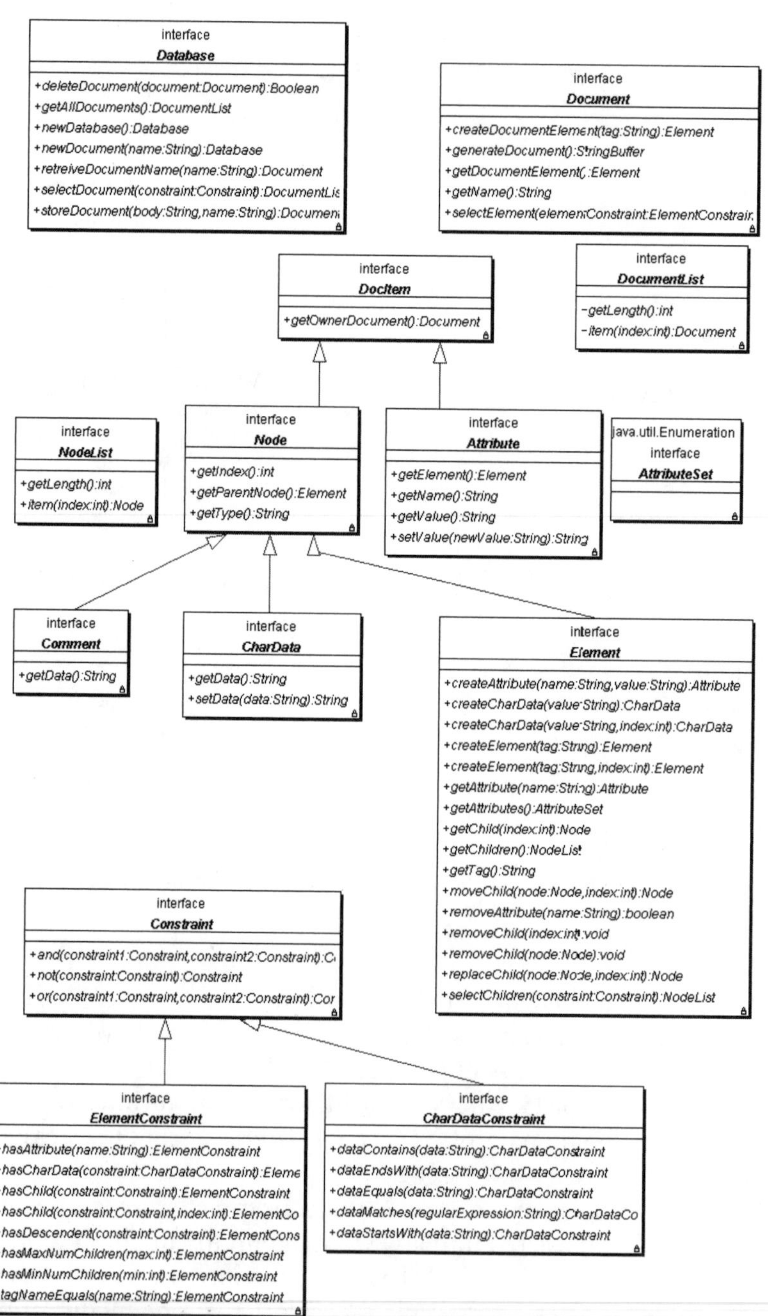

Figure 4–3 UML diagram for object storage of XML

Example 4–2 : Interfaces for XML Storage Objects

```
/*********************** Database.java *********************/
package com.xweave.xmldb.store;

public interface Database {
Boolean deleteDocument(Document document);
DocumentList getAllDocuments();
Database newDatabase();
Database newDocument(String name);
Document retreiveDocumentName(String name);
DocumentList selectDocument(Constraint constraint);
Document storeDocument(String body, String name);
}

/*********************** Document.java *********************/
package com.xweave.xmldb.store;

public interface Document {
Element createDocumentElement(String tag);
StringBuffer generateDocument();
Element getDocumentElement();
String getName();
Element selectElement(ElementConstraint elementConstraint);
}
/*************** DOCUMENT ITEMS (NODES) ********************/

/*********************** DocItem.java **********************/
package com.xweave.xmldb.store;

public interface DocItem {
Document getOwnerDocument();
}

/************************ Node.java ************************/
package com.xweave.xmldb.store;

public interface Node extends DocItem {
int getIndex();
Element getParentNode();
String getType();
}
```

```
/********************** Element.java *********************/
package com.xweave.xmldb.store;

public interface Element extends Node {
Attribute createAttribute(String name, String value);
CharData createCharData(String value);
CharData createCharData(String value, int index);
Element createElement(String tag);
Element createElement(String tag, int index);
Attribute getAttribute(String name);
AttributeSet getAttributes();
Node getChild(int index);
NodeList getChildren();
String getTag();
/* move a node to a new index */
Node moveChild(Node node, int index);
boolean removeAttribute(String name);
void removeChild(int index);
/* Remove the child of <element> which is <node> */
void removeChild(Node node);
/* replace an Element or CharData with an CharData
   equivalent to a delete and move, but more efficient */
Node replaceChild(Node node, int index);
/* returns an Enumeration of DocItem */
NodeList selectChildren(Constraint constraint);

/********************* Attribute.java ********************/
package com.xweave.xmldb.store;

public interface Attribute extends DocItem {
Element getElement();
String getName();
String getValue();
String setValue(String newValue);
}

/********************** CharData.java ********************/
package com.xweave.xmldb.store;

public interface CharData extends Node {
String getData();
String setData(String data);
}
```

```
/*********************** Comment.java **********************/
package com.xweave.xmldb.store;

public interface Comment extends Node {
String getData();
}

/********************* CONSTRAINTS *************************/

/********************* Constraint.java *********************/
package com.xweave.xmldb.store;

public interface Constraint {
Constraint and(Constraint constraint1, Constraint constraint2);
Constraint not(Constraint constraint);
Constraint or(Constraint constraint1, Constraint constraint2);
}

/****************** ElementConstraint.java *****************/
package com.xweave.xmldb.store;

public interface ElementConstraint extends Constraint {
ElementConstraint hasAttribute(String name);
ElementConstraint hasCharData(CharDataConstraint constraint);
ElementConstraint hasChild(Constraint constraint);
ElementConstraint hasChild(Constraint constraint, int index);
ElementConstraint hasDescendent(Constraint constraint);
ElementConstraint hasMaxNumChildren(int max);
ElementConstraint hasMinNumChildren(int min);
ElementConstraint tagNameEquals(String name);
}

/***************** CharDataConstraint.java *****************/
package com.xweave.xmldb.store;

public interface CharDataConstraint extends Constraint {
CharDataConstraint dataContains(String data);
CharDataConstraint dataEndsWith(String data);
CharDataConstraint dataEquals(String data);
CharDataConstraint dataMatches(String regularExpression);
CharDataConstraint dataStartsWith(String data);
}
```

```
/********************** COLLECTIONS ************************/

/********************* AttributeSet.java ******************/
package com.xweave.xmldb.store;

public interface AttributeSet extends java.util.Enumeration {
}

/********************** NodeList.java ********************/
package com.xweave.xmldb.store;

public interface NodeList {
int getLength();
Node item(int index);
}

/********************* DocumentList.java ******************/
package com.xweave.xmldb.store;

public interface DocumentList {
int getLength();
Document item(int index);
}
```

DocItem is created as a superclass of Node and Attribute with the method getOwnerDocument. This makes the objects more useful when using an object-oriented programming language.

You face a trade-off when storing XML data in an object database instead of a relational database. Storing items as objects can impose a burden if many small objects are stored as an instance that has a large memory footprint. For example, consider a relatively small database of 100,000 entities with a shallow hierarchy for each entity of 10 characteristics (as subelements), each with 3 subelements with 2 attributes and 1 character data region. If storage of a small object requires 100 bytes, then 3.11 million elements (at an average of three 100-byte objects per element) and 10 million strings (at an average size of 120 bytes per string object) would require $(3) \cdot (100) \cdot (3110001) + (120) \cdot (9000000) = 2.013$ GB. However, when the object database provides rapid access with a small memory footprint, then the access can be considerably quicker than the relational database. Alternatively, the relational database provides more efficient storage, but will have the different components stored without a direct (memory-managed) connection, which may significantly increase access time.

4.1.3 Relational Database

Developing a relational schema for XML may be the most practical approach to integrating XML into a high-throughput enterprise. Until XML DBMSs reach the stage of maturity of commercial relational DBMSs, leveraging the relational system infrastructure may provide greater benefit than using a recently developed XML DBMS, which may be more effective in some ways but without the robustness, support, or proven business applicability. This approach may be useful later when the enterprise requirements are still primarily captured by the relational model, but also require a tightly-coupled XML DBMS component.

Storing XML in a relational DBMS is described in the remainder of this chapter. The key development decision is *whether* to store the data using this approach. One question that you need to answer before choosing the appropriate technology is: How tightly-coupled does the XML data need to be with other data? If the data to be captured in XML is so integrated with the remainder of the data in a relational form, it may be more effective to use the approach of Chapter 5 to translate data between XML and relational forms. If the XML-oriented data is completely isolated from the relational-oriented data, then a separate XML DBMS may be used, based on the requirements of the specific application. When the coupling is between the two extremes, then storing XML documents in a relational database (as XML) makes the most sense.

Three approaches for storing data in a relational DBMS are described in the following sections. The first is a fine-grained approach where every element and attribute can be individually accessed. The second is a coarse-grained approach where the document is manipulated in its entirety. The third is a medium-grained approach that balances the strengths of the two extremes through a hybrid approach. Any one of the three could serve as the storage facility for a DBMS that implements one of the data models defined in Chapter 3.

4.2 Fine-grained Relational Schema

In the fine-grained approach, every construct in the document is given a unique identity in the relational database. Every element, attribute, and character data region can be individually accessed, modified, or deleted with minimal effect on other document constructs. This provides the most flexibility and ease of access both with the XML DBMS–specific operations as well as through the traditional relational ones. However, regenerating the entire document can be time-consuming when large, and the space required for all the pointers can be significant.

4.2.1 Logical Design

The basic idea of the fine-grained approach is that each type of construct in the document has its own table: elements, attributes, and character data regions. There is also a table for documents and a table for the parent/child relationship between elements and their constituents (subelements or character data). A logical schema in the relational data model is depicted later in this section.

The logical design of the schema consists of two steps. The first step is to create a relational schema in the relational data model. The second step is to normalize that schema. Most database developers will develop a somewhat normalized schema from the beginning, but in this section we start with a schema that is not normalized to first normal form. This simplifies the presentation to those without a lot of relational database design experience and make the section more useful in developing an object-oriented implementation, as described in Section 4.1.2

A logical relational schema is defined in terms of the relation names, column names, and domains. Relation names and column names are familiar to those who have used any relational DBMSs. Domain names are an integral part of the relational data model but are not implemented in a traditional relational DBMS. Instead, the simple data types—such as NUMBER, STRING, and TEXT—are used, often with some variations. Those data types are *pre-defined domains* in the relational data model. Some relational DBMSs with an object-oriented component do implement additional *user-defined* domains to incorporate objects. The user-defined domains may be *atomic* within the schema or refer to relations in the schema (*relation domains*). The relation domain is typically implemented in a DBMS as a foreign key relationship. However, it helps to explicitly define the relational schema by using domains to make explicit the relationship between the XML data models of the previous chapter and the XML storage implementations of the following sections.

The logical schema is specified in the following format:

```
RelationName( columnName1 DOMAIN_NAME_1 , columnName2
    DOMAIN_NAME_2 )
```

A logical schema in the relational data model for the fine-grained schema is

```
Document(name DOC_NAME, root ELEMENT)
Element(doc DOCUMENT, parent ELEMENT, tag ELE_NAME)
Attribute(doc DOCUMENT, element ELEMENT, name
    ATTR_NAME, value ATTR_VALUE)
CharData(doc DOCUMENT, element ELEMENT, value CDATA)
Child(doc DOCUMENT, element ELEMENT, index NUMBER,
    child_class CHILD_CLASS, child CHILD_NODE)
```

The "CHILD_CLASS" and "CHILD_NODE" domains are used to simulate the union of the "ELEMENT" and "CHARDATA" domains.

To normalize the schema into first normal form, the relation domains "DOCUMENT" and "ELEMENT" are eliminated by creating unique identifiers for each relation "doc_id" and "ele_id" in the new atomic user-defined domains "DOC_ID" and "ELE_ID". A normalized logical schema is:

```
Document(doc_id DOC_ID, name DOC_NAME, root
    ELEMENT_ID)
Element(doc_id DOC_ID, ele_id ELE_ID, parent_id
    ELEMENT, tag ELE_NAME)
Attribute(doc_id DOC_ID, ele_id ELE_ID, name
    ATTR_NAME, value ATTR_VALUE)
CharData(doc_id DOC_ID, cdata_id CDATA_ID, ele_id
    ELE_ID, value CDATA)
Child(doc_id DOC_ID, ele_id ELE_ID, index NUMBER,
    child_class CHILD_CLASS, child CHILD_NODE)
```

Figure 4–4 shows a diagram of the normalized logical schema, and Figure 4–5 shows the schema with atomic data types instead of domains.

In the logical schema, the document table contains columns for the name, document ID, and element root. Each entry in the table corresponds to a document in the database. The name provides a unique name for the document for reference by external applications. The document ID provides a unique number identifier that is referenced by the other tables to associate each document construct with the appropriate document. This is necessary for rapid retrieval of the document when performing searches on the document constituents. The element root connects the document table with the element in the element table that is the root of the document element tree.

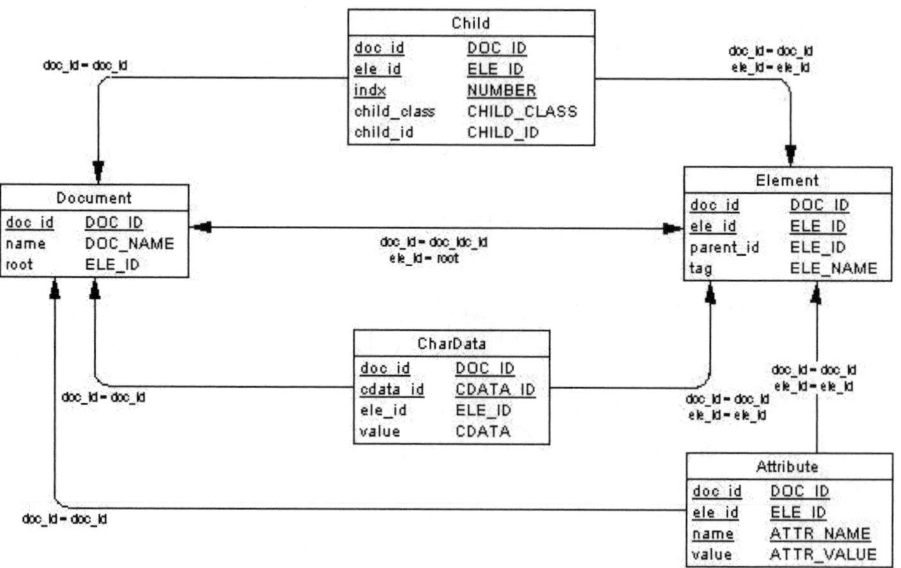

Figure 4–4 Normalized logical schema for fine-grained relational database to store XML data

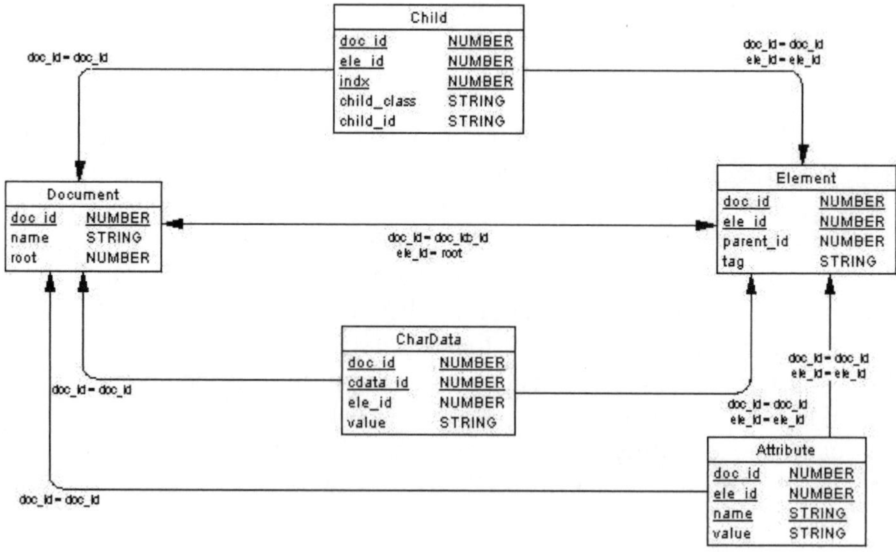

Figure 4–5 Normalized logical schema for fine-grained relational database to store XML data with atomic data types

The element table is central to the design and connects the remaining document constructs. Each element in a document has a unique identifier. The element identifier together with the document identifier serve to uniquely identify the element. Having an element identifier unique to each document simplifies the process of searching and copying documents within the database. The element table also contains columns for the element type (tag) name, the document identifier, and the parent element identifier. The tag name column captures the string value of the element type, and the document identifier refers to the document of which the element is a part.

Every element must be contained in a document. If this constraint were not present, the database could more easily become corrupted should multiple applications simultaneously create elements without documents. The parent element identifier connects the subelements to the parent elements in a tree structure. It provides a method for navigating from the leaves and internal nodes of the tree to the root. Every element in the document should have a parent element except for the root element (which is denoted by a NULL parent identifier). The root element should also be referenced by the root column of the document table.

The attribute table is fairly straightforward. It contains the name and value of the attribute and a reference to the element identifier for which it is an attribute. The element identifier connects the element to its set of attributes. In addition, the attribute has its own unique identifier and has a reference to the document identifier. The attribute identifier is used as an internal reference by database operations that access the attribute directly, such as query, update, and delete.

The child table connects the elements in the element table to their constituents through the element identifier and child identifier columns. It provides a straightforward way to access all the subelements and character data regions that are direct descendants of an element as well as to navigate up the element tree. The child table also provides an ordering of the element constituents with an index column. The index orders both the subelements and character data regions in the one ordering. There is a column called child class that distinguishes between constituent types element and character data. The child table contains a reference to the document identifier, but does not need a unique identifier. The primary key of the child table is the document identifier, element identifier, and index number—this is sufficient to uniquely identify each child relationship in the database.

The child class may also be used to extend the current schema to incorporate other XML constituents, such as comments. This approach may also be used to incorporate data type information from the XML document if that is specified as part of a document type definition (DTD) or XSDL schema. For example, another table may be created for the data type NUMBER, DATE, or user-defined data types.

In some cases more efficient queries may be performed by duplicating the index column of the child table in the Element and CharData tables. For example, this would allow a query of all subelements for a specified element to retrieve only from the Element table without needing to perform a join with the Child table. However, duplicating the index column would require that the application ensure that the index values are kept synchronized or require the use of additional code in the database to keep the values synchronized, such as triggers, SQLJ methods, or PL/SQL procedures. It is also possible to drop the Child table and use only the index column in the Element and CharData tables, but then queries that retrieve based on index number would have to attempt querying from both Element and CharData tables as the data type of the child at a specified index is not explicitly stored. This would probably be okay with only two types of children (Element and CharData), but would not scale-up well if other child types are added. A reasonable compromise for some applications would be to duplicate the index column for the Element table only, which would allow queries of element type names, such as simple XML Path queries, to be executed more efficiently.

4.2.2 Physical Design

The first step in creating a physical schema from the logical schema consists of determining reasonable sizes for the columns. This is best done knowing the particulars of the applications, but reasonable assumptions are made here for a moderate-sized application. Values are chosen to allow for 100 million documents with 100 million elements each, and each element can contain up to 1 million children. Tag and attribute names are limited to 32 characters, and attribute values are limited to 255 characters. The size of the document name was chosen to be 128 characters to allow for a flat collection of named documents, to include path information, or to store URLs.

A physical schema for Oracle is presented in Figure 4–6 and the code that creates it is listed in Example 4–3. When developing a physical schema for Oracle, be aware of the limitation of string sizes to 2000 characters (Oracle 7) or 4000 characters (Oracle 8). It is reasonably likely in many

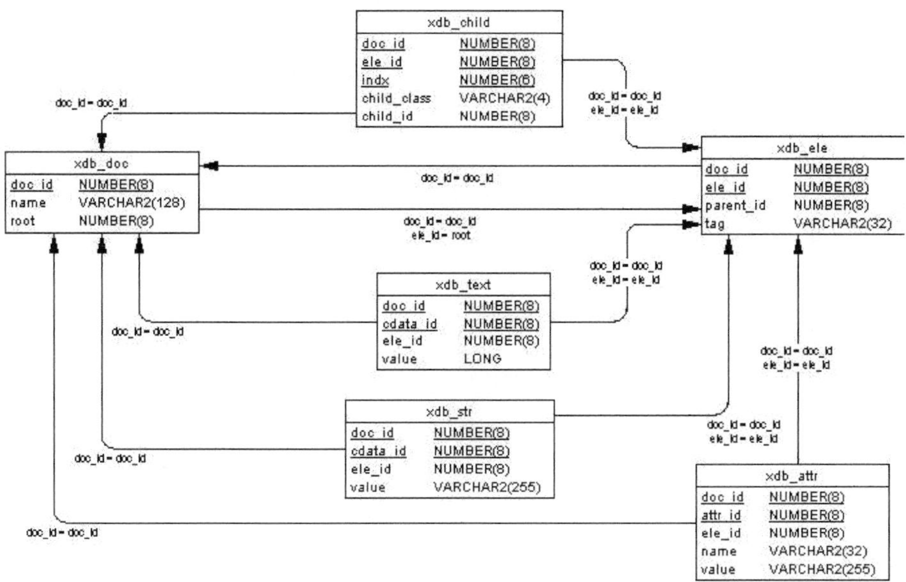

Figure 4–6 Physical schema for fine-grained relational database to store XML data (Oracle)

Example 4–3 : Fine-grained Oracle Schema for Storing XML Documents

```
-- Create fine-grained storage tables and constraints

create table xdb_doc (
   doc_id        NUMBER(8)        NOT NULL,
   name          VARCHAR2(128)    NOT NULL,
   root          NUMBER(8)
);
alter table xdb_doc add primary key (doc_id);

create table xdb_ele (
   doc_id        NUMBER(8)        NOT NULL,
   ele_id        NUMBER(8)        NOT NULL,
   parent_id     NUMBER(8),
   tag           VARCHAR2(32)     NOT NULL
);
alter table xdb_ele add primary key (doc_id, ele_id);

create table xdb_attr (
   doc_id        NUMBER(8)        NOT NULL,
```

```
   attr_id         NUMBER(8)          NOT NULL,
   ele_id          NUMBER(8)          NOT NULL,
   name            VARCHAR2(32)       NOT NULL,
   value           VARCHAR2(255)
);
alter table xdb_attr add primary key (doc_id, attr_id);

create table xdb_child (
   doc_id          NUMBER(8)          NOT NULL,
   ele_id          NUMBER(8)          NOT NULL,
   indx            NUMBER(6)          NOT NULL,
   child_class     VARCHAR2(4)        NOT NULL, -- ELE, STR, or TEXT
   child_id        NUMBER(8)          NOT NULL
);
alter table xdb_child add primary key (doc_id, ele_id, indx);

create table xdb_str (
   doc_id          NUMBER(8)          NOT NULL,
   cdata_id        NUMBER(8)          NOT NULL,
   ele_id          NUMBER(8)          NOT NULL,
   value           VARCHAR2(255)      NOT NULL
);
alter table xdb_str add primary key (doc_id, cdata_id);

create table xdb_text (
   doc_id          NUMBER(8)          NOT NULL,
   cdata_id        NUMBER(8)          NOT NULL,
   ele_id          NUMBER(8)          NOT NULL,
   value           LONG               NOT NULL
);
alter table xdb_text add primary key (doc_id, cdata_id);

-- Foreign Keys
alter table xdb_doc add constraint fk_xdb_doc_root
      foreign key (doc_id, root) references xdb_ele (doc_id, ele_id);
alter table xdb_ele add constraint fk_xdb_ele_doc_id
      foreign key (doc_id) references xdb_doc (doc_id);
alter table xdb_attr add constraint fk_xdb_attr_doc_id
      foreign key (doc_id) references xdb_doc (doc_id);
alter table xdb_attr add constraint fk_xdb_attr_ele_id
      foreign key (doc_id, ele_id) references xdb_ele (doc_id, ele_id);
alter table xdb_child add constraint fk_xdb_child_doc_id
      foreign key (doc_id) references xdb_doc (doc_id);
alter table xdb_child add constraint fk_xdb_child_ele_id
      foreign key (doc_id, ele_id) references xdb_ele (doc_id, ele_id);
```

```
alter table xdb_str add constraint fk_xdb_str_doc_id
      foreign key (doc_id) references xdb_doc (doc_id);
alter table xdb_str add constraint fk_xdb_str_ele_id
      foreign key (doc_id, ele_id) references xdb_ele (doc_id, ele_id);
alter table xdb_text add constraint fk_xdb_text_doc_id
      foreign key (doc_id) references xdb_doc (doc_id);
alter table xdb_text add constraint fk_xdb_text_ele_id
      foreign key (doc_id, ele_id) references xdb_ele (doc_id, ele_id);
```

applications that character data regions may be longer than several hundred characters and thus must be stored separately. Oracle provides the LONG data type that provides relatively unlimited string length (2 GB) but very limited access through relational operations. To address this, it is necessary to modify the schema to provide for both storage mechanisms.

Two approaches to allowing for character and long data types are: (1) to create an additional column or (2) to create an additional table. To create an additional column, the value column in the character data table is replaced with three columns: a VARCHAR2 value column, a LONG value column, and a boolean flag to distinguish which one is filled (the other is null). The Oracle DECODE function can be used to retrieve the data somewhat transparently. To create an additional table, the character data table is replaced with two tables: one where the value is of type VARCHAR2 and one where the value is of type LONG. A flag to distinguish between the two is added to the table(s) that access the character data. In general, adding a column is the best approach; however, because the element child table already distinguishes between constituents of type subelement and character data, the schema becomes cleaner by splitting the character data table and replacing the child class "Character Data" with "String" and "Long". The character data length to split between the two tables becomes a tunable schema parameter. A somewhat arbitrary length of 255 was chosen, which does allow for the creation of an index on the String value column.

A physical schema for other DBMSs can be created similarly. A physical schema for DB2 is shown in Figure 4–7. The code to generate the schema is given in Example 4–4.

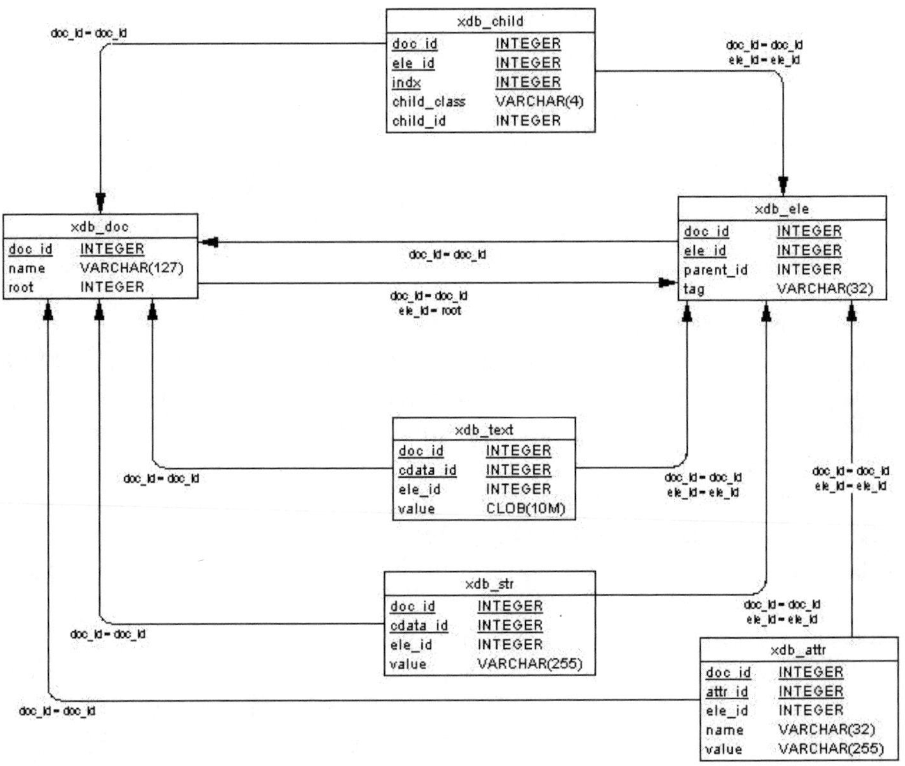

Figure 4–7 Physical schema for fine-grained relational database to store XML data (DB2)

Example 4–4 : Fine-grained DB2 Schema for Storing XML Documents

```
-- Create fine-grained storage tables and constraints

create table xdb_doc (
   doc_id      INTEGER        NOT NULL,
   name        VARCHAR(127)   NOT NULL,
   root        INTEGER
);
alter table xdb_doc add primary key (doc_id);

create table xdb_ele (
   doc_id      INTEGER        NOT NULL,
   ele_id      INTEGER        NOT NULL,
   parent_id   INTEGER,
   tag         VARCHAR(32)    NOT NULL
```

```
);
alter table xdb_ele add primary key (doc_id, ele_id);

create table xdb_attr (
   doc_id        INTEGER          NOT NULL,
   attr_id       INTEGER          NOT NULL,
   ele_id        INTEGER          NOT NULL,
   name          VARCHAR(32)      NOT NULL,
   value         VARCHAR(255)
);
alter table xdb_attr add primary key (doc_id, attr_id);

create table xdb_child (
   doc_id        INTEGER          NOT NULL,
   ele_id        INTEGER          NOT NULL,
   indx          INTEGER          NOT NULL,
   child_class   VARCHAR(4)       NOT NULL,
   child_id      INTEGER          NOT NULL
);
alter table xdb_child add primary key (doc_id, ele_id, indx);

create table xdb_str (
   doc_id        INTEGER          NOT NULL,
   cdata_id      INTEGER          NOT NULL,
   ele_id        INTEGER          NOT NULL,
   value         VARCHAR(255)     NOT NULL
);
alter table xdb_str add primary key (doc_id, cdata_id);

create table xdb_text (
   doc_id        INTEGER          NOT NULL,
   cdata_id      INTEGER          NOT NULL,
   ele_id        INTEGER          NOT NULL,
   value         CLOB(10M)        NOT NULL
);
alter table xdb_text add primary key (doc_id, cdata_id);

-- Foreign Keys
alter table xdb_doc add constraint fk_xdb_doc_root
      foreign key (doc_id, root) references xdb_ele (doc_id,
         ele_id);
alter table xdb_ele add constraint fk_xdb_ele_doc_id
      foreign key (doc_id) references xdb_doc (doc_id);
alter table xdb_attr add constraint fk_xdb_attr_doc_id
      foreign key (doc_id) references xdb_doc (doc_id);
```

```
alter table xdb_attr add constraint fk_xdb_attr_ele_id
      foreign key (doc_id, ele_id) references xdb_ele (doc_id, ele_id);
alter table xdb_child add constraint fk_xdb_child_doc
      foreign key (doc_id) references xdb_doc (doc_id);
alter table xdb_child add constraint fk_xdb_child_ele
      foreign key (doc_id, ele_id) references xdb_ele (doc_id, ele_id);
alter table xdb_str add constraint fk_xdb_str_doc_id
      foreign key (doc_id) references xdb_doc (doc_id);
alter table xdb_str add constraint fk_xdb_str_ele_id
      foreign key (doc_id, ele_id) references xdb_ele (doc_id, ele_id);
alter table xdb_text add constraint fk_xdb_text_doc_id
      foreign key (doc_id) references xdb_doc (doc_id);
alter table xdb_text add constraint fk_xdb_text_ele_id
      foreign key (doc_id, ele_id) references xdb_ele (doc_id, ele_id);
```

The differences between the Oracle schema and DB2 schema are as follows:

- For strings of varying length, Oracle uses the data type name VARCHAR2 and DB2 uses the name VARCHAR.
- The Oracle schema uses NUMBER(8) for identifiers, and the DB2 schema uses INTEGER, which allows for 2^{32} (about 2 billion) identifiers (in DB2 v7.0).
- DB2 only allows for 18 characters in the length of a constraint name, so the foreign key constraint names "fk_xdb_child_doc_id" and "fk_xdb_child_ele_id" were shortened to "fk_xdb_child_doc" and "fk_xdb_child_ele", respectively.
- DB2 does not like the comment in the xdb_child table creation statement, and it is omitted.
- Oracle provides a LONG type for very long character strings up to 2GB. DB2 provides a CLOB (Character Large OBject) type that provides similar functionality, also up to 2GB. However, the DB2 CLOB allows specification of a lower maximum size that is more efficient.

For DB2, a size of 100KB is chosen for the maximum character data region—the maximum length of text without a tag. This is probably enough for most documents, however, some applications may quote a large text region in a CDATA section, which could require an increase in the maximum character data region size.

Additional physical design includes creating indices and tuning the DBMS. Indexes are useful on most of the columns, but indices are best developed within the requirements of the particular application. There are books available on creating appropriate indexes and tuning specific DBMSs, so the remainder of physical design is outside the scope of this book.

4.2.3 Examples

To demonstrate the functionality of the fine-grained approach, a simple system is developed that supports the operations of the Generic Data Model described in Section 3.5.7. To demonstrate the system, some of the tasks from Section 3.4.2 are implemented. Several of the tasks may be performed through SQL statements that are executed against the Oracle database, but other tasks—such as storing and retrieving an entire document—must be developed in a traditional programming language.

A Java system is developed (and described in the next section) that provides storage and retrieval for XML documents captured in the fine-grained relational schema. Although missing much functionality necessary for a complete DBMS, the system allows XML documents to be stored and retrieved in a manner that allows for searching and updating. It also demonstrates the basic operations of an XML DBMS in a form that is comprehendible in a single example and can serve as the basis for more complex systems.

To use the system, a command line application is presented here. The command line interface provides options to store a document, to retrieve by identifier, to list all documents, or to delete by identifier; the retrieved XML documents are written to standard out. Java GUI applications or applets are also possible. An applet is shown in Figure 4–8—where a user may store an XML document by pasting a URL and selecting the "Store" button, and documents may be retrieved by their internal identifier or by selecting from a list of all documents.

After a document is stored in the database, SQL queries may be asked to search for elements or attributes that meet certain constraints, as shown in Example 4–5. Some examples of use are shown in Example 4–6. These examples demonstrate some of the functionality of the system.

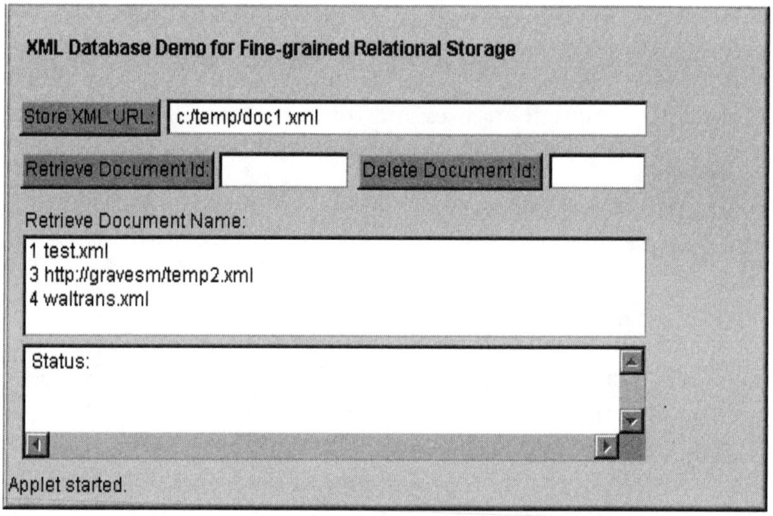

XML Database Demo for Fine-grained Relational Storage

Store XML URL: c:/temp/doc1.xml

Retrieve Document Id: Delete Document Id:

Retrieve Document Name:

1 test.xml
3 http://gravesm/temp2.xml
4 waltrans.xml

Status:

Applet started.

Figure 4–8 Applet for storing and retrieving XML documents

Example 4–5 : Fine-grained Queries for Some XML Database Tasks

```
-- Search for all elements with a given tag name.
select doc_id, ele_id
from xdb_ele
where doc_id = 1
  and tag = 'TagName';

-- Search for all elements with a given attribute name.
select doc_id, attr_id
from xdb_attr
where doc_id = 1
  and name = 'AttrName'
  and value = 'AttrValue';

-- Search for all elements with a given tag name that has a
--  character data child consisting of a given string.
select ele.doc_id, ele.ele_id
from xdb_ele ele, xdb_str str
where ele.doc_id = 1
  and str.doc_id = ele.doc_id
  and ele.tag = 'TagName'
  and ele.ele_id = str.ele_id
  and str.value = 'SearchedForValue';
```

Example 4–6 : Examples of Using a Fine-grained Storage System

```
% # Loading data into fine-grained storage system
%
% ls
fgrel          fgrel.sh       src            waltrans.xml
fgrel.jar      jdbc.jar       test.xml       xml4j.jar
% cat fgrel
java -cp fgrel.jar:jdbc.jar:xml4j.jar com.xweave.xmldb.fgrel.Demo
connect acct/password@localhost:1521:ORCL $*
% fgrel store test.xml
Loaded document 1 from test.xml
% fgrel store http://localhost/temp1.xml
Loaded document 2 from http://localhost/temp1.xml
% fgrel list
1 test.xml
2 http://localhost/temp1.xml

% fgrel store http://anotherhost/temp2.xml
Loaded document 3 from http://anotherhost/temp2.xml
% fgrel store waltrans.xml
Loaded document 4 from waltrans.xml
% fgrel list
1 test.xml
2 http://localhost/temp1.xml
3 http://anotherhost/temp2.xml
4 waltrans.xml

% fgrel delete 2
Deleted document 2
% fgrel list
1 test.xml
3 http://localhost/temp2.xml
4 waltrans.xml

% fgrel retrieve 4
<collection>
<transaction id="400100341">
<customer>
<credit_card number="4234567887654321"/>
</customer>
<store number="4567"/>
<item upc="2460001001" qty="1"/>
<item upc="1600042040" qty="2"/>
<item upc="5928000020" qty="4"/>
<coupon code="5928000100"/>
</transaction>
```

```
<transaction id="400100342">
<customer>
<checking_acct routing="344465456" acct="12345678"/>
</customer>
<store number="4567"/>
<item upc="2460001002" qty="2"/>
<item upc="1600024540" qty="2"/>
</transaction>
<transaction id="400100343">
<customer>
<cash/>
</customer>
<store number="4567"/>
<item upc="2460001001" qty="1"/>
<item upc="1645042940" qty="2"/>
<item upc="5928000020" qty="1"/>
<item upc="1645042876" qty="2"/>
<coupon code="1645081140"/>
</transaction>
</collection>
%
% # Querying data
% sqlplus

SQL> -- Search for all elements with a given tag name.
SQL> select doc_id, ele_id
  2  from xdb_ele
  3  where doc_id = 4
  4    and tag = 'credit_card';

   DOC_ID    ELE_ID
--------- ---------
        4         4

SQL>
SQL> -- Search for all elements with a given attribute name and value.
SQL> select doc_id, attr_id
  2  from xdb_attr
  3  where doc_id = 4
  4    and name = 'upc'
  5    and value = '5928000020';
   DOC_ID   ATTR_ID
--------- ---------
        4         8
        4        25

SQL>
```

4.2.4 Implementation

The Java code that implements the store and retrieve is listed in Example 4–7. Note that the CLASSPATH must contain a JDBC driver and an XML parser (IBM's XML parser is used in the example). A UML diagram for the Java implementation is given in Figure 4–9.

Example 4–7 : Java Implementation of a Fine-grained Storage System

```
/*********************** Demo.java ***********************/
package com.xweave.xmldb.fgrel;

import com.xweave.xmldb.util.rdb.*;
import com.xweave.xmldb.util.io.*;
/**
 * Demonstration of Fine-grained relational storage
 */
public class Demo {
   protected Format format = null;
   protected Load load = null;
   protected Delete delete = null;
   private DocumentList documentList = null;
   private RDB rdb = null;
   protected String rdbAccessString =
com.xweave.xmldb.Default.getXmldbAcct();
   protected final static String DOC_TABLE = "XDB_DOC";
   protected final static String USAGE =
   "demo (help | list | connect <connectstring> | store <url> |
retrieve <id> | delete <id>)*";
   protected Output output = null;
public Demo() {
  super();
}
public void connect() {
  try {
   setRdb(new RDBConnector(new JDBCAcct(rdbAccessString)));
  } catch (java.sql.SQLException ex) {
   ex.printStackTrace();
  }
}
public void connect(String value) {
  this.setRdbAccessString(value);
  connect();
```

```
    }
  public boolean deleteDocumentId(String documentId) {
      boolean status = getDelete().deleteDoc(documentId);
      if (status) {
          status("Deleted document " + documentId);
      } else {
          status("Was unable to delete document " + documentId);
      }
      return status;
  }
  public boolean dispatchArg(String command, String value) {
      if (command.equalsIgnoreCase("RETRIEVE")) {
          this.retrieveDocumentId(value);
          return true;
      }
      if (command.equalsIgnoreCase("RETRIEVEDOC")) {
          this.getOutput().writeln("<?xml version=\"1.0\"?>");
          this.retrieveDocumentId(value);
          return true;
      }
      if (command.equalsIgnoreCase("STORE")) {
          this.storeDocument(value);
          return true;
          }
      if (command.equalsIgnoreCase("DELETE")) {
          this.deleteDocumentId(value);
          return true;
      }
      if (command.equalsIgnoreCase("LIST")) {
          this.writeDocumentList();
          return true;
      }
      if (command.equalsIgnoreCase("CONNECT")) {
          this.connect(value);
          return true;
      }
      if (command.equalsIgnoreCase("HELP")) {
          this.getOutput().writeln(USAGE);
          return true;
      }
      return false;
  }
  /**
   * Get the Delete command object.
   */
```

```
public Delete getDelete() {
   if (delete == null) {
      delete = new Delete(getRdb(), getOutput());
   }
   return delete;
}
/**
 * Get the DocumentList command object.
 */
public DocumentList getDocumentList() {
   if (documentList == null) {
      documentList = new DocumentList(getRdb(), getOutput());
   }
   return documentList;
}
/**
 * Get the Format command object.
 */
public Format getFormat() {
   if (format == null) {
      format = new Format(getRdb(),getOutput());
   }
   return format;
}
/**
 * Get the Load command object.
 */
public Load getLoad() {
   if (load == null) {
      if (getRdb() == null) {
         load = new Load();
      } else {
         load = new Load(getRdb());
      }
   }
   return load;
}
public Output getOutput() {
   if (output == null) {
      setOutput(new Output());
   }
   return output;
}
public RDB getRdb() {
   if (rdb == null) {
```

```
        if (getRdbAccessString() != null) {
            //create a connection to Oracle
            connect();
        }
    }
    return rdb;
}
public String getRdbAccessString() {
    return rdbAccessString;
}
/**
 * Starts the application.
 * Takes database commands as arguments.
 */
public static void main(java.lang.String[] args) {
    if (args.length == 0) {
        System.err.println(USAGE);
    }
    int ctr = 0;
    String command;
    Demo demo = new Demo();
    boolean connected = false;
    while (ctr < args.length) {
        command = args[ctr++];
        if (command.equalsIgnoreCase("HELP")) {
            System.err.println(USAGE);
            continue;
        }
        if (command.equalsIgnoreCase("LIST")) {
            demo.writeDocumentList();
            continue;
        }
        if (command.equalsIgnoreCase("CONNECT")) {
            demo.connect(args[ctr++]);
            connected = true;
            continue;
        }
        if (command.equalsIgnoreCase("STORE")) {
            demo.storeDocument(args[ctr++]);
            continue;
        }
        if (command.equalsIgnoreCase("RETRIEVE")) {
            demo.retrieveDocumentId(args[ctr++]);
            continue;
        }
```

```
        if (command.equalsIgnoreCase("DELETE")) {
                demo.deleteDocumentId(args[ctr++]);
                continue;
            }
        }
        if (connected) {
            try {
                RDB rdb = demo.rdb;
                if (rdb != null) {
                    rdb.close();
                }
            } catch (Throwable e) {
                e.printStackTrace();
            }
        }
    }
    /**
     * Format the XML document with id <documentId>
     */
    public boolean retrieveDocumentId(String documentId) {
        return getFormat().writeDoc(documentId);
    }
    public void setOutput(Output newValue) {
        this.output = newValue;
    }
    protected void setRdb(RDB newValue) {
        this.rdb = newValue;
    }
    public void setRdbAccessString(String newValue) {
        this.rdbAccessString = newValue;
    }
    /**
     * Print a status message
     */
    public void status(String msg) {
        System.err.println(msg);
    }
    /**
     * Store a document from the text <xmlDocText>
     * Should include valid XML processing instruction
     */
    public String storeDocText(String xmlDocText, String name) {
        String documentId = null;
        try {
            documentId = getLoad().parseText(xmlDocText, name);
```

```
    } catch (Throwable ex) {
        status("Error: " + ex.getMessage());
    }
    if (documentId != null) {
        status("Loaded document " + documentId + " from text");
    } else {
        status("Was unable to load document from text");
    }
    return documentId;
}
/**
 * Store a document from the given URL <xmlFile>
 */
public String storeDocument(String xmlFile) {
    return storeDocument(xmlFile, null);
}
/**
 * Store a document from the given URL <xmlFile>
 */
public String storeDocument(String xmlFile, String name) {
    String documentId = null;
    try {
        documentId = getLoad().parse(xmlFile, name);
    } catch (Throwable ex) {
        status("Error: " + ex.getMessage());
    }
    if (documentId != null) {
        status("Loaded document " + documentId + " from " + xmlFile);
    } else {
        status("Was unable to load document from " + xmlFile);
    }
    return documentId;
}
/**
 * Store a document from the given URL <xmlFile>
 */
public String storeDocUrl(String xmlFile, String name) {
    String documentId = null;
    try {
        documentId = getLoad().parseUrl(xmlFile, name);
    } catch (Throwable ex) {
        status("Error: " + ex.getMessage());
    }
    if (documentId != null) {
        status("Loaded document " + documentId + " from " + xmlFile);
```

```
} else {
        status("Was unable to load document from " + xmlFile);
    }
    return documentId;
}
/**
 * Write a list (to out) of all XML documents
 */
public void writeDocumentList() {
    getDocumentList().writeDocumentList();
}
}

/********************** Command.java *********************/
package com.xweave.xmldb.fgrel;

import com.xweave.xmldb.util.io.*;
import com.xweave.xmldb.util.rdb.*;
import java.sql.SQLException;
/**
 * Abstract command
 */

public abstract class Command {
    protected final static String DOC_TABLE = "XDB_DOC";
    protected final static String ELE_TABLE = "XDB_ELE";
    protected final static String ATTR_TABLE = "XDB_ATTR";
    protected final static String CHILD_TABLE = "XDB_CHILD";
    protected final static String STR_TABLE = "XDB_STR";
    protected final static String TEXT_TABLE = "XDB_TEXT";
    private RDB rdb = null;
    private Output output = null;
/**
 * Command constructor comment.
 */
public Command() {
    super();
}
/**
 * Command constructor comment.
 */
public Command(RDB rdb) {
    super();
    setRdb(rdb);
```

```
}
  /**
  * Command constructor comment.
  */
public Command(RDB rdb, Output out) {
    super();
    setRdb(rdb);
    setOutput(out);
}
public Output getOutput() {
    return output;
}
protected RDB getRdb() {
    return rdb;
}
public void rdbExecute(String value) throws SQLException {
    // add a semicolon to print to standard out, omit for JDBC
    if (getRdb() == null) {
        System.out.println(value + ";");
    } else {
        getRdb().executeUpdate(value);
    }
}
public void setOutput(Output newValue) {
    this.output = newValue;
}
protected void setRdb(RDB newValue) {
    this.rdb = newValue;
}
public void write(String value) {
    getOutput().write(value);
}
public void writeln(String value) {
    getOutput().writeln(value);
}
}

/*********************** Format.java **********************/
package com.xweave.xmldb.fgrel;

import com.xweave.xmldb.util.rdb.RDB;
import com.xweave.xmldb.util.io.Output;
import java.util.*;
import java.sql.*;
/**
```

```
 * Format command
 */
public class Format extends Command {
   protected final static int CDATA_SPLIT_LENGTH = 255;
   protected String document;
   protected boolean writeElementId = false;
public Format() {
   super();
}
public Format(RDB rdb) {
   super(rdb);
}
public Format(RDB rdb, Output output) {
   super(rdb, output);
}
public boolean getWriteElementId() {
   return writeElementId;
}
public void setWriteElementId(boolean newValue) {
   this.writeElementId = newValue;
}
public void write(String value, int depth) {
   write(value);
}
protected void writeCdata(String elementId, String cdataId, String
table, int depth) throws SQLException {
   StringBuffer buf = new StringBuffer();
   buf.append("select value from");
   buf.append(" " + table + " ");
   buf.append("where doc_id = " + document);
   buf.append("  and ele_id = " + elementId);
   buf.append("  and cdata_id = " + cdataId);
   String value = getRdb().getDataItem(buf.toString());
   writeln(value, depth);
}
/**
 * Dispatch an element child
 */
protected void writeChild(String childClass, String elementId, String
childId, int childDepth) throws SQLException {
   if (childClass.equalsIgnoreCase("ELE")) {
      //call writeElement recursively
      writeElement(childId,childDepth);
   } else if (childClass.equalsIgnoreCase("STR")) {
      //writeCdata works for STR or TEXT using JDBC
```

```
        writeCdata(elementId, childId, STR_TABLE, childDepth);
    } else if (childClass.equalsIgnoreCase("TEXT")) {
         //writeCdata works for STR or TEXT using JDBC
        writeCdata(elementId, childId,TEXT_TABLE, childDepth);
    } else {
        //have some default in case other classes are added to the database
        writeln("<unknown class=\""+childClass+"\" id=\""+childId+"\"/
>",childDepth);
    }
}
/**
 * Retrieve a document from the database and write it
 */
public boolean writeDoc(String document) {
    this.document = document;
    StringBuffer buf = new StringBuffer();
    buf.append("select root from");
    buf.append(" " + DOC_TABLE + " ");
    buf.append(" where doc_id = " + document);
    try {
        String elementId = getRdb().getDataItem(buf.toString());
        writeElement(elementId, 0);
    } catch (SQLException ex) {
        ex.printStackTrace();
        return false;
    }
    return true;
}
/**
 * Write an element from the database and its children
 */
protected void writeElement(String elementId, int depth) throws
SQLException {
    StringBuffer buf = new StringBuffer();
    buf.append("select tag from");
    buf.append(" " + ELE_TABLE + " ");
    buf.append("where doc_id = " + document);
    buf.append("  and ele_id = " + elementId);
    String tagName = getRdb().getDataItem(buf.toString());
    //write start tag
    write("<" + tagName, depth);
    //maybe write element id
    if (getWriteElementId()) {
        write(" FRAGID=\"" + document + "." + elementId + "\"");
    }
```

```
    //write attributes
    buf = new StringBuffer();
    buf.append("select name, value from");
    buf.append(" " + ATTR_TABLE + " ");
    buf.append("where doc_id = " + document);
    buf.append("  and ele_id = " + elementId);
    ResultSet rset = getRdb().getData(buf.toString());
    while (rset.next()) {
        // for each attribute, write name and value
        write(" " + rset.getString(1) + "=\"" + rset.getString(2) + "\"");
    }
    //close start tag, but first check to see if there are any children
    buf = new StringBuffer();
    buf.append("select indx, child_class, child_id from");
    buf.append(" " + CHILD_TABLE + " ");
    buf.append("where doc_id = " + document);
    buf.append("  and ele_id = " + elementId);
    rset = getRdb().getData(buf.toString());
    boolean moreRows = rset.next();
    if (moreRows) {
        // has children, close start tag and continue
        writeln(">");
    } else {
        // has no children, close tag and return
        writeln("/>");
        return;
    }
    //write children
    // first retrieve all rows, then recurse down
    // to prevent leaving cursor open while recursing deeply
    Vector vec = new Vector();
    int index;
    while(moreRows) {
        //rows are ordered by index
        index = Integer.parseInt(rset.getString(1));
        if (index > vec.size()) {
            vec.setSize(index);
        }
        vec.insertElementAt(new
Child(rset.getString(2),rset.getString(3)), index);
        moreRows = rset.next();
    }
    //write each child
    Enumeration e = vec.elements();
    Child child;
```

```
        String childClass;
        int childDepth = depth + 1;
        while (e.hasMoreElements()) {
            child = (Child) e.nextElement();
            if (child == null) {continue;}
            childClass = child.getClassName();
            writeChild(childClass, elementId, child.getId(), childDepth);
        }
        //write end tag
        writeln("</" + tagName + ">");
    }
    /**
     * Retrieve a fragment (single element) from the database and write it
     */
    public boolean writeFrag(String document, String element) {
        this.document = document;
        try {
            writeElement(element, 0);
        } catch (SQLException ex) {
            ex.printStackTrace();
            return false;
        }
        return true;
    }
    public void writeln(String value, int depth) {
        writeln(value);
    }
}

/************************ Child.java **********************/
package com.xweave.xmldb.fgrel;

/**
 * Used by Format to track Element Child information
 */
public class Child {
    private String className = null;
    private String id = null;
public Child() {
    super();
}
public Child(String className, String id) {
    super();
    setClassName(className);
    setId(id);
```

```
}
/**
 * @return java.lang.String
 */
public String getClassName() {
   return className;
}
/**
 * @return java.lang.String
 */
public String getId() {
   return id;
}
/**
 * @param newValue java.lang.String
 */
public void setClassName(String newValue) {
   this.className = newValue;
}
/**
 * @param newValue java.lang.String
 */
public void setId(String newValue) {
   this.id = newValue;
}
}

/************************* Delete.java ***********************/
package com.xweave.xmldb.fgrel;

import com.xweave.xmldb.util.rdb.RDB;
import com.xweave.xmldb.util.io.Output;
import java.sql.*;
/**
 * Delete command
 */
public class Delete extends Command {
   protected static String[] tables = {
       "XDB_STR",
       "XDB_TEXT",
       "XDB_CHILD",
       "XDB_ATTR",
       "XDB_ELE",
       "XDB_DOC"
   }; //Order is important to avoid violating foreign key constraints
```

```
public Delete() {
    super();
}
public Delete(RDB rdb) {
    super();
    setRdb(rdb);
}
public Delete(RDB rdb, Output output) {
    super(rdb,output);
}
public boolean deleteDoc(String document) {
    boolean status = true;
    try {
    // remove element from doc_table, to break foreign key constraint
        StringBuffer buf = new StringBuffer();
        buf.append("update");
        buf.append(" " + DOC_TABLE + " ");
        buf.append("set root = null");
        buf.append(" where doc_id = " + document);
        rdbExecute(buf.toString());
        int length = this.getTables().length;
        String tables[] = this.getTables();
        for (int i = 0; i < length; i++) {
            rdbExecute("delete from " + tables[i] + " where doc_id = " +
document);
        }
    } catch (SQLException ex) {
        status = false;
        ex.printStackTrace();
    }
    return status;
}
public String[] getTables() {
    return tables;
}
}

/************************* DocumentList.java **********************/
package com.xweave.xmldb.fgrel;

import com.xweave.xmldb.util.io.*;
import com.xweave.xmldb.util.rdb.*;
/**
 * Command to List the document in the database
```

```
 */
public class DocumentList extends Command {
/**
 * DocumentList constructor comment.
 */
public DocumentList() {
   super();
}
/**
 * DocumentList constructor comment.
 * @param rdb com.xweave.xmldb.util.rdb.RDB
 */
public DocumentList(RDB rdb) {
   super(rdb);
}
/**
 * DocumentList constructor comment.
 * @param rdb com.xweave.xmldb.util.rdb.RDB
 * @param out com.xweave.xmldb.util.io.Output
 */
public DocumentList(RDB rdb, Output out) {
   super(rdb, out);
}
/**
 * Retrieve a list (as a formatted String) of all XML documents
 */
public String retrieveDocumentList() {
   StringBuffer buf = new StringBuffer();
   java.util.Enumeration e = retrieveDocumentListVector().elements();
   while (e.hasMoreElements()) {
      buf.append((String) e.nextElement());
      buf.append("\n");
   }
   return buf.toString();
}
/**
 * Retrieve a Vector of all XML documents with their ids
 * as a Vector of Strings with format <id> <space> <name>
 */
public java.util.Vector retrieveDocumentListVector() {
   java.util.Vector vec = new java.util.Vector();
   StringBuffer buf = new StringBuffer();
   buf.append("select doc_id, name from ");
   buf.append(DOC_TABLE);
   buf.append(" order by doc_id");
```

```
    try {
       java.sql.ResultSet rset = getRdb().getData(buf.toString());
       while (rset.next()) {
          // for each document, append <id> <space> <name>
          vec.addElement(rset.getString(1) + " " + rset.getString(2));
       }
       return vec;
    } catch (java.sql.SQLException ex) {
       ex.printStackTrace();
       return null;
    }
}
/**
 * Write a list (to out) of all XML documents
 */
public void writeDocumentList() {
    java.util.Enumeration e = retrieveDocumentListVector().elements();
    Output out = getOutput();
    while (e.hasMoreElements()) {
       out.writeln((String) e.nextElement());
    }
}
/**
 * Write a list (to out) of all XML documents (as select options)
 */
public void writeDocumentSelect() {
    java.util.Enumeration e = retrieveDocumentListVector().elements();
    Output out = getOutput();
    while (e.hasMoreElements()) {
       out.writeln("<option>"+(String) e.nextElement()+"</option>");
    }
}
}

/************************ Load.java **********************/
package com.xweave.xmldb.fgrel;

import com.xweave.xmldb.util.rdb.RDB;
import com.xweave.xmldb.util.io.Output;
import java.sql.*;
import org.xml.sax.*;
import org.xml.sax.helpers.ParserFactory;
import com.ibm.xml.parsers.DOMParser;
import org.w3c.dom.Document;
import java.io.IOException;
```

```
/**
 * Command to Load a document into the database
 */
public class Load extends Command {
public Load() {
   super();
}
public Load(RDB rdb) {
   super(rdb);
}
public Load(RDB rdb, Output output) {
   super(rdb,output);
}
public LoadHandler newHandler() {
   if (getRdb() == null) {
      return new LoadHandler();
   } else {
      return new JDBCLoadHandler(getRdb());
   }
}
/**
 * Parse an XML file using a SAX parser
 * Note: the parser in <parserClass> MUST be included in the Java
CLASSPATH
 */
public String parse(String xmlFile) {
   return parse(xmlFile, null);
}
/**
 * Parse an XML file using a SAX parser
 * Note: the parser in <parserClass> MUST be included in the Java
CLASSPATH
 */
public String parse(String xmlFile, String name) {
   String parserClass = com.xweave.xmldb.Default.getParserClass();
   try {
      Parser parser = ParserFactory.makeParser(parserClass);
      HandlerBase handler = this.newHandler();
      parser.setDocumentHandler(handler);
      parser.setErrorHandler(handler);
      try {
         //determine whether file is document or URL
         String prefix = xmlFile.substring(0,7);
         if (prefix.startsWith("http://") ||
            prefix.startsWith("file://") ||
```

```
            prefix.startsWith("ftp://")) {
            //URL
            if (name == null) {
               ((LoadHandler) handler).setDocumentName(xmlFile);
            } else {
               ((LoadHandler) handler).setDocumentName(name);
            }
            parser.parse(xmlFile);
         } else {
            //File
            if (name != null) {
               ((LoadHandler) handler).setDocumentName(name);
            }
            parser.parse(new InputSource(new java.io.StringReader(xmlFile)));
         }
         return ((LoadHandler) handler).getDocumentId();
      } catch (SAXException se) {
         getOutput().writeln(se.toString());
         se.printStackTrace();
      } catch (IOException ioe) {
         ioe.printStackTrace();
      }
   } catch (ClassNotFoundException ex) {
      ex.printStackTrace();
   } catch (IllegalAccessException ex) {
      ex.printStackTrace();
   } catch (InstantiationException ex) {
      ex.printStackTrace();
   }
   return null;
}
/**
 * Parse an XML file using a SAX parser
 * Note: the parser in <parserClass> MUST be included in the Java
CLASSPATH
 */
public String parseText(String xmlText, String name) {
   String parserClass = com.xweave.xmldb.Default.getParserClass();
   try {
      Parser parser = ParserFactory.makeParser(parserClass);
      HandlerBase handler = this.newHandler();
      parser.setDocumentHandler(handler);
      parser.setErrorHandler(handler);
      try {
         ((LoadHandler) handler).setDocumentName(name);
```

```
            parser.parse(new InputSource(new java.io.StringReader(xmlText)));
            return ((LoadHandler) handler).getDocumentId();
        } catch (SAXException se) {
            getOutput().writeln(se.toString());
            se.printStackTrace();
        } catch (IOException ioe) {
            ioe.printStackTrace();
        }
    } catch (ClassNotFoundException ex) {
        ex.printStackTrace();
    } catch (IllegalAccessException ex) {
        ex.printStackTrace();
    } catch (InstantiationException ex) {
        ex.printStackTrace();
    }
    return null;
}
/**
 * Parse an XML file using a SAX parser
 * Note: the parser in <parserClass> MUST be included in the Java
CLASSPATH
 */
public String parseUrl(String xmlUrl, String name) {
    String parserClass = com.xweave.xmldb.Default.getParserClass();
    try {
        Parser parser = ParserFactory.makeParser(parserClass);
        HandlerBase handler = this.newHandler();
        parser.setDocumentHandler(handler);
        parser.setErrorHandler(handler);
        try {
            ((LoadHandler) handler).setDocumentName(name);
            parser.parse(xmlUrl);
            return ((LoadHandler) handler).getDocumentId();
        } catch (SAXException se) {
            getOutput().writeln(se.toString());
            se.printStackTrace();
        } catch (IOException ioe) {
            ioe.printStackTrace();
        }
    } catch (ClassNotFoundException ex) {
        ex.printStackTrace();
    } catch (IllegalAccessException ex) {
        ex.printStackTrace();
    } catch (InstantiationException ex) {
        ex.printStackTrace();
```

```
    }
    return null;
}
}

/************************ LoadHandler.java **********************/
package com.xweave.xmldb.fgrel;

import org.xml.sax.*;
import java.util.*;
/**
 * SAX Handler which creates SQL to load a document into the database
 */
public class LoadHandler extends HandlerBase {
    protected final static String DOC_TABLE = "XDB_DOC";
    protected final static String ELE_TABLE = "XDB_ELE";
    protected final static String ATTR_TABLE = "XDB_ATTR";
    protected final static String CHILD_TABLE = "XDB_CHILD";
    protected final static String STR_TABLE = "XDB_STR";
    protected final static String TEXT_TABLE = "XDB_TEXT";
    protected final static int CDATA_SPLIT_LENGTH = 255;
    private Element currentElement = null;
    private Stack elementStack = null;
    /* counters for element, attribute, and cdata may be generated
       within the class because they are only unique to the current
       document. The document identifier must come from the database.
    */
    protected int eleCtr = 1;
    protected int attrCtr = 1;
    protected int cdataCtr = 1;
    protected String documentName = null;
    protected String documentId = null;
public LoadHandler() {
    super();
}
public LoadHandler(String documentId) {
    super();
    setDocumentId(documentId);
}
/**
 * Handle character data regions.
 */
public void characters(char[] chars, int start, int length) {
    //Warning: Be sure to use a parser that does not split character data
```

```
//         regions across buffers.
//
// First check to see if characters is whitespace, if so, return
boolean isWhitespace = true;
for (int i = start; i < start+length; i++) {
   if (! Character.isWhitespace(chars[i])) {
      isWhitespace = false;
      break;
   }
}
if (isWhitespace == true) {
   return;
}
// Decide which CDATA table to use
String table;
boolean useStr = true;
if (length <= CDATA_SPLIT_LENGTH) {
   table = STR_TABLE;
} else {
   table = TEXT_TABLE;
   useStr = false;
}
// Create insert statement
int currentId = nextCdataCtrValue();
StringBuffer buf = new StringBuffer();
buf.append("insert into");
buf.append(" " + table + " ");
buf.append("(doc_id, cdata_id, ele_id, value)");
buf.append(" values ");
buf.append("(" + getDocumentId() + ", " +
              currentId + ", " +
             getCurrentElement().getId() + ", ");
if (useStr) {
   buf.append("'");
   buf.append(chars, start, length);
   buf.append("'");
} else {
    //More may need to be done for this to work with some drivers.
    //May need to allow for null values, set this to null, then update
    //   the LONG value in TEXT_TABLE.
   buf.append("'");
   buf.append(chars, start, length);
   buf.append("'");
}
buf.append(")");
```

```
        rdbExecute(buf.toString());
        // create child entry for the new CDATA
        buf = new StringBuffer();
        buf.append("insert into");
        buf.append(" " + CHILD_TABLE + " ");
        buf.append("(doc_id, ele_id, indx, child_class, child_id)");
        buf.append(" values ");
        buf.append("(" + getDocumentId() + ", " +
                    getCurrentElement().getId() + ", " +
                    getCurrentElement().incrIndexCtr() + ", ");
        if (useStr) {
            buf.append("'STR', ");
        } else {
            buf.append("'TEXT', ");
        }
        buf.append(currentId + ")");
        rdbExecute(buf.toString());
    }
    public void endElement(String name) {
        //clear currentElement and pop stack
        if (getElementStack().empty()) {
            this.currentElement = null;
        } else {
            this.currentElement = (Element) getElementStack().pop();
        }
    }
    public Element getCurrentElement() {
        return currentElement;
    }
    public String getDocumentId() {
        return documentId;
    }
    public String getDocumentName() {
        if (documentName == null) {
            setDocumentName("NoName" + getDocumentId());
        }
        return documentName;
    }
    private Stack getElementStack() {
        if (elementStack == null) {
            elementStack = new java.util.Stack();
        }
        return elementStack;
    }
    protected int nextAttrCtrValue() {
```

```
        return attrCtr++;
    }
    protected int nextCdataCtrValue() {
        return cdataCtr++;
    }
    protected int nextEleCtrValue() {
        return eleCtr++;
    }
    /**
     * Write SQL to standard out.
     * All SQL output goes through this method.
     * This method may be changed to use a direct SQL connection.
     */
    public boolean rdbExecute(String value) {
        // add a semicolon to print to standard out, omit for JDBC
        System.out.println(value + ";");
        return true;
    }
    protected void setCurrentElement(String newValue) {
        if (getCurrentElement() != null) {
            //push parent element onto stack
            getElementStack().push(getCurrentElement());
        }
        this.currentElement = new Element(newValue);
    }
    public void setDocumentId(String newValue) {
        this.documentId = newValue;
    }
    public void setDocumentName(String newValue) {
        this.documentName = newValue;
    }
    private void setElementStack(Stack newValue) {
        this.elementStack = newValue;
    }
    /**
     * Initialize the document table when starting a XML document.
     */
    public void startDocument() {
        //create document entry
        StringBuffer buf = new StringBuffer();
        buf.append("insert into");
        buf.append(" " + DOC_TABLE + " ");
        buf.append("(doc_id, name)");
        buf.append(" values ");
        buf.append("(" + getDocumentId() + ", '" + getDocumentName() + "')");
```

```
        rdbExecute(buf.toString());
    }
    /**
     * Handle element, attributes, and the connection from this element
     * to its parent.
     */
    public void startElement(String name, AttributeList attrList) {
        //DEBUG: System.out.println(name);
        //Create new element entry
        Element parent = getCurrentElement();
        String parentId;
        if (parent == null) {
            parentId = "NULL";
        } else {
            parentId = parent.getId();
        }
        setCurrentElement(Integer.toString(nextEleCtrValue()));
        String currentId = getCurrentElement().getId();
        StringBuffer buf = new StringBuffer();
        buf.append("insert into");
        buf.append(" " + ELE_TABLE + " ");
        buf.append("(doc_id, ele_id, parent_id, tag)");
        buf.append(" values ");
        buf.append("(" + getDocumentId() + ", " +
                        currentId + ", " +
                        parentId + ", " +
                        "'" + name + "')");
        rdbExecute(buf.toString());
        if (parent == null) {
            //root element, update document entry
            buf = new StringBuffer();
            buf.append("update");
            buf.append(" " + DOC_TABLE + " ");
            buf.append("set root = " + currentId);
            buf.append(" where doc_id = " + getDocumentId());
            rdbExecute(buf.toString());
        } else {
            // not a root element, create child entry
            buf = new StringBuffer();
            buf.append("insert into");
            buf.append(" " + CHILD_TABLE + " ");
            buf.append("(doc_id, ele_id, indx, child_class, child_id)");
            buf.append(" values ");
            buf.append("(" + getDocumentId() + ", " +
                        parentId + ", " +
```

```
                parent.incrIndexCtr() + ", " +
                "'ELE', " +
                currentId + ")");
        rdbExecute(buf.toString());
    }
    //Create entries for each attribute
    for (int i = 0; i < attrList.getLength(); i++) {
        buf = new StringBuffer();
        buf.append("insert into");
        buf.append(" " + ATTR_TABLE + " ");
        buf.append("(doc_id, attr_id, ele_id, name, value)");
        buf.append(" values ");
        buf.append("(" + getDocumentId() + ", " +
                nextAttrCtrValue() + ", " +
                currentId + ", " +
                "'" + attrList.getName(i) + "', " +
                 "'" + attrList.getValue(i) + "')");
        rdbExecute(buf.toString());
    }
}
}

/*********************** Element.java **********************/
package com.xweave.xmldb.fgrel;

/**
 * Used by LoadHandler to track Element ids
 */
public class Element {
   protected String id = null;
   protected int indexCtr = 1;
public Element(String id) {
   super();
   this.id = id;
}
public String getId() {
   return id;
}
public int getIndexCtr() {
   return indexCtr;
}
public int incrIndexCtr() {
   return this.indexCtr++;
}
protected void setIndexCtr(int newValue) {
```

```
    this.indexCtr = newValue;
}
}

/*********************** JDBCLoadHandler.java *********************/
package com.xweave.xmldb.fgrel;

import com.xweave.xmldb.util.rdb.*;
import java.sql.SQLException;
/**
 * SAX Handler using JDBC to load a document into the database
 */
public class JDBCLoadHandler extends LoadHandler {
    private RDB rdb = null;
public JDBCLoadHandler(RDB rdb) {
    super();
    setRdb(rdb);
}
/**
 * Get document id from instance variable or from database
 */
public String getDocumentId() {
    if (documentId == null) {
        //get next id from Oracle
        //Could use a SEQUENCE, but this will work
        StringBuffer buf = new StringBuffer();
        buf.append("select max(doc_id) from ");
        buf.append(DOC_TABLE);
        try {
            String elementId = getRdb().getDataItem(buf.toString());
            if (elementId == null) {
                //no records in table (or SQL error we may discover later)
                documentId = "1";
            } else {
                documentId = String.valueOf(Integer.parseInt(elementId) + 1);
            }
        } catch (Exception ex) {
            ex.printStackTrace();
            //we will have problems later, so throw out now
            throw new Error("Unable to get new DOC_ID from database.");
        }
    }
    return documentId;
}
```

```
public RDB getRdb() {
   return rdb;
}
public boolean rdbExecute(String value) {
   // add a semicolon to print to standard out, omit for JDBC
   try {
      return getRdb().executeUpdate(value) > 0;
   } catch (SQLException ex) {
      ex.printStackTrace();
      return false;
   }
}
protected void setRdb(RDB newValue) {
   this.rdb = newValue;
}
}
```

The remainder of the section describes the Java code for the readers who wish to better understand the implementation.

The main class for the storage system is "Demo". Each command is implemented by a class, and the "Demo" class keeps an instance of the command classes. "Demo" also keeps an "RDB" class that refers to a connection to the relational database used for storage. The "RDB" class allows for connection and querying of a relational database through a JDBC connection and is described more fully in Appendix A. "Demo" also provides a mechanism for writing the SQL onto standard out for testing or use within a script to access a relational database that does not have a JDBC connection. The "main" method in "Demo" reads the commands from the command line and dispatches them to the appropriate command instance.

The command classes are "Format", "Delete", and "Load". They each access the database through the "RDB" interface and write status messages to the standard error stream.

The primary method for a "Format" instance is the "writeDoc" method that takes a document identifier as its argument and begins to retrieve the data for it from the relational database. It calls "writeElement" on the document element, which then writes out the element, retrieving information as necessary from the relational database. The method "writeElement" writes the element type name and the attributes, then accesses the "xdb_child" table to retrieve a list of children. The method then calls "writeElement" recursively or "writeCdata" as appropriate. The "writeElement" method retrieves all children from the database before writing any child and uses the

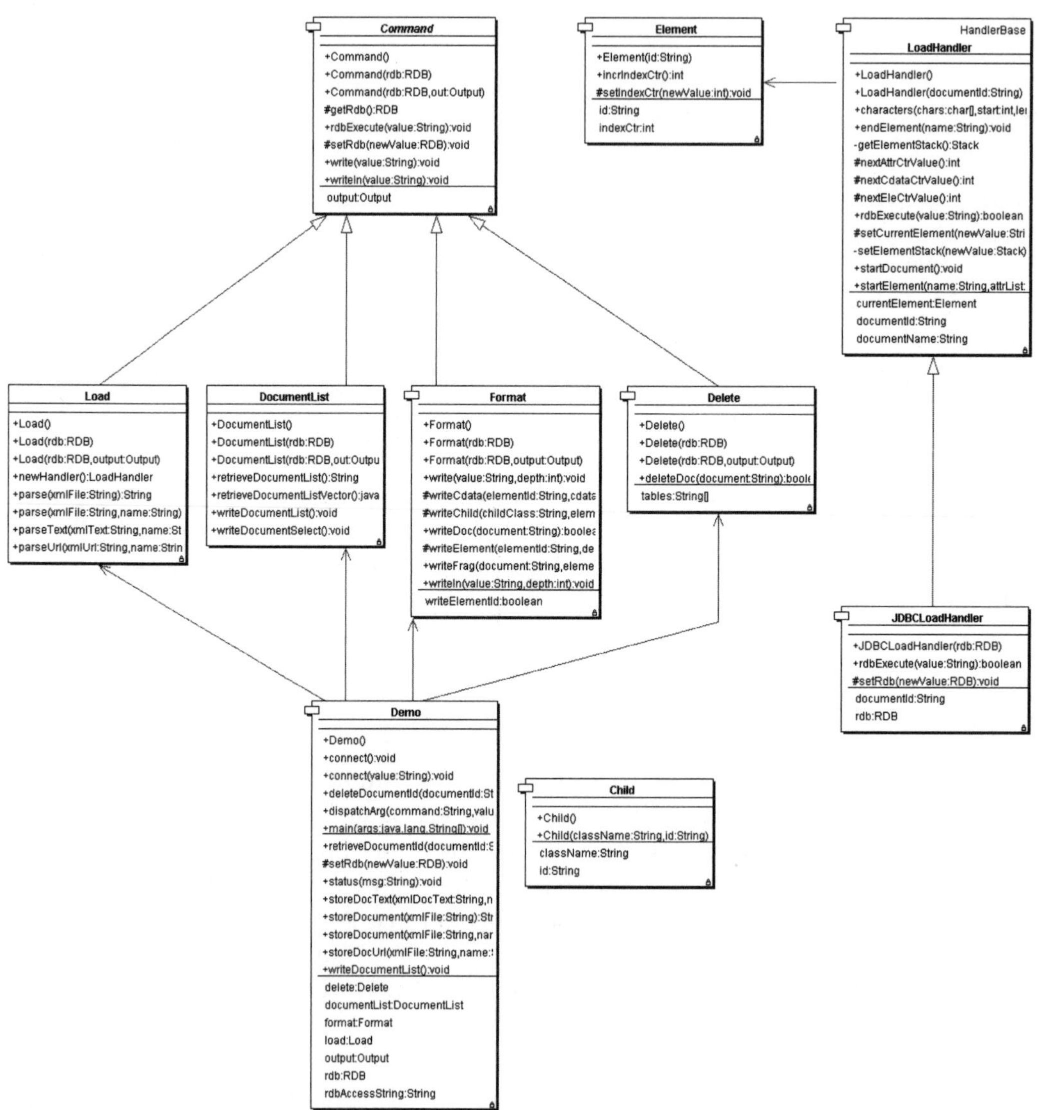

Figure 4–9 UML diagram for fine-grained storage system

"Child" class as a helper object to store the vector of children. All output uses the "writeln" method.

The "Delete" command class has a primary method called "deleteDoc" that takes a document identifier as an argument and deletes all items in all tables with that identifier as the "document_id". The method ensures that foreign key constraints are not broken by deleting from tables in the proper order and by explicitly breaking the circular constraint between the document element entry in the "xdb_element" table and the document entry in the "xdb_document" table. A SQL delete cascade could have been used to simplify the implementation of the delete command.

The "Load" command uses a SAX parser. The parser is described in more detail in Appendix B. The SAX parser uses an instance of the "LoadHandler" class to load each document. The "startElement" method in class "LoadHandler" creates a database entry for the element and each attribute. The counters for the unique identifiers of the element, attributes, and character regions are tracked within the instance as they depend upon the document. An entry in the "xdb_child" table is created between the current element and its parent (as tracked by an instance of the "Element" helper class in the "currentElement" instance variable). The "characters" method of "LoadHandler" creates an entry for the character date region in the "xdb_str" or "xdb_text" table as determined by the "CDATA_SPLIT_LENGTH" class variable. The method also creates an entry in the "xdb_child" table using information in the "currentElement" instance variable. The recursive calls of "startElement" by the SAX parser are handled by keeping a stack of "Element" helper objects with the pertinent information. All output goes through the "out" method of "LoadHandler" that defaults to standard out. For JDBC connections, a subclass of "LoadHandler" is created called "JDBCLoadHandler" that redefines the "out" method to use a "RDB" method and defines that the document ID is obtained from a "RDB" query to add one to the current maximum document identifier.

4.3 Coarse-grained Relational Schema

Another approach to storing the documents in the database is to store them in their entirety. Although similar to storing documents in flat files, this approach has the advantage of allowing the documents to be referred to within other structures in the database. It also provides the security, recovery, and other features of the DBMS in which it is stored. Depending upon the DBMS, there may be built-in operations designed to work on large text documents, which may be useful.

Although some early vendors propose this approach, its primary usefulness is part of a hybrid representation as discussed in the next section. However, it is worth examining independently because it demonstrates a very simple mechanism to capture XML in an existing DBMS. This can be a important step in a phased deployment plan where a flat file database is created, then moved with little modification into a relational database using this coarse-grained approach, then refined making use of the capabilities of the relational DBMS in a fine-grained or medium-grained approach.

A very simple conceptual schema and logical schema is developed here. A document is defined to have a name and a body. The optional "name" provides a unique identifier by which the user may refer to the document. The logical schema consists of one table called document with three columns: a name, a unique numeric identifier, and a body. A unique identifier is added to the schema at this stage to facilitate its integration into other parts of the system and is not strictly needed.

A logical schema for the coarse-grained storage approach is very simple:

```
Document (name STRING, body TEXT)
```

A physical schema for Oracle is presented in Figure 4–10 and SQL code to implement it is given in Example 4–8. The code to implement the database in DB2 is given in Example 4–9.

cgrel_doc	
doc_id	NUMBER(8)
name	VARCHAR2(128)
body	LONG

Figure 4–10 Physical schema for coarse-grained relational database to store XML data (Oracle)

Example 4–8 : Coarse-grained Oracle Schema for Storing XML Documents

```
-- Create coarse-grained storage table and constraint

create table cgrel_doc (
   doc_id      NUMBER(8)        NOT NULL,
   name        VARCHAR2(128),
   body        LONG
);
alter table cgrel_doc add primary key (doc_id);
```

Example 4–9 : Coarse-grained DB2 Schema for Storing XML Documents

```
-- Create coarse-grained storage table and constraint

create table cgrel_doc (
   doc_id        INTEGER          NOT NULL,
   name          VARCHAR(127),
   body          CLOB(10M)
);
alter table cgrel_doc add primary key (doc_id)
```

4.4 Medium-grained Relational Schema

The disadvantage of the fine-granularity approach is that storing and reconstructing a document is very expensive; its advantage is that some queries and modifications are very simple. Evaluating the approaches against the tasks from Section 3.4.2, the fine-grained approach works well to perform tasks that access elements (Tasks c–i), whereas the tasks to store and retrieve an entire document are difficult (Tasks a, b). The coarse-grained approach works well in manipulating entire documents (Tasks a, b) and has difficulty with the element manipulations (Tasks c–i). Task j was to manipulate one element in the context of another, and Task k was to join two elements, which are difficult in either solution.

Another storage approach is to create a medium-granularity approach—a compromise between the fine-granularity and coarse-granularity approaches. The document tree can be sliced into sections where the sub-sections are stored with a coarse-grained approach. This is particularly useful if the sections are accessed individually: for example in reference books such as dictionaries or encyclopedias, a medium-grained approach would be to store each entry separately. Consider the document in Example 4–10. It might be useful to break up the document into 1201 sections: 1 section for the top-level document and 1200 sections for each of the dictionary entries. The medium-grained approach performs better than the fine-grained approach on storing and retrieving documents, and still performs okay on the element manipulating tasks. Task j—to manipulate an element only within the context of another—is still difficult.

Example 4–10 : Dictionary with Many Entries

```
<dictionary>
   <entry number="1" name="aardvark">
   ...
   </entry>
   <entry number="2" name="aadax">
   ...
   </entry>
   .
   .
   .
   <entry number="1200" name="zebra">
   ...
  </entry>
</dictionary>
```

4.4.1 Slice Points

Determining appropriate slice points is a complex issue.

- How many slice points are created?
- How many levels of slicing are created?
- Does the slicing depend upon the element type name or the depth in the tree or the size of the document section?
- Are some sections of the document sliced more finely than other sections?

The fine-grained approach and the coarse-grained approach are actually opposite poles of the medium-grained approach. The fine-grained approach can be described as creating a slice at every tag, and the coarse-grained approach can be described as creating zero slices per document.

One way to approach the slicing granularity is to view slicing as a method to index the database. An index speeds up access for a particular database request by creating an index table that provides quick navigation to the indexed information. Slices can be created on a element type name (or names) for which frequent access is anticipated. A combination of element type names and attribute values can also be used to drive the index slice method. Choosing slice points based on desired indexing will reduce the data access time over the coarse-grained approach for queries or other accesses that involve the indexed tags. Indexes can be created on a few highly requested element type names or on the majority of element type names for which access is anticipated. If most of the directly accessed element type names are indexed, then the access time for those queries approaches the access time under the fine-grained approach while also reducing the document regeneration time because other elements do not need to be regenerated unnecessarily.

Another way to approach the slicing granularity is to view the slicing method as a buffering mechanism. Slices may be determined by physical characteristics, such as size. The slice size can be chosen to efficiently use network communication protocols to reduce the time needed to retrieve a portion of the document when the network response is a critical factor. For example, if the query process or application is on a separate machine or processor from the storage device, and the communication takes place in 8K buffers, then overall efficiency may be improved by sending over portions of the document in slightly less than 8K sections.

Combinations of approaches may also be used for particular applications or documents. For example, a reference book such as the one presented in Example 4–10 essentially combines an index on the dictionary entry with slices of approximately the same size.

One issue that needs to be addressed in this approach is how to represent the slice points in the document. One mechanism is to create a specific element type to represent the necessary information, ensuring that the element type name is unique in the document, possibly by creating it in a new namespace using XML Namespaces. For example, an element type called "slice" or "proxy" could be created with attributes that contain sufficient information to reconstruct the document, namely "document_id" and "element_id". The dictionary document of Example 4–10 is shown in Table 4–1, which illustrates that mechanism.

Table 4–1 Dictionary Document with Many Entries Split for Medium-grained Storage

Document ID	*Element ID*	*Value*
1	1	<dictionary> <proxy document="1" element="2"/> <proxy document="1" element="3"/> ... <proxy document="1" element="1201"/> </dictionary>
1	2	<entry number="1" name="aardvark"> ... </entry>
...	...	...
1	1201	<entry number="1200" name="zebra"> ... </entry>

4.4.2 Database Design

The medium-grained schema is created by adding two relations to the fine-grained schema. The first relation is somewhat similar to the document relation of the coarse-grained schema: It contains identifiers and a body that consists of marked-up text. The second relation serves as an index of what elements are included in which fragment. Although not strictly necessary, having this XML index greatly simplifies performance on some operations. (Note: this relation defines one index in the XML DBMS that is implemented as a relation in a relational DBMS. It is a part of the design of an XML DBMS unlike the relational indexes that may be added later.)

The logical schema of a medium-grained implementation is as follows:

```
Document(name DOC_NAME, root ELEMENT)
Element(doc DOCUMENT, parent ELEMENT, tag ELE_NAME)
Attribute(doc DOCUMENT, element ELEMENT, name
    ATTR_NAME, value ATTR_VALUE)
CharData(doc DOCUMENT, element ELEMENT, value CDATA)
```

```
Child(doc DOCUMENT, element ELEMENT, index NUMBER,
    child_class CHILD_CLASS, child CHILD_NODE)

Fragment(doc DOCUMENT, element ELEMENT, body TEXT)
FragmentReference(doc DOCUMENT, fragment FRAGMENT,
    element_reference ELEMENT)
```

To normalize the schema into first normal form, the relation domains are eliminated by creating unique identifiers for each relation. A normalized logical schema is as follows:

```
Document(doc_id DOCUMENT, name DOC_NAME, root ELEMENT)
Element(doc_id DOCUMENT, ele_id ELEMENT, parent_id
    ELEMENT, tag ELE_NAME)
Attribute(doc_id DOCUMENT, ele_id ELEMENT, name
    ATTR_NAME, value ATTR_VALUE)
CharData(doc_id DOCUMENT, ele_id ELEMENT, value CDATA)
Child(doc_id DOCUMENT, ele_id ELEMENT, index NUMBER,
    child_class CHILD_CLASS, child CHILD_CHILD)

Fragment(doc_id DOCUMENT, frag_id FRAGMENT, ele_id
    ELEMENT, body TEXT)
FragmentReference(doc_id DOCUMENT, frag_id FRAGMENT,
    element_reference ELEMENT)
```

The first five relations in each schema are identical to the fine-grained schema. A physical schema is given in Figure 4–11, and SQL code to implement the design of the two additional tables in Oracle is given in Example 4–11. The SQL for DB2 is given in Example 4–12, and the physical schema is given in Figure 4–12.

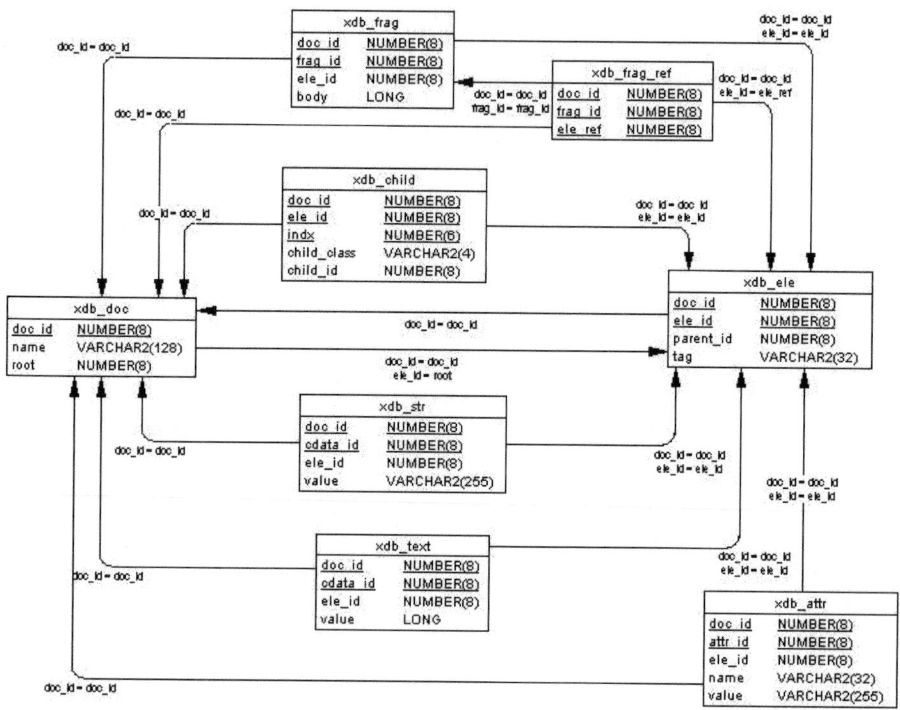

Figure 4–11 Physical schema for medium-grained relational database to store XML data (Oracle)

Example 4–11 : Medium-grained Oracle Schema for Storing XML Documents

```
-- Additional tables and constraints for medium-grained storage

create table xdb_frag (
   doc_id       NUMBER(8)      NOT NULL,
   frag_id      NUMBER(8)      NOT NULL,
   ele_id       NUMBER(8)      NOT NULL,
   body         LONG           NOT NULL
);
alter table xdb_frag add primary key (doc_id, frag_id);

create table xdb_frag_ref (
   doc_id       NUMBER(8)      NOT NULL,
   frag_id      NUMBER(8)      NOT NULL,
   ele_ref      NUMBER(8)      NOT NULL
);
```

```
alter table xdb_frag_ref add primary key (doc_id, frag_id, ele_ref);

alter table xdb_frag add constraint fk_xdb_frag_doc_id
      foreign key (doc_id) references xdb_doc (doc_id);
alter table xdb_frag add constraint fk_xdb_frag_ele_id
      foreign key (doc_id, ele_id) references xdb_ele (doc_id, ele_id);
alter table xdb_frag_ref add constraint fk_xdb_frag_ref_doc_id
      foreign key (doc_id) references xdb_doc (doc_id);
alter table xdb_frag_ref add constraint fk_xdb_frag_ref_ele_ref
      foreign key (doc_id, ele_ref) references xdb_ele (doc_id, ele_id);
alter table xdb_frag_ref add constraint fk_xdb_frag_ref_frag_id
      foreign key (doc_id, frag_id) references xdb_frag (doc_id,
frag_id);
```

Example 4–12 : Medium-grained DB2 Schema for Storing XML Documents

```
-- Additional tables and constraints for medium-grained storage

create table xdb_frag (
   doc_id         INTEGER    NOT NULL,
   frag_id        INTEGER    NOT NULL,
   ele_id         INTEGER    NOT NULL,
   body           CLOB(1M)   NOT NULL
);
alter table xdb_frag add primary key (doc_id, frag_id);

create table xdb_frag_ref (
   doc_id         INTEGER    NOT NULL,
   frag_id        INTEGER    NOT NULL,
   ele_ref        INTEGER    NOT NULL
);
alter table xdb_frag_ref add primary key (doc_id, frag_id, ele_ref);

alter table xdb_frag add constraint fk_xdb_frag_doc_id
      foreign key (doc_id) references xdb_doc (doc_id);
alter table xdb_frag add constraint fk_xdb_frag_ele_id
      foreign key (doc_id, ele_id) references xdb_ele (doc_id, ele_id);
alter table xdb_frag_ref add constraint fk_xdb_frag_ref_do
      foreign key (doc_id) references xdb_doc (doc_id);
alter table xdb_frag_ref add constraint fk_xdb_frag_ref_el
      foreign key (doc_id, ele_ref) references xdb_ele (doc_id, ele_id);
alter table xdb_frag_ref add constraint fk_xdb_frag_ref_fr
      foreign key (doc_id, frag_id) references xdb_frag (doc_id, frag_id)
```

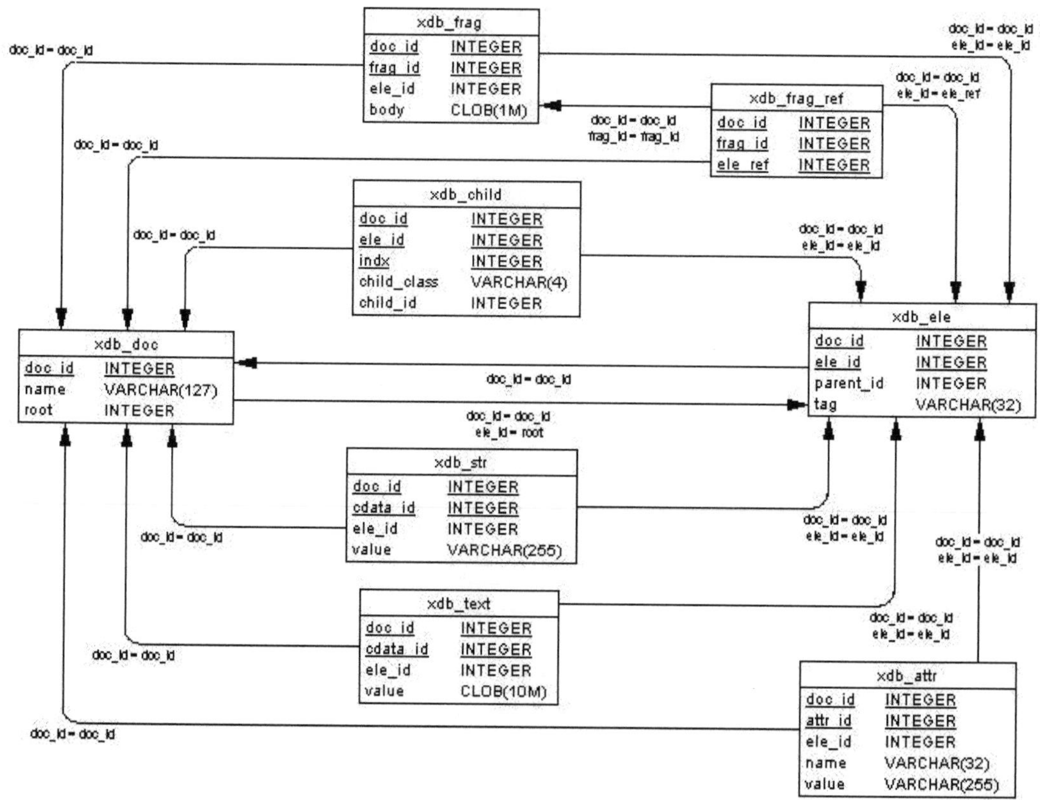

Figure 4–12 Physical schema for medium-grained relational database to store XML data (DB2)

4.4.3 Implementation

Java code that implements storage and retrieval operations for the medium-grained approach is listed in Example 4–13. Note that the CLASSPATH must contain a JDBC driver and an XML parser (IBM's XML parser is used in the example). A UML diagram for the Java implementation is given in Figure 4–13.

Example 4–13 : Java Implementation of a Medium-grained Storage System

```
/************************ Demo.java ***********************/
package com.xweave.xmldb.mgrel;

/**
 * Demonstration of Medium-grained relational storage
 */
public class Demo extends com.xweave.xmldb.fgrel.Demo {
public Demo() {
   super();
}
public boolean addSlicePoint(String name) {
   return ((Load) getLoad()).getSlice().add(name);
}
public void clearSlicePoint() {
   ((Load) getLoad()).setSlice(null);
}
public boolean dispatchArg(String command, String value) {
   if (command.equalsIgnoreCase("ADDSLICE")) {
      this.addSlicePoint(value);
      return true;
   }
   if (command.equalsIgnoreCase("SETSLICE")) {
      this.setSlicePoint(value);
      return true;
   }
   if (command.equalsIgnoreCase("CLEARSLICE")) {
      this.clearSlicePoint();
      return true;
   }
   return super.dispatchArg(command, value);
}
/**
 * Get the Delete command object.
 */
public com.xweave.xmldb.fgrel.Delete getDelete() {
   if (delete == null) {
      delete = new Delete(getRdb(), getOutput());
   }
   return delete;
}
/**
 * Get the Format command object.
```

```
 */
public com.xweave.xmldb.fgrel.Format getFormat() {
   if (format == null) {
      format = new Format(getRdb(),getOutput());
   }
   return format;
}
/**
 * Get the Load command object.
 */
public com.xweave.xmldb.fgrel.Load getLoad() {
   if (load == null) {
      if (getRdb() == null) {
         load = new Load();
      } else {
         load = new Load(getRdb());
      }
   }
   return load;
}
public boolean setSlicePoint(String name) {
   clearSlicePoint();
   return addSlicePoint(name);
}
}

/*********************** Format.java *********************/
package com.xweave.xmldb.mgrel;

import com.xweave.xmldb.util.rdb.RDB;
import com.xweave.xmldb.util.io.Output;
import java.sql.SQLException;
public class Format extends com.xweave.xmldb.fgrel.Format {
   protected final static String FRAG_TABLE = "XDB_FRAG";
public Format() {
   super();
}
public Format(RDB rdb) {
   super(rdb);
}
public Format(RDB rdb, Output output) {
   super(rdb, output);
}
/**
```

```
 * Dispatch an element child
 */
protected void writeChild(String childClass, String elementId, String
childId, int childDepth) throws SQLException {
   if (childClass.equalsIgnoreCase("FRAG")) {
      //call writeElement recursively
      writeFragmentSlice(elementId,childId,childDepth);
   } else {
      super.writeChild(childClass, elementId, childId, childDepth);
   }
}
/**
 * Write a slice of document from FRAG table
 */
protected void writeFragmentSlice(String elementId, String childId,
int childDepth) throws SQLException {
   StringBuffer buf = new StringBuffer();
   buf.append("select body from");
   buf.append(" " + FRAG_TABLE + " ");
   buf.append("where doc_id = " + document);
   buf.append("  and ele_id = " + elementId);
   buf.append("  and frag_id = " + childId);
   String value = getRdb().getDataItem(buf.toString());
   writeln(value, childDepth);
}
}

/************************* Delete.java ***********************/
package com.xweave.xmldb.mgrel;

import com.xweave.xmldb.util.rdb.RDB;
import com.xweave.xmldb.util.io.Output;
public class Delete extends com.xweave.xmldb.fgrel.Delete {
   protected static String[] tables = {
      "XDB_FRAG",
      "XDB_FRAG_REF",
      "XDB_STR",
      "XDB_TEXT",
      "XDB_CHILD",
      "XDB_ATTR",
      "XDB_ELE",
      "XDB_DOC"
   }; //Order is important to avoid violating foreign key constraints
public Delete() {
   super();
```

```
}
public Delete(RDB rdb) {
    super(rdb);
}
public Delete(RDB rdb, Output output) {
    super(rdb, output);
}
public String[] getTables() {
    return tables;
}
}

/************************* Load.java **********************/
package com.xweave.xmldb.mgrel;

import com.xweave.xmldb.util.rdb.RDB;
import com.xweave.xmldb.util.io.Output;
public class Load extends com.xweave.xmldb.fgrel.Load {
    protected Slice slice = null;
/**
 * Load constructor comment.
 */
public Load() {
    super();
}
public Load(RDB rdb) {
    super(rdb);
}
public Load(RDB rdb, Output output) {
    super(rdb, output);
}
public Slice getSlice() {
    if (slice == null) {
        slice = new Slice();
    }
    return slice;
}
public com.xweave.xmldb.fgrel.LoadHandler newHandler() {
    LoadHandler handler;
    if (getRdb() == null) {
        handler = new LoadHandler();
    } else {
        handler = new JDBCLoadHandler(getRdb());
}
```

```
    handler.setSlice(getSlice());
    return handler;
}
public void setSlice(Slice newValue) {
    this.slice = newValue;
}
}

/************************ LoadHandler.java **********************/
package com.xweave.xmldb.mgrel;

import org.xml.sax.*;
import java.util.*;
import com.xweave.xmldb.util.rdb.*;
public class LoadHandler extends com.xweave.xmldb.fgrel.LoadHandler {
    protected final static String FRAG_TABLE = "XDB_FRAG";
    protected Slice slice;
    private boolean inSlice = false;
    private int sliceDepth = 0;
    protected StringBuffer sliceBuf = null;
    /* counters for fragment is generated within the class as it is unique
       to the current document.
    */
    protected int fragCtr = 1;
public LoadHandler() {
    super();
}
public static String attrListToString(AttributeList attrList) {
    StringBuffer buf = new StringBuffer();
    int length = attrList.getLength();
    for (int i=0;i<length;i++) {
       buf.append(attrList.getName(i)+"=\""+attrList.getValue(i)+"\"");
    }
    return buf.toString();
}
public void characters(char[] chars, int start, int length) {
    if (inSlice) {
       getSliceBuf().append(chars, start, length);
    } else {
       super.characters(chars, start, length);
    }
}
public void clearSliceBuf() {
    sliceBuf = new StringBuffer();
}
```

```
public void endElement(String name) {
    if (!inSlice) {
        super.endElement(name);
        return;
    }
    //in slice
    if (sliceDepth > 1) {
        getSliceBuf().append("</"+name+">");
        sliceDepth--;
        return;
    }
    //end tag of slice point
    getSliceBuf().append("</"+name+">");
    setInSlice(false);
    //write sliceBuf to database
    com.xweave.xmldb.fgrel.Element parent = getCurrentElement();
    String parentId;
    if (parent == null) {
        parentId = "NULL";
        //should send error, fragment as root is not allowed
    } else {
        parentId = parent.getId();
    }
    String currentId = Integer.toString(nextFragCtrValue());
    StringBuffer buf = new StringBuffer();
    buf.append("insert into");
    buf.append(" " + FRAG_TABLE + " ");
    buf.append("(doc_id, frag_id, ele_id, body)");
    buf.append(" values ");
    buf.append("(" + getDocumentId() + ", " +
                    currentId + ", " +
                    parentId + ", " +
                    "'" + sliceBuf.toString() + "')");
    rdbExecute(buf.toString());
        //create child entry
    buf = new StringBuffer();
    buf.append("insert into");
    buf.append(" " + CHILD_TABLE + " ");
    buf.append("(doc_id, ele_id, indx, child_class, child_id)");
    buf.append(" values ");
    buf.append("(" + getDocumentId() + ", " +
                parentId + ", " +
                parent.incrIndexCtr() + ", " +
                "'FRAG', " +
                currentId + ")");
```

```
        rdbExecute(buf.toString());
        clearSliceBuf();
    }
    public boolean getInSlice() {
        return inSlice;
    }
    public Slice getSlice() {
        if (slice == null) {
            slice = new Slice();
        }
        return slice;
    }
    public StringBuffer getSliceBuf() {
        if (sliceBuf == null) {
            sliceBuf = new StringBuffer();
        }
        return sliceBuf;
    }
    protected int nextFragCtrValue() {
        return fragCtr++;
    }
    protected void setInSlice(boolean newValue) {
        this.inSlice = newValue;
    }
    public void setSlice(Slice newValue) {
        this.slice = newValue;
    }
    /**
     * Handle subelements and the connection from this element
     * to its parent.
     */
    public void startElement(String name, AttributeList attrList) {
        //DEBUG: System.out.println(name);
        if (inSlice) {
            getSliceBuf().append("<"+name+" "+attrListToString(attrList)+">");
            sliceDepth++;
            return;
        }
        if (!getSlice().sliceElement(name, attrList)) {
            //not a slice point, pass to fgrel to store
            super.startElement(name, attrList);
            return;
        }
        //at start of a slice element
        setInSlice(true);
```

```
sliceDepth = 1;
//slice point, store in medium-grained table
   getSliceBuf().append("<"+name+" "+attrListToString(attrList)+">");
}
}

/********************** JDBCLoadHandler.java *********************/
package com.xweave.xmldb.mgrel;

import com.xweave.xmldb.util.rdb.*;
import java.sql.SQLException;
/**
 * SAX Handler using JDBC to load a document into the database
 * Adds identical functionality to LoadHandler as
com.xweave.xmldb.fgrel.JDBCLoadHandler
 */
public class JDBCLoadHandler extends LoadHandler {
   private RDB rdb = null;
public JDBCLoadHandler(RDB rdb) {
   super();
   setRdb(rdb);
}
/**
 * Get document id from instance variable or from database
 */
public String getDocumentId() {
   if (documentId == null) {
      //get next id from Oracle
      //Could use a SEQUENCE, but this will work
      StringBuffer buf = new StringBuffer();
      buf.append("select max(doc_id) from ");
      buf.append(DOC_TABLE);
      try {
         String elementId = getRdb().getDataItem(buf.toString());
         if (elementId == null) {
            //no records in table (or SQL error we may discover later)
            documentId = "1";
         } else {
            documentId = String.valueOf(Integer.parseInt(elementId) + 1);
         }
      } catch (Exception ex) {
         ex.printStackTrace();
         //we will have problems later, so throw out now
         throw new Error("Unable to get new DOC_ID from database.");
```

```
        }
    }
    return documentId;
}
public RDB getRdb() {
    return rdb;
}
public boolean rdbExecute(String value) {
    // add a semicolon to print to standard out, omit for JDBC
    try {
        return getRdb().executeUpdate(value) > 0;
    } catch (SQLException ex) {
        ex.printStackTrace();
        return false;
    }
}
protected void setRdb(RDB newValue) {
    this.rdb = newValue;
}
}

/************************ Slice.java *********************/
package com.xweave.xmldb.mgrel;

import org.xml.sax.*;
import java.util.*;
public class Slice {
    private Hashtable sliceHash = null;
public Slice() {
    super();
}
public Slice(String name) {
    super();
    this.add(name);
}
public boolean add(String name) {
    //Do preprocessing on name, to check for list
    return addList(name);
}
public boolean addList(String nameList) {
    int spaceIndex = nameList.indexOf(' ');
    if (spaceIndex == -1) {
        //not a list of names
        return addName(nameList);
}
```

```
        int currIndex = 0;
        while (spaceIndex != -1) {
            addName(nameList.substring(currIndex, spaceIndex - 1));
            currIndex = spaceIndex + 1;
            spaceIndex = nameList.indexOf(' ', currIndex);
        }
        addName(nameList.substring(currIndex));
        return true;
    }
    public boolean addName(String name) {
        //Later, can add conditionals to hash entry
        getSliceHash().put(name, Boolean.TRUE);
        return false;
    }
    protected Hashtable getSliceHash() {
        if (sliceHash == null) {
            sliceHash = new Hashtable();
        }
        return sliceHash;
    }
    protected void setSliceHash(Hashtable newValue) {
        this.sliceHash = newValue;
    }
    public boolean sliceElement(String name, AttributeList attrList) {
        return getSliceHash().containsKey(name);
    }
    }
```

The Java code is based on the implementation of the fine-grained approach, and the main class "Demo" is a subclass of the fine-grained "Demo" class, as are the command classes "Load", "Delete", and "Format". The "LoadHandler" class for the medium-grained approach is also a subclass of the "LoadHandler" class for the fine-grained approach, though it adds tracking of the slice points. The slice points are captured in the "Slice" class, which is basically a hashtable of element type names upon which slices are to be performed. The "Slice" class may be extended by modifying the method "sliceElement" to allow for more complex slice points, such as slice points based on attribute values or depth in the tree. The "sliceElement" method determines whether a slice point should be created in the storage of a document and is only called by the "startElement" method of "LoadHandler". The class "JDBCLoadHandler" adds the same JDBC database access functionality to "LoadHandler" as the "JDBCLoadHandler" adds to the "LoadHandler" class in the fine-grained approach.

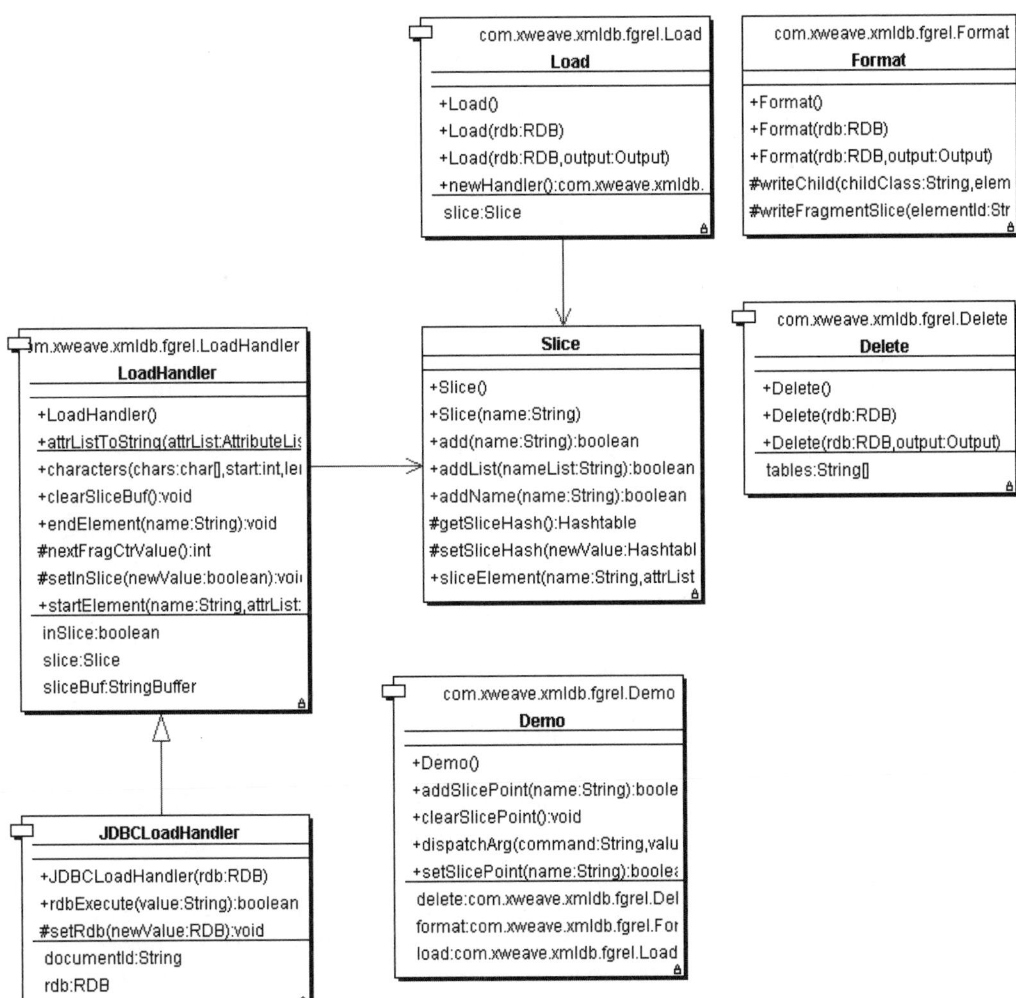

Figure 4–13 UML diagram for medium-grained storage system

4.5 Practical Considerations

The relational database examples in this chapter use Oracle and DB2, but any relational DBMS could be used with minor changes (at most) to the SQL commands in those examples. Postgres and mySQL are two free systems that you can use.

The fine-grained implementation is limited in that when it fully decomposes the document into atomic constituents, it loses data type information (that may be provided by XSDL) and does not make use of structural information stated in XSDL (or DTDs) that could provide more efficient storage. The medium-grained approach improves the efficiency of the decomposition/composition of the document, but also does not take schema information into account.

When the documents being captured in a database are of a specific document type (as defined by a DTD or XSDL schema), the information from the definition of the document type may be used to create a RDBMS schema that captures that specific document type. This can be done manually, by using database design techniques (such as those described in Chapter 2) to create a relational schema from the conceptual description implied by a document type definition (DTD or XSDL). Some of those steps may also be done automatically by translating DTDs or XSDL schemas into relational schema. This only works if the DTD or XSDL schema is fixed (or infrequently modified), as the relational database could need to be modified for every change in the document type.

Several academic conferences provide proceedings with research papers that describe ways to more efficiently store XML in RDBMSs, including:

- ACM SIGMOD Conference on Management of Data
- IEEE Conference on Data Engineering
- Proceedings of the Conference on Very Large Data Bases
- International WWW Conference

Contents of the conferences are available on Web sites for the conferences, and articles from these conferences are often available on the Web (or from the authors of the articles).

Database System Architecture

- How is an XML database used and accessed?
- How does an XML DBMS interact with other systems?
- How can relational data be presented as XML?

5

Because XML is a good language for data exchange, it is often used in communication between systems. System architecture describes how these systems interact. Database system architecture describes how applications and users access and manage data in a DBMS. For XML databases, users and applications need to load XML into a database, transform data using XML, retrieve data from a relational DBMS as XML, retrieve data from an XML DBMS, and combine relational and XML data as XML. Architectures for database systems include client/server architectures where a client application interacts directly with a DBMS and three-tier architectures where a separate server mediates between clients and DBMSs.

5.1 System Architecture

System architecture is the organization of system functionality into interconnected modules. Each *module* is a component of the system that performs several related functions. The goal of good system architecture is to appropriately group functional requirements into modules and to organize the modules into a system that meets all the requirements. System architecture addresses questions such as:

- How many modules?
- How are they connected? *(linear, tree, graph...)*
- What do they do? *(functionality of each module)*

Systems are pervasive, and most scientific fields study systems in some context. Mechanical physics is involved with how objects in a closed system interact, and biology is the in-depth study of a system where the interactions are more "organic." Engineering is concerned more with how to build such large systems and to achieve some functionality through that creation. In construction, architecture is concerned with the design of the building: what it looks like and how it functions. System architecture is thus a potentially broad area concerned with the design of functional components, which through their interaction, perform a global task. In this book, system architecture guides the design of mechanistic, "non-organic" software components of XML DBMSs.

Large systems tend to be organized hierarchically with major subsystems, containing smaller subsystems that contain smaller subsystems on down to packages that contain the basic building blocks of programs: object classes, functions, or procedures. This section addresses the higher (more abstract) levels of granularity particularly with respect to separating processing across machines on a network.

The earliest database systems were *monolithic.* All functionality was contained in one large system, and people connected to the system through "dumb" terminals or punch cards. Later, as end-user workstations gained computing power, some of the processing and functionality was split off of the monolithic system and placed on the end-user (client) machines in a *client-server* architecture. The client subsystem contained formatting and simple processing, whereas the server retained most of the data management functionality. As databases grew and needed to be connected into enterprise systems, a *three-tier* architecture became necessary to simplify client access to multiple databases each with an independent server. The middle-tier enabled client applications to connect to multiple DBMSs through a common interface. Concurrently, developers were struggling with where to put the *business rules,* which describe how the data may be used. The business-rule processing would bog down a server or would require duplication in clients, especially in large systems where business rules were needed by several applications. When business rules are incorporated into the middle-tier, they can be shared across applications without further burdening the efficiency or maintenance of the database server. As the number of databases and applications grows, additional middle-tiers become necessary and that functionality can be reorganized into an *n-tier* architecture.

A Web database system incorporates a Web server as one of the modules in the system and uses a Web transport protocol, such as http, to communicate between tiers. A Web database system may have a client-server, three-tier, or n-tier architecture, with a three-tier architecture being the most prevalent. In the three-tier approach, a DBMS sends data to a Web server that passes the data to a Web browser. In n-tier architectures, a series of databases and application servers send data to one (or more) Web servers that then pass data on to the clients. XML may be used for communication between any of the components in an n-tier architecture. Client/server architectures are possible and usually consist of a Web server embedded within a DBMS.

One of the advantages of Web database systems is that application deployment may be simplified when using Web browsers that support pages with embedded code, such as scripts or Java applets. With Java applets, the Java code is brought over the network when invoked, and the Web browsers provide simple formatting, forms, and scripting, which can be expanded through the use of Java applets. Because of the bandwidth necessary and the desire to put more complicated applications on smaller platforms, functionality that was occurring in client applications sometimes occurs in the server or middle-tier in *thin-client* applications. For example, Java applets may access the database through a JDBC connection instead of native database calls, or they may access statistical analysis programs on a middle-tier instead of performing the computations locally.

The goal of good system architecture is to place functionality into appropriate modules. You can choose from many criteria, such as a desire to isolate technology dependencies or to isolate domain dependencies. These non-functional requirements serve as basic engineering principles to be followed in the earliest design stages. Developing appropriate criteria is a foundation of good system architecture and is essential for successful development. The following non-functional guideposts may be appropriate in particular situations:

- Should DBMS-specific functionality be isolated to one module to facilitate possible porting later?
- Can a company-standard vendor be assumed to be used throughout the system and does not need isolating?

- Should the design be independent of the provider for middle-tier?
- Should the user interface be driven by the database schema to minimize the impact of frequent domain changes?
- Should transfers of data from the database be minimized because of large dataset size?
- Should data access control be isolated to one module to enforce security constraints?

A balance is necessary to incorporate essential requirements without overly constraining the system architecture. A trade-off exists between a flexible system and a timely one—between a creative approach and a realistic one. In critical commercial-software development, much effort is required on the system architecture to anticipate problems and utilize known resources. In rapid prototyping or throw-away systems, little effort is required, and many authors of perl/cgi scripts will mix SQL calls with HTML generation and the domain-specific business rules, resulting in a quickly useful system; unfortunately, the maintenance burden increases dramatically during prolonged use with database-schema changes, Web-browser changes, and business-rule growth.

5.1.1 Client/Server

XML processing can take place in the DBMS server. An XML DBMS or an XML-generation program can be embedded within another DBMS. The solutions provided by commercial relational DBMS systems are described in Section 6.2.2. In addition, server code can be modified to return HTML. One way to do that is to modify a public-domain relational DBMS server such as mysql to generate XML. Another way would be to add objects to an object-oriented DBMS to provide XML (as implemented in eXcelon and as described in Section 4.1.2). This section describes a couple of simple ways to generate XML from within a relational DBMS server. Later sections in this chapter describe data servers in a three-tier architecture, and those data servers may be incorporated in a database server with programming language support, such as a Java virtual machine.

XML can be created within a SQL statement. Given a DEPT table with columns DEPTNO, DNAME, and LOC, (as in Oracle's scott/tiger database) the SQL statement in Example 5–1 will generate XML. To create an XML document, the data must be wrapped in a "<collection>" tag. Doing this requires some support for aggregation functions on the server or in the client application, as shown in Example 5–2. Although not a very general solution, using a SQL statement does demonstrate the ease in which you can generate XML within a relational DBMS and may be a quick solution for very simple applications.

Example 5–1 : SQL Code to Generate XML Fragment for Scott/Tiger Example Database Department Table

```
select '<dept deptno="'||deptno||'" dname="'||dname
  ||'" loc="'||loc||'"/>"'
  from dept
```

Example 5–2 : Shell Script to Generate XML Document for Scott/Tiger Example Database Department Table

```
#!/bin/sh
echo '<?xml version=\"1.0\"?>'
echo '<collection>'
sqlplus scott/tiger <<'EOF'
select '<dept deptno="'||deptno||'" dname="'||dname
  ||'" loc="'||loc||'"/>"'
  from dept
'EOF'
echo '/<collection>'
```

You can develop a more general solution by removing the dependence upon the columns. One way to do that is to create a function on the server that wraps columns with the column name, rows with the table name, and the document with a "<collection>" tag.

A relational record may be formatted either as one element with data as attribute values or as one element with data as embedded elements. Formatting records as attributes is simpler, but formatting records as embedded elements is more general. Embedded elements provide the ability to use CDATA sections for values with reserved characters; they may have attributes with formatting information; and they may be replaced with more complete data in reference to a foreign key constraint. The attribute versus element issue is discussed more fully in Section 2.4.4.

Pseudo-code for formatting the records in a table as attributes is given in Example 5–3, and pseudo-code for formatting the records as embedded elements is given in Example 5–4. Many database vendors provide solutions to query the database and combine the query result with construction of XML documents. Solutions from IBM, Oracle, and Microsoft are introduced in Chapter 6.

Example 5–3 : Procedure to Write Relational Table as XML Attributes

```
procedure writeXMLAttributes(table)
   print "<?xml version=\"1.0\"?>"
   print "<collection>"
   for each row in table
      print "<" tablename ">"
      for each column in row
         print columnname "=" """ value """
      end
      print "/>"
   end
   print "/<collection>"
end
```

Example 5–4 : Procedure to Write Relational Table as XML Embedded Elements

```
procedure writeXMLEmbedElements(table)
   print "<?xml version=\"1.0\"?>"
   print "<collection>"
   for each row in table
      print "<record>"
      for each column in row
      print "<" columnname ">"
      print value
      print "</" columnname ">"
      end
      print "</record>"
   end
   print "</collection>"
end
```

Some of the Java examples from later in the chapter will work in a two-tier architecture, which provides support for expanding foreign-key constraints, retrieving individual records, and query constraints. Supporting XML processing within a database engine in a client/server architecture may be essential for performance with large datasets. However, the software is only described within a three-tier architecture, because understanding the various processing that is needed is simpler when it is thought about within a three-tier architecture rather than a client/server architecture. If a client/server architecture is required, then the functionality in the middle-tier and server in the three-tier architecture may be combined to create a server for a client/server architecture. Also in a client/server architecture, even when the processing takes place within the server, there are still performance issues in communication between the core of the database engine and any extensions that deal with XML; it is just that the performance tradeoffs are of smaller magnitude than with the three-tier solution.

5.1.2 Three-tier

A simple three-tier system architecture for a Web database system is shown in Figure 5–1. The system contains three modules:

- **DBMS**—provides database storage and access. Technology choices for this module include a relational DBMS, an object-oriented DBMS, an XML DBMS, or a file system.
- **Middle-tier**—provides a Web server capable of accessing data from the DBMS and making it available to the client. Technology choices for the middle-tier include a Web server, a Web server with CGI scripts, a Web server with servlets, a Web server with Java Server Pages, a commercial middle-tier with database connectivity, or an application server.
- **Client**—provides a user interface to the functionality made available through the middle-tier. The client may also be another application in, for example, a business-to-business context. Technology choices for the client typically include a browser, a Java applet, or a Java application.

There are technology choices to be made for each module and for inter-module communication. The client communication protocol could be an *ad hoc* language using a TCP/IP protocol, HTML or XML using HTTP, or CORBA. The communication protocol between the database and middle-tier could be JDBC or CORBA. The technology choices are interrelated, and each technology choice is usually restricted by the other choices.

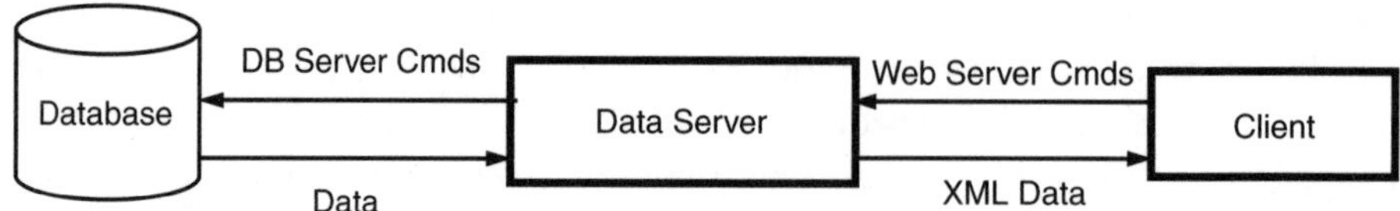

Figure 5–1 Three-tier architecture for Web database system

Other architectures and technology choices are possible, and regardless of the architecture chosen, here are some questions to consider in the system design:

- How is data loaded into the database?
- How is data queried from the database?
- Where does XML generation go?
- Where does XML processing go?

5.2 XML Web Server

An XML Web server provides Web-based access to the data in a DBMS. Support for the DBMS operations are provided, such as storing, retrieving, and updating documents. The underlying DBMS may be any data model, but the retrieved data is formatted as XML. When the data server loads data into a non-XML database, the data server may accept the data as XML and format it as appropriate for the DBMS.

Some implementation options are described in the next section, and Section 5.2.2 describes how the data server can be accessed. Sections 5.2.3 and 5.3, respectively, describe storage and retrieval of relational data as XML using a relational data server. Section 5.4 describes storage and retrieval of XML data using an XML data server. Section 5.5 describes retrieval of relational and XML data through a shared server.

5.2.1 Implementation Options

An XML data server may be built from scratch by modifying a Web server, using a Web server with a CGI script, using a Web server with a servlet, using a Web server that supports Java Server Pages, using an application server, or purchasing a commercial system. To build an XML data server from scratch, a Web server component is needed on top of which one adds the functionality to access the database, format XML, and return XML upon appropriate URL requests. An existing Web server (such as a small open-source server) may be modified or extended to access the database, format XML, and return XML upon appropriate URL requests. To use a Web server with a CGI script, servlet, or application server, the same functionality must be implemented. The advantage of using an application server is that the database connectivity will already be implemented. A good commercial system may provide all the functionality needed.

On top of the data server, additional functionality may be added to perform additional processing before returning, entering, or modifying the XML data in the database. For example, aggregate or statistical manipulations may be needed for some queries, or business rules and validity checks may be required for data inserts or modifications. Being aware of these requirements will guide the choice of data server.

If you can purchase an available commercial XML data server that meets the requirements, then that is the best solution. If you can purchase an application server that is easy to integrate into the development environment and meets the requirements, then it will provide necessary database functionality and should be seriously considered. The disadvantage of some application servers is that sometimes the developer must use limited user interfaces and non-standard database connectivity, which can become burdensome to the overall development effort. However, to develop a database connectivity package from scratch (on top of JDBC, for example) is a considerable effort and should be considered a last resort in a large commercial application (unless your goal is to build an XML data server—then, of course, read on). Database connectivity packages can be simple for small applications that open a database connection, perform a transaction, and close the connection. A simple database connectivity package is described in Appendix A. Connectivity packages become more complex when open connections must be retained for separate transactions in multiple accounts, with pooling of connections to improve efficiency, timeouts, and secure connections.

An important decision to make in implementing a data server is the programming language used.

If you use Java to implement the data server, then a Web server that supports servlets is a good choice. Two options for communicating with a database from a Web server are thin client and thick client, depending upon whether they contain a little or a lot of database capability, respectively. *Thick client* is a complete database application that has direct native access to the database. *Thin client* is a lightweight protocol that allows the Web server to access the database via a protocol but does not typically implement DBMS-specific capabilities. A thick client connection to the database may be implemented using a direct connection in C with a Java wrapper. A typical choice for a thin client connection is JDBC. JDBC—Open Database Connectivity (ODBC) implemented in Java—provides a standard mechanism for accessing relational databases that is supported by most (if not all) database vendors. Some database vendors may provide direct connection within Java (thick client), using JDBC or another protocol. The relative tradeoffs between options can be obtained in a good JDBC book. A thick client may be more efficient. Here, we work with JDBC (thin client) because it is generic, supported by most database vendors, and works in most situations.

An alternative to Java is the scripting language Tcl/tk. Tcl/tk has the advantage of being easy to extend, easy to integrate with C, and easy to combine with a variety of packages. Unfortunately, it is not as well-known as Java or Javascript, but it is worth considering, especially if it is already available in your infrastructure. Tcl/tk is also an excellent prototyping language because it is an untyped, scripting language with flexible data structures and fairly extensive built-in features. Connections to Oracle, Sybase, and other databases are already implemented and available on the Web, and several HTTPD servers are available with source code for free, including one from Scriptics. There are also more robust Web/application servers in Tcl/tk including the one that runs the AOL Web site, which has the advantage of built-in database connectivity. The disadvantages are that because Tcl/tk has a smaller user community there tends to be less support and maintenance of public domain packages, fewer options, and slower response to integrating new technologies. However, if you know Tcl/tk, you can build a reasonable XML data server using open source components that is extensible within the server in a few days. This is a great way to prototype a new XML data server.

Other scripting languages are perl and python. Perl provides a plethora of modules to support CGI and database connectivity. Python has a growing developer community and provides reasonable support within a scripting language for object-oriented programming and sound software engineering practices.

For those wishing to build an XML data server on top of a relational database but without access to a commercial relational database, the public domain DBMS mysql—which is supported by access to several scripting languages—may be useful.

5.2.2 Client Access

When using a Web-based data server, the client applications can access the server through URLs. A URL can be built up to specify most, if not all, of the information necessary for data access and POST-ing to the URL can be used to insert data in the database. There are several questions to address in developing the user or application access to the XML data server:

- How should the Web server be accessed?
- How should URLs be specified to provide appropriate database access?
- What are the design issues?
- Should one URL be used or many?
- What criteria are used to judge the URL design?

Here are three strategies for URL design:

- One URL and pass all information through POST of a single document.
- One URL and pass most information through POST/GET parameters.
- Different URL per function.

All the data and controlling commands may be placed in a document and posted to one URL. The advantage of this approach is that all the information being transported is in XML (and thus compatible with other XML transport in the system). The disadvantage is that at least some parsing of the XML document is required before deciding what to do with the data being sent. For example, if either an update or an insert is possible, the document may need partial parsing to determine the operation and data location before parsing the data to be modified or added. Passing a partially parsed data stream off to another parser is difficult, if not impossible. However, this approach may be useful when the entire document can be processed at one time. Using a single document is likely to be most appropriate when several applications are interacting with the XML data server.

When users are interacting with the XML data server through Web pages and HTML forms, passing information through POST/GET parameters is easier. This is most appropriate when you have a few commands and not much structured data to be passed. For example, if browsing and simple form-based query capabilities are desired, the query parameters may be included in the parameter list. The pedagogical approach taken in this book is to use POST/GET parameters and to pass structured data as XML by specifying the XML source as another URL.

Having a different URL per capability instead of a single URL with parameters to distinguish capabilities is primarily a matter of style, though one choice may be easier to implement depending upon the technology.

The URLs may be defined by having them typed into the Web browser, created in an HTML form, created by an applet, created by an application, created by a CGI script, or defined anywhere that has the capability of accessing data via HTTP.

5.2.3 Data Loading

Loading XML data into an existing relational (or object-oriented database) consists of two challenges: a semantic challenge and a technical challenge. The first challenge is to map the semantics of the XML into the appropriate semantics for the relations—for example, mapping a person element type in the XML to a personnel table in the database. When the XML is designed with the existing relational database in mind, then the mapping should be straightforward. There may also be tags in the XML document that do not map to any concept in the relational database: That data can be ignored or the relational database may be modified as appropriate.

The difficulty in mapping XML data to a relational schema arises when there is partial overlap between the XML and relational semantics. For example, data as XML coming from one system might combine information on permanent, temporary, and contract employees, whereas the relational database stores that information in separate relations. In general, the semantic problem is similar to integration of multiple databases and work in data warehousing and database integration may be useful, with the caveat that the data models are also different.

The second (technical) challenge is how to map hierarchical XML data into flat relations. After the specific semantic mapping is understood, the XML data still needs to be flattened for storage in relations.

5.2.3.1 Restructuring XML Data

You can choose from four approaches that may be useful when you need to store XML in an existing relational (or object-oriented) database.

Custom script—the easiest, but least generic, way is to create a custom program to read and parse an XML document and insert the data into the appropriate tables.

Restricted structure—the XML can be transformed (possibly using XSL) into a structure that is more like the flat relation of a relational database. Embedded elements can be replaced with an appropriate value or identifier and their content placed in another part of the document to be created later. The link from the parent element to the embedded element may be provided by foreign key constraints or linking tables in the relational database. For example, in Example 5–5 micro-array spot records with embedded gene records may be replaced with two collections of flat records where the spot record refers to the appropriate gene record using a unique identifier. Micro-array experiments are similar to the filter hybridization experiments described in Section 2.3.3, with the extension that the quantity of a gene product which hybridizes to the DNA on the array is also measured.

Creating connections—the loader may be able to perform simple queries to more easily load tables that have foreign key constraints.

Bypass—when using a DBMS with a data model other than XML for storage, it may be better to bypass XML when inserting or editing data. In particular, when the client is a user client instead of another application, there may be little benefit in formatting user-specified data as XML before loading it into the database, especially if the data-entry or editing process is interactive with small updates interspersed with small queries. XML's strength in those systems may be in querying. A variety of other technologies exist for creating data entry and editing forms.

For some applications, a generic data loader can be used to load XML data into a relational database. The criteria are that a preprocessor be able to translate the hierarchical XML data into a collection of flat relationships. One mechanism to translate XML is to use XSL stylesheets to translate application-specific XML to a generic, record-oriented XML representation

Example 5–5 : Embedded Records for Loading

```
<?xml version="1.0"?>
<root>
<spot>
  <grid>1</grid>
  <version/>
  <position>1A1</position>
  <gene>
    <name>TYR1</name>
    <description>PREPHENATE DEHYDROGENASE</description>
    <pathway>TYROSINE BIOSYNTHESIS</pathway>
    <organism>yeast</organism>
  </gene>
</spot>
<spot>
  <grid>1</grid>
  <version/>
  <position>1A2</position>
  <gene>
    <name>GRD19</name>
    <description>GOLGI PROTEIN RETENTION</description>
    <pathway>SECRETION</pathway>
    <organism>yeast</organism>
  </gene>
</spot>
</root>
```

that can be loaded using a Java application. However, if there is a large amount of data, it may be necessary to use a mechanism which does not process the data in-memory, such as using an approach based on a SAX parser (described in Appendix B).

The data loading application may be used stand-alone or may be embedded in a server that would allow XML to be posted to a http server and loaded into the database. Two ways to load XML data through a Web interface are via an XML document or via HTTP POST/GET parameters to a Web server. Information about the database and transaction could be specified using parameters to the POST/GET or included in the XML document. The XML document can contain the necessary loading information as elements or attributes, and the data to be loaded may be one of the elements in the document. Using an XML document is a more general solution for loading data created by an application, but using parameters of a HTTPD POST/GET allow the data to be entered manually using HTML forms.

5.2.3.2 Loading Data via URL Parameters

Parameters to a POST can be used to specify the necessary loading information and elements and attributes of a document element. In case of a flat element, the parameters are listed by name. Hierarchical structures are more complicated, but can be created using a naming hierarchy. In a naming hierarchy, the root subelements are listed by name and their subelements named by concatenating their name to their parent's name with a character separator.

Another issue in using HTML forms to pass information through parameters is that some parameters may be needed by the application. For example, the form may set a "Submit" variable and the database account and entry point (such as a tablename or object class) may need to be specified. Four approaches are: to uniquely identify application variables, to uniquely identify user variables, to uniquely identify both, or to not worry about it. Variable names may be uniquely identified by concatenating a unique prefix, such as "_", "var_", "xml_", "app_", or "user_".

XML commands may be embedded in parameter values to simplify the development of a form. For example, if a unique identifier must be created, a command may be used to instruct the data loader to create it, such as "<sequence_generate sequence="transaction_seq">".

5.2.3.3 Loading Data from XML Documents

XML documents to be loaded may come from another application, an external resource (such as database or flat file), or a data entry form. One way to create an XML document from a data entry form is to create a script or program that formats the HTML form data as XML. A Java applet with a graphical user interface may also be used to create an entry form. This is discussed more in Chapter 7.

I have implemented a loader for relational data, called rLoad, in Java that demonstrates the issues in loading XML data into a relational database. The source code for rLoad is given in Example 5–6. The application loads XML data in two steps:

1. Translate the XML data using XSL stylesheets to an XML document consisting of "record" and "field" tags with attributes for the table being loaded and for other load-specific meta-data. For example, the XML document in Example 5–7 can be translated using a stylesheet to a rLoad XML document, such as the one shown in Example 5–8. Stylesheets are discussed more fully in Chapter 7, but a simple stylesheet to translate genes for the micro-array example is given in Example 5–9.
2. Load the "record/field" data into the database using a SAX based parser. The record/field XML document, called a rload XML document, consists of "record" and "field" elements and some additional meta-data to perform the following tasks:
   - Specify into which relation table the record should be loaded. In the document, records to be loaded into different tables may be interspersed. Additionally, a record for one table may be embedded within a record to be loaded into another table. This simplifies the generation of the rload XML document.
   - Specify whether an embedded record should be loaded before or after the record in which it is embedded. Allowing this option increases the flexibility in which records may be defined by the XSL stylesheet translation without concern over foreign key dependencies. For example in an XML document, employees may specify the department to which they belong or a department may list the employees that belong to it. When loading, the independent record can be created first, then the dependent one, regardless of which one occurs as an embedded record in the XML data source.
   - Specify that a field value should be obtained by a DBMS sequence generator to create a unique identifier.
   - Specify that a field value should be the most recently generated value for a given sequence. Thus, a dependent record can refer to the unique identifier generated for the record upon which it depends.
   - Specify that the whitespace should be trimmed or removed from the character data in the field element.

– Specify that a value should be the identifier of a record in another table whose specified column equals the value in the field element. This allows for creation of foreign key constraints on the unique identifiers generated by the DBMS while using alternate keys or columns with unique constraints for date entry and loading.

The Java implementation consists of three classes: the main LoadXML class, a JDBCLoadHandler class for use by the SAX parser, and a Record container class that contains the information for each record to be loaded. The "main" method of LoadXML takes the rload XML file as input and calls a "parse" method that creates a SAX parser with JDBCLoadHandler as the handler. JDBCLoadHandler creates a Record object and fills in the fields as they are parsed. If more than one relational record is needed for an XML "record" element, then multiple Record objects are created and stored on a stack.

Example 5–6 : Java Code for rLoad XML Data Loader

```
/************************* LoadXML.java ***********************/
package com.xweave.xmldb.rload;

/**
 * Main class for loading XML data into a relational database
 */
import org.xml.sax.*;
import org.xml.sax.helpers.ParserFactory;
import com.ibm.xml.parsers.DOMParser;
import org.w3c.dom.Document;
import java.io.IOException;
import com.xweave.xmldb.util.rdb.*;

public class LoadXML {
   public static OracleDB oracleDB = null;
public LoadXML() {
   super();
}
public static OracleDB getOracleDB() {
   if (oracleDB == null) {
      try {
         oracleDB = new OracleDB(new JDBCAcct("mgraves/
mgraves@127.0.0.1"));
         oracleDB.connect();
```

```
        } catch (java.sql.SQLException ex) {
            ex.printStackTrace();
        }
    }
    return oracleDB;
}
public static void main(java.lang.String[] args) {
    // Insert code to start the application here
    if (args.length < 1) {
        System.err.println("XMLLoad: requires <file> as argument");
    }
    (new LoadXML()).parse(args[0]);
}
public void parse(String xmlFile) {
    String parserClass = "com.ibm.xml.parsers.SAXParser";
    try {
        Parser parser = ParserFactory.makeParser(parserClass);
        HandlerBase handler = new JDBCLoadHandler();
            parser.setDocumentHandler(handler);
            parser.setErrorHandler(handler);
try {
            parser.parse(xmlFile);
        } catch (SAXException se) {
            se.printStackTrace();
        } catch (IOException ioe) {
            ioe.printStackTrace();
        }
    } catch (ClassNotFoundException ex) {
        ex.printStackTrace();
    } catch (IllegalAccessException ex) {
        ex.printStackTrace();
    } catch (InstantiationException ex) {
        ex.printStackTrace();
    }
}
public static void setOracleDB(OracleDB newValue) {
    LoadXML.oracleDB = newValue;
}
}
/********************** Record.java *********************/
package com.xweave.xmldb.rload;

/**
 * Contains information about a record
 */
```

```
import java.lang.*;
import com.xweave.xmldb.util.rdb.RDB;
public class Record {
   public String table;
   protected StringBuffer fieldNameBuffer = null;
   protected StringBuffer fieldValueBuffer = null;
   protected StringBuffer subqWhereBuffer = null;
   protected StringBuffer subqFromBuffer = null;
   private int numSubq = 0;
   private boolean inSubq = false;
   private boolean delay = false;
public Record() {
   super();
}
public void addFieldExpr(String value) {
   if (getFieldValueBuffer().length() > 0) {
      getFieldValueBuffer().append(",");
   }
   inSubq = false;
   getFieldValueBuffer().append(value);
}
public void addFieldName(String name) {
   if (getFieldNameBuffer().length() > 0) {
      getFieldNameBuffer().append(",");
   }
   getFieldNameBuffer().append(name);
}
public void addFieldSubq(String value) {
   if (getSubqWhereBuffer().length() > 0) {
      getSubqWhereBuffer().append(" AND ");
      getSubqFromBuffer().append(", ");
   }
   //split keyword at '.'
   int index = value.indexOf((int) '.');
   if (index == -1) {
      getSubqWhereBuffer().append(" ERROR "+value+" not known");
      return;
   }
   String table = value.substring(0,index);
   String column = value.substring(index+1);
   //add to buffers
   numSubq++;
   addFieldExpr("sqt"+Integer.toString(numSubq)+".id");
   inSubq = true;
```

```
getSubqWhereBuffer().append("sqt"+Integer.toString(numSubq)+"."+column+
" = ");
    getSubqFromBuffer().append(table+" sqt"+Integer.toString(numSubq));
}
public void addFieldValue(String value) {
    if (inSubq == true) {
        // note interaction with addFieldSubq
        getSubqWhereBuffer().append("'" + value + "'");
        inSubq = false;
        return;
    }
    if (getFieldValueBuffer().length() > 0) {
        getFieldValueBuffer().append(",");
    }
    // Oracle will correctly interpret a string as a number when
appropriate
    getFieldValueBuffer().append("'" + value + "'");
}
protected boolean getDelay() {
    return delay;
}
protected StringBuffer getFieldNameBuffer() {
    if (fieldNameBuffer == null) {
        fieldNameBuffer = new StringBuffer();
    }
    return fieldNameBuffer;
}
protected StringBuffer getFieldValueBuffer() {
    if (fieldValueBuffer == null) {
        fieldValueBuffer = new StringBuffer();
    }
    return fieldValueBuffer;
}
public static Record getFreeRecord() {
    return new Record();
}
public String getSQLInsertString() {
    StringBuffer buf = new StringBuffer();
    buf.append("insert into");
    buf.append(" " + getTable() + " ");
    buf.append("(" + getFieldNameBuffer() + ")");
    if (numSubq > 0) {
        buf.append(" select ");
        buf.append(getFieldValueBuffer());
```

```
        buf.append(" from " + getSubqFromBuffer());
        buf.append(" where " + getSubqWhereBuffer());
    } else {
        buf.append(" values ");
        buf.append("(" + getFieldValueBuffer() + ")");
    }
    return buf.toString();
}
protected StringBuffer getSubqFromBuffer() {
    if (subqFromBuffer == null) {
        subqFromBuffer = new StringBuffer();
    }
    return subqFromBuffer;
}
protected StringBuffer getSubqWhereBuffer() {
    if (subqWhereBuffer == null) {
        subqWhereBuffer = new StringBuffer();
    }
    return subqWhereBuffer;
}
public String getTable() {
    return table;
}
public void print() {
    System.out.println(getSQLInsertString());
    try {
        if (LoadXML.getOracleDB().executeUpdate(getSQLInsertString()) >
0) {
            System.out.println("...did not work");
        } else {
            System.out.println("...worked");
        }
    } catch (java.sql.SQLException ex) {
        ex.printStackTrace();
        System.out.println("...did not work");
    }
}
protected void setDelay(boolean newValue) {
    this.delay = newValue;
}
protected void setFieldNameBuffer(StringBuffer newValue) {
    this.fieldNameBuffer = newValue;
}
```

```
protected void setFieldValueBuffer(StringBuffer newValue) {
   this.fieldValueBuffer = newValue;
}
protected void setSubqFromBuffer(StringBuffer newValue) {
   this.subqFromBuffer = newValue;
}
protected void setSubqWhereBuffer(StringBuffer newValue) {
   this.subqWhereBuffer = newValue;
}
public void setTable(String newValue) {
   this.table = newValue;
}
}
/********************** JDBCLoadHandler.java **********************/
package com.xweave.xmldb.rload;

/**
 * Load XML data into a Relational Database
 */
import org.xml.sax.*;
import java.util.*;
public class JDBCLoadHandler extends org.xml.sax.HandlerBase {
   private Record currentRecord = null;
   private Stack recordStack = null;
   private Vector printVector = null;
   private boolean inField = false;
   private boolean fieldEmpty = true;
   private short whitespaceOp = 0;
   private final static int WHITESPACE_OP_NONE = 0;
   private final static int WHITESPACE_OP_TRIM = 1;
   private final static int WHITESPACE_OP_REMOVE = 2;
public JDBCLoadHandler() {
   super();
}
public void characters(char[] chars, int start, int length) {
   fieldEmpty = false;
   if (inField) {
      switch (whitespaceOp) {
         case WHITESPACE_OP_TRIM :
            currentRecord.addFieldValue(String.valueOf(chars, start,
length).trim());
            break;
         case WHITESPACE_OP_REMOVE :
            StringBuffer sb = new StringBuffer();
```

```
            for (int i = start; i < start + length; i++) {
               if (!Character.isWhitespace(chars[i])) {
                  sb.append(chars[i]);
               }
            }
            currentRecord.addFieldValue(sb.toString());
            break;
         default :
            // default or NONE is really trim
            currentRecord.addFieldValue(String.valueOf(chars, start,
length).trim());
      }
   }
}
public void endElement(String name) {
   inField = false;
   if (name.equalsIgnoreCase("record")) {
      endRecord();
      return;
   }
   if (name.equalsIgnoreCase("field")) {
      endField();
      return;
}
}
protected void endField() {
   if (inField && fieldEmpty) {
      currentRecord.addFieldValue("");
   }
}
protected void endRecord() {
   if (getCurrentRecord().getDelay()) {
      getPrintVector().addElement(getCurrentRecord());
      setCurrentRecord(null);
      return;
   }
   getCurrentRecord().print();
   setCurrentRecord(null);
   if (! getPrintVector().isEmpty()) {
      //first non-delay record end, so print delayed records
      Enumeration e = getPrintVector().elements();
      while (e.hasMoreElements()) {
         ( (Record) e.nextElement() ).print();
      }
```

```
            getPrintVector().removeAllElements();
        }
    }
    protected Record getCurrentRecord() {
        return currentRecord;
    }
    protected java.util.Vector getPrintVector() {
        if (printVector == null) {
            printVector = new java.util.Vector();
        }
        return printVector;
    }
    protected java.util.Stack getRecordStack() {
        if (recordStack == null) {
            recordStack = new java.util.Stack();
        }
        return recordStack;
    }
    protected void setCurrentRecord(Record newValue) {
        if (newValue == null) {
            //clear currentRecord
            if (getRecordStack().empty()) {
                this.currentRecord = null;
            } else {
                this.currentRecord = (Record) getRecordStack().pop();
            }
            return;
        }
        if (getCurrentRecord() != null) {
            //embedded record
            getRecordStack().push(getCurrentRecord());
        }
        this.currentRecord = newValue;
    }
    protected void setPrintVector(java.util.Vector newValue) {
        this.printVector = newValue;
    }
    protected void setRecordStack(java.util.Stack newValue) {
        this.recordStack = newValue;
    }
    public void startElement(String name, AttributeList attrList) {
        //System.out.println(name);
        inField = false;
        whitespaceOp = WHITESPACE_OP_NONE;
        if (name.equalsIgnoreCase("record")) {
```

```
        startRecord(attrList);
        return;
    }
    if (name.equalsIgnoreCase("field")) {
        startField(attrList);
        return;
    }
}
protected void startField(AttributeList attrList) {
    if (currentRecord == null) {
        System.out.println("Field not in record" + attrList.toString());
    }
    inField = true;
    fieldEmpty = true;
    for (int i = 0; i < attrList.getLength(); i++) {
        if (attrList.getName(i).equalsIgnoreCase("name")) {
            currentRecord.addFieldName(attrList.getValue(i));
        }
        if (attrList.getName(i).equalsIgnoreCase("sequence-generated"))
{
            currentRecord.addFieldExpr(attrList.getValue(i) +
".NextVal");
            inField = false;
        }
        if (attrList.getName(i).equalsIgnoreCase("sequence-value")) {
            currentRecord.addFieldExpr(attrList.getValue(i) + ".CurrVal");
            inField = false;
        }
        if (attrList.getName(i).equalsIgnoreCase("keysearch")) {
            currentRecord.addFieldSubq(attrList.getValue(i));
        }
        if (attrList.getName(i).equalsIgnoreCase("whitespace")) {
            if (attrList.getValue(i).equalsIgnoreCase("none")) {
                whitespaceOp = WHITESPACE_OP_NONE;
            } else
                if (attrList.getValue(i).equalsIgnoreCase("trim")) {
                    whitespaceOp = WHITESPACE_OP_TRIM;
                } else
                    if (attrList.getValue(i).equalsIgnoreCase("remove")) {
                        whitespaceOp = WHITESPACE_OP_REMOVE;
                    }
        }
    }
}
```

```
protected void startRecord(AttributeList attrList) {
   setCurrentRecord(Record.getFreeRecord());
   for (int i = 0; i < attrList.getLength(); i++) {
      if (attrList.getName(i).equalsIgnoreCase("table")) {
         currentRecord.setTable(attrList.getValue(i));
      }
      if (attrList.getName(i).equalsIgnoreCase("delay")) {
         if (! attrList.getValue(i).equalsIgnoreCase("false")) {
            currentRecord.setDelay(true);
         }
      }
   }
}
}
```

Example 5–7 : Example Data for Loading

```
<?xml version="1.0"?>
<root>
<exper_result>
  <spot>
    <grid>1000</grid>
    <version/>
    <position>1A1</position>
    <gene name="p53" organism="human"/>
  </spot>
  <experiment>
     <exper_cond>ts1</exper_cond>
  </experiment>
  <variant>0</variant>
  <value>-0.56</value>
</exper_result>
<exper_result>
  <spot>
    <grid>1000</grid>
    <version/>
    <position>1A2</position>
    <gene name="BRCA1" organism="human"/>
  </spot>
  <experiment>
     <exper_cond>ts1</exper_cond>
  </experiment>
  <variant>0</variant>
  <value>3.25</value>
```

```
</exper_result>
<exper_result>
  <spot>
    <grid>1000</grid>
    <version/>
    <position>1A3</position>
    <gene name="Pak1" organism="human"/>
  </spot>
  <experiment>
     <exper_cond>ts1</exper_cond>
  </experiment>
  <variant>0</variant>
  <value>2.14</value>
</exper_result>
</root>
```

Example 5–8 : Embedded Records for Loading with Values from Database Queries

```
<?xml version="1.0"?>
<ROOT>
<record table="exper_result">
  <field name="id" sequence-generated="exper_result_s"/>
  <record table="spot">
    <field name="id" sequence-generated="spot_s"/>
    <field name="grid>1000</field>
    <field name="version"/>
    <field name="position>1A1</field>
    <field name="gene" keysearch="gene.name">p53<field/>
  </record>
  <record table="experiment">
     <field name="id" sequence-generated="experiment_s"/>
     <field name="exper_cond">ts1</field>
  </record>
  <field name="variant">0</field>
  <field name="value">-0.56</field>
</record>
<record table="exper_result">
  <field name="id" sequence-generated="exper_result_s"/>
  <record table="spot">
    <field name="id" sequence-generated="spot_s"/>
    <field name="grid>1000</grid>
    <field name="version/>
    <field name="position>1A2</field>
    <field name="gene" keysearch="gene.name">BRCA1<field/>
```

```
    </record>
    <field name="experiment" sequence-value="experiment_s"/>
    <field name="variant>0</field>
    <field name="value>3.25</field>
</record>
</ROOT>
```

Example 5–9 : Stylesheet for Translating Example XML Data into rLoad XML

```
<?xml version="1.0"?>
<!-- Stylesheet for Loading Gene data -->
<xsl:stylesheet version="1.0" xmlns:xsl="http://www.w3.org/1999/XSL/
Transform">
  <xsl:output method="xml"/>
  <xsl:template match="/">
    <xsl:apply-templates select="*" />
  </xsl:template>
  <xsl:template match="root">
    <ROOT>
    <xsl:apply-templates select="*" />
    </ROOT>
  </xsl:template>
  <xsl:template match="gene">
    <record table="GENE">
    <field name="id" sequence-generated="gene_s" />
    <xsl:apply-templates select="@*">
    </xsl:apply-templates>
    </record>
  </xsl:template>
    <xsl:template match="@name">
      <field name="name">
        <xsl:value-of select="."/>
      </field>
    </xsl:template>
    <xsl:template match="@description">
      <field name="description">
        <xsl:value-of select="."/>
      </field>
    </xsl:template>
      <xsl:template match="@pathway">
        <field name="pathway">
        <xsl:value-of select="."/>
        </field>
      </xsl:template>
```

```
    <xsl:template match="@organism">
      <field name="organism">
      <xsl:value-of select="."/>
      </field>
    </xsl:template>
</xsl:stylesheet>
```

5.2.4 XML Generation

There are several approaches to generating XML documents from relational data. Five approaches are presented here:

a. An XML document can be generated based on the data in a database table. The table is formatted as an XML document, and the foreign key constraints are used to create a hierarchy of elements for the document. The element type names are taken from the table name(s) and column names. This approach is useful to enable browsing of the data in a database.
b. Similar to the previous approach, in this approach documents are driven by the structures in the database schema, but relational views may also be used. Each view is formatted as an XML document. This provides more flexibility in designing documents because the document structure does not depend upon the tables used for data storage. The element hierarchy can be defined from foreign keys and/or by a relation that explicitly states which values should be expanded and how.
c. *Ad hoc* queries can be used to generate XML documents, as done in the previous approaches. However, the element hierarchy still depends on the structure of the database schema (and/or views).
d. A document template may be defined where parts of the document are specified in terms of a query. The queries are executed and formatted as in the previous approach, but the results are combined into one document.
e. A query is specified with subqueries and the structure of the query determines the structure of the document. This approach works only if the XML rendering is embedded within the database query engine.

Approaches (a)–(c) are supported by the example software in Section 5.3. Approach (d) may be useful when combining XML generation with a Web server that supports server-side document generation, such as Java Server Pages (JSP).

5.3 Relational Data Server

A *relational database adaptor* makes data from a relational DBMS available in XML. It works by querying the database and formatting the report from the relational DBMS as XML. Section 6.2 describes commercial database adaptors. A *relational data server* is a database adaptor combined with a Web server.

The basic process for a user requesting an XML report from a relational DBMS using a Web browser (see Figure 5–2) is as follows:

1. The user specifies a relational query to the Web browser as a URL.
2. The Web browser sends the URL to the data server.
3. The data server parses the URL request and creates a SQL query.
4. The data server passes the SQL query to the database server.
5. The database server executes the query.
6. The database server returns the relational report to the data server.
7. The data server formats the report as XML.
8. The data server returns the XML report to the Web browser.
9. The Web browser parses the XML report and displays it to the user.

When a stylesheet is used, it must also be retrieved and parsed by the Web browser.

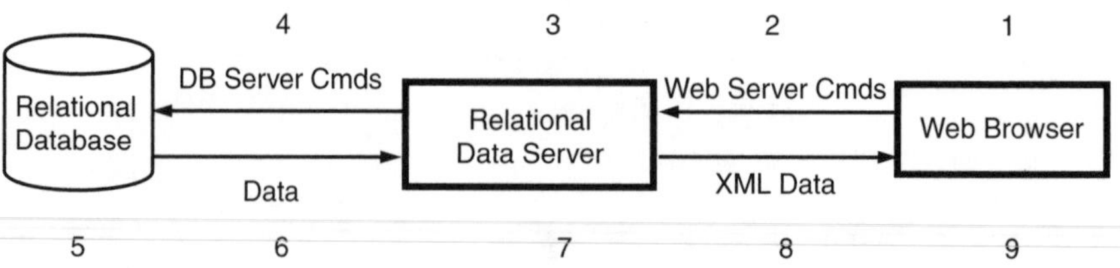

Figure 5–2 Process for a user requesting a report in a three-tier relational data server

Here are some questions to be addressed in developing a relational data server:

- Can relational views be displayed in addition to tables?
- Can data be updated? Or, is data read-only?
- Can data be retrieved from multiple tables?
- How are joins handled?
- How complex can the mapping from relations to XML be?
- Can helper tables or joining tables be recognized and handled differently?
- Can foreign key constraints be followed? To what depth?
- How are cycles in following foreign key constraints handled?
- How are links between tables handled?
- How expressive is the query facility?
- How are large reports returned? One large stream? Small pieces?

These questions are addressed by examining a relational data server implemented in Java, called rServe, which is described in more detail in Section 5.3.5. Example output for the micro-array database is shown in Figure 5–3, which is formatted using an XSL stylesheet (described in Chapter 7). Notice that some of the columns are hypertext links and may be followed to other rServe-generated reports.

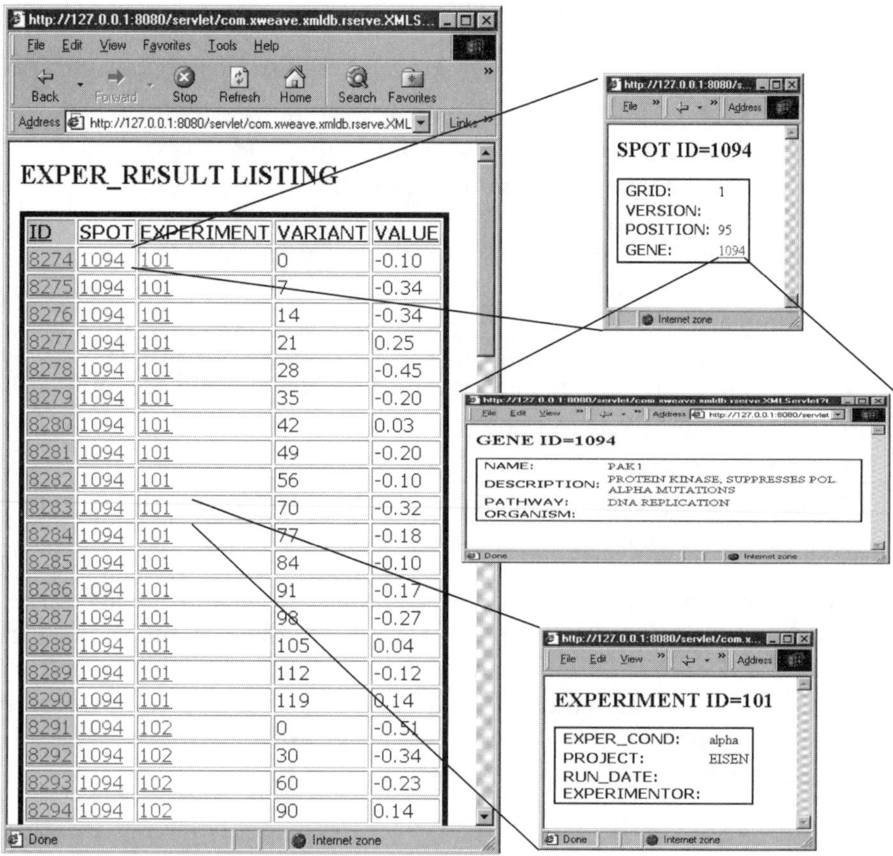

Figure 5–3 Example output of rServe report for micro-array database

5.3.1 Specifying URL Requests

The API to a relational data server may be specified using URL requests. These are described in this section before delving into the internals of rServe.

rServe allows for read-only access of relational data via URLs. A servlet is called with parameters such as the table name, constraints on the columns, and the relational database account to be accessed. An alternative implementation would allow for specifying a SQL statement as part of the URL.

Some example URLs for rServe are

- *http://127.0.0.1/servlets/com.xweave.xmldb.rserve.XMLServlet?tablename=company*—which retrieves all the records in the "company" table.
- *http://127.0.0.1/servlets/com.xweave.xmldb.rserve.XMLServlet?tablename=company&stylesheet=/ss/generic1.xsl*—which retrieves all the records in the "company" table, then formats the data using the stylesheet http://127.0.0.1/ss/generic.xsl.
- *http://127.0.0.1/servlets/com.xweave.xmldb.rserve.XMLServlet?tablename=company&id=12*—which retrieves the record in the "company" table with id equal to "12".
- *http://127.0.0.1/servlets/com.xweave.xmldb.rserve.XMLServlet?tablename=company&stylesheet=/ss/generic1.xsl&name=Acme*—which retrieves the record from the "company" table with name equal to "Acme", then formats the data using the stylesheet http://127.0.0.1/ss/generic.xsl.

There are three main components of the URL: the base, the stylesheet, and the query. The base refers to the servlet (or cgi-script) that provides the data service, in this case the rServe servlet installed on whatever machine the URL requests (as specified by the reserved IP address for localhost 127.0.0.1). The optional stylesheet specifies the XSL stylesheet that should be used to translate the XML to HTML for the browser. The stylesheet and query can occur in any order.

The base is something like

- *http://127.0.0.1/servlets/com.xweave.xmldb.rserve.XMLServlet?*
- *http://mymachine/servlets/com.xweave.xmldb.rserve.XMLServlet?*

with the trailing "?".

The stylesheet is "stylesheet=/ss/generic1.xsl". The stylesheet may also be omitted in a browser, and the default stylesheet for the browser will be used. This will usually show the text and tags of the XML document.

The query is built up from the tablename and column names and the individual name-value pairs are separated by "&".

To retrieve all the records in a table, the query "tablename=<table>" (where <table> is the name of the table) is used. To retrieve a specific entry in the table with a specified id "tablename=<table>&id=<id>" is used. Any column name can be used as part of the query.

In addition, the data server has a facility for specifying the DBMS account to us with the name-value pair "acct=<user>/<password>@<instance>". Any database in the DBMS may be accessed through the URL. For example:

- *http://127.0.0.1/servlets/com.xweave.xmldb.rserve.XMLServlet?tablename=dept&stylesheet=/ss/generic1.xsl&acct=scott/tiger@ORCL*

A couple of other things happen when creating the URL. When using HTML forms, a parameter name such as "Submit" is filled in automatically. The "Submit" parameter is ignored by the data server. URLs are encoded for reserved characters using their hexadecimal ASCII representation or another key; so for example, "/" is encoded "%2F" and spaces are encoded with "+". An actual URL generated by a HTML form looks like

- *http://127.0.0.1/servlets/com.xweave.xmldb.rserve.XMLServlet?tablename=company&stylesheet=%2Fss%2Fgeneric1.xsl&name=Acme&Submit=Find+company*

This is equivalent to

- *http://127.0.0.1/servlets/com.xweave.xmldb.rserve.XMLServlet?tablename=company&stylesheet=/ss/generic1.xsl&name=Acme*

5.3.2 Creating a SQL Query

The relational data server uses the parameters of the URL to build a SQL statement. For example, a request for the contents of a table may be built by adding the value of the "tablename" parameter to the following template:

```
select * from <tablename>
```

More complex queries can be built incrementally by adding column constraints as a "where" clause, by adding sorting constraints as an "ORDER BY" clause, and by adding the columns to be displayed as part of the select statement. These queries result in SQL such as:

```
select <report columns> from <tablename>
  where <conditions>
  order by <sort constraint>
```

Much of the functionality of a SQL statement can be encoded as a URL, though the "where" conditions require a little more creativity. Because the name/value pair must be separated by an "=" sign, the other operations may be encoded by pre-pending the operation to the value. For example:

```
...&partno=1234&quantity=20&... (quantity equal 20)
...&partno=1234&quantity=<20&... (quantity less than 20)
...&partno=1234&quantity=<=20&... (quantity less than or
equal 20)
```

5.3.3 Formatting a Report as XML

One way to format relational data as XML is to use the table names and column names to drive the creation of element type names (and/or attribute names). Information on primary keys and foreign keys can be used to create a document hierarchy. One issue in this approach is that some special characters may be used in table and column names that are not valid as XML element type names. A second issue is that following the foreign keys may cycle (lead to an infinite loop). A cycle forms when a foreign key refers to a table with a foreign key that refers back to the original table, either directly or through intermediate foreign key constraints. This is addressed by keeping track of the tables followed or by limiting the number of foreign key constraints that may be followed.

The process for formatting a report as XML is:

1. Write the header of the document.
2. Write the root element start tag.
3. Retrieve the column names from the meta-data if they are to be used as element type names.
4. Iterate through each record in the relational report.
   - **4.1** Write a start tag for the relation (such as the name of the table, something generic like "record", or a user-specified string).
   - **4.2** Iterate through each column in the record.
     - **4.2.1** If the record value for that column is a string, write it out surrounded by start and end tags.
     - **4.2.2** If that column has a foreign key constraint, consider recursively writing out an element for the record to which this column value refers.
   - **4.3** Write an end tag for the relation.
5. Write an end tag for the root element.

This algorithm may give poor performance on large databases because of the number of queries that are performed. In addition, if the foreign keys are followed for many steps (in effect, the resulting XML tree is deep), then duplicate queries will occur when duplicate foreign key values are retrieved. The algorithm does not take advantage of structural information contained in the relational database, such as foreign key constraints. This additional information may be utilized to create queries that retrieve information from multiple rows (or across multiple tables) in a single query. This allows the data for multiple elements to be retrieved by a single query.

5.3.4 Extracting Dictionary Data

A commercial relational DBMS provides information in its system tables that may be useful to extract in developing a data server. For example, the primary keys of a relation provide a unique index of all the records in the relation and may be used to refer to the records. Foreign keys are references to the primary key of another relation and may be used to link an element with its embedded elements. For example, if a foreign key in a "purchase order" table refers to the primary key of a "customer" table, then the XML that presents the data in a purchase order table may include an XML presentation of the customer record as a subelement. Most relational DBMSs store the information about primary keys and foreign keys in system tables. SQL queries can be used to extract that information from the system tables for use by the data server.

Foreign key constraints may be exploited while *emitting* (i.e., writing out) the relational data as an XML tree. The value of a column (or columns) may consist of values from the primary key of another relation. The primary key uniquely identifies a record in that relation (by definition), and the foreign key value may be substituted with the contents of the record to which it refers.

The data in a relational database can be mapped to XML as a tree by following parent/child relations in the database to create parent/child relationships in the XML tree. The parent/child relations in the relational database are typically encoded as foreign key constraints.

Warning for database developers: A potential point of confusion exists in the parent/child terminology. In relational design, a parent/child functional dependency relationship is being discussed; thus, the child depends upon the parent for information. In trees, the parent is composed of children; thus, the parent depends upon the child for information. Thus, a parent/

child relation in relational terms is the *inverse* relation to the parent/child relation in terms of mapping relational data to an XML tree. For example, in a relational database where employees are employed within a department, the department would be the parent relation and the employee relation would be the child. In formatting the data as XML directly from the employee relation, the employee element is the parent and would have a department element as a child. (See Figure 5–4.)

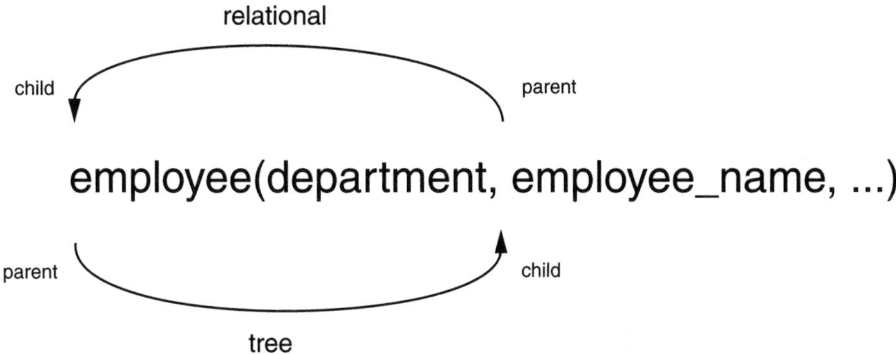

Figure 5–4 Comparison of parent–child relationships in relational design and XML trees

The micro-array relational schema in Figure 5–5 has foreign keys described in Table 5–1. Using those foreign keys, XML may be generated as shown in Example 5–10. The foreign keys in Table 5–1 are followed to create the embedded elements.

Table 5–1 Foreign Keys from Micro-array Database

CHILD_TABLE	*CHILD_COLUMN*	*PARENT_TABLE*	*PARENT_COLUMN*
SPOT	GENE	GENE	ID
EXPER_RESULT	SPOT	SPOT	ID
EXPER_RESULT	EXPERIMENT	EXPERIMENT	ID

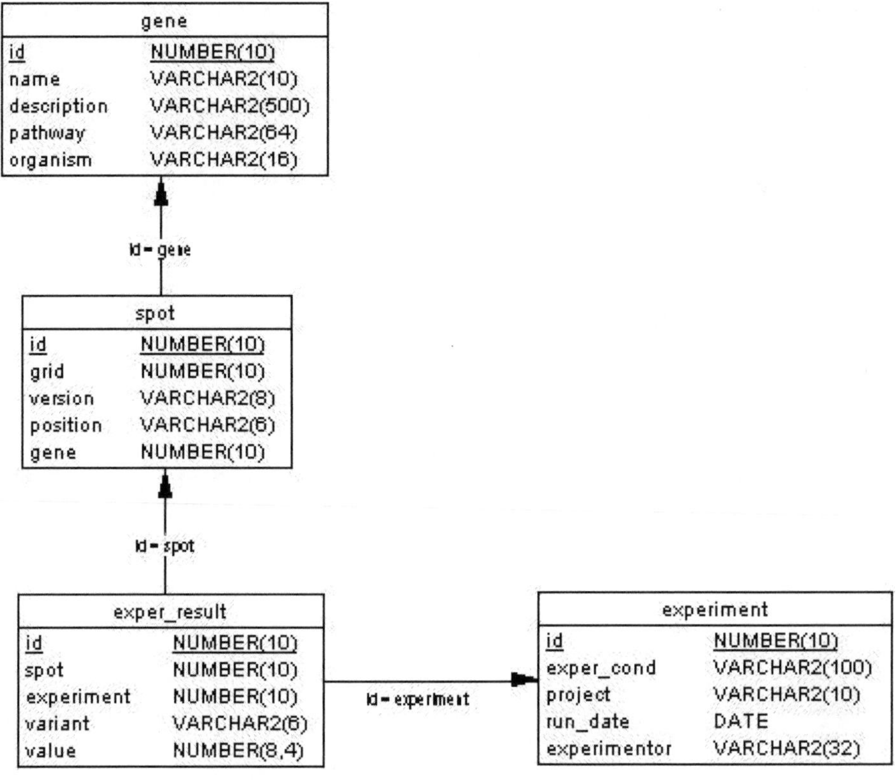

Figure 5–5 Relational schema for micro-array database

Example 5–10 : Example Output from rServe for Micro-array Database

```
<?xml version="1.0"?>
<collection>
<EXPER_RESULT id="8274">
  <SPOT>
    <SPOT id="1094">
      <GRID>1</GRID>
      <VERSION/>
      <POSITION>95</POSITION>
      <GENE>
        <GENE id="1094">
          <NAME>PAK1</NAME>
          <DESCRIPTION>PROTEIN KINASE; </DESCRIPTION>
          <PATHWAY>DNA REPLICATION</PATHWAY>
          <ORGANISM/>
```

```
          </GENE>
        </GENE>
      </SPOT>
    </SPOT>
    <EXPERIMENT>
      <EXPERIMENT id="101">
        <EXPER_COND>alpha</EXPER_COND>
        <PROJECT>EISEN</PROJECT>
        <RUN_DATE/>
        <EXPERIMENTOR/>
      </EXPERIMENT>
    </EXPERIMENT>
    <VARIANT>0</VARIANT>
    <VALUE>-0.10</VALUE>
  </EXPER_RESULT>
</collection>
```

In Oracle, the SQL code in Example 5–11 may be used to extract the foreign key information from the system tables. For example, the foreign keys of the fine-grained relational storage system from Chapter 4 are shown in Table 5–2. The SQL code in Example 5–12 performs a similar function for DB2.

Example 5–11 : SQL Code to Extract Foreign Key Constraints from Oracle

```
select c.table_name child_table,
       c.column_name child_column,
       p.table_name parent_table,
       p.column_name parent_column
  from sys.all_constraints l,
       sys.all_cons_columns c,
       sys.all_cons_columns p
 where l.constraint_type = 'R'
   and l.constraint_name = c.constraint_name
   and l.r_constraint_name = p.constraint_name
   and l.owner = c.owner
   and l.r_owner = p.owner
   and c.position = p.position
```

Table 5–2 Foreign Keys from Fine-grained Relational Storage Database

CHILD_TABLE	*CHILD_COLUMN*	*PARENT_TABLE*	*PARENT_COLUMN*
XDB_ATTR	DOC_ID	XDB_DOC	DOC_ID
XDB_CHILD	DOC_ID	XDB_DOC	DOC_ID
XDB_ELE	DOC_ID	XDB_DOC	DOC_ID
XDB_STR	DOC_ID	XDB_DOC	DOC_ID
XDB_TEXT	DOC_ID	XDB_DOC	DOC_ID
XDB_ATTR	DOC_ID	XDB_ELE	DOC_ID
XDB_CHILD	DOC_ID	XDB_ELE	DOC_ID
XDB_DOC	DOC_ID	XDB_ELE	DOC_ID
XDB_STR	DOC_ID	XDB_ELE	DOC_ID
XDB_TEXT	DOC_ID	XDB_ELE	DOC_ID
XDB_ATTR	ELE_ID	XDB_ELE	ELE_ID
XDB_CHILD	ELE_ID	XDB_ELE	ELE_ID
XDB_DOC	ROOT	XDB_ELE	ELE_ID
XDB_STR	ELE_ID	XDB_ELE	ELE_ID
XDB_TEXT	ELE_ID	XDB_ELE	ELE_ID

Example 5–12 : SQL Code to Extract Foreign Key Constraints from DB2

```
select c.tabname child_table,
       c.colname child_column,
       p.tabname parent_table,
       p.colname parent_column
  from syscat.references l,
       syscat.keycoluse c,
       syscat.keycoluse p
```

```
where l.constname = c.constname
  and l.refkeyname = p.constname
  and l.tabschema = c.tabschema
  and l.reftabschema = p.tabschema
  and c.colseq = p.colseq
```

5.3.5 Implementation

Java code that implements the rServe relational data server is given in Example 5–13. A UML class diagram is given in Figure 5–6.

Example 5–13 : Java Code for rServe Relational Data Server

```
/************************ Demo.java **********************/
package com.xweave.xmldb.rserve;

import com.xweave.xmldb.util.io.Output;

public class Demo extends FormatXML {
/**
 * Demo constructor comment.
 */
public Demo() {
   super();
}
public Demo(Input input, Output output) {
   super(input, output);
}
}
/************************ FormatXML.java *********************/
package com.xweave.xmldb.rserve;

import java.sql.*;
import java.util.*;
import com.xweave.xmldb.util.io.Output;

/**
 * Main generator for formatting relational data as XML
 */
public class FormatXML {
   public Input inputSource = null;
   public Output outputSource = null;
   protected MetaDataRepositoryCol colData = null;
```

```
    protected MetaDataRepositoryTab tableData = null;
    public String defaultAcct =
com.xweave.xmldb.Default.getReldbAcct();
public FormatXML() {
    super();
}
public FormatXML(Input input, Output output) {
    super();
    setInputSource(input);
    setOutputSource(output);
}
public static void dispatchArg(AccessSpec access, String name, String
value) {
    ReportSpec rep = access.getReportSpec();
    QuerySpec query = access.getQuerySpec();
    if (name.equalsIgnoreCase("TABLENAME")) {
        query.setTableName(value);
        return;
    }
    if (name.equalsIgnoreCase("ID")) {
        query.setId(value);
        return;
    }
    if (name.equalsIgnoreCase("ACCT")) {
        access.setAcct(value);
        return;
    }
    if (name.equalsIgnoreCase("DEPTH")) {
        rep.setMaxDepth(Integer.parseInt(value));
        return;
    }
    if (name.equalsIgnoreCase("REPORTARGS")) {
        rep.setReportArgs(value);
        return;
    }
    if (name.equalsIgnoreCase("CONSTRAINTSTR")) {
        query.setConstraintString(value);
        return;
    }
    if (name.equalsIgnoreCase("SQLSTRING")) {
        //throw away query spec and create a SQLQuerySpec
        query = new SQLQuerySpec();
        //keep the tablename to provide FK drill-down
        query.setTableName(access.getQuerySpec().getTableName());
```

```
            access.setQuerySpec(query);
            ((SQLQuerySpec) query).setSqlString(value);
            return;
        }
        if (name.equalsIgnoreCase("STYLESHEET")) {
            access.setStyleSheet(value);
            return;
        }
        if (name.equalsIgnoreCase("SUBMIT")) {
            return;
        }
        if (name.equalsIgnoreCase("ORDERBY")) {
            query.setOrderby(value);
            return;
        }
        if (name.equalsIgnoreCase("ELEMENTNAME")) {
            rep.setElementName(value);
            return;
        }
        query.addConstraint(name, value);
    }
    protected MetaDataRepositoryCol getColData() {
        if (colData == null) {
            colData = new MetaDataRepositoryCol(getInputSource());
        }
        return colData;
    }
    public String getDefaultAcct() {
        return defaultAcct;
    }
    public Input getInputSource() {
        if (inputSource == null) {
            setInputSource(new Input(getDefaultAcct()));
        }
        return inputSource;
    }
    public Output getOutputSource() {
        if (outputSource == null) {
            setOutputSource(new Output());
        }
        return outputSource;
    }
    protected MetaDataRepositoryTab getTableData() {
        if (tableData == null) {
            tableData = new MetaDataRepositoryTab(getInputSource());
```

```
    }
    return tableData;
}
public static void main(String args[]) {
    if (args.length < 1) {
        System.err.println("FormatXML: requires <table> as argument");
    }
    com.xweave.xmldb.Default.init();
    (new FormatXML()).writeDoc(args[0]);
}
public void setInputSource(Input newValue) {
    this.inputSource = newValue;
}
public void setOutputSource(Output newValue) {
    this.outputSource = newValue;
}
public void writeDoc(AccessSpec access) {
//      try {
        getOutputSource().writeln("<?xml version=\"1.0\"?>");
        if (access.getStyleSheet() != null) {
            getOutputSource().writeln("<?xml:stylesheet type=\"text/xsl\"
href=\""+ access.getStyleSheet() +"\"?>");
        }
        getOutputSource().writeln("<collection>");
        writeTable(access, 1);
        getOutputSource().writeln("</collection>");
/*      } catch (Exception Ex) {
        System.out.println("Exception: " + Ex.getMessage());
    }
    */
}
public void writeDoc(String tableName) {
    writeDoc(tableName, null, null);
}
public void writeDoc(String tableName, String idColName, String id) {
    AccessSpec access= new AccessSpec();
    QuerySpec query = new QuerySpec(tableName, idColName, id);
    ReportSpec rep = new ReportSpec();
    access.setQuerySpec(query);
    access.setReportSpec(rep);
    writeDoc(access);
}
public void writeTable(AccessSpec access, int depth) {
    try {
```

```
      QuerySpec query = access.getQuerySpec();
      ReportSpec rep = access.getReportSpec();
      String name;
      String tableName = query.getTableName();
      if (tableName != null) tableName = tableName.toUpperCase();
      if (rep.getElementName() == null) {
         if (tableName == null) {
            name = "RECORD";
         } else {
            name = tableName;
         }
      } else {
         name = rep.getElementName();
      }
      //String id = query.getId();
      String idColName = getTableData().getIdName(tableName);
      ResultSet resultSet = getInputSource().getData(access, depth);
      if (resultSet == null) {
         getOutputSource().writeln("<error msg=\"No data available\"
acct=\""+getInputSource().getCurrentAcct()+"\" query=\""+query+"\"/
>");
         return;
      }
      ResultSetMetaData metaData = resultSet.getMetaData();
      int numCols = metaData.getColumnCount();
      String[] columnLabel = new String[numCols + 1];
      int idColNum = -1;
      for (int i = 1; i <= numCols; i++) {
         columnLabel[i] = metaData.getColumnLabel(i);
         if (columnLabel[i].equalsIgnoreCase(idColName))
            //This condition is also checking that idColName is not
null
            idColNum = i;
      }
      Vector rowCache[] = new Vector[numCols + 1];
      for (int i = 1; i <= numCols; i++)
         rowCache[i] = new Vector();
      String nextId = null;
      boolean moreRows = resultSet.next();
      boolean repeatRowWrite = false;
      String currRow[] = new String[numCols + 1];
      while (moreRows) {
         // for each row, set currRow to contain resultSet
         for (int i = 1; i <= numCols; i++) {
            currRow[i] = resultSet.getString(i);
```

```
        }
        // currRow contains current row, resultSet contains next row
        moreRows = resultSet.next();
        if (idColNum == -1) {
           getOutputSource().writeln("<" + name + ">");
        } else {
           if (moreRows) {
              nextId = resultSet.getString(idColNum);
           } else {
              nextId = null;
           }
           // Note: id may need to be lowercase to avoid conflict
with XML "ID"
           // Warning: id value is not quoted, should be fine for
numbers
           getOutputSource().writeln("<" + name + " " + idColName +
"=" + '"' + currRow[idColNum] + '"' + ">");
        }
        if (idColNum != -1 && currRow[idColNum].equals(nextId)) {
           // join rows with shared id
           repeatRowWrite = true;
           for (int i = 1; i <= numCols; i++) {
              // initialize row cache
              rowCache[i].addElement(currRow[i]);
              // write value
              writeValue(tableName, columnLabel[i], currRow[i],
access, depth + 1);
           }
           while (repeatRowWrite) {
              // update currRow from resultSet
              // we already know this one has a shared id, and needs
to be written
              for (int i = 1; i <= numCols; i++) {
                 currRow[i] = resultSet.getString(i);
              }
              // write value and update cache
              for (int i = 1; i <= numCols; i++) {
                 if (currRow[i] != null &&
!rowCache[i].contains(currRow[i])) {
                    rowCache[i].addElement(currRow[i]);
                    writeValue(tableName, columnLabel[i],
currRow[i], access, depth + 1);
                 }
              }
```

```
                // update resultSet to refer to next row
                moreRows = resultSet.next();
                if (moreRows) {
                   nextId = resultSet.getString(idColNum);
                   repeatRowWrite = currRow[idColNum].equals(nextId);
                } else {
                   // if no more rows after current row, write last
row and break
                   nextId = null;
                   repeatRowWrite = false;
                }
             }
             // free rowCache
             for (int i = 1; i <= numCols; i++)
                rowCache[i].removeAllElements();
          } else {
             // write individual row
             for (int i = 1; i <= numCols; i++) {
                if (i == idColNum)
                   continue;
                writeValue(tableName, columnLabel[i], currRow[i],
access, depth + 1);
             }
          }
          getOutputSource().writeln("</" + name + ">");
       }
    } catch (SQLException Ex) {
       System.out.println("Exception: " + Ex.getMessage());
    }

}
public void writeValue(String tableName, String colName, String value,
AccessSpec access, int depth) {
    if (value == null) {
       getOutputSource().write("  <" + colName + "/>");
       return;
    }
    getOutputSource().write("  <" + colName + ">");
    String recurse = getColData().getRecurse(tableName, colName);
    String idName = getColData().getIdName(tableName, colName);
    if (recurse == null || idName == null) {
       getOutputSource().write(value);
    } else {
       if (depth > access.getReportSpec().getMaxDepth()) {
```

```
            getOutputSource().write("<proxy tablename=\"" + recurse +
"\"");
            if (idName != null) {
                getOutputSource().write(" idname=\"" +
idName.toLowerCase() + "\" idval=\"" + value + "\"");
            }
            getOutputSource().write(">");
            getOutputSource().write(value);
            getOutputSource().write("</proxy>");

        } else {
            AccessSpec newaccess = new AccessSpec();
            newaccess.setQuerySpec(new QuerySpec(recurse, idName,
value));
            newaccess.setReportSpec(access.getReportSpec());
            newaccess.setAcct(access.getAcct());
            writeTable(newaccess, depth);
        }
    }
    getOutputSource().write("</" + colName + ">\n");
}
}
/************************ Input.java **********************/
package com.xweave.xmldb.rserve;

/**
 * Connection to relational database
 */
import com.xweave.xmldb.util.rdb.*;
import java.sql.*;

public class Input {
    protected RDB rdb;
    public String defaultAcct = "scott/tiger@127.0.0.1:1521:ORCL";
    public RDBAcct currentAcct = null;
public Input() {
    super();
    init(new JDBCAcct(com.xweave.xmldb.Default.getReldbAcct()));
}
public Input(RDBAcct acct) {
    super();
    init(acct);
}
```

```
public Input(String acct) {
   super();
   init(new JDBCAcct(acct));
}
public Input(Connection conn) {
   super();
   init(conn);
}
public RDBAcct getCurrentAcct() {
   return currentAcct;
}
public ResultSet getData(AccessSpec access, int depth) {
   if (currentAcct == null ||
!currentAcct.getAcct().equalsIgnoreCase(access.getAcct()))
      if (access.getAcct() != null)
         swapAcct(access.getAcct());
   QuerySpec query = access.getQuerySpec();
   if (query.getClass() == SQLQuerySpec.class) {
      return submitQuery(((SQLQuerySpec) query).getSqlString(),
depth);
   }
   String table = query.getTableName();
   String id = query.getId();
   String idColName = query.getIdColName();
   String constraint = query.getConstraintString();
   String reportargs = access.getReportSpec().getReportArgs();
   String where = null;
   if (constraint != null)
      where = constraint;
   if (id != null) {
      if (idColName == null) {
         //internal error
         System.err.println("getData: no idColName for id " + id);
         //idColName = "id";
      }
      where = idColName + " = " + id;
      }
   String orderby = "";
   if (query.getOrderby() != null) {
      orderby = " ORDER BY " + query.getOrderby();
   }
   if (where == null) {
      return submitQuery("select " + reportargs + " from " + table +
orderby, depth);
```

```
    } else {
        return submitQuery("select " + reportargs + " from " + table + "
where " + where + orderby, depth);
    }
}
public ResultSet getData(String table, int depth) {
    return submitQuery("select * from "+table, depth);
}
public ResultSet getData(String table, String id, int depth) {
    if (id == null) return getData(table, depth);
    return submitQuery("select * from "+table+" where id = "+id,
depth);
}
protected RDB getRDB() {
    return rdb;
}
private void init(RDBAcct acct) {
    try {
        rdb = new RDBConnector();
        rdb.connect(acct);
    } catch (SQLException ex) {
        ex.printStackTrace();
    }
}
private void init(Connection conn) {
    try {
        rdb = new RDBConnector();
        rdb.connect(conn);
    } catch (SQLException ex) {
        ex.printStackTrace();
    }
}
public ResultSet submitQuery(String query, int depth) {
    System.out.println(query);
    return ((RDBConnector) getRDB()).getData(query, depth);
}
public boolean swapAcct(String acctstring) {
    if (acctstring == null)
        return false;
    // Should be smarter about reusing database connections
    if ((getRDB() != null) && !(getRDB().isClosed()))
        getRDB().close();
    RDB newdb;
```

```
   try {
      newdb = new RDBConnector();
      RDBAcct acct = new JDBCAcct(acctstring);
      currentAcct = acct;
      newdb.connect(acct);
      rdb = newdb;
      return true;
   } catch (SQLException ex) {
      ex.printStackTrace();
      return false;
   }
}
}
/************************ XMLServlet.java **********************/
package com.xweave.xmldb.rserve;

import com.xweave.xmldb.util.io.*;
import com.xweave.xmldb.util.ServletBase;
import javax.servlet.http.*;
import javax.servlet.*;
import java.util.*;

public class XMLServlet extends ServletBase {
public XMLServlet() {
   super();
}
public void processRequest(HttpServletRequest req, HttpServletResponse
res) throws ServletException, java.io.IOException {
   ServletOutputStream out = startOutput(res);
   Enumeration enum = req.getParameterNames();
   String pname = null;
   AccessSpec access = new AccessSpec();
   while (enum.hasMoreElements()) {
      pname = (String) enum.nextElement();
      FormatXML.dispatchArg(access, pname, req.getParameter(pname));
   }
   if (access.getQuerySpec().getTableName() == null) {
      log("Error in processRequest: table not defined for:\n  " +
req.getPathTranslated());
      return;
   }
   log("Querying " + access.getQuerySpec().toString());
   FormatXML proc = new FormatXML();
   proc.setOutputSource(new ServletOutput());
```

```
    ((ServletOutput) proc.getOutputSource()).setOut(startOutput(res));
    //((ServletOutput) proc.getOutputSource()).getOut().println("Hello
World 2!!!");
    res.setContentType("text/xml");
    proc.writeDoc(access);
    endOutput(res);
}
}
/********************** SPECIFICATIONS ************************/

/*********************** AccessSpec.java **********************/
package com.xweave.xmldb.rserve;

/**
 * Container of information for database access, query and reporting
 */
public class AccessSpec {
   public String acct = null;
   public QuerySpec querySpec = null;
   public ReportSpec reportSpec = null;
   public String styleSheet = null;
public AccessSpec() {
   super();
}
public String getAcct() {
   return acct;
}
public QuerySpec getQuerySpec() {
   if (querySpec == null)
      querySpec = new QuerySpec();
   return querySpec;
}
public ReportSpec getReportSpec() {
   if (reportSpec == null)
      reportSpec = new ReportSpec();
   return reportSpec;
}
public String getStyleSheet() {
   return styleSheet;
}
public void setAcct(String newValue) {
   this.acct = newValue;
}
```

```
public void setQuerySpec(QuerySpec newValue) {
   this.querySpec = newValue;
}
public void setReportSpec(ReportSpec newValue) {
   this.reportSpec = newValue;
}
public void setStyleSheet(String newValue) {
   this.styleSheet = newValue;
}
}
/************************ QuerySpec.java **********************/
package com.xweave.xmldb.rserve;

/**
 * Specify query parameters
 */
import java.util.*;

public class QuerySpec {
   public String tableName = null;
   public String id = null;
   public String constraintString = null;
   private java.util.Vector constraintSpecVector = null;
   protected String orderby = null;
   public String idColName = null;
public QuerySpec() {
   super();
}
public QuerySpec(String tableName) {
   this();
   setTableName(tableName);
}
public QuerySpec(String tableName, String idColName, String id) {
   this();
   setTableName(tableName);
   setId(id);
   setIdColName(idColName);
}
public void addConstraint(ConstraintSpec constraint) {
   getConstraintSpecVector().addElement(constraint);
}
public void addConstraint(String field, String value) {
   ConstraintSpec constraint = new ConstraintSpec(field, value);
   addConstraint(constraint);
}
```

```
public java.util.Vector getConstraintSpecVector() {
   if (constraintSpecVector == null)
      constraintSpecVector = new Vector(1);
   return constraintSpecVector;
}
public String getConstraintString() {
   StringBuffer buf = new StringBuffer();
   if (constraintString != null) {
      buf.append(constraintString);
   }
   Enumeration enum = getConstraintSpecVector().elements();
   ConstraintSpec constraint = null;
   while (enum.hasMoreElements()) {
      if (buf.length() > 0)
         buf.append(" AND ");
      constraint = (ConstraintSpec) enum.nextElement();
      buf.append(constraint.toString());
   }
   if (buf.length() > 0)
      return buf.toString();
   return null;
}
public String getId() {
   return id;
}
public String getIdColName() {
   return idColName;
}
public String getOrderby() {
   return orderby;
}
public String getTableName() {
   return tableName;
}
public void setConstraintString(String newValue) {
   this.constraintString = newValue;
}
public void setId(String newValue) {
   this.id = newValue;
}
public void setIdColName(String newValue) {
   this.idColName = newValue;
}
public void setOrderby(String newValue) {
   if (newValue.charAt(0) == '-') {
```

```
        newValue = newValue.substring(1) + " DESC";
    }
    this.orderby = newValue;
}
public void setTableName(String newValue) {
    this.tableName = newValue;
}
public String toString() {
    return getTableName() + ":" + getIdColName() + "=" + getId() + ":"
+ getConstraintString();
}
}
/*********************** ConstraintSpec.java ***********************/
package com.xweave.xmldb.rserve;

/**
 * Specify conditional contraints, for where clause
 */
public class ConstraintSpec {
    public String fieldName = null;
    public String value = null;
    public String op = "=";
    protected boolean quoteValue = true;
public ConstraintSpec() {
    super();
}
public ConstraintSpec(String fieldName, String value) {
    this();
    setFieldName(fieldName);
    setValue(value);
}
public String getFieldName() {
    return fieldName;
}
public String getOp() {
    return op;
}
public String getValue() {
    return value;
}
public void setFieldName(String newValue) {
    this.fieldName = newValue;
}
```

```
 public void setOp(String newValue) {
    this.op = newValue;
 }
 public void setValue(String newValue) {
    char char1 = newValue. charAt(0);
    //strip <,>,<=,>=,!= and set op
    if (char1 == '<' || char1 == '>' || char1== '!') {
       char char2 = newValue.charAt(1);
       if (char2 == '=') {
          setOp(String.valueOf(char1)+"=");
          newValue = newValue.substring(2);
       } else {
          setOp(String.valueOf(char1));
          newValue = newValue.substring(1);
       }
       //now check for '@' evaluation
       if (newValue.charAt(0) == '@') {
          this.quoteValue = false;
          newValue = newValue.substring(1);
       }
    } else if (char1 == '%' || newValue.charAt(newValue.length()-1) ==
 '%') {
       //set op to LIKE if string starts and/or ends with '%'
       setOp("LIKE");
    } else if (char1 == '*' || newValue.charAt(newValue.length()-1) ==
 '*') {
       //set op to LIKE if string starts and/or ends with '*'
       // This makes it easier to manually encode a URL
       // and replace '*' with '%'
       setOp("LIKE");
       if (char1 == '*') {
          newValue = "%" + newValue.substring(1);
       }
       if (newValue.charAt(newValue.length()-1) == '*') {
          newValue = newValue.substring(0,newValue.length()-1) + "%";
       }
    } else if (char1 == '@') {
       this.quoteValue = false;
       newValue = newValue.substring(1);
    }
    this.value = newValue;
 }
 public String toString() {
    if (this.quoteValue) {
```

```
        try {
            Integer.parseInt(getValue());
            //value is Integer, use no quotes
        return getFieldName() + " " + getOp() + " " + getValue();
        } catch (NumberFormatException ex) {
            //value is not Integer, use quotes
        }
        return getFieldName() + " " + getOp() + " " + "'" + getValue() +
"'";
    } else {
        return getFieldName() + " " + getOp() + " " + getValue();
    }
}
}
/************************ ReportSpec.java **********************/
package com.xweave.xmldb.rserve;

/**
 * Specify report parameters
 */
public class ReportSpec {
    public int currentDepth = 0;
    public int maxDepth = 1;
    protected String reportArgs = "*";
    protected String elementName = null;
public ReportSpec() {
    super();
}
public String getElementName() {
    return elementName;
}
public int getMaxDepth() {
    return maxDepth;
}
public String getReportArgs() {
    return reportArgs;
}
public void setElementName(String newValue) {
    this.elementName = newValue;
}
public void setMaxDepth(int newValue) {
    this.maxDepth = newValue;
}
public void setReportArgs(String newValue) {
    this.reportArgs = newValue;
```

```
}
}
/********************** META-DATA **************************/

/******************* MetaDataRepositoryTab.java ******************/
package com.xweave.xmldb.rserve;

import java.util.*;
import java.sql.*;
import com.xweave.xmldb.util.rdb.*;

/**
 * Contains Relational Table Meta-Data
 */
public class MetaDataRepositoryTab extends Hashtable {
   public static MetaDataRepositoryTab defaultInstance = null;
   public String primaryKeyQuery = null;
   public final static String TABLE_INFO_TABLE = "XDB_RS_TAB_INFO";
public MetaDataRepositoryTab(int initialCapacity) {
   super(initialCapacity);
}
public MetaDataRepositoryTab(int initialCapacity, float loadFactor) {
   super(initialCapacity, loadFactor);
}
public MetaDataRepositoryTab(Input in) {
   super();
   init(((RDBConnector) in.getRDB()));
}
public void addPK(String table, String idName) {
   get(table).setIdName(idName);
}
public boolean exists(String table) {
   return super.get(table.toUpperCase()) != null;
}
public MetaDataRecordTab get(String table) {
   MetaDataRecordTab rec = (MetaDataRecordTab)
super.get(table.toUpperCase());
   if (rec == null) {
      rec = new MetaDataRecordTab();
      put(table,rec);
   }
   return rec;
}
```

```
public String getIdName(String table) {
   if (table == null) return null;
   String val = get(table).getIdName();
   if (val != null) {
      return val;
   }
   int index = table.indexOf('.');
   String owner = null;
   if (index != -1) {
      //strip owner, and try again
      owner = table.substring(0, index);
      table = table.substring(index + 1);
      val = get(table).getIdName();
      if (val != null) {
         return val;
      }
   }
   if (table.endsWith("_V")) {
      val = get(table.substring(table.length() - 1)).getIdName();
      if (val != null) {
         return val;
      }
   }
   index = table.indexOf("_V_");
   if (index != -1) {
      val = get(table.substring(0, index)).getIdName();
      if (val != null) {
         return val;
      }
   }
   return null;
}
public String getPrimaryKeyQuery(RDB rdb) {
   RDBConnector rdbconn = ((RDBConnector) rdb);
   // should be active, but check first
   if (rdb.isClosed()) {
      //if not open, table remains empty
      System.err.println("Repository is not open for " +
rdbconn.getAcct());
      return null;
   }
   //Check connection for database type
   String dbclass = rdbconn.getConnection().getClass().getName();
   if (dbclass.indexOf("oracle") != -1) {
      return getPrimaryKeyQueryOracle();
```

```
    }
    if (dbclass.indexOf("db2") != -1) {
       return getPrimaryKeyQueryDB2();
    }
    return null;
 }
 public String getPrimaryKeyQueryDB2() {
    StringBuffer buf = new StringBuffer();
    buf.append("select k.tabname as TABLE, ");
    buf.append("       k.colname as PRIMARY_KEY");
    buf.append("  from syscat.tabconst t,");
    buf.append("       syscat.keycoluse k");
    buf.append(" where t.tabname = k.tabname");
    buf.append("   and t.tabschema = k.tabschema");
    buf.append("   and t.constname = k.constname");
    buf.append("   and t.type = 'P'");
//      System.out.println(buf.toString());
    return buf.toString();
 }
 public String getPrimaryKeyQueryOracle() {
    //not correct
    StringBuffer buf = new StringBuffer();
    //Note, this query will give sporadic results if all_constraints
contains
    // table names and column names shared between multiple owners with
    // foreign keys refering to diffent tables. One fix is to use
user_constraints
    // and user_cons_constraints instead.
    buf.append("select c.table_name,    ");
    buf.append("       c.column_name    ");
    buf.append("  from sys.all_constraints l,    ");
    buf.append("       sys.all_cons_columns c    ");
    buf.append(" where l.constraint_type = 'P'   ");
    buf.append("   and l.constraint_name = c.constraint_name");
    buf.append("   and l.owner = c.owner");
    return buf.toString();
 }
 public void init(RDB rdb) {
    ResultSet res;
    ResultSetMetaData metaData;
    String tab;
    //Get foreign keys from system tables
    try {
       res = rdb.getData(getPrimaryKeyQuery(rdb));
       metaData = res.getMetaData();
```

```
         int numCols = metaData.getColumnCount();
         while (res.next()) {
            tab = res.getString(1);
            if (exists(tab)) {
               //most likely a multi-column PK
               //multi-column PK are not handled, delete reference to PK
               addPK(tab, null);
            } else {
               addPK(tab, res.getString(2));
            }
         }
         //this.print();
      } catch (Exception Ex) {
         System.out.println("Exception: " + Ex.getMessage());
      }
      //Get additional drill-downs from user specifications, if available
      try {
         String queryStr = "select * from " + TABLE_INFO_TABLE;
         res = rdb.executeQuery(queryStr);
         metaData = res.getMetaData();
         int numCols = metaData.getColumnCount();
         while (res.next()) {
            addPK(res.getString(1), res.getString(2));
         }
      } catch (Throwable Ex) {
         //no error, if information not available
      }

   }
   public void print() {
      Enumeration e = this.keys();
      String key;
      MetaDataRecordTab rec;
      while (e.hasMoreElements()) {
         key = (String) e.nextElement();
         rec = (MetaDataRecordTab) get(key);
         System.out.println(key +"\t"+ rec.getIdName());
      }
   }
   public Object put(String table, Object value) {
      return super.put(table.toUpperCase(),value);
   }
   public void setPrimaryKeyQuery(String newValue) {
      this.primaryKeyQuery = newValue;
   }
   }
```

```
/********************** MetaDataRecordTab.java *********************/
package com.xweave.xmldb.rserve;

/**
 * Record of Relational Table Meta-Data
 */
public class MetaDataRecordTab {
   public String idName;
public MetaDataRecordTab() {
   super();
}
public String getIdName() {
   return idName;
}
public void setIdName(String newValue) {
   this.idName = newValue;
}
public String toString() {
   return "("+getIdName()+")";
}
}
/******************* MetaDataRepositoryCol.java *******************/
package com.xweave.xmldb.rserve;

import java.util.*;
import java.sql.*;
import com.xweave.xmldb.util.rdb.*;

/**
 * Contains Relational Column Meta-Data
 */
public class MetaDataRepositoryCol extends Hashtable {
   public static MetaDataRepositoryCol defaultInstance = null;
   public String foreignKeyQuery = null;
   public final static String COLUMN_INFO_TABLE = "XDB_RS_COL_INFO";
public MetaDataRepositoryCol(int initialCapacity) {
   super(initialCapacity);
}
public MetaDataRepositoryCol(int initialCapacity, float loadFactor) {
   super(initialCapacity, loadFactor);
}
public MetaDataRepositoryCol(Input in) {
   super();
   init(((RDBConnector) in.getRDB()));
```

```
}
public void addRecurse(String table, String col, String parent, String
id) {
   get(table, col).setRecurse(parent, id);
}
public boolean exists(String table, String col) {
   return get(table.toUpperCase()+"."+col.toUpperCase()) != null;
}
public MetaDataRecordCol get(String table, String col) {
   MetaDataRecordCol rec = (MetaDataRecordCol)
get(table.toUpperCase()+"."+col.toUpperCase());
   if (rec == null) {
      rec = new MetaDataRecordCol();
      put(table,col,rec);
   }
   return rec;
}
public String getForeignKeyQuery(RDB rdb) {
   RDBConnector rdbconn = ((RDBConnector) rdb);
   // should be active, but check first
   if (rdb.isClosed()) {
      //if not open, table remains empty
      System.err.println("Repository is not open for " +
rdbconn.getAcct());
      return null;
   }
   //Check connection for database type
   String dbclass = rdbconn.getConnection().getClass().getName();
   if (dbclass.indexOf("oracle") != -1) {
      return getForeignKeyQueryOracle();
   }
   if (dbclass.indexOf("db2") != -1) {
      return getForeignKeyQueryDB2();
   }
   return null;
}
public String getForeignKeyQueryDB2() {
   StringBuffer buf = new StringBuffer();
   buf.append("select c.tabname child_table,");
   buf.append("       c.colname child_column,");
   buf.append("       p.tabname parent_table,");
   buf.append("       p.colname parent_column");
   buf.append("  from syscat.references l,");
   buf.append("       syscat.keycoluse c,");
   buf.append("       syscat.keycoluse p");
```

```
    buf.append(" where l.constname = c.constname");
    buf.append("   and l.refkeyname = p.constname");
    buf.append("   and l.tabschema = c.tabschema");
    buf.append("   and l.reftabschema = p.tabschema");
    buf.append("   and c.colseq = p.colseq");
    return buf.toString();
}
public String getForeignKeyQueryOracle() {
    StringBuffer buf = new StringBuffer();
    //Note, this query will give sporadic results if all_constraints
contains
    // table names and column names shared between multiple owners with
    // foreign keys referring to different tables. One fix is to use
user_constraints
    // and user_cons_constraints instead.
    buf.append("select c.table_name child_table,");
    buf.append("       c.column_name child_column,       ");
    buf.append("       p.table_name parent_table,        ");
    buf.append("       p.column_name parent_column       ");
    buf.append("  from sys.all_constraints l,    ");
    buf.append("       sys.all_cons_columns c,   ");
    buf.append("       sys.all_cons_columns p    ");
    buf.append(" where l.constraint_type = 'R'   ");
    buf.append("   and l.constraint_name = c.constraint_name");
    buf.append("   and l.r_constraint_name = p.constraint_name");
    buf.append("   and l.owner = c.owner");
    buf.append("   and l.r_owner = p.owner       ");
    buf.append("   and c.position = p.position   ");
    //      buf.append("   and p.column_name = 'ID'      ");
    return buf.toString();
}
public String getIdName(String table, String col) {
    if (table == null) return null;
    String val = get(table, col).getIdName();
    if (val != null) {
       return val;
    }
    return null;
}
public String getRecurse(String table, String col) {
    if (table == null) return null;
    String val = get(table, col).getRecurse();
    if (val != null) {
       return val;
    }
```

```
    int index = table.indexOf('.');
    String owner = null;
    if (index != -1) {
        //strip owner, and try again
        owner = table.substring(0, index);
        table = table.substring(index + 1);
        val = get(table, col).getRecurse();
        if (val != null) {
            if (owner != null) {
                return owner + "." + val;
            }
            return val;
        }
    }
    if (table.endsWith("_V")) {
        val = get(table.substring(table.length() - 1),
col).getRecurse();
        if (val != null) {
            if (owner != null) {
                return owner + "." + val;
            }
            return val;
        }
    }
    index = table.indexOf("_V_");
    if (index != -1) {
        val = get(table.substring(0, index), col).getRecurse();
        if (val != null) {
            if (owner != null) {
                return owner + "." + val;
            }
            return val;
        }
    }
    return null;
}
public void init(RDB rdb) {
    ResultSet res;
    ResultSetMetaData metaData;
    String tab, col;
    //Get foreign keys from system tables
    try {
        res = rdb.getData(getForeignKeyQuery(rdb));
        metaData = res.getMetaData();
        int numCols = metaData.getColumnCount();
```

```
        while (res.next()) {
            tab = res.getString(1);
            col = res.getString(2);
            if (exists(tab, col)) {
                //most likely a multi-column FK
                //multi-column FK are not handled, delete reference to FK
                addRecurse(tab, col, null, null);
            } else {
                addRecurse(tab, col, res.getString(3), res.getString(4));
            }
        }
        //this.print();
    } catch (Exception Ex) {
        System.out.println("Exception: " + Ex.getMessage());
    }
    //Get additional drill-downs from user specifications, if available
    try {
        String queryStr = "select * from " + COLUMN_INFO_TABLE;
        res = rdb.executeQuery(queryStr);
        metaData = res.getMetaData();
        int numCols = metaData.getColumnCount();
        while (res.next()) {
            addRecurse(res.getString(1), res.getString(2),
res.getString(3), res.getString(4));
        }
    } catch (Throwable Ex) {
        //no error, if information not available
    }

}
public void print() {
    Enumeration e = this.keys();
    String key;
    MetaDataRecordCol rec;
    while (e.hasMoreElements()) {
        key = (String) e.nextElement();
        rec = (MetaDataRecordCol) get(key);
        System.out.println(key +"\t"+ rec.getRecurse() +"\t"+
rec.getIdName());
    }
}
public Object put(String table, String col, Object value) {
    return put(table.toUpperCase()+"."+col.toUpperCase(),value);
}
```

```
public void setForeignKeyQuery(String newValue) {
   this.foreignKeyQuery = newValue;
}
}
/********************** MetaDataRecordCol.java ***********************/
package com.xweave.xmldb.rserve;

/**
 * Record of Relational Column Meta-Data
 */
public class MetaDataRecordCol {
   public String idName;
   public String tableName;
public MetaDataRecordCol() {
   super();
}
public String getIdName() {
   return idName;
}
public String getRecurse() {
   return tableName;
}
public String getTableName() {
   return tableName;
}
public void setIdName(String newValue) {
   this.idName = newValue;
}
public void setRecurse(String table, String id) {
   this.tableName = table;
   this.idName = id;
}
public void setTableName(String newValue) {
   this.tableName = newValue;
}
public String toString() {
   return getRecurse()+"("+getIdName()+")";
}
}
```

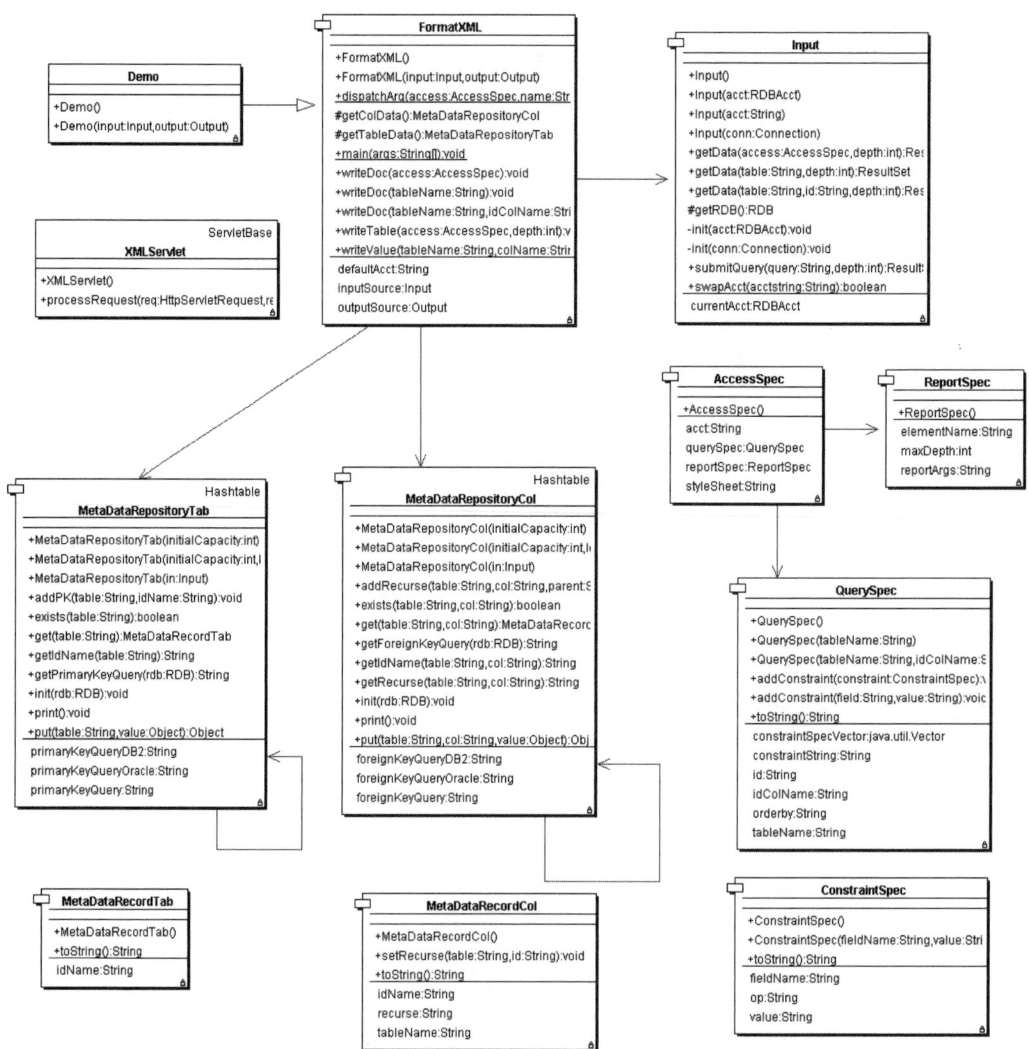

Figure 5–6 UML class diagram for rServe relational data server

The main class in rServe, called Demo, translates relational data from the source specified by the Input class into XML and writes the data on the stream specified by the Output class. The query, account, and report formatting information are captured by the container class AccessSpec and its helper classes QuerySpec and ReportSpec. The QuerySpec class contains the constraints to be used in the "where" clause of the SQL query, making use of a ConstraintSpec helper object to hold each constraint. The Input class formats the SQL query, using the QuerySpec class for formatting the "where" clause, and the Input class interacts with the relational database (using helper classes from com.xweave.xmldb.util.rdb described in Appendix A).

The query is executed by creating an AccessSpec object and passing it to the "writeDoc" method of the FormatXML class. The "writeDoc" method writes the XML document header and root element start and end tags and calls the "writeTable" method. The "writeTable" method implements the algorithm described in Section 5.3.3. It uses the Input object (stored in inputSource field) to retrieve data from the database and the Output object (stored in outputSource field) to write the formatted XML. The "writeTable" method uses the "writeValue" method to write each data item, which may, recursively, call the "writeTable" method again if the data item refers to another table's record as part of a foreign key constraint.

The primary key constraints are contained in an instance of the MetaDataRepositoryTab class. The Meta-Data Repository for Table data contains a collection of MetaDataRecordTab(s). An instance of MetaDataRecordTab contains the information for one primary key constraint. The repository is initialized when it is first accessed. The MetaDataRepositoryTab is a hashtable of MetaDataRecordTab that is keyed off the table name and column name of the primary key. Each MetaDataRecordTab contains the table name and column of the primary key referred to by the hashtable entry. There is also a method in JDBC that could be used to access the primary key system table to initialize the table, but it was not used in this example, to make the approach more applicable to other protocols.

The foreign key constraints are contained in an instance of the MetaDataRepositoryCol class. The Meta-Data Repository for Column data contains a collection of MetaDataRecordCol(s). An instance of MetaDataRecordCol contains the information for one foreign key constraint. The repository is initialized when it is first accessed. The MetaDataRepositoryCol is a hashtable of MetaDataRecordCol, which is keyed off the table name and column name of the foreign key that would be followed to drill down in formatting the report. Each MetaDataRecordCol contains the table name and column of the primary key referred to by the hashtable entry.

5.4 XML Data Server

An XML data server combines an XML DBMS with a Web server. Users and applications can access data in the DBMS via the XML data server, using a Web interface.

I describe an example XML data server in this section called xServe, which stores, edits, and queries an XML database with data stored in a relational database using the relational storage defined in Chapter 4. This data server implements the Chapter 3 data model and specifies an API via URLs similar to the relational data server of the previous section.

In addition to the operations on documents that were defined in Chapter 3, the XML data server provides similar operations on document fragments corresponding to each element in the document. Thus, it is possible to retrieve, delete, and update an element in a document.

The xServe XML data server described in this section demonstrates some of the functionality that could be provided by a Web-accessible XML database system. Although a fairly simple prototype, it may be used to store and retrieve XML documents or to capture hierarchically organized data. The system also demonstrates how to develop an XML database system and some of the functionality that may be necessary in a production environment.

xServe provides the following commands:

- Store a document given its URL.
- Retrieve a document or a document fragment from the database.
- Retrieve any document as a fragment or any fragment as a document. Thus, new documents may be built from other documents and fragments.
- Update a document by replacing a document fragment with a document (or fragment) given a URL (including a URL for xServe).
- Append an XML fragment at a URL reference to a specified fragment.
- Delete a document or document fragment from the database.

Other commands that might be useful, but which are not demonstrated, are to reorder the elements in a document, to search for a document given a constraint, or to perform any other operation described in Chapter 3.

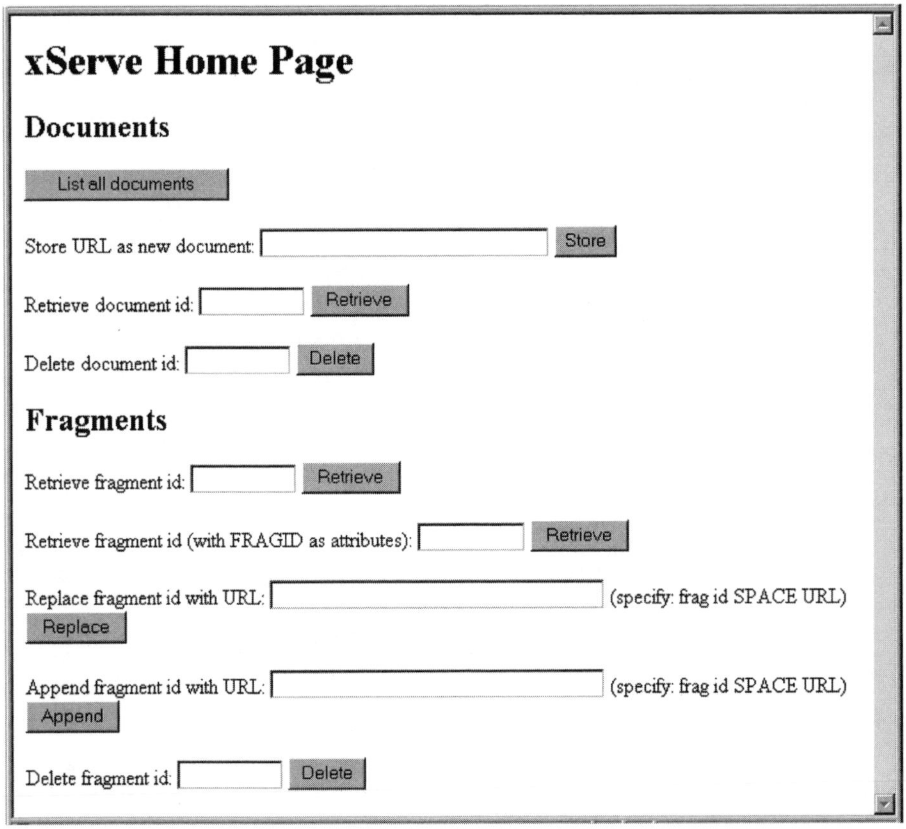

xServe Home Page

Documents

List all documents

Store URL as new document: Store

Retrieve document id: Retrieve

Delete document id: Delete

Fragments

Retrieve fragment id: Retrieve

Retrieve fragment id (with FRAGID as attributes): Retrieve

Replace fragment id with URL: (specify: frag id SPACE URL)
Replace

Append fragment id with URL: (specify: frag id SPACE URL)
Append

Delete fragment id: Delete

Figure 5–7 Home page for xServe

A home page for xServe is shown in Figure 5–7, and its HTML source is listed in Example 5–14. The home page uses HTML forms to create URLs that access the XML database. Some example URLs are

- *http://127.0.0.1/servlets/com.xweave.xmldb.xserve.XMLServlet?list=1*
- *http://127.0.0.1/servlets/com.xweave.xmldb.xserve.XMLServlet?store=http://127.0.0.1/temp1.xml*
- *http://127.0.0.1/servlets/com.xweave.xmldb.xserve.XMLServlet?store=D:\Temp\cancer.xml*
- *http://127.0.0.1/servlets/com.xweave.xmldb.xserve.XMLServlet?getfragdoc=7.1*

- *http://127.0.0.1/servlets/com.xweave.xmldb.xserve.XMLServlet?appendfrag=7.1+http://127.0.0.1/servlets/com.xweave.xmldb.xserve.XMLServlet?retrieve=4*
- *http://127.0.0.1/servlets/com.xweave.xmldb.xserve.XMLServlet?deletefrag=1.2*

Example 5–14 : Home Page for xServe

```
<html>
<head>
<meta http-equiv="Content-Type" content="text/html; charset=iso-8859-1">
<title>xServe Home Page</title>
</head>

<body>
<h1>xServe Home Page</h1>
<h2>Documents</h2>

  <form action=
       "http://127.0.0.1:8080/servlet/com.xweave.xmldb.xserve.XMLServlet"
       method="GET">
    <input type="hidden" name="list" value="1">
    <p><input type="submit" name="ignore" value="List all documents">
  </form>

  <form action=
       "http://127.0.0.1:8080/servlet/com.xweave.xmldb.xserve.XMLServlet"
       method="GET">
  <p> Store URL as new document:
  <input type="input" name="store" size=30>
  <input type="submit" name="ignore" value="Store">
  </form>

  <form action=
       "http://127.0.0.1:8080/servlet/com.xweave.xmldb.xserve.XMLServlet"
       method="GET">
  <p> Retrieve document id:
  <input type="input" name="retrievedoc" size=10>
  <input type="submit" name="ignore" value="Retrieve">
  </form>

  <form action=
       "http://127.0.0.1:8080/servlet/com.xweave.xmldb.xserve.XMLServlet"
       method="GET">
  <p> Delete document id:
  <input type="input" name="delete" size=10>
  <input type="submit" name="ignore" value="Delete">
  </form>
```

```
<h2>Fragments</h2>

  <form action=
      "http://127.0.0.1:8080/servlet/com.xweave.xmldb.xserve.XMLServlet"
      method="GET">
  <p> Retrieve fragment id:
  <input type="input" name="getfragdoc" size=10>
  <input type="submit" name="ignore" value="Retrieve">
  </form>

  <form action=
      "http://127.0.0.1:8080/servlet/com.xweave.xmldb.xserve.XMLServlet"
      method="GET">
  <p> Retrieve fragment id (with FRAGID as attributes):
  <input type="input" name="getfragiddoc" size=10>
  <input type="submit" name="ignore" value="Retrieve">
  </form>

  <form action=
      "http://127.0.0.1:8080/servlet/com.xweave.xmldb.xserve.XMLServlet"
      method="GET">
  <p> Replace fragment id with URL:
  <input type="input" name="setfrag" size=35>
  (specify: frag id SPACE URL)
  <input type="submit" name="ignore" value="Replace">
  </form>

  <form action=
      "http://127.0.0.1:8080/servlet/com.xweave.xmldb.xserve.XMLServlet"
      method="GET">
  <p> Append fragment id with URL:
  <input type="input" name="appendfrag" size=35>
  (specify: frag id SPACE URL)
  <input type="submit" name="ignore" value="Append">
  </form>

  <form action=
      "http://127.0.0.1:8080/servlet/com.xweave.xmldb.xserve.XMLServlet"
      method="GET">
  <p> Delete fragment id:
  <input type="input" name="deletefrag" size=10>
  <input type="submit" name="ignore" value="Delete">
  </form>

</body>
```

5.4.1 Implementation

Java code that implements the xServe relational data server is given in Example 5–15. A UML class diagram is given in Figure 5–8.

Example 5–15 : Java Code for xServe XML Data Server

```
/************************ Demo.java **********************/
package com.xweave.xmldb.xserve;

import com.xweave.xmldb.util.io.*;
import com.xweave.xmldb.util.rdb.*;
import com.xweave.xmldb.fgrel.*;
/**
 * Demonstration of XML Data Server using Fine-grained relational storage
in Oracle
 */
public class Demo extends com.xweave.xmldb.mgrel.Demo {
   private DeleteFrag deleteFrag = null;
   private AppendFrag appendFrag = null;
   private ReplaceFrag replaceFrag = null;
public Demo() {
   super();
}
/**
 * Append the XML fragment at id <documentId>.<elementId><space><xmlFile>
 */
public boolean appendFragment(String argument) {
   String documentId, elementId, xmlFile;
   int dotindex = argument.indexOf('.');
   int spaceindex = argument.indexOf(' ');
   if (spaceindex == -1) {
      return false;
   }
   if (dotindex == -1) {
      documentId = argument.substring(0, spaceindex);
      elementId = "1";
   } else {
      documentId = argument.substring(0, dotindex);
      elementId = argument.substring(dotindex + 1, spaceindex);
   }
   xmlFile = argument.substring(spaceindex + 1);
   return this.appendFragmentUrl(documentId, elementId, xmlFile);
}
/**
 * Append the XML fragment at id <documentId>.<elementId>
 */
```

```
public boolean appendFragment(String fragment, String xmlFile) {
    String documentId, elementId;
    int dotindex = fragment.indexOf('.');
    if (dotindex == -1) {
        documentId = fragment;
        elementId = "1";
    } else {
        documentId = fragment.substring(0, dotindex);
        elementId = fragment.substring(dotindex + 1);
    }
    return this.appendFragmentUrl(documentId, elementId, xmlFile);
}
/**
 * Append the XML fragment at id <documentId> <elementId>
 */
public boolean appendFragmentText(String documentId, String elementId,
String xmlFile) {
    return getAppendFrag().parseText(xmlFile, documentId, elementId);
}
/**
 * Append the XML fragment at id <documentId> <elementId>
 */
public boolean appendFragmentUrl(String documentId, String elementId,
String xmlFile) {
    return getAppendFrag().parseUrl(xmlFile, documentId, elementId);
}
/**
 * Delete the XML fragment with id <documentId>.<elementId>
 */
public boolean deleteFragment(String fragment) {
    String documentId, elementId;
    int dotindex = fragment.indexOf('.');
    if (dotindex == -1) {
        documentId = fragment;
        elementId = "1";
    } else {
        documentId = fragment.substring(0, dotindex);
        elementId = fragment.substring(dotindex + 1);
    }
    return this.deleteFragment(documentId, elementId);
}
/**
 * Delete the XML fragment with id <documentId>.<elementId>
 */
public boolean deleteFragment(String documentId, String elementId) {
    return getDeleteFrag().deleteFrag(documentId, elementId);
}
```

```
public boolean dispatchArg(String command, String value) {
    if (command.equalsIgnoreCase("GETFRAG")) {
        this.retrieveFragment(value);
        return true;
    }
    if (command.equalsIgnoreCase("GETFRAGDOC")) {
        this.getOutput().writeln("<?xml version=\"1.0\"?>");
        this.retrieveFragment(value);
        return true;
    }
    if (command.equalsIgnoreCase("SETFRAG")) {
        this.replaceFragment(value);
        return true;
    }
    if (command.equalsIgnoreCase("APPENDFRAG")) {
        this.appendFragment(value);
        return true;
    }
    if (command.equalsIgnoreCase("DELETEFRAG")) {
        this.deleteFragment(value);
        return true;
    }
    if (command.equalsIgnoreCase("GETFRAGIDDOC")) {
        this.getOutput().writeln("<?xml version=\"1.0\"?>");
        this.getFormat().setWriteElementId(true);
        this.retrieveFragment(value);
        this.getFormat().setWriteElementId(false);
        return true;
    }
    return super.dispatchArg(command, value);
}
/**
 * Get the Append Fragment command object.
 */
public AppendFrag getAppendFrag() {
    if (appendFrag == null) {
        appendFrag = new AppendFrag(getRdb(), getOutput());
    }
    return appendFrag;
}
/**
 * Get the Delete Fragment command object.
 */
public DeleteFrag getDeleteFrag() {
    if (deleteFrag == null) {
        deleteFrag = new DeleteFrag(getRdb(), getOutput());
```

```
    }
    return deleteFrag;
}
/**
 * Get the Replace Fragment command object.
 */
public ReplaceFrag getReplaceFrag() {
    if (replaceFrag == null) {
        replaceFrag = new ReplaceFrag(getRdb(), getOutput());
    }
    return replaceFrag;
}
/**
 * Store the XML fragment at id <documentId>.<elementId><space><xmlFile>
 */
public boolean replaceFragment(String argument) {
    String documentId, elementId, xmlFile;
    int dotindex = argument.indexOf('.');
    int spaceindex = argument.indexOf(' ');
    if (spaceindex == -1) {
        return false;
    }
    if (dotindex == -1) {
        documentId = argument.substring(0, spaceindex);
elementId = "1";
            } else {
        documentId = argument.substring(0, dotindex);
        elementId = argument.substring(dotindex + 1, spaceindex);
    }
    xmlFile = argument.substring(spaceindex + 1);
    return this.replaceFragmentUrl(documentId, elementId, xmlFile);
}
/**
 * Store the XML fragment at id <documentId>.<elementId>
 */
public boolean replaceFragment(String fragment, String xmlFile) {
    String documentId, elementId;
    int dotindex = fragment.indexOf('.');
    if (dotindex == -1) {
        documentId = fragment;
        elementId = "1";
    } else {
        documentId = fragment.substring(0, dotindex);
        elementId = fragment.substring(dotindex + 1);
    }
    return this.replaceFragmentUrl(documentId, elementId, xmlFile);
}
```

```
/**
 * Replace the XML fragment at id <documentId> <elementId>
 */
public boolean replaceFragmentText(String documentId, String elementId,
String xmlText) {
   return getReplaceFrag().parseText(xmlText, documentId, elementId);
}
/**
 * Replace the XML fragment at id <documentId> <elementId>
 */
public boolean replaceFragmentUrl(String documentId, String elementId,
String xmlFile) {
   return getReplaceFrag().parseUrl(xmlFile, documentId, elementId);
}
/**
 * Format the XML fragment with id <documentId>.<elementId>
 */
public boolean retrieveFragment(String fragment) {
   String documentId, elementId;
   int dotindex = fragment.indexOf('.');
   if (dotindex == -1) {
documentId = fragment;
            elementId = "1";
   } else {
      documentId = fragment.substring(0, dotindex);
      elementId = fragment.substring(dotindex + 1);
   }
   return this.retrieveFragment(documentId, elementId);
}
/**
 * Format the XML fragment with id <documentId>.<elementId>
 */
public boolean retrieveFragment(String documentId, String elementId) {
   return getFormat().writeFrag(documentId, elementId);
}
}

/************************ XMLServlet.java **********************/
package com.xweave.xmldb.xserve;

import javax.servlet.*;
import javax.servlet.http.*;
import java.io.*;
import java.util.*;
import com.xweave.xmldb.util.io.ServletOutput;
/**
 * Servlet interface to database.
```

```
 */
public class XMLServlet extends com.xweave.xmldb.util.ServletBase {
/**
 * XMLServlet constructor comment.
 */
public XMLServlet() {
    super();
}
public void processRequest(HttpServletRequest req, HttpServletResponse
res) throws ServletException, java.io.IOException {
    ServletOutputStream out = startOutput(res);
    Enumeration enum = req.getParameterNames();
    String pname, pvalue = null;
    Demo db = new Demo();
    db.setOutput(new ServletOutput(out));
    db.setRdbAccessString(com.xweave.xmldb.Default.getXmldbAcct());
    db.connect();
while (enum.hasMoreElements()) {
        pname = (String) enum.nextElement();
            pvalue = req.getParameter(pname);
        log("Executing " + pname + " " + pvalue);
        db.dispatchArg(pname, pvalue);
    }
    if (db.getRdbAccessString() == null) {
        log("Error in processRequest: access string not defined for:\n  " +
req.getPathTranslated());
    }
    endOutput(res);
}
}

/****************************** COMMANDS **************************/

/************************ AppendFrag.java **********************/
package com.xweave.xmldb.xserve;

import com.xweave.xmldb.fgrel.*;
import com.xweave.xmldb.util.rdb.RDB;
import com.xweave.xmldb.util.io.Output;
import java.sql.*;
import org.xml.sax.*;
import org.xml.sax.helpers.ParserFactory;
import com.ibm.xml.parsers.DOMParser;
import org.w3c.dom.Document;
import java.io.IOException;
```

```
/**
 * Command to Append a fragment in the database
 */
public class AppendFrag extends Command {
public AppendFrag() {
    super();
}
public AppendFrag(RDB rdb) {
    super(rdb);
}
public AppendFrag(RDB rdb, Output out) {
    super(rdb, out);
}
/**
 * Parse an XML file using a SAX parser and store as a fragment
 * Note: the parser in <parserClass> MUST be included in the Java
CLASSPATH
 */
public boolean parseText(String xmlText, String documentId, String
elementId) {
    String parserClass = com.xweave.xmldb.Default.getParserClass();
    try {
        Parser parser = ParserFactory.makeParser(parserClass);
        HandlerBase handler;
        if (getRdb() == null) {
            return false;
        } else {
            handler = new JDBCAppendFragHandler(getRdb());
        }
        parser.setDocumentHandler(handler);
        parser.setErrorHandler(handler);
        try {
            ((LoadHandler)
handler).setDocumentName("Frag"+documentId+"."+"elementId");
            ((JDBCAppendFragHandler) handler).setDocumentId(documentId);
            ((JDBCAppendFragHandler) handler).setFragmentId(elementId);
            parser.parse(new InputSource(new
java.io.StringReader(xmlText)));
            return true;
        } catch (SAXException se) {
            getOutput().writeln(se.toString());
            se.printStackTrace();
        } catch (IOException ioe) {
            ioe.printStackTrace();
        }
```

```
    } catch (ClassNotFoundException ex) {
        ex.printStackTrace();
    } catch (IllegalAccessException ex) {
        ex.printStackTrace();
    } catch (InstantiationException ex) {
        ex.printStackTrace();
    }
    return false;
}
/**
 * Parse an XML file using a SAX parser and store as a fragment
 * Note: the parser in <parserClass> MUST be included in the Java
CLASSPATH
 */
public boolean parseUrl(String xmlFile, String documentId, String
elementId) {
    String parserClass = com.xweave.xmldb.Default.getParserClass();
    try {
        Parser parser = ParserFactory.makeParser(parserClass);
        HandlerBase handler;
        if (getRdb() == null) {
            return false;
        } else {
            handler = new JDBCAppendFragHandler(getRdb());
        }
        parser.setDocumentHandler(handler);
        parser.setErrorHandler(handler);
        try {
            ((LoadHandler) handler).setDocumentName(xmlFile);
            ((JDBCAppendFragHandler) handler).setDocumentId(documentId);
            ((JDBCAppendFragHandler) handler).setFragmentId(elementId);
            parser.parse(xmlFile);
            return true;
        } catch (SAXException se) {
            getOutput().writeln(se.toString());
            se.printStackTrace();
        } catch (IOException ioe) {
            ioe.printStackTrace();
        }
    } catch (ClassNotFoundException ex) {
        ex.printStackTrace();
    } catch (IllegalAccessException ex) {
        ex.printStackTrace();
    } catch (InstantiationException ex) {
        ex.printStackTrace();
    }
    return false;
```

```
}
}

/*********************** DeleteFrag.java **********************/
package com.xweave.xmldb.xserve;

import com.xweave.xmldb.fgrel.*;
import com.xweave.xmldb.util.rdb.RDB;
import com.xweave.xmldb.util.io.Output;
import java.sql.*;
import java.util.*;
/**
 * Delete Fragment command
 */
public class DeleteFrag extends Command {
/**
 * DeleteFrag constructor comment.
 */
public DeleteFrag() {
    super();
}
public DeleteFrag(RDB rdb) {
    super(rdb);
}
public DeleteFrag(RDB rdb, Output out) {
    super(rdb, out);
}
protected void deleteCdata(String document, String elementId, String
cdataId, String table) throws SQLException {
    StringBuffer buf = new StringBuffer();
    buf.append("delete from");
    buf.append(" " + table + " ");
    buf.append("where doc_id = " + document);
    buf.append("  and ele_id = " + elementId);
    buf.append("  and cdata_id = " + cdataId);
    rdbExecute(buf.toString());
}

/**
 * Write an element from the database and its children
 */
protected void deleteElement(String document, String elementId) throws
SQLException {
    StringBuffer buf;
    //delete children
    // check to see if there are any children
```

```
    buf = new StringBuffer();
    buf.append("select indx, child_class, child_id from");
    buf.append(" " + CHILD_TABLE + " ");
    buf.append("where doc_id = " + document);
    buf.append("  and ele_id = " + elementId);
    ResultSet rset = getRdb().getData(buf.toString());
    boolean moreRows = rset.next();
    // retrieve all rows, then recurse down
    // to prevent leaving cursor open while recursing deeply
    Vector vec = new Vector();
int index;
    while(moreRows) {
        //rows are ordered by index
        index = Integer.parseInt(rset.getString(1));
            if (index > vec.size()) {
            vec.setSize(index);
        }
        vec.insertElementAt(new Child(rset.getString(2),rset.getString(3)),
index);
        moreRows = rset.next();
    }
    //delete each child
    Enumeration e = vec.elements();
    Child child;
    String childClass;
    while (e.hasMoreElements()) {
        child = (Child) e.nextElement();
        if (child == null) {continue;}
        childClass = child.getClassName();
        if (childClass.equalsIgnoreCase("ELE")) {
            //call deleteElement recursively
            deleteElement(document, child.getId());
        } else if (childClass.equalsIgnoreCase("STR")) {
             //deleteCdata works for STR or TEXT using JDBC
            deleteCdata(document, elementId, child.getId(), STR_TABLE);
        } else if (childClass.equalsIgnoreCase("TEXT")) {
             //deleteCdata works for STR or TEXT using JDBC
            deleteCdata(document, elementId, child.getId(),TEXT_TABLE);
        } else {
            //need to handle other classes added to the database
        }
    }
    //delete child table entries
    buf = new StringBuffer();
    buf.append("delete from");
    buf.append(" " + CHILD_TABLE + " ");
```

```
    buf.append("where doc_id = " + document);
    buf.append("  and ele_id = " + elementId);
    rdbExecute(buf.toString());
    //delete attributes
    buf = new StringBuffer();
    buf.append("delete from");
    buf.append(" " + ATTR_TABLE + " ");
    buf.append("where doc_id = " + document);
    buf.append("  and ele_id = " + elementId);
    rdbExecute(buf.toString());
    //delete element
    buf = new StringBuffer();
       buf.append("delete from");
    buf.append(" " + ELE_TABLE + " ");
    buf.append("where doc_id = " + document);
    buf.append("  and ele_id = " + elementId);
    rdbExecute(buf.toString());
}
public boolean deleteFrag(String document, String element) {
    // This approach only works with delete cascade,
    // otherwise an explicit recursive delete is necessary
    boolean status = true;
    try {
       //delete child table entry for fragment (in parent)
       StringBuffer buf = new StringBuffer();
       buf.append("delete from");
       buf.append(" " + CHILD_TABLE + " ");
       buf.append("where doc_id = " + document);
       buf.append("  and child_id = " + element);
       rdbExecute(buf.toString());
       //delete element
       deleteElement(document, element);
    } catch (SQLException ex) {
       status = false;
       ex.printStackTrace();
    }
    return status;
}
}

/************************ ReplaceFrag.java **********************/
package com.xweave.xmldb.xserve;

import com.xweave.xmldb.fgrel.*;
import com.xweave.xmldb.util.io.*;
import com.xweave.xmldb.util.rdb.*;
import java.sql.*;
```

```
import org.xml.sax.*;
import org.xml.sax.helpers.ParserFactory;
import com.ibm.xml.parsers.DOMParser;
import org.w3c.dom.Document;
import java.io.IOException;
/**
 * Command to Replace a fragment in the database
 */
public class ReplaceFrag extends Command {
/**
 * ReplaceFrag constructor comment.
 */
public ReplaceFrag() {
    super();
}
/**
 * ReplaceFrag constructor comment.
 * @param rdb com.xweave.xmldb.util.rdb.RDB
 */
public ReplaceFrag(RDB rdb) {
    super(rdb);
}
/**
 * ReplaceFrag constructor comment.
 * @param rdb com.xweave.xmldb.util.rdb.RDB
 * @param out com.xweave.xmldb.util.io.Output
 */
public ReplaceFrag(RDB rdb, Output out) {
    super(rdb, out);
}
/**
 * Parse an XML file using a SAX parser and replace as a fragment
 * Note: the parser in <parserClass> MUST be included in the Java
CLASSPATH
 */
public boolean parseText(String xmlText, String documentId, String
elementId) {
    String parserClass = com.xweave.xmldb.Default.getParserClass();
    try {
        Parser parser = ParserFactory.makeParser(parserClass);
        HandlerBase handler;
        if (getRdb() == null) {
            return false;
        } else {
            handler = new JDBCReplaceFragHandler(getRdb());
        }
```

```
        parser.setDocumentHandler(handler);
        parser.setErrorHandler(handler);
try {
            ((LoadHandler)
handler).setDocumentName("Frag"+documentId+"."+"elementId");
            ((JDBCReplaceFragHandler) handler).setDocumentId(documentId);
            ((JDBCReplaceFragHandler) handler).setFragmentId(elementId);
            parser.parse(new InputSource(new
java.io.StringReader(xmlText)));
                    return true;
        } catch (SAXException se) {
            getOutput().writeln(se.toString());
            se.printStackTrace();
        } catch (IOException ioe) {
            ioe.printStackTrace();
        }
    } catch (ClassNotFoundException ex) {
        ex.printStackTrace();
    } catch (IllegalAccessException ex) {
        ex.printStackTrace();
    } catch (InstantiationException ex) {
        ex.printStackTrace();
    }
    return false;
}
/**
 * Parse an XML file using a SAX parser and replace as a fragment
 * Note: the parser in <parserClass> MUST be included in the Java
CLASSPATH
 */
public boolean parseUrl(String xmlFile, String documentId, String
elementId) {
    String parserClass = com.xweave.xmldb.Default.getParserClass();
    try {
        Parser parser = ParserFactory.makeParser(parserClass);
        HandlerBase handler;
        if (getRdb() == null) {
            return false;
        } else {
            handler = new JDBCReplaceFragHandler(getRdb());
        }
        parser.setDocumentHandler(handler);
        parser.setErrorHandler(handler);
        try {
            ((LoadHandler) handler).setDocumentName(xmlFile);
            ((JDBCReplaceFragHandler) handler).setDocumentId(documentId);
```

```
            ((JDBCReplaceFragHandler) handler).setFragmentId(elementId);
            parser.parse(xmlFile);
return true;
        } catch (SAXException se) {
            getOutput().writeln(se.toString());
            se.printStackTrace();
        } catch (IOException ioe) {
            ioe.printStackTrace();
                    }
    } catch (ClassNotFoundException ex) {
        ex.printStackTrace();
    } catch (IllegalAccessException ex) {
        ex.printStackTrace();
    } catch (InstantiationException ex) {
        ex.printStackTrace();
    }
    return false;
}
}

/*********************** SAX Parser Handlers ****************/

/******************** JDBCFragLoadHandler.java ********************/
package com.xweave.xmldb.xserve;

import com.xweave.xmldb.fgrel.*;
import org.xml.sax.*;
import com.xweave.xmldb.util.rdb.*;
import java.sql.SQLException;
/**
 * SAX Handler using JDBC to load a fragment into the database
 */
public abstract class JDBCFragLoadHandler extends JDBCLoadHandler {
    protected String fragmentId = null;
public JDBCFragLoadHandler(com.xweave.xmldb.util.rdb.RDB rdb) {
    super(rdb);
}
public String getDocumentId() {
    return documentId;
}
public String getFragmentId() {
    return fragmentId;
}
/*
 * Get next id for query result
 */
public int getNextCtr(String query) {
```

```
    //get next id from Oracle
    try {
        java.sql.ResultSet resultSet = getRdb().getData(query);
        if (resultSet == null) {
            //error in query
            //we will have problems later, so throw out now
            throw new Error("Unable to get new id from database:" + query);
        }
        resultSet.next();
        String result = resultSet.getString(1);
        if (result == null) {
            //no records in table
            return 1;
        } else {
            return Integer.parseInt(result) + 1;
        }
    } catch (SQLException ex) {
        ex.printStackTrace();
        //we will have problems later, so throw out now
        throw new Error("Unable to get new id from database:" + query);
    }
}
/**
 * Get document id from instance variable or from database
 */
public void init() {
    String documentId = getDocumentId();
    //get next eleCtr
    StringBuffer buf = new StringBuffer();
    buf.append("select max(ele_id) from ");
    buf.append(ELE_TABLE);
    buf.append(" where doc_id = " + documentId);
    eleCtr = getNextCtr(buf.toString());
    //get next attrCtr
    buf = new StringBuffer();
    buf.append("select max(attr_id) from ");
    buf.append(ATTR_TABLE);
    buf.append(" where doc_id = " + documentId);
    attrCtr = getNextCtr(buf.toString());
    //get next cdataCtr
    buf = new StringBuffer();
    buf.append("select max(child_id) from ");
    buf.append(CHILD_TABLE);
    buf.append(" where doc_id = " + documentId);
    buf.append(" and child_class in ('STR', 'TEXT')");
```

```
    cdataCtr = getNextCtr(buf.toString());
}
public void setFragmentId(String newValue) {
this.fragmentId = newValue;
}
/**
 * Initialize the counters when starting a XML document.
 */
public void startDocument() {
    init();
}
}

/******************** JDBCAppendFragHandler.java **********************/
package com.xweave.xmldb.xserve;

import com.xweave.xmldb.fgrel.*;
import org.xml.sax.*;
import com.xweave.xmldb.util.rdb.*;
import java.sql.SQLException;
/**
 * SAX Handler using JDBC to append a fragment in the database
 */
public class JDBCAppendFragHandler extends JDBCFragLoadHandler {
public JDBCAppendFragHandler(RDB rdb) {
    super(rdb);
}
/**
 * Handle element, attributes, and the connection from this element
 * to its parent.
 */
public void startElement(String name, AttributeList attrList) {
    //DEBUG: System.out.println(name);
    //Create new element entry
    Element parent = getCurrentElement();
    String parentId;
    String indexNum = null;
    if (parent == null) {
        parentId = "NULL";
    } else {
        parentId = parent.getId();
    }
    StringBuffer buf;
    String currentId;
    if (parent == null) {
        //top element, get next index
```

```
        parentId = getFragmentId();
        //get next index
        buf = new StringBuffer();
        buf.append("select max(indx) from ");
        buf.append(CHILD_TABLE);
        buf.append(" where doc_id = " + getDocumentId());
        buf.append(" and ele_id = " + parentId);
        try {
        java.sql.ResultSet resultSet = getRdb().getData(buf.toString());
        if (resultSet == null) {
            //error in query
            //we will have problems later, so throw out now
            throw new Error("Unable to get INDX from database for: " +
                getDocumentId() + "." + parentId + "/n" + buf.toString());
        }
        resultSet.next();
        String ctr = resultSet.getString(1);
        if (ctr == null) {
            //no records in table
            indexNum = "1";
        } else {
            indexNum = String.valueOf(Integer.parseInt(ctr) + 1);
        }
        } catch (SQLException ex) {
            ex.printStackTrace();
            //we will have problems later, so throw out now
            throw new Error("Unable to get INDX from database for: " +
                getDocumentId() + "." + parentId + "/n" + buf.toString());
        }
    }
    //continue with element creation
    setCurrentElement(Integer.toString(nextEleCtrValue()));
    currentId = getCurrentElement().getId();
    buf = new StringBuffer();
    buf.append("insert into");
    buf.append(" " + ELE_TABLE + " ");
    buf.append("(doc_id, ele_id, parent_id, tag)");
    buf.append(" values ");
    buf.append("(" + getDocumentId() + ", " +
                    currentId + ", " +
                    parentId + ", " +
                    "'" + name + "')");
    rdbExecute(buf.toString());
    //create child entry
    buf = new StringBuffer();
    buf.append("insert into");
```

```
    buf.append(" " + CHILD_TABLE + " ");
    buf.append("(doc_id, ele_id, indx, child_class, child_id)");
    buf.append(" values ");
    buf.append("(" + getDocumentId() + ", " + parentId + ", ");
    if (parent == null) {
        //top level element
        buf.append(indexNum);
    } else {
        //sub-element
         buf.append(parent.incrIndexCtr());
    }
    buf.append(", " + "'ELE', " + currentId + ")");
    if (! rdbExecute(buf.toString()) ) {
        throw new Error("Unable to update child table in database: " +
            getDocumentId() + "." + parentId +
            " with element "+ currentId + "/n" + buf.toString());
    }
    //Create entries for each attribute
    for (int i = 0; i < attrList.getLength(); i++) {
        buf = new StringBuffer();
        buf.append("insert into");
        buf.append(" " + ATTR_TABLE + " ");
        buf.append("(doc_id, attr_id, ele_id, name, value)");
        buf.append(" values ");
        buf.append("(" + getDocumentId() + ", " +
                        nextAttrCtrValue() + ", " +
                        currentId + ", " +
                        "'" + attrList.getName(i) + "', " +
                         "'" + attrList.getValue(i) + "')");
        rdbExecute(buf.toString());
    }
}
}

/****************** JDBCReplaceFragHandler.java *******************/
package com.xweave.xmldb.xserve;

import com.xweave.xmldb.fgrel.*;
import org.xml.sax.*;
import com.xweave.xmldb.util.rdb.*;
import java.sql.SQLException;
/**
 * SAX Handler using JDBC to replace a fragment into the database
 */
public class JDBCReplaceFragHandler extends JDBCFragLoadHandler {
/**
 * JDBCReplaceFragHandler constructor comment.
```

```
 * @param rdb com.xweave.xmldb.util.rdb.RDB
 */
public JDBCReplaceFragHandler(RDB rdb) {
    super(rdb);
}
/**
 * Handle element, attributes, and the connection from this element
 * to its parent.
 */
public void startElement(String name, AttributeList attrList) {
    //DEBUG: System.out.println(name);
    //Create new element entry
    Element parent = getCurrentElement();
    String parentId;
    String indexNum = null;
    if (parent == null) {
        parentId = "NULL";
    } else {
        parentId = parent.getId();
    }
    StringBuffer buf;
    String currentId;
    if (parent == null) {
        //first time
        setCurrentElement(getFragmentId());
        currentId = getCurrentElement().getId();
        //get old parent id
        buf = new StringBuffer();
        buf.append("select parent_id from ");
        buf.append(ELE_TABLE);
        buf.append(" where doc_id = " + getDocumentId());
        buf.append(" and ele_id = " + currentId);
        parentId = getRdb().getDataItem(buf.toString());
        if (parentId == null) {
            //we will have problems later, so throw out now
            throw new Error("Unable to get parent id from database: " +
                getDocumentId() + "." + currentId + "/n" + buf.toString());
        }
        //get old index number
        buf = new StringBuffer();
        buf.append("select indx from ");
        buf.append(CHILD_TABLE);
        buf.append(" where doc_id = " + getDocumentId());
        buf.append(" and ele_id = " + parentId);
        buf.append(" and child_id = " + currentId);
        indexNum = getRdb().getDataItem(buf.toString());
```

```
      if (indexNum == null) {
         //we will have problems later, so throw out now
         throw new Error("Unable to get INDX from database: " +
            getDocumentId() + "." + currentId + "/n" + buf.toString());
      }
      //delete old element entry and children
      //create new DeleteFrag Command and use it
      DeleteFrag delFragCmd = new DeleteFrag(getRdb());
      if (! delFragCmd.deleteFrag(getDocumentId(), currentId)) {
         //we will have problems later, so throw out now
         throw new Error("Unable to delete fragment from database: " +
            getDocumentId() + "." + currentId + "/n" + buf.toString());
      }
   } else {
      // not a top element, create new ele entry
      setCurrentElement(Integer.toString(nextEleCtrValue()));
      currentId = getCurrentElement().getId();
   }
   //continue with element creation
   buf = new StringBuffer();
   buf.append("insert into");
   buf.append(" " + ELE_TABLE + " ");
   buf.append("(doc_id, ele_id, parent_id, tag)");
   buf.append(" values ");
   buf.append("(" + getDocumentId() + ", " +
                    currentId + ", " +
                    parentId + ", " +
                    "'" + name + "')");
   rdbExecute(buf.toString());
   //create child entry
   buf = new StringBuffer();
   buf.append("insert into");
   buf.append(" " + CHILD_TABLE + " ");
   buf.append("(doc_id, ele_id, indx, child_class, child_id)");
   buf.append(" values ");
   buf.append("(" + getDocumentId() + ", " + parentId + ", ");
if (parent == null) {
      //top level element
      buf.append(indexNum);
      } else {
      //sub-element
       buf.append(parent.incrIndexCtr());
   }
   buf.append(", " + "'ELE', " + currentId + ")");
   rdbExecute(buf.toString());
   //Create entries for each attribute
   for (int i = 0; i < attrList.getLength(); i++) {
      buf = new StringBuffer();
      buf.append("insert into");
      buf.append(" " + ATTR_TABLE + " ");
```

```
            buf.append("(doc_id, attr_id, ele_id, name, value)");
            buf.append(" values ");
            buf.append("(" + getDocumentId() + ", " +
                             nextAttrCtrValue() + ", " +
                             currentId + ", " +
                             "'" + attrList.getName(i) + "', " +
                              "'" + attrList.getValue(i) + "')");
            rdbExecute(buf.toString());
        }
    }
}
```

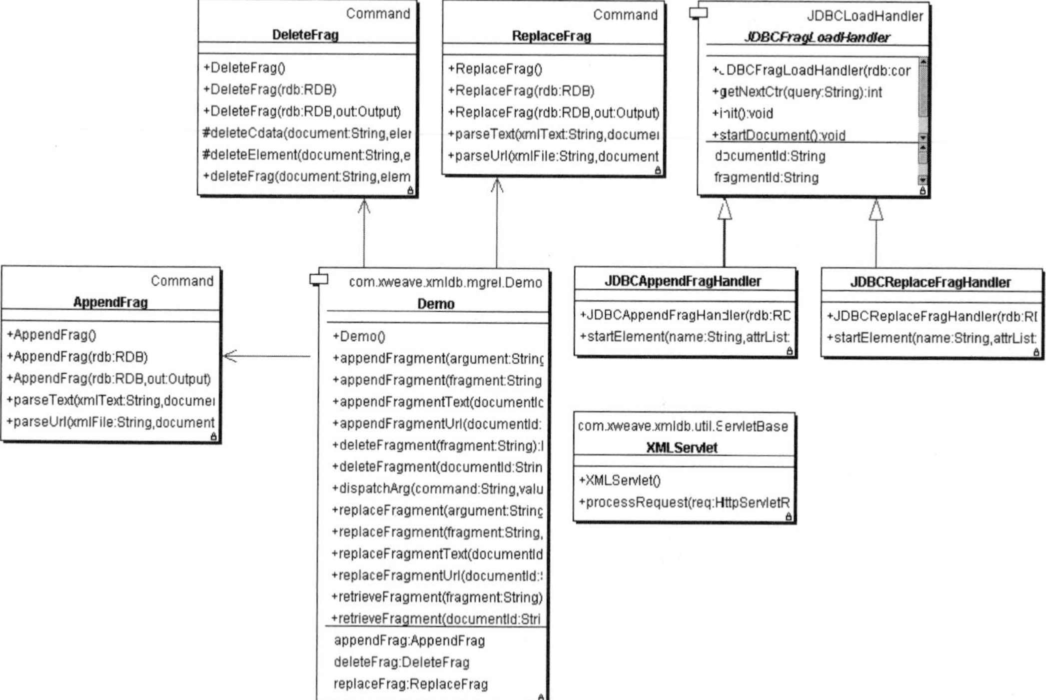

Figure 5–8 UML class diagram for xServe XML data server

The main class in xServe, called Demo, is a subclass of the Demo class of the fine-grained relational storage system described in Section 4.2.4. The xServe Demo class contains fields for each class that implements a command of the data server and executes the command through the "dispatchArg" method. Each command is a subclass of the Command abstract class, which contains a RDB object to connect to the database and an Output object to write the formatted data to the appropriate stream. RDB and Output are described in Appendix A. xServe commands retrieve, append, and replace fragments as well as retrieve, store, and delete documents.

A SAX parser handler is used to append and replace fragments. SAX parsers are described in Appendix B. The abstract class JDBCFragLoadHandler retrieves maximum index values for child, embedded element, and attribute records so the inserts will create appropriate unique identifiers. JDBCReplaceFragHandler uses the DeleteFrag command to delete the old element and then inserts the new XML fragment in its place. JDBCAppendFrag inserts the XML fragment after the last embedded element. Both commands insert data in a manner similar to the load document command JDBCLoadHandler in the fine-grained relational storage system.

5.5 Hybrid Relational/XML Server

Although the relational and XML data servers described in the previous two sections are useful on their own, a hybrid system that provides query access to either would also be useful. A hybrid relational/XML data server can transparently provide access to relational and XML data. Data can be stored in the data model (and DBMS) most appropriate for it; the hybrid data server can provide limited data integration across the data models through connections between the underlying data sources. For example, an XML document may have an embedded "access" element representing a relational query. As the XML document is retrieved, the relational query may be performed and merged into the XML data stream. Similarly, the values in a column in the relational DBMS may refer to documents or fragments in the XML DBMS, and the XML data may be merged with the relational data as it is retrieved and formatted as XML. Thus, the efficiency of relational storage may be combined with the flexibility of an XML DBMS.

One way to build a hybrid relational/XML data server is with an n-tier architecture that calls two backend servers: a traditional relational server and the XML data server. The hybrid server passes URL requests (or uses other protocols) to each of the data servers and merges the documents as they are retrieved.

For demonstration, however, it is probably simpler to create a new data server in a three-tier architecture that accesses the relational DBMS and the XML DBMS. This simplifies the architecture, but does require that the XML and relational data servers reside within the same application. Because the xServe and rServe applications can coexist in the same application, the hybrid system—xrServe—can pass commands directly to the appropriate class. The n-tier architecture would be similar except for intervening steps on the hybrid server to format, post, and retrieve the data from the separate servers.

Additional functionality may be added within the same framework. For example, it may be useful to provide direct access to external URLs within the XML document or relational tables. Another "access" element type may provide information on accessing a resource from files or URLs (as XML).

5.5.1 Implementation

The hybrid server is an expansion of the XML data server of the previous section. The operations of the XML data server are inherited to avoid redundancy and the operations of the relational server are passed to a separate instance. An AccessSpec object is created to contain the query information and is built up in the parsing of the URL. The writeAccess method is then called to pass the command to the appropriate instance: *this* object for xServe or the object in the formatRel field for rServe. Because the only command supported is to write the XML fragment from either source, the code is fairly simple.

Java code that implements the xrServe relational data server is given in Example 5–16. A UML class diagram is given in Figure 5–9.

Example 5–16 : Java Code for xrServer Hybrid Relational/XML Data Server

```
/************************ Demo.java ***********************/
package com.xweave.xmldb.xrserve;

import com.xweave.xmldb.util.io.*;
import com.xweave.xmldb.util.rdb.*;
import com.xweave.xmldb.xserve.*;
import com.xweave.xmldb.rserve.*;
/**
 * Demonstration of Hybrid XML/Relational Data Server
 */
public class Demo extends com.xweave.xmldb.xserve.Demo {
   protected com.xweave.xmldb.rserve.Demo formatRel = null;
public Demo() {
   super();
}
```

```
public void dispatchArg(AccessSpec access, String command, String value) {
    if (command.equalsIgnoreCase("TABLENAME")) {
        access.setTablename(value);
        return;
    }
    if (command.equalsIgnoreCase("ID")) {
        access.setId(value);
        return;
    }
    if (command.equalsIgnoreCase("DOCUMENT")) {
        access.setDocument(value);
        return;
    }
    if (command.equalsIgnoreCase("ACCT")) {
        access.setAcct(value);
        return;
    }
    if (command.equalsIgnoreCase("STYLESHEET")) {
        access.setStyleSheet(value);
        return;
    }
    if (command.equalsIgnoreCase("DOCHEADER")) {
        access.setDocHeader(value);
        return;
    }
    if (command.equalsIgnoreCase("IGNORE") ||
command.equalsIgnoreCase("SUBMIT")) {
        //ignore these arguments
        return;
    }
    //Unknown args are part of query constraint to relational DB
    access.getQuerySpec().addConstraint(command, value);
}
public com.xweave.xmldb.rserve.Demo getFormatRel() {
    if (formatRel == null) {
        formatRel = new com.xweave.xmldb.rserve.Demo();
    }
    return formatRel;
}
public void setFormatRel(com.xweave.xmldb.rserve.Demo newValue) {
    this.formatRel = newValue;
}
public boolean writeAccess(AccessSpec access) {
    if (access.getDocument() != null) {
        //write document
```

```
        com.xweave.xmldb.fgrel.Format formatxml = getFormat();
        formatxml.setOutput(getOutput());
        if (access.getDocHeader() != null) {
            getOutput().writeln("<?xml version=\"1.0\"?>");
        }
        if (access.getStyleSheet() != null) {
            getOutput().writeln("<?xml:stylesheet type=\"text/xsl\" href=\""
+ access.getStyleSheet() + "\"?>");
        }
        if (access.getId() != null) {
            //write fragment
            return formatxml.writeFrag(access.getDocument(),
access.getId());
        } else {
            //write entire document
            return formatxml.writeDoc(access.getDocument());
        }
    } else
        if (access.getTablename() != null) {
            //write table
            com.xweave.xmldb.rserve.Demo formatrel = getFormatRel();
            formatrel.setOutputSource(getOutput());
            com.xweave.xmldb.rserve.QuerySpec query = access.getQuerySpec();
            com.xweave.xmldb.rserve.AccessSpec relaccess = new
com.xweave.xmldb.rserve.AccessSpec();
            relaccess.setQuerySpec(query);
            relaccess.setAcct(access.getAcct());
            if (access.getStyleSheet() != null) {
                relaccess.setStyleSheet(access.getStyleSheet());
            }
            query.setTableName(access.getTablename());
            //Write the appropriate fragment
            //TODO: how to specify a document header
            if (access.getId() != null) {
                //write single record
                query.setId(access.getId());
            } else
                if (access.getQuery() != null) {
                    //write query
                    query.setConstraintString(access.getQuery());
                    //otherwise, write entire table
                    //set no parameters
                }
                //write document or root element
            if (access.getDocHeader() == null) {
                formatrel.writeTable(relaccess, 0);
```

```
            } else {
               formatrel.writeDoc(relaccess);
            }
         } else {
            //information not specified
            return false;
         }
      return true;
   }
}

/************************ AccessSpec.java **********************/
package com.xweave.xmldb.xrserve;

import java.util.*;
import com.xweave.xmldb.rserve.QuerySpec;
/**
 * Access Specification for server
 */
public class AccessSpec {
   public String document = null;
   public String tablename = null;
   public String id = null;
   public String query = null;
   public String acct = com.xweave.xmldb.Default.getXmldbAcct();
   public String styleSheet = null;
   public String docHeader = null;
   public QuerySpec querySpec = null;
public AccessSpec() {
   super();
}
public String getAcct() {
   return acct;
}
public String getDocHeader() {
   return docHeader;
}
public String getDocument() {
   return document;
}
public String getId() {
   return id;
}
public String getQuery() {
   return query;
}
```

```
public QuerySpec getQuerySpec() {
   if (querySpec == null)
      querySpec = new QuerySpec();
   return querySpec;
}
public String getStyleSheet() {
   return styleSheet;
}
public String getTablename() {
   return tablename;
}
public void setAcct(String newValue) {
   this.acct = newValue;
}
public void setDocHeader(String newValue) {
   this.docHeader = newValue;
}
public void setDocument(String newValue) {
   this.document = newValue;
}
public void setId(String newValue) {
   this.id = newValue;
}
public void setQuery(String newValue) {
   this.query = newValue;
}
public void setQuerySpec(QuerySpec newValue) {
   this.querySpec = newValue;
}
public void setStyleSheet(String newValue) {
   this.styleSheet = newValue;
}
public void setTablename(String newValue) {
   this.tablename = newValue;
}
}

/************************ XMLServlet.java ***********************/
package com.xweave.xmldb.xrserve;

import javax.servlet.*;
import javax.servlet.http.*;
import java.io.*;
import java.util.*;
import com.xweave.xmldb.util.io.ServletOutput;

/**
 * Servlet interface to database.
 */
public class XMLServlet extends com.xweave.xmldb.util.ServletBase {
```

```
public XMLServlet() {
    super();
}
public void processRequest(HttpServletRequest req, HttpServletResponse
res) throws ServletException, java.io.IOException {
    ServletOutputStream out = startOutput(res);
    Enumeration enum = req.getParameterNames();
    String pname, pvalue = null;
    Demo db = new Demo();
    db.setOutput(new ServletOutput(out));
    db.setRdbAccessString("mgraves/mgraves@127.0.0.1:1521:ORCL");
    AccessSpec access = new AccessSpec();
    while (enum.hasMoreElements()) {
        pname = (String) enum.nextElement();
        pvalue = req.getParameter(pname);
        log("Dispatching " + pname + " " + pvalue);
        db.dispatchArg(access, pname, pvalue);
    }
    if (access.getAcct() != null) {
        db.setRdbAccessString(access.getAcct());
    }
    if (db.getRdbAccessString() == null) {
        log("Error in processRequest: access string not defined for:\n  " +
req.getPathTranslated());
    }
    db.writeAccess(access);
    endOutput(res);
}
}
```

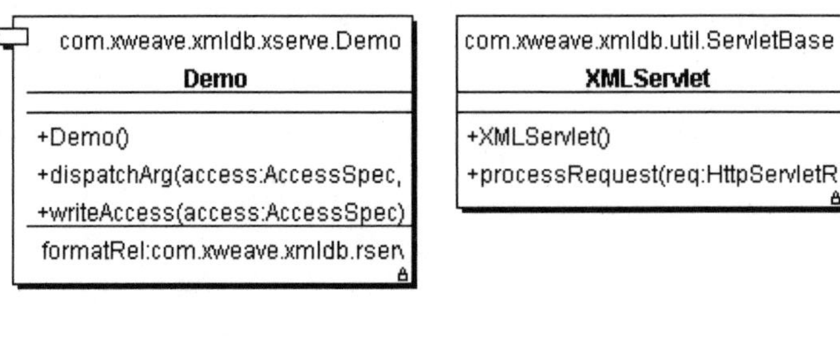

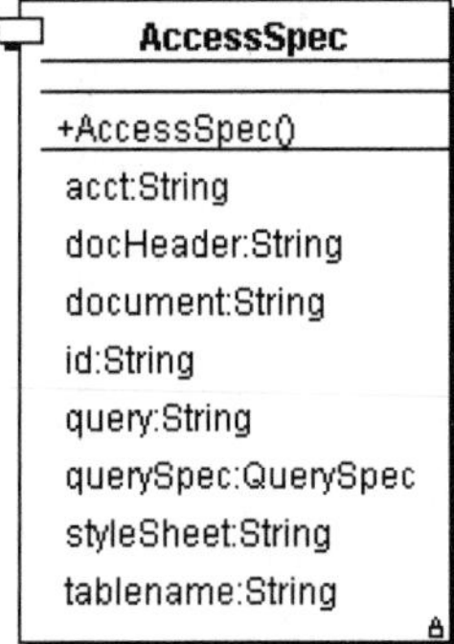

Figure 5–9 UML class diagram for xrServe hybrid relational/XML data server

Commercial Systems

- What commercial XML database solutions are available?
- What functionality do they provide?

6

After a commercial XML database or data server gets through the marketing department (or past the finance gurus), it may sound a lot like an "integrated B2B solution" or new buzzword. This can make it difficult to distinguish XML database solutions from systems that serve and/or produce XML documents.

Commercial systems for XML databases may be divided into four main categories:

- XML query tools and adaptors to a relational database, which generate XML documents from data in the database. They may also have SQL query interfaces that allow query results to be formatted as XML.
- XML DBMSs. They could be built using XML-specific storage or flat files, or built on top of a relational or object-oriented data store. Not all systems perform some of the features needed for a full commercial database system.
- XML data servers that combine an XML database with a Web server.
- XML content management systems, which provide a document-processing-oriented view of the data. These are outside the scope of this book, though I have also included

some XML document servers that provide a document-processing-oriented view and are integrated with Web servers. The ones included are specifically designed to work with XML documents.

The information in this chapter is fairly sparse. The chapter provides an introduction to commercial systems and how to find out about current systems and functionality. The field is changing too rapidly for a published book to be up-to-date, though I hope to provide enough information to help you get started. The information in this chapter comes from several sources, and I have not used most of the products described in this chapter, so check out the products' Web sites for more accurate, up-to-date information.

6.1 Overview

Initially, XML databases were more closely aligned with object-oriented databases. Primarily because the object-oriented technology was more cutting-edge, it tended to be more responsive to new opportunities and could more easily adapt its technology. Object-oriented database products tended to have a smaller customer base than relational databases and could also shift directions without disrupting its customers. Relational databases also lagged behind in integrating XML because of the technical hurdles.

It is fairly easy to generate XML from data in a relational database by formatting the data as XML. It is also fairly straightforward to create a "node" object in an object-oriented database. It is more difficult to expand the relational data model to incorporate the flexibility of XML. Relational databases have tried to incorporate the structure of objects with moderate success, and whether they will incorporate the structures behind XML as required is unclear. A key requirement is the efficient storage and access of variant records.

Whether object-oriented databases will be able to completely support XML is also unclear. The overhead of objects can be fairly high unless sophisticated memory mapping strategies are used, and these depend upon the regularity of the structures of objects. However, XML precisely provides the flexibility that objects do not have, and those memory-mapping strategies may not work for the variant structures of XML.

My opinion of the commercial outlook is that larger relational database companies are not likely to integrate XML at more than a superficial level, whereas smaller, more innovative, relational DBMS will incorporate more features found in XML. As required, additional features will be incorporated into relational databases, and stored procedures (and other object-oriented functionality) will become more integrated into the relational data model. New database ideas will also be incorporated into the relational model. Object-oriented databases will remain a niche market, though the niche will expand.

XML DBMSs will probably be in specific markets, such as scientific databases, some financial services, and electronic publishing. These markets will place a lighter demand on the transaction management of a DBMS and a greater demand on efficient delivery of large documents. XML data stores will be an adjunct to other DBMSs or used alone for less transaction-intensive applications. For example, a relational DBMS might have "plug-ins" for XML data and/or text document management.

XML databases can be integrated with other data storage systems, such as relational or object-oriented. Specialized storage facilities optimized for XML are probably required before efficient, high-volume XML databases will become viable. The techniques described elsewhere in this book provide mechanisms for managing XML databases until robust commercial solutions are available—as well as techniques for developing those solutions.

6.2 Database Adaptors

XML Database Adaptors provide XML access to existing databases. Adaptors consist of middleware, embedded DBMS tools, and query tools. Middleware tools sit between an application and a database to provide data to the application in XML format. Many commercial DBMS companies have incorporated an adaptor directly into their DBMS engines. The middleware tools are components of a n-tier architecture; the DBMS adaptations allow XML to be used in a client-server architecture. Query tools are adaptors that provide additional query or XML reporting capabilities. Some of the commercial DBMS adaptions include query capabilities.

6.2.1 Middleware Tools

BeanStalk (*www.transparency.com*) is a commercial engine that sits between the application and a relational database or other ODBC data source to provide SQL queries via Java/JDBC.

HiT Software (*www.hit.com*) provides a bi-directional adaptor for relational tables with incremental updates. A DOM API is provided to OLE or ODBC-compliant databases, and when the DOM structure is modified, the relational database may be updated based solely on the changed DOM objects.

Merant (*www.merant.com*) provides ODBC access to XML flat files and URLs.

Xaware (*www.xaware.com*) provides a graphical development environment to create bi-directional mappings between XML documents and traditional data sources, including relational (ODBC-compliant) databases and Web servers. The system uses configurable components that support transactions and can join data from multiple data sources.

XML-DB Link (*www.roguewave.com*) is a Web server plug-in that generates XML from parameterized SQL queries.

XML-DBMS (*www.rpbourret.com*) is a Java-based system for transferring data between a relational database and an XML document.

XML Junction (*www.datajunction.com*) is a transformation engine to transform relational data to XML.

XML Shark from InfoShark (*www.infoshark.com*) is a bi-directional adaptor for relational data.

6.2.2 Commercial Relational Databases

Pretty much every large commercial database company has some tools to "XMLize" their database. You can often find tools on a company's main XML page.

- IBM DB2 (*www.ibm.com/developer/xml/*) or the IBM DB2 database site (*www.ibm.com/software/data/db2/*). Their tool is called the DB2 XML Extender. The DB2 XML Data Access Definition lets you define nested XML with user-defined tags.
- Informix (*www.informix.com/xml/*).
- Microsoft SQL Server (*msdn.microsoft.com/xml/default.asp*). SQL Server 2000 allows the user to retrieve data from multiple

relations and join the data in an XML document with arbitrary nesting. Queries can quickly become complex, but the database has a facility to store XML query views. SQL Server 2000 extends SQL by adding a FOR XML clause to the select statement, which formats the report as an XML document from relational data. Options to the FOR XML clause allow formatting of data as an attribute-oriented or element-oriented report.
- Oracle (*technet.oracle.com/tech/xml/*). Oracle provides XSQL to retrieve XML from a relational table, which can then be manipulated using XSLT.
- Sybase (*www.sybase.com*).

6.2.3 Query Tools

No commercial query tools are available, as of this writing, though several research languages have been developed, including XML-QL, XQL, XSQL, and Quilt.

6.3 DBMSs

Birdstep (*www.birdstep.com*) has a small database engine (less than 50K) that has an interface for storing XML documents and fragments in a space-efficient manner. They are currently focusing on the handheld market.

Lore (*www-db.stanford.edu/lore/*) is an academic XML DBMS developed at Stanford. It predates XML but was originally designed to a similar data model.

NeoCore (*www.neocore.com*) uses a sophisticated hashing scheme to index documents and speed up the search in a native store.

Ozone (*ozone-db.org*) is an open-source, object-oriented database with a DOM interface to store XML. It is a pure Java implementation.

XDBM (*www.bowerbird.com.au*) provides an interface to individual flat files. XDBM is a lightweight database manager that provides searching and simple manipulation of XML documents by indexing the documents and storing them as binary files.

XHive (*www.xhive.com*) is an object-oriented XML DBMS that utilizes fine-grained storage of elements.

XYZFind (*www.xyzfind.com*) is an XML repository with search and query capabilities.

6.4 XML Data Servers

XML data servers combine an XML DBMS with a Web server. Three data servers are dbXML, eXcelon, and Tamino.

6.4.1 dbXML

dbXML (*www.dbxml.org*) is an XML server that manages collections of XML documents. It is implemented in Java with some C++ and includes apache connectivity. Three underlying storage facilities are implemented: in-memory, flat file, and a simple hashed bucket indexed storage facility.

6.4.2 eXcelon

eXcelon (*www.exceloncorp.com*) is built on top of Object Design's Object Store database (*www.odi.com*). Each element is represented as an object in the fine-grained data store. Object Store speeds up the access time of each element by caching the elements of a document in the memory of the access server. The fine-grained access allows for efficient access of individual fragments, but as discussed in Chapter 3, there is a large space penalty for modeling each element as an object. The database has an extension that allows it to be plugged into a Web server, which allows URL access of the documents in the database.

eXcelon provides a DOM and XQL interface as well as an XML parser. The data store can also be accessed through an Explorer interface that provides browsing of XML documents, Java extensions, XQL queries, and other objects in the data store. It can also import data from the files system or through ODBC. Documents are retrieved in their entirety through the Explorer, and there is no exploration or browsing of the contents of a document. There is also a design tool and an administrative tool.

6.4.3 Tamino

Tamino (*www.softwareag.com/tamino/*) combines native XML storage with a Web server. The server can access data from an XML data store designed to support XML and from relational data sources. The query language for Tamino is XQL and the server provides URL-based access. Bi-directional access is provided to the relational databases and native XML store within a single document.

6.5 XML Document Servers

DynamiX by Macalla (*www.macalla.com*) is a server for distributing, caching, filtering, and managing XML documents in a distributed environment. It uses a publish/subscribe paradigm to provide XML documents through document channels, which are also XML documents that contains references to the actual sources of XML documents. The document channel maintains an XML document cache, which holds the most recent data for each XML document published on the document channel. The publisher can also publish changes to data in the cache—which is merged into the cache entry—instead of re-publishing complete documents. A security model controls access to the data being delivered at both the document and fragment level and can filter documents by removing sections before delivering them. Macalla focuses on the financial services sector. Although DynamiX is not a DBMS as defined in this book, it uses XSDL and XQL and provides several other features of a data server. If a publisher had storage facility for XML documents, much of the functionality of a data server would be provided, or it might be possible for the caching mechanism to be used for longer-term persistence.

IXIASoft (*www.ixiasoft.com*) provides an XML server that supports searching of indexed XML documents with a repository and configurable indexing module. Each index contains the position within the document for each occurrence. Indexes are recalculated based on user-specified criteria, such as number of documents added, size of data added, or time of day. On the client side, proxies improve performance through the use of caches.

Percussion (*www.percussion.com*) provides tools to support serving of XML content. Their Rhythmyx tool uses XML to retrieve from data repositories and XSL to modify the content depending upon user needs. XSL also is used to format the content as HTML. Rhythmyx can be used as a Web server, servlet, or plug-in.

XPS (*www.sequoiasw.com*) from Sequoia Software is portal software that wraps existing applications and business-to-business services in XML through a personalized Web-based interface.

Bluestone (*www.bluestone.com*) and DataChannel (*www.datachannel.com*) also provide XML services.

6.6 Resources and Sites

To gain more information, the best resource is the Web. Many magazines cover XML and other Web technologies mentioned in Chapter 1. These sometimes have articles on XML databases.

Useful sites for gathering more information about commercial systems are

- *www.alphaworks.ibm.com:* IBM Alphaworks site has many XML products for interacting with databases. Because the products evolve rapidly, it is best to go poke around and see what is there.
- *www.rpbourret.com/xml/XMLDatabaseProds.htm:* A list of XML databases written by the developer of XML-DBMS, a Java-based system for transferring data between a relational database and an XML document. The site lists several product areas including: middleware, XML-enabled databases, XML servers, XML-enabled Web servers, content management systems, and persistent DOM implementations.
- *www.xml.com/pub/Guide/Relational_Databases:* "Information, specifications, and software regarding XML's use in relational databases or for expressing relational database-like data structures."
- *www.xml.com/pub/Guide/Query_Technologies:* "XML-based query languages and non-XML query languages used for querying individual XML documents or XML document repositories."
- *www.xml.com/pub/Guide/Object-Oriented_Databases:* "Information, specifications, and software regarding XML's use in object-oriented databases or for expressing structures that might otherwise be stored in an object database."
- *www.xmlsoftware.com/database/:* Entry to the XMLSoftware listing on XML database systems and utilities.

User Interface

- How is XML data presented to the user?
- What technologies are useful?
- How are they used?

7

Databases eventually get used by people. Web-delivered user interfaces are particularly appropriate for XML databases. Web user interfaces may be used either as clients to present data to end users or at intermediate stages in an application pipeline to examine the XML data stream passing between two applications. In either case, the user may need to query or browse the data.

This chapter describes how to generate HTML forms and reports from the database using XML/XSL for a generic Web browser (such as Microsoft Internet Explorer). A (Java) client architecture is also described for parsing XML and generating generic or custom reports.

7.1 Overview

Two ways to present data via the Web are HTML and Java applets. XML, in conjunction with XSL stylesheets, will generate HTML reports to be viewed through Web browsers. Data entry and query forms can be created by using HTML forms and simple interactions can be created by using Javascript embedded in the HTML pages. For more complex user interfaces, Java applets can be used that parse (and/or generate) the XML and create appropriate reports, forms, and visualizations.

HTML has the advantage of being simple and lightweight. Only a Web browser is necessary, as the client and the user interface is available through the Web browser. HTML is fairly simple to design, and basic data manipulation operations can be implemented using HTML forms. Another advantage is that most users are already familiar with the look and feel of HTML forms, and thus less training or instruction may be required.

Disadvantages of HTML are that it is limited to plain text with hypertext links (and a few pretty pictures) and the user interactions are basic, such as clicking or moving a mouse, filling in a text box, or selecting from a pull-down menu. The layout and rendering of text reports is fairly limited in comparison to what can be developed using a programming language such as Java.

Java can be used to develop fairly sophisticated user interfaces, including all the text manipulations of HTML, as well as graphical displays, rotating 3D images, and incremental interactions with the database. Its disadvantage is that there is more overhead both in development and at run-time: Java code must be written to create and lay out pages to support the more complex interactions, and applets must be downloaded and run on the client within the Web browser.

If current and near-term system requirements can be met using HTML, it is probably better to go ahead and use HTML at least as a prototype. Otherwise, considerable work is required in developing Java interfaces just to duplicate what is already available in HTML. When more interaction is required than HTML, but the full functionality of Java is not required, then JSP or Javascript may be useful. Javascript may be used to increase the interactions available within an HTML page, and JSP allows Java code to be embedded within an HTML document to generate HTML.

The next two sections describe how to use XSL and Java to generate a browsable user interface to a database. Section 7.4 describes how to expand the user interface functionality to include data entry, editing, and searching.

7.2 XSL-based User Interfaces

XSL-based user interfaces can be used to generate HTML. This section introduces XSL stylesheets, describes how to render an XML document as a table or record, and explains how to expand those depictions with drill-downs, proxies, and customizations.

XML with XSL is useful particularly when the presentation of the data needs to vary based on the client. For example, you might use different style sheets to take advantage of features of different Web browsers, or you can use XSL to generate another markup language, such as WML for cell phones or other wireless devices.

7.2.1 XSL Stylesheets

XSL stylesheets are a collection of templates that transform a document. Each template consists of a pattern that is compared to the element of the document and a body that is used to create a fragment in the new document if the pattern matched. For example, the template

```
<xsl:template match="para">
   <p>
</xsl:template>
```

will translate the document

```
<page>
   <para>Welcome to my Web site!</para>
</page>
```

to the document

```
<page>
   <p>Welcome to my Web site!</p>
</page>
```

The pattern part of the template consists of a string representing a set of nodes. Characteristics that can be matched include element type names, element attributes, and properties of children elements. For example:

- emu—matches a node with element type name “emu”
- walrus—matches a node with element type name “walrus”
- frog|fish—matches any node with element type name “frog” or element type name “fish”
- node()—matches any node (it does not match the root node or an attribute)
- /—matches the root node of a document
- circle/coordinate—matches the “coordinate” subelement of a “circle” element
- text()—matches any text
- *—matches any element

- @name—matches the "name" attribute of an element
- @id—matches the "id" attribute of an element
- @*—matches any attribute of an element

The body of the template can be

- an element that is inserted into the target (resulting) document verbatim
- commands to build up the target document using data from the source document, such as character data, elements, and attribute values
- combinations of the preceding items processed using simple programming language constructs such as if-then, iteration, or pattern matching

Some commands that are supported by XSL are

- value-of—emits the text of a node or attribute specified by an expression similar to the patterns used in matching a template
- if—emits the content of the "if" element if the boolean expression is true
- choose—evaluates a series of "when" boolean conditions and emits the content of the first true condition or an (optional) default value if none are true

From these commands, XSL stylesheets can be used to create a variety of HTML documents from a single XML document.

Two versions of XSL stylesheets are described in this book. The first version is the December 1998 version of XSL, which is used by Microsoft Internet Explorer 5.0 (IE5). Currently, this is the only widely available Web browser with native XSL processing. The second version is XSLT 1.0, which is the most recent W3C version. Microsoft provides an XSL processor for XSLT 1.0 at msdn.microsoft.com. Differences include how the stylesheet is introduced; the new version also has additional commands. Most of the examples in this chapter use the IE5 version.

7.2.2 Rendering XML as a Table

XML may be rendered as a table using an XSL stylesheet as shown in Figure 7–1. The example stylesheet document in Example 7–1 renders as a table an XML document of elements with a table-like subelement structure. The stylesheet in Example 7–2 is the same stylesheet using XSLT, and its differences are described at the end of this section.

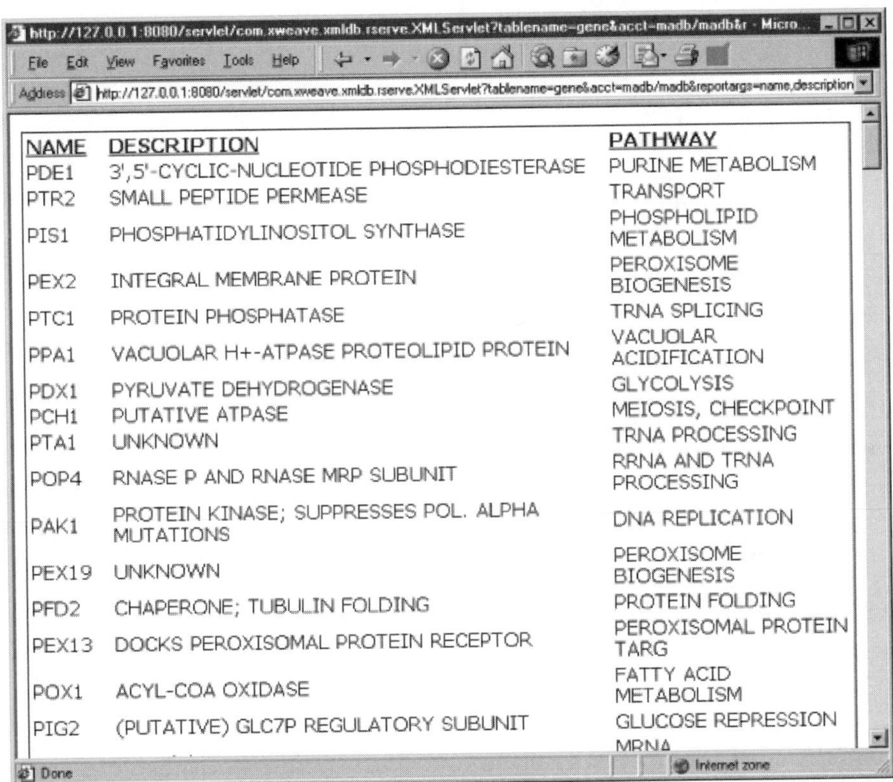

NAME	DESCRIPTION	PATHWAY
PDE1	3',5'-CYCLIC-NUCLEOTIDE PHOSPHODIESTERASE	PURINE METABOLISM
PTR2	SMALL PEPTIDE PERMEASE	TRANSPORT
PIS1	PHOSPHATIDYLINOSITOL SYNTHASE	PHOSPHOLIPID METABOLISM
PEX2	INTEGRAL MEMBRANE PROTEIN	PEROXISOME BIOGENESIS
PTC1	PROTEIN PHOSPHATASE	TRNA SPLICING
PPA1	VACUOLAR H+-ATPASE PROTEOLIPID PROTEIN	VACUOLAR ACIDIFICATION
PDX1	PYRUVATE DEHYDROGENASE	GLYCOLYSIS
PCH1	PUTATIVE ATPASE	MEIOSIS, CHECKPOINT
PTA1	UNKNOWN	TRNA PROCESSING
POP4	RNASE P AND RNASE MRP SUBUNIT	RRNA AND TRNA PROCESSING
PAK1	PROTEIN KINASE; SUPPRESSES POL. ALPHA MUTATIONS	DNA REPLICATION
PEX19	UNKNOWN	PEROXISOME BIOGENESIS
PFD2	CHAPERONE; TUBULIN FOLDING	PROTEIN FOLDING
PEX13	DOCKS PEROXISOMAL PROTEIN RECEPTOR	PEROXISOMAL PROTEIN TARG
POX1	ACYL-COA OXIDASE	FATTY ACID METABOLISM
PIG2	(PUTATIVE) GLC7P REGULATORY SUBUNIT	GLUCOSE REPRESSION

Figure 7–1 Table of biological data generated using XSL

Example 7–1 : Simple Stylesheet to Transform XML Data to HTML Table (IE5)

```
<?xml version="1.0"?>
<xsl:stylesheet xmlns:xsl="http://www.w3.org/TR/WD-xsl">
  <xsl:template match="/">
    <TABLE STYLE="border:1px solid black" BORDER="1">
```

```
        <TR STYLE="font-weight:bold; text-decoration:underline">
          <xsl:for-each select="collection/*[1]/*">
            <TD><xsl:node-name/></TD>
          </xsl:for-each>
        </TR>
        <xsl:apply-templates />
      </TABLE>
    </xsl:template>
    <xsl:template match="collection">
        <xsl:for-each select="*">
          <TR>
            <xsl:for-each select="*">
              <TD><xsl:value-of select="."/></TD>
            </xsl:for-each>
          </TR>
        </xsl:for-each>
    </xsl:template>
  </xsl:stylesheet>
```

Example 7–2 : Simple Stylesheet to Transform XML Data to HTML Table (XSLT)

```
<?xml version="1.0"?>
<xsl:stylesheet version="1.0" xmlns:xsl="http://www.w3.org/1999/XSL/
Transform">
  <xsl:output method="html"/>
  <xsl:template match="/">
    <TABLE STYLE="border:1px solid black" BORDER="1">
      <TR STYLE="font-weight:bold; text-decoration:underline">
        <xsl:for-each select="collection/*[1]/*">
          <TD><xsl:value-of select="name()"/></TD>
        </xsl:for-each>
      </TR>
      <xsl:apply-templates />
    </TABLE>
  </xsl:template>
  <xsl:template match="collection">
      <xsl:for-each select="*">
        <TR>
          <xsl:for-each select="*">
            <TD><xsl:value-of select="."/></TD>
          </xsl:for-each>
        </TR>
      </xsl:for-each>
  </xsl:template>
</xsl:stylesheet>
```

The stylesheet document in Example 7–1 consists of the XML header and an XSL stylesheet element. The stylesheet element consists of an attribute that defines the namespace as the version used by IE5 and two templates as subelements. The first template is executed at the root of the source document (denoted by the slash "/" character), and the second template is executed when it matches any element with the element type name "collection". These sections are outlined here:

```
<?xml version="1.0" ?>
<xsl:stylesheet xmlns:xsl="http://www.w3.org/TR/WD-
    xsl"> <xsl:template match="/">
    ...
   </xsl:template>
   <xsl:template match="collection">
    ...
   </xsl:template>
</xsl:stylesheet>
```

The root template creates an HTML table by interspersing HTML and XSL commands. The "xsl:" namespace prefix distinguishes the XSL commands from the HTML commands. The root template is:

```
<xsl:template match="/">
<TABLE STYLE="border:1px solid black">
  <TR STYLE="font-weight:bold; text-
    decoration:underline">
      <xsl:for-each select="collection/*[1]/*">
        <TD>
          <xsl:node-name />
        </TD>
      </xsl:for-each>
    </TR>
   <xsl:apply-templates />
  </TABLE>
</xsl:template>
```

To understand the template, examine it by looking at the HTML code and the XSL code separately. The HTML code is

```
<TABLE STYLE="border:1px solid black">
  <TR STYLE="font-weight:bold; text-
    decoration:underline"> For each column name,
      <TD>
        The name of the column goes here.
      </TD>
  </TR>
</TABLE>
```

The HTML commands create a “TABLE” with a particular style and create the first row in the table (again with a particular style). The row consists of a collection of element type names that become the names of the columns.

The XSL code is

```
<xsl:template match="/">
  <xsl:for-each select="collection/*[1]/*">
    <xsl:node-name />
  </xsl:for-each>
  <xsl:apply-templates />
</xsl:template>
```

The XSL code is a valid template that without the HTML commands would present the table header as plain text. The template body consists of a “for-each” statement that iterates the names of the columns (intuitively referred to as “collection/*[1]/*”) and an “apply-templates” command that applies any matching templates in the stylesheet at that point (in this case, the “collection” element is executed, emitting the rest of the rows).

The names of the columns are extracted from an XML document such as:

```
<?xml version="1.0"?>
<collection>
<GENE>
  <NAME>PDE1</NAME>
  <DESCRIPTION>PHOSPHODIESTERASE</DESCRIPTION>
  <PATHWAY>PURINE METABOLISM</PATHWAY>
</GENE>
<GENE>
  <NAME>PTR2</NAME>
  <DESCRIPTION>SMALL PEPTIDE PERMEASE</DESCRIPTION>
  <PATHWAY>TRANSPORT</PATHWAY>
</GENE>
</collection>
```

The “collection/*[1]/*” pattern consists of three parts. The entire path refers to an element at the third level of depth in the element tree. Each part refers to an element (or elements) and the slash “/” means to match the next part against the children of the already selected element (or elements). The three parts are:

1. Match the element type “collection”.
2. Match the first child of that element, denoted by “/*[1]”. Literally, of all the children of that element, choose the one that is first in sibling order.
3. Match all children of that element, denoted by “/*”.

Thus, the first step matches:

```
<collection>
 ...
</collection>
```

The second step matches:

```
<GENE>
  <NAME>PDE1</NAME>
  <DESCRIPTION>PHOSPHODIESTERASE</DESCRIPTION>
  <PATHWAY>PURINE METABOLISM</PATHWAY>
</GENE>
```

The third step matches the three elements:

```
<NAME>...</NAME>
<DESCRIPTION>...</DESCRIPTION>
<PATHWAY>...</PATHWAY>
```

Those three elements are iterated over by the "for-each" command and each element type name is extracted using the "node-name" command resulting in the column headings: "Name", "Description", and "Pathway".

The second template in the stylesheet is actually a little simpler. It is:

```
<xsl:template match="collection">
  <xsl:for-each select="*">
    <TR>
      <xsl:for-each select="*">
        <TD>
          <xsl:value-of select="." />
        </TD>
      </xsl:for-each>
    </TR>
  </xsl:for-each>
</xsl:template>
```

The HTML code emits a single row for each element in the collection:

```
For each element in the collection,
  <TR>
    For each subelement (i.e., column element),
      <TD>
        Value of the character data in the column goes
          here.
      </TD>
  </TR>
```

The XSL code is two nested "for" loops:

```
<xsl:template match="collection">
  <xsl:for-each select="*">
    <xsl:for-each select="*">
      <xsl:value-of select="." />
    </xsl:for-each>
  </xsl:for-each>
</xsl:template>
```

The outer "for-each" loop matches all of the elements in the collection, denoted by "*" in the select attribute. For the gene collection example, the loop matches each of the "gene" elements, including the one already used by the root template to extract the column names:

```
<GENE>
 ...
</GENE>
<GENE>
 ...
</GENE>
<GENE>
 ...
</GENE>
```

The inner "for-each" loop matches all of the elements within the "gene" element, for example:

```
<NAME>PDE1</NAME>
<DESCRIPTION>PHOSPHODIESTERASE</DESCRIPTION>
<PATHWAY>PURINE METABOLISM</PATHWAY>
```

The "<xsl:value-of select="." />" command emits the text value of the current node, in effect, the character data between the start and end tags. The current node is denoted by the ".". In this example, the values that are matched in the loop are: "PDE1", "PHOSPHODIESTERASE", and "PURINE METABOLISM".

The entire stylesheet in Example 7–1, when processed with the example data in Example 7–3, results in the HTML given in Example 7–4.

Example 7–3 : Example Biological Data in XML

```
<?xml version="1.0"?>
<?xml:stylesheet type="text/xsl" href="http://127.0.0.1/ss/
simple.xsl"?>
<collection>
<GENE>
  <NAME>PDE1</NAME>
  <DESCRIPTION>3',5'-CYCLIC-NUCLEOTIDE PHOSPHODIESTERASE</DESCRIPTION>
  <PATHWAY>PURINE METABOLISM</PATHWAY>
</GENE>
<GENE>
  <NAME>PTR2</NAME>
  <DESCRIPTION>SMALL PEPTIDE PERMEASE</DESCRIPTION>
  <PATHWAY>TRANSPORT</PATHWAY>
</GENE>
<GENE>
  <NAME>PIS1</NAME>
  <DESCRIPTION>PHOSPHATIDYLINOSITOL SYNTHASE</DESCRIPTION>
  <PATHWAY>PHOSPHOLIPID METABOLISM</PATHWAY>
</GENE>
</collection>
```

Example 7–4 : HTML Table of Biological Data

```
   <TABLE STYLE="border:1px solid black" BORDER="1">
      <TR STYLE="font-weight:bold; text-decoration:underline">
          <TD>NAME</TD>
          <TD>DESCRIPTION</TD>
          <TD>PATHWAY</TD>
      </TR>
        <TR>
            <TD>PDE1</TD>
            <TD>3',5'-CYCLIC-NUCLEOTIDE PHOSPHODIESTERASE</TD>
            <TD>PURINE METABOLISM</TD>
        </TR>
        <TR>
            <TD>PTR2</TD>
            <TD>SMALL PEPTIDE PERMEASE</TD>
            <TD>TRANSPORT</TD>
        </TR>
        <TR>
            <TD>PIS1</TD>
            <TD>PHOSPHATIDYLINOSITOL SYNTHASE</TD>
            <TD>PHOSPHOLIPID METABOLISM</TD>
        </TR>
   </TABLE>
```

The XSLT version Example 7–2 differs from the IE5 XSL version in Example 7–1 in four ways:

- The XSLT namespace is changed to

```
"http://www.w3.org/1999/XSL/Transform".
```

- A version attribute is added to the stylesheet processing command, in effect,

```
<xsl:stylesheet version="1.0"
xmlns:xsl="http://www.w3.org/1999/XSL/Transform">
```

- An output element is defined, which looks like this for HTML output:

```
<xsl:output method="html"/>
```

- The node-name command is replaced with a call to a "name()" function by a "value-of" call; in effect, "<xsl:node-name/>" is replaced with

```
<xsl:value-of select="name()"/>
```

7.2.3 Rendering XML Fragment as a Record

In addition to the table-oriented view of the data, it can be useful to present a record-oriented view when the collection of data contains only one record, or when the user wishes to examine a row of the table in more depth. A record-oriented presentation is especially useful if the table presentation is significantly wider than what the browser can display.

An XSL fragment to create the record presented in Figure 7–2 is given in Example 7–5. To determine whether a collection has more than one element in the IE5 version of XSL, a test is done to see if a second child exists "<xsl:when test="*[1]">". The children are numbered beginning with 0, so the second child is at position 1. The XSLT version has a function, called count, to count the number of children, and XSLT begins number children with "1". The XSLT version of the fragment in Example 7–5 is given in Example 7–6.

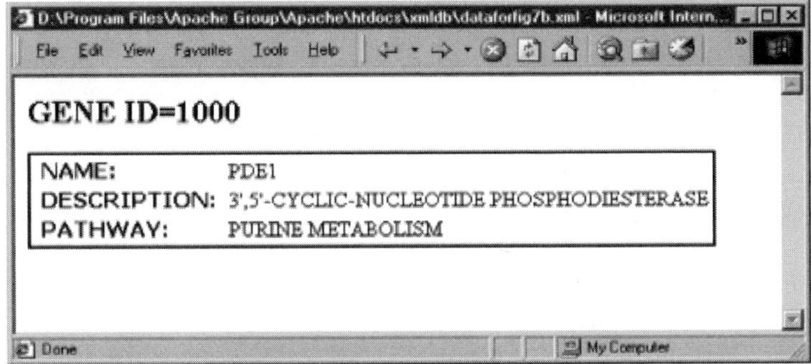

Figure 7–2 Record of biological data generated using XSL

Example 7–5 : Stylesheet to Transform XML Data to HTML Record (IE5)

```
<h2><xsl:for-each select="*[0]"><xsl:node-name/></xsl:for-each></h2>
<TABLE STYLE="border:2px solid black">
   <xsl:for-each select="*[0]/*">
   <TR>
     <TD STYLE="font-weight:bold">
       <xsl:node-name/>:</TD>
       <TD>
         <xsl:value-of select="."/>
      </TD>
   </TR>
   </xsl:for-each>
</TABLE>
```

Example 7–6 : Stylesheet to Transform XML Data to HTML Record (XSLT)

```
<h2><xsl:value-of select="name(*[1])"/> </h2>
<TABLE STYLE="border:2px solid black">
   <xsl:for-each select="*[1]/*">
   <TR>
     <TD STYLE="font-weight:bold">
      <xsl:value-of select="name()"/>:</TD>
       <TD>
         <xsl:value-of select="."/>
      </TD>
   </TR>
   </xsl:for-each>
</TABLE>
```

7.2.4 Rendering Identifiers and Proxies as Hypertext Links

When records in a database have a unique identifier, that identifier may be presented to the user as part of the table to allow for selection and display of only the data in that record. In the stylesheet of Example 7–7, the identifier is assumed to be an "ID" attribute of the corresponding element and is presented as the first column in the table. The stylesheet can be modified to create a hypertext link for the identifier that retrieves the complete record from the database, such as is shown in Figure 7–3. The XSLT version of the stylesheet is in Example 7–8.

Example 7–7 : Stylesheet to Transform XML Data to HTML Table with Identifiers (IE5)

```
<?xml version="1.0"?>
<xsl:stylesheet xmlns:xsl="http://www.w3.org/TR/WD-xsl">
  <xsl:template match="/">
      <xsl:apply-templates />
  </xsl:template>
  <xsl:template match="collection">
    <h2><xsl:for-each select="*[0]"><xsl:node-name/></xsl:for-each>
LISTING</h2>
    <TABLE STYLE="border:5px solid black" BORDER="1">
      <TR STYLE="font-size:12pt; font-family:Verdana; font-
weight:bold; text-decoration:underline">
        <TD STYLE="background-color:lightgrey">ID</TD>
          <xsl:for-each select="*[0]/*">
          <TD><xsl:node-name/></TD>
            </xsl:for-each>
      </TR>
      <xsl:for-each select="*">
        <TR STYLE="font-family:Verdana; font-size:12pt; padding:0px 6px">
          <TD STYLE="background-color:lightgrey">
            <xsl:value-of select="@id"/>
          </TD>
          <xsl:for-each select="*">
                  <TD>
              <xsl:value-of select="."/>
            </TD>
          </xsl:for-each>
        </TR>
      </xsl:for-each>
     </TABLE>
  </xsl:template>
</xsl:stylesheet>
```

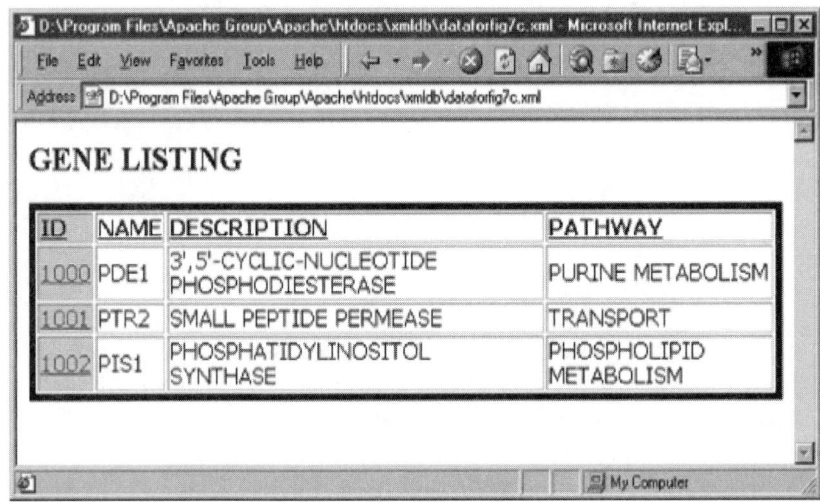

Figure 7–3 Table with identifiers of biological data generated using XSL

Example 7–8 : Stylesheet to Transform XML Data to HTML Table with Identifiers (XSLT)

```
<xsl:stylesheet version="1.0" xmlns:xsl="http://www.w3.org/1999/XSL/
Transform">
  <xsl:output method="html"/>
  <xsl:template match="/">
    <xsl:apply-templates/>
  </xsl:template>
  <xsl:template match="collection">
    <h2><xsl:value-of select="name(*[1])"/> LISTING</h2>
    <TABLE STYLE="border:5px solid black" BORDER="1">
      <TR STYLE="font-size:12pt; font-family:Verdana; font-
weight:bold; text-decoration:underline">
        <TD STYLE="background-color:lightgrey">ID</TD>
          <xsl:for-each select="*[1]/*">
          <TD><xsl:value-of select="name()"/></TD>
            </xsl:for-each>
      </TR>
      <xsl:for-each select="*">
        <TR STYLE="font-family:Verdana; font-size:12pt; padding:0px 6px">
          <TD STYLE="background-color:lightgrey">
            <xsl:value-of select="@id"/>
          </TD>
          <xsl:for-each select="*">
```

```
            <TD>
              <xsl:value-of select="."/>
            </TD>
          </xsl:for-each>
        </TR>
      </xsl:for-each>
    </TABLE>
  </xsl:template>
</xsl:stylesheet>
```

The hypertext link to extract a record for a unique identifier is a special case of using drill-down. *Drill-down* is a mechanism to examine some part of a collection of data in more detail. Drill-down is useful when more data is available than can be presented in a two-dimensional table.

When a document has many levels of embedded elements, it may be wasteful to send all the levels to the user interface, especially if the display presents only the topmost element. A *proxy* element may be used, which substitutes for an XML fragment and contains enough information to retrieve that fragment if needed. For a relational database, the name of the table and a primary key value are sufficient. For an XML database, a unique fragment identifier is used.

A proxy may be expanded by an application while rendering the data in the user interface by retrieving the appropriate fragment as needed. An HTML browser provides a easy mechanism through hypertext links where the user can drill-down into the information contained by the proxies. For example, the XML element

```
<proxy tablename="exper_result" id="1024"/>
```

may be transformed using the following XSL stylesheet template into a hypertext link:

```
<xsl:template match="proxy">
    <xsl:element name="a">
        <xsl:attribute name="href">
        http://127.0.0.1com.xweave.xmldb.rserve.XMLServlet?
          tablename=<xsl:value-of select="@tablename"/>&amp;
          id=<xsl:value-of select="@id">
          &amp;
          stylesheet=
          http://127.0.0.1/ss/generic.xsl
        </xsl:attribute>
```

```
    <xsl:value-of select="@id"/>
      </xsl:element>
    </xsl:template>
```

The template creates an HTML element with element type name "a" and one attribute "href" to create a hypertext link with text value being the value of the "ID" attribute of the proxy. The HTML has the sections for the base URL, tablename, ID, and stylesheet arguments. The "&" encoding is translated to the "&" character and the resulting HTML (with line breaks added to be more readable) looks like this:

```
<a href="http://127.0.0.1/com.xweave.xmldb.rserve.XMLServlet?
tablename=_________&id=________________&
stylesheet=http://127.0.0.1/ss/generic.xsl">
id goes here as text
</a>
```

The HTML results in hypertext links being displayed in the Web browser.

The XSL stylesheet in Example 7–9 emits an HTML table with proxies and drill-down.

Example 7–9 : Stylesheet to Transform XML Data to HTML Table with Drill-down

```
<?xml version="1.0"?>
<xsl:stylesheet xmlns:xsl="http://www.w3.org/TR/WD-xsl">
  <xsl:template match="/">
      <xsl:apply-templates />
  </xsl:template>
  <xsl:template match="collection">
    <h2><xsl:for-each select="*[0]"><xsl:node-name/></xsl:for-each>
LISTING</h2>
    <TABLE STYLE="border:5px solid black" BORDER="1">
      <TR STYLE="font-size:12pt; font-family:Verdana; font-
weight:bold; text-decoration:underline">
        <TD STYLE="background-color:lightgrey">ID</TD>
          <xsl:for-each select="*[0]/*">
          <TD><xsl:node-name/></TD>
            </xsl:for-each>
      </TR>
      <xsl:for-each select="*">
        <TR STYLE="font-family:Verdana; font-size:12pt; padding:0px 6px">
          <TD STYLE="background-color:lightgrey">
             <xsl:element name="a">
```

```
            <xsl:attribute
            name="href">http:/servlets/com.xweave.xmldb.rserve.xmlservlet?
            tablename=<xsl:node-name/>&amp;
            id=<xsl:value-of select="@id"/>&amp;
            stylesheet=http:/ss/generic.xsl
                </xsl:attribute>
                <xsl:value-of select="@id"/>
            </xsl:element>
          </TD>
          <xsl:for-each select="*">
          <TD>
            <xsl:choose>
            <xsl:when test="text()"><xsl:value-of select="."/></xsl:when>
            <xsl:when test="proxy"><xsl:apply-templates /></xsl:when>
            <xsl:when test="node()">
               <xsl:element name="a">
                   <xsl:attribute
name="href">http:/servlets/com.xweave.xmldb.rserve.xmlservlet?
tablename=<xsl:for-each select="*[0]"><xsl:node-name/></xsl:for-each>&amp;
id=<xsl:value-of select="./*/@id"/>&amp;stylesheet=http:/ss/generic.xsl
                </xsl:attribute>
                <xsl:choose>
                <xsl:when test="./*/@id"><xsl:value-of select="./*/@id"/>
                </xsl:when>
                <xsl:otherwise><xsl:value-of select="."/></xsl:otherwise>
                </xsl:choose>
               </xsl:element>
            </xsl:when>
            <xsl:otherwise><xsl:value-of select="."/></xsl:otherwise>
            </xsl:choose>
          </TD>
          </xsl:for-each>
        </TR>
      </xsl:for-each>
     </TABLE>
  </xsl:template>
</xsl:stylesheet>
```

7.2.5 Varying Presentation Based on Content

The stylesheet in Example 7–10 provides a record presentation when there is exactly one record in the collection and a tabular presentation when more than one record is in the collection. It also supports the use of proxies.

Example 7–10 : Generic Stylesheet to Transform XML Data to HTML Record or Table with Drill-down

```
<?xml version="1.0"?>
<xsl:stylesheet xmlns:xsl="http://www.w3.org/TR/WD-xsl">
  <xsl:template match="/">
      <xsl:apply-templates />
  </xsl:template>
  <xsl:template match="collection">
  <xsl:choose>
  <xsl:when test="error">
     <xsl:copy>Error: <xsl:value-of select="*/@msg" /></xsl:copy>
  </xsl:when>
  <xsl:when test="*[1]">
    <h2><xsl:for-each select="*[0]"><xsl:node-name/></xsl:for-each>
LISTING</h2>
    <TABLE STYLE="border:5px solid black" BORDER="1">
      <TR STYLE="font-size:12pt; font-family:Verdana; font-weight:bold;
text-decoration:underline">
        <TD STYLE="background-color:lightgrey">ID</TD>
           <xsl:for-each select="*[0]/*">
          <TD><xsl:node-name/></TD>
            </xsl:for-each>
      </TR>
      <xsl:for-each select="*">
        <TR STYLE="font-family:Verdana; font-size:12pt; padding:0px 6px">
          <TD STYLE="background-color:lightgrey">
             <xsl:element name="a">
                <xsl:attribute
name="href">http:/servlets/com.xweave.xmldb.rserve?
tablename=<xsl:node-name/>&amp;id=<xsl:value-of select="@id"/>&amp;
stylesheet=http:/ss/generic2.xsl
                </xsl:attribute>
                <xsl:value-of select="@id"/>
            </xsl:element>
          </TD>
          <xsl:for-each select="*">
          <TD>
```

```
            <xsl:choose>
            <xsl:when test="text()"><xsl:value-of select="."/></xsl:when>
            <xsl:when test="proxy"><xsl:apply-templates /></xsl:when>
            <xsl:when test="node()">
               <xsl:element name="a">
                   <xsl:attribute
name="href">http:/servlets/com.xweave.xmldb.rserve?
tablename=<xsl:for-each select="*[0]"><xsl:node-name/></xsl:for-each>&amp;
id=<xsl:value-of select="./*/@id"/>&amp;stylesheet=http:/ss/generic2.xsl
                   </xsl:attribute>
                   <xsl:choose>
                    <xsl:when test="./*/@id"><xsl:value-of select="./*/
@id"/>
                    </xsl:when>
                    <xsl:otherwise><xsl:value-of select="."/></
xsl:otherwise>
                   </xsl:choose>
               </xsl:element>
            </xsl:when>
            <xsl:otherwise><xsl:value-of select="."/></xsl:otherwise>
            </xsl:choose>
          </TD>
          </xsl:for-each>
        </TR>
      </xsl:for-each>
     </TABLE>
  </xsl:when>
  <xsl:otherwise>
    <h2><xsl:for-each select="*[0]"><xsl:node-name/></xsl:for-each>
ID=<xsl:value-of
select="*[0]/@id"/></h2>
    <TABLE STYLE="border:2px solid black">
        <xsl:for-each select="*[0]/*">
        <TR>
          <TD STYLE="font-family:Verdana; font-size:12pt; font-weight:bold;
padding:0px 6px">
            <xsl:node-name/>:</TD>
      <TD>
      <xsl:choose>
        <xsl:when test="text()"><xsl:value-of select="."/></xsl:when>
        <xsl:when test="proxy"><xsl:apply-templates /></xsl:when>
        <xsl:when test="node()">
          <xsl:element name="a">
```

```
        <xsl:attribute
name="href">http:/servlets/com.xweave.xmldb.rserve?tablename=<xsl:for-each
select="*[0]"><xsl:node-name/></xsl:for-each>&amp;id=<xsl:value-of
select="./*/@id"/>&amp;stylesheet=http:/ss/generic2.xsl
          </xsl:attribute>
          <xsl:choose>
          <xsl:when test="./*/@id"><xsl:value-of select="./*/@id"/></xsl:when>
          <xsl:otherwise><xsl:value-of select="."/></xsl:otherwise>
           </xsl:choose>
             </xsl:element>
            </xsl:when>
       <xsl:when test="node()">
       <xsl:element name="a">
       <xsl:attribute
name="href">http:/servlets/com.xweave.xmldb.rserve?
tablename=<xsl:value-of select ="./@tablename"/>&amp;
id=<xsl:value-of select="./@id"/>&amp;stylesheet=http:/ss/generic2.xsl
                </xsl:attribute>
           <xsl:value-of select="."/>
             </xsl:element>
            </xsl:when>
           <xsl:otherwise><xsl:value-of select="."/></xsl:otherwise>
           </xsl:choose>
           </TD>
        </TR>
        </xsl:for-each>
     </TABLE>
     </xsl:otherwise>
  </xsl:choose>
  </xsl:template>
  <xsl:template match="proxy">
     <xsl:element name="a">
         <xsl:attribute
name="href">http:/servlets/com.xweave.xmldb.rserve?
tablename=<xsl:value-of select ="@tablename"/>&amp;
id=<xsl:value-of select="@id"/>&amp;stylesheet=http:/ss/generic2.xsl
         </xsl:attribute>
     <xsl:value-of select="@id"/>
     </xsl:element>
  </xsl:template>
</xsl:stylesheet>
```

One of the advantages of using XSL stylesheets with the XML is that customized presentations may be used in addition to the generic rendering. The information in an element may be sufficient to render the data in a graphical form, to plot the data, or to augment the data with additional queries or functionality.

One way to augment the XML is to create an alternative rendering for elements with a specific tag. For example, the presentation of the individual record in the generic stylesheet in Figure 7–2 may be appended with choices based on the element type name of the element to create HTML forms that provide additional functionality via CGI programs. For example, the following XSL fragment can be used to add a comment to an experimental result:

```
<xsl:choose>
  <xsl:when test="EXPER_RESULT">
  <form action="/cgi-bin/add_comment" method="POST">
    <hidden name="tablename" value="EXPER_RESULT" />
    <xsl:element name="hidden">
      <xsl:attribute name="name">id</xsl:attribute>
      <xsl:attribute name="value">
        <xsl:value-of select="EXPER_RESULT/@id"/>
      </xsl:attribute>
    </xsl:element>
    <textarea name="comment" rows="5" cols="60">
    </textarea>
    <p>
    <input type="submit" name="Submit" value="Add
      comment to Experimental Result"/>
    </p>
  </form>
  </xsl:when>
</xsl:choose>
```

The resulting display is shown in Figure 7–4.

Additional information can be added to the display based on information in the database. In addition to CGI scripts, additional information from the schema may be included. For example, the drill-downs based on a foreign key constraint in a relational database provide a link to a detail table, which provides additional information on the value in the current table. Foreign key constraint can be followed in the opposite direction to provide information on tables that refer to the current entry. For example, an employee database in a company may have many tables supporting a variety of applications that refer to the employee ID as a foreign key constraint. The "drill-up" information can be used to examine the applications

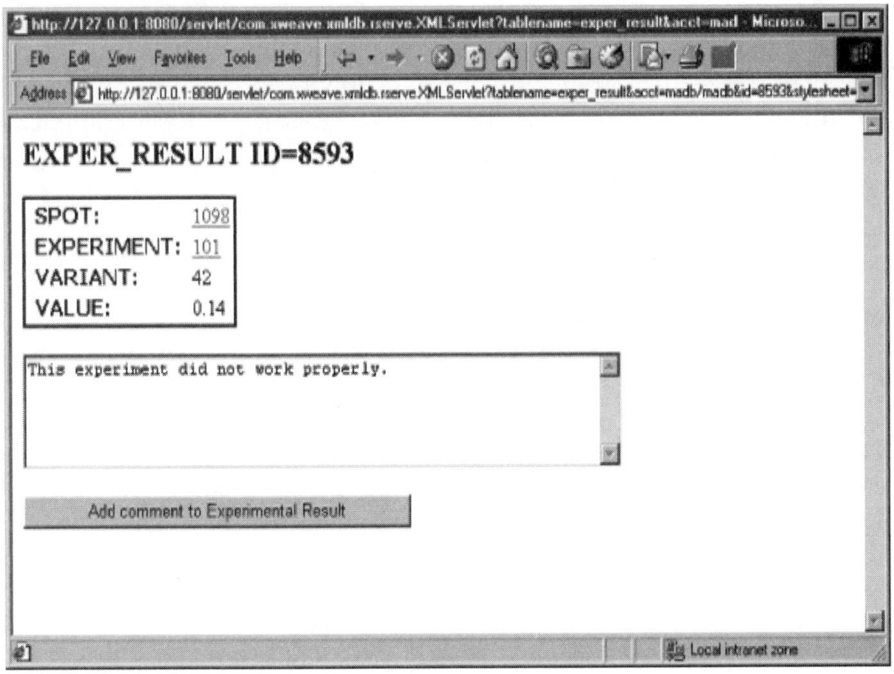

Figure 7–4 Record with form to enter comment

in which a employee is participating, even if the participating application was developed after the current one was implemented. In a biology database, the gene table may be referred to by several other components of the database and browsing the "drill-up" information can illuminate previously unknown relationships.

7.3 Java-based Visualizations

Java-based user interfaces provide another way of interacting with XML databases. Java, or another programming language, can be used to implement editors, data entry applications, visualization tools, report generators, process management software, or other clients that interact with an XML database. Java applets or applications can be used to implement the client depending upon whether the client is to be Web-delivered. Clients interact with the database using commands and XML and with the user via the user interface. The interaction process between a DBMS and client is described in Chapter 5. This chapter focuses on the internal architecture and functionality of the client. This section describes applications that display XML from the database, and the next section describes the creation of applications that interact with the database.

7.3.1 Client Architecture

The simplest client architecture displays XML to the user with no editing or further DBMS interactions. The Java client must first parse the XML before displaying a user interface. There are two major types of XML parsers. The first is a tree-based parser, such as a DOM parser, which would create a tree of the XML document. After parsing is completed, the client creates a display. The second kind of parser is a SAX parser, which is an event-based parser (it creates events while parsing the document). At key locations in the document—such as start and end tags or character data regions—events are created by the parser and passed to an application-specific document handler. The application-specific handler uses the data associated with the event, such as element type name or character data, to create a custom data structure or perform other actions. In the visualization display, the handler would directly create the display without creating a data structure to contain the entire document.

The SAX parser is used in several applications in the book and is explained more fully in Appendix B. The example in Appendix B shows how to immediately print the element type names of the document, which demonstrates a rudimentary display. More realistic displays will need to create a temporary data structure to capture some data from the document to be combined with data occurring later in the document before creating the display. Those data structures can be incorporated into the Document Handler, which the SAX parser uses to handle application-specific code. The SAX parser uses generic code to parse the document, then calls methods in the Document Handler based on the content of the document, as described in Appendix B. For example, a Document Handler that keeps a stack of element type names is presented in Example 7–11. The stack is used to verify the validity of the element type name nesting and to track the depth of the tree. The stack of element type names is defined by the class, pushed in the start element method, popped in the end element method, and accessed in the start element and characters method.

Example 7–11 : SAX-based Application Using a Stack

```
/************************* Test.java ***********************/
package com.xweave.xmldb.ui.test2;

import org.xml.sax.*;
import org.xml.sax.helpers.ParserFactory;
import org.w3c.dom.Document;
import java.io.IOException;
import com.ibm.xml.parsers.*;
// requires IBM XML4j parser in classpath
/*
 * Example class to demonstrate parsing a XML document with
 * a SAX Parser (IBM XML4J is used)
 */
public class Test {
public Test() {
   super();
}
public static void main(java.lang.String[] args) {
   String fileName = null;
   if (args.length < 1) {
      System.err.println("Test: requires <file> as argument");
      //fileName = "file:///C:/Temp/test.xml";
      //fileName = "file:///D:/Temp/test.xml";
      //fileName = "http://127.0.0.1/servlets/
com.xweave.xmldb.rserve.XMLServlet?tablename=emp&acct=scott/tiger";
      fileName = "http://127.0.0.1:8080/servlet/
com.xweave.xmldb.rserve.XMLServlet?tablename=emp&acct=scott/tiger";
      //return;
   } else {
      fileName = args[0];
   }
   (new Test()).parse(fileName);
}
public void parse(String xmlFile) {
   //This class may be any SAX parser, but the classpath
   // must be modified to include it.
   String parserClass = "com.ibm.xml.parsers.SAXParser";
   try {
      Parser parser = ParserFactory.makeParser(parserClass);
      HandlerBase handler = new TreeHandler();
      parser.setDocumentHandler(handler);
      parser.setErrorHandler(handler);
      try {
```

```
            parser.parse(xmlFile);
         } catch (SAXException se) {
            se.printStackTrace();
         } catch (IOException ioe) {
            ioe.printStackTrace();
         }
      } catch (ClassNotFoundException ex) {
         ex.printStackTrace();
      } catch (IllegalAccessException ex) {
         ex.printStackTrace();
      } catch (InstantiationException ex) {
         ex.printStackTrace();
      }
}
}
/************************ TreeHandler.java **********************/
package com.xweave.xmldb.ui.test2;

/**
 * Test Handler that prints debug statements
 */
import org.xml.sax.*;
import java.util.*;
class TreeHandler extends org.xml.sax.HandlerBase implements
org.xml.sax.DocumentHandler {
   protected Stack parentStack = null;
public TreeHandler() {
   super();
}
public void characters(char[] chars, int start, int length) {
   String string = new String(chars, start, length);
   string = string.trim();
   //skip whitespace
   if (string.length() == 0) return;
   int depth = getParentStack().size();
   for (int i = 0; i <= depth; i++)
      System.out.print(' ');
   System.out.println('"'+string+'"');
}
public void endElement(String tag) {
   String currentParent = getCurrentParent();
   if (tag.equalsIgnoreCase(currentParent)) {
      getParentStack().pop();
   } else {
      System.err.println("Error at end tag: expected "+currentParent+"
```

```
found "+tag);
   }
}
public String getCurrentParent() {
   String currentParent;
   try {
      currentParent = (String) getParentStack().peek();
   } catch (EmptyStackException ex) {
      currentParent = null;
   }
   return currentParent;
}
public Stack getParentStack() {
   if (parentStack == null) {
      parentStack = new Stack();
   }
   return parentStack;
}
public void startElement(String tag, AttributeList attrList) {
   String currentParent = getCurrentParent();
   int depth = getParentStack().size();
   for (int i = 0; i <= depth; i++)
      System.out.print(' ');
   System.out.println(tag);
   getParentStack().push(tag);
}
}
```

7.3.2 Tree Example

A more realistic application is given in Example 7–12, which creates a tree representation of an XML document using JTree in Swing. A UML diagram for the Java implementation is given in Figure 7–5. A visualization of the tree is shown in Figure 7–6.

Example 7–12 : SAX-based Application Using Swing to Display Element Tree

```
/************************ Runner.java **********************/
package com.xweave.xmldb.ui.tree;

import org.xml.sax.*;
import org.xml.sax.helpers.ParserFactory;
```

```
import org.w3c.dom.Document;
import java.io.IOException;
import com.ibm.xml.parsers.*;
import com.sun.java.swing.*;
//import javax.swing.*;
import com.sun.java.swing.tree.*;
//import javax.swing.tree.*;
/*
 * Example class to demonstrate parsing a XML document with
 * a SAX Parser (IBM XML4J is used) to create a JTree
 *
 * Note: requires IBM XML4j parser in classpath
 */
public class Runner {
   protected DefaultTreeModel treeModel = null;
   protected JTree treeView = null;
public Runner() {
   super();
}
public void display() {
   JFrame frame = new JFrame();
   JTree tree = getTreeView();
   frame.setSize(400,300);
   frame.getContentPane().add(tree);
   frame.setVisible(true);
}
public DefaultTreeModel getTreeModel() {
   if (treeModel == null) {
      DefaultMutableTreeNode root = new
DefaultMutableTreeNode("Root");
      treeModel = new DefaultTreeModel(root);
   }
   return treeModel;
}
public JTree getTreeView() {
   if (treeView == null) {
      treeView = new JTree(getTreeModel());
   }
   return treeView;
}
public static void main(java.lang.String[] args) {
   // Insert code to start the application here.
   String fileName = null;
   if (args.length < 1) {
      System.err.println("Test: requires <file> as argument");
```

```
      //fileName = "file:///C:/Temp/test.xml";
      //fileName = "file:///D:/Temp/test.xml";
      //fileName = "http://127.0.0.1/servlets/
com.xweave.xmldb.rserve.XMLServlet?tablename=emp&acct=scott/tiger";
      fileName = "http://127.0.0.1:8080/servlet/
com.xweave.xmldb.rserve.XMLServlet?tablename=emp&acct=scott/tiger";
      //return;
   } else {
      fileName = args[0];
   }
   Runner runner = new Runner();
   runner.parse(fileName);
   runner.display();
}
public void parse(String xmlFile) {
   //This class may be any SAX parser, but the classpath
   // must be modified to include it.
   String parserClass = "com.ibm.xml.parsers.SAXParser";
   try {
      Parser parser = ParserFactory.makeParser(parserClass);
      HandlerBase handler = new TreeHandler(getTreeModel());
      parser.setDocumentHandler(handler);
      parser.setErrorHandler(handler);
      try {
         parser.parse(xmlFile);
      } catch (SAXException se) {
         se.printStackTrace();
      } catch (IOException ioe) {
         ioe.printStackTrace();
      }
   } catch (ClassNotFoundException ex) {
      ex.printStackTrace();
   } catch (IllegalAccessException ex) {
      ex.printStackTrace();
   } catch (InstantiationException ex) {
      ex.printStackTrace();
   }
}
}
/************************* TreeHandler.java **********************/
package com.xweave.xmldb.ui.tree;

/**
 * Handler that creates a JTree
 */
```

```
import org.xml.sax.*;
import java.util.*;
import com.sun.java.swing.tree.*;
//import javax.swing.tree.*;
class TreeHandler extends org.xml.sax.HandlerBase implements
org.xml.sax.DocumentHandler {
   protected Stack parentStack = null;
   public DefaultTreeModel treeModel;
public TreeHandler(TreeModel treeModel) {
   super();
   this.treeModel = (DefaultTreeModel) treeModel;
}
public void characters(char[] chars, int start, int length) {
   String string = new String(chars, start, length);
   string = string.trim();
   //skip whitespace
   if (string.length() == 0) return;
   MutableTreeNode currentParent = getCurrentParent();
   MutableTreeNode node = new DefaultMutableTreeNode(string);
   treeModel.insertNodeInto(node, currentParent,
currentParent.getChildCount());
}
public void endElement(String tag) {
   MutableTreeNode currentParent = getCurrentParent();
   if (tag.equalsIgnoreCase(currentParent.toString())) {
      getParentStack().pop();
   } else {
      System.err.println("Error at end tag: expected
"+currentParent.toString()+" found "+tag);
   }
}
public MutableTreeNode getCurrentParent() {
   MutableTreeNode currentParent;
   try {
      currentParent = (MutableTreeNode) getParentStack().peek();
   } catch (EmptyStackException ex) {
      currentParent = (MutableTreeNode) getTreeModel().getRoot();
   }
   return currentParent;
}
public Stack getParentStack() {
   if (parentStack == null) {
      parentStack = new Stack();
   }
   return parentStack;
```

```
}
public TreeModel getTreeModel() {
   return treeModel;
}
public void startElement(String tag, AttributeList attrList) {
   MutableTreeNode currentParent = getCurrentParent();
   MutableTreeNode node = new DefaultMutableTreeNode(tag);
   treeModel.insertNodeInto(node, currentParent,
currentParent.getChildCount());
   getParentStack().push(node);
}
}
```

Runner

+Runner()
+display():void
+main(args:java.lang.String[]):void
+parse(xmlFile:String):void
treeModel:DefaultTreeModel
treeView:JTree

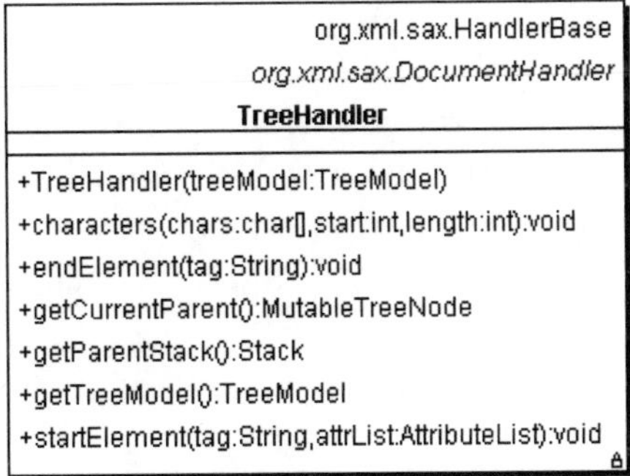

Figure 7–5 UML diagram of an application to display element tree

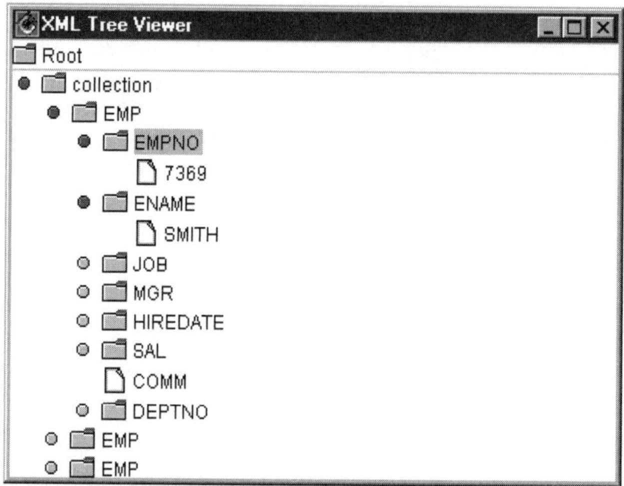

Figure 7–6 XML Tree Viewer display using Swing JTree

The TreeHandler is a subclass of org.xml.sax.HandlerBase and imports a SAX parser (from IBM) and the Swing JTree class from the package "javax.swing.tree.*" for Java 2 or the package "com.sun.java.swing.tree.*" for Java 1.1.x with Swing 1.0.x. It implements the org.xml.sax.DocumentHandler interface and creates a variable to contain an instance of java.util.Stack. It also creates an instance variable for a Swing DefaultTreeModel of which the JTree is a view. Swing uses the model-view-controller paradigm where the data structure capturing the information (model) is isolated from the visualization of the data (view). Thus, to present information using Swing both a model class (DefaultTreeModel) and a view class (JTree) must be created.

In addition to access methods for the instance variables, the methods for the handler are defined: start element, end element, and characters. The start element method creates a node in the tree for the current element as a child of the parent node. The parent node is the top element of the stack or a root node created as the top of the document tree. The current element is then pushed onto the stack. When a character data region occurs in the parsing of the document, the characters method is called that creates a (leaf) node for the character data region. The end element method pops the stack of elements.

There are three parts to the application or applet: User Interface, Parser, and Document Handler. The process consists of

1. Creating an instance of the Parser. The code from Runner#parse (i.e., the parse method of Runner) is

```
String parserClass = "com.ibm.xml.parsers.SAXParser";
Parser parser = ParserFactory.makeParser(parserClass);
```

2. Creating and initializing an instance of the Document Handler. The code from Runner#parse is

```
HandlerBase handler = new TreeHandler(getTreeModel());
```

3. Initializing the Parser to use the Document Handler. The code from Runner#parse is

```
parser.setDocumentHandler(handler);
parser.setErrorHandler(handler);
```

4. Calling the Parser with the XML URL. The code from Runner#parse is

```
public void parse(String xmlFile) {
  ...
  parser.parse(xmlFile);
  ...
}
```

5. The Parser retrieves and parses the document, calling the Handler at

   – The beginning of each element. The code to do that is in TreeHandler#startElement:

   ```
   public void startElement(String tag, AttributeList attrList)
     {
     MutableTreeNode currentParent = getCurrentParent();
     MutableTreeNode node = new
     DefaultMutableTreeNode(tag);
     treeModel.insertNodeInto(node, currentParent,
     currentParent.getChildCount());
     getParentStack().push(node);
   }
   ```

   The method gets the current parent node from the getCurrentParent accessor, creates a node in the tree model, then pushes itself on the stack.

- The end of each character data region. The code to do that is in TreeHandler#characters

```
public void characters(char[] chars, int start, int length)
  {
  String string = new String(chars, start, length);
  string = string.trim();
  //skip whitespace
  if (string.length() == 0) return;
  MutableTreeNode currentParent = getCurrentParent();
  MutableTreeNode node = new DefaultMutableTreeNode(string);
  treeModel.insertNodeInto(node, currentParent,
  currentParent.getChildCount());
}
```

The characters method trims whitespace and creates a node in the tree for the character data region.

- The end of each element. The code to do that is in TreeHandler#endElement:

```
public void endElement(String tag) {
  MutableTreeNode currentParent = getCurrentParent();
  if (tag.equalsIgnoreCase(currentParent.toString()))
  {
    getParentStack().pop();
  } else {
    System.err.println("Error at end tag: expected
      "+currentParent.toString()+" found "+tag);
  }
}
```

The end element pops the stack and verifies that the stack and document are consistent.

6. After the visualization is created, the user interface is displayed to the user. The code to do that is in Runner#display, which is called from Runner#main.

Similar code can be used to generate a table, such as the table provided by JTable in Swing or a commercial widget (possibly implemented as a Java Bean). The table can be augmented to use active buttons to allow for drill-downs, much as hypertext links in HTML do. In addition, some of the default cells may be replaced with custom widgets to provide interactive visualizations of the data, for example, a widget to display a 3D rotating chemical structure that could be used in a chemistry database application.

Widgets can be connected to the type names of the elements either directly in the Java code or through a mapping stored in a repository or database. Although that mapping could be hard-coded, if the applications are undergoing rapid development, it may be useful to have the mappings stored in the database. Thus, new widgets may be added to the user interface without modifying the Java code. In addition, when the XML is schema-driven, a completely new custom interface may be deployed by augmenting the schema and adding an entry to the widget mapping database.

To modify the display to handle widgets, the "startElement" method of the parser is modified to handle specific tags through alternative code. The widget display could be a hard-coded switch statement or a lookup table that was initialized from a database of widget mappings. The widget mapping can occur in one table that contains the element type name and the Java class to use. With a widget mapping database, the widgets may be selected from a predetermined set of Java classes or dynamically loaded using "classForName". For simple widgets, the element type name and attribute list may suffice as parameters. In more complex examples, a temporary data structure may need to be created, in which case the widget display may need to associated with the "endElement" method.

7.4 Instant Applications

One goal of examining the data stream is to work toward supporting instant applications. *Instant applications* are applications that can examine and edit the data in an XML database based solely on the structure of the data. For example, if data is presented on employees in the database, an application may be generated that allows for the addition, deletion, and editing of employee information in the database, as well as querying based on characteristics such as name, years employed, or salary. The application would have no intrinsic information about the employee domain, only the structure of the data in the database and constraints on the fields. Although the development of instant applications is outside the scope of this book, two ways to use XML in these applications are in the transfer of data between database and application and in the specification of data entry and query forms.

Instant applications are particularly important because of the varying structure of XML elements in the database. Unlike the relational database where all the rows of a relation have the same structure or an object-oriented database where all the instances of a class have the same structure, all the elements in an XML document are not required to have the same structure.

For example, consider a Rolodex database of one document that contains contact information for people. All the entries will have a name; most will have a phone number, though some might have only an email address. The phone number could be a work number, home number, cell phone number, and/or pager. There might also be a fax number. Personal contacts might have a birthday, whereas business contacts would have corporate information. There might be notes about the person, and if a business-related contact, the nature of the previous business. There could be multiple physical mail addresses and email addresses, some people might have a Web page, whereas others might have alternate ways of contact, such as an occasionally used phone number. If sales related, or if the person is a client, there could be information about favorite restaurants or previously given gifts.

If the database were modeled as a single concept, it could easily have thirty characteristics. This would lead to a really ugly, non-normalized relational table with 30–50 columns or a normalized database with half a dozen tables. However, an XML document could capture the information using about thirty element type names. To create a traditional data entry editing and query application that would work with the 2^{30} possible layouts could be time-consuming if done manually. However, an instant application would automatically create the appropriate form for each person in the database, regardless of structure.

The application could be implemented to display the form as an HTML form or a Java applet. If a Java applet is used, the applet can dynamically change the user interface based on the characteristics of the XML element. If HTML is used, then a program would need to receive the XML and generate the HTML form. The program can be implemented in Java (as a servlet or JSP) or in XSL, where the data item would be transformed using an XSL stylesheet into the HTML form. In either case, the form would post the new data to the database (as a servlet or CGI script) to execute the update statement (with appropriate validation).

The data used for these applications may be identical to the data presented in browsing the data. Consider the data in Example 7–13. The data may be presented as HTML using an XSL stylesheet, such as the one described in Section 7.2. In addition, an editing application could present the user with a list of names from which to select. A selected name would bring up an HTML form, such as the one shown in Figure 7–7. The HTML form is given in Example 7–14. Other data items would have similar forms with data entry fields that depend upon the element type names of the subelements.

Example 7–13 : Example Rolodex Data

```
<?xml version="1.0"?>
<rolodex>
  <person>
    <name>Tom Joad</name>
    <cell_phone>555-1234</cell_phone>
    <pager>555-9875</pager>
    <Web_site>www.steinbeck.org</Web_site>
    <comments>Don't drink with him.</comments>
  </person>
  <person>
    <name>Rev. Tim Casy</name>
    <home_phone></home_phone>
    <work_phone>555-2906</work_phone>
    <pager>291-8647</pager>
    <email>rev@hotmail.com</email>
    <street_address>1 Grand Ave</street_address>
    <city>Texola</city>
    <state>OK</state>
    <zip>73668</zip>
    <comments>Don't invite to family events.</comments>
  </person>
  <person>
    <name>Muley Graves</name>
    <home_phone>243-1036</home_phone>
    <fax>243-9024</fax>
    <cell_phone>921-5064</cell_phone>
    <pager>555-1036</pager>
    <email>muley@aol.com</email>
    <street_address>3001 Grand Ave</street_address>
    <city>Texola</city>
    <state>OK</state>
    <zip>73668</zip>
    <comments>Family is important.</comments>
  </person>
</rolodex>
```

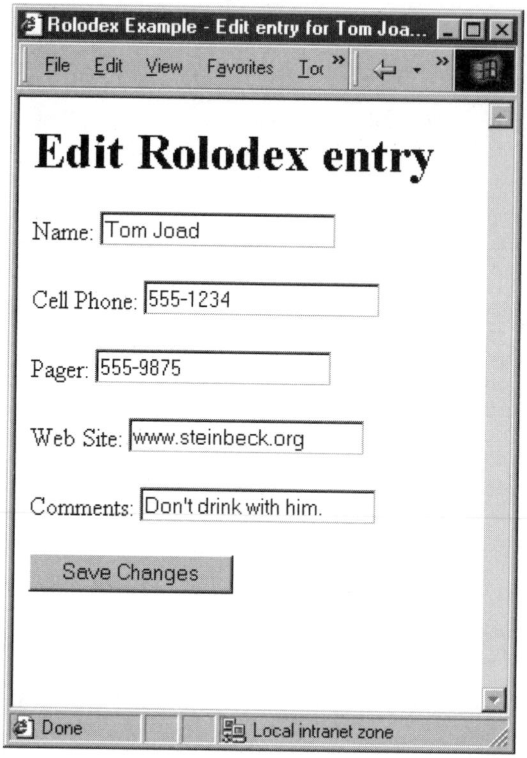

Figure 7–7 Example edit form for Rolodex data

Example 7–14 : Example HTML Form for Editing Rolodex Data

```
<html>
<title>Rolodex Example - Edit entry for Tom Joad</title>
<body>
<h1>Edit Rolodex entry</h1>
<form action="/cgi-bin/edit" method="POST">
  <input type="hidden" name="id" value="7.2"/>
  <p>
  Name:
  <input type="text" name="name" value="Tom Joad"/>
  </p>
  <p>
  Cell Phone:
  <input type="text" name="cell_phone" value="555-1234"/>
  </p>
  <p>
```

```
  Pager:
  <input type="text" name="pager" value="555-9875"/>
  </p>
  <p>
  Web Site:
  <input type="text" name="Web_site" value="www.steinbeck.org"/>
  </p>
  <p>
  Comments:
  <input type="text" name="comments" value="Don't drink with him."/>
  </p>
  <input type="submit" name="Submit" value="Save Changes"/>
</form>
</body>
</html>
```

The pseudo-code to create the form is:

1. Emit the header of the form HTML document.
2. Emit the form start tag and any hidden form elements.
3. Iterate over the subelements, and emit a text box for entry with the subelement's element type name as a text label.
4. Emit the end tag of the form.
5. Emit the end tags for the HTML document.

The same form can be used to create a new data item to be added to the document based on the existing data item.

Element hierarchies can also be supported using this scheme. Each subelement is associated with a part of the form to preserve the hierarchy. For example, the XML in Example 7–15 can be mapped to the HTML form in Example 7–16. Each subelement is grouped in the presentation, but the entire form is updated and the previous element is modified. A possible presentation is shown in Figure 7–8. Other presentations are possible, for example, to group the subelements using HTML tables. When the form is sent to the database, the entire element could be replaced, or a more complex mapping can be used to only update the subelements when they have changed.

Example 7–15 : Example Structured Rolodex Data

```
<?xml version="1.0"?>
<rolodex>
  <person>
    <name>Muley Graves</name>
    <phone>
      <home_phone>243-1036</home_phone>
      <fax>243-9024</fax>
      <cell_phone>921-5064</cell_phone>
      <pager>555-1036</pager>
    </phone>
    <address>
      <street_address>3001 Grand Ave</street_address>
      <city>Texola</city>
      <state>OK</state>
      <zip>73668</zip>
    </address>
    <electronic>
      <email>muley@aol.com</email>
    </electronic>
    <personal>
      <comments>Family is important.</comments>
    </personal>
  </person>
</rolodex>
```

Example 7–16 : Example HTML Form for Editing Structured Rolodex Data

```
<html>
<title>Rolodex Example - Edit entry for Muley Graves</title>
<body>
<h1>Edit Rolodex entry</h1>
<form action="/cgi-bin/edit" method="POST">
  <input type="hidden" name="id" value="7.4"/>
  <p>
  Name:
  <input type="text" name="name" value="Muley Graves"/>
  </p>
  <h2>Phone</h2>
  <p>
  Home Phone:
  <input type="text" name="home_phone" value="243-1036"/>
  </p>
  <p>
```

```
  Fax:
  <input type="text" name="cell_phone" value="243-9024"/>
  </p>
  <p>
  Cell Phone:
  <input type="text" name="cell_phone" value="921-5064"/>
  </p>
  <p>
  Pager:
  <input type="text" name="pager" value="555-1036"/>
  </p>
  <h2>Electronic</h2>
  <p>
  Email:
  <input type="text" name="email" value="muley@aol.com"/>
  </p>
  <h2>Address</h2>
  <p>
  Street Address:
  <input type="text" name="street_address" value="3001 Grand Ave"/>
  </p>
  <p>
  City:
  <input type="text" name="city" value="Texola"/>
  </p>
  <p>
  State:
  <input type="text" name="state" value="OK"/>
  </p>
  <p>
  Zip:
  <input type="text" name="zip" value="73668"/>
  </p>
  <h2>Personal</h2>
  <p>
  Comments:
  <input type="text" name="comments" value="Family is important."/>
  </p>
  <input type="submit" name="Submit" value="Save Changes"/>
</form>
</body>
</html>
```

Figure 7–8 Example edit form for structured Rolodex data

Specialized data entry widgets can be used for particular elements (or subelements), by mapping the element type names to the widgets. This works whether the user interface is in HTML or Java. For example, the phone number data entry widget could be a entry box with a specific number of digits; the birth date data entry box could have restrictions on the values allowed. More complex user interfaces are possible, such as slider bars or a custom user interface. The data entry and query forms may be also specified using the second-generation W3C form language Xforms. If the data restrictions provided by Xforms are used, it may be possible to update data items directly without validating the changes by a separate program.

The power of instant applications occur when a custom user interface can be automatically embedded within another custom interface. For example, if the Rolodex interface can be embedded in other applications, then anytime contact information is needed on a person, a small change to the database schema automatically results in a new user interface being available to all applications that access the personal contact database.

Querying

- How can XML data be queried?
- What query tools and algorithms are useful for querying an XML database?
- What representations support efficient queries of XML databases?
- How can XML links be represented to facilitate cross-document queries?

8

Understanding the type of queries used and how to represent queries and data for efficient querying is important in determining the type of query processing to be included in an XML DBMS or to be used to query XML documents. Section 8.1 describes a classification of queries and Section 8.2 describes how to represent XML data to support more efficient querying. Sections 8.3 and 8.4 describe possible query engines, and Section 8.5 describes query reporting tools.

8.1 Query Classifications

A query can be classified based on the source of the data, the data type of report generated, and the topology of the query. These classifications are not independent and may influence each other. These classifications and some of their interactions are discussed briefly here.

The source of the data to be accessed from an XML database during queries includes an XML document, a fragment of an XML document, character data, or a collection of elements. The data could be an XML element, a string, or a set of elements. This chapter focuses on querying the elements of one or more XML documents (or fragments). Querying from character data is not particular to XML databases and is addressed by techniques for text searching; because it is not specific to XML databases, it is not covered here.

In addition to retrieving data in the representation in which it was stored, data may be combined with other data throughout the database to create novel reports. These reports may take the data type of a string, set of strings, document node, set of document nodes, table, document, or collection of documents.

The data type of the report may depend upon the source of the data. For example:

- An attribute value may be returned as a string.
- A collection of elements with identical structure might be returned as a table.
- One or more elements might be collected together as one document or kept separately as individual elements.
- Character data regions may also be embedded in new elements to construct an XML report.

There are four topologies for the query discussed in this chapter: singleton, path, tree, and graph. Queries can retrieve a single element node from a unique identifier; retrieve one or more nodes from a path as defined in an XML Path Specification; or retrieve a table of nodes from a tree or graph pattern. The distinction between a singleton, path, tree, and graph query is shown in Figure 8–1, where a singleton is shown as a rectangle at a single node, a path is shown from the root node to one of the leaves, a graph is all the edges in the diagram, and a tree is all the edges in the diagram except those labeled as being part of a graph.

The data type of the query results may depend upon the query topology. A query of an individual node by its unique identifier may result in a string or an element, depending upon whether the identifier refers to a character data region or an element, respectively. The path query algorithm described in this chapter formats the result as a set of nodes. The tree and graph query algorithms render the result as a table. Technically, all four query topologies can be thought of as returning a table of results as needed: in the path query, the table has one column (mathematically, a set of 1-tuples), which is equivalent to a set, and in the singleton query, the one column has one row, which is equivalent to a single value.

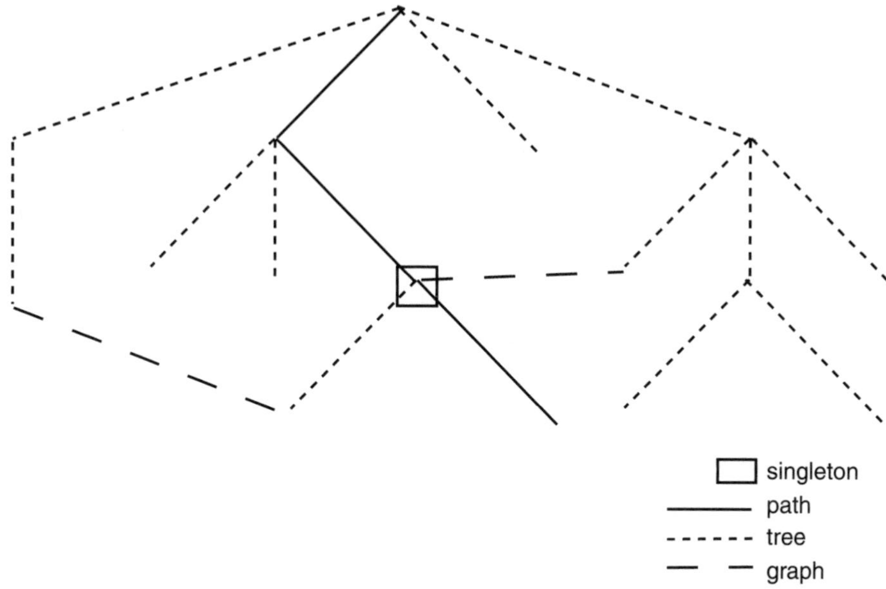

Figure 8–1 Three types of queries

For example, given the schema tree in Figure 8–2, any individual entry in the underlying database may be accessed by a unique identifier. Path queries can be formed that retrieve the entries in the database that satisfy certain logical constraints (or predicates), such as:

- Find all entries by William Shakespeare.
- Find all entries titled Hamlet.
- Find all entries published by Prentice Hall.
- Find all entries containing the character data "Romeo" (regardless of the tag, i.e., either the author or title could contain Romeo).

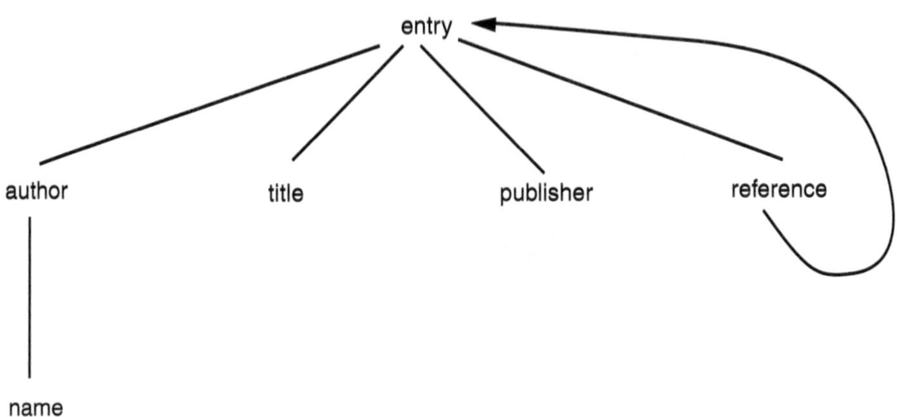

Figure 8–2 Element schema for reference material

Tree queries are used when conjunctions of paths are queried or when multiple results are required, such as:

- Find all entries for Hamlet by William Shakespeare.
- Find all entries that reference an entry for Hamlet by William Shakespeare.
- Find all titles and their publishers for entries by William Shakespeare.

Graph patterns extend the hierarchical queries supported by XML paths, increasing the complexity and flexibility of querying allowed. A tree structure of an XML document becomes a graph when nodes are connected by intradocument links (via IDREF) or interdocument links (via XML Link). Querying with a graph pattern allows an entire (indexed) XML document with links to be examined, and all fragments in the document that match the pattern are returned. Graph pattern queries are also used when two or more paths of a tree must be joined for a query. These queries are especially important for data mining.

An example of graph pattern query is

- Find all entries that refer to an entry by the same author (as shown in Figure 8–3).

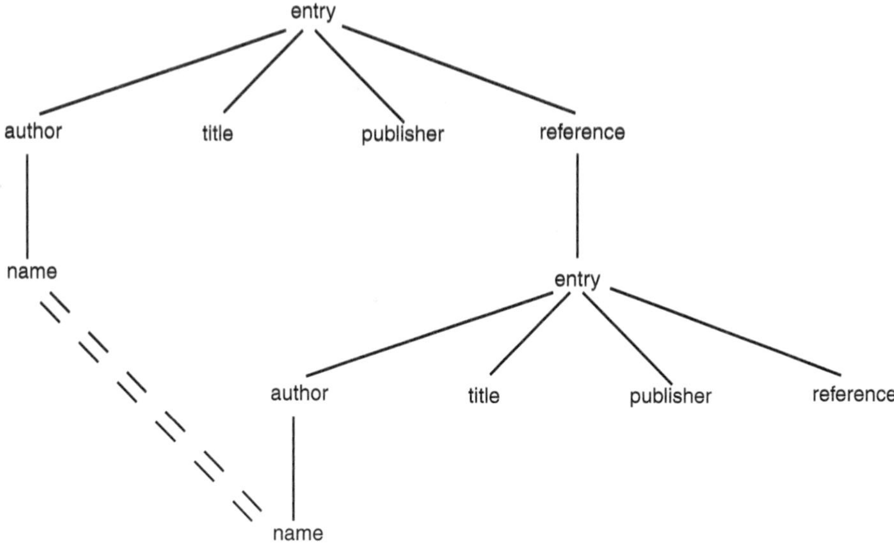

Figure 8–3 Join within element schema for reference material

8.2 Representation

Querying is the process of selecting and synthesizing data from a database by asking questions based on characteristics of the data. The language in which the questions are asked facilitates or limits the answers that can be generated. Because slight variations in a query can yield dramatic differences in the report, it is essential that the query language mimic the structure of the data, capture the features of the domain, and be well understood by the person forming the query.

8.2.1 Organization-centered Documents versus Relationship-centered Data

Section 2.4.2 described how XML could represent documents or data equally well. However, the processing of XML documents requires that you make a decision whether to treat the XML document from a document-processing-oriented perspective or a data-processing-oriented perspective. This is especially crucial in querying, which is a very data-processing-oriented operation.

When presented with a document, or with a piece of data, your primary access is to read it. However, when you want only part of the information in the document or data source, you probably do not want to examine the entire data source to gain the information you need. Retrieval is the process of locating the information in a document or the data in a database that you would like to read. Documents have tables of contents, summaries, and indices to simplify retrieval of desired information, and online documents may be searched for words of interest. Likewise, databases provide query mechanisms and indices to simplify data retrieval.

Retrieval mechanisms depend on whether the information is presented as a document or as a collection of data. Within a document, relationships provided by physical location are very important, but within a collection of data, the semantic relationships between data items are more important than physical relationships. An ATM receipt can have the bank balance above or below the transaction ID, and the two data items would still have the same semantic relationships, but a technical manual describing how an ATM generates a receipt would not make sense if phrases were switched around.

The information storage mechanism used also affects retrieval because the retrieval process is heavily dependent on the model used by the repository. Reading the data dump of a relational database to understand all of its information is painful, and trying to query a book using SQL would be hopeless.

The relevant features for examining a word in a document include the word itself, its physical location, and its connection to other words (or icons). For a word used as a datum, the relevant features include the word and its semantic relationships to other data items. Although physical organization and semantic relationships are important to both document and data processing, frequently document processing has been focused on the physical organization and data processing has been focused on the semantic relationship. There are notable exceptions, for example, object-oriented databases are very good at modeling physical organizations (and thus are often used with CAD/CAM systems), and hypertext systems and GML (a predecessor of SGML) provide support for additional relationships added to the physical structure of a document.

The distinction between an organization-centered approach and a relationship-centered approach becomes more apparent when attempting to query a relation-centered data source with a organization-centered query, or vice versa. To be more concrete, consider the following extreme queries: first a relationship-centered query of an organization-centered data model, and then an organization-centered query of a relationship-centered data model.

1. In the Library of Congress, there is a red book, next to a ten-inch tall book, next to a book by a Russian author, next to a book where "Chaucer" is the seventh word of the sixth chapter. What is the title of the red book?
2. Looking at the vital records and raw census reports of the United States, 1901–2000, who had the most third cousins?

Document processing systems can capture relationships, and relational databases can model physical organizations, but the development of large, realistic applications is much simpler when using the most appropriate representation. In modeling a large system, only part of the information is frequently accessed, and it is more efficient to make the most desired information as explicit as possible in the representation.

It is possible to close the gap between an organization-centric document model and a relationship-centric data model. Unfortunately, the XML standards committees have usually chosen to continue with an organization-centric model rather than narrow the gulf with databases. Luckily, database technology has moved to narrow the gap with the development of graph data models.

8.2.2 Node-centric versus Edge-centric Representations

Graph data models support the representation of organizations and relationships as the nodes and edges of a graph. The organization of documents and the semantic relationships of data may be modeled as either nodes or edges. The different combinations of those have been utilized in different systems. Node-centric representations of physical organization are fairly common in document processing systems and object-oriented databases that support CAD/CAM tools. Node-centric representations of semantic relationships are common in relational databases. Edge-based representations of the organization of inter-linked documents are modeled in Grove, a model that influenced the development of GML, a predecessor of SGML and XML. Edge-centric representations of semantic relationships are modeled in semantic and graph data models.

A graph representation of data clarifies the choices. Consider the text: "The book entitled *Romeo and Juliet* is authored by William Shakespeare."

This may be modeled as a graph as shown in Figure 8–4.

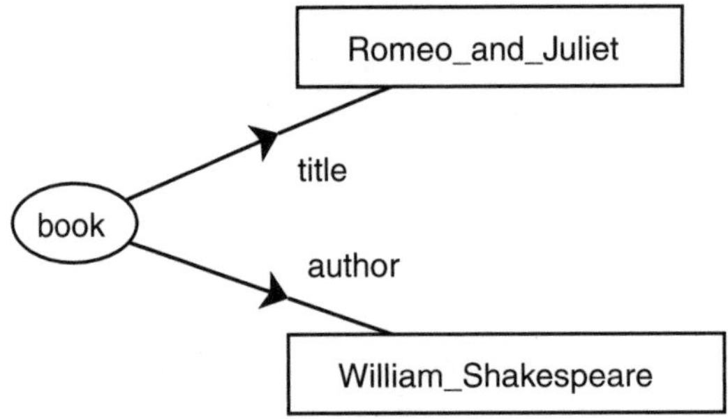

Figure 8–4 Graph of book node and edges

As an edge-centric model, the graph may be captured by the relationships: title and author.

Title

book	*title*
1	Romeo and Juliet

Author

book	*author*
1	William Shakespeare

In a relational database, these two edge relationships could also be combined into a "book" relationship as long as each book has only one author.

In a node-centric model, the graph may be captured by the "book," "Romeo and Juliet" and "William Shakespeare" nodes, for example, as the following object:

```
Book
   title: Romeo and Juliet
   author: William Shakespeare
```

Data in the book example could be presented in a node-centric XML representation, such as follows:

```
<book id="1">
   <title>Romeo and Juliet</title>
   <author>William Shakespeare</author>
</book>
```

Or, in an edge-centric form:

```
<title book="1">Romeo and Juliet</title>
<author book="1">William Shakespeare</author>
```

Typically, the node-centric form is a more common representation for adding data about books to a database. However, the edge-centric form is more amenable to querying based on the characteristics "title" and "author" of a book.

To understand why, consider a collection of 1,000 books stored in either form. To find the book titled "Romeo and Juliet" in the node-centered collection, up to 1,000 books must be retrieved, then for each book, the title must be retrieved, then the title must be compared to "Romeo and Juliet" to see if it matches. In the edge-centric collection, up to 1,000 titles still must be retrieved and compared, but not the 1,000 "book" elements. When the elements have greater subelement depth, then the efficiency of the edge-centric approach increases compared to the node-centric approach.

The node-centric approach could be made more efficient by indexing the "title" element type names within the document. In fact, indexing all the element type names is as efficient as accessing the document in edge-centric form, and this is the approach taken to translate a node-centric document into an edge-centric form amenable to querying.

Edge-centric forms are superior for querying XML because:

- They support queries where an element type name is undefined.
- They cleanly capture in the same framework: element/subelement relationships, intra-document links using IDREFs, and inter-document links using XML Links.
- They support querying documents that have a mutable and frequently changing structure.
- They efficiently support queries with many links between documents.

Efficient querying of XML, especially across XML links, requires translating a node-centric form to an edge-centric form. Either the data must be translated from a node-centric form to an edge-centric form or the query must be translated from an edge-centric form to a node-centric form.

XML has focused on the node-centric form of element, which made sense coming from a document organization perspective. Unfortunately, that means to effectively query an XML database, the underlying gulf between a node-centric data model and an edge-centric data model must be crossed.

Because tools supporting XML technologies are typically node-centric, it is difficult to use XML tools to access relational databases. Instead it is simpler to modify database tools to work with the node-centric operations of XML. This chapter describes how it is possible to view XML elements in an edge-centric form.

8.2.3 Representing Links

This section describes how to create relationships between nodes, thus allowing data in a document to benefit from a more edge-centric approach. Because data in an XML database is stored in a non-linear form (i.e., it is not flat), it is easy to create edges between elements.

There are two possible ways to modify an XML data model to accept edges between existing nodes in a tree (called *links).* The first is to allow multiple parents for a fragment as shown in Figure 8–5. This would change the XML data models in Chapter 3 to graph data models because the one parent per element rule would have to be relaxed. This solution would not allow XML to be used directly for all documents.

The second solution augments the XML data model to include a linking mechanism. Non-hierarchical relationships are captured as links as illustrated in Figure 8–6 by a dashed line, where the ToyotasForSale document root element is linked to each appropriate automobile element. The second

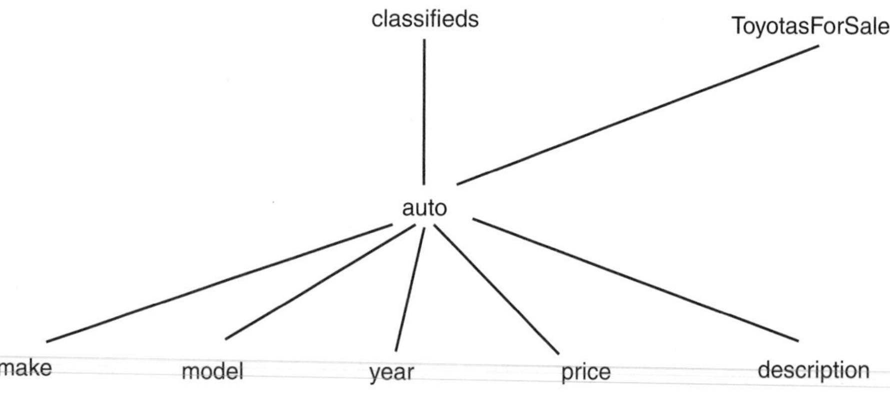

Figure 8–5 Element schema for automobile classifieds with multiple roots

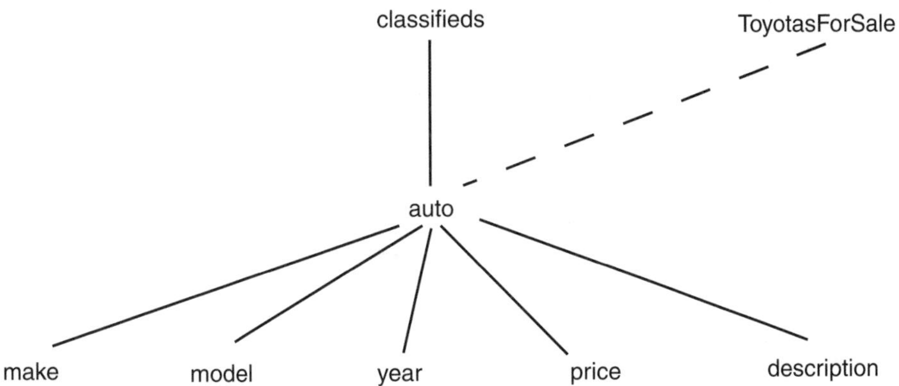

Figure 8–6 Element schema for automobile classifieds with link

solution has been chosen because it is superior for working within the XML framework.

Querying a document with links should integrate link traversal and subelement relationships, supporting the following query against the schema in Figure 8–7:

- Find all URLs for ToyotasForSale possibilities where status is blank.

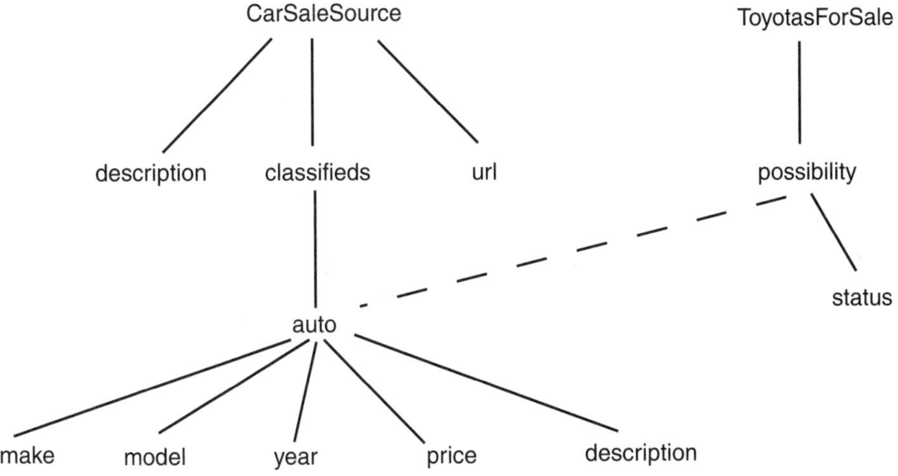

Figure 8–7 Element schema for automobile classifieds and extractions with link

Links also are bi-directional. For example, the following query could be asked against Figure 8–8:

- Find all buyers interested in one-year-old automobiles.

Links are useful for capturing non-hierarchical relationships, such as those discovered during data mining. Because they are bi-directional, queries can be asked from different perspectives, allowing flexible and complex querying.

The biggest advantage of links is that they may span across documents, even at different sites. Because there are storage and security issues associated with links spanning sites, this chapter works with links within a single site. It is easy to have a million URLs to point to *www.cnn.org* (well, theoretically easy), but it would be much more difficult if CNN also had to keep track of all links in which anyone referred to their site. Chapter 9 addresses storage of links that refer to documents at another site.

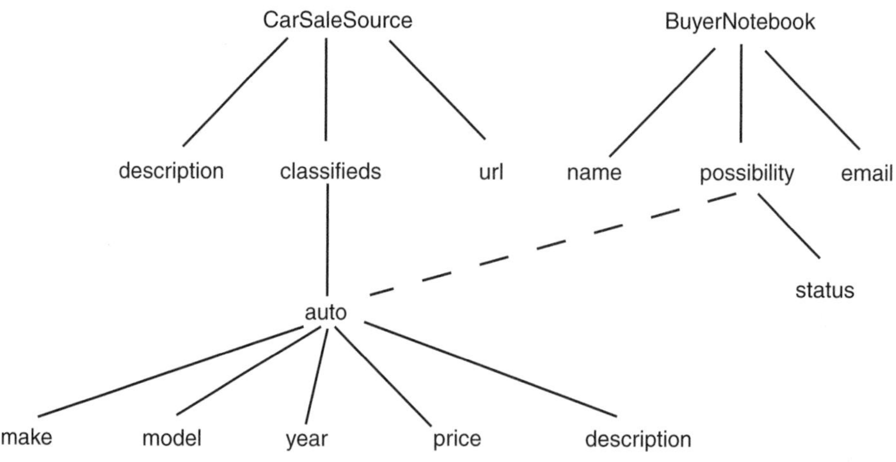

Figure 8–8 Element schema for automobile classifieds and buyers with link

8.2.4 XML Links Presentations of Edges

XML Link Specification provides a mechanism for creating links between XML elements (as a special case of XML documents and other Web resources). Our approach allows most (if not all) likely uses of XML Links and allows the links to be stored and manipulated cleanly with database operations. Database operations can also be expanded to allow for necessary node-centric operations, such as XPath references.

Links can be created in the non-linear database, but must be presented in a flat XML document to be useful. Generically, there are three ways to present any bi-directional link. Bi-directional links may be treated as a separate relationship or as if either element contained the other as a special kind of subelement.

In Figure 8–9, an automobile and a buyer are separate XML documents. The link connecting the representation of buyer with the representation of auto could be presented as a separate link; as a buyer as a subelement of auto; or as an auto as a subelement of buyer. These three possibilities are outlined here.

The separate link presentation could look like this:

```
<auto ID="auto_1">
  <make>Chevy</make>
  <model>Cavalier</model>
  <year>2004</year>
</auto>
<buyer ID="buyer_1">
  <name>Fred Flintstone</name>
</buyer>
<link>
    <auto xlink:href="#auto_1"/>
    <buyer xlink:href="#buyer_1"/>
</link>
```

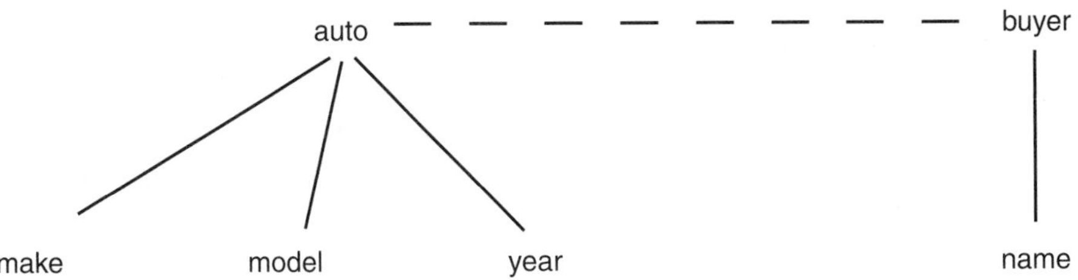

Figure 8–9 Element schema for automobile buyer

where the (slightly simplified) link element refers to the "auto" element by its ID and the "buyer" element by its ID. The "#" hypertext reference refers to the element with the name or ID of "#name" in the specified document, which, in this case, is the default current document.

In the second case, the link relationship between "auto" and "buyer" could also be presented as a subelement of "auto":

```
<auto>
  <make>Chevy</make>
  <model>Cavalier</model>
  <year>2004</year>
  <buyer xlink:href="#buyer_1"/>
</auto>
<buyer ID="buyer_1">
    <name>Fred Flintstone</name>
</buyer>
```

Or, in the third case, the relationship could be presented as a subelement of "buyer" as:

```
<buyer>
  <name>Fred Flintstone</name>
  <auto xlink:href="#auto_1"/>
</buyer>
<auto ID="auto_1">
  <make>Chevy</make>
  <model>Cavalier</model>
  <year>2004</year>
</auto>
```

To keep the use of links compatible with the edge-centered approach needed for querying, the first of the three options is chosen.

8.2.5 Storing Links

The edge-centric data model in Section 3.5.6 describes a mechanism to store XML data in edge-centric form. If a node-centric data model is used, then the queries and relational views of Section 8.4.4.1 may be used to translate the node-centric data model to an edge-centric form. However, in storing a document of XML links, those may be stored more efficiently in an edge-centric form. Because the storage mechanisms of Chapter 4 do not directly address the storage of edge-centric data models, that issue is addressed here briefly in the context of storing the links.

An edge consists of a source, destination, and relation name. Thus, an edge may be stored in a relational database as a single binary relation:

```
Edge(Node source, String relationName, Node destination)
```

To store that relation using the relational DBMS storage mechanisms of Chapter 4 across documents, the nodes will refer to fragment identifiers and will require a specification of document identifiers to support interdocument links. That relation is

```
Link(Document source_doc, Node source,
    String relationName,
    Document destination_doc, Node destination)
```

If the fine-grained or medium-grained storage relational solutions are used, then a table for "link" can be added to the schema as a new type of "child" table. The code to implement this is shown in Example 8–1 for Oracle and Example 8–2 for DB2.

Example 8–1 : Relational Table to Store Links (Oracle)

```
-- Create storage table and constraint for links

create table xdb_link (
   s_doc_id      NUMBER(8)         NOT NULL,
   s_link_id     NUMBER(8)         NOT NULL,
   s_ele_id      NUMBER(8)         NOT NULL,
   name          VARCHAR2(64)      NOT NULL,
   d_doc_id      NUMBER(8)         NOT NULL,
   d_link_id     NUMBER(8)         NOT NULL,
   d_ele_id      NUMBER(8)         NOT NULL
);
alter table xdb_link add primary key (s_doc_id, s_link_id);

alter table xdb_link add constraint uc_xdb_link_d_doc_id
      unique (d_doc_id, d_link_id);

alter table xdb_link add constraint fk_xdb_link_s_doc_id
      foreign key (s_doc_id) references xdb_doc (doc_id);
alter table xdb_link add constraint fk_xdb_link_s_ele_id
      foreign key (s_doc_id, s_ele_id) references xdb_ele (doc_id,
ele_id);
alter table xdb_link add constraint fk_xdb_link_d_doc_id
      foreign key (d_doc_id) references xdb_doc (doc_id);
alter table xdb_link add constraint fk_xdb_link_d_ele_id
      foreign key (d_doc_id, d_ele_id) references xdb_ele (doc_id,
ele_id);
```

Example 8–2 : Relational Table to Store Links (DB2)

```
-- Create storage table and constraint for links

create table xdb_link (
   s_doc_id      INTEGER        NOT NULL,
   s_link_id     INTEGER        NOT NULL,
   s_ele_id      INTEGER        NOT NULL,
   name          VARCHAR(64)    NOT NULL,
   d_doc_id      INTEGER        NOT NULL,
   d_link_id     INTEGER        NOT NULL,
   d_ele_id      INTEGER        NOT NULL
);
alter table xdb_link add primary key (s_doc_id, s_link_id);

alter table xdb_link add constraint uc_xdb_link_d_doc
      unique (d_doc_id, d_link_id);

alter table xdb_link add constraint fk_xdb_link_s_doc
      foreign key (s_doc_id) references xdb_doc (doc_id);
alter table xdb_link add constraint fk_xdb_link_s_ele
      foreign key (s_doc_id, s_ele_id) references xdb_ele (doc_id,
ele_id);
alter table xdb_link add constraint fk_xdb_link_d_doc
      foreign key (d_doc_id) references xdb_doc (doc_id);
alter table xdb_link add constraint fk_xdb_link_d_ele
      foreign key (d_doc_id, d_ele_id) references xdb_ele (doc_id,
ele_id);
```

8.3 Query Engines

Four query algorithms are described in this chapter. The first is a path querying algorithm (Section 8.3.1); the second is a tree querying algorithm (Section 8.3.2); the third is a graph querying algorithm for documents stored in a relational DBMS (Section 8.4.4); and the fourth is a general graph querying algorithm (Section 8.4.5).

8.3.1 Path Querying

Path querying provides a mechanism to retrieve the nodes occurring at some position relative to a starting node. The query engine typically follows

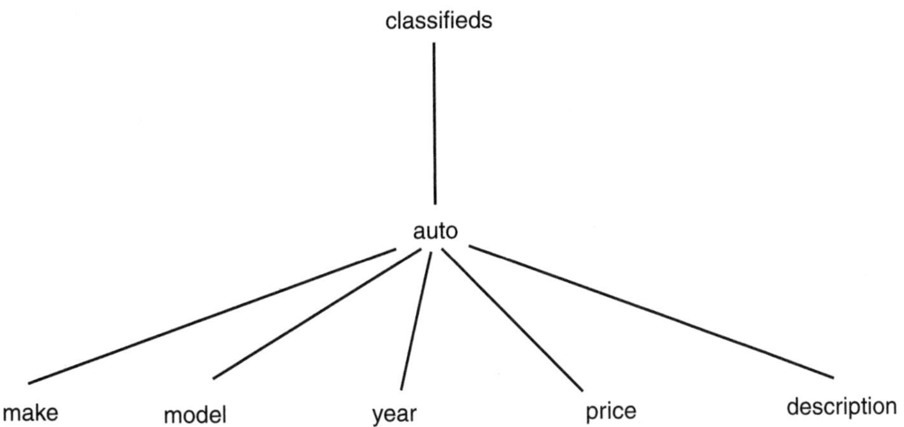

Figure 8–10 Element schema for automobile classifieds

a *path* from the starting node to the ending nodes of the path. For example, in Figure 8–10, following the path query

- Find all makes in the classifieds

would start at the "classified" node, pass through the "auto" node, and end at the "make" nodes. Thus, a query against Example 8–3 would return: "Chevrolet", "Toyota", and "Volkswagen". Starting from the root of the

Example 8–3 : Automobile Classifieds

```
<?xml version="1.0"?>
<classifieds>
  <auto>
    <make>Chevy</make>
    <model>Cavalier</model>
    <year>2004</year>
    <price>8900</price>
    <description>Like new</description>
  </auto>
  <auto>
    <make>Toyota</make>
    <model>Camry</model>
    <year>2000</year>
    <price>7995</price>
```

```
    <description>Has a little rust</description>
  </auto>
  <auto>
    <make>Toyota</make>
    <model>Celica</model>
    <year>2003</year>
    <price>14995</price>
    <description>Runs great</description>
  </auto>
  <auto>
    <make>Volkswagon</make>
    <model>Beetle</model>
    <year>2000</year>
    <price>7435</price>
    <description>Runs good, looks good, stops good</description>
  </auto>
  <auto>
    <make>Volkswagon</make>
    <model>Beetle</model>
    <year>1976</year>
    <price>7435</price>
    <description>Runs good, looks good, stops good</description>
  </auto>
</classifieds>
```

document, the path of the query would be "classifieds/auto/make". The basic algorithm for the path query is as follows:

1. *Begin with the start node.* In this example, the start node would be the root node of Example 8–3.
2. *Retrieve the subelements of the start node with the same element type name as the first type name in the path.* In this case, "classifieds" would be the first type name. There may be more than one subelement node with that element type name.
3. *For each subelement, repeat the previous steps with the remainder of the path, in effect, calling the procedure recursively for each subelement.* Thus, the first time through the procedure would match the (only) "classifieds" node and call the procedure recursively. The second time through, the start node would be the classified node(s) and the path being searched would begin with "auto". This step of the procedure would match

each of the five "auto" elements in the example. The procedure would be called (recursively) five times with path "make", once with each of the "auto" elements. The recursive parameter calls are given in Table 8–1.

4. *If the path is complete, collect the subelements in a list to be returned when all branches have been completed.* The third time through the procedure—with path "make"—the path remainder is empty; so instead of calling the procedure recursively, the elements that matched "make" are added to a result list. Because there are five "auto" nodes and the procedure was called recursively five times in recursion 1, this step will occur five times for the example document.

Table 8–1 Recursive Parameter Calls of Path Querying Algorithm for Automobile Classifieds

Pass	*Recursion level*	*Start node*	*Path*	*Match element type*
1	0	root	classifieds/auto/make	classifieds
2	1	classifieds	auto/make	auto
3	2	auto (5 times)	make	make

In theoretical terms, the algorithm is a depth-first search of the part of the document tree corresponding to the path.

When executing the path query, it is possible to optimize the query based on additional information, if indices are available and a complete search is not required. For example, consider a database of one document that contains basic geographic, political, and economic information about the countries in the world. A query to find the population of each country might be "country/demographics/population" and proceed efficiently in the top-down manner described in the algorithm. However, a query to obtain the production of yak milk by a country might be "country/agriculture/yak_milk" and be more efficiently executed by first searching all "agriculture" elements for those that have the "yak_milk" subelement, assuming that the "agriculture" elements were indexed. These optimizations are similar to optimizing join paths in queries of relational databases.

In addition to following a completely specified path, any node in an XML Path may be a wildcard or constrained with a node constraint. For example, if the "auto" node were split between types for "auto" or "truck," the name of those nodes in the path could be replaced with a wildcard, such as "classifieds/*/make". A node in the path could also be constrained, such as "classifieds/auto[price<10000]/make", which would refer to makes of all autos with a price subelement with value less than 10,000. The algorithm is modified in these cases to use a more general retrieval of the subelement nodes in Step 2 and/or to filter those nodes based on the constraint.

In addition to following paths down the subelement tree, it is useful to follow paths up the tree or to follow paths up or down without specifying all the intermediate steps. For example, the path "classifieds//make" would find the make subelements without regard for the number of intermediate nodes (called the descendent nodes).

The XML Path Specification provides for thirteen dimensions in which a path may follow from a given context. Eight of the dimensions are geared toward navigating the subelements of the document tree.

- Child—contains the children of the context node.
- Parent—contains the single parent node, if there is one.
- Descendent—contains all the descendent nodes. These are all the subelement nodes, their subelement nodes, their subelement nodes, and so on.
- Ancestor—contains the parent node, its parent node, and so on, up to and including the root node.
- Preceding sibling—contains the previous siblings of the context node.
- Following sibling—contains the following siblings of the context node.
- Preceding—contains all the nodes preceding the context node, excluding any ancestor nodes.
- Following—contains all the nodes following the context node, excluding any descendent nodes.

Three of the dimensions include the context node within the document tree navigation. These dimensions may simplify some queries.

- Self—contains only the context node itself.

- Descendent-or-self—contains the context node and descendents.
- Ancestor-or-self—contains the context node and ancestors.

The remaining two dimensions of the XML Path Specification are to handle attributes and namespaces in the same framework as subelements.

- Attribute—contains the attributes of the context node.
- Namespace—contains the namespace node of the context node.

8.3.2 Tree Querying

Tree querying depends upon the data model chosen to represent the tree. Primarily tree data models may be either node-centric (as described in Section 3.5.5) or edge-centric (as described in Section 3.5.6).

Much of the XML activity has taken a node-centric approach to data modeling, which has historically been appropriate for a document-processing-oriented view of XML. However, an edge-centric approach is probably superior for querying.

In the short term, the use of node-centric querying facilitates the rapid development of a query data model and tools and ensures compatibility with other XML standards. However, it ultimately limits the integration and interoperability of XML and relational data. Relational data is already compatible with edge-centric queries because the edges of a tree are easily modeled as binary relations in a relational database.

Tree querying provides a mechanism to retrieve the nodes occurring at multiple positions relative to a starting root node. The query engine typically follows a *tree* from the starting node to the ending nodes of the path. For example, in Figure 8–10, following the tree query

- Find all makes and models in the classifieds.

would start at the "classified" node, pass through the "auto" node, and end at the "make" and "model" nodes. Thus, a query against Example 8–3, would return: "Chevrolet Cavalier", "Toyota Camry", Toyota Celica", and "Volkswagen Bug".

Tree querying is a special case of graph querying, which is described in the next section. A simple tree querying algorithm is presented here:

1. *Begin with the start node.* In this example, the start node would be the root node of Example 8–3.
2. *For each subelement of the tree pattern, retrieve the subelements of the start node with the same element type name as the type name in the tree pattern.* In this case, “classifieds” would be the first type name. There may be more than one subelement node with that element type name.
3. *For each subelement, repeat the previous steps, in effect, calling the procedure recursively for each subelement.* Thus, the first time through the procedure would match the (only) “classifieds” node and call the procedure recursively. The second time through, the start node would be the classified node(s) and the tree being searched would begin with “auto”. This step of the procedure would match each of the five “auto” elements in the example. The procedure would be called (recursively) for each matching subelement of the “auto” elements, in effect, five times with tree “make” interspersed with five calls with tree "model".
4. *If the subtree is complete, collect the subelements in a table to be returned when all branches have been completed.* The table is associated with the root node of each tree in the pattern and these tables are joined (Cartesian product) after the completion of each subtree in the pattern.

In theoretical terms, the algorithm is a depth-first search of the part of the document tree corresponding to the tree pattern.

When executing the tree query, it is possible to optimize the query based on additional information, such as indices, as was mentioned for the path query. Indexing is discussed in Chapter 9.

8.4 Graph Querying

Graph querying matches a graph pattern that describes a query against the documents in the database. Graph patterns are described in Section 8.4.2, and Section 8.4.4 and Section 8.4.5 describe in detail two graph query algorithms.

Graph querying may be used across the subelement and link relationships that occur within a document as well as across links that span documents and databases. The subelement relationships and links can be viewed as a graph, where each subelement relationship or link is an edge in the graph. Although some cases exist where a complex link may be mapped to multiple edges in the graph, those may be addressed by creating a new node in the graph to connect the link components as individual edges.

The graph query algorithm is related to and more general than the path following algorithm or the tree querying algorithm. The path following algorithm follows a collection of linearly-connected edges from one start node to one end node. A tree querying algorithm follows a hierarchical collection of edges from one start node (the root) to several destination nodes (the leaves). The query algorithm "follows" an arbitrary collection of edges without concern for start or end nodes. For example, the graph in Figure 8–11 may be followed in any order. In terms of result, it does not matter whether the make, model, or name edges are retrieved first. In general, the six edges may be matched in any of the 6! (=720) orders, but hopefully with the one leading to the most efficient query.

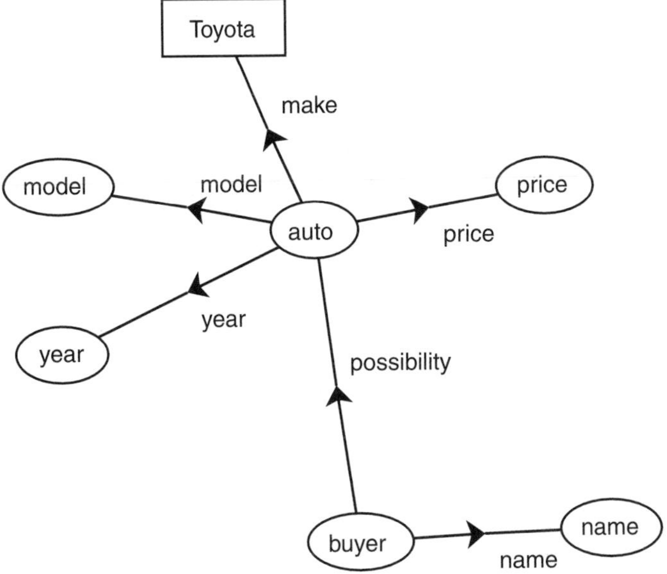

Figure 8–11 Graph pattern for an automobile buyer

8.4.1 Graph Data Model

A graph is a set of vertices and labeled edges. Labeled edges connect two vertices and have a type name. The vertices are the nodes in a document and the edges are the link names or element type names. A graph may be represented as a list of edges. The following document fragments can be represented as the graph shown in Figure 8–12 where the vertices are rectangles and the edges are lines.

```
<auto id="auto_1">
      <make>Toyota</make>
      <model>Celica</model>
      <year>2003</year>
      <price>14995</price>
      <description>Runs great</description>
</auto>

<BuyerNotebook id="BuyerNotebook_1">
      <name>Fred Flintstone</name>
      <possibility xlink:type="simple" xlink:href="#auto_1"/>
</BuyerNotebook>
```

The edges are also listed in Table 8–2.

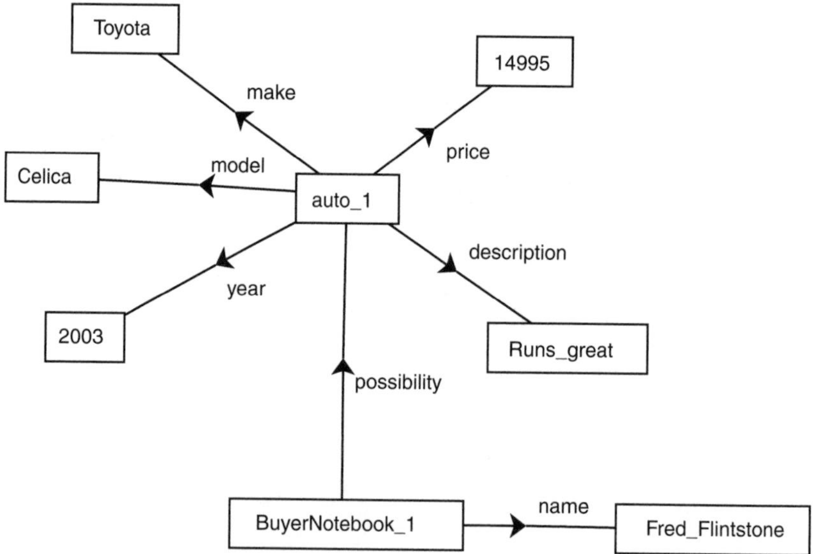

Figure 8–12 Graph of an automobile buyer fragment

Table 8–2 Edges in Graph of Automobile Classifieds

Source	*Name*	*Destination*
#auto_1	make	Toyota
#auto_1	model	Celica
#auto_1	year	2003
#auto_1	price	14995
#auto_1	description	Runs great
#BuyerNotebook_1	name	Fred Flintstone
#BuyerNotebook_1	possibility	#auto_1

A data model was given in Section 3.5.6 that supports accessing subelement (child) relationships and attributes of a document. To support links, the edge-centric data model is extended to contain a new dimension called "link" and to allow edges to refer to nodes in different documents. The simple binary links can be captured directly as edges.

8.4.2 Graph Patterns

Just as the subelement or link relationships may be represented as a graph with vertices and edges, the patterns that would match them may be represented as a graph with vertices, edges, and variables. For example, the pattern corresponding to an automobile with its make and model can be diagrammed using the graph pattern in Figure 8–13, where auto, make, and model are variables, denoted by ovals in the diagram.

A graph pattern is described in terms of its edges. The edges in Figure 8–13 are listed in Table 8–3. The graph pattern consists of two edge patterns that can be denoted as (?auto make ?make) and (?auto model ?model) where "?name" denotes a variable and "make" and "model" are the edge label names. A graph pattern consists of a collection of edge patterns.

In practice, it may be useful for a graph pattern to contain report information, such as a name of the pattern for the title of a report, and an

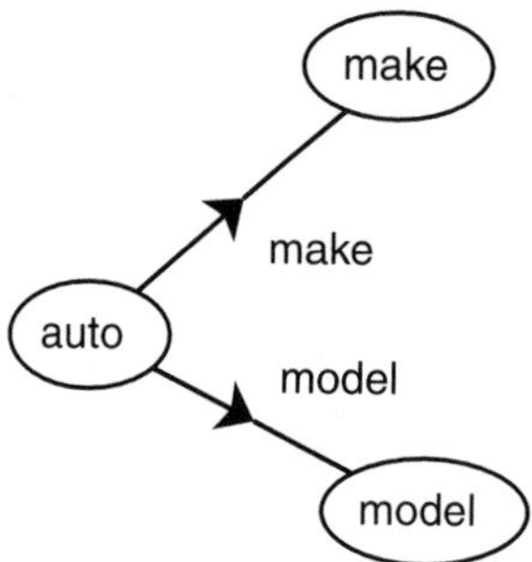

Figure 8–13 Graph pattern for an automobile

Table 8–3 Edges in Graph Pattern of Automobile Classifieds

Source	*Name*	*Dest*
?auto	make	?make
?auto	model	?model

ordered list of variables in the pattern whose order serves as the order for the columns of a report.

To contain the edge patterns and report information, a graph pattern can be rendered as an XML document, such as the one in Example 8–4, which is an XML representation of the graph in Figure 8–11.

Example 8–4 : Graph Pattern for an Automobile Buyer

```
<?xml version="1.0"?>
<pattern name="ToyotaBuyers">
  <edge>
    <source><var name="auto"/></source>
    <label>make</label>
    <dest>Toyota</dest>
  </edge>
  <edge>
    <source><var name="auto"/></source>
    <label>model</label>
    <dest><var name="model"/></dest>
```

```
  </edge>
  <edge>
    <source><var name="auto"/></source>
    <label>year</label>
    <dest><var name="year"/></dest>
  </edge>
  <edge>
    <source><var name="auto"/></source>
    <label>price</label>
    <dest><var name="price"/></dest>
  </edge>
  <edge>
    <source><var name="buyer"/></source>
    <label>possibility</label>
    <dest><var name="auto"/></dest>
  </edge>
  <edge>
    <source><var name="buyer"/></source>
    <label>name</label>
    <dest><var name="name"/></dest>
  </edge>
</pattern>
```

8.4.3 Visualization Tools

A simple way to visually define a graph pattern is to draw a graph. The tool should support the creation of the variable and constant nodes and the edges in the graph. One such tool is shown in Figure 8–14 to illustrate some of the requirements for a graph pattern drawing tool. It shows how a graph pattern for the make, model, and year of an automobile can be drawn. The resulting pattern can be stored or queried against the database. One way to store a pattern is as an XML document, either in a flat file or into the database as a separate document. When querying the database, the pattern can be compared against the documents and the result returned as a text report or an XML document.

When creating queries from edges with a fixed set of labels, having a list of labels from which to select is useful. The edge labels can be retrieved from the documents being queried, which simplifies the creation of the edges by the user.

Figure 8–15 shows the process of creating edges visually. Edges can be created by creating parameter and constant nodes, dragging them around the screen, and connecting them by selecting the source with the mouse

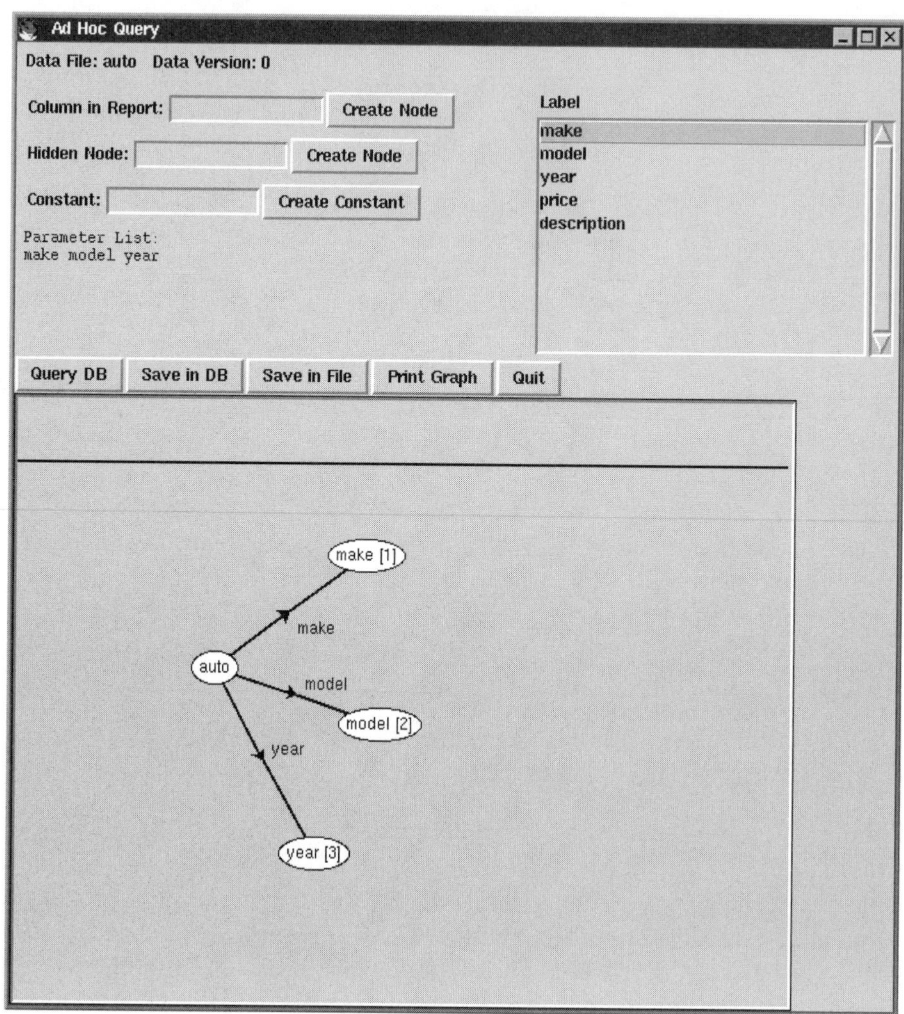

Figure 8–14 Visualization tool for automobile graph pattern

and then clicking the destination to create an edge with the previously selected edge label.

A graph query visualization tool should also support selecting and ordering the parameters for the report. The tool shown distinguishes between parameters that are displayed in a report and those that are hidden. The order of the parameters can be changed by moving the mouse over the graphical nodes and using the "+" and "-" key to shift the parameters.

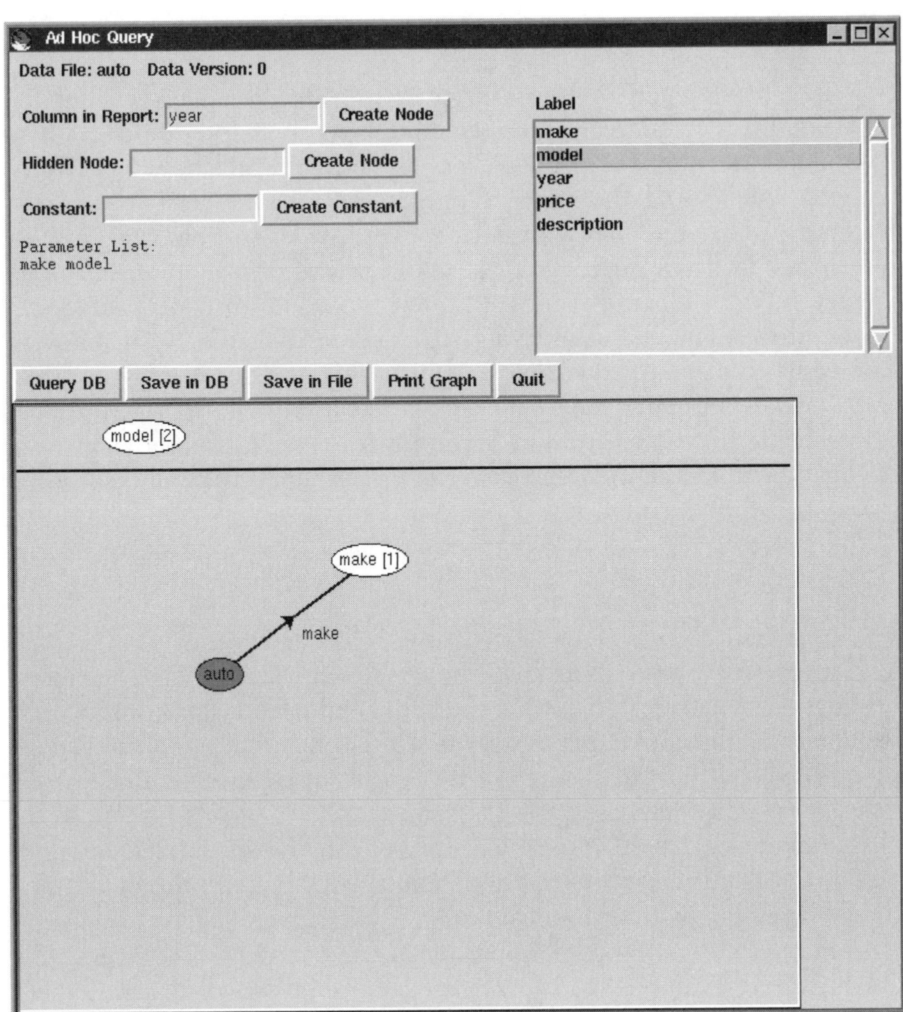

Figure 8–15 Visualization tool while creating automobile graph pattern

8.4.4 SQL Implementation

An XML DBMS must provide access to data as edges to support path or graph querying. Path querying simplifies the access because each edge is traversed linearly; thus, the edge retrieval always specifies one of the nodes and the edge label and requests the other node. Graph querying requires more general access, as the edges may be requested in any order; thus, the edge retrieval may have any combination of source node, edge label, or destination node unspecified.

Chapter 9 describes how to efficiently provide the edge access of the DBMS to support querying. The remainder of this chapter describes how to support querying when those edges are available and how to perform querying when using the storage approach of Chapter 3. The indexing strategies in Chapter 9 are particularly useful when storing XML in custom storage facilities (such as a new XML DBMS) or on top of an object-oriented DBMS. When a relational DBMS is used to store the XML documents, then completely indexing the relational tables may provide reasonably efficient query support, which this section describes. When larger queries are performed or a storage facility other than a relational DBMS is used, the algorithm in Section 8.4.5 is necessary. In either case, information from the indexed database, such as data distribution, can be used to optimize the queries.

8.4.4.1 Retrieving Edges

To compare graph patterns against edges retrieved from the XML database, the database must support viewing the nodes and relationships of the XML document as edges. The mechanism to do that depends upon the storage system used. If a relational database is used to store the XML documents, then a relational view can be created on the XML storage tables. If an object-oriented database is used for storage or a custom implementation, then the mechanism would need to be implemented within that system.

For the fine-grained relational storage system described in Chapter 4, edges may be viewed by combining information stored in the tables. The Oracle SQL in Example 8–5 shows the relationships between each element and its subelements, and Example 8–6 has the equivalent SQL for DB2. The result of those queries on the Example 8–3 document is given in Table 8–4. Example 8–7 is the (Oracle and DB2) query that shows the relationships between elements and their character data regions stored as strings. A similar query could be formed to show the relationships between elements and their character data regions stored as Oracle Longs or DB2 CLOBs. The Example 8–7 query shows the character data sections that occur as the first child of an element and thus assumes that a data-processing-oriented approach has been taken for the documents where each character data region is individually embedded in a element. Table 8–5 is the result for the query against Example 8–3.

Example 8–5 : Query to Retrieve Subelement Relationships (Oracle)

```
select s.ele_id source, d.tag name, c.child_id dest_ref,
       null dest_val, s.doc_id doc
from xdb_ele s,
     xdb_child c,
     xdb_ele d
where s.doc_id = c.doc_id and
      s.ele_id = c.ele_id and
      c.child_class = 'ELE' and
      d.doc_id = c.doc_id and
      d.ele_id = c.child_id;
```

Example 8–6 : Query to Retrieve Subelement Relationships (DB2)

```
select s.ele_id source, d.tag name, c.child_id dest_ref,
     cast (null as varchar(1))  dest_val, s.doc_id doc
from xdb_ele s,
     xdb_child c,
     xdb_ele d
where s.doc_id = c.doc_id and
      s.ele_id = c.ele_id and
      c.child_class = 'ELE' and
      d.doc_id = c.doc_id and
      d.ele_id = c.child_id;
```

Table 8–4 Subelement Relationships in Automobile Classifieds

SOURCE	*NAME*	*DEST_REF*	*DEST_VAL*	*DOC*
1	auto	2		7
1	auto	8		7
1	auto	14		7
1	auto	20		7
1	auto	26		7
2	make	3		7
2	model	4		7
2	year	5		7

Table 8–4 Subelement Relationships in Automobile Classifieds(continued)

2	price	6	7
2	description	7	7
8	make	9	7
8	model	10	7
8	year	11	7
8	price	12	7
8	description	13	7
14	make	15	7
14	model	16	7
14	year	17	7
14	price	18	7
14	description	19	7
20	make	21	7
20	model	22	7
20	year	23	7
20	price	24	7
20	description	25	7
26	make	27	7
26	model	28	7
26	year	29	7
26	price	30	7
26	description	31	7

Example 8–7 : Query to Retrieve Subelement Relationships of CDATA Region

```
select s.ele_id source, 'CDATA' CDATA, -1 dest_ref, d.value dest_val,
       s.doc_id doc
from xdb_ele s,
     xdb_child c,
     xdb_str d
where s.doc_id = c.doc_id and
      s.ele_id = c.ele_id and
      c.child_class = 'STR' and
      c.indx = 1 and
      d.doc_id = c.doc_id and
      d.ele_id = c.ele_id and
      d.cdata_id = c.child_id;
```

Table 8–5 Character Data Relationships in Automobile Classifieds

SOURCE	*CDATA*	*DEST_REF*	*DEST_VAL*	*DOC*
3	CDATA	-1	Chevy	7
4	CDATA	-1	Cavalier	7
5	CDATA	-1	2004	7
6	CDATA	-1	8900	7
7	CDATA	-1	Like new	7
9	CDATA	-1	Toyota	7
10	CDATA	-1	Camry	7
11	CDATA	-1	2000	7
12	CDATA	-1	7995	7
13	CDATA	-1	Has a little rust	7
15	CDATA	-1	Toyota	7
16	CDATA	-1	Celica	7
17	CDATA	-1	2003	7
18	CDATA	-1	14995	7
19	CDATA	-1	Runs great	7

Table 8–5 Character Data Relationships in Automobile Classifieds(continued)

21	CDATA	-1	Volkswagen	7
22	CDATA	-1	Beetle	7
23	CDATA	-1	2000	7
24	CDATA	-1	7435	7
25	CDATA	-1	Runs good, looks good, stops good	7
27	CDATA	-1	Volkswagen	7
28	CDATA	-1	Beetle	7
29	CDATA	-1	1976	7
30	CDATA	-1	7435	7
31	CDATA	-1	Runs good, looks good, stops good	7

A relational view can be created that combines the two queries; however, there would be some overlap as the leaf-most subelement relationship is redundant. This can be filtered from the view by eliminating those relationships from the subelement part of the query and including only subelement relationships that also contain a subelement relationship. Example 8–8 for Oracle is such a relational view and the (sorted) view of the document in Example 8–3 is given in Table 8–6. Example 8–9 shows the equivalent DB2 view.

Example 8–8 : View to Retrieve Subelement Relationships (Oracle)

```
create or replace view xdb_ele_edges_help_v as
select s.ele_id source, d.tag name, c.child_id dest_ref,
       null dest_val, s.doc_id doc
from xdb_ele s,
     xdb_child c,
     xdb_ele d,
     xdb_child dc
where s.doc_id = c.doc_id and
      s.ele_id = c.ele_id and
      c.child_class = 'ELE' and
```

```
      d.doc_id = c.doc_id and
      d.ele_id = c.child_id and
      dc.doc_id = d.doc_id and
      dc.ele_id = d.ele_id and
      dc.child_class = 'ELE' and
      dc.indx = 1
union
select s.parent_id source, s.tag name, -1 dest_ref, d.value dest_val,
       s.doc_id doc
from xdb_ele s,
     xdb_child c,
     xdb_str d
where s.doc_id = c.doc_id and
      s.ele_id = c.ele_id and
      c.child_class = 'STR' and
      c.indx = 1 and
      d.doc_id = c.doc_id and
      d.ele_id = c.ele_id and
      d.cdata_id = c.child_id;
```

Table 8–6 Filtered Subelement and Character Data Relationships in Automobile Classifieds

SOURCE	*NAME*	*DEST_REF*	*DEST_VAL*	*DOC*
1	auto	2		7
1	auto	8		7
1	auto	14		7
1	auto	20		7
1	auto	26		7
2	description	-1	Like new	7
2	make	-1	Chevy	7
2	model	-1	Cavalier	7
2	price	-1	8900	7
2	year	-1	2004	7
8	description	-1	Has a little rust	7
8	make	-1	Toyota	7

Table 8–6 Filtered Subelement and Character Data Relationships in Automobile Classifieds (continued)

8	model	-1	Camry	7
8	price	-1	7995	7
8	year	-1	2000	7
14	description	-1	Runs great	7
14	make	-1	Toyota	7
14	model	-1	Celica	7
14	price	-1	14995	7
14	year	-1	2003	7
20	description	-1	Runs good, looks good, stops good	7
20	make	-1	Volkswagen	7
20	model	-1	Beetle	7
20	price	-1	7435	7
20	year	-1	2000	7
26	description	-1	Runs good, looks good, stops good	7
26	make	-1	Volkswagen	7
26	model	-1	Beetle	7
26	price	-1	7435	7
26	year	-1	1976	7

Example 8–9 : View to Retrieve Subelement Relationships (DB2)

```
create view xdb_ele_edges_help_v as
select s.ele_id source, d.tag name, c.child_id dest_ref,
       CAST (NULL AS VARCHAR(10)) dest_val, s.doc_id doc
from xdb_ele s,
     xdb_child c,
     xdb_ele d,
```

```
     xdb_child dc
where s.doc_id = c.doc_id and
      s.ele_id = c.ele_id and
      c.child_class = 'ELE' and
      d.doc_id = c.doc_id and
      d.ele_id = c.child_id and
      dc.doc_id = d.doc_id and
      dc.ele_id = d.ele_id and
      dc.child_class = 'ELE' and
      dc.indx = 1
union
select s.parent_id source, s.tag name, -1 dest_ref, d.value dest_val,
       s.doc_id doc
from xdb_ele s,
     xdb_child c,
     xdb_str d
where s.doc_id = c.doc_id and
      s.ele_id = c.ele_id and
      c.child_class = 'STR' and
      c.indx = 1 and
      d.doc_id = c.doc_id and
      d.ele_id = c.ele_id and
      d.cdata_id = c.child_id;
```

Such a filtered view provides a way to retrieve binary relationships for a specific document. For example, the SQL in Example 8–10 for Oracle (and Example 8–11 for DB2) retrieves the binary relationships for the "make" relationships in document "7". To retrieve relationships across documents, the view in Example 8–12 for Oracle (and Example 8–13 for DB2) combines the document and element identifiers as a fragment identifier. When retrieving relationships across documents, it may be useful to sort the result by document and element identifier. The SQL to perform that query is given in Example 8–14 for Oracle (and Example 8–15 for DB2), and the result of that query for Example 8–3 is given in Table 8–7.

Example 8–10 : Query for Binary Relationships for Automobile Make (Oracle)

```
select source source, name name,
       decode(dest_ref,-1,dest_val,dest_ref) dest
from xdb_ele_edges_help_v
where name = 'make'
  and doc = 7;
```

Example 8–11: Query for Binary Relationships for Automobile Make (DB2)

```
select source source, name name,
CASE
         WHEN dest_ref = -1
                THEN dest_val
                 ELSE char(dest_ref)
      END AS dest
from xdb_ele_edges_help_v
where name = 'make'
  and doc = 7;
```

Example 8–12 : View to Retrieve Subelement Relationships as Binary Relationships (Oracle)

```
create or replace view xdb_ele_edges_user_v as
select doc||'.'||source source, name name,
       decode(dest_ref,-1,dest_val,doc||'.'||dest_ref) dest
from xdb_ele_edges_help_v v
```

Example 8–13 : View to Retrieve Subelement Relationships as Binary Relationships (DB2)

```
select
     CASE
         WHEN t1.dest_ref = -1
                THEN t1.dest_val
                 ELSE char(t1.dest_ref)
      END AS make,
      CASE
         WHEN t2.dest_ref = -1
                THEN t2.dest_val
                 ELSE char(t2.dest_ref)
      END AS model,
      CASE
         WHEN t3.dest_ref = -1
                THEN t3.dest_val
                 ELSE char(t3.dest_ref)
      END AS year
from xdb_ele_edges_help_v t1,
     xdb_ele_edges_help_v t2,
     xdb_ele_edges_help_v t3
```

```
where t1.name = 'make'
  and t2.name = 'model'
  and t3.name = 'year'
  and t1.doc = t2.doc
  and t1.source = t2.source
  and t2.doc = t3.doc
  and t2.source = t3.source;
```

Example 8–14 : Query to Order Subelement Binary Relationships (Oracle)

```
select doc||'.'||source source, name name,
       decode(dest_ref,-1,dest_val,doc||'.'||dest_ref) dest
from xdb_ele_edges_help_v v
order by doc, v.source;
```

Example 8–15 : Query to Order Subelement Binary Relationships (DB2)

```
select
    rtrim(char(doc))||'.'||rtrim(char(source)) as source,
    name as name,
    CASE
       WHEN dest_ref = -1
          THEN dest_val
            ELSE rtrim(char(doc))||'.'||rtrim(char(dest_ref))
    END AS dest
from xdb_ele_edges_help_v v
order by doc, v.source;
```

Table 8–7 Binary Relationships across Documents Including Relationships in Automobile Classifieds

SOURCE	*NAME*	*DEST*
7.1	auto	7.2
7.1	auto	7.8
7.1	auto	7.14
7.1	auto	7.20
7.1	auto	7.26
7.2	description	Like new

Table 8–7 Binary Relationships across Documents Including Relationships in Automobile Classifieds (continued)

7.2	make	Chevy
7.2	model	Cavalier
7.2	price	8900
7.2	year	2004
7.8	description	Has a little rust
7.8	make	Toyota
7.8	model	Camry
7.8	price	7995
7.8	year	2000
7.14	description	Runs great
7.14	make	Toyota
7.14	model	Celica
7.14	price	14995
7.14	year	2003
7.20	description	Runs good, looks good, stops good
7.20	make	Volkswagen
7.20	model	Beetle
7.20	price	7435
7.20	year	2000
7.26	description	Runs good, looks good, stops good
7.26	make	Volkswagen
7.26	model	Beetle
7.26	price	7435
7.26	year	1976

If the link table of Section 8.2.5 is added to the database, then the query algorithm would need to include a query of the link table as well as the relational views of the element/subelement relationships. This could be done by creating a new view that combines element queries with link queries or by modifying the algorithm to allow either or both to be specified as part of the query.

8.4.4.2 Relational Query Algorithm

For small queries, a simple algorithm can be used where the edge patterns are joined together. This algorithm is especially amenable to implementation when the documents are stored in a relational database. The algorithm generates a SQL statement that will result in executing a graph pattern query.

For example, consider the graph pattern in Figure 8–16, which retrieves the make, model, and year of an automobile. The SQL that performs the query is in Example 8–16 for Oracle (and Example 8–17 for DB2), and the result of the query on Example 8–3 is given in Table 8–8.

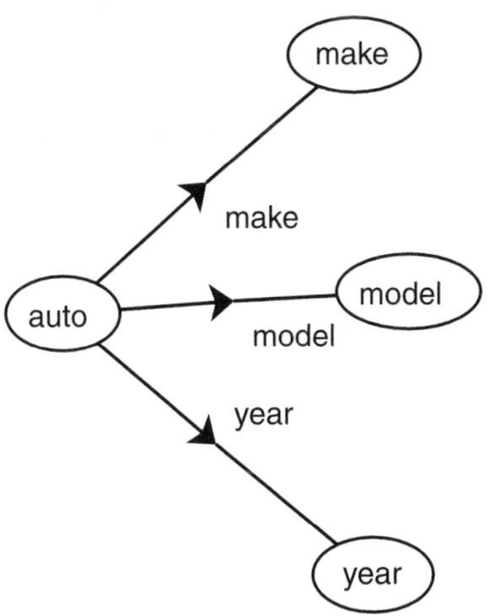

Figure 8–16 Graph pattern for an automobile

Example 8–16 : Query for Automobile Make, Model, and Year (Oracle)

```
select decode(t1.dest_ref,-1,t1.dest_val,t1.dest_ref) make,
       decode(t2.dest_ref,-1,t2.dest_val,t2.dest_ref) model,
       decode(t3.dest_ref,-1,t3.dest_val,t3.dest_ref) year
from xdb_ele_edges_help_v t1,
     xdb_ele_edges_help_v t2,
     xdb_ele_edges_help_v t3
where t1.name = 'make'
  and t2.name = 'model'
  and t3.name = 'year'
  and t1.doc = t2.doc
  and t1.source = t2.source
  and t2.doc = t3.doc
  and t2.source = t3.source;
```

Example 8–17 : Query for Automobile Make, Model, and Year (DB2)

```
                                                ex8o.sql
create or replace view xdb_ele_edges_user_v as
select doc||'.'||source source, name name,
       decode(dest_ref,-1,dest_val,doc||'.'||dest_ref) dest
from xdb_ele_edges_help_v v
```

Table 8–8 Automobile Make, Model, and Year

MAKE	*MODEL*	*YEAR*
Chevy	Cavalier	2004
Toyota	Camry	2000
Toyota	Celica	2003
Volkswagen	Beetle	2000
Volkswagen	Beetle	1976

The pseudo-code to create an SQL query from a graph pattern is as follows:

1. For each edge in the graph pattern
   1.1 Create a *table alias* of the database edge table to be included in the "from" clause, such as the table alias "xdb_ele_edges_help_v t1".
   1.2 Create a "where" constraint for the *source variable*. The name of the variable in the SQL is "<table_alias>.source". The name should be stored in a local repository of variable names, such as an associative array or hashtable. If the variable has occurred before (and thus it is already in the repository), a "where" constraint is created where the current variable is constrained to be equal to the variable name from the repository. For example, if the variable "auto" occurs in the first three edge patterns, its name would be "t1.source" in the repository, and constraints would be added for the second and third edge patterns that "t1.source = t2.source" and "t1.source = t3.source". If a variable has not occurred in the graph pattern, no "where" constraint is needed.
   1.3 Create a "where" constraint for the *edge label.* The relation name column in the table is constrained to be the relation mentioned in the edge pattern. For example, if the label of the first edge is "make", a constraint is added where "t1.rel = 'make'".
   1.4 Create a "where" constraint for the *destination*. If the destination of the edge is a variable, it is treated the same as the source variable, and the same repository is used for the source and destination variables. If the destination is a constant, it is handled in the same way as the constant edge label, and a constraint is created to specify that the destination column have that value. For example, if the destination of the first edge is the variable "make", the name "t1.dest" would be associated with the name "make" in the repository. If the destination of the first edge is the constant "Toyota", a constraint is added where "t1.dest = 'Toyota'".
2. Emit the "SELECT".

3. For each variable in the parameter list of the graph pattern, retrieve its SQL name from the repository. Emit it as part of the select list, with the name of the variable as a column alias. For example, if the parameters were "make, model, year", the select list would be "t1.dest make, t2.dest model, t3.source dest".
4. Emit the collection of table aliases created in Step 1.1 as the "from" clause.
5. Emit the collection of "where" constraints created in Steps 1.2–1.4.

The SQL code in Example 8–16 is slightly more complicated than the algorithm described in the pseudo-code because the Oracle and DB2 views contain multiple documents and split destination into two columns: the numeric fragment reference and the string character data value. The variable constraints added in Steps 1.2 and 1.4 can be augmented to constrain the document columns in addition to the source or destination columns. The view described in Example 8–12 for Oracle (and Example 8–13 for DB2) eliminates the need in user queries for the "decode" statement in Oracle SQL (or "case" statement in DB2 SQL).

8.4.4.3 Relational Query Algorithm Implementation

Example 8–18 is the Java code to read an XML graph pattern and create a SQL statement. A UML diagram for the Java implementation is given in Figure 8–17. The program takes a graph pattern, such as the one in Example 8–19, creates SQL (as given in Example 8–20 for Oracle and Example 8–21 for DB2), executes the SQL against the database, and returns the result as an XML report, shown in Example 8–22.

Example 8–18 : Relational Query Algorithm Implementation

```
/************************ Test.java **********************/
package com.xweave.xmldb.rgquery;

import org.xml.sax.*;
import org.xml.sax.helpers.ParserFactory;
import org.w3c.dom.Document;
import java.io.IOException;
import com.ibm.xml.parsers.*;
import com.xweave.xmldb.rserve.*;
// requires IBM XML4j parser in classpath
```

```
/*
 * Example class to demonstrate parsing a XML document with
 * a SAX Parser (IBM XML4J is used)
 */
public class Test {
   GraphPattern pattern = null;
   protected AccessSpec accessSpec = null;
public Test() {
   super();
}
public AccessSpec getAccessSpec() {
   if (accessSpec == null) {
      accessSpec = new AccessSpec();
   }
   return accessSpec;
}
public GraphPattern getPattern() {
   return pattern;
}
public static void main(java.lang.String[] args) {
   String fileName = null;
   String doc = null;
   if (args.length < 1) {
      System.err.println("Test: requires <file> as argument");
      //fileName = "file:///C:/Temp/test.xml";
      //fileName = "file:///D:/Temp/test.xml";
      //fileName = "http://127.0.0.1/xmldb/tbpattern.xml";
      //doc = "6";
      return;
   } else {
      fileName = args[0];
      if (args.length > 1) {
         doc = args[1];
      }
   }
   Test parser = new Test();
   parser.parse(fileName);
   StatementBuilder sbuild = new StatementBuilder();
   sbuild.setPattern(parser.getPattern());
   sbuild.setAccessSpec(parser.getAccessSpec());
   sbuild.build(doc);
FormatXML format = new FormatXML();
   format.setInputSource(new Input("xmldb/xmldb"));
// format.setInputSource(new Input("madb/madb"));
   format.writeDoc(parser.getAccessSpec());
}
```

```
public void parse(String xmlFile) {
    //This class may be any SAX parser, but the classpath
    // must be modified to include it.
    String parserClass = "com.ibm.xml.parsers.SAXParser";
    try {
        Parser parser = ParserFactory.makeParser(parserClass);
        HandlerBase handler = new PatternHandler();
        parser.setDocumentHandler(handler);
parser.setErrorHandler(handler);
        try {
            parser.parse(xmlFile);
            pattern = ((PatternHandler) handler).getPattern();
        } catch (SAXException se) {
            se.printStackTrace();
        } catch (IOException ioe) {
            ioe.printStackTrace();
        }
    } catch (ClassNotFoundException ex) {
        ex.printStackTrace();
    } catch (IllegalAccessException ex) {
        ex.printStackTrace();
    } catch (InstantiationException ex) {
        ex.printStackTrace();
    }
}
}
/********************* StatementBuilder.java **********************/
package com.xweave.xmldb.rgquery;

import com.xweave.xmldb.rserve.*;
import java.util.*;
public class StatementBuilder {
    protected GraphPattern pattern;
    protected AccessSpec accessSpec = null;
    static String EDGE_VIEW = "xdb_ele_edges_help_v";
    protected Hashtable varNameHash = null;
public StatementBuilder() {
    super();
}
protected void addVarName(String name, String value) {
    getVarNameHash().put(name, value);
}
public boolean build(String doc) {
    accessSpec = getAccessSpec();
    QuerySpec querySpec = getAccessSpec().getQuerySpec();
    Enumeration e = getPattern().getEdges().elements();
```

```
    StringBuffer select = new StringBuffer();
    StringBuffer from = new StringBuffer();
    EdgePattern edge;
    String tableAlias, key, destcol;
    PatternNode source, label, dest;
    int ctr = 1;
while (e.hasMoreElements()) {
        tableAlias = "t"+ctr++;
        from.append(EDGE_VIEW+" "+ tableAlias +", ");
        if (doc != null) {
            querySpec.addConstraint(tableAlias+".doc",doc);
        }
        edge = (EdgePattern) e.nextElement();
        source = edge.getSource();
        if (source.getType() != 'V') {
            System.err.println("Source should be a variable in "+edge);
            return false;
        }
        if (existsVarName(source.getName())) {

querySpec.addConstraint(tableAlias+".source","@"+getVarName(source.getName
()));
        } else {
            addVarName(source.getName(),tableAlias+".source");
        }
        label = edge.getLabel();
        if (label.getType() != 'C') {
            System.err.println("Label should be a constant in "+edge);
            return false;
        }
        querySpec.addConstraint(tableAlias+".name",label.getName());
        dest = edge.getDest();
        switch (com.xweave.xmldb.Default.DBProduct) {
            case com.xweave.xmldb.Default.ORACLE:
            destcol = "decode("+tableAlias+".dest_ref,-
1,"+tableAlias+".dest_val,"
                +tableAlias+".dest_ref)";
            break;
            case com.xweave.xmldb.Default.DB2:
destcol = "CASE WHEN "+tableAlias+".dest_ref = -1 THEN "
                +tableAlias+".dest_val ELSE char("+tableAlias+".dest_ref)
END";
            break;
            default:
            destcol = "CASE WHEN "+tableAlias+".dest_ref = -1 THEN "
                +tableAlias+".dest_val ELSE "+tableAlias+".dest_ref END";
```

```
        }
        switch (dest.getType()) {
            case 'C':
            //in RDB view, no constants are references, so use dest_val
            querySpec.addConstraint(tableAlias+".dest_val",dest.getName());
            break;
            case 'V':
if (existsVarName(dest.getName())) {

querySpec.addConstraint(destcol,"@"+getVarName(dest.getName()));
            } else {
                addVarName(dest.getName(),destcol);
            }
        }
    }
    if (ctr == 1) {return false;}
    from.setCharAt(from.length()-2,' '); //trim the trailing ','; trailing
spaces okay
    querySpec.setTableName(from.toString());
    //build report args
    e = getVarNameHash().keys();
    while (e.hasMoreElements()) {
        key = (String) e.nextElement();
        select.append(((String)getVarNameHash().get(key)) + " AS " + key +
", ");
    }
    if (select.length() == 0) {
        //No variables in query
        return false;
    }
    select.setCharAt(select.length()-2,' '); //trim the trailing ',';
trailing spaces okay
    //build accessSpec
    accessSpec.getReportSpec().setReportArgs(select.toString());
    accessSpec.getReportSpec().setElementName(pattern.getName());
    return true;
}
protected boolean existsVarName(String name) {
    return getVarNameHash().containsKey(name);
}
public AccessSpec getAccessSpec() {
    if (accessSpec == null) {
        accessSpec = new AccessSpec();
    }
    return accessSpec;
}
```

```
public GraphPattern getPattern() {
   return pattern;
}
protected String getVarName(String name) {
   return (String) getVarNameHash().get(name);
}
protected Hashtable getVarNameHash() {
if (varNameHash == null) {
      varNameHash = new Hashtable();
   }
   return varNameHash;
}
public void setAccessSpec(AccessSpec newValue) {
   this.accessSpec = newValue;
}
public void setPattern(GraphPattern newValue) {
   this.pattern = newValue;
}
}

/*********************** PatternHandler.java **********************/
package com.xweave.xmldb.rgquery;

/**
 * Pattern Handler that creates a GraphPattern
 */
import org.xml.sax.*;
import java.util.*;
class PatternHandler extends HandlerBase implements DocumentHandler {
   protected GraphPattern pattern = null;
   protected EdgePattern edge = null;
   protected PatternNode node = null;
public PatternHandler() {
   super();
}
public void characters(char[] chars, int start, int length) {
   String string = new String(chars, start, length);
   string = string.trim();
//skip whitespace
   if (string.length() == 0) return;
   setNode(new PatternConstant(string));
}
public void endElement(String tag) {
   if (tag.equalsIgnoreCase("SOURCE")) {
      getEdge().setSource(getNode());
      node = null;
```

```
    } else if (tag.equalsIgnoreCase("LABEL")) {
        getEdge().setLabel(getNode());
        node = null;
    } else if (tag.equalsIgnoreCase("DEST")) {
        getEdge().setDest(getNode());
node = null;
    } else if (tag.equalsIgnoreCase("EDGE")) {
        getPattern().addEdge(edge);
        edge = null;
    }
}
protected EdgePattern getEdge() {
    return edge;
}
protected PatternNode getNode() {
    return node;
}
protected GraphPattern getPattern() {
    return pattern;
}
protected void setEdge(EdgePattern newValue) {
    this.edge = newValue;
}
protected void setNode(PatternNode newValue) {
    this.node = newValue;
}
protected void setPattern(GraphPattern newValue) {
    this.pattern = newValue;
}
public void startElement(String tag, AttributeList attrList) {
    if (tag.equalsIgnoreCase("PATTERN")) {
        //graph pattern
        setPattern(new GraphPattern(attrList.getValue("name")));
    } else if (tag.equalsIgnoreCase("EDGE")) {
        setEdge(new EdgePattern());
} else if (tag.equalsIgnoreCase("VAR")) {
        setNode(new PatternVar(attrList.getValue("name")));
    }
}
}

/************************ GraphPattern.java **********************/
package com.xweave.xmldb.rgquery;

import java.util.*;
```

```
public class GraphPattern {
   public String name = null;
   private Vector edges = null;
public GraphPattern() {
super();
}
public GraphPattern(String name) {
   super();
   setName(name);
}
protected void addEdge(EdgePattern edge) {
   getEdges().addElement(edge);
}
protected Vector getEdges() {
   if (edges == null) {
      edges = new Vector();
   }
   return edges;
}
public String getName() {
   return name;
}
public void setName(String newValue) {
   this.name = newValue;
}
public String toString() {
   Enumeration e = getEdges().elements();
   StringBuffer buf = new StringBuffer();
   while (e.hasMoreElements()) {
      buf.append(e.nextElement().toString());
   }
   return buf.toString();
}
}

/************************** EdgePattern.java ***********************/
package com.xweave.xmldb.rgquery;

public class EdgePattern {
   public PatternNode source = null;
   public PatternNode dest = null;
   public PatternNode label = null;
public EdgePattern() {
   super();
}
public PatternNode getDest() {
   return dest;
```

```
}
public PatternNode getLabel() {
    return label;
}
public PatternNode getSource() {
    return source;
}
public void setDest(PatternNode newValue) {
    this.dest = newValue;
}
public void setLabel(PatternNode newValue) {
    this.label = newValue;
}
public void setSource(PatternNode newValue) {
    this.source = newValue;
}
public String toString() {
    return "("+ getSource() + " " + getLabel() + " " + getDest() + ")";
}
}

/*********************** PatternNode.java **********************/
package com.xweave.xmldb.rgquery;

public abstract class PatternNode {
    public String name;
public PatternNode() {
    super();
}
public PatternNode(String name) {
    super();
    setName(name);
}
public String getName() {
    return name;
}
public abstract char getType();
public void setName(String newValue) {
    this.name = newValue;
}
public String toString() {
    return name;
}
}
```

```
/********************** PatternConstant.java ************************/
package com.xweave.xmldb.rgquery;

public class PatternConstant extends PatternNode {
public PatternConstant() {
    super();
}
public PatternConstant(String name) {
    super(name);
}
public char getType() {
    return 'C';
}
}

/************************** PatternVar.java **************************/
package com.xweave.xmldb.rgquery;

public class PatternVar extends PatternNode {
public PatternVar() {
    super();
}
public PatternVar(String name) {
    super(name);
}
public char getType() {
    return 'V';
}
public String toString() {
    return "?" + name;
}
}
```

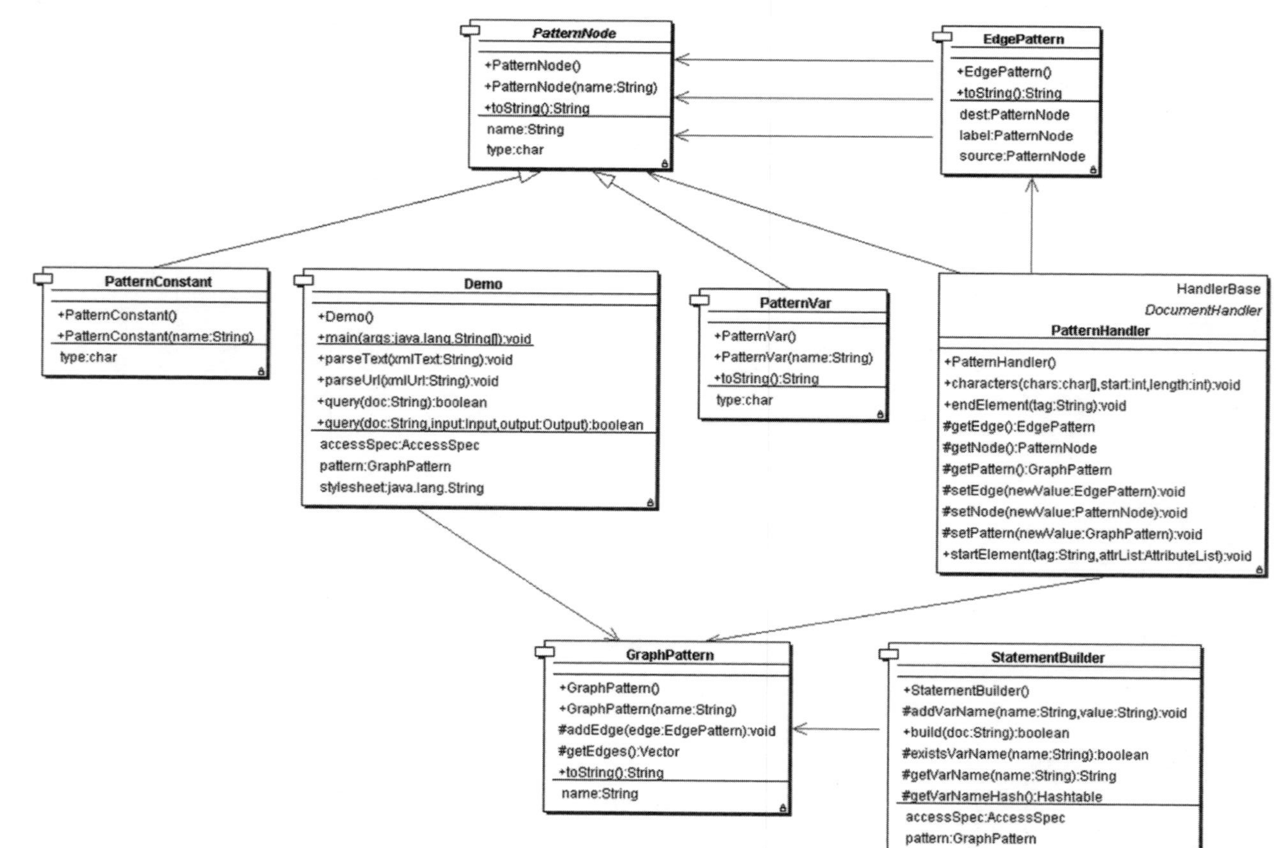

Figure 8–17 UML diagram for relational query algorithm implementation

Example 8–19 : Graph Pattern for an Automobile for Sale

```
<?xml version="1.0"?>
<pattern name="ToyotaForSell">
  <edge>
    <source><var name="auto"/></source>
    <label>make</label>
    <dest>Toyota</dest>
  </edge>
  <edge>
    <source><var name="auto"/></source>
    <label>model</label>
    <dest><var name="model"/></dest>
  </edge>
  <edge>
    <source><var name="auto"/></source>
    <label>year</label>
    <dest><var name="year"/></dest>
  </edge>
  <edge>
    <source><var name="auto"/></source>
    <label>price</label>
    <dest><var name="price"/></dest>
  </edge>
</pattern>
```

Example 8–20 : Generated SQL Query of Graph Pattern (Oracle)

```
select decode(t3.dest_ref,-1,t3.dest_val,t3.dest_ref) year,
       decode(t4.dest_ref,-1,t4.dest_val,t4.dest_ref) price,
       t1.source auto,
       decode(t2.dest_ref,-1,t2.dest_val,t2.dest_ref) model
 from xdb_ele_edges_help_v t1,
      xdb_ele_edges_help_v t2,
      xdb_ele_edges_help_v t3,
      xdb_ele_edges_help_v t4
 where t1.doc = '6' AND
       t1.name = 'make' AND
       t1.dest_val = 'Toyota' AND
       t2.doc = '6' AND
       t2.source = t1.source AND
       t2.name = 'model' AND
       t3.doc = '6' AND
       t3.source = t1.source AND
       t3.name = 'year' AND
       t4.doc = '6' AND
       t4.source = t1.source AND
       t4.name = 'price';
```

Example 8–21 : Generated SQL Query of Graph Pattern (DB2)

```
select
  CASE WHEN t4.dest_ref = -1
       THEN t4.dest_val
  ELSE char(t4.dest_ref)
      END AS price,
     CASE WHEN t2.dest_ref = -1
  THEN t2.dest_val
  ELSE char(t2.dest_ref)
      END AS model,
     CASE WHEN t3.dest_ref = -1
  THEN t3.dest_val
  ELSE char(t3.dest_ref)
      END AS year, t1.source auto
  from xdb_ele_edges_help_v t1,
       xdb_ele_edges_help_v t2,
       xdb_ele_edges_help_v t3,
       xdb_ele_edges_help_v t4
 where t1.doc = 2 AND
       t1.name = 'make' AND
       t1.dest_val = 'Toyota' AND
       t2.doc = 2 AND
       t2.source = t1.source AND
       t2.name = 'model' AND
       t3.doc = 2 AND
       t3.source = t1.source AND
       t3.name = 'year' AND
       t4.doc = 2 AND
       t4.source = t1.source AND
       t4.name = 'price'
```

Example 8–22 : Result of Graph Pattern Query

```
<?xml version="1.0"?>
<collection>
<ToyotaForSell>
  <YEAR>2000</YEAR>
  <PRICE>7995</PRICE>
  <AUTO>8</AUTO>
  <MODEL>Camry</MODEL>
</ToyotaForSell>
<ToyotaForSell>
  <YEAR>2003</YEAR>
```

```
  <PRICE>14995</PRICE>
  <AUTO>14</AUTO>
  <MODEL>Celica</MODEL>
</ToyotaForSell>
</collection>
```

The Java implementation consists of a Test class whose main method calls the XML parser, builds the SQL, and executes it against the database. The building and execution of the SQL uses the RServe package from Chapter 5.

The parser uses a PatternHandler instance, which is a SAX handler that creates a GraphPattern object for the graph pattern in the XML file. A GraphPattern consists of a name and an EdgePattern for each edge. The EdgePattern has a source, label, or destination that can be either a PatternConstant or PatternVar (variable). The PatternConstant and PatternVar are both subclasses of the PatternNode abstract class.

After the GraphPattern object is created from the XML graph pattern file by the XML parser, a StatementBuilder object is created to build a SQL statement from the GraphPattern. The SQL statement is built using the AccessSpec class of the RServe package. Query and constraint objects are created as part of the AccessSpec that are used to generate the SQL string after all parts of the query are specified. The SQL string is generated and sent to the database using the Input class of RServe, and the resulting data is rendered using RServe's FormatXML object.

8.4.5 Graph Query Algorithm

Graph querying provides a mechanism to retrieve all nodes that match a graph pattern. The *graph query engine* iteratively retrieves matching edges from the database and joins those results to previous intermediate query results following a set of join rules.

The general process of the algorithm is as follows:

1. Iterate through the edge patterns of the graph pattern. For each edge pattern

  1.1 Match an edge pattern against the database, retrieving all matching edges.

1.2 Using the appropriate join rule, add the edge results to the intermediate results from matching the previous edges.

2. Return the final result.

When including a new edge pattern in the intermediate query results, the edges corresponding to the pattern are joined to the intermediate results. If the variable(s) used in the pattern already occur in the intermediate query result, the effect is to restrict the intermediate query result to only contain values that also satisfy the new edge pattern. If the variable(s) used in the pattern do not occur in the intermediate query result, the effect is to perform a Cartesian product.

The graph querying algorithm is defined as a collection of join rules. As each edge is processed by the query engine, it is combined with the existing intermediate results based on the appropriate join rule. There are join rules for including an edge with

- No variables.
- One variable, when the variable *does not* already occur in the intermediate results.
- One variable, when the variable *does* occur in the intermediate results.
- Two variables, when the variables *do not* occur in the intermediate results.
- Two variables, when one variable *does* occur and one variable *does not* occur in the intermediate results.
- Two variables, when both variables *do* occur in the intermediate results. There are two subcases to this rule that depend upon the relationship between the two variables with respect to the rest of the query.

To efficiently store the intermediate results of joins, Cartesian products are not calculated directly, but the terms are stored separately. Thus, the intermediate result data structure consists of a set of tables, which—if combined in a Cartesian product—would result in the current intermediate result. The advantage of suspending Cartesian products is that it reduces space for disjoint patterns, increases performance for unoptimized queries, and improves the efficiency of the query optimization.

Query optimization is performed by sorting the edges in the query based on the number of matches in the database. Although counting the number of edges in an unindexed database is expensive, the indexing strategy described in Chapter 9 simplifies the optimization by storing the count that each edge pattern would match within the indexing structure.

The join rules are described in the next section, and examples of the rules are given in the section after that one.

8.4.5.1 Join Rules

The join rules are

1. If an intermediate query result is empty, the final query result is empty.
2. If no variables are in the edge pattern:
   - **2.1** If the edge occurs in the database, the query continues with the next edge pattern.
   - **2.2** Otherwise, the query result is empty.
3. If the edge pattern has any variables and does not match any edges in the database, then the query result is empty.
4. If there is one variable in the edge pattern and the variable does not occur in the intermediate result, then the variable values of the edges matched by the edge pattern are added to a new intermediate result table. Later, the edges will be joined to another edge result set or be part of the Cartesian product at the end of the query.
5. If one variable is in the edge pattern and the variable does occur in the intermediate result, then restrict the intermediate result table that contains the variable to the values occurring in the edges for that variable. In effect, the existing values for the variable are deleted if the value does not occur in the new edges, and the rows in the internal table that used the deleted variable values are also deleted.
6. If the edge pattern has two variables and neither variable occurs in the intermediate result table, then the edge results are added to a new intermediate result table.
7. If the edge pattern has two variables and one variable occurs in the intermediate result table and one variable does not, then the values from the edge patterns are joined to the intermediate query result.

8. If the edge pattern has two variables and both are in the intermediate result table, there are two subcases: this join rule and the next one. If both variables are in the same internal table, the internal table is restricted by the values from the edge patterns. Rows are retained in the internal table only if they contain a value pair that occurs in the edges.
9. If the variables are in different internal tables, the two internal tables and edge results are joined.
10. If the edge pattern has three variables, the internal tables and edges are joined.

8.4.5.2 Examples

The following examples illustrate the join rules. Consider the graph in Figure 8–18. Its edges are in Table 8–9.

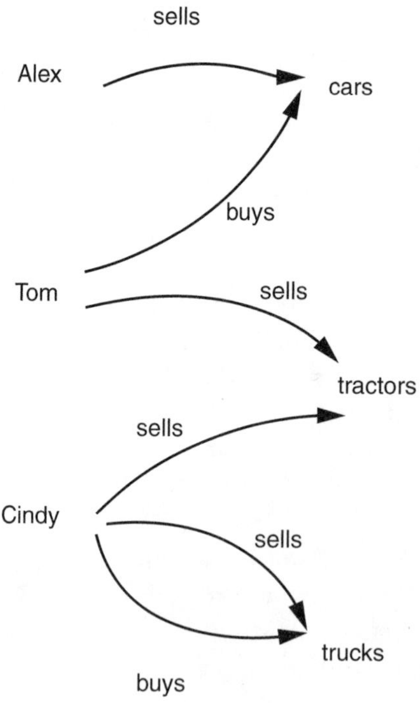

Figure 8–18 Simple graph of car, truck, and tractor dealers

Table 8–9 Edges in Graph of Vehicle Traders

SOURCE	*NAME*	*DEST*
Alex	sells	cars
Tom	buys	cars
Tom	sells	tractors
Cindy	sells	tractors
Cindy	sells	trucks
Cindy	buys	trucks

It may be queried to answer the following questions:

- What does Cindy sell? *(Rule 3)*
  The edge pattern (Cindy sell ?x) against the graph in Figure 8–18 results in binding the variable ?x to "trucks" and "tractors", because the database only contains two edges that match the pattern: (Cindy sells trucks) and (Cindy sells tractors). An intermediate binding result is created with one table using Rule 4 (which is also the final result):

?x
trucks
tractors

- Who sells and buys trucks? *(Rules 4,5)*
  The edge patterns (?x sell trucks) and (?x buy trucks) must both be compared against the database in Figure 8–8. The intermediate result of querying the first edge pattern (?x sell trucks) is

?x
Cindy

Comparing the edge pattern (?x buy trucks) against the database also returns the value "Cindy" and the intermediate result remains the same after applying Rule 5.

- What is sold by the person who also buys trucks? *(Rule 6 followed by 5)*
  The edge patterns (?x sells ?y) and (?x buys trucks) are compared against the database. The intermediate result after querying (?x sells ?y) is

?x	*?y*
Alex	cars
Cindy	trucks
Cindy	tractors
Tom	trucks

Because the query of (?x buys trucks) against the database returns "Cindy", the intermediate result is restricted using Rule 5 to eliminate the first and last row and result in

?x	*?y*
Cindy	Trucks
Cindy	Tractors

- Who buys and sells the same thing? *(Rules 6, 8)*
  The edge patterns (?x buys ?y) and (?x sells ?y) are compared against the database. The result of the edge pattern (?x buys ?y) is

?x	*?y*
Cindy	Trucks
Tom	Cars

The result of the edge pattern (?x sells ?y) is

?x	*?y*
Alex	Cars
Cindy	Trucks
Cindy	Tractors
Tom	Trucks

The edges are added to the intermediate query result using Rule 8 because the variables "?x" and "?y" are both in the previous table. The result of the join is

?x	*?y*
Cindy	trucks

The result of the query is that "Cindy" buys and sells "trucks".

- What else is sold by anyone who buys what Alex sells? *(Rules 6, 4, then 9)*
  Consider the edge patterns (?x sells ?y), (Alex sells ?z), (?x buys ?z) in that order. The edge pattern (?x sells ?y) returns the following values:

?x	*?y*
Alex	cars
Cindy	trucks
Cindy	tractors
Tom	tractors

The edge pattern (Alex sells ?z) returns the value "cars", which results in an intermediate query result with two tables (from Rule 5):

?x	*?y*
Alex	cars
Cindy	trucks
Cindy	tractors
Tom	trucks

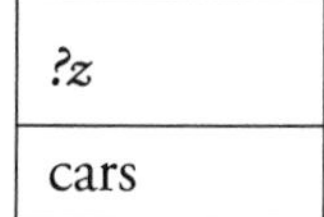

?z
cars

The third edge (?x buys ?z) has the following values:

?x	*?z*
Cindy	trucks
Tom	cars

These values are joined with the intermediate query result via application of Rule 9, and the resulting binding table is:

?x	*?y*	*?z*
Tom	trucks	cars

The answer to the query is that "cars" are sold by "Tom", who also buys trucks.

8.4.5.3 Mathematics

The expressions to build the intermediate result table can be represented as relational operations on the internal tables. The operations are presented in Figure 8–19.

If σ is a sequence of edge patterns with n conjuncts, consider the computation series

$$S_0\sigma_1S_1\sigma_2S_2\cdots\sigma_nS_n$$

where σ_i is the ith edge pattern in σ, S_i is a binding set, and the final result $query(\sigma)$ is given by S_n. The following are true of each computation $S_{i-1}\sigma_iS_i$ where $llquery(\sigma_i)$ refers to the result of the edge pattern:

1) If $S_{i-1} = \emptyset$, then $S_i = \emptyset$, thus $S_i, \ldots, S_n = \emptyset$ and $query(\sigma) = \emptyset$.
2) If σ_i has *no* variables,
   a) If $llquery(\sigma_i) \neq \emptyset$, then $S_i = S_{i-1}$, i.e, the binding set remains unchanged.
   b) If the result of σ_i is empty, i.e., there is no such conjunct in the data store $llquery(\sigma_i) = \emptyset$, then the query fails, i.e., $S_i, \ldots, S_n = \emptyset$.
3) If σ_i has one or two variables and the conjunct matches no atomic sentence in the data store, i.e. $llquery(\sigma_i) = \emptyset$, then the query fails.
4) If σ_i has one variable which *does not* already occur in S_{i-1}, call it x, then

   $$S_i = S_{i-1} \cup \{ \langle x, llquery(\sigma_i)_x \rangle \}$$

   where $llquery(\sigma_i)_x$ denotes the values specified by $llquery(\sigma_i)$ for the variable x, and $\langle x, \{t_1, t_2, \ldots\} \rangle$ is the linear notation for a binding relationship for x with values $\{t_1, t_2, \ldots\}$.
5) If σ_i has one variable which *does* already occur in S_{i-1}, call it x, then

   $$S_i = (S_{i-1} - R^x_{i-1}) \cup R^x_{i-1}|_{x \in llquery(\sigma_i)_x}$$

   where R^x_{i-1} denotes the binding relationship for x (along with the binding for any other variables in that relationship). The notation $\langle binding\ relationship \rangle |_{\langle restriction \rangle}$ is a selection operation — select tuples from R^x_{i-1} where $x \in llquery(\sigma_i)_x$.
6) If σ_i has two variables, say x and y, *neither* of which occur in S_{i-1}, then

   $$S_i = S_{i-1} \cup \{ \langle xy, llquery(\sigma_i)_{xy} \rangle \}$$

7) If σ_i has two variables, *one* of which occurs in S_{i-1}, say x, and the other does not, say y, then

   $$S_i = (S_{i-1} - R^x_{i-1}) \cup \left[\left(R^x_{i-1}|_{x \in llquery(\sigma_i)_x} \right) \times \left(\langle xy, llquery(\sigma_i)_{xy} \rangle |_{x \in R^x_{i-1}} \right) \right]$$

   The new binding relationship is the same as the old one cross the *llquery* result where the x's occur in both the old binding relationship and the query. This can be written as a natural join:

   $$S_i = (S_{i-1} - R^x_{i-1}) \cup (R^x_{i-1} \bowtie \langle xy, llquery(\sigma_i)_{xy} \rangle)$$

8) If σ_i has two variables, say x and y, *both* of which occur in S_{i-1}, and they are in the *same* binding relationship, i.e., $R^x_{i-1} = R^y_{i-1}$, then

   $$S_i = (S_{i-1} - R^{xy}_{i-1}) \cup (R^{xy}_{i-1}|_{(x\ y) \in llquery(\sigma_i)_{xy}})$$

9) If σ_i has two variables, say x and y, *each* of which occur in S_{i-1}, but in *separate* binding relationships, i.e., $R^x_{i-1} \neq R^y_{i-1}$, then

   $$S_i = (S_{i-1} - R^x_{i-1} - R^y_{i-1}) \cup ((R^x_{i-1} \bowtie \langle xy, llquery(\sigma_i)_{xy} \rangle) \bowtie R^y_{i-1})$$

   which is equivalent to

   $$S_i = (S_{i-1} - R^x_{i-1} - R^y_{i-1}) \cup ((R^x_{i-1} \times R^y_{i-1}) \bowtie \langle xy, llquery(\sigma_i)_{xy} \rangle)$$

   which is equivalent to

   $$S_i = (S_{i-1} - R^x_{i-1} - R^y_{i-1}) \cup ((R^x_{i-1} \times R^y_{i-1})|_{(x\ y) \in \langle xy, llquery(\sigma_i)_{xy} \rangle})$$

Figure 8–19 Formulas for graph algorithm join rules

8.5 Query Report Tools

There are path and graph query tools that implement the algorithms discussed in this chapter. Path query tools are discussed in Section 8.5.1 using XSL to provide formatted reports. Section 8.5.2 describes graph query tools and how to produce an XML report from a graph query.

Path and graph querying tools may be used to query the database. Path querying tools may be stand-alone or integrated with XSL processing to provide formatted reports. A graph querying tool implements an algorithm to compare graph patterns to the database, such as the algorithm of the previous section.

8.5.1 Path Querying with XSL

The templates in XSL match paths in a document before executing the body of the template. The same form can be used to combine path querying in an XML database with report generation using XSL. One approach to supporting path querying in an XML database is to modify an XSL query engine to perform path queries against the documents in the database.

Although it is possible to retrieve the entire document before performing the match, it is more efficient to retrieve only the nodes that are specified in the path patterns. The nodes may be accessed directly from the database when needed. Caching and database indexing may improve performance of the database request.

A useful extension to the XSL query engine would support querying across documents in a database. XSL supports pattern matching against the elements of a document but not across the collection of documents in a database. There are three possible solutions:

- **a.** To match against all the elements in all the documents.
- **b.** To restrict querying to only one document.
- **c.** To store additional information about the documents, which could then be filtered to limit the documents, against which the querying is performed.

Solutions (a) and (b) are problematic. Solution (a) is time-consuming and potentially uninformative, and Solution (b) is overly restrictive. Solution (c) addresses those issues by allowing filtering appropriate to the query.

For Solution (c), information you can store about a document includes some of the following:

- Name of the document.
- Descriptive features of the document that are defined by the user.
- Any element type names used in the document.
- The person who created the document.
- The owner of the document (if different from the creator).
- When the document was created and last accessed.
- Summary information defined by the user. For example, in the automobile buyer examples, the summary information might include the source of the classifieds and in the Wal-Mart example, the summary information might include the store.

Any of this information can be used to filter the documents to be included in the query. A query would be performed only on documents that met those specific restrictions.

The information can be stored in a specialized form in the database. The storage structures in Chapter 4 support storage of the name of the document. The indexing strategies in Chapter 9 address ways in which the element type names might be associated with a document. A specialized data structure can also be created for the descriptive features of the document defined by the user, or that data may be stored as a summary or meta-data document in XML. The summary or meta-data document can also be searched using the XSL path querying. It may also be possible to store some of that information as a fragment within the document.

XPath, XSLT, or other path-centric querying tools are most useful with a document-processing-oriented view of the data. Graph querying is more useful when taking a data-processing-oriented approach.

8.5.2 Graph Querying

Graph querying consists of two steps. The first step is to compare the graph pattern with the documents in the database. The second step is to generate a report from the result of the query.

The graph pattern is compared with the documents in the database via the graph query algorithm described in Section 8.4. The query algorithm has two parameters: The first is the graph pattern, as described in Section

8.4.2; the second is the document (or documents) against which the query pattern is to be compared. The document (or documents) may be specified directly or using some of the ways described in Section 8.5.1 to select documents to be queried.

The result of the graph query is a collection of graphs. The graphs consist of the graph pattern and the variable bindings in the query result. The variable bindings are presented as a table. The table may be rendered as a tabular report, as would occur with a relational database query, or it may be rendered as an XML document. In either case, only some of the variables would be desired for the report. A simple XML document can be created from the query result table by creating a single element for each record in the table. For example, the report of the query in Figure 8–11 might result in a document such as this:

```
<buyers>
  <auto>
        <model>Camry</model>
        <year>2000</year>
        <price>7995</price>
        <name>Fred Flintstone</name>
  </auto>
  <auto>
        <model>Celica</model>
        <year>2003</year>
        <price>14995</price>
        <name>George Jetson</name>
  </auto>
<buyers>
```

The document could be returned to the user as is or could be processed further. For example, the graph pattern could also be used in some cases to generate a document that has a similar structure to the source document, though that would be difficult if the graph pattern was not a strict tree. A more useful report may be generated by using an XSL stylesheet on the query result document to further transform the data into a custom report.

If a Web architecture for the XML database is used—such as one described in Chapter 5—the query tool may be embedded within a Web server, which would result in an XML report being returned for the query.

Indexing

- How can XML data be efficiently accessed in a database?
- What data structures are necessary to support queries of XML documents?
- How can those data structures be organized to support interdocument links?
- How can intradocument and interdocument links be efficiently retrieved?

9

9.1 Overview

Indexing XML documents share many issues with indexes for relational and object-oriented databases. Rapid access of information is desired and a tradeoff is chosen between access time and storage space used. By using storage space to track the location of data items in a way that reduces access time, faster querying can be performed. Indexes can be created on the data values in the database, such as numbers and strings, as well as on the structural connections.

XML documents are fairly unique in that there is a shared, though variant, structure that can be navigated across multiple dimensions, such as element/subelement, element/attribute, element/character data, and node/sibling. Each dimension can be treated separately in developing the data structures to support rapid access. In a relational database, the only structural dimension that can be navigated is across joins, such as between the primary key and foreign key constraints. Structural indexing in a relational database consists primarily of creating data structures to most efficiently access the table records (rows) given a primary key value (or value from a unique constraint). In an object-oriented database, objects have an *ad hoc* interconnection structure that depends upon the definition of each class.

Although similar to the joins of a relational database, the access patterns may vary widely because the access occurs in the methods of the object-oriented database programming language and not in a declarative language, such as SQL. An object-oriented database may create indexes similar to the kind created for a relational database but often indexing is focused on virtual memory addressing schemes that map object identifiers to the most efficient physical storage, given the likely accessions. XML documents may be navigated through parent/child subelement relationships, element sibling relationships, document order, or links.

Several database indexing books and articles are available for relational and object-oriented databases, and other sources describe indexing of documents. Rather than duplicate the information in those sources, this chapter focuses primarily on aspects of XML databases that are not covered by those sources.

9.2 Element Data Structures

The element data structures of XML require different index strategies than relational or object-oriented databases because the element data structures have a more flexible internal structure.

An element's structure information can vary, so building a static indexing structure for an element is not feasible, unlike indexing structures for object classes. The structure of an element is not fixed, though the element type name provides some type information. Although the regularities in XML are exploited by the user interface and query tools of the previous chapters, low-level indexing requires a rigid framework. That framework is provided by decomposing element structures into a collection of binary relationships.

Binary relations are relations with two attributes (or columns). Because the named relationships of an element have both a source and a destination, they are a binary relation. For example, attributes have a name and subelements have an element type name. Binary relationships and graph edges are equivalent in the context of this book. Indexing in this chapter is focused on storage and access of the individual binary relation.

Indexing of element data structures requires creating indexing data structures to access the subelement relationships based on element and element type, attributes, and link relationships. There may also be a need to index on the character data regions that occur within a document.

One unique aspect of XML databases is the bi-directional navigation of documents by element type, attributes, and link relationships. Starting from a database, a collection of documents, a document root, or the element node of a fragment, an efficient mechanism is desired to get to another specified node. In other words, indexing addresses the following questions:

- What is an efficient way to get to the desired destination node(s) given a query?
- Can interdocument relationships be efficiently created within and across databases?
- Given the Web of information available in XML databases, what techniques can be used to efficiently search the data without resulting in inefficient, exhaustive searches?

9.3 Indexing Strategies

Three indexing strategies are described for indexing bi-directional links within an XML database: no indexing, complete indexing, and partial indexing. Indexing may not always be appropriate, and it is important to recognize those situations. Some situations may benefit from completely indexing the binary relations in a database, whereas other situations should use a partial indexing strategy.

9.3.1 No Indexing

No indexing may be appropriate in several situations: when data is rapidly changing and when queries access a small number of nodes. When the data source is rapidly changing, keeping the index up to date may be more expensive than performing the queries. Time spent indexing should be substantially less than the time spent answering queries; if not, then less indexing should be performed. When the database is large relative to the number of nodes accessed during a query, then indexing may be less efficient than direct access. For example, if the queries typically access only the parent and child nodes of an element, then indexing across all ancestors and descendents in a large database would be wasteful. Indexing is also inappropriate when there is not direct physical access to the individual nodes—for example, if an entire document is stored in a flat file.

9.3.2 Complete Indexing

Complete indexing is most appropriate when a relatively small, unchanging database is frequently accessed. Every possible query (within some space) is made more efficient by indexing structures. Complete indexing of the links and subelement relationships within a document may increase performance. Capturing the relationships between documents can also provide performance gains when performed at an appropriate level of granularity.

To completely index the subelement and link relationships, a common store of subelement and link relationships is assumed as described in Chapter 8. The subelement relationships are indexed on the element type name and the link relationships are indexed on the binary relation name (equivalent to a pair of XML link roles). For example, the subelement and link relationships in the fragment

```
<customer id="1.112">
    <item id="1.456">
      <upc xlink:type="simple" xlink:href="#1.4532"/>
    </item>
</customer>
```

can be encoded by the following relationships:

source	*name*	*destination*
customer:1.112	item	item:1.456
item:1.456	upc	upc:1.4532

To simplify the description of the link structure, both subelement and link relationships are treated the same. If needed in practice, the type of relationship can be encoded in a record structure (such as an object); in the name, such as "ele_item" and "lnk_upc"; or by using namespaces, such as "ele:item" and "lnk:upc".

To access the relationships in the most time-efficient manner, a complete index of the table can be performed. Binary relations can be completely indexed using seven indexes in addition to the storage of the complete relation. The indexes are keyed off the following:

- Source only
- Name only
- Destination only

- Source and name
- Source and destination
- Name and destination
- Source, name, and destination

If the binary relations are stored in a RDBMS, then these indexes can be created using the RDBMS indexing facility. However, for native store or implementation in an OODB, specialized data structures for indexing are valuable. Some of the possible indexing data structures are discussed here.

9.3.2.1 Indexing Data Structure

The seven indexes can be stored in a hierarchical data structure that is accessed as shown in Figure 9–1 depending upon which of the three pieces of information is known. For a document there is one Initial Index. For each binary relation name, there is a Name Index; for each unique source, there is a Source Index; and for each unique destination, there is a unique Name-Source Store. Within the Name Index, there is a Name-Source Index for every source that occurs with that binary relation name in the document, and there is a Source Store for every destination that occurs with that binary relation name in the document. Within the Name-Source Index, there is a pointer from each destination that occurs with the specified name and source to the binary relationship in which it occurs. The information is retrieved from the index structure as follows:

- No information—All relationships in the document are retrieved from the database.
- Source only—The Source Index structure for the source provides all names and destinations for a given source.
- Name only—The Name Index structure for the name provides all source and destinations for a given name.
- Destination only—The Name-Source Store for the destination provides all name and sources for a given destination.
- Source and name—The appropriate Name Index is chosen based on the name known. Within the Name Index, an index of sources is followed to the appropriate Name-Source Index, which has all destinations for a given name and source.

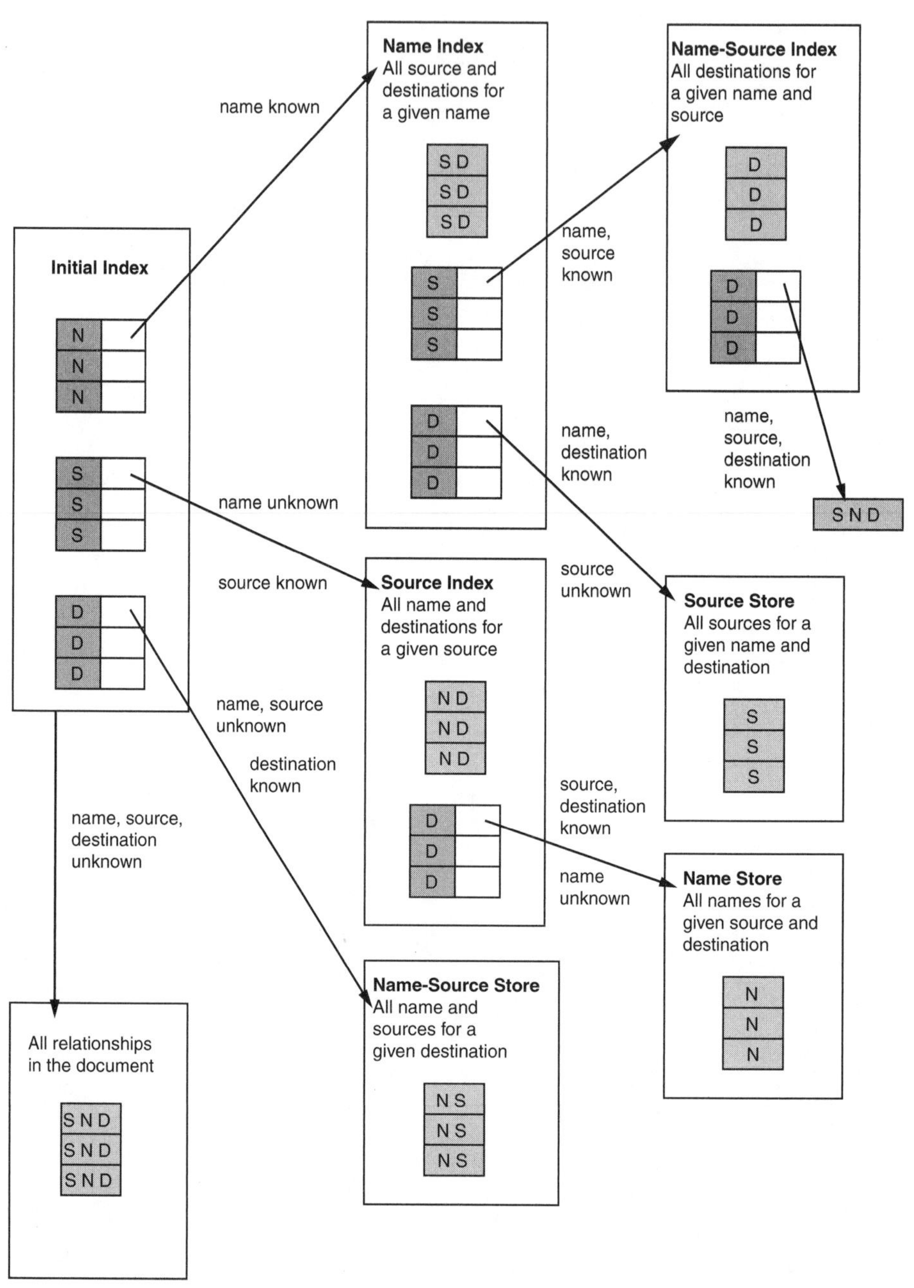

Figure 9–1 Data structure for complete indexing of binary relationships

- Source and destination—The appropriate Source Index is chosen based on the source known. Within the Source Index, an index of destinations is followed to the appropriate Name Store, which has all names for a given source and destination.
- Name and destination—The appropriate Name Index is chosen based on the name known. Within the Name Index, an index of destinations is followed to the appropriate Source Store, which has all sources for a given name and destination.
- Source, name, and destination—To verify that a binary relationship with a given source, name, and destination are in the database, the appropriate Name Index is chosen based on the name known. Within the Name Index, an index of sources is followed to the appropriate Name-Source Index, and within the Name-Source Index, an index of destinations is followed to the appropriate binary relationship in the database, if it exists.

The complete index can be used to store all binary relationships of a document in the database. Section 9.3.3 describes how to select which names and nodes should be included in the indexing. Section 9.3.4 describes how to generalize the index tables to cover multiple documents, and Section 9.4 describes how to index multiple documents in multiple databases and multiple sites.

9.3.2.2 Attribute Indexing

The indexing of attribute values depends upon the queries supported. If attribute values are queried only within the context of an element, then additional indexing is probably not needed—for example, if all queries are of the form "Find element with type name X and attribute Y with value Z." However, if attributes may be queried without specifying element type names, then indexing may be useful. Take, for example, a query of the form "Find all elements with an attribute named 'href'." In that case, it would be useful to have a bi-directional indexing structure keyed off the element type name and the attribute name, as is shown in Figure 9–2. It is unlikely that queries would be asked that depend on unnamed attribute values, but those can be addressed by indexing the underlying data structures that store the attribute value strings (e.g., the attribute table in the fine-grained relational storage of Section 4.2). If the elements have substantial information in attributes, which are queried in a variety of forms, the nested index store

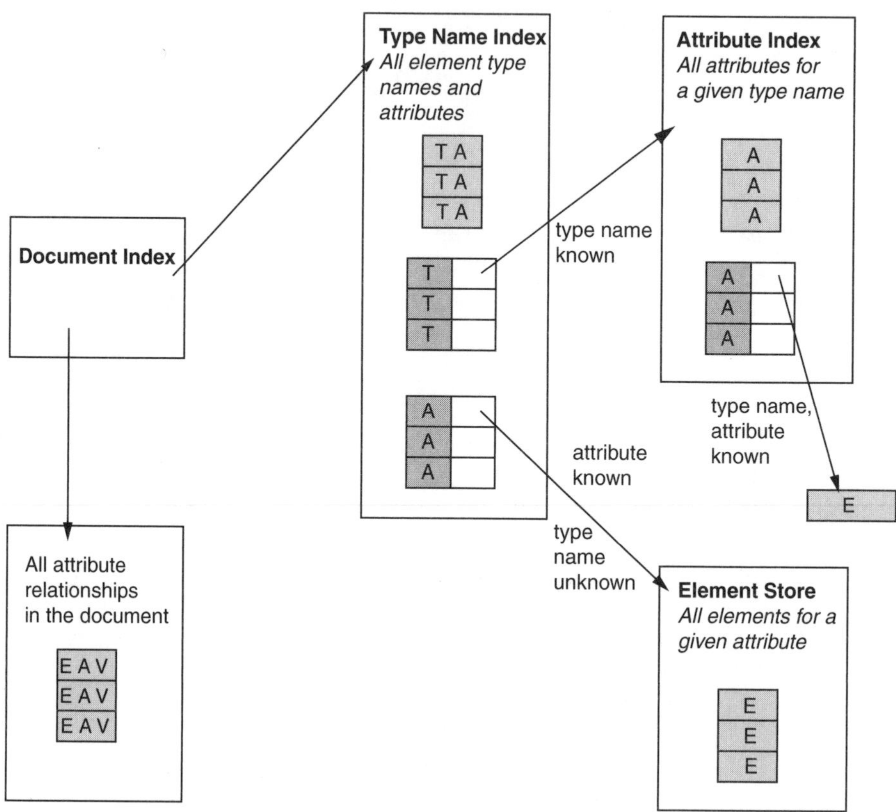

Figure 9–2 Indexing data structure for element type names and attributes

described earlier may be appropriate. In that case, the attribute names can be treated the same as the element type names or link names.

Indexing of the underlying data structures that store the data can also be appropriate, for example, if the documents have a unique name (as described in Chapter 4), the unique names may be indexed to speed up access of entire documents. If character data regions are to be queried against, then text indexing of the character data regions may also increase performance of those queries. Text indexing is described in other indexing resources and is not covered here.

Complete indexing may be combined with caching of intermediate query results to substantially increase the speed of query processing.

9.3.3 Partial Indexing

Indexing on only some of the elements, such as those with certain type names, will reduce the amount of indexing required. This strategy is similar to the slicing strategies described in Section 4.4.1. Indexing can also be reduced by supporting indexing on only some of the possible queries.

Partial indexing reduces the number of indexing structures created in complete indexing. Some queries are supported by indexing and others are not. Hopefully, the most frequently asked, time-consuming queries are the ones supported by indexing structures, and the least frequently asked, quickly answered queries are not indexed. Choosing the best indexing strategy depends upon knowing the kinds of queries that are likely to be asked.

One way to reduce the space needed for indexing is to eliminate some of the indexing structures used in complete indexing. A combination of indexing with search can respond rapidly to the most frequently asked queries and provide reasonable response to the less frequently asked queries. The eight kinds of low-level queries can be reduced to four as follows:

- No information known—For each binary relation name in the database (stored in the Initial Index), combine all the source/destination pairs for the name from its Name Index. This results in a recreation of all the binary relationships.
- Source known—Retrieve the name/destination pairs from the Name-Destination Store.
- Name known—Retrieve the source/destination pairs from the Name Index.
- Destination known—For each binary relation name, access its Name Index, and from there, access the Source Store for the specified destination. Combine all the sources in that Source Store with the binary relation name to create the name/source pairs.
- Source and name known—Retrieve the destinations from the Destination Store.
- Source and destination known—Search the Name-Destination Store associated with the specified source for all the name/destination pairs that contain the specified destination and return the list of binary relation names that occur with the specified destination.
- Name and destination known—Retrieve the sources from the Source Store.

- Source, name, and destination known—Search the Destination Store associated with the specified name and source for the specified destination.

This corresponds to the indexing structure in Figure 9–3, which stores four pointers for each binary relationship instead of eight.

When processing speed is at a premium, an extra pointer may be used to rapidly perform the low-level query that verifies a binary relationship with a specified source, name, and destination when that query is frequently asked. In that case, the partial indexing data structure can be modified to replace the Destination Store with a Name-Source Index as described in the previous data structure and shown in Figure 9–4. This structure stores five pointers for each binary relationship.

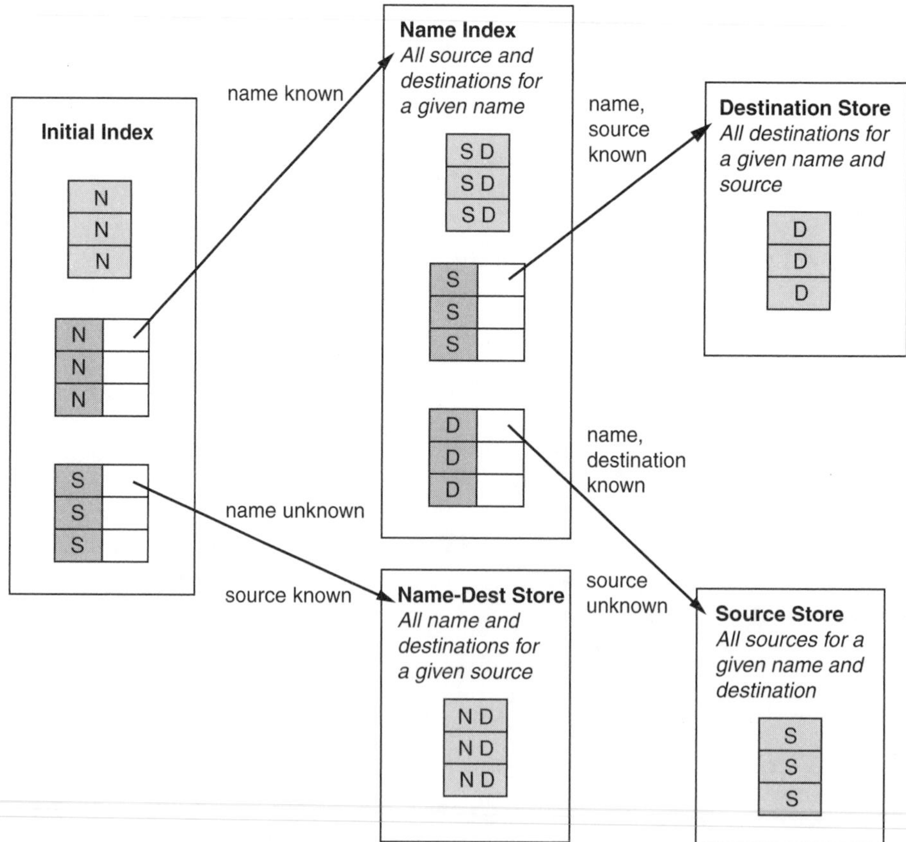

Figure 9–3 Data structure for partial indexing of binary relationships

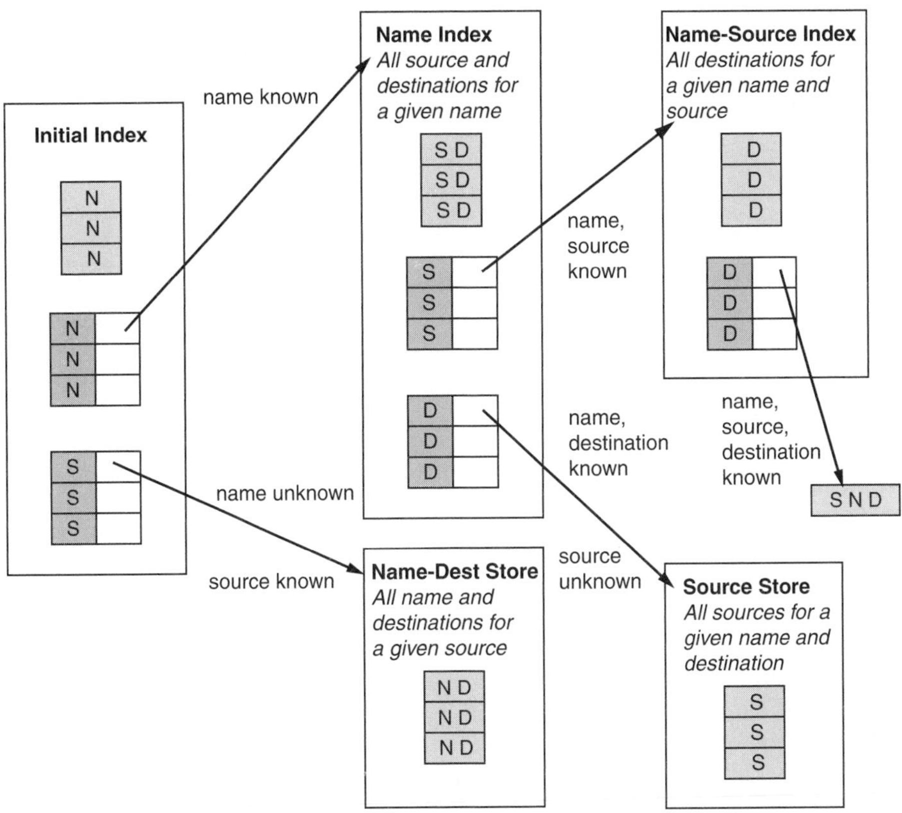

Figure 9–4 Alternate data structure for partial indexing of binary relationships

Alternatively, when space is at a premium, the indexing structures may be combined to three low-level queries as follows:

- No information known—For each binary relation name in the database (stored in the Initial Index), combine all the source/destination pairs for the name from its Name Index. This results in a recreation of all the binary relationships.
- Source known—For each binary relation name, access its Name Index, and from there, access the Destination Store for the specified source. Combine all the destinations in that Destination Store with the binary relation name to create the name/destination pairs.

- Name known—Retrieve the source/destination pairs from the Name Index.
- Destination known—For each binary relation name, access its Name Index, and from there, access the Source Store for the specified destination. Combine all the sources in that Source Store with the binary relation name to create the name/source pairs.
- Source and name known—Retrieve the destinations from the Destination Store.
- Source and destination known—For each binary relation name, access its Name Index, and from there, access the Destination Store for the specified source. Search through the Destination Store for the specified destination, and if it is found, include the binary relation name in the result. Alternately, the Source Store for the specified destination may be searched more efficiently for the specified source, if the Source Store is smaller.
- Name and destination known—Retrieve the sources from the Source Store.
- Source, name, and destination known—Search the Destination Store associated with the specified name and source for the specified destination.

This corresponds to the indexing structure in Figure 9–5, which stores three pointers for each binary relationship.

9.3.4 Cross-document Indexing

Indexing and querying discussion has primarily focused on a single document, though the same methods directly apply across documents that are stored in the same database. In storing links that cross documents, however, it may be more efficient to index only the referenced document rather than the referenced fragment. The referenced document's index is then searched for the appropriate fragment. This allows the internal storage structure of the document to be encapsulated and changed as needed, without modifying extra-document indexes. For example, if there is a link between fragment 1.234 (i.e., fragment 234 in document number 1) and fragment 2.456, then the index for document 1 would refer to the link involving 1.234 as a reference to document 2 without direct reference to the fragment 2.456. Conversely, the index for document 2 would refer to the link as a

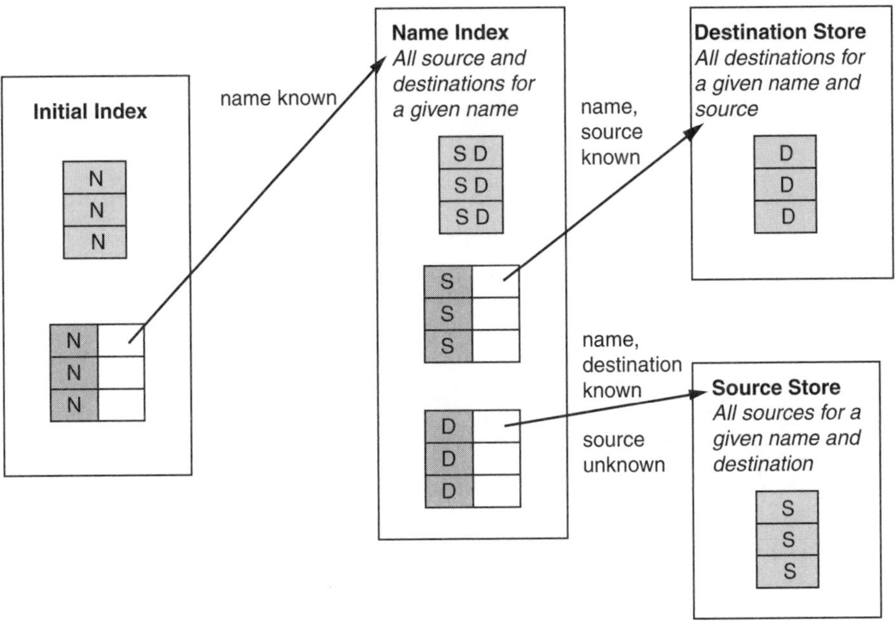

Figure 9–5 Data structure for compact partial indexing of binary relationships

reference to document 1 without referring to the fragment in document 1. The link would still contain the two fragments, but the index would be simplified. An advantage is that the index structures are smaller; for example, fragment 1.234 could refer to a hundred links in document 2 without changing the document 1 index, and the document 2 index would only change for those fragments that are not already referring to a fragment in document 1. A disadvantage is that querying cross-document links require two lookups: The first lookup is in the local index structure to find the external documents referred to by the link, and the second lookup is in the index structure of the other document(s) to find the appropriate link reference. A second disadvantage is that it may be more time-consuming to delete links when the indexes are updated. The two lookup steps for a cross-database link are illustrated shortly for the query "Find all purchases that refer to UPC 1600042040." For this query, it is assumed that the database schema contains the conceptual relationships shown in Figure 9–6 and sup-

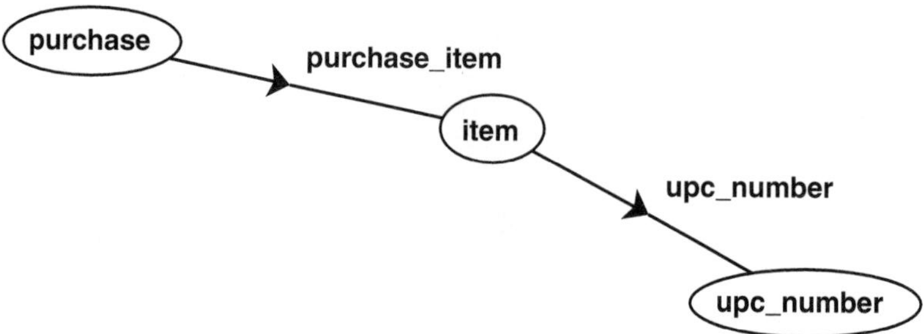

Figure 9–6 Partial conceptual schema for item purchases

ports the two binary relation query (?x upc_number 1600042040);(?y purchase_item ?x). Document 1 contains the items as follows:

```
<items fragment="1.1">
...
    <item fragment="1.789">
      <upc_number>1600042040</upc_number>
      ...
    </item>
</items>
```

There is a slight simplification because the character data region of the "upc_number" is assumed to be the value stored in the index instead of a fragment that refers to the upc_number, such as binary relationship (1.790 cdata_value 1600042040).

Document 2 contains the following items:

```
<purchases fragment="2.1"/>
    ...
    <purchase fragment="2.5049">
      <purchase_item
        xlink:type="simple"
        xlink:href="items.xml#1.789"
        xlink:title="UPC 1600042040"/>
      ...
    </purchase>
    ...
    <purchase fragment="2.6136">
      <purchase_item
        xlink:type="simple"
        xlink:href="items.xml#1.789"
        xlink:title="UPC 1600042040"/>
```

```
      ...
    </purchase>
    ...
    <purchase fragment="2.9045">
      <purchase_item
        xlink:type="simple"
        xlink:href="items.xml#1.789"
        xlink:title="UPC 1600042040"/>
      ...
    </purchase>
    ...
</purchases>
```

The relevant index links for Document 1 are

source	*name*	*destination*
1.789	upc_number	"1600042040"
2.x	purchase_item	1.789

The relevant index links for Document 2 are

source	*name*	*destination*
2.5049	purchase_item	1.789
2.6136	purchase_item	1.789
2.9045	purchase_item	1.789

In performing the query (?x upc_number 1600042040);(?y purchase_item ?x), the index for Document 1 would be searched for links participating in the relation "upc_number" with a destination value of "1600042040". The result would be the fragment "1.789". The second binary relationship would be queried and joined to the previous values, resulting in a binding of the "?y" variable to Document 2, denoted "2.x" in the table above. The Document 2 relationships would be expanded by querying the Document 2 index links with the constraining query (?y purchase_item ?x) to retrieve fragments "2.5049", "2.6136", and "2.9045".

A subtle indexing requirement is the need to map from the "upc_number" name to Document 1. This can occur by either searching each document for the binary relation name "upc_number", using the document-level index, or by indexing all of the binary relation names in the database to map each name to the documents in which it is used.

The document-level indexing of links only affects the indexing in one direction. The alternative direction index remains the same. For example, a query for the item purchased in the transactions "2.5049", "2.6136", and "2.9045" would immediately return the fragment "1.789" for the UPC item. There is an assumption in this method that either the source or the destination "owns" the link.

In some cases, it may be useful to have a separate document (or documents) that owns the links in a database. For example, the purchase elements might contain only the general information about a purchase transaction and a separate document would link the purchase with the item. In that case, the purchase index link would refer to a third document, say Document 3; the third document would contain the link between the two fragments, say "1.789" and "2.5049". The Document 1, with the items, would have a reference in the index links to Document 3. The disadvantage is that all queries would need to access two indexing structures. The advantage is that all links are stored in one (or more) document(s), and the other document indexes are much smaller.

A similar method to the cross-document indexing may be used to index links across databases. A cross-database query would require lookups of three index structures: in the current document to find the external database reference, in the external database to find the document reference, and in the external document to find the appropriate link.

A similar method can also be used to link documents across sites, assuming that read-write privileges to the external databases are allowed. It is also possible to have a different indexing strategy at the database or site level than the document level. For example, a document might "own" its links, but links across databases or sites might be stored in a separate document.

9.4 Document Identification

For complex applications, XML databases may exchange data between multiple sites. It may be more efficient if trusted sites can exchange references to documents and fragments rather than the entire data item. To provide efficient access to items in another database, the indexing strategy must be generalized.

One mechanism to index documents at another site is to create an indexing structure for the link roles and element type names of interest. For example, if another site provided read-only access to historical stock quotes, then a local document could be created for the stocks of interest with links to the external database. The local index could be created that refers to the external element types of interest—such as price, date, and volume—as links. Local queries may be formed that would transparently access the external data as the links are followed.

If more information from the external site is desired to form local queries, then some limited, external information may be locally mirrored to provide more rapid access. For example, the recent price and date of stocks might be locally mirrored, but volume and older information might not be. The information that is not central to the queries can still be captured as links, even if not mirrored or indexed.

So far, fragments have been referred to with their unique identifier. In accessing documents—and databases—it can be useful to have unique names for the documents and databases. Chapter 4 describes support for the unique naming of documents within a database, and a similar mechanism can be used to create unique names for databases within a site. Most sites already have a unique name, encoded within a internet domain name or IP address. When site identifiers are combined with database and document names, it is possible to uniquely identify every fragment in an XML database regardless of site. Exchanging data across sites within an enterprise may use a simpler addressing scheme, but still provide unique identifiers to every XML fragment.

Fragments may also be identified with unique names, for example, the UPC number in the example above could be the name of the item. A unique name of "UPC1600042040" could be mapped uniquely to fragment "789" within Document 1, thus simplifying the creation of cross-document links between fragments.

Mechanisms can be used to simplify the numbering of sites, databases, documents, and fragments to simplify linking and indexing across databases when the sites have specific data-exchange policies—for example, within e-commerce relationships or scientific projects. One simple mechanism is to encode the site by a number based on the IP address using a formula to translate the four-part base 256 address into a decimal number. One simple (invertible) encoding is

```
site = ((((d1 · 256) + d2) · 256 + d3) · 256 + d4)
```

where the sections of the IP address are mapped as d1.d2.d3.d4. The databases can be uniquely numbered as are the documents and fragments. This mechanism does not depend up the choice of XML database system, but only requires that the databases, documents, and fragments have a unique identifier.

A symbolic mechanism can be overlaid on the numeric mechanism above, to provide the naming of databases and documents within a site, much as the Internet DNS service protocol provides resolution from domain names to IP addresses. The symbolic names can be encoded within URLs to be compatible with W3C standards, for example

http://www.xweave.com/xmldb/retrieve?db_name="walmart"& doc_name= "items"&frag_ name="UPC1600040240"

or

http://www.xweave.com/xmldb/retrieve/walmart/items/UPC1600040240

This URL could map to a unique identifier for site.database.document.fragment such as "2130706433.4.1.179" that could be shared between sites.

The same mechanism can also be used to link between XML documents and relational or object-oriented databases that present data as XML, as described in Chapter 5. The database identifiers for a site can vary across flat-file documents and the relational or object-oriented databases.

In internet search applications, the same mechanism can be used to uniquely identify XML documents and fragments of interest regardless of their storage mechanism. For example, if a search is performed that captures elements with type name of "stylesheet" in the W3C XSL namespace, then those documents can be locally mapped to a unique identifier, based on site and document. If the "xsl:include" or "xsl:import" elements within those documents are also to be indexed, they can be mapped to unique fragment identifiers within the document. After all the documents references have been found, an indexing structure can be created as described above. The resulting index structure may be queried to find relationships between stylesheets, and the mapping between document identifier and URL can be used to navigate to the external sites to retrieve additional information. In this case, the database identifier would probably remain unused, unless a site provided HTTP access through multiple ports.

9.5 Search Technologies

How can the indexing strategies described be applied to internet searching where numerous large data sources provide read-only access?

One way to apply the querying and indexing strategies to internet searching is to create local index structures for external documents. The documents may remain on the external site, but the local indices provide efficient access for querying. The documents are retrieved; the index data structures are created; and the documents may be deleted. Whether to delete the documents depends upon the type of queries to be performed, the index strategy chosen, the size of the documents, the number of documents, the frequency in which they are accessed, the time taken to retrieve the document from the external site, and the space available. In many cases, space will not be available to store all the documents.

The factors may be quantified as follows.

Probability of a document being required can be calculated as:

$p_j = \Sigma_i$ p(query$_i$ occurring) · p(query$_i$ accessing document$_j$) · p(document$_j$ will need to be retrieved from external source to answer query$_i$ given the index strategy chosen)

Relative time taken to retrieve a document compared to other documents is

t_j = (time taken to retrieve document$_j$) / (average of all document retrieval times)

Relative space taken to store a document locally compared to average space available is

s_j = (size of document$_j$) / ((total space available) / (number of documents to be stored))

These three factors can be combined into a score capturing the benefit of storing a document locally as follows:

$$b_j = (p_j \cdot t_j)/s_j$$

The higher the score, the greater the relative benefit of storing the document locally.

One strategy to using the benefit score would be to create probabilities and benefit scores for each document, then start storing the documents beginning with those that have the most benefit until the available space is consumed. A more realistic strategy is to group the documents into classes based on estimated probability of being accessed and use the benefit score to make decisions about those classes, relative to their time and space. In many cases, no real information about the probability of access is available, and then the documents may be treated uniformly.

For example, if only certain kinds of queries are to be performed on the documents, such as queries on element types or link relationships, then partial indexing may be appropriate. These queries may be answered using binary relation queries and there may be sufficient information in the index structure to answer those queries without retrieving the document. Thus, those documents would have a zero probability of being retrieved. However, the user may occasionally wish to see the answer to the query in the context of the document. So, occasionally, some documents may need to be retrieved, but the probability of retrieval is uniform across the documents; thus, the relative time and relative space components of the benefit score predominate.

Because the documents need to be initially retrieved to create the index, a cache of the documents can be created during the indexing where documents with the lowest benefit score are dropped to make space for new documents with higher benefit scores. The access time can be estimated from the single retrieval necessary to create an index, and the space needed for the document is available after retrieval. The only information not available is the average space available per document and the average retrieval time. These must be estimated to obtain the relative weight of the time and space components. The information may be available from previous knowledge or it may be estimated from the sample of documents retrieved before the cache fills, assuming no systematic bias in the retrieval process; for example, that documents with quicker access times are retrieved first.

In some cases, a more accurate estimate of probability of access may be available. When the index is being created to answer a certain kind of query, traversing link, or finding a specific element type name or namespace, then the quantity of relevant information in the document may be proportional to its probability of being accessed. For example, if all internet documents are searched for sites that have an XML link to a site in your domain for later querying, then the number of those links that occur in a document may be proportional to the probability it would be part of a query result and need to be retrieved. In that case, the probability could be estimated as the number of links in a document divided by the total number of links found.

In practice, the external documents should be periodically checked to see if they have been modified and the index re-created. This can also occur incrementally as documents are retrieved in response to queries.

Implementation

- How is an XML DBMS built?
- What are basic features specific to an XML DBMS?
- What is required for a robust XML DBMS?

10

To integrate the concepts and systems of the previous chapters, I describe a simple notebook system that supports storing, retrieving, and querying of genes and gene relationships. The system illustrates some of the basic functionality required of an XML database system with emphasis on the design and data linking aspects. XML databases provide greater flexibility than other databases in domain modeling, conceptual design, and capturing complex relationships. Those aspects are illustrated by describing a relatively static system for a domain focused on a single concept with complex interrelationships. Less emphasis is placed on the dynamic aspects of transactions, security, and recovery. Those dynamic aspects are very similar to the aspects required by any modern DBMS and are not particular to XML databases. Thus, the system described in this chapter does not illustrate the complete functionality needed for an XML DBMS but only the functionality that differs from traditional DBMSs.

10.1 Notebook System

The requirements for a generic *notebook system* are that it captures information about the following:

- A specific entity (in this chapter, a gene)
- Annotations on those entities
- Pair-wise relationships between those entities
- Collections of entities and pair-wise relationships

The focus is on a system that captures peripheral information about one complex type of data. Although limited in scope, focusing on a central data type is useful in a variety of domains. The notebook framework can be used to describe information in domains, such as resume tracking, auto parts, Web pages, or molecular biology.

A resume database has information about job candidates: their names and contact information. The job candidate entry is annotated with information based on interviews and resume scanning, such as previous experience, job skills, and education.

Other databases may have pair-wise relationships, such as interactions. An auto parts database has information about parts: their part number and description. The auto parts are annotated with the vehicle in which it occurs, the price of the parts, and their location within the vehicle. The part relationship database contains the part–part relationships that describe how the auto parts are assembled or if one part may be substituted for another one. Collections of part–part relationships define subsystems of the automobile.

A Web page database has information about Web pages and their URLs. The Web page entry is annotated with summary information, words occurring in the page, user feedback scores, and whether that site has paid money to have the page occur at the top of search results. There are Web page relationships; for example, that one page links to another or that two pages have similar content (based on statistics of word overlap). Collections of Web pages can be created that cover similar content, geographical area, and so on.

Collections capture information in the same structure as XML and are represented as an XML fragment. There are no *a priori* constraints on the types of collections or their XML representations, thus most (if not all) related information can be captured within the framework. All information could be captured as collections, but the annotations and (binary) relationships are useful because the shared structure is made explicit and can be exploited in designing user interfaces and downstream processing.

The user interface should allow browsing of intrinsic information about the key entity and add annotations to it or relationships that include it. That data is stored in the database. In addition, configuration information must be captured on the types of annotations or relationships possible.

From the components described in the previous chapters, the notebook system built in this chapter is developed to capture biological information about genes. Applying the development of a notebook to a specific domain will better illustrate the steps than a generic presentation. Hopefully, because only the design and data storage aspects are fully realized in a notebook system, the intricacies of developing a complex database application for a specific domain will be avoided.

10.2 Biological Motivation

To appreciate some of the decisions made in design of the gene notebook and to apply that process in developing a system for a different domain, it may be useful to understand some of the biology that is being captured. It might also be interesting.

The collection of all genes in an individual is called its *genome.* The genome is often broken up into several long stretches of DNA, called *chromosomes,* and DNA is represented as a string of the characters A, C, T, and G, which represent the four bases of DNA. Many genes occur on a chromosome. Genes are shorter sequences of DNA, and in multicelled organisms, gene sequences are composed of even shorter stretches of DNA called *exons* and *introns.* The typical process is that the exons are transcribed and spliced together by the cellular machinery to create a messenger RNA (mRNA). The mRNA is translated into *proteins* that perform some function in the cell by interacting with other proteins. There are several kinds of interactions including, but not limited to, enzymatic, structural, or transportation. Proteins are often expressed specifically in certain cell types or locations within a cell. For example, cell structure proteins typically are found in and around the cell wall, splicing enzymes are found in the cell nucleus, and muscle fiber proteins are typically found in muscle cells.

The gene notebook captures the information about genes, their DNA and protein sequence, their sequence similarities, and their protein interaction and functions. It may also relate to information about the expression of the protein in certain cells under certain experimental conditions. An example of such expression information would be that the quantity of one protein is ten times greater in a cancer cell than a normal cell. The sequence of a gene may also be similar to the sequence of another gene whose protein performs a similar function. For example, a protein that provides connectivity in a heart muscle may be very similar, but not identical to, a protein that provides connectivity in a skeletal muscle.

Genes may also have similarities across organisms when they encode for proteins with similar function. After genes are translated to proteins, the linear protein sequence of amino acids folds into a 3D shape. The protein that makes up the heart muscle fiber of a cat is more similar to a protein in the heart muscles of pig that has a similar function than to a protein used in making red blood cells in a cat.

Some of the basic cell transport mechanisms have proteins that are similar across many organisms including yeast, fruit flies, and mammals. Understanding how the proteins interact in one organism can help scientists understand how they interact in another organism.

To track the relationships between the thousands or tens of thousands of genes in an organism and their relationships to each other and to similar genes in other organisms requires a database that captures and manipulates highly interconnected data. XML databases can provide that functionality, especially when augmented with the graph-like structure provided by XML Links.

10.3 User Requirements

The requirements for the gene notebook are that the user be able to store, retrieve, query, delete, and update entries for genes, gene annotations, gene pair-wise relationships, and more complex gene relationships. A gene has a name and occurs within the *genome* (collection of all genes) of a particular organism. Gene annotations include additional information about the gene: its chromosome location, DNA sequence, protein sequence, cellular location, tissue specificity, and function. These annotations describe the gene through indirect evidence but are not definitive *a priori*. Almost all information about genes is discovered through indirect experiments, because they are used in molecular processes occurring in dynamic, easily perturbed systems. Annotation information is supported by experimental evidence produced by an experiment or obtained from results published by other scientists in the literature. Because biology is focused on how gene products interact, it is useful to explicitly capture similarities or interactions between two genes. More complex relationships between collections of genes are also captured, such as collections of genes on a chromosome, in a region of a chromosome, in a pathway, in a literature reference, or in a family of similar sequences.

The gene notebook application manipulates entries for each gene. Each gene has annotations that augment the entry. There are many types of annotations, and new types can be added often, so the gene concept is kept as a light-weight entity and annotations refer to the gene. Two genes may be compared using a comparison relationship based on either an intrinsic property—such as name of the gene—or its annotations. For example, the DNA sequence of two genes may be compared for similarities, or the literature references of two genes may be compared for keyword overlap. Collections of genes and gene–gene relationships can also be captured.

The Gene Notebook constrains all information to be explicitly associated with genes. At times, there may be information that is gene-related, but the relevant gene is not known or does not need to be explicitly stated to be useful. This information can be captured in the collection section associated with an empty set of genes.

10.4 Conceptual Model

The domain to be captured in the gene notebook is described using a conceptual model. The process defined in Chapter 2 describes the steps of listing the major concepts, fleshing out the descriptions, choosing central concepts, diagramming their relationships as a conceptual schema, adding detail to the conceptual schema from the domain, and reviewing and revising the schema as necessary.

The major concepts to be captured in the gene notebook are

- Genes—defining characteristics such as name and organism
- Gene annotations—properties and descriptions of genes, such as chromosome location, DNA sequence, protein sequence, cellular location, and known or presumed function
- Similarities—similarity between two genes based on overall sequence similarity or similarity of functional subsequences
- Interactions—two genes interact in some biological way, such as their proteins physically interact, one regulates the other through intermediate mechanisms, or they are both regulated by a shared construct

- Chromosomes—identified as one of the biological constructs containing the DNA sequence of genes
- Regions of chromosomes—their location within a chromosome
- Literature references

The second step is to add more information about the concepts:

- Genes—consist of name and organism
- Gene annotations—chromosome location, DNA sequence, protein sequence, cellular location, tissue specificity, and known or presumed function
- Similarities—two genes, the type of similarity comparison, a value quantifying their similarity, and supporting information
- Interactions—two genes, the type of their interaction, details of the interaction, and supporting evidence
- Chromosomes—chromosome identifier
- Regions of chromosomes—chromosome and start and end of the region
- Literature references—source, author, and other citation information

The central concepts are the following:

- Gene
- Gene annotation
- Gene similarities
- Gene interactions

A conceptual schema can be developed from these primary concepts and filled in with details from the domain. In addition, because the domain description is being incorporated into a notebook application, it is useful to add a concept of the notebook. A conceptual schema is shown in Figure 10–1.

Logical design of the database schema consists of creating an XML document from the conceptual schema. Genes are the fundamental entity captured in the notebook and being manipulated by the application. All other major entities will refer to them.

All information about genes, gene interactions, and gene relationships are stored in a Gene Notebook XML document. The document consists of three sections: genes, interactions, and relationships. An empty Notebook is

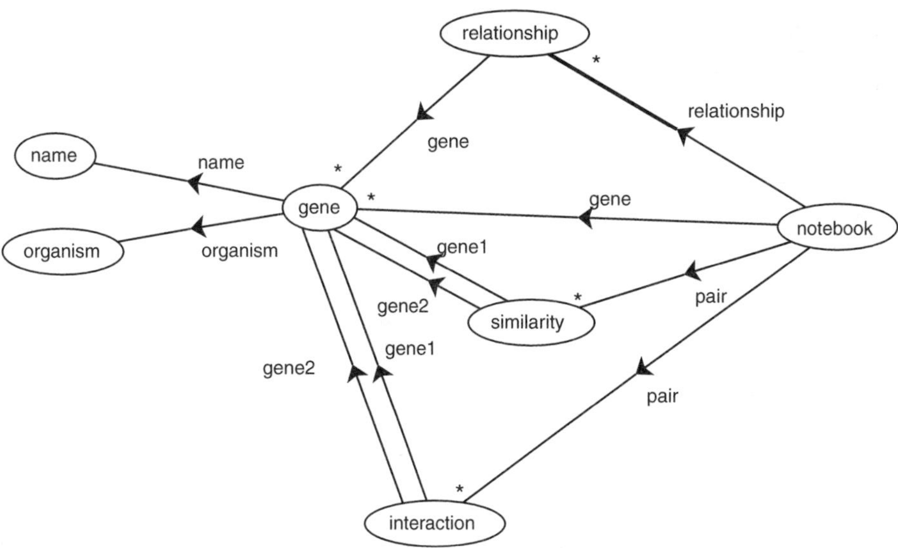

Figure 10–1 Conceptual schema for gene notebook

shown in Example 10–1. The document has three sections: "genes", "interactions", and "relationships". All the primary information for a Notebook is contained in one document, though the notebook may also contain links to other documents. An example XML document with data is given in Example 10–2.

In performing the logical design, the decision is made to isolate the gene elements into a "genes" element that will be at the top level of the document. As the annotations are dependent upon only one gene, they are associated with the gene that they annotate. The "gene" element gains an "annotations" element that contains all the annotations for that gene. The pair-wise and more complex relationships depend upon more than one gene, so are collected in the remainder of the document. The gene similarities and interactions share many characteristics, are manipulated similarly by the application and can be collected together as pair-wise relationships, as was described in the user requirements section above. Thus, they are collected into an "interactions" element. The remaining n-ary relationships can be collected together into another section of the document called "relationships".

Example 10–1 : Empty Gene Notebook Template Document

```
<?xml version="1.0"?>
<GeneNotebook>
<genes>
</genes>
<interactions>
</interactions>
<relationships>
</relationships>
</GeneNotebook>
```

Example 10–2 : Example Gene Notebook Document

```
<?xml version="1.0"?>
<GeneNotebook>
<genes>
 <gene id="531">
  <name>ANGPT1</name>
  <organism>Human</organism>
  <annotations>
   <protein_sequence>
    MPEPKKVFCNMDVNGG
   </protein_sequence>
  </annotations>
 </gene>
 <gene id="532">
  <name>ANGPT2</name>
  <organism>Human</organism>
  <family>angiopoietin</family>
  <annotations>
   <protein_sequence>
    MWQIVFFTLSCDLV
   </protein_sequence>
  </annotations>
 </gene>
</genes>
<interactions>
 <sequence_similarity id="10001" gene1="531" gene2="532">
  <score>
   89
  </score>
 </sequence_similarity>
</interactions>
<relationships/>
</GeneNotebook>
```

10.5 Application Description

The Gene Notebook has a three-tier system architecture with a Web browser client, Web server middle-tier with a Java servlet, and a relational DBMS back-end that stores XML documents. The client consists of an HTML home page and an XSL stylesheet and contains the biology-specific part of the application. The middle-tier is not domain-specific and would work for a variety of applications. The back-end is a storage system from Chapter 4 to capture XML documents, and the Gene Notebook consists of one XML document stored in the database.

The biology-specific aspects of the Gene Notebook consist of an HTML home page, an XSL stylesheet, and a single XML document stored in the database. The home page and HTML document generated by the stylesheet interact with a generic Java servlet that implements basic notebook functionality. The Java servlet is driven by commands to store, retrieve, delete, query, or modify a document. Modification of a document takes place with commands that retrieve, replace, append, or delete a fragment of a document.

10.5.1 Client

The Gene Notebook home page consists of forms to load and retrieve the XML document into the XML database. It also has a facility to set the relational database instance used for storage. When retrieving a Notebook document from the home page, the document is viewed using an XSL stylesheet. The home page is shown in Figure 10–2, and the HTML that generates it is in Example 10–3. Note the use of hidden variables and input boxes to build up the URLs that access the database, as was described in Chapter 7.

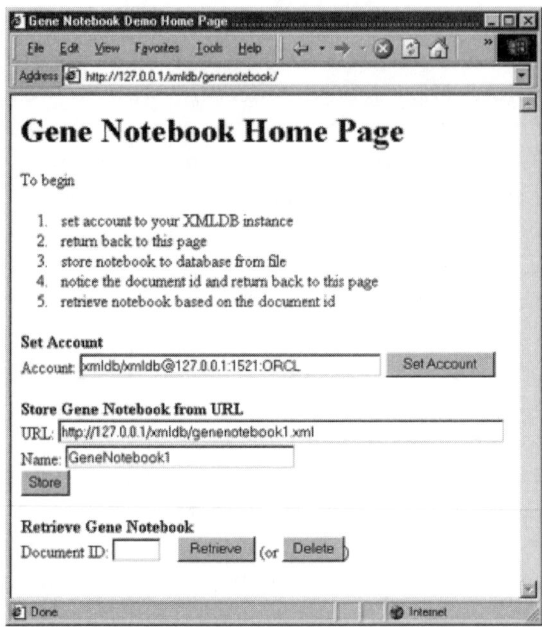

Figure 10–2 Home page for gene notebook

Example 10–3 : Home Page for Gene Notebook

```
<html>
<head>
<meta http-equiv="Content-Type" content="text/html; charset=iso-8859-1">
<title>Gene Notebook Demo Home Page</title>
</head>

<body>
<h1>Gene Notebook Home Page</h1>

To begin
<ol>
<li>set account to your XMLDB instance</li>
<li>return back to this page</li>
<li>store notebook to database from file</li>
<li>notice the document id and return back to this page</li>
<li>retrieve notebook based on the document id</li>
</ol>
```

```
  <form action=
        "http://127.0.0.1/servlets/com.xweave.xmldb.demo.XMLServlet"
        method="GET">
  <b>Set Account</b><br/>
  Account: <input type="input" name="setacct" size="40"
        value="xmldb/xmldb@127.0.0.1:1521:ORCL"/>
  <input type="submit" name="ignore" value="Set Account"/>
  </form>

  <form action=
        "http://127.0.0.1/servlets/com.xweave.xmldb.demo.XMLServlet"
        method="GET">
  <b>Store Gene Notebook from URL</b><br/>
  URL: <input type="input" name="url" size="60"
        value="http://127.0.0.1/xmldb/genenotebook1.xml"/><br/>
  Name: <input type="input" name="name" size="30"
value="GeneNotebook1"/><br/>
  <input type="submit" name="cmd" value="Store"/>
  </form>

  <form action="http://127.0.0.1/servlets/
com.xweave.xmldb.demo.XMLServlet"
        method="GET">
  <b>Retrieve Gene Notebook</b><br/>
  Document ID:
  <input type="input" name="doc" size=5/>
  <input type="hidden" name="includefragid" value="1"/>
  <input type="hidden" name="head" value="1"/>
  <input type="hidden" name="ss" value="/ss/genenotebook.xsl"/>
  <input type="submit" name="cmd" value="Retrieve"/>
  (or <input type="submit" name="cmd" value="Delete"/>)
  </form>

</body>
```

An example Notebook document is shown in Figure 10–3, and the XSL stylesheet which generates it is given in Example 10–4 and consists of four main collections of templates: templates for initialization and default processing, templates for genes, templates for interactions, and templates for relationships. Each major section of the XML Notebook is handled by a different collection of templates allowing the presentation to be tailored to the kinds of information being displayed. For example, the individual genes

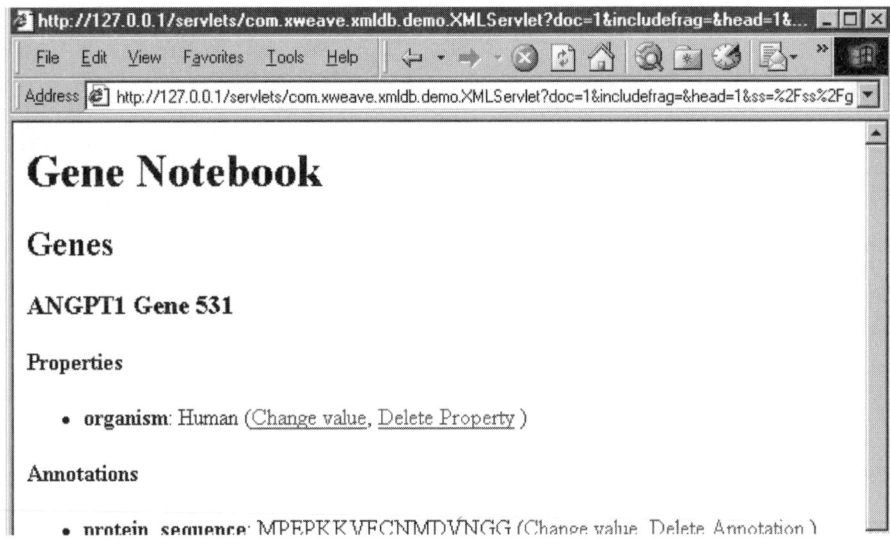

Figure 10–3 Example gene notebook

Example 10–4 : Stylesheet for Gene Notebook

```
<?xml version="1.0"?>
<!-- Stylesheet for viewing GeneNotebook document -->
<xsl:stylesheet xmlns:xsl="http://www.w3.org/TR/WD-xsl">

<xsl:template match="/">
<xsl:apply-templates />
</xsl:template>

<!-- Default templates -->

<xsl:template match="*">
  <DIV STYLE="margin-left:1em; color:gray">
    &lt;<xsl:node-name/><xsl:apply-templates select="@*"/>/&gt;
  </DIV>
</xsl:template>

<xsl:template match="*[node()]">
  <DIV STYLE="margin-left:1em">
    <SPAN STYLE="color:gray">
    &lt;<xsl:node-name/><xsl:apply-templates select="@*"/>&gt;
    </SPAN>
    <xsl:apply-templates select="node()"/>
    <SPAN STYLE="color:gray">&lt;/<xsl:node-name/>&gt;</SPAN>
```

```
  </DIV>
</xsl:template>

<xsl:template match="@*">
  <SPAN STYLE="color:navy">
  <xsl:node-name/>=
  "<SPAN STYLE="color:black"><xsl:value-of /></SPAN>"
  </SPAN>
</xsl:template>


<xsl:template match="cdata()">
  <pre>&lt;![CDATA[<xsl:value-of />]]&gt;</pre>
  </xsl:template>

<xsl:template match="textNode()"><xsl:value-of /></xsl:template>

<!-- GeneNotebook templates -->

<xsl:template match="GeneNotebook">
<h1>Gene Notebook</h1>
<xsl:apply-templates />
</xsl:template>

<xsl:template match="genes">
<h2>Genes</h2>
<xsl:apply-templates />
</xsl:template>

<xsl:template match="interactions">
<h2>Gene Interactions</h2>
<table STYLE="border:2px solid black"  BORDER="1">
  <tr>
    <td STYLE="padding:0px 6px; font-weight:bold">Gene 1</td>
    <td STYLE="padding:0px 6px; font-weight:bold">Gene 2</td>
    <td STYLE="padding:0px 6px; font-weight:bold">Interaction</td>
    <td STYLE="padding:0px 6px; font-weight:bold">ID</td>
    <td STYLE="padding:0px 6px; font-weight:bold">Values</td>
  </tr>
  <xsl:for-each select="*">
    <tr>
    <td STYLE="padding:0px 6px"><xsl:value-of select="@gene1"/></td>
    <td STYLE="padding:0px 6px"><xsl:value-of select="@gene2"/></td>
    <td STYLE="padding:0px 6px"><xsl:node-name/></td>
    <td STYLE="padding:0px 6px"><xsl:value-of select="@id"/></td>
    <td>
```

```
        <xsl:apply-templates select="*">
          <!-- This could handle the interaction data a lot better.
          For example, it does not handle nested elements well
          and it uses gene identifiers instead of names
          and those should be hypertext links to the gene -->
          <xsl:template match="*[node()]">
              <SPAN STYLE="color:navy">
              <xsl:node-name/>:<xsl:apply-templates select="@*"/>
              </SPAN>
              <xsl:apply-templates select="node()"/>
          </xsl:template>
          <xsl:template match="@*">
            <SPAN STYLE="color:navy">
            <xsl:node-name/>=
            "<SPAN STYLE="color:black"><xsl:value-of /></SPAN>"
            </SPAN>
          </xsl:template>
          <xsl:template match="cdata()">
          <pre><xsl:value-of /></pre>
          </xsl:template>
          <xsl:template match="textNode()">
          <xsl:value-of />
          </xsl:template>
        </xsl:apply-templates>
      </td>
      </tr>
    </xsl:for-each>
  </table>
  </xsl:template>

  <xsl:template match="relationships">
  <!-- Handled by default templates -->
  <h2>Gene Relationships</h2>
  <xsl:apply-templates />
  </xsl:template>

  <xsl:template match="gene">
  <h3><xsl:value-of select="name"/> Gene <xsl:value-of select="@id"/></h3>
    <h4>Properties</h4>
    <xsl:apply-templates select="*">
      <!-- apply templates for sub-elements of gene -->
      <xsl:template match="*">
        <ul>
        <li><b><xsl:node-name/></b>: <xsl:value-of select="."/>
          (<xsl:element name="a">
          <xsl:attribute name="href">
          com.xweave.xmldb.demo.XMLServlet?
```

```
      cmd=store&amp;
      frag=<xsl:value-of select="@FRAGID"/>&amp;
      texttag=<xsl:node-name/>
      </xsl:attribute>
      Change value
      </xsl:element>,
      <xsl:element name="a">
      <xsl:attribute name="href">
      com.xweave.xmldb.demo.XMLServlet?
      cmd=delete&amp;
      frag=<xsl:value-of select="@FRAGID"/>&amp;
      </xsl:attribute>
      Delete Property
      </xsl:element>
    )</li>
    </ul>
  </xsl:template>
  <xsl:template match="name|annotations">
    <!-- already grabbed name, annotations so ignore it this time -->
  </xsl:template>
</xsl:apply-templates>
<!-- Begin annotation section -->
<h4>Annotations</h4>
<!-- apply templates for gene annotations -->
<ul>
<xsl:apply-templates select="annotations/*">
  <xsl:template match="*">
    <li><b><xsl:node-name/></b>: <xsl:value-of select="."/>
      (<xsl:element name="a">
      <xsl:attribute name="href">
      com.xweave.xmldb.demo.XMLServlet?
      cmd=store&amp;
      frag=<xsl:value-of select="@FRAGID"/>&amp;
      texttag=<xsl:node-name/>
      </xsl:attribute>
      Change value
      </xsl:element>,
      <xsl:element name="a">
      <xsl:attribute name="href">
      com.xweave.xmldb.demo.XMLServlet?
      cmd=delete&amp;
      frag=<xsl:value-of select="@FRAGID"/>
      </xsl:attribute>
      Delete Annotation
      </xsl:element>
      )
    </li>
```

```
    </xsl:template>
  </xsl:apply-templates>
  </ul>
  <!-- Emit commands on properties and annotations -->
  <h4>Commands</h4>
  <div style="margin-left:2em">
  <!-- Changing of gene name -->
  <xsl:element name="a">
  <xsl:attribute name="href">
  com.xweave.xmldb.demo.XMLServlet?
  cmd=store&amp;
  frag=<xsl:value-of select="name/@FRAGID"/>&amp;
  texttag=name
  </xsl:attribute>
  Change name of gene
  </xsl:element>
  <!-- Create new properties -->
  <form action="com.xweave.xmldb.demo.XMLServlet" method="GET">
    Add property:
    type:
    <select name="texttag">
      <xsl:for-each select="/GeneNotebook/genes/gene/*">
        <!-- STUB: either make unique or replace with fixed set of names -->
        <option><xsl:node-name/></option>
      </xsl:for-each>
    </select>
    value:
    <input type="input" name="text" size="30"/>
    <xsl:element name="input">
      <xsl:attribute name="type">hidden</xsl:attribute>
      <xsl:attribute name="name">frag</xsl:attribute>
      <xsl:attribute name="value">
      <xsl:value-of select="@FRAGID"/>
      </xsl:attribute>
    </xsl:element>
    <input type="hidden" name="cmd" value="Append"/>
    <input type="submit" name="ignore" value="Add"/>
  </form>
  <!-- Create new annotations -->
  <form action="com.xweave.xmldb.demo.XMLServlet" method="GET">
    Add annotation:
    type:
    <input type="input" name="texttag" size="20"/>
    value:
    <input type="input" name="text" size="30"/>
    <xsl:element name="input">
```

```
      <xsl:attribute name="type">hidden</xsl:attribute>
      <xsl:attribute name="name">frag</xsl:attribute>
      <xsl:attribute name="value">
      <xsl:value-of select="annotations/@FRAGID"/>
      </xsl:attribute>
    </xsl:element>
    <input type="hidden" name="cmd" value="Append"/>
    <input type="submit" name="ignore" value="Add"/>
  </form>
  </div>
  <!-- Emit external links -->
  <h4>Additional Information</h4>
  <div style="margin-left:2em">
  <!-- Link to Microarray Data -->
  <xsl:element name="a">
  <xsl:attribute name="href">
  com.xweave.xmldb.demo.XMLServlet?
  cmd=rdb&amp;
  name=<xsl:value-of select="name"/>&amp;
  tablename=gene&amp;
  stylesheet=/ss/generic1.xsl
  </xsl:attribute>
  View Microarray Data
  </xsl:element>
  </div>
</xsl:template>

</xsl:stylesheet>
```

are rendered as separate sections in the HTML display while gene interactions are collected together in a table. Commands to manipulate the data are encoded as HTML forms and links, for example as shown in Figure 10–4 where a new property is added to the database by building a URL to append data to the appropriate gene's element. The updated page is shown in Figure 10–5.

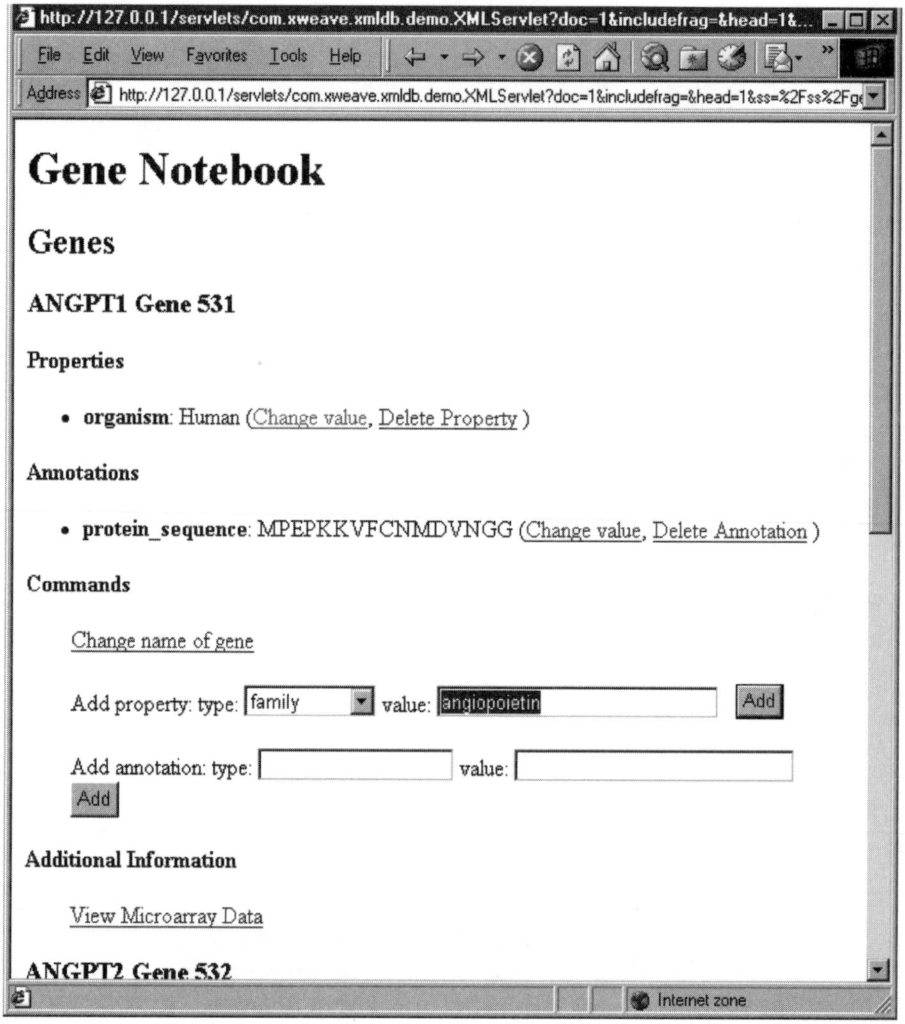

Figure 10–4 Adding protein family to a gene notebook entry

http://127.0.0.1/servlets/com.xweave.xmldb.demo.XMLServlet?doc=1&includefragid=1&head...

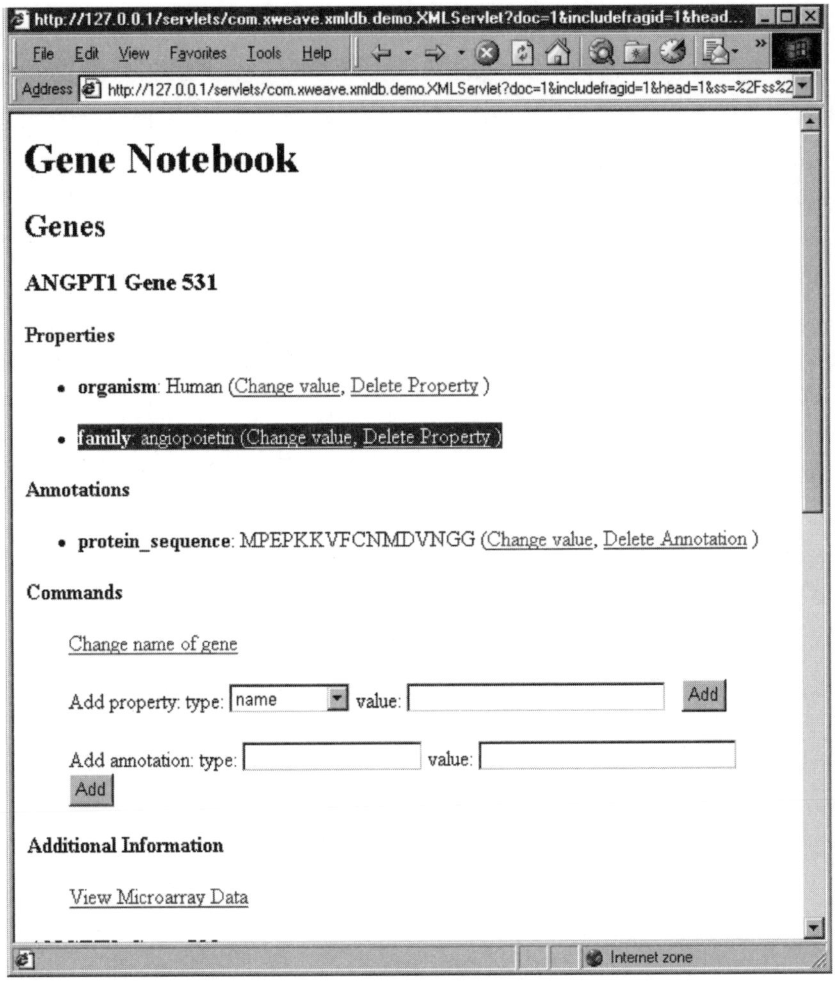

File Edit View Favorites Tools Help

Address http://127.0.0.1/servlets/com.xweave.xmldb.demo.XMLServlet?doc=1&includefragid=1&head=1&ss=%2Fss%2

Gene Notebook

Genes

ANGPT1 Gene 531

Properties

- **organism**: Human (Change value, Delete Property)
- **family**: angiopoietin (Change value, Delete Property)

Annotations

- **protein_sequence**: MPEPKKVFCNMDVNGG (Change value, Delete Annotation)

Commands

Change name of gene

Add property: type: name value: Add

Add annotation: type: value: Add

Additional Information

View Microarray Data

Internet zone

Figure 10–5 Updated gene notebook entry

To support searching the data, the user interface could also use a query tool. The query tool retrieves genes and gene information from which the user can begin to browse. The information about properties, annotations, interactions, and relationships are extracted from the document using XSL. Complex queries can also be asked of the database. For example, the query in Figure 10–6 can be created as a graph query in XML and retrieved from the database, as was described in Chapter 8. The XML documents for queries may also be stored in the XML database.

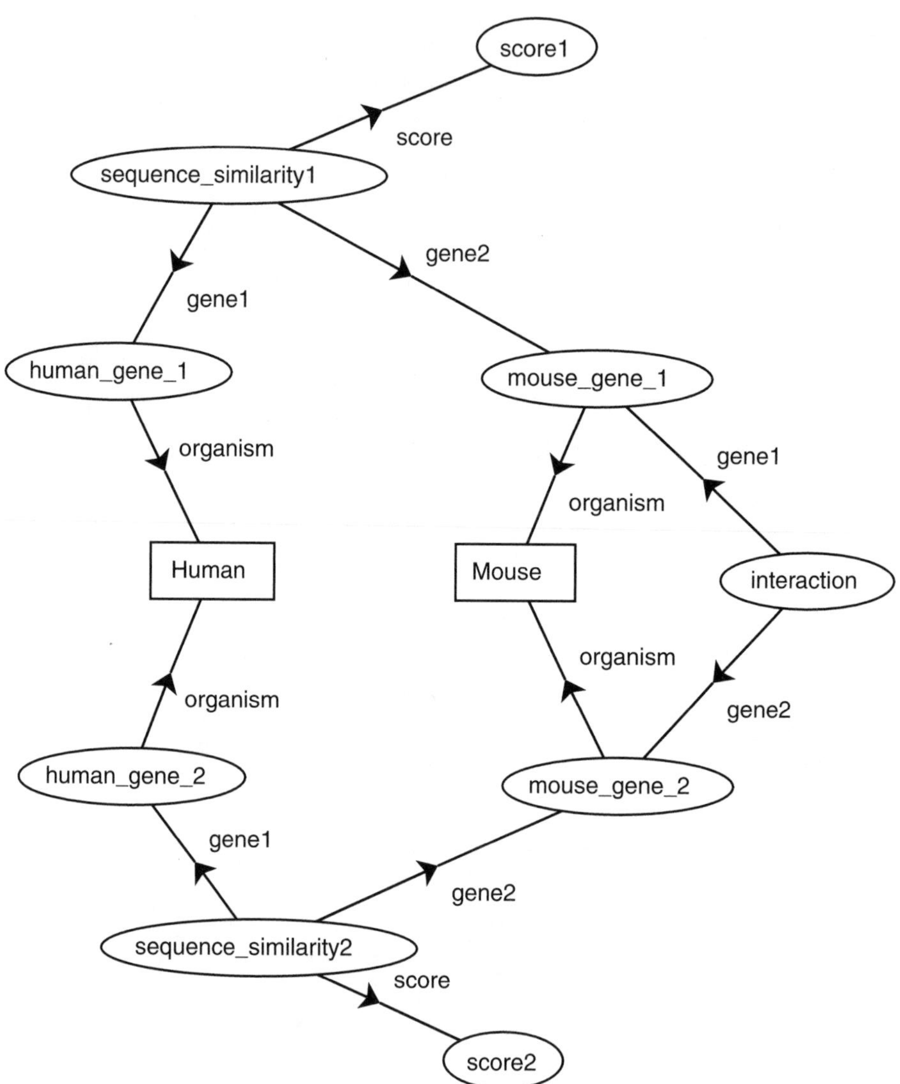

Figure 10–6 Graph query to retrieve possible gene interactions

10.5.2 Middle-tier

The Java servlet for the Gene Notebook reimplements the hybrid relational/XML data server of Chapter 5 to allow more flexibility in the commands that can be defined for the server. Figure 10–7 shows a UML diagram for the sys-

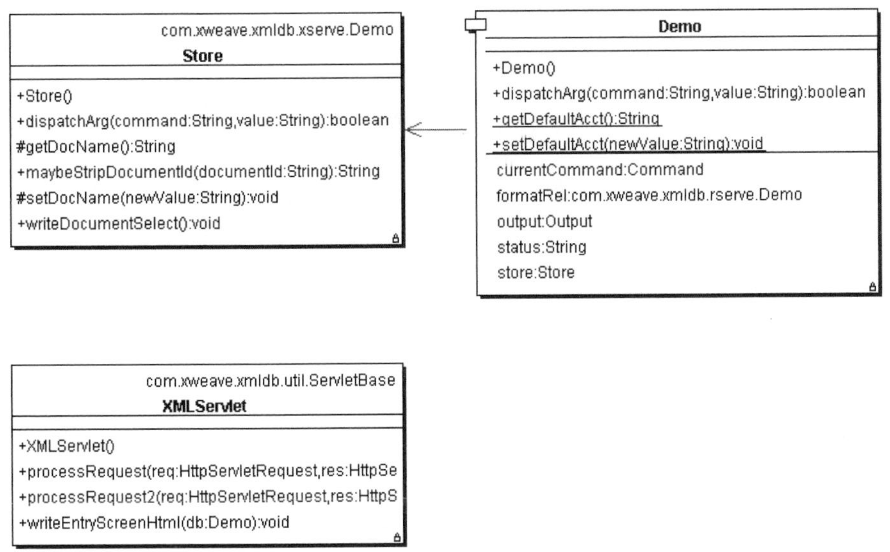

Figure 10–7 UML diagram for demo system

tem, and Figure 10–8 shows a UML diagram for the classes that implement database commands. Commands are defined as objects to allow them to take arguments and perform more complex processing. The inheritance hierarchy for commands is shown in Figure 10–9. All commands inherit from the abstract class com.xweave.xmldb.demo.cmd.Command. Primarily, two abstract commands are used to define the functionality of subsequent commands: "dispatchArg" and "execute". The method "dispatchArg" takes two arguments: the name of a parameter to the command and its value. The method stores the values in the appropriate instance variables of the command. For example, the "store" command dispatches the parameters "text" and "url" that contain either the text of an XML document to be stored or a URL referring to an XML document, respectively. The "execute" method is called after the parameters have been processed and performs the functionality of the command. The servlet also has a method "XMLServlet#writeEntryScreenHtml" that generates a generic home page to display a list of documents in the database and to allow simple commands to be performed, such as to retrieve, store, or delete a document as shown in Figure 10–10. The code for the Java servlet is given in Example 10–5.

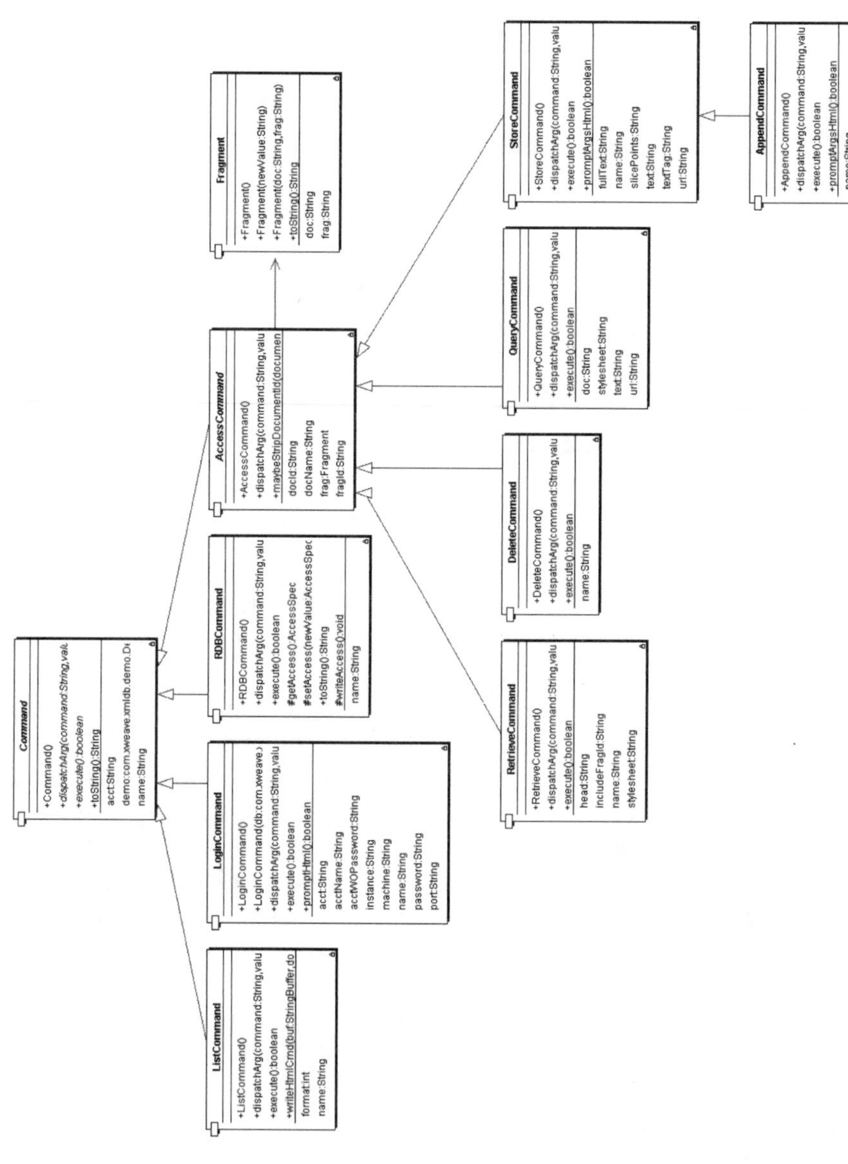

Figure 10–8 UML diagram for demo system commands

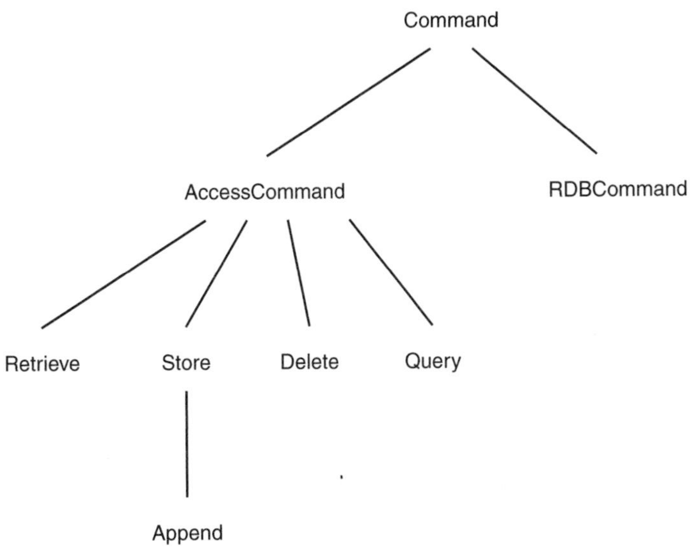

Figure 10–9 Inheritance hierarchy for demo system commands

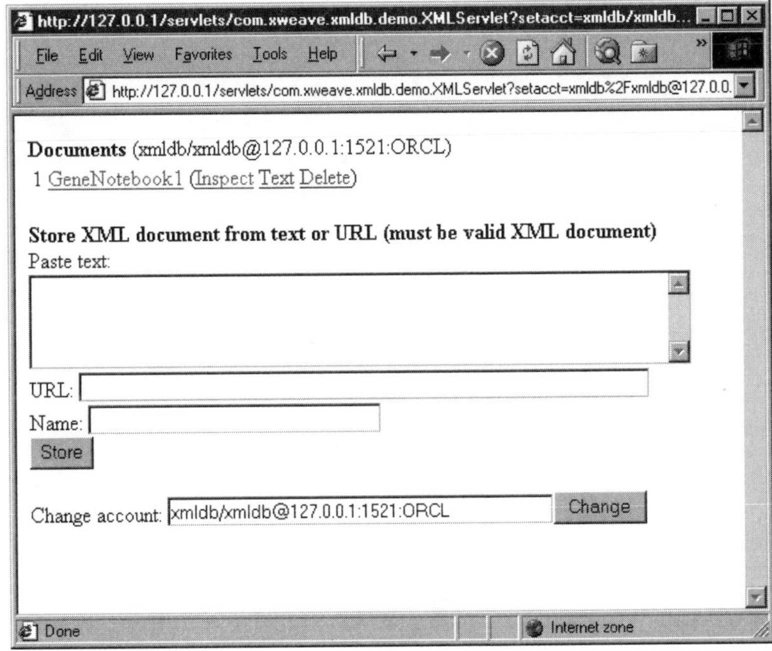

Figure 10–10 Home page for XMLDB demo

Example 10–5 : Gene Notebook Servlet

```
/***************** Demo Application  *****************/

/*********************** Demo.java **********************/
package com.xweave.xmldb.demo;

import com.xweave.xmldb.util.io.*;
import com.xweave.xmldb.util.rdb.*;
import com.xweave.xmldb.xserve.*;
import com.xweave.xmldb.rserve.*;
import com.xweave.xmldb.demo.cmd.*;

/**
 * Demonstration of XML Data Server
 */
public class Demo {
   protected Output output = null;
   protected com.xweave.xmldb.rserve.Demo formatRel = null;
   private Store store = null;
   private StringBuffer status = null;
   private Command currentCommand = null;
   //private static String defaultAcct = "jdbc:oracle:thin:xmldb/
xmldb@127.0.0.1:1521:ORCL";
   private static String defaultAcct =
com.xweave.xmldb.Default.getXmldbAcct();
public Demo() {
   super();
}
public boolean dispatchArg(String command, String value) {
   if (value.equals("")) {
      //ignore empty arguments
      return true;
   }
   if (command.equalsIgnoreCase("IGNORE") ||
command.equalsIgnoreCase("SUBMIT")) {
      //ignore these arguments
      return true;
   }
   if (command.equalsIgnoreCase("CMD")) {
      if (value.equalsIgnoreCase("RETRIEVE")) {
         setCurrentCommand(new RetrieveCommand());
      } else if (value.equalsIgnoreCase("STORE")) {
         setCurrentCommand(new StoreCommand());
      } else if (value.equalsIgnoreCase("APPEND")) {
setCurrentCommand(new AppendCommand());
      } else if (value.equalsIgnoreCase("QUERY")) {
```

```
setCurrentCommand(new QueryCommand());
        } else if (value.equalsIgnoreCase("RDB")) {
            setCurrentCommand(new RDBCommand());
        } else if (value.equalsIgnoreCase("DELETE")) {
            setCurrentCommand(new DeleteCommand());
        } else if (value.equalsIgnoreCase("LIST")) {
            setCurrentCommand(new ListCommand());
        } else if (value.equalsIgnoreCase("LOGIN")) {
            setCurrentCommand(new LoginCommand());
        } else {
            return false;
        }
        getCurrentCommand().setDemo(this);
        return true;
    }
    if (getCurrentCommand() != null) {
        return getCurrentCommand().dispatchArg(command, value);
    }
    return false;
}
public Command getCurrentCommand() {
    return currentCommand;
}
public static String getDefaultAcct() {
    return Demo.defaultAcct;
}
public com.xweave.xmldb.rserve.Demo getFormatRel() {
    if (formatRel == null) {
        formatRel = new com.xweave.xmldb.rserve.Demo();

formatRel.getInputSource().swapAcct(getStore().getRdbAccessString());
        formatRel.setOutputSource(getOutput());
    }
    return formatRel;
}
public Output getOutput() {
    if (output == null) {
        setOutput(new Output());
    }
    return output;
}
public String getStatus() {
    String currentStatus = status.toString();
    status = null;
    return currentStatus;
}
```

```
public Store getStore() {
    if (store == null) {
        store = new Store();
        store.setRdbAccessString(Demo.getDefaultAcct());
        store.setOutput(getOutput());
    }
    return store;
}
public void setCurrentCommand(Command newValue) {
    this.currentCommand = newValue;
}
public static void setDefaultAcct(String newValue) {
    Demo.defaultAcct = newValue;
}
public void setFormatRel(com.xweave.xmldb.rserve.Demo newValue) {
    this.formatRel = newValue;
}
public void setOutput(Output newValue) {
    this.output = newValue;
}
public void setStatus(String newValue) {
    if (status == null) {
        status = new StringBuffer();
    }
    status.append(newValue);
    status.append("/n");
}
public void setStore(Store newValue) {
    this.store = newValue;
}
}

/************************ Store.java **********************/
package com.xweave.xmldb.demo;

public class Store extends com.xweave.xmldb.xserve.Demo {
    private String docName = null;
public Store() {
    super();
}
public boolean dispatchArg(String command, String value) {
    if (command.equalsIgnoreCase("RETRIEVE")) {
        value = this.maybeStripDocumentId(value);
        this.retrieveDocumentId(value);
        return true;
    }
```

```
    if (command.equalsIgnoreCase("RETRIEVEDOC")) {
        this.getOutput().writeln("<?xml version=\"1.0\"?>");
        value = this.maybeStripDocumentId(value);
        this.retrieveDocumentId(value);
        return true;
    }
    if (command.equalsIgnoreCase("STORE")) {
        this.storeDocument(value, getDocName());
        return true;
        }
    if (command.equalsIgnoreCase("STOREDOCTEXT")) {
        this.storeDocument(value, getDocName());
        return true;
        }
    if (command.equalsIgnoreCase("STOREURL")) {
        this.storeDocument(value, getDocName());
        return true;
        }
    if (command.equalsIgnoreCase("NAME")) {
        this.setDocName(value);
        return true;
        }
    if (command.equalsIgnoreCase("DELETE")) {
        value = this.maybeStripDocumentId(value);
        this.deleteDocumentId(value);
        return true;
    }
    if (command.equalsIgnoreCase("LISTSELECT")) {
        this.writeDocumentSelect();
        return true;
    }
    return super.dispatchArg(command, value);
}
protected String getDocName() {
    return docName;
}
/**
 * Maybe strip additional information that was passed in as part of
documentId
 */
public String maybeStripDocumentId(String documentId) {
    if (documentId.indexOf(' ') != -1) {
        //additional information was passed in as part of documentId, ignore it
        documentId = documentId.substring(0,documentId.indexOf(' '));
    }
    return documentId;
}
```

```
protected void setDocName(String newValue) {
    this.docName = newValue;
}
/**
 * Write a list (to out) of all XML documents (as select options)
 */
public void writeDocumentSelect() {
    getDocumentList().writeDocumentSelect();
}
}

/************************* XMLServlet.java **********************/
package com.xweave.xmldb.demo;

import javax.servlet.*;
import javax.servlet.http.*;
import java.io.*;
import java.util.*;
import com.xweave.xmldb.util.io.ServletOutput;
/**
 * Servlet interface to database.
 */
public class XMLServlet extends com.xweave.xmldb.util.ServletBase {
public XMLServlet() {
    super();
}
public void processRequest(HttpServletRequest req, HttpServletResponse
res) throws ServletException, java.io.IOException {
    ServletOutputStream out = startOutput(res);
    Enumeration enum = req.getParameterNames();
    String pname, pvalue = null;
    String cmd = null;
    String val = null;
    boolean statusFlag;
    //process servlet arguments
    if (req.getParameter("setacct") != null) {
        Demo.setDefaultAcct(req.getParameter("setacct"));
    }
    //init
    Demo db = new Demo();
    db.getStore().setRdbAccessString(Demo.getDefaultAcct());
    db.getStore().connect();
    db.setOutput(new ServletOutput(out));
    db.getStore().setOutput(db.getOutput());
    //handle command
```

```
    if (req.getParameter("cmd") != null) {
        //if cmd parameter exists, do it first
        pvalue = req.getParameter("cmd");
        log("Initializing Command: " + pvalue);
        statusFlag = db.dispatchArg("cmd", pvalue);
        if (!statusFlag) {
            log("...was in error.");
        }
    } else {
        writeEntryScreenHtml(db);
        if (!db.getStore().getRdb().isClosed()) {
            db.getStore().getRdb().close();
        }
        endOutput(res);
        return;
    }
    //process command arguments
    while (enum.hasMoreElements()) {
        pname = (String) enum.nextElement();
        pvalue = req.getParameter(pname);
        if (pname.equalsIgnoreCase("cmd") ||
pname.equalsIgnoreCase("setacct") || pname.equalsIgnoreCase("successurl"))
{
            continue;
        }
        if (pvalue.length() < 120) {
            log("  arg " + pname + " = " + pvalue);
        } else {
            log("  arg " + pname + "[truncated from " + pvalue.length() + "
chars] = " + pvalue.substring(0, 119) + "...");
        }
        statusFlag = db.dispatchArg(pname, pvalue);
        if (!statusFlag) {
            log("...was in error.");
        }
    }
    log("Executing " + db.getCurrentCommand());
    statusFlag = db.getCurrentCommand().execute();
    if ((req.getParameter("successurl") != null) && statusFlag) {
        //Note: does not work if res is already written to
        res.sendRedirect(req.getParameter("successurl"));
    }
    if (!db.getStore().getRdb().isClosed()) {
        db.getStore().getRdb().close();
    }
    endOutput(res);
}
```

```
public void writeEntryScreenHtml(Demo db) {
    Vector vec =
db.getStore().getDocumentList().retrieveDocumentListVector();
    if (vec == null) {
        return;
    }
    StringBuffer buf = new StringBuffer();
    java.util.Enumeration e = vec.elements();
    buf.append("<html>\n<body>\n");
    buf.append("<b>Documents</b>
("+db.getStore().getRdbAccessString()+")<br/>\n");
    buf.append("<table>\n");
    String pair;
    int index;
    String id, name;
    while (e.hasMoreElements()) {
        pair = (String) e.nextElement();
        index = pair.indexOf(' ');
        id = pair.substring(0, index);
        name = pair.substring(index + 1);
        if (index == -1) {
            return;
        }
        buf.append("<TR><TD>");
        buf.append(id);
        //retrieve
        buf.append("</TD><TD><A HREF=\"com.xweave.xmldb.demo.XMLServlet?
            cmd=retrieve&amp;head=1&amp;doc=");
        buf.append(id);
        buf.append("\">");
        buf.append(name);
        buf.append("</A>");
        //inspect
        buf.append(" (<A HREF=\"com.xweave.xmldb.demo.XMLServlet?
            cmd=retrieve&amp;head=1&amp;includefragid=1&amp;doc=");
        buf.append(id);
        buf.append("\">Inspect</A>");
        //text
        buf.append(" <A HREF=\"com.xweave.xmldb.demo.XMLServlet?
            cmd=retrieve&amp;doc=");
        buf.append(id);
        buf.append("\">Text</A>");
        //delete
        buf.append(" <A HREF=\"com.xweave.xmldb.demo.XMLServlet?
            cmd=delete&amp;doc=");
        buf.append(id);
```

```
        buf.append("\">Delete</A>");
        buf.append(")</TD></TR>\n");
    }
    buf.append("</table>\n");
    //store
    buf.append("<form action=\"com.xweave.xmldb.demo.XMLServlet\"
method=\"POST\">");
    buf.append("<b>Store XML document from text or URL (must be valid XML
document)</b><br/>");
    buf.append("Paste text:<br/>");
    buf.append("<textarea name=\"text\" rows=\"6\" cols=\"60\"></
textarea></br>");
    buf.append("URL: <input type=\"input\" name=\"url\" size=60><br/>");
    buf.append("Name: <input type=\"input\" name=\"name\" size=30></br>");
    buf.append("Slice Points: <input type=\"input\" name=\"addslice\"
size=30> (space delimited)</br>");
    buf.append("<input type=\"submit\" name=\"cmd\" value=\"Store\">");
    buf.append("</form>");
    //change acct
    buf.append("<form action=\"com.xweave.xmldb.demo.XMLServlet\"
method=\"GET\">");
    buf.append("Change account: <input type=\"input\" name=\"setacct\"
size=40 value=\""+db.getStore().getRdbAccessString()+"\">");
    buf.append("<input type=\"submit\" name=\"ignore\" value=\"Change\"></
br>");
    buf.append("</form>");

    buf.append("</html>\n</body>\n");
    db.getOutput().writeln(buf.toString());
}
}

/****************** Commands  **************************/

/************************** cmd/Command.java ***********************/
package com.xweave.xmldb.demo.cmd;
public abstract class Command {
    protected String acct = null;
    protected com.xweave.xmldb.demo.Demo demo = null;
public Command() {
    super();
}
public abstract boolean dispatchArg(String command, String value);
public abstract boolean execute();
public String getAcct() {
    return acct;
}
```

```
public com.xweave.xmldb.demo.Demo getDemo() {
    return demo;
}
public String getName() {
    return "Unknown";
}
public void setAcct(String newValue) {
    this.acct = newValue;
}
public void setDemo(com.xweave.xmldb.demo.Demo newValue) {
    this.demo = newValue;
}
public String toString() {
    return getName();
}
}
/****************** XML Access Commands  ***************/

/********************** cmd/AccessCommand.java *********************/
package com.xweave.xmldb.demo.cmd;

public abstract class AccessCommand extends Command {
    protected String docName = null;
    protected Fragment frag = null;
public AccessCommand() {
    super();
}
public boolean dispatchArg(String command, String value) {
if (command.equalsIgnoreCase("DOC")) {
        this.setDocId(value);
        return true;
    }
    if (command.equalsIgnoreCase("FRAG")) {
        this.setFragId(value);
        return true;
    }
    if (command.equalsIgnoreCase("NAME")) {
        this.setDocName(value);
        return true;
    }
    return false;
}
public String getDocId() {
    if ((frag == null || frag.getDoc() == null) && docName != null) {
        //STUB: get id from docname using Demo
    }
    return getFrag().getDoc();
```

```
}
public String getDocName() {
   return docName;
}
public Fragment getFrag() {
   if (frag == null) {
      frag = new Fragment();
   }
   return frag;
}
public String getFragId() {
   return getFrag().getFrag();
}
/**
 * Maybe strip additional information that was passed in as part of
documentId
 */
public String maybeStripDocumentId(String documentId) {
   if (documentId.indexOf(' ') != -1) {
      //additional information was passed in as part of documentId, ignore it
      documentId = documentId.substring(0,documentId.indexOf(' '));
   }
   return documentId;
}
public void setDocId(String newValue) {
   getFrag().setDoc(maybeStripDocumentId(newValue));
}
public void setDocName(String newValue) {
   this.docName = newValue;
}
public void setFragId(String newValue) {
   getFrag().setFrag(newValue);
}
}

/************************* cmd/Fragment.java **********************/
package com.xweave.xmldb.demo.cmd;

public class Fragment {
   protected String doc = null;
   protected String frag = null;
public Fragment() {
   super();
}
public Fragment(String newValue) {
   super();
```

```
    setDoc(newValue);
}
public Fragment(String doc, String frag) {
    super();
    this.doc = doc;
    this.frag = frag;
}
public String getDoc() {
    return doc;
}
public String getFrag() {
    return frag;
}
public void setDoc(String newValue) {
    int dotindex = newValue.indexOf('.');
    if (dotindex == -1) {
        this.doc = newValue;
    } else {
        this.doc = newValue.substring(0, dotindex);
        this.frag = newValue.substring(dotindex + 1);
    }
}
public void setFrag(String newValue) {
    int dotindex = newValue.indexOf('.');
    if (dotindex == -1) {
        this.frag = newValue;
    } else {
        this.doc = newValue.substring(0, dotindex);
        this.frag = newValue.substring(dotindex + 1);
    }
}
public String toString() {
    if (frag != null) {
        return doc+"."+frag;
    } else {
        return doc;
    }
}
}

/********************* cmd/DeleteCommand.java *********************/
package com.xweave.xmldb.demo.cmd;

public class DeleteCommand extends AccessCommand {
public DeleteCommand() {
    super();
}
```

```
public boolean dispatchArg(String command, String value) {
   return super.dispatchArg(command, value);
}
public boolean execute() {
   String msg = null;
   boolean resultFlag = false;
   if (getFragId() == null) {
      //delete document
      resultFlag = getDemo().getStore().deleteDocumentId(getDocId());
      if (resultFlag) {
         msg = "Deleted document " + getFrag();
      } else {
         msg = "Error in deleting document " + getFrag();
      }
   } else {
      //delete fragment
      resultFlag = getDemo().getStore().deleteFragment(getDocId(),
getFragId());
      if (resultFlag) {
         msg = "Deleted fragment " + getFrag();
      } else {
         msg = "Error in deleting fragment " + getFrag();
      }
   }
   getDemo().setStatus(msg);
   getDemo().getOutput().writeln(msg);
   return resultFlag;
}
public String getName() {
   return "Delete";
}
}

/********************* cmd/QueryCommand.java **********************/
package com.xweave.xmldb.demo.cmd;

/*
 * Queries the pattern specified in <text> or <url> against the document
in the
 * database specified by <doc> id. Will add <sylesheet> to stylesheet
processing
 * instruction, if specified.
 */
public class QueryCommand extends AccessCommand {
   public String text = null;
   public String doc = null;
```

```
    public String url = null;
    public String stylesheet = null;
public QueryCommand() {
    super();
}
public boolean dispatchArg(String command, String value) {
    if (command.equalsIgnoreCase("DOC")) {
        this.setDoc(value);
        return true;
    }
    if (command.equalsIgnoreCase("TEXT")) {
        this.setText(value);
        return true;
    }
    if (command.equalsIgnoreCase("URL")) {
        this.setUrl(value);
        return true;
    }
if (command.equalsIgnoreCase("STYLESHEET") ||
command.equalsIgnoreCase("SS")) {
        this.setStylesheet(value);
        return true;
    }
    return super.dispatchArg(command, value);
}
public boolean execute() {
    String msg = null;
    boolean resultFlag = false;
    com.xweave.xmldb.rgquery.Demo rgdemo = new
com.xweave.xmldb.rgquery.Demo();
    if (getStylesheet() != null) {
        rgdemo.setStylesheet(getStylesheet());
    }
    if (getUrl() != null) {
        rgdemo.parseUrl(getUrl());
    } else if (getText() != null) {
        rgdemo.parseText(getText());
    } else {

        msg = "No query pattern specified.";
    }
    java.sql.Connection conn = ((com.xweave.xmldb.util.rdb.RDBConnector)
getDemo().getStore().getRdb()).getConnection();
    rgdemo.query(getDoc(), new com.xweave.xmldb.rserve.Input(conn),
getDemo().getOutput());
    return true;
```

```
}
public String getDoc() {
   return doc;
}
public String getStylesheet() {
   return stylesheet;
}
public String getText() {
   return text;
}
public String getUrl() {
   return url;
}
public void setDoc(String newDoc) {
   doc = newDoc;
}
public void setStylesheet(String newStylesheet) {
   stylesheet = newStylesheet;
}
public void setText(String newText) {
   text = newText;
}
public void setUrl(String newUrl) {
   url = newUrl;
}
}

/******************** cmd/RetrieveCommand.java **********************/
package com.xweave.xmldb.demo.cmd;

public class RetrieveCommand extends AccessCommand {
   public String head = null;
   protected String doc = null;
   protected String frag = null;
   protected String includeFragId = null;
   public String stylesheet = null;
public RetrieveCommand() {
   super();
}
public boolean dispatchArg(String command, String value) {
   if (command.equalsIgnoreCase("HEAD")) {
      this.setHead(value);
      return true;
   }
   if (command.equalsIgnoreCase("STYLESHEET") ||
command.equalsIgnoreCase("SS")) {
```

```
        this.setStylesheet(value);
        return true;
    }
    if (command.equalsIgnoreCase("INCLUDEFRAGID")) {
        this.setIncludeFragId(value);
        return true;
    }
    return super.dispatchArg(command, value);
}
public boolean execute() {
    String msg = null;
    boolean resultFlag = false;
    if (getHead() != null) {
        getDemo().getOutput().writeln("<?xml version=\"1.0\"?>");
    }
    if (getStylesheet() != null) {
        getDemo().getOutput().writeln("<?xml:stylesheet type=\"text/xsl\"
href=\""+ getStylesheet() +"\"?>");
    }
    if (getFragId() != null) {
        //write fragment
        if (getIncludeFragId() != null) {
            //STUB: should modify format to use specified name
            getDemo().getStore().getFormat().setWriteElementId(true);
            resultFlag =
getDemo().getStore().retrieveFragment(getDocId(),getFragId());
            getDemo().getStore().getFormat().setWriteElementId(false);
        } else {
            resultFlag =
getDemo().getStore().retrieveFragment(getDocId(),getFragId());
        }
    } else {
        //write document
        //write fragment
        if (getIncludeFragId() != null) {
            //STUB: should modify format to use specified name
            getDemo().getStore().getFormat().setWriteElementId(true);
            resultFlag =
getDemo().getStore().retrieveFragment(getDocId(),"1");
            getDemo().getStore().getFormat().setWriteElementId(false);
        } else {
            resultFlag =
getDemo().getStore().retrieveDocumentId(getDocId());
        }
    }
    if (resultFlag) {
        msg = "Retrieved " + getFrag();
```

```
    } else {
        msg = "Error in retrieving fragment " + getFrag();
    }
    getDemo().setStatus(msg);
    return resultFlag;
}
public String getHead() {
    return head;
}
public String getIncludeFragId() {
    return includeFragId;
}
public String getName() {
    return "Retrieve";
}
public String getStylesheet() {
    return stylesheet;
}
public void setHead(String newValue) {
    if (newValue.equalsIgnoreCase("1")) {
        this.head = "<?xml version=\"1.0\"?>";
        return;
    }
    this.head = newValue;
}
public void setIncludeFragId(String newValue) {
    if (newValue.equalsIgnoreCase("1")) {
        includeFragId = "FRAGID";
        return;
    }
    this.includeFragId = newValue;
}
public void setStylesheet(String newValue) {
    this.stylesheet = newValue;
}
}

/********************** cmd/StoreCommand.java **********************/
package com.xweave.xmldb.demo.cmd;

public class StoreCommand extends AccessCommand {
    public String text = null;
    public String url = null;
    public String textTag = null;
    public String slicePoints = null;
public StoreCommand() {
    super();
```

```
}
public boolean dispatchArg(String command, String value) {
    if (command.equalsIgnoreCase("TEXT")) {
        this.setText(value);
        return true;
    }
    if (command.equalsIgnoreCase("URL")) {
        this.setUrl(value);
        return true;
    }
    if (command.equalsIgnoreCase("TEXTTAG")) {
        this.setTextTag(value);
        return true;
    }
    if (command.equalsIgnoreCase("ADDSLICE")) {
        this.setSlicePoints(value);
        return true;
    }
    return super.dispatchArg(command, value);
}
public boolean execute() {
    String id = null;
    String msg = null;
    boolean resultFlag = false;
    if ( (getText() == null) && (getUrl() == null) ) {
        return promptArgsHtml();
    }
    if (getSlicePoints() != null) {
        try {
            //put in catch, in case slice points are not supported
            //This allows fine-grained, medium-grained, or coarse-grained to
be used
            //should really be called indirectly
            getDemo().getStore().addSlicePoint(getSlicePoints());
        } catch (Exception ex) {
            getDemo().getOutput().writeln("Slice points not added: " +
getSlicePoints());
        }
    }
    if (getFragId() != null) {
        //set fragment
        if (getUrl() != null) {
            resultFlag = getDemo().getStore().replaceFragmentUrl(getDocId(),
                getFragId(), getUrl());
            if (resultFlag) {
                msg = "Stored fragment " + getFrag() + " from " + getUrl();
```

```
            } else {
                msg = "Error in storing fragment " + getFrag() + " from " +
getUrl();
            }
        } else if (getText() != null) {
            resultFlag =
getDemo().getStore().replaceFragmentText(getDocId(),
                getFragId(), getFullText());
            if (resultFlag) {
                msg = "Stored fragment " + getFrag();
            } else {
                msg = "Error in storing fragment " + getFrag();
            }
        } else {
            msg = "No data specified to store in fragment " + getFrag();
        }
    } else if (getDocName() != null) {
        //store document
        if (getUrl() != null) {
            id = getDemo().getStore().storeDocUrl(getUrl(), getDocName());
            if (id != null) {
                msg = "Stored document " + getDocName() + " as document " +
id;
                resultFlag = true;
            } else {
                msg = "Error in storing document " + getDocName();
            }
        } else if (getText() != null) {
            id = getDemo().getStore().storeDocText(getFullText(),
getDocName());
            if (id != null) {
                msg = "Stored document " + getDocName() + " as document " +
id;
                resultFlag = true;
            } else {
                msg = "Error in storing document " + getDocName();
            }
        } else {
            msg = "No data specified to store as document " + getDocName();
        }
    } else {
        msg = "Not enough information specified for store.";
    }
    getDemo().setStatus(msg);
    getDemo().getOutput().writeln(msg);
    return resultFlag;
}
```

```
public String getFullText() {
    //surrounds text with textTag element for parsing
    if (getTextTag() == null) {
        return getText();
    } else {
        return "<?xml version=\"1.0\"?>\n<" + getTextTag() + ">" + getText()
+ "</" + getTextTag() + ">";
    }
}
public String getName() {
    return "Store";
}
public String getSlicePoints() {
    return slicePoints;
}
public String getText() {
    return text;
}
public String getTextTag() {
    return textTag;
}
public String getUrl() {
    return url;
}
public boolean promptArgsHtml() {
    StringBuffer buf = new StringBuffer();
    buf.append("<html>\n<body>\n");
    buf.append("<form action =\"com.xweave.xmldb.demo.XMLServlet\"
method=\"POST\">\n");
    buf.append("<input type=\"hidden\" name=\"cmd\" value=\"Store\"/>\n");
    if (getTextTag() == null) {
        buf.append("<b>Store document text (or URL)</b><br/>\n");
        buf.append("Paste text:<br/>\n");
        buf.append("<textarea name=\"text\" rows=\"6\" cols=\"60\"></
textarea></br>\n");
        buf.append("URL: <input type=\"input\" name=\"url\" size=\"60\"/
><br/>\n");
    } else {
        buf.append("<b>Enter value for " + getTextTag() + "</b><br/>\n");
        buf.append(getTextTag() + ": <input name=\"text\" size=\"60\"/></
br>\n");
        buf.append("(Text will be wrapped in &lt;" + getTextTag() + "&gt;
element)</br>\n");
        buf.append("<input type=\"hidden\" name=\"texttag\" value=\"" +
getTextTag() + "\"/>\n");
    }
```

```
    if (getFrag() == null) {
        if (getDocName() == null) {
            buf.append("Name: <input type=\"input\" name=\"name\"
size=\"30\"/></br>\n");
        } else {
            buf.append("Name: " + getDocName() + "<br/>\n");
            buf.append("<input type=\"hidden\" name=\"name\" value=\"" +
getDocName() + "\"/>\n");
        }
        buf.append("<input type=\"submit\" name=\"ignore\" value=\"Store\"/
>\n");
} else {
        if (getFragId() == null) {
            buf.append("Replace Document: " + getDocId() + "<br/>\n");
            buf.append("<input type=\"hidden\" name=\"doc\" value=\"" +
getDocId() + "\"/>\n");
        } else {
            buf.append("Replace Fragment: " + getFrag() + "<br/>\n");
            buf.append("<input type=\"hidden\" name=\"doc\" value=\"" +
getDocId() + "\"/>\n");
            buf.append("<input type=\"hidden\" name=\"frag\" value=\"" +
getFragId() + "\"/>\n");
        }
        buf.append("<input type=\"submit\" name=\"ignore\"
value=\"Replace\"/>\n");
    }
    buf.append("</form>\n</body>\n</html>\n");
    getDemo().getOutput().writeln(buf.toString());
    return true;
}
public void setSlicePoints(String newSlicePoints) {
    slicePoints = newSlicePoints;
}
public void setText(String newValue) {
    this.text = newValue;
}
public void setTextTag(String newValue) {
    this.textTag = newValue;
}
public void setUrl(String newValue) {
    this.url = newValue;
}
}

/********************* cmd/AppendCommand.java *********************/
package com.xweave.xmldb.demo.cmd;
```

```
public class AppendCommand extends StoreCommand {
public AppendCommand() {
   super();
}
public boolean dispatchArg(String command, String value) {
   return super.dispatchArg(command, value);
}
public boolean execute() {
   String id = null;
   String msg = null;
   boolean resultFlag = false;
   if ((getText() == null) && (getUrl() == null)) {
      return promptArgsHtml();
   }
   if (getDocId() != null && getFragId() == null) {
      //append to top-level element, by default
      setFragId("1");
   }
   if (getDocId() != null) {
      //append fragment
      if (getUrl() != null) {
         resultFlag = getDemo().getStore().appendFragmentUrl(getDocId(),
getFragId(), getUrl());
         if (resultFlag) {
            msg = "Appended fragment " + getFrag() + " from " + getUrl();
         } else {
            msg = "Error in appending fragment " + getFrag() + " from " +
getUrl();
         }
      } else
         if (getText() != null) {
            resultFlag =
getDemo().getStore().appendFragmentText(getDocId(), getFragId(),
getFullText());
            if (resultFlag) {
               msg = "Appended fragment " + getFrag();
            } else {
               msg = "Error in appending fragment " + getFrag();
            }
         } else {
            msg = "No data specified to append to fragment " + getFrag();
         }
   } else {
      msg = "Not enough information specified for append.";
   }
   getDemo().setStatus(msg);
   getDemo().getOutput().writeln(msg);
```

```
        return resultFlag;
    }
    public String getName() {
        return "Append";
    }
    public boolean promptArgsHtml() {
        if (getDocId() != null && getFragId() == null) {
            //append to top-level element, by default
            setFragId("1");
        }
        StringBuffer buf = new StringBuffer();
        buf.append("<html>\n<body>\n");
        buf.append("<form action =\"com.xweave.xmldb.demo.XMLServlet\"
method=\"POST\">\n");
        buf.append("<input type=\"hidden\" name=\"cmd\" value=\"Append\"/>\n");
        buf.append("<b>Append document text (or URL) to fragment</b><br/>\n");
        buf.append("Paste text:<br/>\n");
        buf.append("<textarea name=\"text\" rows=\"6\" cols=\"60\"></
textarea></br>\n");
        if (getTextTag() != null) {
            buf.append("(Text will be wrapped in &lt;" + getTextTag() + "&gt;
element)</br>\n");
            buf.append("<input type=\"hidden\" name=\"texttag\" value=\"" +
getTextTag() + "\"/>\n");
        }
        buf.append("URL: <input type=\"input\" name=\"url\" size=\"60\"/><br/
>\n");
        if (getFragId() == null) {
            buf.append("Append Fragment: ");
            buf.append("Document ID: <input type=\"input\" name=\"doc\"
size=\"10\"/>\n");
            buf.append("Fragment ID: <input type=\"input\" name=\"frag\"
size=\"10\"/></br>\n");
        } else {
            buf.append("Append Fragment: " + getFrag());
            buf.append("<input type=\"hidden\" name=\"doc\" value=\"" +
getDocId() + "\"/>\n");
            buf.append("<input type=\"hidden\" name=\"frag\" value=\"" +
getFragId() + "\"/></br>\n");
        }
        buf.append("<input type=\"submit\" name=\"ignore\" value=\"Append\"/
>\n");
        buf.append("</form>\n</body>\n</html>\n");
        getDemo().getOutput().writeln(buf.toString());
        return true;
    }
    }
```

```
/***************** Other Commands  *******************/

/*********************** cmd/RDBCommand.java **********************/
package com.xweave.xmldb.demo.cmd;

import com.xweave.xmldb.rserve.*;
public class RDBCommand extends Command {
    protected AccessSpec access = null;
public RDBCommand() {
    super();
}
public boolean dispatchArg(String command, String value) {
    getDemo().getFormatRel().dispatchArg(getAccess(), command, value);
    return true;
}
public boolean execute() {
/* Write document from access spec when rserve args have been set */
/* Warning: this may also execute when bogus args are included in command
*/
    if (access != null) {
        //check <access> instance variable directly to avoid
        //lazy initialization
        getDemo().getFormatRel().writeDoc(getAccess());
        return true;
    }
    return false;
}
protected AccessSpec getAccess() {
    if (access == null) {
        access = new com.xweave.xmldb.rserve.AccessSpec();
    }
    return access;
}
public String getName() {
    return "RDB";
}
protected void setAccess(AccessSpec newValue) {
    this.access = newValue;
}
public String toString() {
    return super.toString();
}
/* Write document from access spec when rserve args have been set */
/* Warning: this may also execute when bogus args are included in command
*/
```

```
protected void writeAccess() {
   if (access != null) {
      //check <access> instance variable directly to avoid
      //lazy initialization
      getDemo().getFormatRel().writeDoc(getAccess());
   }
}
}

/********************** cmd/ListCommand.java **********************/
package com.xweave.xmldb.demo.cmd;

import java.util.*;
public class ListCommand extends Command {
   public int format = 1;
   public final static int TEXT = 1;
   public final static int HTML = 2;
   public final static int XML = 3;
   public final static int HTML_CMD = 4;
public ListCommand() {
   super();
}
public boolean dispatchArg(String command, String value) {
   if (command.equalsIgnoreCase("FORMAT")) {
      if (value.equalsIgnoreCase("TEXT")) {
         this.setFormat(TEXT);
         return true;
      }
      if (value.equalsIgnoreCase("HTML")) {
         this.setFormat(HTML);
         return true;
      }
      if (value.equalsIgnoreCase("XML")) {
         this.setFormat(XML);
         return true;
      }
      if (value.equalsIgnoreCase("HTML_CMD") ||
value.equalsIgnoreCase("HTML-CMD")) {
         this.setFormat(HTML_CMD);
         return true;
      }
   }
   return false;
}
public boolean execute() {
   String msg = null;
   Vector vec =
```

```
getDemo().getStore().getDocumentList().retrieveDocumentListVector();
    if (vec == null) {
        return false;
    }
    StringBuffer buf = new StringBuffer();
    java.util.Enumeration e = vec.elements();
    if (getFormat() == HTML_CMD) {
        writeHtmlCmd(buf, e);
    }
    //TODO: other formats
    msg = buf.toString();
    //getDemo().setStatus(msg);
    getDemo().getOutput().writeln(msg);
    return true;
}
public int getFormat() {
    return format;
}
public String getName() {
    return "List";
}
public void setFormat(int newValue) {
    this.format = newValue;
}
public boolean writeHtmlCmd(StringBuffer buf, Enumeration docEnum) {
    buf.append("<html>\n<body>\n");
    buf.append("<b>Documents</b>
("+getDemo().getStore().getRdbAccessString()+")<br/>\n");
    buf.append("<table>\n");
    String pair;
    int index;
    String id, name;
    while (docEnum.hasMoreElements()) {
        pair = (String) docEnum.nextElement();
        index = pair.indexOf(' ');
        id = pair.substring(0, index);
        name = pair.substring(index + 1);
        if (index == -1) {
            return false;
        }
        buf.append("<TR><TD>");
        buf.append(id);
        //retrieve
        buf.append("</TD><TD><A HREF=\"com.xweave.xmldb.demo.XMLServlet?
            cmd=retrieve&amp;head=1&amp;doc=");
```

```
        buf.append(id);
        buf.append("\">");
        buf.append(name);
        buf.append("</A>");
        //inspect
        buf.append(" (<A HREF=\"com.xweave.xmldb.demo.XMLServlet?
            cmd=retrieve&amp;head=1&amp;includefragid=1&amp;doc=");
        buf.append(id);
        buf.append("\">Inspect</A>");
        //text
        buf.append(" <A HREF=\"com.xweave.xmldb.demo.XMLServlet?
            cmd=retrieve&amp;doc=");
        buf.append(id);
        buf.append("\">Text</A>");
        //delete
        buf.append(" <A
HREF=\"com.xweave.xmldb.demo.XMLServlet?cmd=delete&amp;doc=");
        buf.append(id);
        buf.append("\">Delete</A>");
        buf.append(")</TD></TR>\n");
    }
    buf.append("</table>\n");
    //store
    buf.append("<form action=\"com.xweave.xmldb.demo.XMLServlet\"
method=\"POST\">");
    buf.append("<b>Store XML document from text or URL [must be valid XML
document]</b><br/>");
    buf.append("Paste text:<br/>");
    buf.append("<textarea name=\"text\" rows=\"6\" cols=\"60\"></
textarea></br>");
    buf.append("URL: <input type=\"input\" name=\"url\" size=60><br/>");
    buf.append("Name: <input type=\"input\" name=\"name\" size=30></br>");
    buf.append("<input type=\"submit\" name=\"cmd\" value=\"Store\">");
    buf.append("</form>");
    buf.append("</html>\n</body>\n");
    return true;
}
}

/********************* cmd/LoginCommand.java **********************/
package com.xweave.xmldb.demo.cmd;

public class LoginCommand extends Command {
    public String acctName = "xmldb";
    public String password = "xmldb";
    public String machine = "127.0.0.1";
```

```
    public String port = "1521";
    public String instance = "ORCL";
public LoginCommand() {
    super();
}
public LoginCommand(com.xweave.xmldb.demo.Demo db) {
    super();
    setDemo(db);
}
public boolean dispatchArg(String command, String value) {
    if (command.equalsIgnoreCase("NAME")) {
        this.setAcctName(value);
        return true;
    }
    if (command.equalsIgnoreCase("PASSWORD")) {
        this.setPassword(value);
        return true;
    }
    if (command.equalsIgnoreCase("MACHINE")) {
        this.setMachine(value);
        return true;
    }
    if (command.equalsIgnoreCase("PORT")) {
        this.setPort(value);
        return true;
    }
    if (command.equalsIgnoreCase("INSTANCE")) {
        this.setInstance(value);
        return true;
    }
    return false;
}
public boolean execute() {
    //getDemo().setRdbAccessString(getAcct());
    getDemo().setStore(new com.xweave.xmldb.demo.Store());
    getDemo().getStore().setOutput(getDemo().getOutput());
    getDemo().getStore().setRdbAccessString(getAcct());
    getDemo().getStore().connect();
    //getDemo().setCurrentAcctName(getAcctWOPassword());
    return (! getDemo().getStore().getRdb().isClosed());
}
public String getAcct() {
    return getAcctName() + "/"
    + getPassword() + "@"
    + getMachine() + ":"
    + getPort() + ":"
    + getInstance();
```

```
}
public String getAcctName() {
   return acctName;
}
public String getAcctWOPassword() {
   return getAcctName() + "@"
   + getMachine() + ":"
   + getPort() + ":"
   + getInstance();
}
public String getInstance() {
   return instance;
}
public String getMachine() {
   return machine;
}
public String getName() {
   return "Login";
}
public String getPassword() {
   return password;
}
public String getPort() {
   return port;
}
public boolean promptHtml() {
   StringBuffer buf = new StringBuffer();
   buf.append("<html>\n<body>\n");
   buf.append("<form action =\"com.xweave.xmldb.demo.XMLServlet\"
method=\"POST\">\n");
   buf.append("<input type=\"hidden\" name=\"cmd\" value=\"Login\"/>\n");
   buf.append("<h1>Login to XML DB</h1><br/>\n");
   buf.append("Name: <input type=\"input\" name=\"name\" size=\"15\"
value=\"" + getAcctName() + "\"/></br>\n");
   buf.append("Password: <input type=\"password\" name=\"password\"
size=\"15\" value=\"" + getPassword() + "\"/><br/>\n");
   buf.append("Machine: <input type=\"input\" name=\"machine\" size=\"15\"
value=\"" + getMachine() + "\"/><br/>\n");
   buf.append("Port: <input type=\"input\" name=\"port\" size=\"6\"
value=\"" + getPort() + "\"/><br/>\n");
   buf.append("Instance: <input type=\"input\" name=\"instance\"
size=\"15\" value=\"" + getInstance() + "\"/><br/>\n");
   buf.append("<input type=\"hidden\" name=\"successurl\"
value=\"com.xweave.xmldb.demo.XMLServlet?cmd=list&format=html_cmd\"/><br/
>\n");
```

```
    buf.append("<input type=\"submit\" name=\"ignore\" value=\"Login\"/
>\n");
    buf.append("</form>\n</body>\n</html>\n");
    getDemo().getOutput().writeln(buf.toString());
    return true;
}
public void setAcctName(String newValue) {
    this.acctName = newValue;
}
public void setInstance(String newValue) {
    this.instance = newValue;
}
public void setMachine(String newValue) {
    this.machine = newValue;
}
public void setPassword(String newValue) {
    this.password = newValue;
}
public void setPort(String newValue) {
    this.port = newValue;
}
}
```

The Java servlet also provides dynamic HTML pages to prompt the user when some required parameters are not specified in the URL. This feature is used in the Gene Notebook to allow modification of data in the Notebook without specifying a complete data entry form as part of the user interface. For example, to change the name of a gene, a link is followed that specifies the identifier associated with the element for the gene as part of a URL, but not the new name. The user is prompted by generic code in the servlet to fill in the missing information, as shown in Figure 10–11.

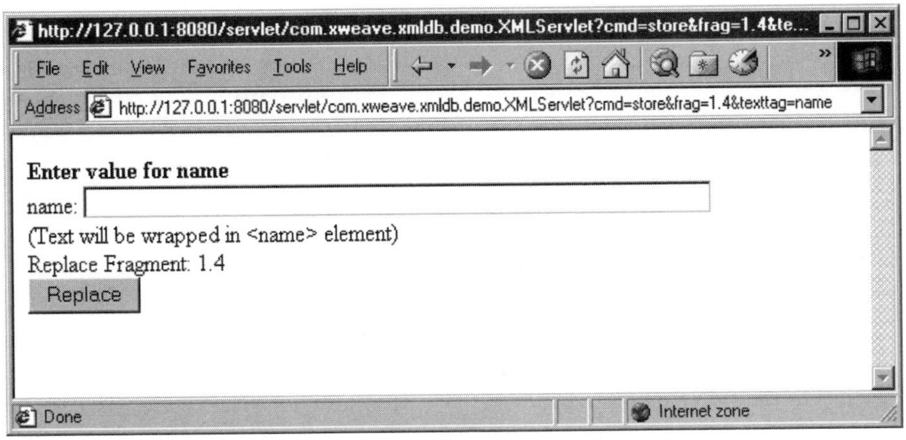

Figure 10–11 Entering a new name for a gene in gene notebook

Each fragment in the database is identified by a unique identifier consisting of the numeric document identifier and a numeric fragment identifier. The fragment identifier initially is the position of the element in the document in text order (i.e., *document order)*, though inserted elements are assigned the next higher ID number in the document, regardless of the location in document order. An identifier does not change until that element is deleted. The command to retrieve a document takes as a flag whether to include the unique fragment identifier as an additional attribute on each element. That "includefragid" option is set for the Gene Notebook retrievals, and the XSL stylesheet extracts that identifier and uses it in creating URL commands to the database to modify the XML document.

10.6 Limitations and Extensions

Currently, the implementation is limited in its use of links. As XML Linking becomes more integrated into Web browsers, many of the interactions described using the stylesheets can be captured using links. The element types for annotations, relationships, and collections can be modified to have default and explicit attributes that are used by the XML Linking processor.

10.7 Practical Considerations

The example Gene Notebook captures all the information in a single document. Having one document simplifies the processing and maintenance, but may become unwieldy as the document grows toward its goal of capturing all known genes. It may be useful to create separate documents for larger annotations, relationships, and collections broken out, or in particular the references that validate that information that might already be a document in XML form.

There may also need to be other sections (or documents) to support the various kinds of analysis and each gene-specific run of an analysis tool may create an entire XML document as part of the processing. From this document, key information can be extracted and summarized and stored associated with each gene.

Medium-grained storage can be used efficiently by deciding which splice points are needed. A simple user interface can present the element type names of a document being imported into the database. The user (or administrator) can select the element type names that should be indexed and which form the slice points. By judicious use of slice points, traditional relational schemas, and XML flat files, a large flexible system can be developed and maintained that provides efficient access to a variety of data sources and analysis results.

10.8 Scaling Up

The notebook system may be expanded to a DBMS. Requirements that the notebook system would need to be a DBMS include transaction management, security features, recovery mechanisms, and optimizations. Additional operations may also be necessary or desired, such as features to support database navigation.

10.8.1 Transaction Management

Transaction management has not been worked out for XML DBMSs, though some possible starting places are included in this section.

When a document is being updated, it may be necessary to lock the document or part of the document to prevent other users from attempting changes that would interact with the current change in an inconsistent manner. For example, if one user tried to reorder the elements in a document while another user tried to delete one of the elements, the database could be left in an inconsistent state depending upon the order in which parts of the two transactions were executed: The element might not have been deleted, the wrong element might be deleted, or the order might not be what the first user requested.

In some cases, it may be necessary to lock the entire document, but in other cases only part of the document needs to be locked. If two users make changes on separate parts of the document, and it is clear by the nature of the operations and the parameters to the operations that no interaction is possible, then both operations can take place simultaneously and locking the entire document would slow down system performance.

Borrowing from locking mechanisms that have been developed for relational and object-oriented DBMSs, levels of locking that may be useful for an XML DBMS are: document, element tree, and element. In addition, it may be useful to lock an element type of a document if there are operations that modify some aspect of all elements with a given element type.

So far, applications that use XML databases have not required sophisticated transaction management and when the XML DBMS is built on top of a robust DBMS, the transaction management system of that DBMS may provide sufficient transaction management for most applications.

Transaction management is not currently as important for XML DBMSs as it is for other DBMSs. The application areas in which XML DBMSs are most currently used are not heavily transaction-oriented. However, if robust transaction management were available, new application areas could be discovered.

In practice, if an existing DBMS is used for storage, then some of the locking mechanisms of that system may be used. If a generic persistent storage system is used, it may provide operations that simplify building an XML DBMS. If a from-scratch implementation is attempted, then the specific requirements for that system would need to be developed.

10.8.2 Security

Access control may be needed to read, write, edit, or link to an element, element tree, element type, or document. Editing may include adding, deleting, modifying, or reordering subelement. File systems have a similar structure to XML documents, and many of the access control features of a file system are also useful for XML documents.

Locking individual attributes or character data regions does not appear to be necessary, though scenarios can be imagined where that would be useful. However, most of those can be implemented with a slight change in document structure and element or element type locking and to support locking at a finer granularity than element could be expensive.

10.8.3 Recovery

Recovery restores the database to a state presumed to be correct after some failure. Two aspects of recovery are: logging, which tracks the transactions that have occurred; and rollback, which reverts the state of the database to a previous state.

Logging records the operations that have taken place on a database that can be used to recover from a system failure or to roll back a transaction. Theoretically, logging in an XML DBMS is not much different than logging in a relational database. In practice, logging may be more complicated because a node in the XML tree could contain a data item (as a character data region) or a subelement (which could be quite large). Thus, the overall size of the data in an update operation may be quite large and have a complex structure.

Rollback allows operations to be undone from a transaction that was not successfully completed. In practice, changes to the database are kept in a buffer and only written to the physical storage when the transaction is committed. Theoretically, rollback in an XML DBMS is not substantially different than rollback in a relational DBMS.

10.8.4 Optimization

Both access time and storage space efficiency are critical for DBMSs. Optimization of efficiency of operations that access the database must be possible as well as efficient use of space. Query optimization was discussed in Chapters 8 and 9, and indexing improves the performance of all operations that retrieve data from the database. Mechanisms to reduce the space needed for storage were described in Chapter 4.

Appendix A
Java Utilities

Most of the examples in the book require a connection to a relational database as well as output to a servlet. Rather than duplicate the description of those utilities where used, they are presented in this appendix. Also presented in the appendix is a "Default" class for the systems in the book. This class collects together the system parameters that can be set to make the software examples work together in a system.

The access utilities consist of three parts: a relational database connection, classes that provide output streams, and an interface that defines interaction with both a relational database and output source. The Java examples in the book use only these classes for interacting with the database and output source, which provides a simple way to change the RDBMS used or the output source.

The only other Java packages used are a JDBC client and a SAX parser.

A.1 System Defaults

The code for the class is in the class com.xweave.xmldb.Default. The class contains values for four (static) variables. The variables are

- DBProduct—defines the relational DBMS used for storage
- xmldbAcct—defines the account within the DBMS that contains XML documents in a form defined in Chapter 4
- reldbAcct—defines the account that contains any relational tables for access by the system described in Chapter 5
- parserClass—describes the SAX parser used (as described in Appendix B)

The variables are accessed by the system via getter/setter methods. The default values are

- DBProduct = ORACLE

The format for the access string for the variables xmldbacct and reldbacct is: "jdbc:oracle:thin:acct/password@machine:port:instance" for Oracle JDBC or "jdbc:db2:instance" for IBM DB2 via JDBC. Their defaults are

- xmldbAcct = "jdbc:oracle:thin:xmldb/xmldb@127.0.0.1 :1521:ORCL";
- xmldbAcct = "jdbc:db2:XMLDB";

The default value for "reldbAcct" is null, which means that the same value as the "xmldbAcct" is used.

The default value for the SAX parser is the IBM xml4j parser:

- parserClass = "com.ibm.xml.parsers.SAXParser";

The entire code for the class is:

```
package com.xweave.xmldb;

/**
 * Contains defaults for system
 */
public class Default {
   //access string is acct/password@machine:port:instance
for Oracle JDBC
   public static String xmldbAcct = "jdbc:oracle:thin:xmldb/
xmldb@127.0.0.1:1521:ORCL";
   //public static String xmldbAcct = "jdbc:db2:XMLDB";
   public static String reldbAcct = null;
   //public static String reldbAcct =
```

```
"jdbc:oracle:thin:scott/tiger@127.0.0.1:1521:ORCL";
   public static String parserClass =
"com.ibm.xml.parsers.SAXParser";
public Default() {
   // do not instantiate
}
public static String getParserClass() {
   return parserClass;
}
public static String getReldbAcct() {
   if (reldbAcct == null) {
      return getXmldbAcct();
   }
   return reldbAcct;
}
public static String getXmldbAcct() {
   return xmldbAcct;
}
public static void setParserClass(String newValue) {
   Default.parserClass = newValue;
}
public static void setReldbAcct(String newValue) {
   Default.reldbAcct = newValue;
}
public static void setXmldbAcct(String newValue) {
   Default.xmldbAcct = newValue;
}
}
```

A.2 Relational Database Connection

Several pieces of software in the book require a connection to a relational database. They all use a simple utility written in Java to connect to a relational DBMS using JDBC. There are many commercial and free systems that provide the same functionality and often provide much more. Some of these are integrated with Web servers as an application server. The utility in this appendix is used because it provides only the functionality required for the examples in the book and is simple to understand.

The RDB utility consists of two interfaces and two classes. The interface RDB provides access to a relational database with methods to open, close, query, and modify the database. The interface RDBAcct encapsulates the account information needed to access the relational DBMS. The class DBConnector implements the RDB interface and provides access to a DBMS through JDBC. The class JDBCAcct implements the RDBAcct interface for JDBC access. The classes OracleDB and DB2DB are subclasses of DBConnector.

The code for RDB interface is

```
package com.xweave.xmldb.util.rdb;

import java.sql.*;
/**
 * Interface to access a Relational Database
 */
public interface RDB {
void close();
public boolean connect(RDBAcct acct);
public boolean connect(Connection conn);
ResultSet executeQuery(String statement) throws
SQLException;
int executeUpdate(String statement) throws SQLException;
ResultSet getData(String query);
String getDataItem(String query);
public boolean isClosed();
}
```

The code for the interface RDBAccess is

```
package com.xweave.xmldb.util.rdb;

/**
 * Account and access for relational database.
 */
public interface RDBAcct {
String getAcct();
void setAcct(String acct);
String toString();
}
```

The code for the class JDBCAccess is

```
package com.xweave.xmldb.util.rdb;

/**
 * Captures acct and access information for connection to RDB.
```

```
 */
public class JDBCAcct implements RDBAcct {
    protected String jdbcaccess = null;
public JDBCAcct() {
    super();
}
public JDBCAcct(String acct) {
    super();
    setAcct(acct);
}
public String getAcct() {
    return jdbcaccess;
}
public void setAcct(String acct) {
    this.jdbcaccess = acct;
}
public String toString() {
    return getAcct();
}
}
```

The code for the class DBConnector is

```
package com.xweave.xmldb.util.rdb;

import java.sql.*;
/**
 * Implements access to a relational database
 * Requires JDBC Thin Driver in the class path.
 *
 * Drivers are registered from the array driverArray.
 * Connection string is connectStringPrefix + acct +
       connectStringSuffix
 */
public class RDBConnector implements RDB {
    protected Statement[] statement = new Statement[32];
    protected RDBAcct acct = null;
    protected Connection conn = null;
    // If you always use the same DBMS, set
       connectStringPrefix
    // to be the appropriate URL prefix. Then only the
       account
    // is needed as part of the connect string.
    // public String connectStringPrefix =
       "jdbc:oracle:thin:";
```

```
        public String connectStringPrefix = "";
    // If you always use the same machine and instance, set
        connectStringSuffix
    // to be the appropriate URL suffix. Then only the
        account
    // is needed as part of the connect string.
    public String connectStringSuffix = "";
    public String[] driverArray = {
        "oracle.jdbc.driver.OracleDriver",
        "COM.ibm.db2.jdbc.app.DB2Driver"
    };
public RDBConnector() throws SQLException {
    super();
    register();
}
public RDBConnector(RDBAcct acct) throws SQLException {
    super();
    setAcct(acct);
    register();
    connect();
}
public void close() {
    try {
      if (conn.isClosed()) {
        return;
    } else {
        conn.close();
    }
  } catch (SQLException ex) {
    ex.printStackTrace();
  }
}
public boolean connect() {
    try {
        if (conn != null) {
            return true;
        }
        conn =
    DriverManager.getConnection(getConnectString());
        return true;
    } catch (SQLException ex) {
      ex.printStackTrace();
      return false;
    }
}
```

```
public boolean connect(RDBAcct acct) {
    setAcct(acct);
    return connect();
}
public boolean connect(Connection newconn) {
    conn = newconn;
    return true;
}
public ResultSet executeQuery(String query) throws
    SQLException
    {
    return executeQuery(query,0);
}
public ResultSet executeQuery(String query, int
    statementNum)
    throws SQLException {
    if (statement[statementNum] == null) {
        if (conn == null) {
            System.err.println("Database is closed for " +
    query);
            return null;
      }
      statement[statementNum] = conn.createStatement();
    }
    return
    statement[statementNum].executeQuery(query.trim());
}
/**
 * execute a sql statement that does not return a result
 * return the number of rows modified, or 0 if no result
 */
public int executeUpdate(String sql) throws SQLException {
    try {
        if (statement[0] == null) {
            if (conn == null) {
                System.err.println("Database is closed for
    " + sql);
                return 0;
            }
            statement[0] = conn.createStatement();
        }
        return statement[0].executeUpdate(sql.trim());
    } catch (SQLException ex) {
        ex.printStackTrace();
        return 0;
```

```
    }
}
public RDBAcct getAcct() {
    return acct;
}
public java.sql.Connection getConnection() {
    // Provide direct access to RDB Connection. This
       typically
    will not be needed.
    return conn;
}
public String getConnectString() {
    return getConnectStringPrefix() + getAcct() +
    getConnectStringSuffix();
}
public String getConnectStringPrefix() {
    return connectStringPrefix;
}
public String getConnectStringSuffix() {
    return connectStringSuffix;
}
public ResultSet getData(String query) {
    return getData(query,0);
}
public ResultSet getData(String query, int statementNum) {
    try {
        return executeQuery(query, statementNum);
    } catch (SQLException ex) {
      ex.printStackTrace();
      return null;
    }
}
/**
 * Get the singleton value of a query
 */
public String getDataItem(String query) {
    // returns the value of the first column of the first row
    try {
    ResultSet resultSet = getData(query);
    if (resultSet == null) {
        //error in query
        //we may have problems later, but return null
        //throw new Error("Error in query: " + query);
        return null;
      }
```

```
        resultSet.next();
        return resultSet.getString(1);
      } catch (SQLException ex) {
        ex.printStackTrace();
        return null;
      }
  }
  public Statement getStatement() {
      return statement[0];
  }
  public Statement getStatement(int statementNum) {
      return statement[statementNum];
  }
  public boolean isClosed() {
      if (conn == null) {
         return true;
      } else {
         try {
              return conn.isClosed();
         } catch (SQLException ex) {
              ex.printStackTrace();
              return true;
         }
      }
  }
  public void register() {
      //registers all the drivers in driverArray
      for (int i = 0; i < driverArray.length; i++) {
          try {
              Class.forName(driverArray[i]);
          } catch (Exception ex) {
              //ignore failed drivers
              //ex.printStackTrace();
          }
      }
  }
  public void setAcct(JDBCAcct newValue) {
      this.acct = newValue;
  }
  public void setAcct(RDBAcct newValue) {
      this.acct = newValue;
  }
  public void setConnectStringPrefix(String newValue) {
      this.connectStringPrefix = newValue;
  }
```

```
public void setConnectStringSuffix(String newValue) {
    this.connectStringSuffix = newValue;
}
}
```

The code for OracleDB is

```
package com.xweave.xmldb.util.rdb;

import java.sql.*;
/**
 * Implements access to Oracle
 * Requires JDBC Thin Driver in the class path.
 */
public class OracleDB extends RDBConnector implements RDB {
public OracleDB() throws SQLException {
    super();
    setConnectStringPrefix("jdbc:oracle:thin:");
}
public OracleDB(RDBAcct acct) throws SQLException {
    super();
    setAcct(acct);
    setConnectStringPrefix("jdbc:oracle:thin:");
    connect();
}
}
```

The code for DB2DB is

```
package com.xweave.xmldb.util.rdb;

import java.sql.*;
/**
 * Implements access to DB2
 * Requires JDBC Thin Driver in the class path.
 */
public class DB2DB extends RDBConnector implements RDB {
public DB2DB() throws SQLException {
    super();
}
public DB2DB(RDBAcct acct) throws SQLException {
    super();
    setAcct(acct);
    connect();
```

```
}
public boolean connect() {
    try {
        if (conn != null) {
            return true;
        }
        conn = DriverManager.getConnection("jdbc:db2:xmldb",
    "", "");
        return true;
    } catch (SQLException ex) {
      ex.printStackTrace();
      return false;
    }
}
}
```

A.3 Servlet Output

Three classes provide output for the software described in this book: the Output class, which writes to standard output; ServletOutput, which inherits from the Output class and provides the ability to write to a ServletOutputStream; and JSPOutput, which inherits from the Output class and provides the ability to write to a JSPWriter.

The code for Output is

```
package com.xweave.xmldb.util.io;

import java.io.*;
/**
 * Handles output to an output source.
 */
public class Output {
public Output() {
    super();
}
public void write(String s) {
    System.out.print(s);
}
public void writeln(String s) {
    System.out.println(s);
}
}
```

The code for ServletOutput is

```
package com.xweave.xmldb.util.io;

import javax.servlet.*;
import javax.servlet.http.*;
/**
 * Handles Servlet output
 */
public class ServletOutput extends Output {
    protected ServletOutputStream out = null;
public ServletOutput() {
    super();
}
public ServletOutput(ServletOutputStream newValue) {
    super();
    setOut(newValue);
}
public ServletOutputStream getOut() {
    return out;
}
public void setOut(ServletOutputStream newValue) {
    this.out = newValue;
}
public void write(String s) {
    try {
      out.print(s);
    } catch (Exception ex) {
      ex.printStackTrace();
    }
}
public void writeln(String s) {
    try {
      out.println(s);
    } catch (Exception ex) {
      ex.printStackTrace();
    }
}
}
```

The code for JSPOutput is

```
package com.xweave.xmldb.util.io;
```

```
import javax.servlet.jsp.*;
public class JSPOutput extends Output {
    protected javax.servlet.jsp.JspWriter out = null;
public JSPOutput() {
    super();
}
public JSPOutput(JspWriter newValue) {
    super();
    setOut(newValue);
}
public JspWriter getOut() {
    return out;
}
public void setOut(JspWriter newOut) {
    out = newOut;
}
public void write(String s) {
    try {
      out.print(s);
    } catch (Exception ex) {
      ex.printStackTrace();
    }
}
public void writeln(String s) {
    try {
      out.println(s);
    } catch (Exception ex) {
      ex.printStackTrace();
    }
}
}
```

A.4 Interactive Access Interface

The RDBInteractor class combines functionality from the RDB interface and Output class. The code for RDBInteractor is

```
package com.xweave.xmldb.util.rdb;

import com.xweave.xmldb.util.rdb.*;
import com.xweave.xmldb.util.io.*;
/**
```

```
 * Basic RDB interactor.
 */
public abstract class RDBInteractor {
    private RDB rdb = null;
    //access string is acct/password@machine:port:instance
    for JDBC, or null for stdout
    protected String rdbAccessString =
    "xmldb/xmldb@127.0.0.1:1521:ORCL";
    protected Output output = null;
public RDBInteractor() {
    super();
}
public void connect() {
    try {
        setRdb(new OracleDB(new JDBCAcct(rdbAccessString)));
    } catch (java.sql.SQLException ex) {
        ex.printStackTrace();
    }
}
public void connect(String value) {
    this.setRdbAccessString(value);
    connect();
}
public Output getOutput() {
    if (output == null) {
        setOutput(new Output());
    }
    return output;
}
public RDB getRdb() {
    if (rdb == null) {
        if (getRdbAccessString() != null) {
            //create a connection to Oracle
            connect();
        }
    }
    return rdb;
}
public String getRdbAccessString() {
    return rdbAccessString;
}
public void setOutput(Output newValue) {
    this.output = newValue;
}
protected void setRdb(RDB newValue) {
```

```
    this.rdb = newValue;
}
public void setRdbAccessString(String newValue) {
    this.rdbAccessString = newValue;
}
}
```

Appendix B
SAX Parser

Several applications in the book use SAX parsers (Simple API for XML), and an introduction is presented here. More detail on using the SAX parser is discussed in Chapter 7.

There are two major types of XML parsers: tree-based parsers and event-based parsers. A tree-based parser creates an internal tree structure (like the one described in Chapter 3). The tree structure is navigated by the application to extract information. The DOM (Domain Object Model) parser is a tree-based parser that creates objects for each element and character data region in the document. An event-based parser reports parsing events, such as the start and end of an element and does not build an internal tree structure. The SAX parser is an event-based parser that may be more efficient for extracting data from large documents.

The SAX parser calls a user-defined method at the beginning and end of each element and for each character data region. The user-defined methods can create an alternative data structure more efficiently than DOM that meets the requirements of the application. For example, if the application is only extracting part of the data from an XML stream, then the parsing may be much faster using SAX than creating the DOM objects that would not be used. However, the event-based parsing may require the creation of additional, temporary data structures to retain parsed information before placing it in the final data structure. For example, character data may be associated with the containing element. In that case, a stack of elements is necessary to facilitate the association.

XML parsers are often created using a "factory" pattern. A string of the class name for the parser is passed to the parser factory to create a parser. Many companies—including IBM, Sun, and Oracle—provide parsers that can be created using this approach. An advantage of using a parser factory is that the parser can be easily replaced if a more efficient one is found. The main caveat when using the factory pattern is to be sure to include the specified parser class in the class path.

The process of creating a SAX parser consists of the following:

1. Creating an instance of the Parser.
2. Creating and initializing an instance of the Parser Handler.
3. Initializing the Parser to use the Parser Handler.
4. Calling the Parser with the XML URL.
5. The Parser retrieves and parses the document, calling the Handler at
   - The beginning of the document.
   - The beginning of each element.
   - The end of each character data region.
   - The end of each element.
   - The end of the document.

There are two versions of the SAX parser currently available. The code in this chapter uses the original SAX classes and methods. There is also a SAX2 parser framework that includes support for namespaces (among other things). The methods described here are still included in SAX2, but these SAX1 methods may also be switched over to the new methods in SAX2 (with the same names) if you desire. Also, the classes in this appendix refer to an IBM parser, while the code delivered in the CD uses a more recent Apache parser, which is based on the IBM parser. Code to create a parser is

```
String parserClass = "com.ibm.xml.parsers.SAXParser";
Parser parser = ParserFactory.makeParser(parserClass);
```

The parser class is defined and then the parser factory is used to create a parser. After the parser is created, a document handler is created, and the parser is set to use that handler:

```
HandlerBase handler = new DebugHandler();
parser.setDocumentHandler(handler);
```

```
parser.setErrorHandler(handler);
```

The parser is called by passing a URL to the parser, such as:

```
parser.parse(xmlFile);
```

The entire code is wrapped in exception handlers to catch exceptions, and the result as a method is

```
public void parse(String xmlFile) {
    String parserClass = "com.ibm.xml.parsers.SAXParser";
    try {
      Parser parser = ParserFactory.makeParser(parserClass);
      HandlerBase handler = new DebugHandler();
      parser.setDocumentHandler(handler);
      parser.setErrorHandler(handler);
      try {
          parser.parse(xmlFile);
      } catch (SAXException se) {
          se.printStackTrace();
      } catch (IOException ioe) {
          ioe.printStackTrace();
      }
    } catch (ClassNotFoundException ex) {
      ex.printStackTrace();
    } catch (IllegalAccessException ex) {
      ex.printStackTrace();
    } catch (InstantiationException ex) {
      ex.printStackTrace();
    }
}
```

A simple class to execute the parser is

```
package com.xweave.xmldb.ui.test1;

import org.xml.sax.*;
import org.xml.sax.helpers.ParserFactory;
import org.w3c.dom.Document;
import java.io.IOException;
import com.ibm.xml.parsers.*;

public class Test {
public Test() {
```

```
    super();
}
public static void main(java.lang.String[] args) {
    String fileName = null;
    if (args.length < 1) {
      System.err.println("Test: requires <file> as
    argument");
      return;
    } else {
      fileName = args[0];
    }
    (new Test()).parse(fileName);
}
public void parse(String xmlFile) {
    //code given above
}
}
```

A simple handler can be created as

```
package com.xweave.xmldb.ui.test1;

/**
 * Test Handler that prints debug statements
 */
import org.xml.sax.*;
class DebugHandler extends org.xml.sax.HandlerBase implements
    org.xml.sax.DocumentHandler {
public DebugHandler() {
    super();
}
public void characters(char[] chars, int start, int length) {
    String string = new String(chars, start, length);
    System.out.println("chars="+string+"!");
}
public void endDocument() {
    System.out.println("end document");
}
public void endElement(String tag) {
    System.out.println("end: "+tag);
}
public void startDocument() {
    System.out.println("start document");
}
public void startElement(String tag, AttributeList attrList)
```

```
{    System.out.println("start: "+tag);
}
}
```

The DebugHandler class implements the DocumentHandler SAX interface and has methods for the following:

- The beginning of the document—emits "start document"
- The beginning of each element—emits "start: <name>"
- The end of each character data region—emits the character data region (ended with a "!" to delimit white space)
- The end of each element—emits "end: <name>"
- The end of the document—emits "end document"

When executing the test procedure on a simple document like the following:

```
<?xml version="1.0"?>
<doc>
<body>Hello world!!!</body>
</doc>
```

The handler will create output something like this:

```
start document
start: doc
start: body
chars=Hello world!!!!
end: body
end: doc
end document
```

The phrase "something like" is somewhat misleading because the output will be this:

```
start document
start: doc
chars=
!
start: body
chars=Hello world!!!!
end: body
chars=
```

```
!
end: doc
end document
```

Actually, two extra character data regions surround the element with type name “body”. The character data consists of a carriage return. In practice, character data regions may be trimmed of white space and empty regions can be ignored. A document that would give the former output is

```
<?xml version="1.0"?>
<doc><body>Hello world!!!</body></doc>
```

A tree-based parser, such as DOM, would filter such occurrences, but because the SAX event-based parser is at a lower level, the application that uses it must filter those occurrences.

Appendix C
XML Schema Part 0: Primer
W3C Recommendation, 2 May 2001

This version:
http://www.w3.org/TR/2001/REC-xmlschema-0-20010502/

Latest version:
http://www.w3.org/TR/xmlschema-0/

Previous version:
http://www.w3.org/TR/2001/PR-xmlschema-0-20010330/

Editor:
David C. Fallside (IBM) *fallside@us.ibm.com*

ABSTRACT XML Schema Part 0: Primer is a non-normative document intended to provide an easily readable description of the XML Schema facilities, and is oriented towards quickly understanding how to create schemas using the XML Schema language. XML Schema Part 1: Structures and XML Schema Part 2: Datatypes provide the complete normative description of the XML Schema language. This primer describes the language features through numerous examples which are complemented by extensive references to the normative texts.

STATUS OF THIS DOCUMENT *This section describes the status of this document at the time of its publication. Other documents may supersede this document. The latest status of this document series is maintained at the W3C.*

This document has been reviewed by W3C Members and other interested parties and has been endorsed by the Director as a W3C Recommendation. It is a stable document and may be used as reference material or cited as a normative reference from another document. W3C's role in making the Recommendation is to draw attention to the specification and to promote its widespread deployment. This enhances the functionality and interoperability of the Web.

This document has been produced by the W3C XML Schema Working Group as part of the W3C XML Activity. The goals of the XML Schema language are discussed in the XML Schema Requirements document. The authors of this document are the members of the XML Schema Working Group. Different parts of the document have different editors.

This version of this document incorporates some editorial changes from earlier versions.

Please report errors in this document to *www-xml-schema-comments@w3.org* (archive). The list of known errors in this specification is available at *http://www.w3.org/2001/05/xmlschema-errata.*

The English version of this specification is the only normative version. Information about translations of this document is available at *http://www.w3.org/2001/05/xmlschema-translations.*

A list of current W3C Recommendations and other technical documents can be found at *http://www.w3.org/TR/.*

Table of Contents

1 Introduction

This document, XML Schema Part 0: Primer, provides an easily approachable description of the XML Schema definition language, and should be used alongside the formal descriptions of the language contained in Parts 1 and 2 of the XML Schema specification. The intended audience of this document includes application developers whose programs read and write schema documents, and schema authors who need to know about the features of the language, especially features that provide functionality above and beyond what is provided by DTDs. The text assumes that you have a basic understanding of XML 1.0 and XML-Namespaces. Each major section of the primer introduces new features of the language, and describes those features in the context of concrete examples.

Section 2 covers the basic mechanisms of XML Schema. It describes how to declare the elements and attributes that appear in XML documents, the distinctions between simple and complex types, defining complex types, the use of simple types for element and attribute values, schema annotation, a simple mechanism for re-using element and attribute definitions, and nil values.

Section 3, the first advanced section in the primer, explains the basics of how namespaces are used in XML and schema documents. This section is important for understanding many of the topics that appear in the other advanced sections.

Section 4, the second advanced section in the primer, describes mechanisms for deriving types from existing types, and for controlling these derivations. The section also describes mechanisms for merging together fragments of a schema from multiple sources, and for element substitution.

Section 5 covers more advanced features, including a mechanism for specifying uniqueness among attributes and elements, a mechanism for using types across namespaces, a mechanism for extending types based on namespaces, and a description of how documents are checked for conformance.

In addition to the sections just described, the primer contains a number of appendices that provide detailed reference information on simple types and a regular expression language.

The primer is a non-normative document, which means that it does not provide a definitive (from the W3C's point of view) specification of the XML Schema language. The examples and other explanatory material in this document are provided to help you understand XML Schema, but they may not always provide definitive answers. In such cases, you will need to refer to the XML Schema specification, and to help you do this, we provide many links pointing to the relevant parts of the specification. More specifically, XML Schema items mentioned in the primer text are linked to an index of element names and attributes, and a summary table of datatypes, both in the primer. The table and the index contain links to the relevant sections of XML Schema parts 1 and 2.

2 Basic Concepts: The Purchase Order

The purpose of a schema is to define a class of XML documents, and so the term "instance document" is often used to describe an XML document that conforms to a particular schema. In fact, neither instances nor schemas need to exist as documents *per se*—they may exist as streams of bytes sent between applications, as fields in a database record, or as collections of XML Infoset "Information Items"—but to simplify the primer, we have chosen to always refer to instances and schemas as if they are documents and files.

Let us start by considering an instance document in a file called `po.xml`. It describes a purchase order generated by a home products ordering and billing application:

The Purchase Order, `po.xml`

```
<?xml version="1.0"?>
 <purchaseOrder orderDate="1999-10-20">
     <shipTo country="US">
         <name>Alice Smith</name>
         <street>123 Maple Street</street>
         <city>Mill Valley</city>
         <state>CA</state>
         <zip>90952</zip>
     </shipTo>
     <billTo country="US">
         <name>Robert Smith</name>
         <street>8 Oak Avenue</street>
         <city>Old Town</city>
         <state>PA</state>
         <zip>95819</zip>
     </billTo>
     <comment>Hurry, my lawn is going wild!</comment>
     <items>
         <item partNum="872-AA">
             <productName>Lawnmower</productName>
             <quantity>1</quantity>
             <USPrice>148.95</USPrice>
             <comment>Confirm this is electric</comment>
         </item>
         <item partNum="926-AA">
             <productName>Baby Monitor</productName>
             <quantity>1</quantity>
             <USPrice>39.98</USPrice>
```

```
            <shipDate>1999-05-21</shipDate>
        </item>
    </items>
</purchaseOrder>
```

The purchase order consists of a main element, `purchaseOrder`, and the subelements `shipTo`, `billTo`, `comment`, and `items`. These subelements (except `comment`) in turn contain other subelements, and so on, until a subelement such as `USPrice` contains a number rather than any subelements. Elements that contain subelements or carry attributes are said to have complex types, whereas elements that contain numbers (and strings, and dates, etc.) but do not contain any subelements are said to have simple types. Some elements have attributes; attributes always have simple types.

The complex types in the instance document, and some of the simple types, are defined in the schema for purchase orders. The other simple types are defined as part of XML Schema's repertoire of built-in simple types.

Before going on to examine the purchase order schema, we digress briefly to mention the association between the instance document and the purchase order schema. As you can see by inspecting the instance document, the purchase order schema is not mentioned. An instance is not actually required to reference a schema, and although many will, we have chosen to keep this first section simple, and to assume that any processor of the instance document can obtain the purchase order schema without any information from the instance document. In later sections, we will introduce explicit mechanisms for associating instances and schemas.

2.1 The Purchase Order Schema

The purchase order schema is contained in the file `po.xsd`:

The Purchase Order Schema, `po.xsd`

```
<xsd:schema xmlns:xsd="http://www.w3.org/2001/XMLSchema">

  <xsd:annotation>
   <xsd:documentation xml:lang="en">
    Purchase order schema for Example.com.
    Copyright 2000 Example.com. All rights reserved.
   </xsd:documentation>
  </xsd:annotation>
  <xsd:element name="purchaseOrder" type="PurchaseOrderType"/>
```

```
  <xsd:element name="comment" type="xsd:string"/>

  <xsd:complexType name="PurchaseOrderType">
   <xsd:sequence>
    <xsd:element name="shipTo" type="USAddress"/>
    <xsd:element name="billTo" type="USAddress"/>
    <xsd:element ref="comment" minOccurs="0"/>
    <xsd:element name="items"  type="Items"/>
   </xsd:sequence>
   <xsd:attribute name="orderDate" type="xsd:date"/>
  </xsd:complexType>

  <xsd:complexType name="USAddress">
   <xsd:sequence>
    <xsd:element name="name"   type="xsd:string"/>
    <xsd:element name="street" type="xsd:string"/>
    <xsd:element name="city"   type="xsd:string"/>
    <xsd:element name="state"  type="xsd:string"/>
    <xsd:element name="zip"    type="xsd:decimal"/>
   </xsd:sequence>
   <xsd:attribute name="country" type="xsd:NMTOKEN"
      fixed="US"/>
  </xsd:complexType>

  <xsd:complexType name="Items">
   <xsd:sequence>
    <xsd:element name="item" minOccurs="0" maxOccurs="unbounded">
     <xsd:complexType>
      <xsd:sequence>
       <xsd:element name="productName" type="xsd:string"/>
       <xsd:element name="quantity">
        <xsd:simpleType>
         <xsd:restriction base="xsd:positiveInteger">
          <xsd:maxExclusive value="100"/>
         </xsd:restriction>
        </xsd:simpleType>
       </xsd:element>
       <xsd:element name="USPrice"  type="xsd:decimal"/>
       <xsd:element ref="comment"   minOccurs="0"/>
       <xsd:element name="shipDate" type="xsd:date"
minOccurs="0"/>
      </xsd:sequence>
      <xsd:attribute name="partNum" type="SKU" use="required"/>
     </xsd:complexType>
    </xsd:element>
   </xsd:sequence>
  </xsd:complexType>
```

```
 <!-- Stock Keeping Unit, a code for identifying products -->
 <xsd:simpleType name="SKU">
  <xsd:restriction base="xsd:string">
   <xsd:pattern value="\d{3}-[A-Z]{2}"/>
  </xsd:restriction>
 </xsd:simpleType>

</xsd:schema>
```

The purchase order schema consists of a `schema` element and a variety of subelements, most notably `element`, `complexType`, and `simpleType` which determine the appearance of elements and their content in instance documents.

Each of the elements in the schema has a prefix `xsd:` which is associated with the XML Schema namespace through the declaration, `xmlns:xsd="http://www.w3.org/2001/XMLSchema"`, that appears in the `schema` element. The prefix `xsd:` is used by convention to denote the XML Schema namespace, although any prefix can be used. The same prefix, and hence the same association, also appears on the names of built-in simple types, e.g., `xsd:string`. The purpose of the association is to identify the elements and simple types as belonging to the vocabulary of the XML Schema language rather than the vocabulary of the schema author. For the sake of clarity in the text, we just mention the names of elements and simple types (e.g., `simpleType`), and omit the prefix.

2.2 Complex Type Definitions, Element & Attribute Declarations

In XML Schema, there is a basic difference between complex types which allow elements in their content and may carry attributes, and simple types which cannot have element content and cannot carry attributes. There is also a major distinction between definitions which create new types (both simple and complex), and declarations which enable elements and attributes with specific names and types (both simple and complex) to appear in document instances. In this section, we focus on defining complex types and declaring the elements and attributes that appear within them.

New complex types are defined using the `complexType` element and such definitions typically contain a set of element declarations, element references, and attribute declarations. The declarations are not themselves types, but rather an association between a name and the constraints which govern the appearance of that name in documents governed by the associated schema. Elements are declared using the `element` element, and attributes are declared using the `attribute` element. For example, `USAddress` is defined as a complex type, and within the definition of `USAddress` we see five element declarations and one attribute declaration:

Defining the USAddress Type

```
<xsd:complexType name="USAddress" >
  <xsd:sequence>
    <xsd:element name="name"   type="xsd:string"/>
    <xsd:element name="street" type="xsd:string"/>
    <xsd:element name="city"   type="xsd:string"/>
    <xsd:element name="state"  type="xsd:string"/>
    <xsd:element name="zip"    type="xsd:decimal"/>
  </xsd:sequence>
  <xsd:attribute name="country" type="xsd:NMTOKEN" fixed="US"/>
</xsd:complexType>
```

The consequence of this definition is that any element appearing in an instance whose type is declared to be `USAddress` (e.g., `shipTo` in `po.xml`) must consist of five elements and one attribute. These elements must be called `name`, `street`, `city`, `state` and `zip` as specified by the values of the declarations' `name` attributes, and the elements must appear in the same sequence (order) in which they are declared. The first four of these elements will each contain a string, and the fifth will contain a number. The element whose type is declared to be `USAddress` may appear with an attribute called `country` which must contain the string `US`.

The `USAddress` definition contains only declarations involving the simple types: `string`, `decimal` and `NMTOKEN`. In contrast, the `PurchaseOrderType` definition contains element declarations involving complex types, e.g., `USAddress`, although note that both declarations use the same `type` attribute to identify the type, regardless of whether the type is simple or complex.

Defining PurchaseOrderType

```
<xsd:complexType name="PurchaseOrderType">
  <xsd:sequence>
   <xsd:element name="shipTo" type="USAddress"/>
   <xsd:element name="billTo" type="USAddress"/>
   <xsd:element ref="comment" minOccurs="0"/>
   <xsd:element name="items"  type="Items"/>
  </xsd:sequence>
  <xsd:attribute name="orderDate" type="xsd:date"/>
 </xsd:complexType>
```

In defining PurchaseOrderType, two of the element declarations, for `shipTo` and `billTo`, associate different element names with the same complex type, namely `USAddress`. The consequence of this definition is that any element appearing in an instance document (e.g., `po.xml`) whose type is declared to be `PurchaseOrderType` must consist of elements named `shipTo` and `billTo`, each containing the five subelements (`name`, `street`, `city`, `state` and `zip`) that were declared as part of `USAddress`. The `shipTo` and `billTo` elements may also carry the `country` attribute that was declared as part of `USAddress`.

The `PurchaseOrderType` definition contains an `orderDate` attribute declaration which, like the `country` attribute declaration, identifies a simple type. In fact, all attribute declarations must reference simple types because, unlike element declarations, attributes cannot contain other elements or other attributes.

The element declarations we have described so far have each associated a name with an existing type definition. Sometimes it is preferable to use an existing element rather than declare a new element, for example:

```
<xsd:element ref="comment" minOccurs="0"/>
```

This declaration references an existing element, `comment`, that was declared elsewhere in the purchase order schema. In general, the value of the `ref` attribute must reference a global element, i.e., one that has been declared under `schema` rather than as part of a complex type definition. The consequence of this declaration is that an element called `comment` may appear in an instance document, and its content must be consistent with that element's type, in this case, `string`.

2.2.1 Occurrence Constraints

The `comment` element is optional within `PurchaseOrderType` because the value of the `minOccurs` attribute in its declaration is 0. In general, an element is required to appear when the value of `minOccurs` is 1 or more. The maximum number of times an element may appear is determined by the value of a `maxOccurs` attribute in its declaration. This value may be a positive integer such as 41, or the term unbounded to indicate there is no maximum number of occurrences. The default value for both the `minOccurs` and the `maxOccurs` attributes is 1. Thus, when an element such as `comment` is declared without a `maxOccurs` attribute, the element may not occur more than once. Be sure that if you specify a value for only the `minOccurs` attribute, it is less than or equal to the default value of `maxOccurs`, i.e., it is 0 or 1. Similarly, if you specify a value for only the `maxOccurs` attribute, it must be greater than or equal to the default value of `minOccurs`, i.e., 1 or more. If both attributes are omitted, the element must appear exactly once.

Attributes may appear once or not at all, but no other number of times, and so the syntax for specifying occurrences of attributes is different than the syntax for elements. In particular, attributes can be declared with a `use` attribute to indicate whether the attribute is `required` (see for example, the `partNum` attribute declaration in `po.xsd`), `optional`, or even `prohibited`.

Default values of both attributes and elements are declared using the `default` attribute, although this attribute has a slightly different consequence in each case. When an attribute is declared with a default value, the value of the attribute is whatever value appears as the attribute's value in an instance document; if the attribute does not appear in the instance document, the schema processor provides the attribute with a value equal to that of the `default` attribute. Note that default values for attributes only make sense if the attributes themselves are optional, and so it is an error to specify both a default value and anything other than a value of `optional` for `use`.

The schema processor treats defaulted elements slightly differently. When an element is declared with a default value, the value of the element is whatever value appears as the element's content in the instance document; if the element appears without any content, the schema processor provides the element with a value equal to that of the `default` attribute. However, if the element does not appear in the instance document, the schema processor does not provide the element at all. In summary, the differences between element and attribute defaults can be stated as: Default attribute values apply when attributes are missing, and default element values apply when elements are empty.

The `fixed` attribute is used in both attribute and element declarations to ensure that the attributes and elements are set to particular values. For example, `po.xsd` contains a declaration for the `country` attribute, which is declared with a `fixed` value `US`. This declaration means that the appearance of a `country` attribute in an instance document is optional (the default value of `use` is `optional`), although if the attribute does appear, its value must be `US`, and if the attribute does not appear, the schema processor will provide a `country` attribute with the value `US`. Note that the concepts of a fixed value and a default value are mutually exclusive, and so it is an error for a declaration to contain both `fixed` and `default` attributes.

The values of the attributes used in element and attribute declarations to constrain their occurrences are summarized in Table 1.

Table 1 Occurrence Constraints for Elements and Attributes

Elements (`minOccurs`, `maxOccurs`) `fixed`, `default`	*Attributes* `use`, `fixed`, `default`	*Notes*
(1, 1) -, -	required, -, -	element/attribute must appear once, it may have any value
(1, 1) 37, -	required, 37, -	element/attribute must appear once, its value must be 37
(2, unbounded) 37, -	n/a	element must appear twice or more, its value must be 37; in general, `minOccurs` and `maxOccurs` values may be positive integers, and `maxOccurs` value may also be "unbounded"
(0, 1) -, -	optional, -, -	element/attribute may appear once, it may have any value
(0, 1) 37, -	optional, 37, -	element/attribute may appear once, if it does appear its value must be 37, if it does not appear its value is 37
(0, 1) -, 37	optional, -, 37	element/attribute may appear once; if it does not appear its value is 37, otherwise its value is that given

Table 1 Occurrence Constraints for Elements and Attributes (continued)

(0, 2) -, 37	n/a	element may appear once, twice, or not at all; if the element does not appear it is not provided; if it does appear and it is empty, its value is 37; otherwise its value is that given; in general, `minOccurs` and `maxOccurs` values may be positive integers, and `maxOccurs` value may also be "unbounded"
(0, 0) -, -	prohibited, -, -	element/attribute must not appear

Note that neither `minOccurs`, `maxOccurs`, nor `use` may appear in the declarations of global elements and attributes.

2.2.2 Global Elements & Attributes

Global elements, and global attributes, are created by declarations that appear as the children of the `schema` element. Once declared, a global element or a global attribute can be referenced in one or more declarations using the `ref` attribute as described above. A declaration that references a global element enables the referenced element to appear in the instance document in the context of the referencing declaration. So, for example, the `comment` element appears in `po.xml` at the same level as the `shipTo`, `billTo` and `items` elements because the declaration that references `comment` appears in the complex type definition at the same level as the declarations of the other three elements.

The declaration of a global element also enables the element to appear at the top level of an instance document. Hence `purchaseOrder`, which is declared as a global element in `po.xsd`, can appear as the top-level element in `po.xml`. Note that this rationale will also allow a `comment` element to appear as the top-level element in a document like `po.xml`.

There are a number of caveats concerning the use of global elements and attributes. One caveat is that global declarations cannot contain references; global declarations must identify simple and complex types directly. Put concretely, global declarations cannot contain the `ref` attribute, they must use the `type` attribute (or, as we describe shortly, be followed by an anonymous type definition). A second caveat is that cardinality constraints cannot be placed on global declarations, although they can be placed on local declarations that reference global declarations. In other words, global declarations cannot contain the attributes `minOccurs`, `maxOccurs`, or `use`.

2.2.3 Naming Conflicts

We have now described how to define new complex types (e.g., `PurchaseOrderType`), declare elements (e.g., `purchaseOrder`) and declare attributes (e.g., `orderDate`). These activities generally involve naming, and so the question naturally arises: What happens if we give two things the same name? The answer depends upon the two things in question, although in general the more similar are the two things, the more likely there will be a conflict.

Here are some examples to illustrate when same names cause problems. If the two things are both types, say we define a complex type called USStates and a simple type called USStates, there is a conflict. If the two things are a type and an element or attribute, say we define a complex type called USAddress and we declare an element called USAddress, there is no conflict. If the two things are elements within different types (i.e., not global elements), say we declare one element called name as part of the USAddress type and a second element called name as part of the Item type, there is no conflict. (Such elements are sometimes called local element declarations.) Finally, if the two things are both types and you define one and XML Schema has defined the other, say you define a simple type called decimal, there is no conflict. The reason for the apparent contradiction in the last example is that the two types belong to different namespaces. We explore the use of namespaces in schema in a later section.

2.3 Simple Types

The purchase order schema declares several elements and attributes that have simple types. Some of these simple types, such as `string` and `decimal`, are built in to XML Schema, while others are derived from the built-ins. For example, the `partNum` attribute has a type called `SKU` (Stock Keeping Unit) that is derived from `string`. Both built-in simple types and their derivations can be used in all element and attribute declarations. Table 2 lists all the simple types built in to XML Schema, along with examples of the different types.

Table 2 Simple Types Built In to XML Schema

Simple Type	*Examples (delimited by commas)*	*Notes*
`string`	Confirm this is electric	
`normalizedString`	Confirm this is electric	see (3)
`token`	Confirm this is electric	see (4)
`byte`	-1, 126	see (2)
`unsignedByte`	0, 126	see (2)
`base64Binary`	GpM7	
`hexBinary`	0FB7	
`integer`	-126789, -1, 0, 1, 126789	see (2)
`positiveInteger`	1, 126789	see (2)
`negativeInteger`	-126789, -1	see (2)
`nonNegativeInteger`	0, 1, 126789	see (2)
`nonPositiveInteger`	-126789, -1, 0	see (2)
`int`	-1, 126789675	see (2)
`unsignedInt`	0, 1267896754	see (2)
`long`	-1, 12678967543233	see (2)
`unsignedLong`	0, 12678967543233	see (2)
`short`	-1, 12678	see (2)
`unsignedShort`	0, 12678	see (2)
`decimal`	-1.23, 0, 123.4, 1000.00	see (2)
`float`	-INF, -1E4, -0, 0, 12.78E-2, 12, INF, NaN	equivalent to single-precision 32-bit floating point, NaN is "not a number", see (2)
`double`	-INF, -1E4, -0, 0, 12.78E-2, 12, INF, NaN	equivalent to double-precision 64-bit floating point, see (2)

Table 2 Simple Types Built In to XML Schema (continued)

Simple Type	*Examples (delimited by commas)*	*Notes*
`boolean`	true, false 1, 0	
`time`	13:20:00.000, 13:20:00.000-05:00	see (2)
`dateTime`	1999-05-31T13:20:00.000-05:00	May 31st 1999 at 1.20pm Eastern Standard Time which is 5 hours behind Co-Ordinated Universal Time, see (2)
`duration`	P1Y2M3DT10H30M12.3S	1 year, 2 months, 3 days, 10 hours, 30 minutes, and 12.3 seconds
`date`	1999-05-31	see (2)
`gMonth`	--05--	May, see (2) (5)
`gYear`	1999	1999, see (2) (5)
`gYearMonth`	1999-02	the month of February 1999, regardless of the number of days, see (2) (5)
`gDay`	---31	the 31st day, see (2) (5)
`gMonthDay`	--05-31	every May 31st, see (2) (5)
`Name`	shipTo	XML 1.0 Name type
`QName`	po:USAddress	XML Namespace QName
`NCName`	USAddress	XML Namespace NCName, i.e., a QName without the prefix and colon
`anyURI`	http://www.example.com/, http://www.example.com/doc.html#ID5	

Table 2 Simple Types Built In to XML Schema (continued)

Simple Type	*Examples (delimited by commas)*	*Notes*
`language`	en-GB, en-US, fr	valid values for xml:lang as defined in XML 1.0
`ID`		XML 1.0 ID attribute type, see (1)
`IDREF`		XML 1.0 IDREF attribute type, see (1)
`IDREFS`		XML 1.0 IDREFS attribute type, see (1)
`ENTITY`		XML 1.0 ENTITY attribute type, see (1)
`ENTITIES`		XML 1.0 ENTITIES attribute type, see (1)
`NOTATION`		XML 1.0 NOTATION attribute type, see (1)
`NMTOKEN`	US, BrÈsil	XML 1.0 NMTOKEN attribute type, see (1)
`NMTOKENS`	US UK, BrÈsil Canada Mexique	XML 1.0 NMTOKENS attribute type, i.e., a whitespace separated list of NMTOKEN's, see (1)

Notes: (1) To retain compatibility between XML Schema and XML 1.0 DTDs, the simple types `ID`, `IDREF`, `IDREFS`, `ENTITY`, `ENTITIES`, `NOTATION`, `NMTOKEN`, `NMTOKENS` should only be used in attributes. (2) A value of this type can be represented by more than one lexical format, e.g., 100 and 1.0E2 are both valid float formats representing "one hundred". However, rules have been established for this type that define a canonical lexical format, see XML Schema Part 2. (3) Newline, tab and carriage-return characters in a normalizedString type are converted to space characters before schema processing. (4) As normalizedString, and adjacent space characters are collapsed to a single space character, and leading and trailing spaces are removed. (5) The "g" prefix signals time periods in the Gregorian calender.

New simple types are defined by deriving them from existing simple types (built-in's and derived). In particular, we can derive a new simple type by restricting an existing simple type, in other words, the legal range of values for the new type are a subset of the existing type's range of values. We use the `simpleType` element to define and name the new simple type. We use the `restriction` element to indicate the existing (base) type, and to identify the "facets" that constrain the range of values. A complete list of facets is provided in Appendix B.

Suppose we wish to create a new type of integer called `myInteger` whose range of values is between 10000 and 99999 (inclusive). We base our definition on the built-in simple type `integer`, whose range of values also includes integers less than 10000 and greater than 99999. To define `myInteger`, we restrict the range of the `integer` base type by employing two facets called `minInclusive` and `maxInclusive`:

Defining myInteger, Range 10000-99999

```
<xsd:simpleType name="myInteger">
  <xsd:restriction base="xsd:integer">
    <xsd:minInclusive value="10000"/>
    <xsd:maxInclusive value="99999"/>
  </xsd:restriction>
</xsd:simpleType>
```

The example shows one particular combination of a base type and two facets used to define `myInteger`, but a look at the list of built-in simple types and their facets (Appendix B) should suggest other viable combinations.

The purchase order schema contains another, more elaborate, example of a simple type definition. A new simple type called `SKU` is derived (by restriction) from the simple type `string`. Furthermore, we constrain the values of `SKU` using a facet called `pattern` in conjunction with the regular expression `"\d{3}-[A-Z]{2}"` that is read "three digits followed by a hyphen followed by two upper-case ASCII letters":

Defining the Simple Type "SKU"

```
<xsd:simpleType name="SKU">
  <xsd:restriction base="xsd:string">
    <xsd:pattern value="\d{3}-[A-Z]{2}"/>
  </xsd:restriction>
</xsd:simpleType>
```

This regular expression language is described more fully in Appendix D.

XML Schema defines fifteen facets which are listed in Appendix B. Among these, the `enumeration` facet is particularly useful and it can be used to constrain the values of almost every simple type, except the `boolean` type. The `enumeration` facet limits a simple type to a set of distinct values. For example, we can use the `enumeration` facet to define a new simple type called `USState`, derived from `string`, whose value must be one of the standard US state abbreviations:

Using the Enumeration Facet

```
<xsd:simpleType name="USState">
  <xsd:restriction base="xsd:string">
    <xsd:enumeration value="AK"/>
    <xsd:enumeration value="AL"/>
    <xsd:enumeration value="AR"/>
    <!-- and so on ... -->
  </xsd:restriction>
</xsd:simpleType>
```

`USState` would be a good replacement for the `string` type currently used in the `state` element declaration. By making this replacement, the legal values of a `state` element, i.e., the `state` subelements of `billTo` and `shipTo`, would be limited to one of `AK`, `AL`, `AR`, etc. Note that the enumeration values specified for a particular type must be unique.

2.3.1 List Types

XML Schema has the concept of a list type, in addition to the so-called atomic types that constitute most of the types listed in Table 2. (Atomic types, list types, and the union types described in the next section are collectively called simple types.) The value of an atomic type is indivisible from XML Schema's perspective. For example, the `NMTOKEN` value `US` is indivisible in the sense that no part of `US`, such as the character "S", has any meaning by itself. In contrast, list types are comprised of sequences of atomic types and consequently the parts of a sequence (the "atoms") themselves are meaningful. For example, `NMTOKENS` is a list type, and an element of this type would be a white-space delimited list of `NMTOKEN`'s, such as "US UK FR". XML Schema has three built-in list types, they are `NMTOKENS`, `IDREFS`, and `ENTITIES`.

In addition to using the built-in list types, you can create new list types by derivation from existing atomic types. (You cannot create list types from existing list types, nor from complex types.) For example, to create a list of `myInteger`'s:

Creating a List of myInteger's

```
<xsd:simpleType name="listOfMyIntType">
   <xsd:list itemType="myInteger"/>
 </xsd:simpleType>
```

And an element in an instance document whose content conforms to `listOfMyIntType` is:

```
<listOfMyInt>20003 15037 95977 95945</listOfMyInt>
```

Several facets can be applied to list types: `length`, `minLength`, `maxLength`, and `enumeration`. For example, to define a list of exactly six US states (`SixUSStates`), we first define a new list type called `USStateList` from `USState`, and then we derive `SixUSStates` by restricting `USStateList` to only six items:

List Type for Six US States

```
<xsd:simpleType name="USStateList">
  <xsd:list itemType="USState"/>
 </xsd:simpleType>

 <xsd:simpleType name="SixUSStates">
  <xsd:restriction base="USStateList">
   <xsd:length value="6"/>
  </xsd:restriction>
 </xsd:simpleType>
```

Elements whose type is `SixUSStates` must have six items, and each of the six items must be one of the (atomic) values of the enumerated type `USState`, for example:

```
<sixStates>PA NY CA NY LA AK</sixStates>
```

Note that it is possible to derive a list type from the atomic type `string`. However, a `string` may contain white space, and white space delimits the items in a list type, so you should be careful using list types whose base type is `string`. For example, suppose we have defined a list type with a `length` facet equal to 3, and base type `string`, then the following 3 item list is legal:

```
Asie Europe Afrique
```

But the following 3 "item" list is illegal:

```
Asie Europe Amérique Latine
```

Even though "Amérique Latine" may exist as a single string outside of the list, when it is included in the list, the whitespace between Amérique and Latine effectively creates a fourth item, and so the latter example will not conform to the 3-item list type.

2.3.2 Union Types

Atomic types and list types enable an element or an attribute value to be one or more instances of one atomic type. In contrast, a union type enables an element or attribute value to be one or more instances of one type drawn from the union of multiple atomic and list types. To illustrate, we create a union type for representing American states as singleton letter abbreviations or lists of numeric codes. The `zipUnion` union type is built from one atomic type and one list type:

Union Type for Zipcodes

```
<xsd:simpleType name="zipUnion">
  <xsd:union memberTypes="USState listOfMyIntType"/>
</xsd:simpleType>
```

When we define a union type, the `memberTypes` attribute value is a list of all the types in the union.

Now, assuming we have declared an element called `zips` of type `zipUnion`, valid instances of the element are:

```
<zips>CA</zips>
<zips>95630 95977 95945</zips>
<zips>AK</zips>
```

Two facets, `pattern` and `enumeration`, can be applied to a union type.

2.4 Anonymous Type Definitions

Schemas can be constructed by defining sets of named types such as `PurchaseOrderType` and then declaring elements such as `purchase-Order` that reference the types using the `type=` construction. This style of schema construction is straightforward but it can be unwieldy, especially if you define many types that are referenced only once and contain very few constraints. In these cases, a type can be more succinctly defined as an anonymous type which saves the overhead of having to be named and explicitly referenced.

The definition of the type `Items` in `po.xsd` contains two element declarations that use anonymous types (`item` and `quantity`). In general, you can identify anonymous types by the lack of a `type=` in an element (or attribute) declaration, and by the presence of an un-named (simple or complex) type definition:

Two Anonymous Type Definitions

```
<xsd:complexType name="Items">
 <xsd:sequence>
  <xsd:element name="item" minOccurs="0" maxOccurs="unbounded">
   <xsd:complexType>
    <xsd:sequence>
     <xsd:element name="productName" type="xsd:string"/>
     <xsd:element name="quantity">
      <xsd:simpleType>
       <xsd:restriction base="xsd:positiveInteger">
        <xsd:maxExclusive value="100"/>
       </xsd:restriction>
      </xsd:simpleType>
     </xsd:element>
     <xsd:element name="USPrice"  type="xsd:decimal"/>
     <xsd:element ref="comment"   minOccurs="0"/>
     <xsd:element name="shipDate" type="xsd:date" minOccurs="0"/>
    </xsd:sequence>
    <xsd:attribute name="partNum" type="SKU" use="required"/>
   </xsd:complexType>
  </xsd:element>
 </xsd:sequence>
</xsd:complexType>
```

In the case of the `item` element, it has an anonymous complex type consisting of the elements `productName`, `quantity`, `USPrice`, `comment`, and `shipDate`, and an attribute called `partNum`. In the case of the `quantity` element, it has an anonymous simple type derived from `integer` whose value ranges between 1 and 99.

2.5 Element Content

The purchase order schema has many examples of elements containing other elements (e.g., `items`), elements having attributes and containing other elements (e.g., `shipTo`), and elements containing only a simple type of value (e.g., `USPrice`). However, we have not seen an element having attributes but containing only a simple type of value, nor have we seen an element that contains other elements mixed with character content, nor have we seen an element that has no content at all. In this section we'll examine these variations in the content models of elements.

2.5.1 Complex Types from Simple Types

Let us first consider how to declare an element that has an attribute and contains a simple value. In an instance document, such an element might appear as:

```
<internationalPrice currency="EUR">423.46</internationalPrice>
```

The purchase order schema declares a `USPrice` element that is a starting point:

```
<xsd:element name="USPrice" type="decimal"/>
```

Now, how do we add an attribute to this element? As we have said before, simple types cannot have attributes, and `decimal` is a simple type. Therefore, we must define a complex type to carry the attribute declaration. We also want the content to be simple type `decimal`. So our original question becomes: How do we define a complex type that is based on the simple type `decimal`? The answer is to *derive* a new complex type from the simple type `decimal`:

Deriving a Complex Type from a Simple Type

```
<xsd:element name="internationalPrice">
  <xsd:complexType>
   <xsd:simpleContent>
    <xsd:extension base="xsd:decimal">
```

```
      <xsd:attribute name="currency" type="xsd:string"/>
     </xsd:extension>
    </xsd:simpleContent>
   </xsd:complexType>
  </xsd:element>
```

We use the `complexType` element to start the definition of a new (anonymous) type. To indicate that the content model of the new type contains only character data and no elements, we use a `simpleContent` element. Finally, we derive the new type by extending the simple `decimal` type. The extension consists of adding a `currency` attribute using a standard attribute declaration. (We cover type derivation in detail in Section 4.) The `internationalPrice` element declared in this way will appear in an instance as shown in the example at the beginning of this section.

2.5.2 Mixed Content

The construction of the purchase order schema may be characterized as elements containing subelements, and the deepest subelements contain character data. XML Schema also provides for the construction of schemas where character data can appear alongside subelements, and character data is not confined to the deepest subelements.

To illustrate, consider the following snippet from a customer letter that uses some of the same elements as the purchase order:

Snippet of Customer Letter

```
<letterBody>
 <salutation>Dear Mr.<name>Robert Smith</name>.</salutation>
 Your order of <quantity>1</quantity> <productName>Baby
 Monitor</productName> shipped from our warehouse on
 <shipDate>1999-05-21</shipDate>. ....
 </letterBody>
```

Notice the text appearing between elements and their child elements. Specifically, text appears between the elements `salutation`, `quantity`, `productName` and `shipDate` which are all children of `letterBody`, and text appears around the element name which is the child of a child of `letterBody`. The following snippet of a schema declares `letterBody`:

Snippet of Schema for Customer Letter

```
<xsd:element name="letterBody">
 <xsd:complexType mixed="true">
  <xsd:sequence>
   <xsd:element name="salutation">
    <xsd:complexType mixed="true">
     <xsd:sequence>
      <xsd:element name="name" type="xsd:string"/>
     </xsd:sequence>
    </xsd:complexType>
   </xsd:element>
   <xsd:element name="quantity"    type="xsd:positiveInteger"/>
   <xsd:element name="productName" type="xsd:string"/>
   <xsd:element name="shipDate"    type="xsd:date" minOccurs="0"/>
   <!-- etc. -->
  </xsd:sequence>
 </xsd:complexType>
</xsd:element>
```

The elements appearing in the customer letter are declared, and their types are defined using the `element` and `complexType` element constructions we have seen before. To enable character data to appear between the child-elements of `letterBody`, the `mixed` attribute on the type definition is set to true.

Note that the `mixed` model in XML Schema differs fundamentally from the `mixed` model in XML 1.0. Under the XML Schema mixed model, the order and number of child elements appearing in an instance must agree with the order and number of child elements specified in the model. In contrast, under the XML 1.0 mixed model, the order and number of child elements appearing in an instance cannot be constrained. In summary, XML Schema provides full validation of mixed models in contrast to the partial schema validation provided by XML 1.0.

2.5.3 Empty Content

Now suppose that we want the `internationalPrice` element to convey both the unit of currency and the price as attribute values rather than as separate attribute and content values. For example:

```
<internationalPrice currency="EUR" value="423.46"/>
```

Such an element has no content at all; its content model is empty. To define a type whose content is empty, we essentially define a type that allows only elements in its content, but we do not actually declare any elements and so the type's content model is empty:

An Empty Complex Type

```
<xsd:element name="internationalPrice">
  <xsd:complexType>
   <xsd:complexContent>
    <xsd:restriction base="xsd:anyType">
     <xsd:attribute name="currency" type="xsd:string"/>
     <xsd:attribute name="value"    type="xsd:decimal"/>
    </xsd:restriction>
   </xsd:complexContent>
  </xsd:complexType>
 </xsd:element>
```

In this example, we define an (anonymous) type having `complexContent`, i.e., only elements. The `complexContent` element signals that we intend to restrict or extend the content model of a complex type, and the `restriction` of `anyType` declares two attributes but does not introduce any element content (see Section 4.4 for more details on restriction). The `international-Price` element declared in this way may legitimately appear in an instance as shown in the example above.

The preceding syntax for an empty-content element is relatively verbose, and it is possible to declare the `internationalPrice` element more compactly:

Shorthand for an Empty Complex Type

```
<xsd:element name="internationalPrice">
  <xsd:complexType>
   <xsd:attribute name="currency" type="xsd:string"/>
   <xsd:attribute name="value"    type="xsd:decimal"/>
  </xsd:complexType>
 </xsd:element>
```

This compact syntax works because a complex type defined without any `simpleContent` or `complexContent` is interpreted as shorthand for complex content that restricts `anyType`.

2.5.4 anyType

The `anyType` represents an abstraction called the `ur-type` which is the base type from which all simple and complex types are derived. An `anyType`

type does not constrain its content in any way. It is possible to use `anyType` like other types, for example:

```
<xsd:element name="anything" type="xsd:anyType"/>
```

The content of the element declared in this way is unconstrained, so the element value may be 423.46, but it may be any other sequence of characters as well, or indeed a mixture of characters and elements. In fact, `anyType` is the default type when none is specified, so the above could also be written as follows:

```
<xsd:element name="anything"/>
```

If unconstrained element content is needed, for example in the case of elements containing prose which requires embedded markup to support internationalization, then the default declaration or a slightly restricted form of it may be suitable. The `text` type described in Section 5.5 is an example of such a type that is suitable for such purposes.

2.6 Annotations

XML Schema provides three elements for annotating schemas for the benefit of both human readers and applications. In the purchase order schema, we put a basic schema description and copyright information inside the `documentation` element, which is the recommended location for human readable material. We recommend you use the `xml:lang` attribute with any `documentation` elements to indicate the language of the information. Alternatively, you may indicate the language of all information in a schema by placing an `xml:lang` attribute on the `schema` element.

The `appInfo` element, which we did not use in the purchase order schema, can be used to provide information for tools, stylesheets and other applications. An interesting example using `appInfo` is a schema that describes the simple types in XML Schema Part 2: Datatypes. Information describing this schema, e.g., which facets are applicable to particular simple types, is represented inside `appInfo` elements, and this information was used by an application to automatically generate text for the XML Schema Part 2 document.

Both `documentation` and `appInfo` appear as subelements of `annotation`, which may itself appear at the beginning of most schema constructions. To illustrate, the following example shows `annotation` elements appearing at the beginning of an element declaration and a complex type definition:

Annotations in Element Declaration & Complex Type Definition

```
<xsd:element name="internationalPrice">
  <xsd:annotation>
   <xsd:documentation xml:lang="en">
       element declared with anonymous type
   </xsd:documentation>
  </xsd:annotation>
  <xsd:complexType>
   <xsd:annotation>
    <xsd:documentation xml:lang="en">
        empty anonymous type with 2 attributes
    </xsd:documentation>
   </xsd:annotation>
   <xsd:complexContent>
    <xsd:restriction base="xsd:anyType">
     <xsd:attribute name="currency" type="xsd:string"/>
     <xsd:attribute name="value"    type="xsd:decimal"/>
    </xsd:restriction>
   </xsd:complexContent>
  </xsd:complexType>
 </xsd:element>
```

The `annotation` element may also appear at the beginning of other schema constructions such as those indicated by the elements `schema`, `simpleType`, and `attribute`.

2.7 Building Content Models

The definitions of complex types in the purchase order schema all declare sequences of elements that must appear in the instance document. The occurrence of individual elements declared in the so-called content models of these types may be optional, as indicated by a 0 value for the attribute `minOccurs` (e.g., in `comment`), or be otherwise constrained depending upon the values of `minOccurs` and `maxOccurs`. XML Schema also provides constraints that apply to groups of elements appearing in a content model. These constraints mirror those available in XML 1.0 plus some additional constraints. Note that the constraints do not apply to attributes.

XML Schema enables groups of elements to be defined and named, so that the elements can be used to build up the content models of complex types (thus mimicking common usage of parameter entities in XML 1.0). Un-named groups of elements can also be defined, and along with elements in named groups, they can be constrained to appear in the same order (sequence) as they are declared. Alternatively, they can be constrained so that only one of the elements may appear in an instance.

To illustrate, we introduce two groups into the `PurchaseOrderType` definition from the purchase order schema so that purchase orders may contain either separate shipping and billing addresses, or a single address for those cases in which the shippee and billee are co-located:

Nested Choice and Sequence Groups

```
<xsd:complexType name="PurchaseOrderType">
  <xsd:sequence>
   <xsd:choice>
    <xsd:group   ref="shipAndBill"/>
    <xsd:element name="singleUSAddress" type="USAddress"/>
   </xsd:choice>
   <xsd:element ref="comment" minOccurs="0"/>
   <xsd:element name="items"  type="Items"/>
  </xsd:sequence>
  <xsd:attribute name="orderDate" type="xsd:date"/>
 </xsd:complexType>

 <xsd:group name="shipAndBill">
   <xsd:sequence>
     <xsd:element name="shipTo" type="USAddress"/>
     <xsd:element name="billTo" type="USAddress"/>
   </xsd:sequence>
 </xsd:group>
```

The `choice` group element allows only one of its children to appear in an instance. One child is an inner `group` element that references the named group `shipAndBill` consisting of the element sequence `shipTo`, `billTo`, and the second child is a `singleUSAddress`. Hence, in an instance document, the `purchaseOrder` element must contain either a `shipTo` element followed by a `billTo` element or a `singleUSAddress` element. The `choice` group is followed by the `comment` and `items` element declarations, and both the `choice` group and the element declarations are children of a `sequence` group. The effect of these various groups is that the address element(s) must be followed by `comment` and `items` elements in that order.

There exists a third option for constraining elements in a group: All the elements in the group may appear once or not at all, and they may appear in any order. The `all` group (which provides a simplified version of the SGML &-Connector) is limited to the top-level of any content model. Moreover, the group's children must all be individual elements (no groups), and no element in the content model may appear more than once, i.e., the permissible values of `minOccurs` and `maxOccurs` are 0 and 1. For example, to allow the child elements of `purchaseOrder` to appear in any order, we could redefine `PurchaseOrderType` as:

An 'All' Group

```
<xsd:complexType name="PurchaseOrderType">
   <xsd:all>
     <xsd:element name="shipTo" type="USAddress"/>
     <xsd:element name="billTo" type="USAddress"/>
     <xsd:element ref="comment" minOccurs="0"/>
     <xsd:element name="items"  type="Items"/>
   </xsd:all>
   <xsd:attribute name="orderDate" type="xsd:date"/>
 </xsd:complexType>
```

By this definition, a `comment` element may optionally appear within `purchaseOrder`, and it may appear before or after any `shipTo`, `billTo` and `items` elements, but it can appear only once. Moreover, the stipulations of an `all` group do not allow us to declare an element such as `comment` outside the group as a means of enabling it to appear more than once. XML Schema stipulates that an `all` group must appear as the sole child at the top of a content model. In other words, the following is illegal:

Illegal Example with an 'All' Group

```
<xsd:complexType name="PurchaseOrderType">
 <xsd:sequence>
  <xsd:all>
    <xsd:element name="shipTo" type="USAddress"/>
    <xsd:element name="billTo" type="USAddress"/>
    <xsd:element name="items"  type="Items"/>
  </xsd:all>
  <xsd:sequence>
   <xsd:element ref="comment" minOccurs="0"
     maxOccurs="unbounded"/>
  </xsd:sequence>
 </xsd:sequence>
 <xsd:attribute name="orderDate" type="xsd:date"/>
</xsd:complexType>
```

Finally, named and un-named groups that appear in content models (represented by `group` and `choice`, `sequence`, `all` respectively) may carry `minOccurs` and `maxOccurs` attributes. By combining and nesting the various groups provided by XML Schema, and by setting the values of `minOccurs` and `maxOccurs`, it is possible to represent any content model expressible with an XML 1.0 DTD. Furthermore, the `all` group provides additional expressive power.

2.8 Attribute Groups

Suppose we want to provide more information about each item in a purchase order, for example, each item's weight and preferred shipping method. We can accomplish this by adding `weightKg` and `shipBy` attribute declarations to the `item` element's (anonymous) type definition:

Adding Attributes to the Inline Type Definition

```
<xsd:element name="Item" minOccurs="0" maxOccurs="unbounded">
   <xsd:complexType>
    <xsd:sequence>
     <xsd:element   name="productName" type="xsd:string"/>
     <xsd:element   name="quantity">
      <xsd:simpleType>
       <xsd:restriction base="xsd:positiveInteger">
        <xsd:maxExclusive value="100"/>
       </xsd:restriction>
      </xsd:simpleType>
     </xsd:element>
     <xsd:element name="USPrice"  type="xsd:decimal"/>
     <xsd:element ref="comment"   minOccurs="0"/>
     <xsd:element name="shipDate" type="xsd:date" minOccurs="0"/>
    </xsd:sequence>
    <xsd:attribute name="partNum"  type="SKU" use="required"/>
    <!-- add weightKg and shipBy attributes -->
    <xsd:attribute name="weightKg" type="xsd:decimal"/>
    <xsd:attribute name="shipBy">
     <xsd:simpleType>
      <xsd:restriction base="xsd:string">
       <xsd:enumeration value="air"/>
       <xsd:enumeration value="land"/>
       <xsd:enumeration value="any"/>
      </xsd:restriction>
     </xsd:simpleType>
    </xsd:attribute>
```

```
  </xsd:complexType>
 </xsd:element>
```

Alternatively, we can create a named attribute group containing all the desired attributes of an `item` element, and reference this group by name in the `item` element declaration:

Adding Attributes Using an Attribute Group

```
<xsd:element name="item" minOccurs="0" maxOccurs="unbounded">
  <xsd:complexType>
   <xsd:sequence>
    <xsd:element name="productName" type="xsd:string"/>
    <xsd:element name="quantity">
     <xsd:simpleType>
      <xsd:restriction base="xsd:positiveInteger">
       <xsd:maxExclusive value="100"/>
      </xsd:restriction>
     </xsd:simpleType>
    </xsd:element>
    <xsd:element name="USPrice"  type="xsd:decimal"/>
    <xsd:element ref="comment"   minOccurs="0"/>
    <xsd:element name="shipDate" type="xsd:date" minOccurs="0"/>
   </xsd:sequence>

   <!-- attributeGroup replaces individual declarations -->
   <xsd:attributeGroup ref="ItemDelivery"/>
  </xsd:complexType>
 </xsd:element>

 <xsd:attributeGroup name="ItemDelivery">
   <xsd:attribute name="partNum"  type="SKU" use="required"/>
   <xsd:attribute name="weightKg" type="xsd:decimal"/>
   <xsd:attribute name="shipBy">
     <xsd:simpleType>
      <xsd:restriction base="xsd:string">
       <xsd:enumeration value="air"/>
       <xsd:enumeration value="land"/>
       <xsd:enumeration value="any"/>
      </xsd:restriction>
     </xsd:simpleType>
   </xsd:attribute>
 </xsd:attributeGroup>
```

Using an attribute group in this way can improve the readability of schemas, and facilitates updating schemas because an attribute group can be defined and edited in one place and referenced in multiple definitions and declarations. These characteristics of attribute groups make them similar to parameter entities in XML 1.0. Note that an attribute group may contain other attribute groups. Note also that both attribute declarations and attribute group references must appear at the end of complex type definitions.

2.9 Nil Values

One of the purchase order items listed in `po.xml`, the `Lawnmower`, does not have a `shipDate` element. Within the context of our scenario, the schema author may have intended such absences to indicate `items` not yet shipped. But in general, the absence of an element does not have any particular meaning: It may indicate that the information is unknown, or not applicable, or the element may be absent for some other reason. Sometimes it is desirable to represent an unshipped `item`, unknown information, or inapplicable information *explicitly* with an element, rather than by an absent element. For example, it may be desirable to represent a "null" value being sent to or from a relational database with an element that is present. Such cases can be represented using XML Schema's nil mechanism which enables an element to appear with or without a non-nil value.

XML Schema's nil mechanism involves an "out of band" nil signal. In other words, there is no actual nil value that appears as element content, instead there is an attribute to indicate that the element content is nil. To illustrate, we modify the `shipDate` element declaration so that nils can be signalled:

```
<xsd:element name="shipDate" type="xsd:date" nillable="true"/>
```

And to explicitly represent that `shipDate` has a nil value in the instance document, we set the nil attribute (from the XML Schema namespace for instances) to true:

```
<shipDate xsi:nil="true"></shipDate>
```

The `nil` attribute is defined as part of the XML Schema namespace for instances, `http://www.w3.org/2001/XMLSchema-instance`, and so it must appear in the instance document with a prefix (such as `xsi:`) associated with that namespace. (As with the `xsd:` prefix, the `xsi:` prefix is used by convention only.) Note that the nil mechanism applies only to element values, and not to attribute values. An element with `xsi:nil="true"` may not have any element content but it may still carry attributes.

3 Advanced Concepts I: Namespaces, Schemas & Qualification

A schema can be viewed as a collection (vocabulary) of type definitions and element declarations whose names belong to a particular namespace called a target namespace. Target namespaces enable us to distinguish between definitions and declarations from different vocabularies. For example, target namespaces would enable us to distinguish between the declaration for `element` in the XML Schema language vocabulary, and a declaration for `element` in a hypothetical chemistry language vocabulary. The former is part of the *http://www.w3.org/2001/XMLSchema* target namespace, and the latter is part of another target namespace.

When we want to check that an instance document conforms to one or more schemas (through a process called schema validation), we need to identify which element and attribute declarations and type definitions in the schemas should be used to check which elements and attributes in the instance document. The target namespace plays an important role in the identification process. We examine the role of the target namespace in the next section.

The schema author also has several options that affect how the identities of elements and attributes are represented in instance documents. More specifically, the author can decide whether or not the appearance of locally declared elements and attributes in an instance must be qualified by a namespace, using either an explicit prefix or implicitly by default. The schema author's choice regarding qualification of local elements and attributes has a number of implications regarding the structures of schemas and instance documents, and we examine some of these implications in the following sections.

3.1 Target Namespaces & Unqualified Locals

In a new version of the purchase order schema, `po1.xsd`, we explicitly declare a target namespace, and specify that both locally defined elements and locally defined attributes must be unqualified. The target namespace in `po1.xsd` is `http://www.example.com/PO1`, as indicated by the value of the `targetNamespace` attribute.

Qualification of local elements and attributes can be globally specified by a pair of attributes, `elementFormDefault` and `attributeFormDefault`, on the `schema` element, or can be specified separately for each local declaration using the `form` attribute. All such attributes' values may each be set to `unqualified` or `qualified`, to indicate whether or not locally declared elements and attributes must be unqualified.

In `po1.xsd` we globally specify the qualification of elements and attributes by setting the values of both `elementFormDefault` and `attributeFormDefault` to `unqualified`. Strictly speaking, these settings are unnecessary because the values are the defaults for the two attributes; we make them here to highlight the contrast between this case and other cases we describe later.

Purchase Order Schema with Target Namespace, po1.xsd

```
<schema xmlns="http://www.w3.org/2001/XMLSchema"
        xmlns:po="http://www.example.com/PO1"
        targetNamespace="http://www.example.com/PO1"
        elementFormDefault="unqualified"
        attributeFormDefault="unqualified">

  <element name="purchaseOrder" type="po:PurchaseOrderType"/>
  <element name="comment"       type="string"/>

  <complexType name="PurchaseOrderType">
   <sequence>
    <element name="shipTo"    type="po:USAddress"/>
    <element name="billTo"    type="po:USAddress"/>
    <element ref="po:comment" minOccurs="0"/>
    <!-- etc. -->
   </sequence>
   <!-- etc. -->
  </complexType>

  <complexType name="USAddress">
   <sequence>
    <element name="name"   type="string"/>
    <element name="street" type="string"/>
    <!-- etc. -->
   </sequence>
  </complexType>

  <!-- etc. -->

 </schema>
```

To see how the target namespace of this schema is populated, we examine in turn each of the type definitions and element declarations. Starting from the end of the schema, we first define a type called `USAddress` that consists of the elements `name`, `street`, etc. One consequence of this type definition is that the `USAddress` type is included in the schema's target namespace. We next define a type called `PurchaseOrderType` that consists of the elements `shipTo`, `billTo`, `comment`, etc. `PurchaseOrderType` is also included in the schema's target namespace. Notice that the type references in the three element declarations are prefixed, i.e., `po:USAddress`, `po:USAddress` and `po:comment`, and the prefix is associated with the namespace `http://www.example.com/PO1`. This is the same namespace as the schema's target namespace, and so a processor of this schema will know to look within this schema for the definition of the type `USAddress` and the declaration of the element `comment`. It is also possible to refer to types in another schema with a different target namespace, hence enabling re-use of definitions and declarations between schemas.

At the beginning of the schema `po1.xsd`, we declare the elements `purchaseOrder` and `comment`. They are included in the schema's target namespace. The `purchaseOrder` element's type is prefixed, for the same reason that `USAddress` is prefixed. In contrast, the `comment` element's type, `string`, is not prefixed. The `po1.xsd` schema contains a default namespace declaration, and so unprefixed types such as `string` and unprefixed elements such as `element` and `complexType` are associated with the default namespace `http://www.w3.org/2001/XMLSchema`. In fact, this is the target namespace of XML Schema itself, and so a processor of `po1.xsd` will know to look within the schema of XML Schema—otherwise known as the "schema for schemas"—for the definition of the type `string` and the declaration of the element called `element`.

Let us now examine how the target namespace of the schema affects a conforming instance document:

A Purchase Order with Unqualified Locals, po1.xml

```
<?xml version="1.0"?>
 <apo:purchaseOrder xmlns:apo="http://www.example.com/PO1"
                    orderDate="1999-10-20">
     <shipTo country="US">
         <name>Alice Smith</name>
         <street>123 Maple Street</street>
         <!-- etc. -->
     </shipTo>
```

```
    <billTo country="US">
        <name>Robert Smith</name>
        <street>8 Oak Avenue</street>
        <!-- etc. -->
    </billTo>
    <apo:comment>Hurry, my lawn is going wild!</apo:comment>
    <!-- etc. -->
</apo:purchaseOrder>
```

The instance document declares one namespace, `http://www.example.com/PO1`, and associates it with the prefix `apo:`. This prefix is used to qualify two elements in the document, namely `purchaseOrder` and `comment`. The namespace is the same as the target namespace of the schema in `po1.xsd`, and so a processor of the instance document will know to look in that schema for the declarations of `purchaseOrder` and `comment`. In fact, target namespaces are so named because of the sense in which there exists a target namespace for the elements `purchaseOrder` and `comment`. Target namespaces in the schema therefore control the validation of corresponding namespaces in the instance.

The prefix `apo:` is applied to the global elements `purchaseOrder` and `comment` elements. Furthermore, `elementFormDefault` and `attributeFormDefault` require that the prefix is *not* applied to any of the locally declared elements such as `shipTo`, `billTo`, `name` and `street`, and it is *not* applied to any of the attributes (which were all declared locally). The `purchaseOrder` and `comment` are global elements because they are declared in the context of the schema as a whole rather than within the context of a particular type. For example, the declaration of `purchaseOrder` appears as a child of the `schema` element in `po1.xsd`, whereas the declaration of `shipTo` appears as a child of the `complexType` element that defines `PurchaseOrderType`.

When local elements and attributes are not required to be qualified, an instance author may require more or less knowledge about the details of the schema to create schema valid instance documents. More specifically, if the author can be sure that only the root element (such as `purchaseOrder`) is global, then it is a simple matter to qualify only the root element. Alternatively, the author may know that all the elements are declared globally, and so all the elements in the instance document can be prefixed, perhaps taking advantage of a default namespace declaration. (We examine this approach in Section 3.3.) On the other hand, if there is no uniform pattern of global and local declarations, the author will need detailed knowledge of the schema to correctly prefix global elements and attributes.

3.2 Qualified Locals

Elements and attributes can be independently required to be qualified, although we start by describing the qualification of local elements. To specify that all locally declared elements in a schema must be qualified, we set the value of `elementFormDefault` to `qualified`:

Modifications to `po1.xsd` for Qualified Locals

```
<schema xmlns="http://www.w3.org/2001/XMLSchema"
        xmlns:po="http://www.example.com/PO1"
        targetNamespace="http://www.example.com/PO1"
        elementFormDefault="qualified"
        attributeFormDefault="unqualified">

  <element name="purchaseOrder" type="po:PurchaseOrderType"/>
  <element name="comment"       type="string"/>

  <complexType name="PurchaseOrderType">
   <!-- etc. -->
  </complexType>

  <!-- etc. -->

 </schema>
```

And in this conforming instance document, we qualify all the elements explicitly:

A Purchase Order with Explicitly Qualified Locals

```
<?xml version="1.0"?>
 <apo:purchaseOrder xmlns:apo="http://www.example.com/PO1"
                    orderDate="1999-10-20">
     <apo:shipTo country="US">
         <apo:name>Alice Smith</apo:name>
         <apo:street>123 Maple Street</apo:street>
         <!-- etc. -->
     </apo:shipTo>
     <apo:billTo country="US">
         <apo:name>Robert Smith</apo:name>
         <apo:street>8 Oak Avenue</apo:street>
         <!-- etc. -->
     </apo:billTo>
     <apo:comment>Hurry, my lawn is going wild!</apo:comment>
     <!-- etc. -->
 </apo:purchaseOrder>
```

Alternatively, we can replace the explicit qualification of every element with implicit qualification provided by a default namespace, as shown here in po2.xml:

A Purchase Order with Default Qualified Locals, po2.xml

```
<?xml version="1.0"?>
 <purchaseOrder xmlns="http://www.example.com/PO1"
                orderDate="1999-10-20">
     <shipTo country="US">
         <name>Alice Smith</name>
         <street>123 Maple Street</street>
         <!-- etc. -->
     </shipTo>
     <billTo country="US">
         <name>Robert Smith</name>
         <street>8 Oak Avenue</street>
         <!-- etc. -->
     </billTo>
     <comment>Hurry, my lawn is going wild!</comment>
     <!-- etc. -->
 </purchaseOrder>
```

In po2.xml, all the elements in the instance belong to the same namespace, and the namespace statement declares a default namespace that applies to all the elements in the instance. Hence, it is unnecessary to explicitly prefix any of the elements. As another illustration of using qualified elements, the schemas in Section 5 all require qualified elements.

Qualification of attributes is very similar to the qualification of elements. Attributes that must be qualified, either because they are declared globally or because the attributeFormDefault attribute is set to qualified, appear prefixed in instance documents. One example of a qualified attribute is the xsi:nil attribute that was introduced in Section 2.9. In fact, attributes that are required to be qualified must be explicitly prefixed because the XML-Namespaces specification does not provide a mechanism for defaulting the namespaces of attributes. Attributes that are not required to be qualified appear in instance documents without prefixes, which is the typical case.

The qualification mechanism we have described so far has controlled all local element and attribute declarations within a particular target namespace. It is also possible to control qualification on a declaration by declaration basis using the form attribute. For example, to require that the locally declared attribute publicKey is qualified in instances, we declare it in the following way:

Requiring Qualification of Single Attribute

```
<schema xmlns="http://www.w3.org/2001/XMLSchema"
        xmlns:po="http://www.example.com/PO1"
        targetNamespace="http://www.example.com/PO1"
        elementFormDefault="qualified"
        attributeFormDefault="unqualified">
  <!-- etc. -->
  <element name="secure">
   <complexType>
    <sequence>
     <!-- element declarations -->
    </sequence>
    <attribute name="publicKey" type="base64Binary"
form="qualified"/>
   </complexType>
  </element>
 </schema>
```

Notice that the value of the `form` attribute overrides the value of the `attributeFormDefault` attribute for the `publicKey` attribute only. Also, the `form` attribute can be applied to an element declaration in the same manner. An instance document that conforms to the schema is:

Instance with a Qualified Attribute

```
<?xml version="1.0"?>
 <purchaseOrder xmlns="http://www.example.com/PO1"
                xmlns:po="http://www.example.com/PO1"
                orderDate="1999-10-20">
     <!-- etc. -->
     <secure po:publicKey="GpM7">
         <!-- etc. -->
     </secure>
 </purchaseOrder>
```

3.3 Global vs. Local Declarations

Another authoring style, applicable when all element names are unique within a namespace, is to create schemas in which all elements are global. This is similar in effect to the use of <!ELEMENT> in a DTD. In the example below, we have modified the original `po1.xsd` such that all the elements are declared globally. Notice that we have omitted the `elementFormDefault` and `attributeFormDefault` attributes in this example to emphasize that their values are irrelevant when there are only global element and attribute declarations.

Modified version of `po1.xsd` *using only global element declarations*

```
<schema xmlns="http://www.w3.org/2001/XMLSchema"
        xmlns:po="http://www.example.com/PO1"
        targetNamespace="http://www.example.com/PO1">

  <element name="purchaseOrder" type="po:PurchaseOrderType"/>
  <element name="shipTo"  type="po:USAddress"/>
  <element name="billTo"  type="po:USAddress"/>
  <element name="comment" type="string"/>

  <element name="name" type="string"/>
  <element name="street" type="string"/>

  <complexType name="PurchaseOrderType">
   <sequence>
    <element ref="po:shipTo"/>
    <element ref="po:billTo"/>
    <element ref="po:comment" minOccurs="0"/>
    <!-- etc. -->
   </sequence>
  </complexType>

  <complexType name="USAddress">
   <sequence>
    <element ref="po:name"/>
    <element ref="po:street"/>
    <!-- etc. -->
   </sequence>
  </complexType>

  <!-- etc. -->

 </schema>
```

This "global" version of `po1.xsd` will validate the instance document `po2.xml` which, as we described previously, is also schema valid against the "qualified" version of `po1.xsd`. In other words, both schema approaches can validate the same, namespace defaulted, document. Thus, in one respect the two schema approaches are similar, although in another important respect the two schema approaches are very different. Specifically, when all elements are declared globally, it is not possible to take advantage of local names. For example, you can only declare one global element called "title". However, you can locally declare one element called "title" that has a string type, and is a subelement of "book". Within the same schema (target namespace) you can declare a second element also called "title" that is an enumeration of the values "Mr Mrs Ms".

3.4 Undeclared Target Namespaces

In Section 2 we explained the basics of XML Schema using a schema that did not declare a target namespace and an instance document that did not declare a namespace. So the question naturally arises: What is the target namespace in these examples and how is it referenced?

In the purchase order schema, `po.xsd`, we did not declare a target namespace for the schema, nor did we declare a prefix (like `po:` above) associated with the schema's target namespace with which we could refer to types and elements defined and declared within the schema. The consequence of not declaring a target namespace in a schema is that the definitions and declarations from that schema, such as `USAddress` and `purchaseOrder`, are referenced without namespace qualification. In other words there is no explicit namespace prefix applied to the references nor is there any implicit namespace applied to the reference by default. So for example, the `purchaseOrder` element is declared using the type reference `PurchaseOrderType`. In contrast, all the XML Schema elements and types used in `po.xsd` are explicitly qualified with the prefix `xsd:` that is associated with the XML Schema namespace.

In cases where a schema is designed without a target namespace, it is strongly recommended that all XML Schema elements and types are *explicitly* qualified with a prefix such as `xsd:` that is associated with the XML Schema namespace (as in `po.xsd`). The rationale for this recommendation is that if XML Schema elements and types are associated with the XML Schema namespace by default, i.e., without prefixes, then references to XML Schema types may not be distinguishable from references to user-defined types.

Element declarations from a schema with no target namespace validate unqualified elements in the instance document. That is, they validate elements for which no namespace qualification is provided by either an explicit prefix or by default (`xmlns:`). So, to validate a traditional XML 1.0 document which does not use namespaces at all, you must provide a schema with no target namespace. Of course, there are many XML 1.0 documents that do not use namespaces, so there will be many schema documents written without target namespaces; you must be sure to give to your processor a schema document that corresponds to the vocabulary you wish to validate.

4 Advanced Concepts II: The International Purchase Order

The purchase order schema described in Chapter 2 was contained in a single document, and most of the schema constructions—such as element declarations and type definitions—were constructed from scratch. In reality, schema authors will want to compose schemas from constructions located in multiple documents, and to create new types based on existing types. In this section, we examine mechanisms that enable such compositions and creations.

4.1 A Schema in Multiple Documents

As schemas become larger, it is often desirable to divide their content among several schema documents for purposes such as ease of maintenance, access control, and readability. For these reasons, we have taken the schema constructs concerning addresses out of `po.xsd`, and put them in a new file called `address.xsd`. The modified purchase order schema file is called `ipo.xsd`:

The International Purchase Order Schema, ipo.xsd

```
<schema targetNamespace="http://www.example.com/IPO"
        xmlns="http://www.w3.org/2001/XMLSchema"
        xmlns:ipo="http://www.example.com/IPO">

  <annotation>
   <documentation xml:lang="en">
    International Purchase order schema for Example.com
    Copyright 2000 Example.com. All rights reserved.
   </documentation>
  </annotation>

  <!-- include address constructs -->
```

```
<include
 schemaLocation="http://www.example.com/schemas/address.xsd"/>

<element name="purchaseOrder" type="ipo:PurchaseOrderType"/>

<element name="comment" type="string"/>

<complexType name="PurchaseOrderType">
 <sequence>
  <element name="shipTo"     type="ipo:Address"/>
  <element name="billTo"     type="ipo:Address"/>
  <element ref="ipo:comment" minOccurs="0"/>
  <element name="items"      type="ipo:Items"/>
 </sequence>
 <attribute name="orderDate" type="date"/>
</complexType>

<complexType name="Items">
 <sequence>
  <element name="item" minOccurs="0" maxOccurs="unbounded">
   <complexType>
    <sequence>
     <element name="productName" type="string"/>
     <element name="quantity">
      <simpleType>
       <restriction base="positiveInteger">
        <maxExclusive value="100"/>
       </restriction>
      </simpleType>
     </element>
     <element name="USPrice"    type="decimal"/>
     <element ref="ipo:comment" minOccurs="0"/>
     <element name="shipDate"   type="date" minOccurs="0"/>
    </sequence>
    <attribute name="partNum" type="ipo:SKU" use="required"/>
   </complexType>
  </element>
 </sequence>
</complexType>

<simpleType name="SKU">
 <restriction base="string">
  <pattern value="\d{3}-[A-Z]{2}"/>
 </restriction>
</simpleType>

</schema>
```

The file containing the address constructs is:

Addresses for International Purchase Order schema, address.xsd

```
<schema targetNamespace="http://www.example.com/IPO"
        xmlns="http://www.w3.org/2001/XMLSchema"
        xmlns:ipo="http://www.example.com/IPO">

  <annotation>
   <documentation xml:lang="en">
    Addresses for International Purchase order schema
    Copyright 2000 Example.com. All rights reserved.
   </documentation>
  </annotation>

  <complexType name="Address">
   <sequence>
    <element name="name"   type="string"/>
    <element name="street" type="string"/>
    <element name="city"   type="string"/>
   </sequence>
  </complexType>

  <complexType name="USAddress">
   <complexContent>
    <extension base="ipo:Address">
     <sequence>
      <element name="state" type="ipo:USState"/>
      <element name="zip"   type="positiveInteger"/>
     </sequence>
    </extension>
   </complexContent>
  </complexType>
   <complexType name="UKAddress">
   <complexContent>
    <extension base="ipo:Address">
     <sequence>
      <element name="postcode" type="ipo:UKPostcode"/>
     </sequence>
     <attribute name="exportCode" type="positiveInteger"
fixed="1"/>
    </extension>
   </complexContent>
  </complexType>

  <!-- other Address derivations for more countries -->
```

```
 <simpleType name="USState">
  <restriction base="string">
   <enumeration value="AK"/>
   <enumeration value="AL"/>
   <enumeration value="AR"/>
   <!-- and so on ... -->
  </restriction>
 </simpleType>

 <!-- simple type definition for UKPostcode -->

</schema>
```

The various purchase order and address constructions are now contained in two schema files, `ipo.xsd` and `address.xsd`. To include these constructions as part of the international purchase order schema, in other words to include them in the international purchase order's namespace, `ipo.xsd` contains the `include` element:

```
<include schemaLocation="http://www.example.com/schemas/
address.xsd"/>
```

The effect of this `include` element is to bring in the definitions and declarations contained in `address.xsd`, and make them available as part of the international purchase order schema target namespace. The one important caveat to using `include` is that the target namespace of the included components must be the same as the target namespace of the including schema, in this case `http://www.example.com/IPO`. Bringing in definitions and declarations using the `include` mechanism effectively adds these components to the existing target namespace. In Section 4.5, we describe a similar mechanism that enables you to modify certain components when they are brought in.

In our example, we have shown only one including document and one included document. In practice it is possible to include more than one document using multiple `include` elements, and documents can include documents that themselves include other documents. However, nesting documents in this manner is legal only if all the included parts of the schema are declared with the same target namespace.

Instance documents that conform to schema whose definitions span multiple schema documents need only reference the 'topmost' document and the common namespace, and it is the responsibility of the processor to gather together all the definitions specified in the various included documents. In our example above, the instance document `ipo.xml` (see Section 4.3) references only the common target namespace, `http://www.example.com/IPO`, and (by implication) the one schema file `http://www.example.com/schemas/ipo.xsd`. The processor is responsible for obtaining the schema file `address.xsd`.

In Section 5.4 we describe how schemas can be used to validate content from more than one namespace.

4.2 Deriving Types by Extension

To create our address constructs, we start by creating a complex type called `Address` in the usual way (see `address.xsd`). The `Address` type contains the basic elements of an address: a name, a street and a city. (Such a definition will not work for all countries, but it serves the purpose of our example.) From this starting point we derive two new complex types that contain all the elements of the original type plus additional elements that are specific to addresses in the US and the UK. The technique we use here to derive new (complex) address types by extending an existing type is the same technique we used in in Section 2.5.1, except that our base type here is a complex type whereas our base type in the previous section was a simple type.

We define the two new complex types, `USAddress` and `UKAddress`, using the `complexType` element. In addition, we indicate that the content models of the new types are complex, i.e., contain elements, by using the `complexContent` element, and we indicate that we are extending the base type `Address` by the value of the `base` attribute on the `extension` element.

When a complex type is derived by extension, its effective content model is the content model of the base type plus the content model specified in the type derivation. Furthermore, the two content models are treated as two children of a sequential group. In the case of `UKAddress`, the content model of `UKAddress` is the content model of `Address` plus the declarations for a `postcode` element and an `exportCode` attribute. This is like defining the `UKAddress` from scratch as follows:

Example

```
<complexType name="UKAddress">
  <sequence>
   <!-- content model of Address -->
   <element name="name"   type="string"/>
   <element name="street" type="string"/>
```

```
    <element name="city"   type="string"/>

    <!-- appended element declaration -->
    <element name="postcode" type="ipo:UKPostcode"/>
   </sequence>

   <!-- appended attribute declaration -->
   <attribute name="exportCode" type="positiveInteger" fixed="1"/>
  </complexType>
```

4.3 Using Derived Types in Instance Documents

In our example scenario, purchase orders are generated in response to customer orders which may involve shipping and billing addresses in different countries. The international purchase order, `ipo.xml` below, illustrates one such case where goods are shipped to the UK and the bill is sent to a US address. Clearly it is better if the schema for international purchase orders does not have to spell out every possible combination of international addresses for billing and shipping, and even more so if we can add new complex types of international address simply by creating new derivations of `Address`.

XML Schema allows us to define the `billTo` and `shipTo` elements as `Address` types (see `ipo.xsd`) but to use instances of international addresses in place of instances of `Address`. In other words, an instance document whose content conforms to the `UKAddress` type will be valid if that content appears within the document at a location where an `Address` is expected (assuming the `UKAddress` content itself is valid). To make this feature of XML Schema work, and to identify exactly which derived type is intended, the derived type must be identified in the instance document. The type is identified using the `xsi:type` attribute which is part of the XML Schema instance namespace. In the example, `ipo.xml`, use of the `UKAddress` and `USAddress` derived types is identified through the values assigned to the `xsi:type` attributes.

An International Purchase order, ipo.xml

```
<?xml version="1.0"?>
 <ipo:purchaseOrder
   xmlns:xsi="http://www.w3.org/2001/XMLSchema-instance"
   xmlns:ipo="http://www.example.com/IPO"
   orderDate="1999-12-01">
```

```
      <shipTo exportCode="1" xsi:type="ipo:UKAddress">
          <name>Helen Zoe</name>
          <street>47 Eden Street</street>
          <city>Cambridge</city>
          <postcode>CB1 1JR</postcode>
      </shipTo>

      <billTo xsi:type="ipo:USAddress">
          <name>Robert Smith</name>
          <street>8 Oak Avenue</street>
          <city>Old Town</city>
          <state>PA</state>
          <zip>95819</zip>
      </billTo>

      <items>
          <item partNum="833-AA">
              <productName>Lapis necklace</productName>
              <quantity>1</quantity>
              <USPrice>99.95</USPrice>
              <ipo:comment>Want this for the holidays!</
ipo:comment>
              <shipDate>1999-12-05</shipDate>
          </item>
      </items>
 </ipo:purchaseOrder>
```

In Section 4.8 we describe how to prevent derived types from being used in this sort of substitution.

4.4 Deriving Complex Types by Restriction

In addition to deriving new complex types by extending content models, it is possible to derive new types by restricting the content models of existing types. Restriction of complex types is conceptually the same as restriction of simple types, except that the restriction of complex types involves a type's declarations rather than the acceptable range of a simple type's values. A complex type derived by restriction is very similar to its base type, except that its declarations are more limited than the corresponding declarations in the base type. In fact, the values represented by the new type are a subset of the values represented by the base type (as is the case with restriction of simple types). In other words, an application prepared for the values of the base type would not be surprised by the values of the restricted type.

For example, suppose we want to update our definition of the list of `items` in an international purchase order so that it must contain *at least* one `item` on order; the schema shown in `ipo.xsd` allows an `items` element to appear without any child `item` elements. To create our new `ConfirmedItems` type, we define the new type in the usual way, indicate that it is derived by restriction from the base type `Items`, and provide a new (more restrictive) value for the minimum number of `item` element occurrences. Notice that types derived by restriction must repeat all the components of the base type definition that are to be included in the derived type:

Deriving ConfirmedItems by Restriction from Items

```
<complexType name="ConfirmedItems">
 <complexContent>
  <restriction base="ipo:Items">
   <sequence>

    <!-- item element is different than in Items -->
    <element name="item" minOccurs="1" maxOccurs="unbounded">

     <!-- remainder of definition is same as Items -->
     <complexType>
      <sequence>
       <element name="productName" type="string"/>
       <element name="quantity">
        <simpleType>
         <restriction base="positiveInteger">
          <maxExclusive value="100"/>
         </restriction>
        </simpleType>
       </element>
       <element name="USPrice"    type="decimal"/>
       <element ref="ipo:comment" minOccurs="0"/>
       <element name="shipDate"   type="date" minOccurs="0"/>
      </sequence>
      <attribute name="partNum" type="ipo:SKU" use="required"/>
     </complexType>
    </element>

   </sequence>
  </restriction>
 </complexContent>
</complexType>
```

This change, requiring at least one child element rather than allowing zero or more child elements, narrows the allowable number of child elements from a minimum of 0 to a minimum of 1. Note that all `ConfirmedItems` type elements will also be acceptable as `Item` type elements.

To further illustrate restriction, Table 3 shows several examples of how element and attribute declarations within type definitions may be restricted (the table shows element syntax although the first three examples are equally valid attribute restrictions).

Table 3 Restriction Examples

Base	*Restriction*	*Notes*
	default="1"	setting a default value where none was previously given
	fixed="100"	setting a fixed value where none was previously given
	type="string"	specifying a type where none was previously given
(`minOccurs`, `maxOccurs`)	(`minOccurs`, `maxOccurs`)	
(0, 1)	(0, 0)	exclusion of an optional component; this may also be accomplished by omitting the component's declaration from the restricted type definition
(0, unbounded)	(0, 0) (0, 37)	
(1, 9)	(1, 8) (2, 9) (4, 7) (3, 3)	
(1, unbounded)	(1, 12) (3, unbounded) (6, 6)	
(1, 1)	-	cannot restrict `minOccurs` or `maxOccurs`

4.5 Redefining Types & Groups

In Section 4.1 we described how to include definitions and declarations obtained from external schema files having the same target namespace. The `include` mechanism enables you to use externally created schema components "as-is", that is, without any modification. We have just described how to derive new types by extension and by restriction, and the `redefine` mechanism we describe here enables you to redefine simple and complex types, groups, and attribute groups that are obtained from external schema files. Like the `include` mechanism, `redefine` requires the external components to be in the same target namespace as the redefining schema, although external components from schemas that have no namespace can also be redefined. In the latter cases, the redefined components become part of the redefining schema's target namespace.

To illustrate the `redefine` mechanism, we use it instead of the `include` mechanism in the International Purchase Order schema, `ipo.xsd`, and we use it to modify the definition of the complex type `Address` contained in `address.xsd`:

Using redefine in the International Purchase Order

```
<schema targetNamespace="http://www.example.com/IPO"
        xmlns="http://www.w3.org/2001/XMLSchema"
        xmlns:ipo="http://www.example.com/IPO">

  <!-- bring in address constructs -->
  <redefine
   schemaLocation="http://www.example.com/schemas/address.xsd">

   <!-- redefinition of Address -->
   <complexType name="Address">
    <complexContent>
      <extension base="ipo:Address">
       <sequence>
        <element name="country" type="string"/>
       </sequence>
      </extension>
    </complexContent>
   </complexType>

  </redefine>

  <!-- etc. -->

 </schema>
```

The `redefine` element acts very much like the `include` element as it includes all the declarations and definitions from the `address.xsd` file. The complex type definition of `Address` uses the familiar extension syntax to add a `country` element to the definition of `Address`. However, note that the base type is also `Address`. Outside of the `redefine` element, any such attempt to define a complex type with the same name (and in the same namespace) as the base from which it is being derived would cause an error. But in this case, there is no error, and the extended definition of `Address` becomes the only definition of `Address`.

Now that `Address` has been redefined, the extension applies to all schema components that make use of `Address`. For example, `address.xsd` contains definitions of international address types that are derived from `Address`. These derivations reflect the redefined `Address` type, as shown in the following snippet:

Snippet of `ipo.xml` *using Redefined Address*

```
 ....
  <shipTo exportCode="1" xsi:type="ipo:UKAddress">
   <name>Helen Zoe</name>
   <street>47 Eden Street</street>
   <city>Cambridge</city>
   <!-- country was added to Address which is base type of
UKAddress -->
   <country>United Kingdom</country>
   <!-- postcode was added as part of UKAddress -->
   <postcode>CB1 1JR</postcode>
  </shipTo>
  ....
```

Our example has been carefully constructed so that the redefined `Address` type does not conflict in any way with the types that are derived from the original `Address` definition. But note that it would be very easy to create a conflict. For example, if the international address type derivations had extended `Address` by adding a `country` element, then the redefinition of `Address` would be adding an element of the same name to the content model of `Address`. It is illegal to have two elements of the same name (and in the same target namespace) but different types in a content model, and so the attempt to redefine `Address` would cause an error. In general, `redefine` does not protect you from such errors, and it should be used cautiously.

4.6 Substitution Groups

XML Schema provides a mechanism, called substitution groups, that allows elements to be substituted for other elements. More specifically, elements can be assigned to a special group of elements that are said to be substitutable for a particular named element called the head element. (Note that the head element must be declared as a global element.) To illustrate, we declare two elements called `customerComment` and `shipComment` and assign them to a substitution group whose head element is `comment`, and so `customerComment` and `shipComment` can be used anyplace that we are able to use `comment`. Elements in a substitution group must have the same type as the head element, or they can have a type that has been derived from the head element's type. To declare these two new elements, and to make them substitutable for the `comment` element, we use the following syntax:

Declaring Elements Substitutable for comment

```
<element name="shipComment" type="string"
         substitutionGroup="ipo:comment"/>
 <element name="customerComment" type="string"
          substitutionGroup="ipo:comment"/>
```

When these declarations are added to the international purchase order schema, `shipComment` and `customerComment` can be substituted for `comment` in the instance document, for example:

Snippet of ipo.xml with Substituted Elements

```
....
  <items>
    <item partNum="833-AA">
      <productName>Lapis necklace</productName>
      <quantity>1</quantity>
      <USPrice>99.95</USPrice>
      <ipo:shipComment>
        Use gold wrap if possible
      </ipo:shipComment>
      <ipo:customerComment>
        Want this for the holidays!
      </ipo:customerComment>
      <shipDate>1999-12-05</shipDate>
    </item>
  </items>
 ....
```

Note that when an instance document contains element substitutions whose types are derived from those of their head elements, it is *not* necessary to identify the derived types using the `xsi:type` construction that we described in Section 4.3.

The existence of a substitution group does not require any of the elements in that class to be used, nor does it preclude use of the head element. It simply provides a mechanism for allowing elements to be used interchangeably.

4.7 Abstract Elements and Types

XML Schema provides a mechanism to force substitution for a particular element or type. When an element or type is declared to be "abstract", it cannot be used in an instance document. When an element is declared to be abstract, a member of that element's substitution group must appear in the instance document. When an element's corresponding type definition is declared as abstract, all instances of that element must use `xsi:type` to indicate a derived type that is not abstract.

In the substitution group example we described in Section 4.6, it would be useful to specifically disallow use of the `comment` element so that instances must make use of the `customerComment` and `shipComment` elements. To declare the `comment` element abstract, we modify its original declaration in the international purchase order schema, `ipo.xsd`, as follows:

```
<element name="comment" type="string" abstract="true"/>
```

With `comment` declared as abstract, instances of international purchase orders are now only valid if they contain `customerComment` and `shipComment` elements.

Declaring an element as abstract requires the use of a substitution group. Declaring a type as abstract simply requires the use of a type derived from it (and identified by the `xsi:type` attribute) in the instance document. Consider the following schema definition:

Schema for Vehicles

```
<schema xmlns="http://www.w3.org/2001/XMLSchema"
        targetNamespace="http://cars.example.com/schema"
        xmlns:target="http://cars.example.com/schema">
```

```
  <complexType name="Vehicle" abstract="true"/>

  <complexType name="Car">
   <complexContent>
    <extension base="target:Vehicle"/>
   </complexContent>
  </complexType>

  <complexType name="Plane">
   <complexContent>
    <extension base="target:Vehicle"/>
   </complexContent>
  </complexType>

  <element name="transport" type="target:Vehicle"/>
 </schema>
```

The `transport` element is not abstract, therefore it can appear in instance documents. However, because its type definition is abstract, it may never appear in an instance document without an `xsi:type` attribute that refers to a derived type. That means the following is not schema-valid:

```
<transport xmlns="http://cars.example.com/schema"/>
```

because the `transport` element's type is abstract. However, the following is schema-valid:

```
 <transport xmlns="http://cars.example.com/schema"
       xmlns:xsi="http://www.w3.org/2001/XMLSchema-instance"
       xsi:type="Car"/>
```

because it uses a non-abstract type that is substitutable for `Vehicle`.

4.8 Controlling the Creation & Use of Derived Types

So far, we have been able to derive new types and use them in instance documents without any restraints. In reality, schema authors will sometimes want to control derivations of particular types, and the use of derived types in instances.

XML Schema provides a couple of mechanisms that control the derivation of types. One of these mechanisms allows the schema author to specify that for a particular complex type, new types may not be derived from it, either (a) by restriction, (b) by extension, or (c) at all. To illustrate, suppose we want to prevent any derivation of the `Address` type by restriction because we intend for it only to be used as the base for extended types such as `USAddress` and `UKAddress`. To prevent any such derivations, we slightly modify the original definition of `Address` as follows:

Preventing Derivations by Restriction of Address

```
<complexType name="Address" final="restriction">
  <sequence>
   <element name="name"   type="string"/>
   <element name="street" type="string"/>
   <element name="city"   type="string"/>
  </sequence>
 </complexType>
```

The `restriction` value of the `final` attribute prevents derivations by restriction. Preventing derivations at all, or by extension, are indicated by the values `#all` and `extension` respectively. Moreover, there exists an optional `finalDefault` attribute on the `schema` element whose value can be one of the values allowed for the `final` attribute. The effect of specifying the `finalDefault` attribute is equivalent to specifying a `final` attribute on every type definition and element declaration in the schema.

Another type-derivation mechanism controls which facets can be applied in the derivation of a new simple type. When a simple type is defined, the `fixed` attribute may be applied to any of its facets to prevent a derivation of that type from modifying the value of the fixed facets. For example, we can define a `Postcode` simple type as:

Preventing Changes to Simple Type Facets

```
<simpleType name="Postcode">
   <restriction base="string">
     <length value="7" fixed="true"/>
   </restriction>
 </simpleType>
```

Once this simple type has been defined, we can derive a new postal code type in which we apply a facet not fixed in the base definition, for example:

Legal Derivation from Postcode

```
<simpleType name="UKPostcode">
   <restriction base="ipo:Postcode">
     <pattern value="[A-Z]{2}\d\s\d[A-Z]{2}"/>
   </restriction>
 </simpleType>
```

However, we cannot derive a new postal code in which we re-apply any facet that was fixed in the base definition:

Illegal Derivation from Postcode

```
<simpleType name="UKPostcode">
  <restriction base="ipo:Postcode">
   <pattern value="[A-Z]{2}\d\d[A-Z]{2}"/>
   <!-- illegal attempt to modify facet fixed in base type -->
   <length value="6" fixed="true"/>
  </restriction>
 </simpleType>
```

In addition to the mechanisms that control type derivations, XML Schema provides a mechanism that controls which derivations and substitution groups may be used in instance documents. In Section 4.3, we described how the derived types, `USAddress` and `UKAddress`, could be used by the `shipTo` and `billTo` elements in instance documents. These derived types can replace the content model provided by the `Address` type because they are derived from the `Address` type. However, replacement by derived types can be controlled using the `block` attribute in a type definition. For example, if we want to block any derivation-by-restriction from being used in place of `Address` (perhaps for the same reason we defined `Address` with `final="restriction"`), we can modify the original definition of `Address` as follows:

Preventing Derivations by Restriction of Address in the Instance

```
<complexType name="Address" block="restriction">
  <sequence>
   <element name="name"   type="string"/>
   <element name="street" type="string"/>
   <element name="city"   type="string"/>
  </sequence>
 </complexType>
```

The restriction value on the block attribute prevents derivations-by-restriction from replacing Address in an instance. However, it would not prevent UKAddress and USAddress from replacing Address because they were derived by extension. Preventing replacement by derivations at all, or by derivations-by-extension, are indicated by the values #all and extension respectively. As with final, there exists an optional blockDefault attribute on the schema element whose value can be one of the values allowed for the block attribute. The effect of specifying the blockDefault attribute is equivalent to specifying a block attribute on every type definition and element declaration in the schema.

5 Advanced Concepts III: The Quarterly Report

The home-products ordering and billing application can generate ad-hoc reports that summarize how many of which types of products have been billed on a per region basis. An example of such a report, one that covers the fourth quarter of 1999, is shown in 4Q99.xml.

Notice that in this section we use qualified elements in the schema, and default namespaces where possible in the instances.

Quarterly Report, 4Q99.xml

```
<purchaseReport
   xmlns="http://www.example.com/Report"
   period="P3M" periodEnding="1999-12-31">

  <regions>
   <zip code="95819">
    <part number="872-AA" quantity="1"/>
    <part number="926-AA" quantity="1"/>
    <part number="833-AA" quantity="1"/>
    <part number="455-BX" quantity="1"/>
   </zip>
   <zip code="63143">
    <part number="455-BX" quantity="4"/>
   </zip>
  </regions>

  <parts>
   <part number="872-AA">Lawnmower</part>
   <part number="926-AA">Baby Monitor</part>
```

```
  <part number="833-AA">Lapis Necklace</part>
  <part number="455-BX">Sturdy Shelves</part>
 </parts>

</purchaseReport>
```

The report lists, by number and quantity, the parts billed to various zip codes, and it provides a description of each part mentioned. In summarizing the billing data, the intention of the report is clear and the data is unambiguous because a number of constraints are in effect. For example, each zip code appears only once (uniqueness constraint). Similarly, the description of every billed part appears only once although parts may be billed to several zip codes (referential constraint), see for example part number `455-BX`. In the following sections, we'll see how to specify these constraints using XML Schema.

The Report Schema, report.xsd

```
<schema targetNamespace="http://www.example.com/Report"
        xmlns="http://www.w3.org/2001/XMLSchema"
        xmlns:r="http://www.example.com/Report"
        xmlns:xipo="http://www.example.com/IPO"
        elementFormDefault="qualified">

 <!-- for SKU -->
 <import namespace="http://www.example.com/IPO"/>

 <annotation>
  <documentation xml:lang="en">
   Report schema for Example.com
   Copyright 2000 Example.com. All rights reserved.
  </documentation>
 </annotation>

 <element name="purchaseReport">
  <complexType>
   <sequence>
    <element name="regions" type="r:RegionsType">
     <keyref name="dummy2" refer="r:pNumKey">
      <selector xpath="r:zip/r:part"/>
      <field xpath="@number"/>
     </keyref>
    </element>

    <element name="parts" type="r:PartsType"/>
```

```
  </sequence>
  <attribute name="period"       type="duration"/>
  <attribute name="periodEnding" type="date"/>
 </complexType>

 <unique name="dummy1">
  <selector xpath="r:regions/r:zip"/>
  <field xpath="@code"/>
 </unique>

 <key name="pNumKey">
  <selector xpath="r:parts/r:part"/>
  <field xpath="@number"/>
 </key>
</element>

<complexType name="RegionsType">
 <sequence>
  <element name="zip" maxOccurs="unbounded">
   <complexType>
    <sequence>
     <element name="part" maxOccurs="unbounded">
      <complexType>
       <complexContent>
        <restriction base="anyType">
         <attribute name="number"   type="xipo:SKU"/>
         <attribute name="quantity" type="positiveInteger"/>
        </restriction>
       </complexContent>
      </complexType>
     </element>
    </sequence>
    <attribute name="code" type="positiveInteger"/>
   </complexType>
  </element>
 </sequence>
</complexType>

<complexType name="PartsType">
 <sequence>
  <element name="part" maxOccurs="unbounded">
   <complexType>
    <simpleContent>
     <extension base="string">
      <attribute name="number" type="xipo:SKU"/>
     </extension>
    </simpleContent>
```

```
      </complexType>
    </element>
  </sequence>
 </complexType>

</schema>
```

5.1 Specifying Uniqueness

XML Schema enables us to indicate that any attribute or element value must be unique within a certain scope. To indicate that one particular attribute or element value is unique, we use the `unique` element first to "select" a set of elements, and then to identify the attribute or element "field" relative to each selected element that has to be unique within the scope of the set of selected elements. In the case of our report schema, `report.xsd`, the selector element's `xpath` attribute contains an XPath expression, `regions/zip`, that selects a list of all the `zip` elements in a report instance. Likewise, the `field` element's `xpath` attribute contains a second XPath expression, `@code`, that specifies that the `code` attribute values of those elements must be unique. Note that the XPath expressions limit the scope of what must be unique. The report might contain another `code` attribute, but its value does not have to be unique because it lies outside the scope defined by the XPath expressions. Also note that the XPath expressions you can use in the `xpath` attribute are limited to a subset of the full XPath language defined in XML Path Language 1.0.

We can also indicate combinations of fields that must be unique. To illustrate, suppose we can relax the constraint that zip codes may only be listed once, although we still want to enforce the constraint that any product is listed only once within a given zip code. We could achieve such a constraint by specifying that the combination of zip code and product number must be unique. From the report document, `4Q99.xml`, the combined values of zip `code` and `number` would be: {`95819 872-AA`}, {`95819 926-AA`}, {`95819 833-AA`}, {`95819 455-BX`}, and {`63143 455-BX`}. Clearly, these combinations do not distinguish between zip `code` and `number` combinations derived from single or multiple listings of any particular zip, but the combinations would unambiguously represent a product listed more than once within a single zip. In other words, a schema processor could detect violations of the uniqueness constraint.

To define combinations of values, we simply add `field` elements to identify all the values involved. So, to add the part number value to our existing definition, we add a new `field` element whose `xpath` attribute value, `part/@number`, identifies the `number` attribute of `part` elements that are children of the `zip` elements identified by `regions/zip`:

A Unique Composed Value

```
<unique name="dummy1">
  <selector xpath="r:regions/r:zip"/>
  <field    xpath="@code"/>
  <field    xpath="r:part/@number"/>
</unique>
```

5.2 Defining Keys & Their References

In the 1999 quarterly report, the description of every billed part appears only once. We could enforce this constraint using `unique`, however, we also want to ensure that every part-quantity element listed under a zip code has a corresponding part description. We enforce the constraint using the `key` and `keyref` elements. The report schema, `report.xsd`, shows that the `key` and `keyref` constructions are applied using almost the same syntax as `unique`. The key element applies to the `number` attribute value of `part` elements that are children of the `parts` element. This declaration of `number` as a key means that its value must be unique and cannot be set to nil (i.e., is not nillable), and the name that is associated with the key, `pNumKey`, makes the key referenceable from elsewhere.

To ensure that the part-quantity elements have corresponding part descriptions, we say that the `number` attribute (`<field>@number</field>`) of those elements (`<selector>zip/part</selector>`) must reference the `pNumKey` key. This declaration of `number` as a `keyref` does not mean that its value must be unique, but it does mean there must exist a `pNumKey` with the same value.

As you may have figured out by analogy with `unique`, it is possible to define combinations of `key` and `keyref` values. Using this mechanism, we could go beyond simply requiring the product numbers to be equal, and define a combination of values that must be equal. Such values may involve combinations of multiple value types (`string`, `integer`, `date`, etc.), provided that the order and type of the `field` element references is the same in both the `key` and `keyref` definitions.

5.3 XML Schema Constraints vs. XML 1.0 ID Attributes

XML 1.0 provides a mechanism for ensuring uniqueness using the ID attribute and its associated attributes IDREF and IDREFS. This mechanism is also provided in XML Schema through the `ID`, `IDREF`, and `IDREFS` simple types which can be used for declaring XML 1.0-style attributes. XML Schema also introduces new mechanisms that are more flexible and powerful. For example, XML Schema's mechanisms can be applied to any element and attribute content, regardless of its type. In contrast, ID is a type of *attribute* and so it cannot be applied to attributes, elements or their content. Furthermore, Schema enables you to specify the scope within which uniqueness applies whereas the scope of an ID is fixed to be the whole document. Finally, Schema enables you to create `keys` or a `keyref` from combinations of element and attribute content whereas ID has no such facility.

5.4 Importing Types

The report schema, `report.xsd`, makes use of the simple type `xipo:SKU` that is defined in another schema, and in another target namespace. Recall that we used `include` so that the schema in `ipo.xsd` could make use of definitions and declarations from `address.xsd`. We cannot use `include` here because it can only pull in definitions and declarations from a schema whose target namespace is the same as the including schema's target namespace. Hence, the `include` element does not identify a namespace (although it does require a `schemaLocation`). The import mechanism that we describe in this section is an important mechanism that enables schema components from different target namespaces to be used together, and hence enables the schema validation of instance content defined across multiple namespaces.

To import the type `SKU` and use it in the report schema, we identify the namespace in which `SKU` is defined, and associate that namespace with a prefix for use in the report schema. Concretely, we use the `import` element to identify `SKU`'s target namespace, `http://www.example.com/IPO`, and we associate the namespace with the prefix `xipo` using a standard namespace declaration. The simple type `SKU`, defined in the namespace `http://www.example.com/IPO`, may then be referenced as `xipo:SKU` in any of the report schema's definitions and declarations.

In our example, we imported one simple type from one external namespace, and used it for declaring attributes. XML Schema in fact permits multiple schema components to be imported, from multiple namespaces, and they can be referred to in both definitions and declarations. For example in `report.xsd` we could additionally reuse the `comment` element declared in `ipo.xsd` by referencing that element in a declaration:

```
<element ref="xipo:comment"/>
```

Note however, that we cannot reuse the `shipTo` element from `po.xsd`, and the following is not legal because only *global* schema components can be imported:

```
<element ref="xipo:shipTo"/>
```

In `ipo.xsd`, `comment` is declared as a global element, in other words it is declared as an element of the `schema`. In contrast, `shipTo` is declared locally, in other words it is an element declared inside a complex type definition, specifically the `PurchaseOrderType` type.

Complex types can also be imported, and they can be used as the base types for deriving new types. Only named complex types can be imported; local, anonymously defined types cannot. Suppose we want to include in our reports the name of an analyst, along with contact information. We can reuse the (globally defined) complex type `USAddress` from `address.xsd`, and extend it to define a new type called `Analyst` by adding the new elements `phone` and `email`:

Defining Analyst by Extending USAddress

```
<complexType name="Analyst">
  <complexContent>
   <extension base="xipo:USAddress">
    <sequence>
     <element name="phone" type="string"/>
     <element name="email" type="string"/>
    </sequence>
   </extension>
  </complexContent>
 </complexType>
```

Using this new type we declare an element called `analyst` as part of the `purchaseReport` element declaration (declarations not shown) in the report schema. Then, the following instance document would conform to the modified report schema:

Instance Document Conforming to Report Schema with Analyst Type

```
<purchaseReport
   xmlns="http://www.example.com/Report"
   period="P3M" periodEnding="1999-12-31">
   <!-- regions and parts elements omitted -->
    <analyst>
         <name>Wendy Uhro</name>
         <street>10 Corporate Towers</street>
         <city>San Jose</city>
         <state>CA</state>
         <zip>95113</zip>
         <phone>408-271-3366</phone>
         <email>uhro@example.com</email>
    </analyst>
 </purchaseReport>
```

When schema components are imported from multiple namespaces, each namespace must be identified with a separate `import` element. The `import` elements themselves must appear as the first children of the `schema` element. Furthermore, each namespace must be associated with a prefix, using a standard namespace declaration, and that prefix is used to qualify references to any schema components belonging to that namespace. Finally, `import` elements optionally contain a `schemaLocation` attribute to help locate resources associated with the namespaces. We discuss the `schemaLocation` attribute in more detail in a later section.

5.4.1 Type Libraries

As XML schemas become more widespread, schema authors will want to create simple and complex types that can be shared and used as building blocks for creating new schemas. XML Schemas already provides types that play this role, in particular, the types described in the Simple Types appendix and in an introductory type library.

Schema authors will undoubtedly want to create their own libraries of types to represent currency, units of measurement, business addresses, and so on. Each library might consist of a schema containing one or more definitions, for example, a schema containing a currency type:

Example Currency Type in Type Library

```
<schema targetNamespace="http://www.example.com/Currency"
        xmlns:c="http://www.example.com/Currency"
        xmlns="http://www.w3.org/2001/XMLSchema">

  <annotation>
   <documentation xml:lang="en">
    Definition of Currency type based on ISO 4217
   </documentation>
  </annotation>

  <complexType name="Currency">
   <simpleContent>
    <extension base="decimal">
     <attribute name="name">
      <simpleType>
       <restriction base="string">

         <enumeration value="AED">
          <annotation>
           <documentation xml:lang="en">
            United Arab Emirates: Dirham (1 Dirham = 100 Fils)
           </documentation>
          </annotation>
         </enumeration>

         <enumeration value="AFA">
          <annotation>
           <documentation xml:lang="en">
            Afghanistan: Afghani (1 Afghani = 100 Puls)
           </documentation>
          </annotation>
         </enumeration>

         <enumeration value="ALL">
          <annotation>
           <documentation xml:lang="en">
            Albania, Lek (1 Lek = 100 Qindarka)
           </documentation>
          </annotation>
         </enumeration>

         <!-- and other currencies -->

       </restriction>
      </simpleType>
```

```
      </attribute>
    </extension>
   </simpleContent>
  </complexType>

 </schema>
```

An example of an element appearing in an instance and having this type:

```
<convertFrom name="AFA">199.37</convertFrom>
```

Once we have defined the currency type, we can make it available for re-use in other schemas through the `import` mechanism just described.

5.5 Any Element, Any Attribute

In previous sections we have seen several mechanisms for extending the content models of complex types. For example, a mixed content model can contain arbitrary character data in addition to elements, and for example, a content model can contain elements whose types are imported from external namespaces. However, these mechanisms provide very broad and very narrow controls respectively. The purpose of this section is to describe a flexible mechanism that enables content models to be extended by any elements and attributes belonging to specified namespaces.

To illustrate, consider a version of the quarterly report, `4Q99html.xml`, in which we have embedded an HTML representation of the XML parts data. The HTML content appears as the content of the element `htmlExample`, and the default namespace is changed on the outermost HTML element (`table`) so that all the HTML elements belong to the HTML namespace, `http://www.w3.org/1999/xhtml`:

Quarterly Report with HTML, 4Q99html.xml

```
<purchaseReport
   xmlns="http://www.example.com/Report"
   period="P3M" periodEnding="1999-12-31">

  <regions>
    <!-- part sales listed by zip code, data from 4Q99.xml -->
  </regions>

  <parts>
    <!-- part descriptions from 4Q99.xml -->
```

```
 </parts>

 <htmlExample>
  <table xmlns="http://www.w3.org/1999/xhtml"
         border="0" width="100%">
   <tr>
     <th align="left">Zip Code</th>
     <th align="left">Part Number</th>
     <th align="left">Quantity</th>
   </tr>
   <tr><td>95819</td><td> </td><td> </td></tr>
   <tr><td> </td><td>872-AA</td><td>1</td></tr>
   <tr><td> </td><td>926-AA</td><td>1</td></tr>
   <tr><td> </td><td>833-AA</td><td>1</td></tr>
   <tr><td> </td><td>455-BX</td><td>1</td></tr>
   <tr><td>63143</td><td> </td><td> </td></tr>
   <tr><td> </td><td>455-BX</td><td>4</td></tr>
  </table>
 </htmlExample>

</purchaseReport>
```

To permit the appearance of HTML in the instance document we modify the report schema by declaring a new element `htmlExample` whose content is defined by the `any` element. In general, an `any` element specifies that any well-formed XML is permissible in a type's content model. In the example, we require the XML to belong to the namespace `http://www.w3.org/1999/xhtml`, in other words, it should be HTML. The example also requires there to be at least one element present from this namespace, as indicated by the values of `minOccurs` and `maxOccurs`:

Modification to purchaseReport Declaration to Allow HTML in Instance

```
<element name="purchaseReport">
  <complexType>
   <sequence>
    <element name="regions" type="r:RegionsType"/>
    <element name="parts"   type="r:PartsType"/>
    <element name="htmlExample">
     <complexType>
      <sequence>
       <any namespace="http://www.w3.org/1999/xhtml"
            minOccurs="1" maxOccurs="unbounded"
            processContents="skip"/>
```

```
      </sequence>
     </complexType>
    </element>
   </sequence>
   <attribute name="period"       type="duration"/>
   <attribute name="periodEnding" type="date"/>
  </complexType>
 </element>
```

The modification permits some well-formed XML belonging to the namespace `http://www.w3.org/1999/xhtml` to appear inside the `htmlExample` element. Therefore `4Q99html.xml` is permissible because there is one element which (with its children) is well-formed, the element appears inside the appropriate element (`htmlExample`), and the instance document asserts that the element and its content belongs to the required namespace. However, the HTML may not actually be valid because nothing in `4Q99html.xml` by itself can provide that guarantee. If such a guarantee is required, the value of the `processContents` attribute should be set to `strict` (the default value). In this case, an XML processor is obliged to obtain the schema associated with the required namespace, and validate the HTML appearing within the `htmlExample` element.

In another example, we define a `text` type which is similar to the text type defined in XML Schema's introductory type library (see also Section 5.4.1), and is suitable for internationalized human-readable text. The text type allows an unrestricted mixture of character content and element content from any namespace, for example Ruby annotations, along with an optional `xml:lang` attribute. The `lax` value of the `processContents` attribute instructs an XML processor to validate the element content on a can-do basis: It will validate elements and attributes for which it can obtain schema information, but it will not signal errors for those it cannot obtain any schema information.

Text Type

```
<xsd:complexType name="text">
  <xsd:complexContent mixed="true">
   <xsd:restriction base="xsd:anyType">
    <xsd:sequence>
     <xsd:any processContents="lax" minOccurs="0"
maxOccurs="unbounded"/>
    </xsd:sequence>
    <xsd:attribute ref="xml:lang"/>
   </xsd:restriction>
```

```
  </xsd:complexContent>
 </xsd:complexType>
```

Namespaces may be used to permit and forbid element content in various ways depending upon the value of the `namespace` attribute, as shown in Table 4.

Table 4 Namespace Attribute in Any

Value of Namespace Attribute	*Allowable Element Content*
##any	Any well-formed XML from any namespace (default)
##local	Any well-formed XML that is not qualified, i.e., not declared to be in a namespace
##other	Any well-formed XML that is not from the target namespace of the type being defined
"http://www.w3.org/1999/xhtml ##targetNamespace"	Any well-formed XML belonging to any namespace in the (whitespace separated) list; ##targetNamespace is shorthand for the target namespace of the type being defined

In addition to the `any` element which enables element content according to namespaces, there is a corresponding `anyAttribute` element which enables attributes to appear in elements. For example, we can permit any HTML attribute to appear as part of the `htmlExample` element by adding `anyAttribute` to its declaration:

Modification to htmlExample Declaration to Allow HTML Attributes

```
<element name="htmlExample">
  <complexType>
   <sequence>
    <any namespace="http://www.w3.org/1999/xhtml"
         minOccurs="1" maxOccurs="unbounded"
         processContents="skip"/>
```

```
    </sequence>
    <anyAttribute namespace="http://www.w3.org/1999/xhtml"/>
  </complexType>
 </element>
```

This declaration permits an HTML attribute, say `href`, to appear in the `htmlExample` element. For example:

An HTML attribute in the htmlExample Element

```
....
   <htmlExample xmlns:h="http://www.w3.org/1999/xhtml"
                h:href="http://www.example.com/reports/
4Q99.html">
      <!-- HTML markup here -->
   </htmlExample>
 ....
```

The `namespace` attribute in an `anyAttribute` element can be set to any of the values listed in Table 4 for the `any` element, and `anyAttribute can be specified with a processContents` attribute. In contrast to an `any` element, `anyAttribute` cannot constrain the number of attributes that may appear in an element.

5.6 schemaLocation

XML Schema uses the `schemaLocation` and `xsi:schemaLocation` attributes in three circumstances.

1. In an instance document, the attribute `xsi:schemaLocation` provides hints from the author to a processor regarding the location of schema documents. The author warrants that these schema documents are relevant to checking the validity of the document content, on a namespace by namespace basis. For example, we can indicate the location of the Report schema to a processor of the Quarterly Report:

Using schemaLocation in the Quarterly Report, 4Q99html.xml

```
<purchaseReport
   xmlns="http://www.example.com/Report"
   xmlns:xsi="http://www.w3.org/2001/XMLSchema-instance"
   xsi:schemaLocation="http://www.example.com/Report
```

```
  http://www.example.com/Report.xsd"
  period="P3M" periodEnding="1999-12-31">

 <!-- etc. -->

</purchaseReport>
```

The schemaLocation attribute contains pairs of values: The first member of each pair is the namespace for which the second member is the hint describing where to find to an appropriate schema document. The presence of these hints does not require the processor to obtain or use the cited schema documents, and the processor is free to use other schemas obtained by any suitable means, or to use no schema at all.
A schema is not required to have a namespace (see Section 3.4) and so there is a noNamespaceSchemaLocation attribute which is used to provide hints for the locations of schema documents that do not have target namespaces.

2. In a schema, the include element has a required schemaLocation attribute, and it contains a URI reference which must identify a schema document. The effect is to compose a final effective schema by merging the declarations and definitions of the including and the included schemas. For example, in Section 4, the type definitions of Address, USAddress, UKAddress, USState (along with their attribute and local element declarations) from address.xsd were added to the element declarations of purchaseOrder and comment, and the type definitions of PurchaseOrderType, Items and SKU (along with their attribute and local element declarations) from ipo.xsd to create a single schema.

3. Also in a schema, the import element has optional namespace and schemaLocation attributes. If present, the schemaLocation attribute is understood in a way which parallels the interpretation of xsi:schemaLocation in (1). Specifically, it provides a hint from the author to a processor regarding the location of a schema document that the author warrants supplies the required components for the namespace identified by the namespace attribute. To import components that are not in any target namespace, the import element is used without a namespace attribute (and with or without a

schemaLocation attribute). References to components imported in this manner are unqualified.

Note that the schemaLocation is only a hint and some processors and applications will have reasons to not use it. For example, an HTML editor may have a built-in HTML schema.

5.7 Conformance

An instance document may be processed against a schema to verify whether the rules specified in the schema are honored in the instance. Typically, such processing actually does two things, (1) it checks for conformance to the rules, a process called schema validation, and (2) it adds supplementary information that is not immediately present in the instance, such as types and default values, called infoset contributions.

The author of an instance document, such as a particular purchase order, may claim, in the instance itself, that it conforms to the rules in a particular schema. The author does this using the schemaLocation attribute discussed above. But regardless of whether a schemaLocation attribute is present, an application is free to process the document against any schema. For example, a purchasing application may have the policy of always using a certain purchase order schema, regardless of any schemaLocation values.

Conformance checking can be thought of as proceeding in steps, first checking that the root element of the document instance has the right contents, then checking that each subelement conforms to its description in a schema, and so on until the entire document is verified. Processors are required to report what checking has been carried out.

To check an element for conformance, the processor first locates the declaration for the element in a schema, and then checks that the targetNamespace attribute in the schema matches the actual namespace URI of the element. Alternatively, it may determine that the schema does not have a targetNamespace attribute and the instance element is not namespace-qualified.

Supposing the namespaces match, the processor then examines the type of the element, either as given by the declaration in the schema, or by an xsi:type attribute in the instance. If the latter, the instance type must be an allowed substitution for the type given in the schema; what is allowed is controlled by the `block` attribute in the element declaration. At this same time, default values and other infoset contributions are applied.

Next the processor checks the immediate attributes and contents of the element, comparing these against the attributes and contents permitted by the element's type. For example, considering a `shipTo` element such as the one in Section 2.1, the processor checks what is permitted for an `Address`, because that is the `shipTo` element's type.

If the element has a simple type, the processor verifies that the element has no attributes or contained elements, and that its character content matches the rules for the simple type. This sometimes involves checking the character sequence against regular expressions or enumerations, and sometimes it involves checking that the character sequence represents a value in a permitted range.

If the element has a complex type, then the processor checks that any required attributes are present and that their values conform to the requirements of their simple types. It also checks that all required subelements are present, and that the sequence of subelements (and any mixed text) matches the content model declared for the complex type. Regarding subelements, schemas can either require exact name matching, permit substitution by an equivalent element or permit substitution by any element allowed by an 'any' particle.

Unless a schema indicates otherwise (as it can for 'any' particles) conformance checking then proceeds one level more deeply by looking at each subelement in turn, repeating the process described above.

A Acknowledgements

Many people have contributed ideas, material and feedback that has improved this document. In particular, the editor acknowledges contributions from David Beech, Paul Biron, Don Box, Allen Brown, David Cleary, Dan Connolly, Roger Costello, Martin Dürst, Martin Gudgin, Dave Hollander, Joe Kesselman, John McCarthy, Andrew Layman, Eve Maler, Ashok Malhotra, Noah Mendelsohn, Michael Sperberg-McQueen, Henry Thompson, Misha Wolf, and Priscilla Walmsley for validating the examples.

B Simple Types & Their Facets

The legal values for each simple type can be constrained through the application of one or more facets. Tables B1.a and B1.b list all of XML Schema's built-in simple types and the facets applicable to each type. The names of the simple types and the facets are linked from the tables to the corresponding descriptions in XML Schema Part 2: Datatypes.

Table B1.a Simple Types & Applicable Facets

Simple Types	*Facets*					
	length	*minLength*	*maxLength*	*pattern*	*enumeration*	*whiteSpace*
`string`	y	y	y	y	y	y
`normalized-String`	y	y	y	y	y	y
`token`	y	y	y	y	y	y
`byte`				y	y	y
`unsignedByte`				y	y	y
`base64Binary`	y	y	y	y	y	y
`hexBinary`	y	y	y	y	y	y
`integer`				y	y	y
`positiveInteger`				y	y	y
`negativeInteger`				y	y	y
`nonNegativeInteger`				y	y	y
`nonPositiveInteger`				y	y	y
`int`				y	y	y
`unsignedInt`				y	y	y
`long`				y	y	y

Table B1.a Simple Types & Applicable Facets (continued)

Simple Types	*Facets*					
	length	*minLength*	*maxLength*	*pattern*	*enumeration*	*whiteSpace*
`unsignedLong`				y	y	y
`short`				y	y	y
`unsignedShort`				y	y	y
`decimal`				y	y	y
`float`				y	y	y
`double`				y	y	y
`boolean`				y		y
`time`				y	y	y
`dateTime`				y	y	y
`duration`				y	y	y
`date`				y	y	y
`gMonth`				y	y	y
`gYear`				y	y	y
`gYearMonth`				y	y	y
`gDay`				y	y	y
`gMonthDay`				y	y	y
`Name`	y	y	y	y	y	y
`QName`	y	y	y	y	y	y
`NCName`	y	y	y	y	y	y
`anyURI`	y	y	y	y	y	y
`language`	y	y	y	y	y	y

Table B1.a Simple Types & Applicable Facets (continued)

Simple Types	*Facets*					
	length	*minLength*	*maxLength*	*pattern*	*enumeration*	*whiteSpace*
`ID`	y	y	y	y	y	y
`IDREF`	y	y	y	y	y	y
`IDREFS`	y	y	y		y	y
`ENTITY`	y	y	y	y	y	y
`ENTITIES`	y	y	y		y	y
`NOTATION`	y	y	y	y	y	y
`NMTOKEN`	y	y	y	y	y	y
`NMTOKENS`	y	y	y		y	y

The facets listed in Table B1.b apply only to simple types which are ordered. Not all simple types are ordered and so B1.b does not list all of the simple types.

Table B1.b Simple Types & Applicable Facets

Simple Types	*Facets*					
	max Inclusive	*max Exclusive*	*min Inclusive*	*min Exclusive*	*total Digits*	*fraction-Digits*
`byte`	y	y	y	y	y	y
`unsignedByte`	y	y	y	y	y	y
`integer`	y	y	y	y	y	y
`positiveInteger`	y	y	y	y	y	y
`negativeInteger`	y	y	y	y	y	y

Table B1.b Simple Types & Applicable Facets (continued)

Simple Types	*Facets*					
	max Inclusive	*max Exclusive*	*min Inclusive*	*min Exclusive*	*total Digits*	*fraction-Digits*
nonNegativeInteger	y	y	y	y	y	y
nonPositiveInteger	y	y	y	y	y	y
int	y	y	y	y	y	y
unsignedInt	y	y	y	y	y	y
long	y	y	y	y	y	y
unsignedLong	y	y	y	y	y	y
short	y	y	y	y	y	y
unsignedShort	y	y	y	y	y	y
decimal	y	y	y	y	y	y
float	y	y	y	y		
double	y	y	y	y		
time	y	y	y	y		
dateTime	y	y	y	y		
duration	y	y	y	y		
date	y	y	y	y		
gMonth	y	y	y	y		
gYear	y	y	y	y		
gYearMonth	y	y	y	y		
gDay	y	y	y	y		
gMonthDay	y	y	y	y		

C Using Entities

XML 1.0 provides various types of entities which are named fragments of content that can be used in the construction of both DTD's (parameter entities) and instance documents. In Section 2.7, we noted how named groups mimic parameter entities. In this section we show how entities can be declared in instance documents, and how the functional equivalents of entities can be declared in schemas.

Suppose we want to declare and use an entity in an instance document, and that document is also constrained by a schema. For example:

Declaring and referencing an entity in an instance document.

```
<?xml version="1.0" ?>
 <!DOCTYPE PurchaseOrder [
 <!ENTITY eacute "È">
 ]>
 <purchaseOrder xmlns="http://www.example.com/PO1"
                orderDate="1999-10-20>
  <!-- etc. -->
   <city>Montr&eacute;al</city>
  <!-- etc. -->
 </purchaseOrder>
```

Here, we declare an entity called `eacute` as part of an internal (DTD) subset, and we reference this entity in the content of the `city` element. Note that when this instance document is processed, the entity will be dereferenced before schema validation takes place. In other words, a schema processor will determine the validity of the `city` element using `MontrÈal` as the element's value.

We can achieve a similar but not identical outcome by declaring an element in a schema, and by setting the element's content appropriately:

```
<xsd:element name="eacute" type="xsd:token" fixed="È"/>
```

And this element can be used in an instance document:

Using an Element instead of an Entity in an Instance Document

```
<?xml version="1.0" ?>
 <purchaseOrder xmlns="http://www.example.com/PO1"
                xmlns:c="http://www.example.com/
characterElements"
                orderDate="1999-10-20>
```

```
  <!-- etc. -->
   <city>Montr<c:eacute/>al</city>
  <!-- etc. -->
</purchaseOrder>
```

In this case, a schema processor will process two elements, a `city` element, and an `eacute` element for the contents of which the processor will supply the single character `È`. Note that the extra element will complicate string matching; the two forms of the name "MontrÈal" given in the two examples above will not match each other using normal string-comparison techniques.

D Regular Expressions

XML Schema's `pattern` facet uses a regular expression language that supports Unicode. It is fully described in XML Schema Part 2. The language is similar to the regular expression language used in the Perl Programming language, although expressions are matched against entire lexical representations rather than user-scoped lexical representations such as line and paragraph. For this reason, the expression language does not contain the metacharacters ^ and $, although ^ is used to express exception, e.g., [^0-9]x.

Table D1 Examples of Regular Expressions

Expression	*Match(s)*
Chapter \d	Chapter 0, Chapter 1, Chapter 2 ....
Chapter\s\d	Chapter followed by a single whitespace character (space, tab, newline, etc.), followed by a single digit
Chapter\s\w	Chapter followed by a single whitespace character (space, tab, newline, etc.), followed by a word character (XML 1.0 Letter or Digit)
Espanñola	EspaÒola
\p{Lu}	any uppercase character, the value of \p{} (e.g., "Lu") is defined by Unicode

Table D1 Examples of Regular Expressions (continued)

Expression	*Match(s)*
\p{IsGreek}	any Greek character, the 'Is' construction may be applied to any block name (e.g., "Greek") as defined by Unicode
\P{IsGreek}	any non-Greek character, the 'Is' construction may be applied to any block name (e.g., "Greek") as defined by Unicode
a*x	x, ax, aax, aaax ....
a?x	ax, x
a+x	ax, aax, aaax ....
(a|b)+x	ax, bx, aax, abx, bax, bbx, aaax, aabx, abax, abbx, baax, babx, bbax, bbbx, aaaax ....
[abcde]x	ax, bx, cx, dx, ex
[a-e]x	ax, bx, cx, dx, ex
[-ae]x	-x, ax, ex
[ae-]x	ax, ex, -x
[^0-9]x	any non-digit character followed by the character x
\Dx	any non-digit character followed by the character x
.x	any character followed by the character x
.*abc.*	1x2abc, abc1x2, z3456abchooray ....
ab{2}x	abbx
ab{2,4}x	abbx, abbbx, abbbbx
ab{2,}x	abbx, abbbx, abbbbx ....
(ab){2}x	ababx

E Index

XML Schema Elements. Each element name is linked to a formal XML description in either the Structures or Datatypes parts of the XML Schema specification. Element names are followed by one or more links to examples (identified by section number) in the Primer.

- `simpleContent`: 2.5.1
- `simpleType`: 2.3
- `union`: 2.3.2
- `unique`: 5.1

XML Schema Attributes. Each attribute name is followed by one or more pairs of references. Each pair of references consists of a link to an example in the Primer, plus a link to a formal XML description in either the Structures or Datatypes parts of the XML Schema specification.

- `abstract`: element declaration [Structures], complex type definition [Structures]
- `attributeFormDefault`: `schema` element [Structures]
- `base`: simple type definition [Datatypes], complex type definition [Structures]
- `block`: complex type definition [Structures]
- `blockDefault`: `schema` element [Structures]
- `default`: attribute declaration [Structures]
- `default`: element declaration [Structures]
- `elementFormDefault`: `schema` element [Structures]
- `final`: complex type definition [Structures]
- `finalDefault`: `schema` element [Structures]
- `fixed`: attribute declaration [Structures]
- `fixed`: element declaration [Structures]
- `fixed`: simple type definition [Datatypes]
- `form`: element declaration [Structures], attribute declaration [Structures]
- `itemType`: list type definition [Datatypes]
- `memberTypes`: union type definition [Datatypes]
- `maxOccurs`: element declaration [Structures]
- `minOccurs`: element declaration [Structures]
- `mixed`: complex type definition [Structures]
- `name`: element declaration [Structures], attribute declaration [Structures], complex type definition [Structures], simple type definition [Datatypes]
- `namespace`: `any` element [Structures], include element [Structures]
- `noNamespaceSchemaLocation`: instance element [Structures]

- `xsi:nil`: instance element [Structures]
- `nillable`: element declaration [Structures]
- `processContents`: any element [Structures], `anyAttribute` element [Structures]
- `ref`: element declaration [Structures]
- `schemaLocation`: include specification [Structures], redefine specification [Structures], import specification [Structures]
- `xsi:schemaLocation`: instance attribute [Structures]
- `substitutionGroup`: element declaration [Structures]
- `targetNamespace`: `schema` element [Structures]
- `type`: element declaration [Structures], attribute declaration [Structures]
- `xsi:type`: `instance` element [Structures]
- `use`: attribute declaration [Structures]
- `xpath`: `selector` & `field` elements [Structures]

XML Schema's simple types are described in Table 2.

Index

Page numbers ending in "f" refer to figures.
Page numbers ending in "t" refer to tables.

A

B

C

D

H

I

J

L

M

N

O

P

Q

R

W

X

LICENSE AGREEMENT AND LIMITED WARRANTY

READ THE FOLLOWING TERMS AND CONDITIONS CAREFULLY BEFORE OPENING THIS SOFTWARE MEDIA PACKAGE. THIS LEGAL DOCUMENT IS AN AGREEMENT BETWEEN YOU AND PRENTICE-HALL, INC. (THE "COMPANY"). BY OPENING THIS SEALED SOFTWARE MEDIA PACKAGE, YOU ARE AGREEING TO BE BOUND BY THESE TERMS AND CONDITIONS. IF YOU DO NOT AGREE WITH THESE TERMS AND CONDITIONS, DO NOT OPEN THE SOFTWARE MEDIA PACKAGE. PROMPTLY RETURN THE UNOPENED SOFTWARE MEDIA PACKAGE AND ALL ACCOMPANYING ITEMS TO THE PLACE YOU OBTAINED THEM FOR A FULL REFUND OF ANY SUMS YOU HAVE PAID.

1. **GRANT OF LICENSE:** In consideration of your payment of the license fee, which is part of the price you paid for this product, and your agreement to abide by the terms and conditions of this Agreement, the Company grants to you a nonexclusive right to use and display the copy of the enclosed software program (hereinafter the "SOFTWARE") on a single computer (i.e., with a single CPU) at a single location so long as you comply with the terms of this Agreement. The Company reserves all rights not expressly granted to you under this Agreement.

2. **OWNERSHIP OF SOFTWARE:** You own only the magnetic or physical media (the enclosed software media) on which the SOFTWARE is recorded or fixed, but the Company retains all the rights, title, and ownership to the SOFTWARE recorded on the original software media copy(ies) and all subsequent copies of the SOFTWARE, regardless of the form or media on which the original or other copies may exist. This license is not a sale of the original SOFTWARE or any copy to you.

3. **COPY RESTRICTIONS:** This SOFTWARE and the accompanying printed materials and user manual (the "Documentation") are the subject of copyright. You may not copy the Documentation or the SOFTWARE, except that you may make a single copy of the SOFTWARE for backup or archival purposes only. You may be held legally responsible for any copying or copyright infringement which is caused or encouraged by your failure to abide by the terms of this restriction.

4. **USE RESTRICTIONS:** You may not network the SOFTWARE or otherwise use it on more than one computer or computer terminal at the same time. You may physically transfer the SOFTWARE from one computer to another provided that the SOFTWARE is used on only one computer at a time. You may not distribute copies of the SOFTWARE or Documentation to others. You may not reverse engineer, disassemble, decompile, modify, adapt, translate, or create derivative works based on the SOFTWARE or the Documentation without the prior written consent of the Company.

5. **TRANSFER RESTRICTIONS:** The enclosed SOFTWARE is licensed only to you and may not be transferred to any one else without the prior written consent of the Company. Any unauthorized transfer of the SOFTWARE shall result in the immediate termination of this Agreement.

6. **TERMINATION:** This license is effective until terminated. This license will terminate automatically without notice from the Company and become null and void if you fail to comply with any provisions or limitations of this license. Upon termination, you shall destroy the Documentation and all copies of the SOFTWARE. All provisions of this Agreement as to warranties, limitation of liability, remedies or damages, and our ownership rights shall survive termination.

7. **MISCELLANEOUS:** This Agreement shall be construed in accordance with the laws of the United States of America and the State of New York and shall benefit the Company, its affiliates, and assignees.

8. **LIMITED WARRANTY AND DISCLAIMER OF WARRANTY:** The Company warrants that the SOFTWARE, when properly used in accordance with the Documentation, will operate in substantial conformity with the description of the SOFTWARE set forth in the Documentation. The Company does not warrant that the SOFTWARE will meet your requirements or that the operation of the SOFTWARE will be uninterrupted or error-free. The Company warrants that the media on which the SOFTWARE is delivered shall be free from defects in materials and workmanship under normal use for a period of thirty (30) days from the date of your purchase. Your only remedy and the Company's only obligation under these limited warranties is, at the Company's option, return of the warranted item for a refund of any amounts paid by you or replacement of the item. Any replacement of SOFTWARE or media under the warranties shall not extend the original warranty period. The limited warranty set forth above shall not apply to any SOFTWARE which the Company determines in good faith has been subject to misuse, neglect, improper installation, repair, alteration, or dam-

age by you. EXCEPT FOR THE EXPRESSED WARRANTIES SET FORTH ABOVE, THE COMPANY DISCLAIMS ALL WARRANTIES, EXPRESS OR IMPLIED, INCLUDING WITHOUT LIMITATION, THE IMPLIED WARRANTIES OF MERCHANTABILITY AND FITNESS FOR A PARTICULAR PURPOSE. EXCEPT FOR THE EXPRESS WARRANTY SET FORTH ABOVE, THE COMPANY DOES NOT WARRANT, GUARANTEE, OR MAKE ANY REPRESENTATION REGARDING THE USE OR THE RESULTS OF THE USE OF THE SOFTWARE IN TERMS OF ITS CORRECTNESS, ACCURACY, RELIABILITY, CURRENTNESS, OR OTHERWISE.

IN NO EVENT, SHALL THE COMPANY OR ITS EMPLOYEES, AGENTS, SUPPLIERS, OR CONTRACTORS BE LIABLE FOR ANY INCIDENTAL, INDIRECT, SPECIAL, OR CONSEQUENTIAL DAMAGES ARISING OUT OF OR IN CONNECTION WITH THE LICENSE GRANTED UNDER THIS AGREEMENT, OR FOR LOSS OF USE, LOSS OF DATA, LOSS OF INCOME OR PROFIT, OR OTHER LOSSES, SUSTAINED AS A RESULT OF INJURY TO ANY PERSON, OR LOSS OF OR DAMAGE TO PROPERTY, OR CLAIMS OF THIRD PARTIES, EVEN IF THE COMPANY OR AN AUTHORIZED REPRESENTATIVE OF THE COMPANY HAS BEEN ADVISED OF THE POSSIBILITY OF SUCH DAMAGES. IN NO EVENT SHALL LIABILITY OF THE COMPANY FOR DAMAGES WITH RESPECT TO THE SOFTWARE EXCEED THE AMOUNTS ACTUALLY PAID BY YOU, IF ANY, FOR THE SOFTWARE.

SOME JURISDICTIONS DO NOT ALLOW THE LIMITATION OF IMPLIED WARRANTIES OR LIABILITY FOR INCIDENTAL, INDIRECT, SPECIAL, OR CONSEQUENTIAL DAMAGES, SO THE ABOVE LIMITATIONS MAY NOT ALWAYS APPLY. THE WARRANTIES IN THIS AGREEMENT GIVE YOU SPECIFIC LEGAL RIGHTS AND YOU MAY ALSO HAVE OTHER RIGHTS WHICH VARY IN ACCORDANCE WITH LOCAL LAW.

ACKNOWLEDGMENT

YOU ACKNOWLEDGE THAT YOU HAVE READ THIS AGREEMENT, UNDERSTAND IT, AND AGREE TO BE BOUND BY ITS TERMS AND CONDITIONS. YOU ALSO AGREE THAT THIS AGREEMENT IS THE COMPLETE AND EXCLUSIVE STATEMENT OF THE AGREEMENT BETWEEN YOU AND THE COMPANY AND SUPERSEDES ALL PROPOSALS OR PRIOR AGREEMENTS, ORAL, OR WRITTEN, AND ANY OTHER COMMUNICATIONS BETWEEN YOU AND THE COMPANY OR ANY REPRESENTATIVE OF THE COMPANY RELATING TO THE SUBJECT MATTER OF THIS AGREEMENT.

Should you have any questions concerning this Agreement or if you wish to contact the Company for any reason, please contact in writing at the address below.

Robin Short
Prentice Hall PTR
One Lake Street
Upper Saddle River, New Jersey 07458

About the CD

The CD-ROM included with *Designing XML Databases* contains Apache Tomcat, Xerces XML parser, and practical examples to build your own XML database.

The CD-ROM can be used on Microsoft® Windows® 95/98/NT® 4.x/2000, UNIX, and Linux.

To download the latest updates, go to http://www.phptr.com/graves/.

License Agreement

Use of the software accompanying *Designing XML Databases* is subject to the terms of the License Agreement and Limited Warranty, found on the previous two pages.

Technical Support

Prentice hall does not offer technical support for this software. However, if there is a problem with the media, you may obtain a replacement copy by emailing us with your problem at: disc_exchange@prenhall.com.